Communications
in Computer and Information Science

412

Linqiang Pan   Gheorghe Păun
Mario J. Pérez-Jiménez   Tao Song (Eds.)

Bio-Inspired Computing – Theories and Applications

9th International Conference, BIC-TA 2014
Wuhan, China, October 16-19, 2014
Proceedings

 Springer

Volume Editors

Linqiang Pan
Huazhong University of Science and Technology
School of Automation
Wuhan 430074, China
E-mail: lqpan@mail.hust.edu.cn

Gheorghe Păun
Institute of Mathematics of the Romanian Academy
014700 Bucuresti, Romania
E-mail: gpaun@us.es

Mario J. Pérez-Jiménez
University of Sevilla
Department of Computer Science and Artificial Intelligence
Avda. Reina Mercedes s/n., 41012 Sevilla, Spain
E-mail: marper@us.es

Tao Song
Huazhong University of Science and Technology
School of Automation
Wuhan 430074, China
E-mail: songtao0608@hotmail.com

ISSN 1865-0929   e-ISSN 1865-0937
ISBN 978-3-662-45048-2   e-ISBN 978-3-662-45049-9
DOI 10.1007/978-3-662-45049-9
Springer Heidelberg New York Dordrecht London

Library of Congress Control Number: 2014950076

Typesetting: Camera-ready by author, data conversion by Scientific Publishing Services, Chennai, India

Printed on acid-free paper

Springer is part of Springer Science+Business Media (www.springer.com)

Preface

Bio-inspired computing is a field of study that abstracts computing ideas (data structures, operations with data, ways to control operations, computing models, etc.) from the living phenomena or biological systems such as evolution, cells, tissues, neural networks, immune system, and ant colonies. Bio-Inspired Computing: Theories and Applications (BIC-TA) is a series of conferences that aims to bring together researchers working in the main areas of natural computing inspired from biology, for presenting their recent results, exchanging ideas and cooperating in a friendly framework. The conference has four main topics: evolutionary computing, neural computing, DNA computing, and membrane computing.

Since 2006, the conference has taken place at Wuhan (2006), Zhengzhou (2007), Adelaide (2008), Beijing (2009), Liverpool and Changsha (2010), Penang (2011), Gwalior (2012), and Anhui (2013). Following the success of previous editions, the 9th International Conference on Bio-Inspired Computing: Theories and Applications (BIC-TA 2014) was organized by Huazhong University of Science and Technology and Zhengzhou University of Light Industry, in Wuhan, China, during October 16–19, 2014.

BIC-TA 2014 attracted a wide spectrum of interesting research papers on various aspects of bio-inspired computing with a diverse range of theories and applications. We received 204 submissions and 109 papers were selected for this volume of *Communications in Computer and Information Science*.

We gratefully acknowledge the financial support of the National Natural Science Foundation of China. We thank Huazhong University of Science and Technology and Zhengzhou University of Light Industry for extensive assistance in organizing the conference. We also thank PhD student Cheng He and all other volunteers, whose efforts ensured a smooth running of the conference.

The editors warmly thank the Program Committee members for their prompt and efficient support in reviewing the papers, and the authors of the submitted papers for their interesting papers.

Special thanks are due to Springer for the efficient cooperation in the timely production of this volume.

August 2014

Linqiang Pan
Gheorghe Păun
Mario J. Pérez-Jiménez
Tao Song

Organization

Steering Committee

Guangzhao Cui	Zhengzhou University of Light Industry, China
Kalyanmoy Deb	Indian Institute of Technology Kanpur, India
Miki Hirabayashi	National Institute of Information and Communications Technology (NICT), Japan
Joshua Knowles	University of Manchester, UK
Thom LaBean	North Carolina State University, USA
Jiuyong Li	University of South Australia, Australia
Kenli Li	University of Hunan, China
Giancarlo Mauri	Università di Milano-Bicocca, Italy
Yongli Mi	Hong Kong University of Science and Technology, SAR China
Atulya K. Nagar	Liverpool Hope University, UK
Linqiang Pan	Huazhong University of Science and Technology, China
Gheorghe Păun	Romanian Academy, Bucharest, Romania
Mario J. Pérez-Jiménez	University of Seville, Spain
K.G. Subramanian	Universiti Sains Malaysia, Malaysia
Robinson Thamburaj	Madras Christian College, India
Jin Xu	Peking University, China
Hao Yan	Arizona State University, USA

Organizing Committee

Guangzhao Cui	Zhengzhou University of Light Industry, China (Co-chair)
Linqiang Pan	Huazhong University of Science and Technology, China (Chair)
Xiaolong Shi	Huazhong University of Science and Technology, China
Tao Song	Huazhong University of Science and Technology, China (Co-chair)
Zheng Zhang	Huazhong University of Science and Technology, China
Zhiqiang Zhang	Huazhong University of Science and Technology, China
Keqin Jiang	Huazhong University of Science and Technology, China

Program Committee

Rosni Abdullah, Malaysia
Muhammad Abulaish, Saudi Arabia
Chang Wook Ahn, South Korea
Adel Al-Jumaily, Australia
Bahareh Asadi, Iran
Li He, USA
Eduard Babulak, European
  Commission, Community Research
  and Development Information
Mehdi Bahrami, Iran
Soumya Banerjee, India
Jagdish Chand Bansal, India
Debnath Bhattacharyya, India
Monowar H. Bhuyan, India
Kavita Burse, India
Michael Chen, China
Tsung-Che Chiang, Taiwan, China
Sung-Bae Cho, South Korea
Kadian Davis, Jamaica
Sumithra Devi K.A., India
Ciprian Dobre, Romania
Amit Dutta, India
Carlos Fernandez-Llatas, Spain
Pierluigi Frisco, UK
Shan He, UK
Jer Lang Hong, Malaysia
Tzung-Pei Hong, Taiwan, China
Wei-Chiang Hong, Taiwan, China
Mo Hongwei, China
Sriman Narayana Iyengar, India
Antonio J. Jara, Spain
Sunil Kumar Jha, India
Guoli Ji, China
Mohamed Rawidean Mohd Kassim,
  Malaysia
M. Ayoub Khan, India
Razib Hayat Khan, Norway
Joanna Kolodziej, Poland
Ashwani Kush, India
Shyam Lal, India
Kenli Li, China
Chun-Wei Lin, China
Wenjian Luo, China

Mario J. Pérez-Jiménez, Spain
  (Co-chair)
Vittorio Maniezzo, Italy
Francesco Marcelloni, Italy
Hasimah Mohamed, Malaysia
Chilukuri K. Mohan, USA
Abdulqader Mohsen, Malaysia
Holger Morgenstern, Germany
Andres Muñoz, Spain
G.R.S. Murthy, India
Akila Muthuramalingam, India
Atulya Nagar, UK
Asoke Nath, India
Linqiang Pan, China (Chair)
Mrutyunjaya Panda, India
Manjaree Pandit, India
Gheorghe Păun, Romania (Co-chair)
Andrei Păun, USA
Yoseba Penya, Spain
Ninan Sajeeth Philip, India
Hugo Proença, Portugal
Balwinder Raj, India
Balasubramanian Raman, India
Nur' Aini Abdul Rashid, Malaysia
Mehul Raval, India
Rawya Rizk, Egypt
Thamburaj Robinson, India
Samrat Sabat, India
S.M. Sameer, India
Rajesh Sanghvi, India
Aradhana Saxena, India
Sonia Schulenburg, UK
G. Shivaprasad, India
K.K. Shukla, India
Madhusudan Singh, South Korea
Pramod Kumar Singh, India
Ravindra Singh, India
Sanjeev Singh, India
Satvir Singh, India
Don Sofge, USA
Tao Song, China
Kumbakonam Govindarajan
  Subramanian, Malaysia

Ponnuthurai Suganthan, Singapore
S.R. Thangiah, USA
Nikolaos Thomaidis, India
D.G. Thomas, India
Ravi Sankar Vadali, India
Ibrahim Venkat, Malaysia

Sudhir Warier, India
Ram Yadav, USA
Umi Kalsom Yusof, Malaysia
Sotirios Ziavras, USA
Pan Zheng, Malaysia

Sponsors

National Natural Science Foundation of China
Huazhong University of Science and Technology
Zhengzhou University of Light Industry

Table of Contents

Worst-Case Execution Time Test Generation for Solutions of the Knapsack Problem Using a Genetic Algorithm

Maxim Buzdalov and Anatoly Shalyto

ITMO University
49 Kronverkskiy prosp.
Saint-Petersburg, Russia, 197101
mbuzdalov@gmail.com, shalyto@mail.ifmo.ru

Abstract. Worst-case execution time test generation can be hard if tested programs use complex heuristics. This is especially true in the case of the knapsack problem, which is often called "the easiest NP-complete problem". For randomly generated test data, the expected running time of some algorithms for this problem is linear. We present an approach for generation of tests against algorithms for the knapsack problem. This approach is based on genetic algorithms. It is evaluated on five algorithms, including one simple branch-and-bound algorithm, two algorithms by David Pisinger and their partial implementations. The results show that the presented approach performs statistically better than generation of random tests belonging to certain classes. Moreover, a class of tests that are especially hard for one of the algorithms was discovered by the genetic algorithm.

Keywords: knapsack problem, test generation, genetic algorithms, worst-case execution time.

1 Introduction

What is the input data which makes your program work too long? What is the maximum delay between an input event and an output action? These questions are related to the problem of determining the worst-case execution time of a program or a procedure.

It is impossible to write a program that determines the worst-case execution time of an arbitraty program, as follows from the Rice theorem [17]. However, one may hope to find an approximate answer. This makes it reasonable to apply search-based optimization techniques, such as genetic algorithms, to the problem of worst-case execution time test generation [3,4].

Many works on evolutionary worst-case execution time test generation consider the case of real-time software testing [2,10–12,18,19]. Another application where worst-case execution time matters is test generation for programming challenge tasks [7]. There are some papers on related topics of testing discrete mathematics algorithms [5,6] and SAT solvers [13].

L. Pan et al. (Eds.): BIC-TA 2014, CCIS 472, pp. 1–10, 2014.

In many papers on worst-case execution time test generation, the execution time is optimized directly. However, measurements of the execution time contain noise introduced by the operating system scheduling and the measured time is often proportional to a certain time quantity [7]. To overcome these difficulties, paper [7] advises to instrument the tested code with special counters. Each of these counters is associated with a loop or a procedure and incremented each time the loop is entered or the procedure is called. The values of these counters, as well as the execution time, serve as optimization objectives.

The *0-1 knapsack problem* (will be referred to as simply *knapsack problem* in the rest of the paper) is a well-known combinatorial optimization problem. N items are given, each characterized by weight w_i and profit p_i, and a knapsack with a weight capacity of W. One needs to find a subset of items of the maximum total profit that can be placed into the knapsack, i.e. to determine $x_i \in \{0, 1\}$ such that $\sum_{i=1}^{N} w_i x_i \leq W$ and $\sum_{i=1}^{N} p_i x_i$ is maximum possible.

The knapsack problem is weakly NP-hard [9], and is often called "the easiest NP-problem", because there exist algorithms that solve a large fraction of big instances in polynomial (even linear) time [15]. In [8], a way to construct hard test cases (in terms of the number of elementary operations) for a certain class of algorithms is given as follows:

$$p_j = w_j = 2^{K+N+1} + 2^{K+j} + 1,$$

where N is the number of items, $K = \lfloor \log 2N \rfloor$, $1 \leq j \leq N$.

In the test case construction scheme given above, weights and profits of items are exponential in the size of the problem. However, it may happen that in a particular setup weights and profits are bound by a constant, so such test cases are no longer valid.

We present an approach based on genetic algorithms to generate test cases against algorithms for the knapsack problem. The approach is compared with random test generation according to some known patterns [15] and it is shown that the evolutionary approach works statistically better. For one of the algorithms, the genetic algorithm discovered a new class of hard test cases.

The rest of the paper is structured as follows. In Section 2, the algorithms for the knapsack problem are described along with the fitness functions used to measure their performance. Section 3 outlines the ways to generate random test data for the knapsack problem, known from [15]. In Section 4, the genetic algorithm is described that is used to generate tests against the algorithms for the knapsack problem. Section 5 contains experimental results both for the genetic algorithm from Section 4 and for random tests from Section 3. Some analysis of the generated tests is included as well, which leads to a new class of knapsack problems that are hard for one of the algorithms. Section 6 concludes.

2   Algorithms for the Knapsack Problem

This section describes the algorithms for the knapsack problem that are tested in this paper. The first algorithm is a simple branch-and-bound algorithm, called SIM-PLEBRANCH in this paper. The second one is the algorithm EXPKNAP from [15].

The third one is the partial implementation of the EXPKNAP, that is, an implementation with several heuristics omitted, which makes it run slower than EXP-KNAP under certain circumstances. The fourth one is the algorithm HARDKNAP, also from [15]. The fifth one is the partial implementation of HARDKNAP.

Below, we describe the SIMPLEBRANCH algorithm, outline the algorithms EX-PKNAP and HARDKNAP and partial implementations of the two latter algorithms. Performance measures of all these algorithms, which are used as fitness functions, are also discussed.

2.1   Simple Branch-and-Bound Algorithm

We start with an algorithm which we call SIMPLEBRANCH. The ideas of the algorithm are very simple and mostly come from common sense:

- sort the items in decreasing order of their profit-per-weight ratio (as is commonly done [15]);
- store the best known solution in a dedicated variable (initially an empty solution);
- for each item, starting from the first one, first try to put it to the knapsack, second try to put it aside;
- return from the current branch if the current profit plus the profit of the yet-to-consider items is less than or equal to the profit of the best known solution;
- don't ignore an item if the maximum possible weight for the current state does not exceed the knapsack capacity.

The algorithm is implemented as a single recursive function and a small number of preparation utilities. The amount of work for a single call to this function is constant, however, the number of calls can be large. The performance measure used for this algorithm is the number of calls to this function.

2.2   ExpKnap

The EXPKNAP algorithm is described in detail in [15]. The name of the algorithm comes from the concept of *expanding core*. Consider all items in decreasing order of their profit-per-weight ratio. Let G be a solution to the knapsack problem constructed by taking items to the knapsack starting from the first one while the items can fit into the knapsack. The first item that does not fit is called the *break item*.

The algorithm EXPKNAP considers solutions to the knapsack problem encoded as differences from solution G (i.e. a set of elements that are present in G but not present in the solution, or vice versa). The idea of the algorithm comes from the fact that in most problem instances the elements that differ from solution G are concentrated in a small area around the break item. This area is called the *core* [15]. Enumerating all the possible solutions with a small fixed core size is cheap. However, guessing the correct core size is a difficult problem, and the EXPKNAP algorithm solves it by expanding the core when needed.

The partial implementation of the EXPKNAP algorithm, which is used in this paper along with the original EXPKNAP algorithm, uses a simple core expansion procedure, which just adds to the core the items that are adjacent to it. The original algorithm uses a more complicated procedure, which may change the order of elements to achieve better performance. It is thus expected to see the cases when the partial implementation performs worse than the original algorithm.

Implementations of EXPKNAP, similarly to SIMPLEBRANCH, contain a recursive procedure which performs almost all computations. In both partial and full implementations of EXPKNAP, the performance measure is the number of calls to this procedure.

2.3   HardKnap

The HARDKNAP algorithm is described in detail in [15]. This is an algorithm from the dynamic programming family. It solves the knapsack problem by solving subproblems of the following kind: enumerate all sets of items, which have indices from L to R, such that no set is dominated by any other set. Set A dominates set B if the profit of A is not smaller than the profit of B, while the weight of A is not larger than the weight of B. A subproblem $[L; R]$ can be solved by solving two subproblems $[L; M]$ and $[M + 1; R]$ and then merging the sets. For the top-level problem $[1; N]$, one does not need to find all the sets — it is enough to find a set with the larges profit and with a weight not exceeding the knapsack capacity, which can be done in linear time.

The original HARDKNAP algorithm constructs upper bounds on the possible solutions to the knapsack problem for each set and eliminates the sets for which this bound is too low, thus reducing the number of considered sets and decreasing the running time. The partial implementation of the HARDKNAP algorithm, which is considered in this paper along with the original one, does not do this kind of elimination. Effectively, this is an implementation of the Nemhauser and Ullmann algorithm [14].

The performance measure for both HARDKNAP implementations is the number of set merge events. Each time the upper bound construction and filtering, which is present in the original implementation but is missing in the partial implementation, makes the difference, the number of set merge events decreases, so we can compare both implementations by comparing their performance measures.

3   Tests for the Knapsack Problem

There are several strategies to generate tests for the knapsack problems. We consider three of them [15]:

- **Uncorrelated Tests.** In these tests, no dependency between weights and profits of items is specified. To generate random tests of this sort, one may set the weight w to a random integer between 1 and the maximum weight W_{max}, and set the profit p to a random integer between 1 and the maximum profit P_{max}.

- **Strongly Correlated Tests.** The difference between the profit and the weight of an item is equal to a small number d. To generate random tests of this sort, one may set the weight w to a random integer between $\max(1, 1-d)$ and $\min(W_{max}, P_{max} - d)$ and set the profit $p = w + d$.
- **Subset Sum Tests.** These are the tests where weights are equal to profits. Such instances of the knapsack problem are also the instances of the *subset sum* problem. To generate random tests of this sort, set the weight w to a random integer between 1 and $\min(W_{max}, P_{max})$ and set the profit $p = w$.

It should be noted that uncorrelated tests correspond to the general case, i.e. no constraints are put on tests. As in [15], we choose the capacity of the knapsack to be half the sum of weights of all items.

4 Genetic Algorithm

This section describes the encoding of a problem instance as an individual of the genetic algorithm, the evolutionary operators that are used, and some other settings of the genetic algorithm. The fitness functions to be used with different algorithms for the knapsack problem have been described in the corresponding subsections of Section 2.

We perform three series of experiments with the genetic algorithm, corresponding to three considered types of tests (Section 3). The new individual creation procedure and the mutation operator are different for each test type, all other operators and settings remain the same.

There are three parameters imposed by the knapsack problem: the number of items N, the maximum item weight W_{max} and the maximum item profit P_{max}. For the strongly correlated test type, the difference parameter d is also used. All these parameters are fixed during each run of an algorithm.

The **individual** is encoded as a list of items, where each item has a specified weight and profit. As said in Section 3, the capacity of the knapsack is chosen to be half the sum of weights.

The procedure of **new individual creation** creates a list of N items, where each item is generated at random as specified in Section 3 for the corresponding type of test.

The **mutation operator** works as follows. It selects a random item and mutates it according to the procedure described below. Then it terminates with the probability of 0.5, otherwise it repeats the process. Such operator is capable of making an arbitrarily large mutation, but prefers small mutations. The single item mutation procedure, depending on the test type, does the following:

- for uncorrelated tests — adds $d_w \sim \lfloor N(0, 1) \cdot W_{max}/3 \rfloor$ to the weight, $d_p \sim \lfloor N(0, 1) \cdot P_{max}/3 \rfloor$ to the profit, and then fits the weight to the $[1; W_{max}]$ interval and the profit to the $[1; P_{max}]$ interval.
- for strongly correlated tests — adds $d_w \sim \lfloor N(0, 1) \cdot \min(W_{max}, P_{max})/3 \rfloor$ to the weight w, fits it to the $[\max(1, 1-d); \min(W_{max}, P_{max} + d)]$ interval and sets the profit to $w + d$.

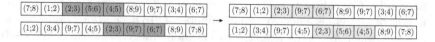

Fig. 1. Illustration of the two-point crossover with shift

- for subset sum tests — adds $d_w \sim \lfloor N(0,1) \cdot \min(W_{max}, P_{max})/3 \rfloor$ to the weight, fits it to the $[1; \min(W_{max}, P_{max})]$ interval and sets the profit equal to the weight.

The mutation operator is applied with a probability of 0.1.

The **crossover operator** is a two-point crossover with shift similar to the one proposed in [5]. This variant of crossover also performed well in [7] on a problem which is similar to the knapsack problem. This operator takes two individuals and returns also two individuals. It selects an exchange length L randomly from 1 to $N-1$. Then it selects offsets O_1 and O_2 for the first and second individuals randomly and independently from 1 to $N - L$. After that, the subsequences of length L at offset O_1 in the first individual and at offset O_2 in the second individual are exchanged (see Fig. 1). The crossover operator is applied with a probability of 1.0.

It is worth noting that, in the case of subset sum tests and strongly correlated tests both mutation and crossover operators always produce tests of the type that is equal to the type of the arguments. For example, a mutation test will produce a strongly correlated test if a strongly correlated test is given. This means that if the genetic algorithm is initialized with, for example, strongly correlated tests, the results will be strongly correlated as well. In the case of uncorrelated tests, that is, in the general case, tests can become structured spontaneously during the evolution.

The **reproduction selection** is a variant of tournament selection. For each individual to be selected, eight individuals are selected at random. Then the individuals are grouped in pairs, and in each pair a tournament is conducted — with a probability of 0.9, the individual with higher fitness wins. The process is repeated with the winning individuals until only one is left. We borrow this selection operator from [7]. The **survival selection** is the elitist selection with the elite rate of 20%.

5   Experiments

This section describes the experiment setup and results.

5.1   Setup

In our experiments we considered three types of tests described in Section 3. For each type and each algorithm for the knapsack problem, we compared the genetic algorithm with random test generation. To do that, we performed 100 runs of each algorithm, and the number of fitness evaluations was limited to 500 000. Thus, the computational budget was the same for random test generation and for the genetic algorithm. For each run, the best individual is considered to be the result.

The generation size in the genetic algorithm was set to 50. The knapsack problem parameters were $N = 20$, $W_{max} = P_{max} = 10000$, the difference for strongly correlated tests $d = 5$. We chose such a small problem size because we wanted even the weakest algorithms to terminate in reasonable time.

The source code is available on GitHub [1].

5.2 Results

The minima, maxima, averages and means of best fitness values are presented in Table 1 for all considered configurations. To measure statistical difference between results for different configurations, the Wilcoxon rank sum test implemented in the R system [16] is used with the alternative hypothesis set to "greater" when the mean of the results for the first configuration is greater than the mean for the second one, and to "less" otherwise. We reject the null hypothesis if the p-value is less than 0.001.

Randomly Generated Tests. First, it can be seen that random uncorrelated tests are very simple for all considered algorithms. Even for SIMPLEBRANCH the average fitness value for random uncorrelated tests is approximately 10 times smaller than for the hardest test found. On the other hand, random strongly correlated tests and random subset sum tests are rather hard. Note that for SIM-PLEBRANCH strongly correlated tests are noticeably (p-value less than $2.2 \cdot 10^{-16}$, as reported by R) harder than subset sum tests, while for other algorithms subset sum tests are harder (p-value less than $2.2 \cdot 10^{-16}$ for EXPKNAP, partial EXP-KNAP and partial HARDKNAP; p-value equal to $1.785 \cdot 10^{-14}$ for HARDKNAP).

Random Tests vs. Genetic Algorithm. For each algorithm for the knapsack problem and for each type of tests, we compared statistically the results for random test generation and for genetic algorithms. For all configurations except for two, the p-value was reported to be less than $2.2 \cdot 10^{-16}$. For HARDKNAP and strongly correlated tests, it was equal to $1.717 \cdot 10^{-15}$, and for partial HARDKNAP and subset sum tests, it was equal to 0.01209.

This means that the genetic algorithm consistently produces statistically better results than random test generation. It seems that the small difference for the last configuration can be explained by the fact that the hardest possible problem instances (fitness value 15 119) were generated with high probability.

Table 1. Experimental results

Optimizer	Individual	Min	Max	Median	Mean	Deviation
SimpleBranch						
best of random	uncorrelated	90882	211530	108851.0	112820.74	17516.91
	strongly correlated	773333	881402	804713.0	809474.83	23793.61
	subset sum	671104	784717	708195.5	714033.65	27280.72
genetic	uncorrelated	520685	1048576	1048576.0	984013.90	157357.85
	strongly correlated	1048576	1048613	1048576.0	1048584.09	8.77
	subset sum	1048576	1048604	1048576.0	1048580.81	6.92
ExpKnap						
best of random	uncorrelated	393	1269	539.0	583.51	165.13
	strongly correlated	62627	156475	76391.5	84656.27	21268.04
	subset sum	176555	447333	348194.5	337375.98	64381.87
genetic	uncorrelated	428298	688129	447746.0	496336.91	81824.28
	strongly correlated	428298	512278	429182.0	459105.40	32676.90
	subset sum	696321	699041	698881.0	698603.88	419.75
Partial implementation of ExpKnap						
best of random	uncorrelated	492	2223	683.0	724.38	199.72
	strongly correlated	63915	164171	80573.5	86059.53	21265.52
	subset sum	154812	445699	322171.0	312934.88	77359.58
genetic	uncorrelated	369226	688129	447746.0	487032.44	72677.54
	strongly correlated	428298	541348	485316.0	465577.64	32425.55
	subset sum	698369	699009	698881.0	698726.52	260.21
HardKnap						
best of random	uncorrelated	771	1252	941.0	963.03	104.89
	strongly correlated	13700	14401	13789.0	13811.16	103.32
	subset sum	13068	15113	15022.5	14645.37	756.27
genetic	uncorrelated	3686	11457	8075.5	7892.86	1885.56
	strongly correlated	13682	15113	14062.5	14205.19	449.63
	subset sum	15113	15113	15113.0	15113.00	0.00
Partial implementation of HardKnap						
best of random	uncorrelated	5660	6970	6230.5	6278.98	333.20
	strongly correlated	15054	15074	15054.0	15054.35	2.29
	subset sum	15114	15119	15119.0	15118.80	0.94
genetic	uncorrelated	9859	13790	12318.5	12219.61	699.25
	strongly correlated	15060	15114	15114.0	15113.46	5.37
	subset sum	15119	15119	15119.0	15119.00	0.00

Partial Implementations. We cannot compare algorithms from different families by performance, but we can compare algorithms with their partial implementations. In this section, unlike the others, we use the two-sided alternative hypothesis.

For EXPKNAP algorithms, statistic analysis reports surprising results — it is possible to distinguish the full and the partial implementations only at uncorrelated random tests (p-value is $1.83 \cdot 10^{-12}$). For subset sum tests, p-values are 0.02643 and 0.01595 for random tests and the genetic algorithm correspondingly.

For strongly correlated tests by the genetic algorithm it is 0.1346, and for other configurations it exceeds 0.5. It can be deduced that the difference between the implementations improves the average-case performance, but does not influence the worst case.

For HARDKNAP algorithms, however, full and partial versions are always distinguishable ($p < 2.2 \cdot 10^{-16}$).

Hard Test Analysis. We analyzed the hard test cases for EXPKNAP, because the genetic algorithm constructs tests that are much harder than random tests.

The hardest test for EXPKNAP with a fitness value of 699041 belongs to the group of subset sum tests. It consists of five items with weight and value of 1, three items of 34, one item of 83, two items of 265, one item of 335, two items of 614, one item of 1696, two items of 3842, one item of 5887, and two items of 10 000. Many other hard tests from the same group feature many items of 1 and of 10 000, but no particular structure is seen.

One of the hardest tests for EXPKNAP among the strongly correlated tests (fitness value 512278) has only two types of items: one item with weight 9596 and profit 9601 and 19 items with weight 3030 and profit 3035.

A small experiment was performed to test if the latter type of tests is hard enough. For each algorithm, ten runs were performed, each for 100 000 fitness evaluations. The best fitness for each algorithm was the same for all runs. For SIMPLEBRANCH it was 1048576, for EXPKNAP family — 541348, for HARD-KNAP — 799 and for partial HARDKNAP — 803. It appears that such tests are hard, but not the hardest, for SIMPLEBRANCH and the EXPKNAP family and easy for HARDKNAP.

6 Conclusion

We presented an approach to worst-case execution time test generation for algorithms solving the knapsack problem. This approach is based on genetic algorithms. Statistical analysis of the experimental results showed that the genetic algorithm consistently produces harder tests than random test generation.

A new class of tests for the knapsack problem was also found — tests with two types of items — that appeared to be very hard for the EXPKNAP algorithm family, but they are easy for another algorithm, HARDKNAP.

This work was partially financially supported by the Government of Russian Federation, Grant 074-U01.

References

1. Source code for experiments (a part of this paper),
   https://github.com/mbuzdalov/papers/tree/master/2014-bicta-knapsacks
2. Alander, J.T., Mantere, T., Moghadampour, G.: Testing Software Response Times Using a Genetic Algorithm. In: Proceedings of the 3rd Nordic Workshop on Genetic Algorithms and their Applications, pp. 293–298 (1997)

3. Alander, J.T., Mantere, T., Turunen, P.: Genetic Algorithm based Software Testing. In: Proceedings of the 3rd International Conference on Artificial Neural Networks and Genetic Algorithms, Norwich, UK, pp. 325–328 (April 1997)
4. Alander, J.T., Mantere, T., Turunen, P., Virolainen, J.: GA in Program Testing. In: Proceedings of the 2nd Nordic Workshop on Genetic Algorithms and their Applications, Vaasa, Finland, August 19-23, pp. 205–210 (1996)
5. Arkhipov, V., Buzdalov, M., Shalyto, A.: Worst-Case Execution Time Test Generation for Augmenting Path Maximum Flow Algorithms using Genetic Algorithms. In: Proceedings of the International Conference on Machine Learning and Applications, vol. 2, pp. 108–111. IEEE Computer Society (2013)
6. Buzdalov, M.: Generation of Tests for Programming Challenge Tasks on Graph Theory using Evolution Strategy. In: Proceedings of the International Conference on Machine Learning and Applications, vol. 2, pp. 62–65. IEEE Computer Society (2012)
7. Buzdalova, A., Buzdalov, M., Parfenov, V.: Generation of Tests for Programming Challenge Tasks Using Helper-Objectives. In: Ruhe, G., Zhang, Y. (eds.) SSBSE 2013. LNCS, vol. 8084, pp. 300–305. Springer, Heidelberg (2013)
8. Chvatal, V.: Hard Knapsack Problems. Operations Research 28(6), 1402–1411 (1980)
9. Garey, M.R., Johnson, D.S.: Computers and Intractability: A Guide to the Theory of NP-Completeness. W. H. Freeman & Co., New York (1979)
10. Gross, H.G.: A Prediction System for Evolutionary Testability Applied to Dynamic Execution Time Analysis. Information and Software Technology 43(14), 855–862 (2001)
11. Gross, H.G., Jones, B.F., Eyres, D.E.: Structural Performance Measure of Evolutionary Testing Applied to Worst-Case Timing of Real-Time Systems. IEEE Proceedings - Software 147(2), 25–30 (2000)
12. Gross, H.G., Mayer, N.: Search-based Execution-Time Verification in Object-Oriented and Component-Based Real-Time System Development. In: Proceedings of the 8th IEEE International Workshop on Object-Oriented Real-Time Dependable Systems, pp. 113–120 (2003)
13. Moreno-Scott, J.H., Ortíz-Bayliss, J.C., Terashima-Marín, H., Conant-Pablos, S.E.: Challenging Heuristics: Evolving Binary Constraint Satisfaction Problems. In: Proceedings of Genetic and Evolutionary Computation Conference, pp. 409–416. ACM (2012)
14. Nemhauser, G., Ullmann, Z.: Discrete dynamic programming and capital allocation. Management Science 15(9), 494–505 (1969)
15. Pisinger, D.: Algorithms for Knapsack Problems. Ph.D. thesis, University of Copenhagen (February 1995)
16. R Core Team: R: A Language and Environment for Statistical Computing. R Foundation for Statistical Computing, Vienna, Austria (2013), http://www.R-project.org/
17. Rice, H.G.: Classes of recursively enumerable sets and their decision problems. Transactions of the American Mathematical Society 74(2), 358–366 (1953)
18. Tlili, M., Wappler, S., Sthamer, H.: Improving Evolutionary Real-Time Testing. In: Proceedings of Genetic and Evolutionary Computation Conference, pp. 1917–1924. ACM (2006)
19. Wegener, J., Mueller, F.: A Comparison of Static Analysis and Evolutionary Testing for the Verification of Timing Constraints. Real-Time Systems 21(3), 241–268 (2001)

The Application of Spiking Neural P Systems for PLC Programming

Ke Chen, Jun Wang, Zhang Sun, Juan Luo, and Tao Liu

School of Electrical and Information Engineering,
Xihua University, Chengdu 610039, Sichuan, China
2511198132@qq.com

Abstract. In this paper, five basic logic relationships are built by spiking neural P systems (SN P systems, for short). A method that uses spiking neural P systems to build a PLC control system model is proposed and implemented through the PLC programming application of a typical water level control system. Example shows that PLC programming process has been simplified and readability of the program has been enhanced after the introduction of SN P systems. Therefore, the upgraded and maintenance of PLC program can be effectively improved.

Keywords: Membrane computing, Spiking Neural P Systems, PLC technology, Ladder Diagram.

1 Introduction

Membrane computing is a theoretical model that simulates the structure and function of the biological tissue. SN P systems belong to membrane computing. At present, many scholars have turned to the study of its applications (e.g., [9], [12], [13]). PLC technology has developed rapidly nowadays. PLC programming languages are varied. Scholars devote to the study of them (e.g., [10],[11]). Ladder diagram is the most widely used PLC programming languages currently. To simplify the programming process, domestic and foreign scholars attempts to develop a new design idea constantly (e.g., [1], [14]).

In this paper, five basic logic relationships are built by SN P systems. A method that uses SN P systems to build a PLC control system model is proposed for the first time. It is implemented through the PLC programming application of a typical water level control system. Example shows that PLC programming process can be simplified.

2 The Application of Spiking Neural P Systems for PLC Programming

2.1 Build Basic Logical Relationships by SN P Systems

Three types of neurons are defined as: status neurons, condition neurons and module neurons. The detailed analysis how the models of the basic logic relationships are built by SN P systems is show in Figure 1 as follow.

L. Pan et al. (Eds.): BIC-TA 2014, CCIS 472, pp. 11–15, 2014.

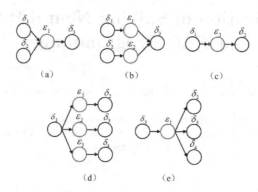

Fig. 1. Basic logical relationships built by SN P system. (a) "AND"; (b) "OR"; (c) "NOT"; (d) "Competition Control"; (e) "Concurrency Control".

2.2   An Application of SN P Systems on PLC Programming of a Typical Water Level Control System

2.2.1   The Theory of the Water Level Control System

An example to demonstrate the feasibility and reliability of the proposed method is introduced in this section. As shown in Fig. 2(a). PLC schematic is shown in Fig. 2(b).

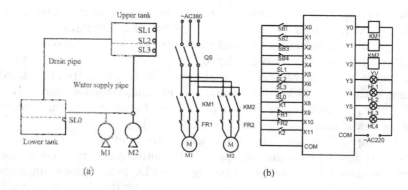

Fig. 2. The water level control system. (a) control system; (b) schematic.

2.2.2   SN P Systems Model

Status neurons (black) is represented by $\alpha_1 \sim \alpha_{23}$, condition neurons (blue) is represented by $\sigma_1 \sim \sigma_{20}$, and module neurons (red) is represented by $\beta_1 \sim \beta_3$. Then, we will use five basic logic relationships to built complex logical relationships for this water level control system.

The overall water level control system model built by SN P system is expressed in Fig. 3. It reflects the design philosophy of the whole system. It consists of three modules neurons. Fig. 4 expresses the internal structure of the module neuron β_1. It reflects the connection relationships in β_1. The input of β_1 is the system start signal, and the output of β_1 is neuron α_{11}. Similarly, according to this method, we can build a model of β_2 and β_3. Here we will not go into details. Finally, logic expressions are built by these SN P system models.

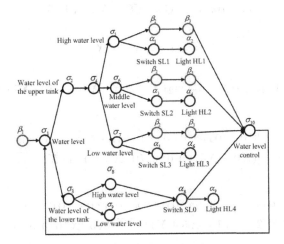

Fig. 3. Overall SN P system model

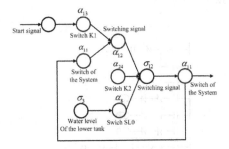

Fig. 4. The system model of module neuron β_1

2.2.3   Assign I/O Ports and Writing Logical Expressions

As stated previously, we have defined that status neurons express the current states of sensors, relays, contactors, switches and other devices. On this basis, the corresponding status neurons are assigned to the PLC I/O ports. The logic expressions of the water level control system can be written by the spiking neural system model and the allocation I/O ports. The following Eq. (1) ∼(7) is derived. Specific derived as follows:

$$\alpha_2 = \alpha_1 \cdot \overline{\alpha_3} \cdot \overline{\alpha_5} \Leftrightarrow Y3 = X4 \cdot \overline{X5} \cdot \overline{X6} \tag{1}$$

$$\alpha_4 = \alpha_3 \cdot \overline{\alpha_1} \cdot \overline{\alpha_5} \Leftrightarrow Y4 = X5 \cdot \overline{X4} \cdot \overline{X6} \tag{2}$$

$$\alpha_6 = \alpha_5 \cdot \overline{\alpha_1} \cdot \overline{\alpha_3} \Leftrightarrow Y5 = X6 \cdot \overline{X4} \cdot \overline{X5} \tag{3}$$

$$\alpha_9 = \alpha_8 \Leftrightarrow Y6 = X7 \tag{4}$$

$$\alpha_{15} = (\alpha_{11} + \alpha_{13}) \cdot \alpha_8 \cdot \alpha_{24} \Leftrightarrow M0 = (X8 + M0) \cdot X7 \cdot X11 \tag{5}$$

$$\alpha_{15} = [(\alpha_1 + \alpha_{10} + \alpha_{15}) \cdot \alpha_1 \cdot \alpha_{11} + \alpha_{19}] \cdot \alpha_{14} \cdot \alpha_{16} \Leftrightarrow$$
$$Y0 = [(X0 + X4 + Y0) \cdot M0 \cdot X4 + Y1] \cdot \overline{X2} \cdot \overline{X9} \tag{6}$$

$$\alpha_{19} = \alpha_{23} = \alpha_3 \cdot \alpha_{11} \cdot \alpha_{20} \cdot \alpha_{21} \cdot \alpha_{22} \cdot \alpha_{15} \cdot \alpha_{19} \Leftrightarrow$$
$$Y1/Y2 = (X1 + X5 + Y1) \cdot \overline{X3} \cdot X5 \cdot \overline{X10} \cdot Y0 \cdot M0 \tag{7}$$

2.2.4   Program the Ladder Diagram

According to equations (1)∼(7), Ladder Diagram of the water level control system is drawn and shown in Fig. 5.

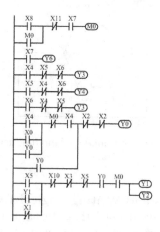

Fig. 5. The Ladder Diagram of the water level control system

3   Conclusion

In this paper, a typical water level control system as an example expresses how the SN P system model is built to achieve the PLC programming. It proves the idea that introduces spiking neural P systems into PLC programming is feasible. Experimental results show that the introduction of SN P systems simplifies the process of the PLC programming, increases the readability of the program and facilitates the upgrades and maintenance of the program.

Acknowledgments. This work was partially supported by the Research Fund of Sichuan Provincial Education Department(No. 12ZZ007), the National Natural Science Foundation of China (Grant No. 61170030), and Foundation for International Cooperation of Ministry of Science and Technology, China (No: SQ2011ZOF000004), and the Ministry of Education Chunhui Project of China (No. Z2012025).

References

1. Peng, S.S., Zhou, M.C.: Ladder Diagram And Petri-Net-Based Discrete-Event Control Design Methods. IEEE T. Syst. Man. Cy. C. Appl. Rev. 34(4), 523–531 (2004)
2. Wang, J., Peng, H.: Fuzzy Knowledge Representation Based on An Improving Spiking Neural P System. In: Proceedings of the 6th International Conference on Natural Computation (2010)
3. Peng, S.S., Zhou, M.C.: Petri Net based PLC Stage Programming for Discrete-event Control Design. In: Proceedings of the 2001 International Conference on IEEE International Conference on Systems, Man and Cybernetics, vol. 4, pp. 2706–2710 (2001)
4. Minas, M., Frey, G.: Visual PLC-Programming using Signal Interpreted Petri Nets. In: Proceedings of the 2002 American Control Conference, vol. 6, pp. 5019–5024 (2002)
5. Fagarăsan, I., Iliescu, S.S., Dumitru, I.: Process Simulator Using PLC Technology Series C: Electrical Engineering. UPB Scientific Bulletin 72, 17–26 (2010)
6. Song, T., Pan, L., Wang, J., Ibrahim, V., Subramanian, K.G., Rosni, A.: Normal Forms of Spiking Neural P Systems with Anti-Spikes. IEEE Trans. on Nanobioscience 11(4), 352–359 (2012)
7. Păun, G.: Introduction to Membrane Computing. In: Appl. Membr. Comput., pp. 1–42. Springer, Heidelberg (2006)
8. Syropoulos, A.: Fuzzifying P Systems. Comput. J. 49(5), 619–628 (2006)
9. Peng, H., Wang, J., Pérez-Jiménez, M.J.: Fuzzy Reasoning Spiking Neural P System for Fault Diagnosis. Inform. Sciences 235, 106–116 (2012)
10. Wang, D., Qian, C.Z., Ma, X.C.: OPC-based PLC Program Automated Testing. Comput. Syst. Appl. 28(10), 100–104 (2011)
11. Chen, X., Liu, Y.Z., Xu, E.S.: The Design and Implementation of Editing Software for Qt-Based Soft-Plc Ladder Diagram. Comput. Syst. Appl. 20(12), 64–69 (2012)
12. Song, T., Pan, L., Păun, G.: Asynchronous Spiking Neural P Systems with Local Synchronization. Information Sciences 219, 197–207 (2013)
13. Wang, J., Shi, P., Peng, H., et al.: Weighted Fuzzy Spiking Neural P Systems. IEEE T. Fuzzy Syst. 21(2), 209–220 (2013)
14. Lin, H.B., Jiao, Z.G.: PLC Ladder Design Method based on the Petri Nets with the Restraining Arc. Mech. Electr. Eng. Technol. 40(4), 73–75 (2011)

Criteria for Nonsingular $H-$Matrices

Qi Chen and Min Li*

School of Mathematics and Statistics, Beihua University, Jilin, 132013, China
bhulimin@163.com

Abstract. In order to achieve further investigation, new extended criteria of nonsingular $H-$matrix are introduced. In the recent paper, several simple criteria, as well as some necessary conditions for nonsingular $H-$matrix, have been obtained. Inspired by these results, we partition the row and column index set of square matrix, construct a positive diagonal matrix according to the elements and row sum, column sum of the matrix as well, then obtain a set of criteria for the nonsingular $H-$matrix, and extend the criteria of nonsingular $H-$matrix. Finally, a few numerical examples are given to illustrate relative merits of the proposed criteria.

Keywords: Diagonally dominant matrices, $\alpha-$diagonally Dominant Matrices, $H-$matrices.

1   Introduction

As is well known, $H-$matrices is a special class of matrices with wide applications in engineering, scientific computation, etc. (e.g., [1, 2]). But it is difficult to determine nonsingular $H-$matrices in practice. The problem is investigated in some papers, (see [3-10]). In this paper, we will present a set of practical criteria of $H-$matrices. The advantages of the criteria of nonsingular $H-$matrices are illustrated by two numerical examples.

It is well known that A is a nonsingular $H-$matrix if and only if A is a generalized strictly diagonally dominant matrix. In this paper, we always assume that all diagonal entries of A are nonzero. Let $N = \{1, 2, \cdots, n\}$ and $C^{n \times n}$ be the set of all n by n complex matrices. Let $A = (a_{ij}) \in C^{n \times n}$ and

$$R_i(A) = \sum_{j \in N \setminus \{i\}} |a_{ij}|, \ C_i(A) = \sum_{j \in N \setminus \{i\}} |a_{ji}|, \ \forall i, j \in N.$$

Definition 1. *Let $A = (a_{ij}) \in C^{n \times n}$. If $|a_{ii}| > R_i(A)$, $\forall i \in N$, then A is said strictly diagonally dominant matrix and denoted $A \in D$. If there exists a positive diagonal matrix X such that $AX \in D$, then A is said a generalized strictly diagonally dominant matrix (i.e., nonsingular $H-$ matrix) and denoted $A \in D^*$.*

---

* Corresponding author.

L. Pan et al. (Eds.): BIC-TA 2014, CCIS 472, pp. 16–23, 2014.
© Springer-Verlag Berlin Heidelberg 2014

Definition 2. Let $A = (a_{ij}) \in C^{n \times n}$. If $\exists \alpha \in [0, 1]$, such that $|a_{ii}| > \alpha R_i(A) + (1 - \alpha)C_i(A)$, $\forall i \in N$, then A is said strictly $\alpha-$diagonally dominant matrix and denoted $A \in D(\alpha)$. If there exists a positive diagonal matrix X such that $AX \in D(\alpha)$, then A is said a generalized strictly $\alpha-$diagonally dominant matrix and denoted $A \in D^*(\alpha)$.

Definition 3. Let $A = (a_{ij}) \in C^{n \times n}$ be irreducible. If $\exists \alpha \in [0, 1]$, such that $|a_{ii}| \geq \alpha R_i(A) + (1 - \alpha)C_i(A)$, $\forall i \in N$ and a strict inequality holds for at least one $i \in N$, then A is said an irreducibly $\alpha-$diagonally dominant matrix.

Definition 4. Let $A = (a_{ij}) \in C^{n \times n}$. If $\exists \alpha \in [0, 1]$, such that $|a_{ii}| \geq \alpha R_i(A) + (1 - \alpha)C_i(A)$, $\forall i \in N$, at least one strict inequality holds and for every i with $|a_{ii}| = \alpha R_i(A) + (1 - \alpha)C_i(A)$, there exists a nonzero elements chain $a_{ij_1} a_{j_1 j_2} \cdots a_{j_{k-1} j_k} \neq 0$ such that $|a_{j_k j_k}| > \alpha R_{j_k}(A) + (1 - \alpha)C_{j_k}(A)$. Then A is said an $\alpha-$diagonally dominant matrix with nonzero elements chain.

Lemma 1. from [5]. Let $A = (a_{ij}) \in C^{n \times n}$. Then A is a generalized strictly $\alpha-$diagonally dominant matrix if and only if A is a generalized strictly diagonally dominant matrix.

Lemma 2. from [6]. Let $A = (a_{ij}) \in C^{n \times n}$. If A is an irreducible $\alpha-$diagonally dominant matrix, or A is an $\alpha-$diagonally dominant matrix with nonzero elements chain, then A is a nonsingular $H-$matrix.

For $\alpha \in [0, 1]$, we define

$$N_1 = \{i \in N \mid 0 < |a_{ii}| = \alpha R_i(A) + (1 - \alpha)C_i(A)\},$$

$$N_2 = \{i \in N \mid 0 < |a_{ii}| < \alpha R_i(A) + (1 - \alpha)C_i(A)\},$$

$$N_3 = \{i \in N \mid |a_{ii}| > \alpha R_i(A) + (1 - \alpha)C_i(A) \geqslant 0\}.$$

If we have not specific explanation, we denote $R_i(A) = R_i$, $C_i(A) = C_i$, $i \in N$, and

$$M_i = \frac{\sum_{t \in N_1} |a_{it}| + \sum_{t \in N_2} |a_{it}| \dfrac{(\alpha R_t + (1 - \alpha)C_t) - |a_{tt}|}{\alpha R_t + (1 - \alpha)C_t}}{R_i - \sum_{t \in N_3 \setminus \{i\}} |a_{it}| \dfrac{\alpha R_t + (1 - \alpha)C_t}{|a_{tt}|}}, i \in N_3,$$

$$K_i = \frac{\alpha \left(\sum_{t \in N_2} |a_{it}| \dfrac{(\alpha R_t + (1 - \alpha)C_t) - |a_{tt}|}{\alpha R_t + (1 - \alpha)C_t} + \sum_{t \in N_3} |a_{it}| \dfrac{\alpha R_t + (1 - \alpha)C_t}{|a_{tt}|} \right)}{|a_{ii}| - \alpha \sum_{t \in N_1 \setminus \{i\}} |a_{it}| - (1 - \alpha)C_i}, i \in N_1.$$

If $|a_{ii}| = \alpha \sum_{t \in N_1 \setminus \{i\}} |a_{it}| + (1 - \alpha)C_i$, $i \in N_1$, then we take $K_i = 1$, $i \in N_1$.

Obviously $0 \leq M_i \leq 1$, $\forall i \in N_3$, and $0 < K_i \leq 1$, $\forall i \in N_1$.

2 Main Results

Theorem 1. *Let* $A = (a_{ij}) \in C^{n \times n}$. $I_1(A) = \{i \mid R_i = \sum\limits_{t \in N_1 \backslash \{i\}} |a_{it}|, i \in N_1\} = \emptyset$. *If* $\exists \alpha \in [0, 1]$ *and* $\forall i \in N_2$, *such that*

$$
\begin{aligned}
|a_{ii}| \geq &\frac{\alpha R_i + (1-\alpha)C_i}{(\alpha R_i + (1-\alpha)C_i) - |a_{ii}|} \cdot \alpha \Big(\sum_{t \in N_1} |a_{it}| + \sum_{t \in N_2 \backslash \{i\}} |a_{it}| \frac{(\alpha R_t + (1-\alpha)C_t) - |a_{tt}|}{\alpha R_t + (1-\alpha)C_t} \\
&+ (\max_{i \in N_3} M_i) \sum_{t \in N_3} |a_{it}| \frac{\alpha R_t + (1-\alpha)C_t}{|a_{tt}|} \Big) + (1-\alpha)C_i.
\end{aligned}
\tag{1}
$$

Denote $T_1(A) = \{i \mid i \in N_2$ *and make the equality of* (1) *holds*$\} \bigcup I_1(A)$. *If A satisfies one of the following conditions: (i)* $T_1(A) = \emptyset$;
(ii) A is an irreducible matrix and $N_2 \backslash T_1(A) \neq \emptyset$;
(iii) $\forall i \in T_1(A) \bigcup N_3$, *there exists a nonzero elements chain* $a_{ii_1} a_{i_1 i_2} \cdots a_{i_k, j}$, *such that* $j \in (N_1 \bigcup N_2) \backslash T_1(A) \neq \emptyset$.
A is a nonsingular H−matrix.

Proof. For $\forall i \in N_2$, denote

$$
m_i = \frac{(|a_{ii}| - (1-\alpha)C_i)\frac{(\alpha R_i + (1-\alpha)C_i) - |a_{ii}|}{\alpha(\alpha R_i + (1-\alpha)C_i)} - \sum\limits_{t \in N_2 \backslash \{i\}} |a_{it}| \frac{(\alpha R_t + (1-\alpha)C_t) - |a_{tt}|}{\alpha R_t + (1-\alpha)C_t}}{\sum\limits_{t \in N_3} |a_{it}| \frac{\alpha R_t + (1-\alpha)C_t}{|a_{tt}|}}
$$
$$
- \frac{\sum\limits_{t \in N_1} |a_{it}|}{\sum\limits_{t \in N_3} |a_{it}| \frac{\alpha R_t + (1-\alpha)C_t}{|a_{tt}|}}.
$$

If $\sum\limits_{t \in N_3} |a_{it}| = 0$, denote $m_i = +\infty$. From (1), then there exists a nonnegative constant q, such that

$$
\min_{i \in N_2} m_i \geq q \geq \max_{i \in N_3} M_i.
\tag{2}
$$

Construct a positive diagonal matrix $X = diag\{d_1, \cdots, d_n\}$, where

$$
d_i = \begin{cases}
1, & i \in N_1; \\
\frac{(\alpha R_i + (1-\alpha)C_i) - |a_{ii}|}{\alpha R_i + (1-\alpha)C_i}, & i \in N_2; \\
q \frac{\alpha R_i + (1-\alpha)C_i}{|a_{ii}|}, & i \in N_3.
\end{cases}
$$

Let $B = AX = (b_{ij}) \in C^{n \times n}$.
(i) If $T_1(A) = \emptyset$, from (2), $\min\limits_{i \in N_2} m_i > \max\limits_{i \in N_3} M_i$. We can take the constant q that satisfies

$$
\max_{i \in N_3} M_i < q < \min\{\min_{i \in N_3} \frac{|a_{ii}|}{\alpha R_i + (1-\alpha)C_i}, \min_{i \in N_2} m_i\}.
\tag{3}
$$

For $\forall i \in N_1$, if $\sum\limits_{t \in N_3} |a_{it}| = 0$, then

$$\alpha R_i(B) + (1 - \alpha)C_i(B)$$
$$= \alpha\Big(\sum_{t \in N_1 \backslash \{i\}} |a_{it}| + \sum_{t \in N_2} |a_{it}| \frac{(\alpha R_t + (1-\alpha)C_t) - |a_{tt}|}{\alpha R_t + (1-\alpha)C_t} + q \sum_{t \in N_3} |a_{it}| \frac{\alpha R_t + (1-\alpha)C_t}{|a_{tt}|} \Big)$$
$$+ (1 - \alpha)C_i$$
$$= \alpha\Big(\sum_{t \in N_1 \backslash \{i\}} |a_{it}| + \sum_{t \in N_2} |a_{it}| \frac{(\alpha R_t + (1-\alpha)C_t) - |a_{tt}|}{\alpha R_t + (1-\alpha)C_t} \Big) + (1 - \alpha)C_i$$
$$< \alpha\Big(\sum_{t \in N_1 \backslash \{i\}} |a_{it}| + \sum_{t \in N_2} |a_{it}| \Big) + (1 - \alpha)C_i$$
$$= \alpha R_i + (1 - \alpha)C_i = |a_{ii}| = |b_{ii}|.$$

If $\sum\limits_{t \in N_3} |a_{it}| \neq 0$, from the second inequality of (3), we have $\frac{\alpha R_t + (1-\alpha)C_t}{|a_{tt}|} q < 1$, $\forall t \in N_3$. Then

$$\alpha R_i(B) + (1 - \alpha)C_i(B)$$
$$= \alpha\Big(\sum_{t \in N_1 \backslash \{i\}} |a_{it}| + \sum_{t \in N_2} |a_{it}| \frac{(\alpha R_t + (1-\alpha)C_t) - |a_{tt}|}{\alpha R_t + (1-\alpha)C_t} + q \sum_{t \in N_3} |a_{it}| \frac{\alpha R_t + (1-\alpha)C_t}{|a_{tt}|} \Big)$$
$$+ (1 - \alpha)C_i$$
$$< \alpha\Big(\sum_{t \in N_1 \backslash \{i\}} |a_{it}| + \sum_{t \in N_2} |a_{it}| + \sum_{t \in N_3} |a_{it}| \Big) + (1 - \alpha)C_i$$
$$= \alpha R_i + (1 - \alpha)C_i = |a_{ii}| = |b_{ii}|.$$

For $\forall i \in N_2$, from the second inequality of (3), we know $q < m_i$, $\forall i \in N_2$. That implies

$$q \sum_{t \in N_3} |a_{it}| \frac{\alpha R_t + (1-\alpha)C_t}{|a_{tt}|}$$
$$< (|a_{ii}| - (1-\alpha)C_i) \frac{(\alpha R_i + (1-\alpha)C_i) - |a_{ii}|}{\alpha(\alpha R_i + (1-\alpha)C_i)} - \sum_{t \in N_2 \backslash \{i\}} |a_{it}| \frac{(\alpha R_t + (1-\alpha)C_t) - |a_{tt}|}{\alpha R_t + (1-\alpha)C_t}$$
$$- \sum_{t \in N_1} |a_{it}|.$$

Then $\forall i \in N_2$,

$$\alpha R_i(B) + (1 - \alpha)C_i(B)$$
$$= \alpha\Big(\sum_{t \in N_1} |a_{it}| + \sum_{t \in N_2 \backslash \{i\}} |a_{it}| \frac{(\alpha R_t + (1-\alpha)C_t) - |a_{tt}|}{\alpha R_t + (1-\alpha)C_t} + q \sum_{t \in N_3} |a_{it}| \frac{\alpha R_t + (1-\alpha)C_t}{|a_{tt}|} \Big)$$
$$+ \frac{(\alpha R_i + (1-\alpha)C_i) - |a_{ii}|}{\alpha R_i + (1-\alpha)C_i}(1 - \alpha)C_i$$
$$< \alpha\Big(\sum_{t \in N_1} |a_{it}| + \sum_{t \in N_2 \backslash \{i\}} |a_{it}| \frac{(\alpha R_t + (1-\alpha)C_t) - |a_{tt}|}{\alpha R_t + (1-\alpha)C_t} \Big)$$
$$+ (|a_{ii}| - (1-\alpha)C_i) \frac{(\alpha R_i + (1-\alpha)C_i) - |a_{ii}|}{\alpha(\alpha R_i + (1-\alpha)C_i)} - \sum_{t \in N_1} |a_{it}|$$
$$- \sum_{t \in N_2 \backslash \{i\}} |a_{it}| \frac{(\alpha R_t + (1-\alpha)C_t) - |a_{tt}|}{\alpha R_t + (1-\alpha)C_t}) + \frac{(\alpha R_i + (1-\alpha)C_i) - |a_{ii}|}{\alpha R_i + (1-\alpha)C_i}(1 - \alpha)C_i$$
$$= \frac{(\alpha R_i + (1-\alpha)C_i) - |a_{ii}|}{\alpha R_i + (1-\alpha)C_i} |a_{ii}| = |b_{ii}|.$$

From the first inequality of (3), i.e., $q > \max\limits_{i \in N_3} M_i$. This implies $\forall i \in N_3$,

$$q \sum_{t \in N_3 \backslash \{i\}} |a_{it}| \frac{\alpha R_t + (1-\alpha)C_t}{|a_{tt}|} < qR_i - \sum_{t \in N_1} |a_{it}| - \sum_{t \in N_2} |a_{it}| \frac{(\alpha R_t + (1-\alpha)C_t) - |a_{tt}|}{\alpha R_t + (1-\alpha)C_t}.$$

Then $\forall i \in N_3$,

$$
\begin{aligned}
&\alpha R_i(B) + (1-\alpha)C_i(B) \\
&= \alpha\Big(\sum_{t\in N_1} |a_{it}| + \sum_{t\in N_2} |a_{it}| \frac{(\alpha R_t+(1-\alpha)C_t)-|a_{tt}|}{\alpha R_t+(1-\alpha)C_t} + q \sum_{t\in N_3\setminus\{i\}} |a_{it}| \frac{\alpha R_t+(1-\alpha)C_t}{|a_{tt}|} \Big) \\
&\quad + q\frac{\alpha R_i+(1-\alpha)C_i}{|a_{ii}|}(1-\alpha)C_i \\
&< \alpha\Big(qR_i - \sum_{t\in N_1} |a_{it}| - \sum_{t\in N_2} |a_{it}| \frac{(\alpha R_t+(1-\alpha)C_t)-|a_{tt}|}{\alpha R_t+(1-\alpha)C_t} + \sum_{t\in N_1} |a_{it}| \\
&\quad + \sum_{t\in N_2} |a_{it}| \frac{(\alpha R_t+(1-\alpha)C_t)-|a_{tt}|}{\alpha R_t+(1-\alpha)C_t} \Big) + q\frac{\alpha R_i+(1-\alpha)C_i}{|a_{ii}|}(1-\alpha)C_i \\
&= \alpha qR_i + q\frac{\alpha R_i+(1-\alpha)C_i}{|a_{ii}|}(1-\alpha)C_i \\
&< \alpha qR_i + q(1-\alpha)C_i \\
&= q\frac{\alpha R_i+(1-\alpha)C_i}{|a_{ii}|}|a_{ii}| = |b_{ii}|.
\end{aligned}
$$

Therefore B is a strictly α−diagonally dominant matrix, according to the Lemma 1, then B is a nonsingular H−matrix. So A is a nonsingular H−matrix.

(ii) By the irreducibility of A, we have $0 < M_i < 1$, $\forall i \in N_3$. From (1), we can take the constant q, such that $q < \min\limits_{i\in N_3} \frac{|a_{ii}|}{\alpha R_i+(1-\alpha)C_i}$ and

$$
0 < \max_{i\in N_3} M_i \le q \le \min_{i\in N_2} m_i. \tag{4}
$$

For $\forall i \in N_1$,

$$
\begin{aligned}
&\alpha R_i(B) + (1-\alpha)C_i(B) \\
&= \alpha\Big(\sum_{t\in N_1\setminus\{i\}} |a_{it}| + \sum_{t\in N_2} |a_{it}| \frac{(\alpha R_t+(1-\alpha)C_t)-|a_{tt}|}{\alpha R_t+(1-\alpha)C_t} + q \sum_{t\in N_3} |a_{it}| \frac{\alpha R_t+(1-\alpha)C_t}{|a_{tt}|} \Big) \\
&\quad + (1-\alpha)C_i \\
&< \alpha\Big(\sum_{t\in N_1\setminus\{i\}} |a_{it}| + \sum_{t\in N_2} |a_{it}| + \sum_{t\in N_3} |a_{it}| \Big) + (1-\alpha)C_i \\
&= \alpha R_i + (1-\alpha)C_i = |a_{ii}| = |b_{ii}|.
\end{aligned} \tag{5}
$$

For $\forall i \in N_2$, from the third inequality of (4), we have

$$
\begin{aligned}
&\alpha R_i(B) + (1-\alpha)C_i(B) \\
&= \alpha\Big(\sum_{t\in N_1} |a_{it}| + \sum_{t\in N_2\setminus\{i\}} |a_{it}| \frac{(\alpha R_t+(1-\alpha)C_t)-|a_{tt}|}{\alpha R_t+(1-\alpha)C_t} + q \sum_{t\in N_3} |a_{it}| \frac{\alpha R_t+(1-\alpha)C_t}{|a_{tt}|} \Big) \\
&\quad + \frac{(\alpha R_i+(1-\alpha)C_i)-|a_{ii}|}{\alpha R_i+(1-\alpha)C_i}(1-\alpha)C_i \\
&\le \alpha\Big(\sum_{t\in N_1} |a_{it}| + \sum_{t\in N_2\setminus\{i\}} |a_{it}| \frac{(\alpha R_t+(1-\alpha)C_t)-|a_{tt}|}{\alpha R_t+(1-\alpha)C_t} \\
&\quad + m_i \sum_{t\in N_3} |a_{it}| \frac{\alpha R_t+(1-\alpha)C_t}{|a_{tt}|} \Big) + \frac{(\alpha R_i+(1-\alpha)C_i)-|a_{ii}|}{\alpha R_i+(1-\alpha)C_i}(1-\alpha)C_i \\
&= \frac{(\alpha R_i+(1-\alpha)C_i)-|a_{ii}|}{\alpha R_i+(1-\alpha)C_i}|a_{ii}| = |b_{ii}|.
\end{aligned} \tag{6}
$$

Because of $N_2 \setminus T_1(A) \ne \emptyset$, we know at least one inequality of (1) holds. Therefore according to the above inequality, there exists $r \in N_2$, such that $|b_{rr}| > \alpha R_r(B) + (1-\alpha)C_r(B)$.

For $\forall i \in N_3$, from the second inequality of (4), we have

$$
\begin{aligned}
&\alpha R_i(B) + (1-\alpha)C_i(B) \\
&= \alpha \Big(\sum_{t\in N_1} |a_{it}| + \sum_{t\in N_2} |a_{it}| \frac{(\alpha R_t+(1-\alpha)C_t)-|a_{tt}|}{\alpha R_t+(1-\alpha)C_t} + q \sum_{t\in N_3\backslash\{i\}} |a_{it}| \frac{\alpha R_t+(1-\alpha)C_t}{|a_{tt}|} \Big) \\
&\quad + q\frac{\alpha R_i+(1-\alpha)C_i}{|a_{ii}|}(1-\alpha)C_i \\
&\leq \alpha \Big(\sum_{t\in N_1} |a_{it}| + \sum_{t\in N_2} |a_{it}| \frac{(\alpha R_t+(1-\alpha)C_t)-|a_{tt}|}{\alpha R_t+(1-\alpha)C_t} + qR_i - \sum_{t\in N_1} |a_{it}| \\
&\quad - \sum_{t\in N_2} |a_{it}| \frac{(\alpha R_t+(1-\alpha)C_t)-|a_{tt}|}{\alpha R_t+(1-\alpha)C_t} \Big) + q\frac{\alpha R_i+(1-\alpha)C_i}{|a_{ii}|}(1-\alpha)C_i \\
&= \alpha qR_i + q\frac{\alpha R_i+(1-\alpha)C_i}{|a_{ii}|}(1-\alpha)C_i < q(\alpha R_i + (1-\alpha)C_i) \\
&= q\frac{\alpha R_i+(1-\alpha)C_i}{|a_{ii}|}|a_{ii}| = |b_{ii}|.
\end{aligned}
\tag{7}
$$

Notice AX can not change the irreducibility of A, therefore B is a irreducible $\alpha-$diagonally dominant matrix. According to the Lemma 2, we obtain that B is a nonsingular $H-$matrix, so A is a nonsingular $H-$matrix.

(iii) Based on the condition of (iii), we know $\sum_{t\in N_1 \bigcup N_2} |a_{it}| > 0$. Furthermore, according to the definition of M_i, we have $0 < M_i \leq 1, \forall i \in N_3$. So we can take a nonnegative constant q, such that $q < \min_{i\in N_3} \frac{|a_{ii}|}{\alpha R_i+(1-\alpha)C_i}$ and $0 < \max_{i\in N_3} M_i \leq q \leq \min_{i\in N_2} m_i$. Similar to the above proof, let $B = AX = (b_{ij}) \in C^{n\times n}$, we have $|b_{ii}| \geq \alpha R_i(B) + (1-\alpha)C_i(B)$, $\forall i \in N$. Notice $(N_1 \bigcup N_2) \backslash T_1(A) \neq \emptyset$, if $N_1 \backslash I_1(A) \neq \emptyset$, from (5) we know $|b_{rr}| > \alpha R_r(B) + (1-\alpha)C_r(B)$, $\forall r \in N_1 \backslash I_1(A)$. If $N_2 \backslash I_1(A) \neq \emptyset$, from (6) we know $|b_{rr}| > \alpha R_r(B)+(1-\alpha)C_r(B)$, $\forall r \in N_2 \backslash I_1(A)$. In a word, B is an $\alpha-$diagonal dominant matrix with nonzero elements chain. Based on the Lemma 2, we obtain that B is a nonsingular $H-$matrix, so A is a nonsingular $H-$matrix.

Similar to the proof of Theorem 1, we can obtain following theorem:

Theorem 2. *Let $A = (a_{ij}) \in C^{n\times n}$. $I_1(A) = \{i \mid R_i = \sum_{t\in N_1\backslash\{i\}} |a_{it}|, i \in N_1\} = \emptyset$, $\exists \alpha \in [0,1]$ and $\forall i \in N_2$, such that*

$$
\begin{aligned}
|a_{ii}| \geq \ & \frac{\alpha R_i+(1-\alpha)C_i}{(\alpha R_i+(1-\alpha)C_i)-|a_{ii}|} \cdot \alpha \Big(\sum_{t\in N_2\backslash\{i\}} |a_{it}| \frac{(\alpha R_t+(1-\alpha)C_t)-|a_{tt}|}{\alpha R_t+(1-\alpha)C_t} \\
& + \sum_{t\in N_3} |a_{it}| \frac{\alpha R_t+(1-\alpha)C_t}{|a_{tt}|} + (\max_{i\in N_1} K_i) \sum_{t\in N_1} |a_{it}| \Big) + (1-\alpha)C_i.
\end{aligned}
\tag{8}
$$

Denote $T_2(A) = \{i \mid i \in N_2$ and make the equality of (8) holds$\}$. If A satisfies one of the following conditions:
(i) $T_2(A) = \emptyset$;
(ii) A is an irreducible matrix and $N_2 \setminus T_2(A) \neq \emptyset$;
(iii) $\forall i \in T_2(A) \bigcup N_1$, there exists a nonzero elements chain $a_{ii_1} a_{i_1 i_2} \cdots a_{i_k,j}$, such that $j \in (N_2 \bigcup N_3) \setminus T_2(A) \neq \emptyset$.
Then A is a nonsingular $H-$matrix.

3 Examples

Example 1. Let

$$A = \begin{pmatrix} 1.5 & 1 & 0 & 1 & 0 \\ 1 & 2.5 & 1.5 & 5.5 & 0 \\ 0 & 1 & 3 & 2 & 0 \\ 0 & 0 & 0.5 & 120 & 3.5 \\ 0 & 0.5 & 0 & 4 & 8 \end{pmatrix}.$$

Taking $\alpha = \frac{1}{2}$, then we have $R_1 = 2, R_2 = 8, R_3 = 3, R_4 = 4, R_5 = 4.5, C_1 = 1,$ $C_2 = 2.5, C_3 = 2, C_4 = 12.5, C_5 = 3.5,$ and

$$N_1 = \{1\}, N_2 = \{2\}, N_3 = \{3,4,5\}, \max_{i \in N_3} M_i = \max\{0.1830, 0, 0.0620\} = 0.1830.$$

$$\begin{aligned} |a_{22}| &= 2.5 \\ &> \frac{\alpha R_2 + (1-\alpha)C_2}{(\alpha R_2 + (1-\alpha)C_2) - |a_{22}|} \cdot \alpha(|a_{21}| + (\max_{i \in N_3} M_i)(|a_{23}| \frac{\alpha R_3 + (1-\alpha)C_3}{|a_{33}|} \\ &\quad + |a_{24}| \frac{\alpha R_4 + (1-\alpha)C_4}{|a_{44}|} + |a_{25}| \frac{\alpha R_5 + (1-\alpha)C_5}{|a_{55}|})) + (1-\alpha)C_2 \qquad (9) \\ &= \frac{5.25}{5.25 - 2.5} \times \frac{1}{2}(1 + 0.1830(1.5 \times \frac{2.5}{3} + 5.5 \times \frac{8.25}{120} + 0 \times \frac{4}{8})) + \frac{1}{2} \times 2.5 \\ &\approx 2.4889. \end{aligned}$$

We know that A satisfies the conditions of the Theorem 1, so A is a nonsingular $H-$matrix.

But $|a_{22}| = 2.5 < 2.6111 = \frac{R_2}{R_2 - |a_{22}|}(|a_{23}| + |a_{21}| \frac{R_1 - |a_{11}|}{R_1} + (\max_{i \in N_3} M_i)(|a_{24}| \frac{R_4}{|a_{44}|}$ $+ |a_{25}| \frac{R_5}{|a_{55}|}))$, so A does not satisfy the corresponding conditions of the Theorem 1 in [10].

Example 2. Let

$$A = \begin{pmatrix} 1.5 & 1 & 1 & 0 & 0 \\ 1 & 2.5 & 0 & 0.5 & 4.5 \\ 0 & 1 & 10 & 0 & 10 \\ 0 & 0 & 2 & 12 & 2 \\ 0 & 0.5 & 0 & 4 & 160 \end{pmatrix}.$$

Taking $\alpha = \frac{1}{2}$, then we have $R_1 = 2, R_2 = 6, R_3 = 11, R_4 = 4, R_5 = 4.5, C_1 = 1,$ $C_2 = 2.5, C_3 = 3, C_4 = 4.5, C_5 = 16.5,$ and

$$N_1 = \{1\}, N_2 = \{2\}, N_3 = \{3,4,5\}, \max_{i \in N_1} K_i = \max\{0.5559\} = 0.5559.$$

Since

$$\begin{aligned} |a_{22}| &= 2.5 \\ &> \frac{\alpha R_2 + (1-\alpha)C_2}{(\alpha R_2 + (1-\alpha)C_2) - |a_{22}|} \cdot \alpha(|a_{23}| \frac{\alpha R_3 + (1-\alpha)C_3}{|a_{33}|} + |a_{24}| \frac{\alpha R_4 + (1-\alpha)C_4}{|a_{44}|} \\ &\quad + |a_{25}| \frac{\alpha R_5 + (1-\alpha)C_5}{|a_{55}|} + (\max_{i \in N_1} K_i)|a_{21}|) + (1-\alpha)C_2 \\ &= \frac{4.25}{4.25 - 2.5} \times \frac{1}{2}(0 \times \frac{7}{10} + 0.5 \times \frac{4.25}{12} + 4.5 \times \frac{10.5}{160} + 0.5559 \times 1) + \frac{1}{2} \times 2.5 \\ &\approx 2.4986. \end{aligned}$$

We know that A satisfies the conditions of the Theorem 2, so A is a nonsingular $H-$matrix. But A does not satisfy the corresponding conditions of the Theorem 2 in [10].

Acknowledgement. This work was supported by the National Science Foundation of China (Project No. 11171103) and the Scientific Research Fund of Jilin Provincial Education Department of China (Project No. 2012-152). Corresponding author: Min Li, Department of Mathematics, Beihua University, Jilin, 132013, China.

References

1. Berman, A., Plemmons, R.J.: Nonnegative matrices in the mathematical sciences. SIAM Press, Philadelphia (1994)
2. Varga, R.S.: On recurring theorems on diagonal dominance. Linear Algebra Appl., pp. 1–9 (1976)
3. Wang, J., Xu, Z., Lu, Q.: A set of new criteria conditions for generalized strictly diagonally dominany matrices. Mathematica Numerica Sinica 33, 225–232 (2011)
4. Jiang, R.: New criteria for nonsingular H−matrix. Chinese Journal of Engineering Mathematics 28, 393–400 (2011)
5. Sun, Y.X.: An improvment on a theorem by Ostrowski and its applications. Northeastern Mathematical Journal 7, 497–502 (1991)
6. Sun, Y.X.: Sufficient conditions for generalized diagonally dominant matrices. Numerical Mathematics a Journal of Chinese Universities 19, 216–223 (1997)
7. Fang, X.F., Huang, T.Z.: α−Connective diagonally dominant matrices and M−matrices. Chinese Journal of Engineering Mathematics 22, 123–127 (2005)
8. Li, M., Li, Q.C.: New criteria for nonsingular H−matrices. Chinese Journal of Engineering Mathematics 29, 715–719 (2012)
9. Chen, Q., Li, M.: Criteria for nonsingular H−matrices. Computer Science and Electronics Engineering 2, 582–585 (2013)
10. Huang, R., Liu, J.Z.: New practical determinate conditions for nonsingular H−matrices. Applied Mathematics a Journal of Chinese Universities 22, 111–119 (2007)

Molecular Dynamic Simulation for Heat Capacity of $MgSiO_3$ Perovskite

Qiong Chen

College of Electrical Engineering, Northwest University for Nationalities,
Lanzhou 730124, Gansu, China
531428908@qq.com

Abstract. The interaction potential plays an important role in molecular dynamics (MD) simulations of $MgSiO_3$ perovskite. A new set of potential parameters is developed by means of combining two fitting potential parameters of previous studies. The constant-pressure heating capacity of $MgSiO_3$ are simulated by using the new set of potential parameters. It is shown that the heating capacity of $MgSiO_3$ perovskite are close to the experimental data.

Keywords: Interaction potential parameter, Molecular dynamics, Heat capacity.

1 Introduction

The most common mineral in the Earths lower mantle is $MgSiO_3$ with the perovskite structure. An understanding of its thermodynamic properties is important to describe the Earths evolution. Therefore the physical properties of $MgSiO_3$ perovskite under extreme pressure and temperature conditions have attracted the attention of geophysicists [1–3].

The thermodynamic properties of $MgSiO_3$ perovskite has not yet been well understood. The experimental data on material properties at high pressures is still limited, especially under the conditions of both high temperature and high pressure. Computer modeling is particularly useful and powerful for problems that may be inaccessible to direct experiment study, such as extremes in temperature and pressure prevailing deep in the Earth.

The previous studies in [4, 5] have chosen the same pair-potential model, but with different potential parameters. In this work, a new set of potential parameters is developed by means of combining two fitting potential parameters of [4] and [5]. The new set of parameters is employed to calculate the equations of state, the constant-pressure heating capacity and the constant-pressure thermal expansivity which have not been calculated in studies [4, 5]. The results are compared with experimental data.

L. Pan et al. (Eds.): BIC-TA 2014, CCIS 472, pp. 24–28, 2014.
© Springer-Verlag Berlin Heidelberg 2014

2 Method

2.1 Simulation Technique

MD simulation is a well-established technique to determine the properties of materials. This method has been applied extensively in previous works [6–8]. Normally, as is often the case in MD calculation, periodic boundary conditions (PBC) are applied. The electrostatic interactions are evaluated both in real and reciprocal space according to the Ewalds method.

The present calculations are performed with the shell-dynamo code. Simulations in NTP (constant N is the number of particles, T is the temperature, and P is the pressure) ensemble in [9] are applied. Simulation runs are carried out with 360 particules (72 Mg, 72 Si, 216 O atoms). The results of molecular dynamics simulations in the NTP ensemble with chosen model of the interatomic interaction depend on, apart from the initial arrangement of particles, the size of the time step (Δt), the number of particles (N), and the temperature of windows (T_{win}). The influence of these parameters was studied by carrying out test runs at various temperatures and pressures. The correct results could be obtained with Δt=0.001ps, T_{win}=23K. Usually, the system was re-equilibrated at the required temperature and pressure for 3 ps and then temperature, pressure and volume were measured over a further 6 ps. Typically, the actual temperature differed from the required temperature by less than 1K, the actual pressure differed from the required pressure by less than 1MPa, and the discrepancy in the volume was less than 0.002cm^3/mol.

The constant-pressure heat capacity C_p and thermal expansivity α_P are calculated from the following definitions.

$$C_p = (\frac{\partial H}{\partial T})_p \tag{1}$$

Here, H and T are enthalpy, temperature, respectively.

2.2 Interaction Potential

In this study, the interaction potential is pair potential, and has the following form:

$$U(r_{ij}) = \frac{Z_i Z_j e^2}{r_{ij}} + A_{ij} exp(-\frac{r_{ij}}{\rho_{ij}}) - \frac{C_{ij}}{r_{ij}^6} \tag{2}$$

where the first part is the long-range Coulomb term and the rest are the short-range terms in the form of a Buckingham potential in [10]. The Buckingham potential is a rather traditional model that has been performed sufficiently well in [11–13] and, therefore is widely used for modeling of various oxides. The advantages and shortcomings of this kind of model are known from [14]. Here Z_i or Z_j is an effective charge, e is the electronic unit charge, r_{ij} is the interatomic distance between atoms i and j, A_{ij} and ρ_{ij} are the parameters for the repulsive interaction, and C_{ij} is the van der Waals constant.

3   Results and Discussion

3.1   Derivation of the New of Potential Parameters

In the crystal structure of $MgSiO_3$ perovskite, there are two distinct oxygen sites at octahedral corners. Silicons lie in the octahedral centers. Each Si atom is octahedrally coordinated by O atoms. Magnesiums are isolated, compare to silicons and oxygens. The octahedral structure is rather stable. Consequently, the Si-O and O-O interaction may be more important for the properties of $MgSiO_3$ perovskite than the Mg-O interaction. To further investigate the influence of potential parameters on the MD simulation, the authors design a new set of potential parameters. In the new set of potential parameters, the Si-O and O-O potential parameters, shell charges and spring constants are kept at the values used in the study in [5], the Mg-O potential parameters are taken from the study in [4]. The method that transforming the potential parameters of one system into another similar system is available in the other literatures. For example, in the study in [15], the potential parameters representing short-range interactions between Al^{3+} and O^{2-} in Al_2O_3 were used in the MD stimulation of $MgAl_2O_4$.

As shown in [16], the technique generated a set of potential parameters for $ZnAl_2O_4$ and $ZnGa_2O_4$: The Oxygen-Oxygen short range potential were taken from the work of Bush et al. in [17]; Zn-O potential were fitted to the hexagonal polymorph of ZnO (wurtzite); and the Al-O and Ga-O potential parameters were determined by fitting to $-Al_2O_3/ZnAl_2O_4$ and $Ga_2O_3/ZnGa_2O_4$ respectively. Consequently, the potential parameters used in the present study are derived using this technique, the parameters are: $A_{Mg-O} = 1041.435ev$; $\rho_{Mg-O} = 0.2673\text{Å}$; $A_{Si-O} = 7363.45ev$; $\rho_{Si-O} = 0.1900\text{Å}$; $A_{O-O} = 1621.68ev$; $\rho_{O-O} = 0.3000\text{Å}$; $C_{O-O} = 1621.68ev\text{Å}^6$; $Z_{Mg} = +1.565$; $Z_{Si} = +2.329$; $Z_o = -1.298$.

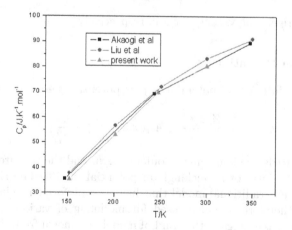

Fig. 1. Heat capacity MgSiO3 perovskite. The closed squares are from the present study. The closed triangles are experimental data of Akaogi et al.[18]. The closed circles are from the study of Ref.[4].

3.2 Heat Capacity of $MgSiO_3$ Perovskite

Fig.1 shows that the specific heat capacity at ambient pressure calculated from the present study is closer to the experimental data [18] than the study of Ref.[5]. The importance of thermal expansivity to the Earths mantle is well recognized, but it has not been calculated in previous studies [4, 5].

4 Summary

In this paper, A new set of potential parameters based on adopting fitting empirical potential parameters is used to simulate the thermodynamic properties of $MgSiO_3$ perovskite. The resulting constant-pressure heating capacity is close to the experimental data. The validity of the new set of potential parameters has been confirmed.

Acknowledgment. This work was supported by the Fundamental Research Funds for the Central Universities (No.31920130014).

References

1. Oganov, A.R., Brodholt, J.P., Price, G.D.: Ab Initio Elasticity and Thermal Equation of State of MgSiO3 Perovskite. Earth Planet. Sci. Lett. 184, 555–560 (2001)
2. Fiquet, G., Dewaele, A., Andrault, D., Kunz, M.: Thermoelastic Properties and Crystal Structure of MgSiO3 Perovskite at Lower Mantle Pressure and Temperature Conditions. Geophys. Res. Lett. 27, 21–24 (2000)
3. Shim, S.H., Duffy, T.S., Shen, G.Y.: Stability and Structure of MgSiO3 Perovskite to 2300-Kilometer Depth in Earth's Mantle. Science 293, 2437–2440 (2001)
4. Liu, Z.J., Cheng, X.L., Yang, X.D., Zhang, H., Cai, L.C.: Molecular Dynamics of MgSiO3 Perovskite Melting. Chin. Phys. 15, 224–228 (2006)
5. Liu, Z.J., Sun, X.W., Yang, X.D., Cheng, X.L., Guo, Y.D.: Simulation of Melting Behavior of The MgSiO3 Perovskite under Lower Mantle Conditions. Chin. J. Chem. Phys. 19, 311–314 (2006)
6. Gu, T.K., Qi, Y.H., Qin, Y.J.: Molecular Dynamics Simulations of Solidification of Liquid NiAl. Chin. J. Chem. Phys. 16, 385–389 (2003)
7. Liu, Z.J., Cheng, X.L., Chen, X.R., Zhang, F.P.: Molecular Dynamics Simulations for Melting Temperatures of CaF2. Chin. J. Chem. Phys. 18, 193–196 (2005)
8. Liu, Z.J., Cheng, X.L., Zhang, F.P.: Simulated Equations of State of MgSiO3 Perovskite. Chin. J. Chem. Phys. 19, 65–68 (2006)
9. Hoover, W.G.: Canonical Dynamics: Equilibrium phase-space distributions. Phys. Rev. A. 31, 1695–1697 (1985)
10. Catlow, C.R.A.: Mott–Littleton Calculations in Solid-State Chemistry and Physics. J. Chem. Soc. Faraday Trans. 85(2), 335–340 (1989)
11. Belonoshko, A.B.: Molecular Dynamics of MgSiO3 Perovskite at High Pressures: Equation of state, Structure, and Melting Transition. Geochim. Cosmochim. Atca. 58, 4039–4047 (1994)
12. Belonoshko, A.B., Dubrovinski, L.S.: Molecular Dynamics of NaCl (B1 and B2) and MgO (B1) Melting; Two-Phase Simulation. Am. Mineral. 81, 303–316 (1996)

13. Kuklju, M.M.: Defects in Yttrium Aluminium Perovskite and Garnet Crystals: Atomistic Study. J. Phys.: Condens. Matter 12, 2953–2967 (2000)
14. Kramer, G.J., Farragher, N.P., van Beest, B.W.H.: Interatomic Force Fields for Silicas, Aluminophosphates, and Zeolites: Derivation based Onab Initio Calculations. Phys. Rev. B. 43, 5068–5080 (1991)
15. Lewis, G.V., Catlow, C.R.A.: Potential Model for Ionic Oxides. J. Phys. C: Solid State Phys. 18, 1149–1161 (1985)
16. Pandey, R., Gale, J.D., Sampth, S.K., Recio, J.M.: Atomistic Simulation Study of Spinel Oxides: Zinc Aluminate and Zinc Gallate. J. Am. Ceram. Soc. 82, 3337–3341 (1999)
17. Bush, T.S., Gale, J.D., Catlow, C.R.A., Battle, P.D.: Self-Consistent Interatomic Potentials for The Simulation of Binary and Ternary Oxides. J. Mater. Chem. 4, 831–837 (1994)
18. Akaogi, M., Ito, E.: Heat Capacity of MgSiO3 Perovskite. Geophys. Res. Lett. 20, 105–108 (1993)

Molecular Model for Information Addressing and Transporting Based on DNA Nanotechnology

Zhihua Chen[1], Xiaoli Qiang[2,*], and Kai Zhang[3]

[1] Key Laboratory of Image Information Processing and Intelligent Control,
School of Automation, Huazhong University of Science and Technology,
Wuhan 430074, Hubei, P.R. China
[2] College of Computer Science, South-Central University for Nationalities,
Wuhan 430074, Hubei, P.R. China
[3] School of Computer Science,
Wuhan University of Science and Technology,
Wuhan 430081, Hubei, P.R. China
chenzhihua@hust.edu.cn, qiangxl@mail.scuec.edu.cn,
zhangkai@wust.edu.cn

Abstract. DNA-based information processing includes storage, addressing, transporting and error-correction, etc. Here we describe a feasible model that can extract and transport the information from specified sources to targeted destinations. This model is established based on the DNA nanotechnologies of hybridization, DNA strand displacement and nanoparticle aggregation reactions. By adding the extracting strands, the data strands of specified sources can be extracted, and then transported to the targets by the transporting strands. The result could be detected by observing the change of color through the naked eyes. Theoretical analysis indicates that this model could achieve the parallel information extracting and transporting from different specified sources to different targeted destination, which offers a realistic technology for the flexibility of managing information.

Keywords: DNA strand displacement, Nanoparticle aggregation, Information addressing.

1 Introduction

DNA molecule has been used as a computing substrate, since it is used to solve a seven-city Hamilton path problem in 1994[1]. Because of its advantages of stability and specificity, DNA molecules have been used for the construction of nano-scale structures[2, 3], logic gates[4], information storage[5], and even nano-machines[6] through the programmed hybridization of complementary strands. With the development of DNA molecule self-assembly strategy, lots

---

* Corresponding author.

L. Pan et al. (Eds.): BIC-TA 2014, CCIS 472, pp. 29–34, 2014.

of programmable DNA tiles and DNA devices, including circuits, catalytic amplifiers, autonomous molecular motors and reconfigurable nanostructures, were constructed, and DNA nanotechnology is becoming increasingly attractive for engineering applications[4, 7–10]. The new methods and experimental results have greatly inspired us to design a model to implement the information addressing and retrieval in DNA nanotechnology.

Addressing and retrieval plays an important part in communication and storage, which implement the targeted information retrieval and transportation. Addressing is the key technology to locate, store and retrieve the specific data in computer science. In this work, we design a model to complete information addressing and targeted transporting by DNA strand displacement and nanoparticles[11, 12].In the model, the specified DNA data can be retrieved by specified source strand displacement, and the obtained DNA data can also be transported to specified destination by specified destination strand hybridization.

2   DNA-Based Information Addressing Model

In this section, we will discuss three technology used for information addressing first, and then, explain our information addressing model based on several DNA molecules. Here, DNA is represented as directional lines, and the different domains as reaction units are in different colors and denoted by different lowercase letters. The same color lines represent the complementary domain and different color lines mean the single strands which are not complementary (e.g. the yellow line c and the green line d shown in Fig. 1). An apostrophe is used as a superscript to distinguish the complementary single strand (e.g. the blue line a is complementary to the blue line a.)

2.1   The Technology Used in This Model

Hybridization, the process of joining two complementary strands of DNA, is an routine technology and has already been used in many DNA computing models. Here, hybridization reaction is used to control the process of addressing.

DNA Strand Displacement, an important technique that allowed the construction of the dynamic assemblies, has already been used to construct a variety of DNA devices, including logic gates, catalysts, and motors[13]. In a DNA strand displacement system, a substrate complex (two strands hybridized with partial complementary regions) should be constructed at first, and then a special single strand DNA molecules will be mixed with the substrate complex and initiates the strand displacement reaction. Just as shown in Fig. 1, after adding strand C to substrate complex S, the domain c of strand C will react with toe-hold regions (a short single-stranded overhang region) of strand A (unhybridized regions). In order to minimize system free energy, the strand C will gradually occupy the binding site of strand A, and displace strand B at the same time. By highly specific recognition, this process can be triggered in parallel and in multiple levels.

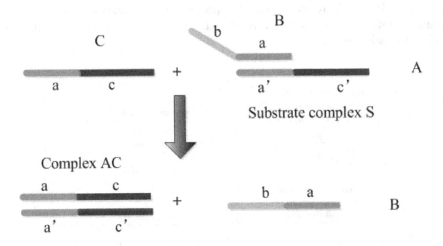

Fig. 1. The principle of strand displacement reaction

DNA/AuNP conjugates (DNA fractionalized gold nanoparticles) have shown great potential and exciting opportunities for DNA computing and disease diagnostics and treatment[14]. Here, we use the DNA/AuNP conjugates as detection DNA molecules because of the optical properties of the aggregation of DNA/AuNP conjugates. For AuNP (quantum size, nanosurface), as the distance between nanoparticles changes, the absorption of the whole system will change accordingly.

2.2   The Information Addressing Model

The model, proposed here, is divided into three layers according to the information transporting state: source layer, destination layer and addressing layer, as shown in Figure 2A. The source layer is used to store messages, with their respective unique addresses encoded by DNA strand. The destination layer is used to accept the data strands from addressing layer, and the structure is similar as the source layer. The transporting layer consists of free data strands. There are two interfaces to communicate with source layer and destination layer respectively. The input interface can extract the data strands from the specified source, while the output interface can transport the data strands to the specified destination. Messages can be managed with a clear hierarchy in this model. The Figure 2B shows the implementations in DNA molecules. The source layer and destination layer may be constructed by molecule complex, such as DNA tile sticken to magnetic beads, nanoparticle or DNA chip, etc.

In this model two steps are consisted : DNA information extracting and addressing. By given data extracting strands with specified source address, the data strands are released via DNA strand displacement. After the data strands are freed fully, the transporting strands with specified source and destination address are put in. By DNA hybridization, the specified data strands are bound to the targeted destination by the given transporting strands with specified destination and source address.

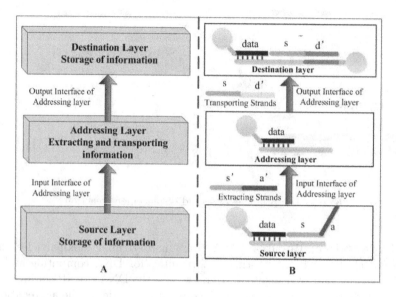

Fig. 2. The diagram of DNA-based information addressing model (A) and the corresponding DNA molecules for different layers (B)

3   The Process of Information Addressing

Once the input DNA molecules trigger the DNA strand displacement reaction, the information addressing starts. The steps of the addressing are as follows.

Step 1. Input the the strand sa and release the data strand stored at source s.

Step 2. Collect all released data strands and transport them to the transporting layer where the data strand will be caught by transmitter strand and transported to the destination layer.

Step 3. Observing the destinations state. If the color is changed, we can estimate that the data stored at source s is transported to the right destination. If not, no data arrives.

As a result, the messages stored at source s can be transported to the proper destination d. By using the method, we can use several tubes, labeled by D_1, D_2, D_3, $\cdots$ as different destination. If the color of D_i tube is changed, we can estimate that the information is transported to destination D_i.

4   Discussion and Conclusion

In this paper, a DNA-based addressing and transporting model was constructed using strand displacement and hybridization. There are three layers in the model: source layer, addressing layer and destination layer. The addressing layer, which is the middle layer, manages the data through two interfaces: extracting strand (input interface) and transporting strand (output interface). By the input interface and output interface, two functions are achieved in the proposed model. DNA information extracting can be carried out based on strand displacement and targeted information transporting based on strand hybridization.

The model proposed may give a way to communicate between different DNA devices, which can promote the development of large-scale logic circuits or complex nanorobot in DNA nanotechnology.

Acknowledgments. The authors thank the financial support for the work from Chinese National Natural Science Foundation (61370105, 61379059, 61272071, 61100055), the Fundamental Research Funds for the Central Universities (HUST-2013TS124, CZZ13003), and Natural Science Foundation of Hubei Province (Grant No. 2013CFB159).

References

1. Adleman, L.M.: Molecular computation of solutions to combinatorial problems. Science 266, 1021–1024 (1994)
2. Ke, Y., Ong, L.L., Shih, W.M., et al.: Three-Dimensional Structures Self-Assembled from DNA Bricks. Science 6111(338), 1177–1183 (2012)
3. Han, D., Pal, S., Nangreave, J., et al.: DNA Origami with Complex Curvatures in Three-dimensional Space. Science 6027(332), 342–346 (2011)
4. Qian, L., Winfree, E.: Scaling up Digital Circuit Computation with DNA Strand Displacement Cascades. Science 6034(332), 1196–1201 (2011)
5. Goldman, N., Bertone, P., Chen, S., et al.: Towards Practical, High-capacity, Low-maintenance Information Storage in Synthesized DNA. Nature, doi:10.1038/nature11875
6. Douglas, S.M., Bachelet, I., Church, G.M.: A Logic-Gated Nanorobot for Targeted Transport of Molecular Payloads. Science 6070(335), 831–834 (2012)
7. Lee, I.H., Yang, K.A., Lee, J.H., et al.: The use of gold nanoparticle aggregation for DNA computing and logic-based biomolecular detection. Nanotechnology 19(39), 395103 (2008)
8. Liu, Q.H., Wang, L.M., Frutos, A.G., et al.: DNA Computing on surfaces. Nature 403, 175 (2000)
9. Elbaz, J., Lioubashevski, O., Wang, F., et al.: DNA computing circuits using libraries of DNAzyme subunits. Nature Nanotechnology 5(6), 417–422 (2010)
10. Shi, X., Lu, W., Wang, Z., et al.: Programmable DNA tile self-assembly using a hierarchical subtile strategy. Nanotechnology 25(7), 75602 (2014)
11. Motornov, M., Zhou, J., Pita, M., et al.: "Chemical transformers" from nanoparticle ensembles operated with logic. Nano Letters 8(9), 2993–2997 (2008)

12. Liu, D., Chen, W., Sun, K., et al.: Resettable, Multi Readout Logic Gates Based on Controllably Reversible Aggregation of Gold Nanoparticles. Angewandte Chemie International Edition 50(18), 4103–4107 (2011)
13. Zhang, D.Y., Winfree, E.: Control of DNA strand displacement kinetics using toehold exchange. Journal of the American Chemical Society 131(47), 17303–17314 (2009)
14. Zhang, C., Yang, J., Xu, J.: Molecular logic computing model based on self-assembly of DNA nanoparticles. Chinese Sci. Bull. 56(27), 2276–2282 (2011)

Real-Coded Genetic Algorithm with Oriented Search towards Promising Region for Parameter Optimization

Zhiqiang Chen*, Yun Jiang, and Xudong Chen

School of Computer Science and Information Engineering,
Chongqing Technology and Business University, 19, Xuefu Avenue,
Nan'an, Chongqing, 400067, China
wilber_chen@hotmail.com

Abstract. In this paper, a novel real-coded genetic algorithm is presented to generate offspring towards a promising polygon field with $k+1$ vertexes, which represents a set of promising points in the entire population at a particular generation. A set of 13 test problems available in the global parameter optimization literature is used to test the performance of the proposed real-coded genetic algorithms. Simulations show the proposed approach is a significant evolutionary computing to efficiently solve parameter optimization problems.

Keywords: Genetic Algorithm, Real-coded, Oriented Search, Parameter Optimization.

1 Introduction

Most of the population-based search algorithms try to balance between two contradictory aspects of their performance: exploration and exploitation. The first one means the ability of the algorithm to "explore" or search every region of the feasible search space, while the second denotes the ability to converge to the near-optimal solutions as quickly as possible [1,2]. Practical experience, however, shows that existing RCGAs still may occasionally stop proceeding toward the global optimum even though the population has not converged to a local optimum or any other point. In fact, it is impossible there is a general tractable algorithm that could efficiently and effectively solve all possible complexities of real-life optimization problems [2], which motivates researchers to develop better algorithms that yield better approximate solutions. In the context, we develop a new real-coded genetic algorithm to attempt to make a balanced use of the exploration and exploitation abilities of the search mechanism and to be therefore more likely to avoid false or premature convergence in many cases. In the proposed algorithm, a promising polygon field with $k+1$ vertexes is defined, which represents a set of promising points in the entire population at a particular generation, and offspring is generated towards the centroid of the polygon

---

* Corresponding author.

L. Pan et al. (Eds.): BIC-TA 2014, CCIS 472, pp. 35–39, 2014.

field. We call the proposed RCGA as real-coded genetic algorithm with oriented search towards promising region (OSGA). In this paper, a set of 13 test problems available in the global optimization literature including unimodal, multimodal, parameter dependency, and ill-scale parameter optimization problems are used to evaluate the performance of OSGA.

2   Real-Coded Genetic Algorithm with Oriented Search towards Promising Region

In the proposed real-coded genetic algorithm, a new recombination operator is designed as follows:

$$\boldsymbol{X}_c = \boldsymbol{X}_p + \mathcal{W}(\boldsymbol{X}_g - \boldsymbol{X}_p) + \xi|\boldsymbol{X}_p - \boldsymbol{X}_r|$$
$$\mathcal{W} = diag(\omega_1^t, \omega_2^t, ..., \omega_n^t) \tag{1}$$
$$\omega_i^t \sim u(0, t)$$

$$\xi = \begin{cases} -b\log_e(r) & if \ \ r \leq 0.5 \\ b\log_e(r) & if \ \ r > 0.5 \end{cases} \tag{2}$$

$$\boldsymbol{X}_g = \frac{\sum\limits_{i=1}^{k} \boldsymbol{X}_{B,i} + \boldsymbol{X}_O}{k+1} \tag{3}$$

$$f(x) = \frac{1}{2b}\exp(-\frac{|x|}{b}), \tag{4}$$

where $\boldsymbol{X}_p$ and $\boldsymbol{X}_c$ represents parent and offspring, respectively; $\boldsymbol{X}_{B,i}$ is i^{th} best promising point; $\boldsymbol{X}_O$ is the champion found on the fitness landscape through iterations; $\boldsymbol{X}_r$ is an individual selected randomly from the mating pool P_M; t is a parameter defined by user which decides the movement towards the promising search direction $\boldsymbol{X}_g - \boldsymbol{X}_p$; ξ is a random generated number using Laplace(0, b) distribution with probability density function Eq.(4); k express k promising points from the mating pool P_M.

In Equation (1), the first and second items decide the exploring direction; the third item strengthens the exploiting ability of the algorithm following the direction. The $\boldsymbol{X}_{B,i}$ in Eq.(3) are obtained using following subprocedure:

SubStep 1. Create mating pool $P_M = \{\boldsymbol{X}_{M,1}, ..., \boldsymbol{X}_{M,N_m}\}$ as follows:
    For i to N_m
        Generate cluster C_i with C_s individuals selected randomly from the current population P_G;
        Assign the champion of cluster C_i to $\boldsymbol{X}_{M,i}$.
    End

SubStep 2. Sort the mating pool P_M: k best individuals in the mating pool P_M are as $\boldsymbol{X}_{B,i}(i = 1, 2, ..., k)$, respectively.

In order to further strengthen the exploring ability of the algorithm and increase the potential diversity of the population, we define a mutation behavior as follows: a solution is randomly selected from the population P_G and is mutated by given probability in each iteration. In this paper, we use MPTM (Makinen, periaux and toivanen mutation) mutation operator defined by Makinen et al. [3]. The detail of the proposed scheme is intertwined in the following manner:

Step 1. Set the generation number $G = 0$ and randomly initialize a population (P_G) of N_P individuals, and each individual uniformly distributed in the range $[\boldsymbol{X}_{Min}, \boldsymbol{X}_{Max}]$.

Step 2. Create mating pool $P_M = \{\boldsymbol{X}_{M,1}, ..., \boldsymbol{X}_{M,N_m}\}$ and obtain Promising Points Set $\boldsymbol{X}_{B,i}(i = 1, 2, ..., k)$.

Step 3. Calculate the centroid $\boldsymbol{X}_g$ of the polygon formed by the promising points using Eq. (3).

Step 4. Select randomly N_C individuals $(\boldsymbol{X}_{p,1}, ..., \boldsymbol{X}_{p,N_c})$ from the mating pool P_M and generate N_C offspring $X_C = \{\boldsymbol{X}_{c,1}, ..., \boldsymbol{X}_{c,N_C}\}$ using Eq. (1).

Step 5. Evaluate X_C.

Step 6. Replace randomly an individual of the population P_G using the best offspring $\boldsymbol{X}_{best}$ in the X_C in the fitness landscape.

Step 7. Mutate an individual selected randomly from the population P_G using MPTM mutation operator by probability r_M.

Step 8. $G = G + 1$, repeat Step 2~Step 7 until the stopping criterion is not satisfied.

3 Simulations

We used a test-bed of 9 traditional benchmark functions including unimodal, multimodal, parameter dependency, and ill-scale parameter optimization problems. The 13 traditional benchmarks have been reported in the Appendix, where D represents the number of dimensions $D=25$ to 100. They apparently belong to the difficult class of problems for many optimization algorithms.

In this section, we perform a serial of experiments to evaluate the performance of the proposed approach. The study focuses on three important aspects of OSGA: 1) The speed of convergence measured in terms of the number of FEs required by an algorithm to reach a predefined threshold value of the objective function; 2) the frequency of hitting the optima (or success rate) measured in terms of the number of runs of an algorithm that converge to a threshold value within a predetermined number of FEs; 3) the issue of scalability, i.e., how the performance of an algorithm changes with the growth of the search-space dimensionality. The dimension of the variable in the entire problems is fixed to 30, 50 and 100, respectively. The number of FEs required by OSGA to reach two predefined thresholds (10^{-7} and 10^{-21}) are reported for all the problems with different dimensionality. A lower number of FEs corresponds to a faster algorithm. 25 independent runs are carried out for every problem. It is considered

Table 1. Number of FEs Achieving the Fixed Accuracy Level Using OSGA

Func.	D	N_P	Threshold value=10^{-7}			Threshold value=10^{-20}		
			Least no. of FEs	Most no. of FEs	Mean no. of FEs	Least no. of FEs	Most no. of FEs	Mean no. of FEs
f_1	30	300	14100	18414	15930.88	31658	35934	33821.92
	100	300	74798	117690	85161.20	166282	196968	180516.96
f_2	30	1500	95870	238682	157541.68	248524	573778	358490.40
	100	2000	1151432	2191700	1594944.64	-	-	-
f_3	30	600	21584	42354	27405.84	56644	83610	64310.48
	100	1500	307474	414642	358309.04	669412	764318	712000.40
f_4	30	1500	306260	428714	358330.72	697338	876414	805848.48
	50	1500	845512	1042796	903468.08	3501782	4559988	3998598.64
f_5	30	500	26174	45170	29816.32	-	-	-
	100	500	146430	212110	183115.52	-	-	-
f_6	30	1200	35704	43056	37843.12	65480	79980	68213.44
	100	1500	151066	1791544	288506.24	250666	785878	303656.48
f_7	30	900	84150	177304	123383.68	89918	205892	132924.64
	100	900	357528	724248	494553.84	494403	857538	625887.00
f_8	30	900	24568	27414	26194.40	42934	49088	46047.28
	100	900	98584	132908	112053.20	176982	943206	290975.36
f_9	30	1500	167164	180278	173016.48	374636	384600	379528.80
	50	2000	442260	716374	480956.64	954182	1904664	1054012.96

to be successful if a run achieves to reach the predefined threshold. A run is terminated before reaching the max number of function evaluations if the error value $f(x) - f(x^*)$ is less than the given accuracy, where x^* is the global optimal solution. These experimental results are reported in Table 1.

As shown in Table 1, the proposed OSGA is enable to solve efficiently the function optimization with ill-scale, strong dependence among variables or multi-model. The proposed approach almost achieves the accuracy level 10^{-7} for all the tested problems except f_4 and f_{13} of D=100, 10^{-20} for all the tested problems except f_2 and f_5. Performance of most of the evolutionary algorithms deteriorates with the growth of the dimensionality of the search space. Increase of dimensions implies a rapid growth of the hypervolume of the search space and this in turn slows down the convergence speed of most of the global optimizers. Table 1 shows the proposed approach can efficiently solve all the problem of D=100 except f_4 and f_{13}.

4   Conclusions

The empirical study showed the proposed OSGA is an efficiently scheme for solving parameter optimization problem. This, however, does not lead us to claim that the OSGA may outperform their contestants over every possible objective function since it is impossible to model all possible complexities of real-life optimization problems with the limited test-suite that we used for testing the algorithms.

Acknowledgments. This work was supported by Natural Science Foundation Project of CQ CSTC (No.cstc2012jjA40041, No. cstc2012jjA40059). Science Research Fund of Chongqing Technology and Business University (No. 2011-56-05, No. 2013-56-01)

References

1. Qin, A.K., Huang, V.L., Suganthan, P.N.: Differential evolution algorithm with strategy adaptation for global numerical optimization. IEEE Transactions on Evolutionary Computations 13(2), 298–417 (2009)
2. Das, S., Abraham, A.: Differential evolution using a neighborhood-based mutation operator. IEEE Transactions on Evolutionary Computation 13(3), 522–553 (2009)
3. Makinen, R.A.E., Periaux, J., Toivanen, J.: Multidisciplinary shape optimization in aerodynamics and electromagnetic using genetic algorithms. International Journal for Numerical Methods in Fluids 30(2), 149–159 (1999)

Appendix: Test Bed

f_1: $\min\limits_{x} f(x) = \sum\limits_{i=1}^{n} x_i^2$, $-100 \le x_i \le 100$, $x^* = (0, 0, ..., 0)$, $f(x^*) = 0$.

f_2: $\min\limits_{x} f(x) = \sum\limits_{i=1}^{n-1} (100(x_{i+1} - x_i^2)^2 + (1 - x_i)^2)$, $-30 \le x_i \le 30$, $x^* = (0, 0, ..., 0)$, $f(x^*) = 0$.

f_3: $\min\limits_{x} f(x) = \sum\limits_{i=1}^{n} |x_i| + \prod\limits_{i=1}^{n} |x_i|$, $-10 \le x_i \le 10$, $x^* = (0, 0, ..., 0)$, $f(x^*) = 0$.

f_4: $\min\limits_{x} f(x) = \max\limits_{x} \{|x_i|, 1 \le i \le n\}$, $-100 \le x_i \le 100$, $x^* = (0, 0, ..., 0)$, $f(x^*) = 0$.

f_5: $\min\limits_{x} f(x) = -20 \exp(-0.2\sqrt{\frac{1}{n} \sum\limits_{i=1}^{n} x_i^2}) - \exp(\frac{1}{n} \sum\limits_{i=1}^{n} \cos(2\pi x_i)) + 20 + e$,
$-32 \le x_i \le 32$, $x^* = (0, 0, ..., 0)$, $f(x^*) = 0$.

f_6: $\min\limits_{x} f(x) = 1 + \frac{1}{4000} \sum\limits_{i=1}^{n} x_i^2 - \prod\limits_{i=1}^{n} \cos(\frac{x_i}{\sqrt{i}})$, $-600 \le x_i \le 600$, $x^* = (0, 0, ..., 0)$, $f(x^*) = -0.1n$.

f_7: $\min\limits_{x} f(x) = 10n + \sum\limits_{i=1}^{n} (x_i^2 - 10 \cos(2\pi x_i))$, $-5.12 \le x_i \le 5.12$, $x^* = (0, 0, ..., 0)$, $f(x^*) = 0$.

f_8: $\min\limits_{x} f(x) = \sum\limits_{i=1}^{n-1} (x_i^2 + 2x_{i+1}^2) - \sum\limits_{i=1}^{n-1} (0.3 \cos(3\pi x_i) - 0.4 \cos(4\pi x_{i+1} + 0.7))$,
$-5.12 \le x_i \le 5.12$, $x^* = (0, 0, ..., 0)$, $f(x^*) = 0$.

f_9: $\min\limits_{x} f(x) = \sum\limits_{i=1}^{n-1} [(x_i^2 + x_{i+1}^2)(\sin^2(50(x_i^2 + x_{i+1}^2)^{0.1}) + 1.0)]$,
$-100 \le x_i \le 100$, $x^* = (0, 0, ..., 0)$, $f(x^*) = 0$.

A Population-P-Systems-Inspired Membrane Algorithm for Multi-objective Optimization

Jixiang Cheng[1], Gexiang Zhang[1], and Yanhui Qin[2]

[1]School of Electrical Engineering, Southwest Jiaotong University, Chengdu 610031, P.R. China
[2]State Grid Xinjiang Electric Power Corporation Electric Power Research Institute, Urumqi, 830011, P.R. China
{chengjixiang0106,zhgxdylan}@126.com

Abstract. This paper proposes a Population-P-Systems-inspired Membrane Algorithm (PPSMA) for multi-objective optimization. In the algorithm, the cells of population P systems are divided into two groups to implement different functions and the communications among cells are performed at two levels in order to obtain well converged and distributed solution set. Moreover, differential evolution is employed as search operator in PPSMA. Twelve multi-objective benchmark problems are utilized to test algorithm performance. Experimental results show that PPSMA performs better than five compared algorithms.

Keywords: Membrane Algorithm, Population P Systems, Multi-objective Optimization.

1 Introduction

In recent years, membrane algorithms (MAs), which hybridize membrane computing with evolutionary computation, have attracted much attention in both methodological aspects and practical applications. At present, several membrane structures, such as nested membrane structure [1], one level membrane structure [2], dynamic membrane structure [3], statistic network structure [4] and dynamic network structure [5], have been combined with various evolutionary algorithms to design many MAs. A comprehensive review of MAs can be found in the survey paper by Zhang et, al. [6].

To date, the research on MAs mainly focuses on the use of structures of cell-like P systems. In our previous work [5], population P systems [7] were applied to construct a MA for single-objective optimization. In this paper, we push the work forward and propose a Population-P-Systems-inspired MA for multi-objective optimization called PPSMA. In the algorithm, population P systems are used to organize individuals; cells in the system are divided into two groups with different functions; communications among cells are performed at local and global levels; and differential evolution (DE)[8] is applied as search operator. Experimental results show that PPSMA outperforms five peer algorithms in terms of three performance metrics.

2 PPSMA

To obtain uniformly distributed solutions, we can first define a set of uniformly distributed directions and then search for one solution that converges well along each

L. Pan et al. (Eds.): BIC-TA 2014, CCIS 472, pp. 40–44, 2014.
© Springer-Verlag Berlin Heidelberg 2014

direction. Hence, the problem is transformed to a set of sub-problems with different goals. To ensure good convergence performance, efficient search operators like DE should be applied and the information of a sub-problem should be shared by others. Population P systems are quite suitable for solving multi-objective optimization problems (MOPs). In PPSMA, the cells are divided into two groups. The first group called evolving cells, including cells C_k, $k = 1, 2, \ldots, NP$, focuses on searching individuals toward Pareto front; while the second group called surviving cell, consisting of only one cell C_{NP+1}, aims at surviving individuals and re-scattering them across the evolving cells for next generation, where NP is the population size. Hence, there are $NP+1$ cells involved in the system.

In PPSMA, we first generate NP uniformly distributed direction vectors, one for each evolving cell, and then define the neighboring cells of each evolving cell. Specifically, each direction vector $\mathbf{r} = (r_1, r_2, \ldots, r_M)$ should satisfy

$$r_m \in \left\{ \tfrac{0}{H}, \tfrac{H}{H}, \ldots, \tfrac{H}{H} \right\}, m = 1, 2, \ldots, M, \sum_{m=1}^{M} r_m = 1 \tag{1}$$

where M is the number of objectives and H is a positive integer. The total number of available direction vectors is C_{H+M-1}^{M-1}. Then, each evolving cell i is associated with a unique direction vector, denoted as $\mathbf{r}_i$. The neighboring cells of evolving cell i are the evolving cells whose direction vectors are the $\lfloor R \cdot NP \rfloor$ closest vectors to $\mathbf{r}_i$, denoted as $N(i)$, where $R \in (0, 1)$ is a pre-defined parameter.

Based on the above description, the population P systems in PPSMA can be formulated as the following construct

$$P = (V, \gamma, \alpha, \omega_e, C_1, C_2, \ldots, C_{NP}, C_{NP+1}, c_o)$$

where

(i) $V = \{\mathbf{x}_1, \mathbf{x}_2, \ldots, \mathbf{x}_{NP}\}$, where $\mathbf{x}_i = (x_{i,1}, x_{i,2}, \ldots, x_{i,D})$ is a real-valued string;

(ii) $\gamma = (\{1, 2, \ldots, NP+1\}, E)$ with $E = E_1 \cup E_2$ is a finite directed graph, where $E_1 = \{(i, j) | 1 \leq i \leq NP, j \in N(i)\}$, $E_2 = \{(i, j) | 1 \leq i \leq NP, j = NP+1, \text{or } i = NP+1, 1 \leq j \leq NP\}$;

(iii) α is a finite set of bond making rule $(i, x_1; x_2, j), (i, j) \in E$;

(iv) $\omega_e = \lambda$;

(v) $C_k = (\omega_k, S_k, R_k)$, for each evolving cell k, $1 \leq k \leq NP$,

    (a) $\omega_k = \{\mathbf{x}_1, \mathbf{x}_2, \ldots, \mathbf{x}_{n_k}\}$, where n_k is the number of individuals in cell C_k, satisfying $\sum_{k=1}^{NP} n_k = NP$;

    (b) S_k is a finite set of communication rules of the form $(\lambda; b, in), b \in V$;

    (c) R_k is a finite set of transformation rules of the form $x \rightarrow y$, consisting of the mutation, crossover, and selection operators of DE;

    and for surviving cell k, $k = NP+1$,

    (a) $\omega_k = \{\mathbf{x}_1, \mathbf{x}_2, \ldots, \mathbf{x}_{NP}\}$;

    (b) S_k is a finite set of communication rules of the forms $(\lambda; b, in)$ and $(b, exit)$, $b \in V$;

    (c) $R_k = \emptyset$;

(vi) $c_o = NP+1$ is the label of the output cell.

In what follows we describe the procedures of PPSMA step by step.

Step 1: *Initialization*. A population P system with $NP + 1$ cells is created. Each evolving cell k is associated with a direction vector $\mathbf{r}_k$. An initial population with NP individuals is generated and each individual is sent to a random selected evolving cell. Hence, each evolving cell has n_k individuals with $0 \le n_k \le NP$ and $\sum_{k=1}^{NP} n_k = NP$.

Step 2: *Parameter setting*. In PPSMA, DE is applied as search operator. As scaling factor F and crossover rate Cr of DE have great influence on algorithm performance, we adapt the two parameters according to their recent successful values using the strategy in [9]. At generation g, the values F_i and Cr_i for the ith individual are generated by

$$F_i = randc(\mu_F, 0.1), \mu_F = \sum_{F \in sF} F^2 \Big/ \sum_{F \in sF} F \qquad (2)$$

$$Cr_i = randn(\mu_{Cr}, 0.1), \mu_{Cr} = \sum_{Cr \in sCr} Cr \Big/ W \qquad (3)$$

where, $randc(\mu_F, 0.1)$ is a cauchy distribution with location parameter μ_F and scale parameter 0.1; $randn(\mu_{Cr}, 0.1)$ is a normal distribution of mean μ_{Cr} and standard deviation 0.1; sF and sCr are the sets of most recent W values of F and Cr which produce offspring entering the next generation.

Step 3: *Individual evolution*. Transformation rules of the form $x \to y$ is utilized to evolve the objects in each of non-empty evolving cells (i.e., $n_k \ne 0$). The rules are the mechanisms of DE. Instead of evolving individuals in each cell independently, individuals from neighboring cells are used through local communication. Specifically, for each individual $\mathbf{x}_i$ in an evolving cell $k, i = 1, 2, \ldots, n_k$, three individuals $\mathbf{x}_{r1}, \mathbf{x}_{r2}$ and $\mathbf{x}_{r3}$ randomly selected from evolving cells k_{r1}, k_{r2} and k_{r3} are used to generate a trail vector $\mathbf{v}_i$, where k_{r1}, k_{r2} and $k_{r3} \in \{k\} \bigcup \{N(k) | n_k \ne 0\}$. If $\mathbf{f}(\mathbf{v}_i)$ dominates $\mathbf{f}(\mathbf{x}_i)$, $\mathbf{x}_i$ is replaced by $\mathbf{v}_i$; otherwise, $\mathbf{x}_i$ is kept unchanged and $\mathbf{v}_i$ is stored in the current cell temporally. The values of k_{r1}, k_{r2} and k_{r3} determine what membrane structure will be created and used to perform local communication.

Step 4: Global communication. In this step, surviving cell c_o receives all individuals (including $\mathbf{x}_i$ and temporally stored $\mathbf{v}_i$) from all evolving cells using rule $(\lambda; b, in)$, forming a temporary population P' with size N, $N \in [NP, 2NP]$. The population P' is then divided into fronts $\mathscr{F}_1, \mathscr{F}_2, \ldots, \mathscr{F}_L$ through non-dominated sorting. The individuals in $\mathscr{F}_1, \mathscr{F}_2, \ldots, \mathscr{F}_{l-1}, l \le L$ are first survived, satisfying $\sum_{i=1}^{l-1} |\mathscr{F}_i| \le NP$ and $\sum_{i=1}^{l} |\mathscr{F}_i| > NP$. Then for each individual $\mathbf{x}$ in fronts $\mathscr{F}_1, \mathscr{F}_2, \ldots, \mathscr{F}_l$, we determine an evolving cell k that $\mathbf{x}$ could enter according to the closest perpendicular distance between $\mathbf{f}(\mathbf{x})$ and $\mathbf{r}_i$, i.e.,

$$k = \operatorname*{argmin}_{i \in \{1, \ldots, NP\}} d(\mathbf{f}(\mathbf{x}), \mathbf{r}_i) = \operatorname*{argmin}_{i \in \{1, \ldots, NP\}} \mathbf{f}(\mathbf{x}) - \mathbf{r}_i^T \mathbf{f}(\mathbf{x}) \mathbf{r}_i \qquad (4)$$

Thirdly, we send all individuals in $\mathscr{F}_1, \mathscr{F}_2, \ldots, \mathscr{F}_{l-1}$ to corresponding cells. Afterwards, we scan all evolving cells in ascending order of the number of individuals in evolving cells. Specifically, if an evolving cell has the fewest individuals in it and there exists an individual in F_l that could enter into this evolving cell, the corresponding individual is sent to this cell and the number of individuals in this cell is incremented by 1; otherwise, the next evolving cell with the fewest individuals is checked. If all evolving cells with the fewest individuals have been checked and there are still some individuals need to be survived, then the evolving cells with the second fewest individuals are checked. The scanning procedure is repeated until $NP - \sum_{i=1}^{l-1} |\mathscr{F}_i|$ individuals have been survived from $\mathscr{F}_l$. At the end of re-scattering procedure, the most recently adopted F_i and Cr_i values which produce the survived individuals are stored in sF and sCr for updating μ_F and μ_{Cr} at next generation.

Step 5: Termination condition. The algorithm stops when a prescribed number of evolutionary generations or function evaluations is attained. Otherwise, go to Step 2.

Step 6: Output. For cell c_o, rule $(\lambda; b, in)$ is performed to collect all individuals from evolving cells. These individuals constitute the final solution set.

3 Experimental Results

Twelve benchmark MOPs, including five two-objective problems (ZDT1-ZDT4, ZDT6) and seven three-objective problems (DTLZ1-DTLZ7) are employed to conduct experiment. To quantify algorithm performance, three performance metrics including generational distance (GD), inverted generational distance (IGD) and hypervolume (HV) are used. To show the advantage of PPSMA, five compared algorithms are considered, i.e., NSGA-II [10], GDE3 [11], DEMO [12], ε-MyDE [13] and MOEA/D-DE [14]. The maximal number of function evaluations is set to 30,000 as the stopping criterion. The population size NP is set to 100, except for PPSMA and MOEA/D-DE when solving three-object problems, where NP is set to 105 because it is impossible to generate exact 100 uniformly distributed weight vectors or direction vectors for the two algorithms when solving three-objective problems. In PPSMA, R and W are set to 0.3 and 80, respectively, according to a parameter analysis procedure. The other parameters for each compared algorithms are set the same as in their original papers. In addition, 25 independent runs for each algorithm on each test problem are performed.

Due to space limitation, we do not list the mean and standard deviation values of GD, IGD and HV. Instead, we give the statistical test results with respect to Wilcoxon's rank sum test at a 0.05 significance level, shown in Table 1. From the table, we can see that the numbers of problems where PPSMA performs significantly better than five compared algorithms are much larger than the number of problems where PPSMA performs significantly worse, which demonstrates PPSMA is superior to five compared algorithms.

Table 1. Statistical test results in terms of GD, IGD and HV

Algorithms	GD			IGD			HV		
	+	=	−	+	=	−	+	=	−
NSGA-II	11	0	1	10	1	1	9	1	2
GDE3	8	2	2	7	2	3	8	2	2
DEMO	6	2	4	7	1	4	8	2	2
ε-MyDE	9	0	3	10	1	1	10	1	1
MOEA/D-DE	12	0	0	11	1	0	11	1	0

4 Conclusion

This paper proposed a multi-objective MA called PPSMA. In the algorithms, two kinds of cells with different functions are used and the communications are performed at both local and global levels. Experimental results show that PPSMA outperforms five peer algorithms in terms of three performance metrics. Our future work will focus on designing multi-objective MAs by exploiting the features of other advanced P systems and applying these algorithms to solving real-word problems.

Acknowledgement. This work was supported by the National Natural Science Foundation of China (No. 61170016, No.61373047), the Program for New Century Excellent Talents in University (No.NCET-11-0715) and SWJTU supported project (No.SWJTU12CX008), and the 2014 Doctoral Innovation Funds of southwest Jiaotong University.

References

1. Nishida, T.Y.: An Approximate Algorithm for NP-complete Optimization Problems Exploiting P Systems. In: BWMC, pp. 185–192 (2004)
2. Zhang, G., Gheorghe, M., Wu, C.Z.: A Quantum-Inspired Evolutionary Algorithm based on P Systems for Knapsack Problem. Fund. Inform. 87, 93–116 (2008)
3. Liu, C., Zhang, G., Liu, H., Gheorghe, M., Ipate, F.: An Improved Membrane Algorithm for Solving Time-Frequency Atom Decomposition. In: Păun, G., Pérez-Jiménez, M.J., Riscos-Núñez, A., Rozenberg, G., Salomaa, A. (eds.) WMC 2009. LNCS, vol. 5957, pp. 371–384. Springer, Heidelberg (2010)
4. Zhang, G., Cheng, J., Gheorghe, M., Meng, Q.: A Hybrid Approach based on Differential Evolution and Tissue Membrane Systems for Solving Constrained Manufacturing Parameter Optimization Problems. Appl. Soft Comput. 13, 1528–1542 (2013)
5. Zhang, G., Rong, H., Cheng, J., Qin, Y.: A Population-Membrane-System-Inspired Evolutionary Algorithm for Distribution Network Reconfiguration. Chinese J. Electron. 23, 437–441
6. Zhang, G., Gheorghe, M., Pan, L., Pérez-Jiménez, M.J.: Evolutionary Membrane Computing: A Comprehensive Survey. Inform Sciences 279, 528–551 (2014)
7. Bernardini, F., Gheorghe, M.: Population P systems. J. Univers. Comput. Sci. 10, 509–539 (2004)
8. Storn, R., Price, K.: Differential evolution - A Simple and Efficient Heuristic for Global Optimization over Continuous Spaces. J. Global Optim. 11, 341–359 (1997)
9. Zhang, J.Q., Sanderson, A.C.: JADE: Adaptive Differential Evolution with Optional External Archive. IEEE T. Evolut. Comput. 13, 945–958 (2009)
10. Deb, K., Pratap, A., Agarwal, S., Meyarivan, T.: A Fast and Elitist Multiobjective Genetic Algorithm: NSGA-II. IEEE T. Evolut. Comput. 6, 182–197 (2002)
11. Kukkonen, S., Lampinen, J.: GDE3: The Third Evolution Step of Generalized Differential Evolution. In: IEEE CEC, pp. 443–450 (2005)
12. Robic, T., Filipic, B.: DEMO: Differential Evolution for Multiobjective Optimization. In: Coello Coello, C.A., Hernández Aguirre, A., Zitzler, E. (eds.) EMO 2005. LNCS, vol. 3410, pp. 520–533. Springer, Heidelberg (2005)
13. Deb, K., Mohan, M., Mishra, S.: Evaluating the ε-domination based Multi-objective Evolutionary Algorithm for a Quick Computation of Pareto-optimal Solutions. Evol. Comput. 13, 501–525 (2005)
14. Li, H., Zhang, Q.F.: Multiobjective optimization problems with complicated Pareto sets, MOEA/D and NSGA-II. IEEE T. Evolut. Comput. 13, 284–302 (2009)

The Algorithms and Composition of a Travel System Based on Geographical Information

Wen Cheng and Zheng Zhang*

School of Automation
Huazhong University of Science and Technology, Hubei, China
boyweb@163.com, leaf@hust.edu.cn

Abstract. The purpose of GIS is trying to tell people the environment around them, and providing the needed information to them, and it is widely used in Location Based Service (LBS) applications, and LBS have little processing on the direction information. In this paper, a travel system based on GIS is presented, which has a relationship with the direction and attitude angle information, for more convenient communication in the crowd of the tourists. People can see the doodles which are created by the man who was in the same place before through our system. The algorithms of the system are discussed, one algorithm is used for matching the best data from the request of users, which is based on *k-Nearest Neighbor (KNN)* algorithm, and the other one is supported by the concept of spherical coordinate system. The simulation results of the algorithms are presented, and show that the algorithms are reasonable and acceptable in the environment of the system.

Keywords: Travel System, Geographical Information System, KNN, Spherical Coordinate.

1 Introduction

There is a situation that GIS is used widely, and it exists in many terminals and applications. And generally, GIS is defined as

> A system of hardware, software, data, people, organizations and institutional arrangements for collecting, storing, analyzing and disseminating information about areas of the earth. (Dueker and Kjerne 1989, pp. 7-8) [1]

The purpose of a GIS can be involved in a lot of aspect, such as LBS and those applications based on it, or some policies of agriculture and industry, even military affairs. Leave those functions alone, the most close to our life is GPS, which makes our life more convenient since it is created. However, it still has the large potential.

---

* Corresponding author.

L. Pan et al. (Eds.): BIC-TA 2014, CCIS 472, pp. 45–56, 2014.
© Springer-Verlag Berlin Heidelberg 2014

Noticed the usefulness of GPS, an idea was proposed to bring GPS into a travel system, and make more convenient and interesting communication between the tourists.

With the advent of modern society, people attach more importance to the protection of the attractions and the cultural relics. In the past, when some travelers stood in front the attractions, they usually took out their pens, and left their emotions and names on it, such as "XXX have a visit", or maybe a poem created by a passionate visitor. But now, those behaviors are considered as a kind of vandalism. The travelers become more civilized and the doodles in the attractions gradually reduced. A lot of applications were created because of that situation, the developers hope that tourists could communicate with others through their software by sharing photos and their status, however it lacks of the immersive feelings, and disappoint us somehow.

What if those doodles are moved into the Internet and stay in the phones? A system are designed that can help the tourists communicate with each other with the immersive feelings. The tourist can take a photo in an attraction, and then doodle on it, and the system will record the geographical information of it. The information will be sent to the server of the system, and be reserved in the databases. When another tourist comes to the same place, raises his/her phone and aims to the same direction, he/she will see the doodles which the people left before.

2   Composition of system

This system consists of two parts, the server and the client, and the Internet connection between the two parts is needed for the data transferring, and all of the data will be reserved in databases of the server, also some caches will be saved in the client and need to be cleaned periodically. See Figure 1.

2.1   Client

The client is defined as an application on the mobile devices platform such as iOS, Android and Windows Phone. The application will interact with the user to meet their demands. The functions of the client could be simple and easy to use, and there are only a few features of it.

- Users can take the photo with the application, and doodle on the pictures. The doodles can be sent to the server to share with other people if they like.
- Users can see the doodles that are created by other users when they raise their devices and look at the attractions.
- Users can report some inappropriate doodles to the system, and those doodles will be removed if necessary.

2.2 Server

The server consists of three components: database, HTTP server, and data processing module. Database, naturally, is the storage of the data and will reserve vast amount of data that contains the specific geographical information. The pattern of the data is KEY-VALUE pairs and each one shows a connection between a doodle and its geographical information, the KEY is the geographical information, which is used for searching and locating, and the VALUE is the doodle information, which is created by the user on this specific position. *(see Data structure)*

HTTP server acts as a role that receives the requests from the user, invoke the data processing module to get appropriate result, and then response it to the client. This component will open up some APIs, and provide the authentication that can protect the privacy of the users.

Data processing module is the most important component in the server. The request from the user passes through the HTTP server, and then will be disposed in this workflow. The module needs to get the location of the data at first, and searches in the database to find that whether there are some valid data *(see Data validation algorithm)*. Then it will pick up the appropriate data from the valid data, which can best meet the conditions of the users and the doodles can be displayed on the client suitably *(see Data searching algorithm)*. At last, the module returns the final result to the HTTP server.

3 Structure and Algorithms

3.1 Data Structure

The data has been defined in the previous chapters, and its form is a KEY-VALUE pair.

The KEY contains the geographical information, which should be something unique in the earth. The earth can be regard as a sphere, and there is a kind of coordinate system called Spherical Coordinate System [2], which can represent a point in the space in a different way from the Rectangular Coordinate System.

A point in the Spherical Coordinate System can be represented as follow

$$P = \{r, \beta, \epsilon\} \tag{1}$$

Setting the center of the sphere as the origin of the coordinate system, creating a Rectangular Coordinate System from it, and then drawing three rays OX, OY, OZ. Value r represents the distance between the point P and the origin, value β represents the angle between OP and OZ, and value ϵ represents the angle between OX and the projection of the OP on the plane XOY. As those values of a point are known, the position of it in the space can be determined. See Figure 2.

However, actually we live on the surface of the earth, and what we need is not only the value of our location, but also the direction of our sight. We should

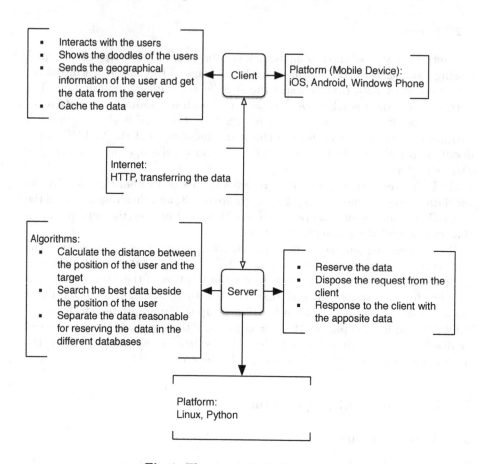

Fig. 1. The structure of the system

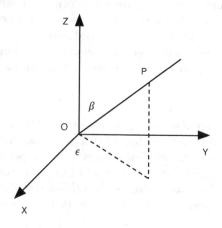

Fig. 2. Spherical Coordinate System

make a little change on this coordinate system, and find out a way to represent a ray in the space.

We can reference the concept of the spherical coordinate system, and move it into the surface of the earth. When we stand on the earth, our sight could be a ray, its origin is the position of us, and its direction is the path we see. So, the data structure of the KEY is defined as follow

$$K = \{P, \theta, \alpha\} \tag{2}$$

Value P represents the coordinate of the user, which is presented by the latitude (β) and the longitude (ϵ), value θ represents the direction angle, which means the angle between the sight direction and the north direction, and value α is the attitude angle, which equals the angle between the sight direction and horizon direction. With these values, a ray that represents our sight on the earth can be determined.

Those values can be get very conveniently with the devices of the mobile phones. With the GPS, the latitude and the longitude (P) can be known, and the direction angle (θ) can be get through the compass. As for the attitude angle, we need to do some calculation. According to the accelerometer of the phone, there are three values can be obtained, and those are the acceleration in the three directions.

$$A = \{A_X, A_Y, A_Z\} \tag{3}$$

And the attitude angle (α) can be calculated with these values.

$$\alpha = \begin{cases} tan^{-1}(\frac{A_Z}{A_X}) \\ tan^{-1}(\frac{A_Z}{A_Y}) \end{cases} \tag{4}$$

3.2   Data Validation Algorithm

The request that contains the geographical information needs to be validated when it comes to the data processing module. The information tells the position the users, and the requirements from them. The algorithm should exclude the invalidate data in the database, and pick up the validate ones for the next step (*see Data searching algorithm*). Thus, the computation of the searching algorithm can be reduced largely, and the efficiency of it will be improved.

The range of the direction angle and the attitude angle are very small for the latitude and the longitude. So, the algorithm should filter the data with the distance first. The data should be ruled out if the distance between it and the user are far larger than the *Acceptable Distance*.

Denoting ΔD as the *Acceptable Distance*. K represents the KEY from the user

$$\begin{cases} K = \{P, \theta, \alpha\} \\ P = \{\beta, \epsilon\} \end{cases} \tag{5}$$

And K_i represents the KEY of one data in the database is

$$\begin{cases} K_i = \{P_i, \theta_i, \alpha_i\} \\ P_i = \{\beta_i, \epsilon_i\} \end{cases} \tag{6}$$

Earth is a near-standard ellipsoid, its equatorial radius of 6378.140 km, polar radius of 6356.755 km and an average radius of 6,371.004 km. If we assume that the Earth is a perfect sphere, then its radius is the average radius of it, denoted R.

Setting the 0 degrees longitude as the benchmark, and do some transformation on the data. Denoting B and L as the new latitude and longitude after the transformation. [3]

$$B = \begin{cases} 90 - \beta, & latitude\ in\ the\ north \\ 90 + \beta, & latitude\ in\ the\ south \end{cases}$$

$$\tag{7}$$

$$L = \begin{cases} -\epsilon, & longitude\ in\ the\ west \\ +\epsilon, & longitude\ in\ the\ east \end{cases}$$

According to the trigonometric functions, the formula of calculating the distance can be get

$$\begin{aligned} C_i &= sin(B) * sin(B_i) * cos(L - L_i) + cos(B) * cos(B_i) \\ D_i &= R * cos^{-1}(C_i) * \pi/180 \end{aligned} \tag{8}$$

For the computer system, we need to change the latitude and the longitude into the radians. Thus, the formula should be changed as follow

$$\begin{aligned} rad(\alpha) &= \alpha * \pi/180 \\ C_i &= sin(rad(B)) * sin(rad(B_i)) * cos(rad(L) - rad(L_i)) \\ &\quad + cos(rad(B)) * cos(rad(B_i)) \\ D_i &= R * cos^{-1}(C_i) \end{aligned} \tag{9}$$

While D_i is far larger than ΔD ($D_i \gg \Delta D$), data i should be regarded as invalid data. The rest of the data will be sent to the searching algorithm to pick up the appropriate ones.

3.3   Data Searching Algorithm

The purpose of searching algorithm is to find the highest similarity data with the one of the user, and the variable which is reserved in the database is the KEY. The algorithm should search the K nearest neighbors of the KEY of user data, and return those K data to present on the phone, and it is based on KNN algorithm. [4,5]

According to the *Euclidean Distance*, the distance of the three-dimension data should be calculated by the formula

$$\begin{aligned} x &= (x_1, x_2, x_3) \\ y &= (y_1, y_2, y_3) \\ d(x, y) &= \sqrt{(x_1 - y_1)^2 + (x_2 - y_2)^2 + (x_3 - y_3)^2} \end{aligned} \tag{10}$$

However, the parameters of the KEY is not simple as the normal numbers. ΔP represents the distance of the latitude and the longitude. $\Delta\theta$ represents the difference between the direction angles, and $\Delta\alpha$ represents the difference between the attitude angles.

$$d(x,y) = \sqrt{\Delta P^2 + \Delta\theta^2 + \Delta\alpha^2} \qquad (11)$$

The algorithm above (*see Data validation algorithm*) can be used to calculate ΔP, and we will not repeat here. For the θ and the α, the values of them are the looping numbers, so the normal subtraction is useless. The range θ is $[0, 360)$, and the range of α is $[-180, 180)$. The method of calculating them is as follows:

Calculate the distance of θ and α

```
function calculate(x, y) {
    var maxDistance = 180;
    var d = abs(x - y);
    if (d > maxDistance) {
        d = d - 2 * maxDistance;
    }
    return d;
}
```

In the algorithm above, one point which must be paid attention is that when we calculate the distance between two KEYs, the data should be normalized [6,7]. The parameters have different units, and the value of them could be very large or small. The method of calculation is base on *Euclidean Distance*, so the range of the parameters could influence the result, and normalization should be processed depends on their weight. In the formula above, three parameters are the same important, and they have the same weight. The formula should be modified into another way.

$$N(v) = \frac{v}{v_{max} - v_{min}}$$

$$d(x,y) = \sqrt{N(\Delta P)^2 + N(\Delta\theta)^2 + N(\Delta\alpha)^2} \qquad (12)$$

And be represented as the following code:

Calculate the distance of KEYs

```
function normalized(v, v_diff_max){
    return v / v_diff_max;
}

function calculateDistance(x, y) {
  var d = sqrt(pow(normalized(x.c - y.c, COORDINATE_DIFF_MAX), 2)
            + pow(normalized(x.a - y.a, ATTITUDE_DIFF_MAX), 2)
            + pow(normalized(x.d - y.d, DIRECTION_DIFF_MAX), 2));
    return d;
}
```

After calculating the distances, the next step is to find the top K nearest values. A large number of invalidate data have been filtered before, so the calculation will not be so large. The Maximum Heap algorithm is choosed to reach the goal.

Build a heap of K capacity first, and calculate the distance between the data and the KEY of user. The heap is empty at the beginning, so the first K distance can be insert into the heap directly. After the heap is full, do a *HEAPSORT* to it, and now the distance remained should be processed one by one. The root of the heap is the maximal number in it. When a new number is generated, it should compared with the root. If it is smaller than the root, it means that the root is not the K smallest number any more, and it must be replaced by the new number. The next step is to do the *HEAPSORT* again to make sure the new root is the largest in the new heap [8]. After all the data are processed, the K smallest distance to the data of user can be get, also means the nearest data around the user. The whole algorithm code is as follows:

Select the k nearest data

```
// u - the KEY of user
// k - the size of the required data
// data - the data to be processed
function kNearest(u, k, data) {
    h = new heap(k);
    length = data.size();
    for (var i = 0; i < length; i ++) {
        d = calculateDistance(u, data[i]);
        if (h.size() < k) {
            h.push({d, i});
            if (h.size() == k) {
                h.sort();
            }
        } else {
            if (d > h.head().d) {
                h.head() = {d, i};
                h.sort();
            }
        }
    }
    h.reverse();
    return h;
}
```

3.4   Analysis and Simulation

We have make the simulations for the algorithm. Because the mount and the range of the real data could be very large, we just generate the simulative data in a small zone, and analyze the algorithm through these data.

- We pick up a small zone, and the range of its longitude is from 103.5 to 103.6, the range of its latitude is from 120.5 to 120.6. This field covers about 100 square kilometers. We generate some simulative data in this field averagely as the test data. We denote N as the size of the test data.
- We set the *Acceptable Distance* as 2 kilometers, and pick up the appropriate data as a new collection. We denote V as the collection.
- Use the searching algorithm to get the nearest K data around the user in V.

Simulation 1. The data of this simulation are as follows:

The data of user: Latitude = 120.554490; Longitude = 103.581840; Attitude angle = 58.320000; Direction angle = -148.283997.

Parameters: K = 200; N = 10000000.

Running result: Running time = 2386 ms; Size of V = 1146965.

Table 1. Top 20 of V in the simulation 1

Latitude	Longitude	Attitude angle	Direction angle
120.555550	103.583020	60.264000	-148.571991
120.553670	103.582150	59.688004	-153.828003
120.553430	103.583200	58.752003	-151.307999
120.553000	103.582000	56.952000	-151.776001
120.554670	103.583750	58.392002	-145.115997
120.553820	103.581890	64.187996	-144.612000
120.554180	103.579780	62.099998	-149.076004
120.553080	103.582380	64.080002	-147.708008
120.553820	103.580120	62.136002	-144.035995
120.556650	103.582240	58.752003	-149.039993
120.554610	103.584110	60.407997	-144.684006
120.555530	103.581800	52.667999	-142.559998
120.554420	103.583430	64.260002	-152.748001
120.552940	103.582740	52.811996	-145.584000
120.553500	103.581140	60.371998	-140.472000
120.555430	103.579720	60.444000	-144.216003
120.555650	103.582060	50.472000	-145.152008
120.552770	103.581480	64.980003	-148.500000
120.554710	103.580120	52.163998	-142.703995
120.556640	103.581020	54.792000	-144.936005

Simulation 2. The data of this simulation are as follows:

The data of user: Latitude = 120.540020; Longitude = 103.525890; Attitude angle = 57.527996; Direction angle = -102.851997.

Parameters: K = 300; N = 10000000.

Running result: Running time = 2289 ms; Size of V = 1179922.

Table 2. Top 20 of V in the simulation 2

Latitude	Longitude	Attitude angle	Direction angle
120.540140	103.526100	55.691998	-106.451996
120.539830	103.526760	59.652000	-101.124001
120.539190	103.525580	53.855999	-100.727997
120.539510	103.526320	52.883999	-101.195999
120.540130	103.526250	50.975998	-101.520004
120.541130	103.526070	62.568001	-102.203995
120.539880	103.525880	57.203999	-110.159996
120.540380	103.527560	61.776001	-101.699997
120.541560	103.525190	57.959999	-99.612000
120.540960	103.524840	52.236000	-102.059998
120.539740	103.527230	56.051998	-97.092003
120.541680	103.526260	60.984001	-102.671997
120.541050	103.527460	57.492001	-106.848000
120.541210	103.527720	56.484001	-104.435997
120.540960	103.527210	53.208000	-99.071999
120.540190	103.523940	61.667999	-105.515999
120.541020	103.527190	58.032001	-109.008003
120.540610	103.526600	64.835999	-99.503998
120.539590	103.527770	52.596001	-100.403999
120.540370	103.526910	49.536003	-101.951996

Simulation 3. The data of this simulation are as follows:

The data of user: Latitude = 120.503150; Longitude = 103.578150; Attitude angle = 107.063995; Direction angle = 26.891998.

Parameters: K = 1000; N = 10000000.

Running result: Running time = 2176 ms; Size of V = 720466.

According to the simulation results above, we can see that the deviation between the nearest data and the user data can be acceptable. The deviation of the longitude and the latitude are both ±0.002 degrees, which means that the position distance between the user and each response data will be up to 282 meters. The deviation of the attitude angle and the direction angle are both ±6 degrees.

With the analysis, we can see that the response data are more reasonable and more consistent in their direction and the direction of the request from the user, and the distance between them are not far away. So it is easier to reproduce the scene before, and achieve better interaction effects.

Table 3. Top 20 of V in the simulation 3

Latitude	Longitude	Attitude angle	Direction angle
120.503940	103.578890	107.063995	29.628006
120.502960	103.576400	107.063995	24.984009
120.502560	103.575870	106.307999	25.740005
120.503370	103.578200	102.960007	31.895996
120.502070	103.576700	109.296005	23.112000
120.501070	103.577540	108.360001	27.359985
120.502690	103.576580	107.747993	21.780014
120.502760	103.576310	102.636002	25.595993
120.501540	103.577240	102.671997	26.459991
120.503150	103.576740	101.699997	24.263992
120.501690	103.576200	105.264000	28.692001
120.504960	103.576710	105.480003	29.376007
120.505120	103.577790	104.436005	30.060013
120.501920	103.578680	101.879997	30.599991
120.505200	103.577370	104.040001	28.944000
120.502450	103.579220	105.875992	20.304001
120.501430	103.577940	111.420006	30.167999
120.504770	103.577040	111.887993	25.343994
120.504140	103.575940	109.476006	30.779999
120.505120	103.579730	106.667999	23.651993

4 Conclusion and Discussion

The GIS has been paid great attention in many fields, and especially in the GPS. A lot of companies are involved in the mobile map service application, and also trying to make the applications more humanized. Thus, those IT companies should gather more ideas from the normal life. For this system, it also have some aspects to be improved.

4.1 Include the 3D Model of the Objects

In this system, the information is still fuzzy, and the object that the user is looking at is not sure yet. The information we have can only build a ray in the earth, not a vector, however, this ray can pass through more than one objects. If the 3D models are included, the system can take the more accurate information about the user, and it is more accurate when the user request the doodles, too.

4.2 Combine with the Cloud Calculation

While the amount of data is so large, the burden of the server could be so large, too. Especially in the processing data module. The system need an algorithm to separate the operations, distribute the data to the different machines, and handle the result from the machines at last. The efficiency will be improved largely by using the cloud calculation.

Acknowledgement. This work is supported by National Natural Science Foundation of China No.61100145.

References

1. Chrisman, N.R., Cowen, D.J., Fisher, P.F., Goodchild, M.F., Mark, D.M.: Geographic information systems. Geography in America, 353–375 (1989)
2. Busche, J.R., Hillier, D.J.: An efficient short characteristic solution for the transfer equation in axisymmetric geometries using a spherical coordinate system. The Astrophysical Journal 531(2), 1071 (2000)
3. Byers, J.A.: Surface distance between two points of latitude and longitude. USDA, Agricultural Research Service (1997),
   http://www.chemical-ecology.net/java/lat-long.htm
   (accessed November 3, 2006)
4. Keller, J.M., Gray, M.R., Givens, J.A.: A fuzzy k-nearest neighbor algorithm. IEEE Transactions on Systems, Man and Cybernetics (4), 580–585 (1985)
5. Dudani, S.A.: The distance-weighted k-nearest-neighbor rule. IEEE Transactions on Systems, Man and Cybernetics (4), 325–327 (1976)
6. Kim, Y., Kim, W., Kim, U.: Mining Frequent Itemsets with Normalized Weight in Continuous Data Streams. JIPS 6(1), 79–90 (2010)
7. Marzal, A., Vidal, E.: Computation of normalized edit distance and applications. IEEE Transactions on Pattern Analysis and Machine Intelligence 15(9), 926–932 (1993)
8. Mouratidis, K., Yiu, M.L., Papadias, D., Mamoulis, N.: Continuous nearest neighbor monitoring in road networks. In: Proceedings of the 32nd International Conference on Very Large Data Bases, pp. 43–54. VLDB Endowment (September 2006)

The Modular Inversion in $GF(p)$ by Self-assembling and Its Application to Elliptic Curve Diffie-Hellman Key Exchange

Zhen Cheng* and Yufang Huang

School of Computer Science and Technology, Zhejiang University of Technology,
Hangzhou 310023, China
College of Maths, Southwest Jiaotong University, Chengdu 610031, China
chengzhen0716@163.com

Abstract. The study of tile self-assembly model shows the development of self-assembling systems for solving complex computational problems. In this paper, we show the method of performing modular inversion in $GF(p)$ by self-assembling with $\Theta(p)$ computational tile types in $\Theta(p)$ steps. Then, we discuss how the self-assembling systems for computing modular inversion in $GF(p)$ apply to elliptic curve Diffie-Hellman key exchange algorithm. The self-assembled architectures provide the feasibility of cryptanalysis for this algorithm.

Keywords: Modular inversion, Self-assembling, Elliptic curve, Diffie-Hellman key exchange.

1 Introduction

In recent years, DNA computing is extensively and deeply investigated [1–4]. Our work focuses on tile self-assembly model [5] which is an important model of DNA computing. Barish et al. [6] experimentally performed patterns of binary counters to create crystals. Rothemund [7] first used the technology of folding DNA to design nanoscale shapes and patterns. On this basis, such as Sierpinski triangles [8] and 3D nanostructure [9] can also be created. Mao et al. experimentally implemented a logical computation based on the algorithmic tile self-assembly model [10]. The computational power of this model has embodied in the work of Brun [11]. Furthermore, this model is also used to solve NP-complete problem by using nondeterministic algorithm [12]. It has potential applications in the cryptography. Cheng proposed nondeterministic algorithm to break Diffie-Hellman key exchange using tile self-assembly model [13]. The modular inversion [14] is essential for point operation computations on elliptic curve cryptosystems [15] defined in $GF(p)$. Here we mainly focus on the computation of the modular inversion in $GF(p)$ by self-assembling with $\Theta(p)$ basic tile types in $\Theta(p)$ steps.

The main content of this paper is as follows: Section 2 will show the process of implementing modular inversion in $GF(p)$ by self-assembling, and we will

---

* Corresponding author.

L. Pan et al. (Eds.): BIC-TA 2014, CCIS 472, pp. 57–62, 2014.
© Springer-Verlag Berlin Heidelberg 2014

discuss how it applies to elliptic curve Diffie-Hellman key exchange algorithm. The complexity analysis and conclusion are given in Section 3.

2   The Modular Inversion in $GF(p)$ Using Tile Self-assembly Model

In this section, the definition of modular inversion in $GF(p)$ is given. Then, the computation of modular inversion can be converted into modular multiplications.

The classical definition of the modular inversion states that the inversion of an integer $x \in [1, p-1]$ modulus p, is defined as an integer $y \in [1, p-1]$ such that $x * y \equiv 1 (\bmod p)$. This translates to the following equation $y = x^{-1} (\bmod p)$.

Format theory: Suppose p be prime and x be an integer, $x^p \equiv x \bmod p$. Especially, when $gcd(x, p) = 1$, $x^{p-1} \equiv 1 \bmod p$.

Therefore, according to the Format theory, the modular inversion can be computed by a serial of modular multiplications which can be represented as $x^{-1} \bmod p = x^{p-2} \bmod p$. Then we can get $x^{i+1} \bmod p = (x * x^i \bmod p) \bmod p (0 \le i \le p - 2)$. Thus the modular inversion in $GF(p)$ can be converted into $(p - 3)$ modular multiplications. We first consider the computation of modular multiplication. For the integers x, p with $(0 \le i \le p-2)$, in order to get the result of $x^2 \bmod p$, the method of interleaved modular multiplication is as follows: (1) $M = 0$; (2) for ($i = n-1; i \ge 0; i = i-1$) (3) $M = 2 * M$; (4) $M = M + x_i * x$; (5) if $(M \ge p) M = M - p$; (6) if $(M \ge p)$ $M = M - p$. Here, n is the number of bits of x. x_i is denoted as the i-th bit of x. M is the intermediate results and p is the modulus. For every $x_i (0 \le i \le n - 2)$, there is a left shift, a partial product computation, an addition, and at most two subtractions.

Addition Operation. The addition operation can make the sum between two positive integers. When the comparison result at the previous step is $<$ which means the value of M is smaller than p, the addition operation between two integers M and x is carried out. The value of M, p, x are arranged in the seed configuration from the lowest bit to the highest bit represented as b, c, d respectively, and one of the other x denoted as a is set from the highest to the lowest bit. Here, $a, b, c, d, e, f, g \in \{0, 1\}$. The basic tile set of this operation is as follows in Fig.1. For the tiles in the first row in Fig.1, the initial value of M is set as 0. The highest bit of x denoted as x_{n-1} is 1, so the first addition operation only needs to pass the value of x to M for the corresponding bits. The number 1 as the input, and output of the tile is the value of x_{n-1} which is assigned to 1. The numbers of bits of M and p are more than x, so bc in the first tile of the tile types are represented as the higher bits of M and p respectively. a' is used to label the highest bit of x which should be passed to the lowest bit. For the tiles in second and third rows, if $x_i = 0 \le i \le n - 2$, the lowest bit of M is 0, and the result of the addition operation is $2 * M$. If $x_i = 1 \le i \le n - 2$, the lowest bit of M is the corresponding lowest bit of x, then the addition is made between M and x. If the carry bit from the lower bit is f^*, and the shifted bit from is g, the addition result e and the carry bit k^* can be generated at this step, synchronously the bit of M and x labeled as b and 1 respectively should be passed to the higher bit. The tiles in the fourth row in Fig.1 can determine

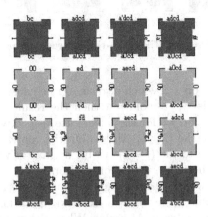

Fig. 1. The basic tile set of the addition operation

whether and what the bit of x is passed to the next addition operation. If the lowest bit of x has been completed the addition operation, it is passed to the final result. Otherwise, the value of x_i should be passed to the lower bit x_{i-1} to make it do the next round addition. So if the input on the right of the tiles including f' can determine the value of x_{i-1} denoted as a' will be passed to the next addition system.

Subtraction Operation. When the comparison result at the previous step is $>$ or $=$ which means the value of M is bigger than or equal to p, then the subtraction operation will make the difference between the two integers M and p. The basic tile set of this operation is as follows in Fig.2. Fig.2 shows the formulas of one bit subtraction. Here, the value of a, b, c, d at the bottom of the tile is denoted as x, M, p, x respectively, and $a, b, c, d, e, f, g \in \{0, 1\}$. The subtraction operation begins from the lowest bit to the highest bit with the label $*$. a' is the value of x with the label which is passed to the addition system. The representation f^* is the borrow bit from the lower bit and g^* is the borrow bit which is generated at this step. The value of e is the result which can be computed by the sum of b and c minus f.

Comparing Operation. The comparing operation compares two input numbers which are represented as M at each step and p respectively bit-by-bit from the highest bit to the lowest bit until the relationship which is less than ($<$), greater than ($>$) or equal to ($=$) is determined. Fig.3 shows the basic tile set of this operation. In each tile, the value of a, b, c, d is denoted as x, M, p, x respectively. When the $(i + 1)$−th bit of M is smaller then or equal to p, then

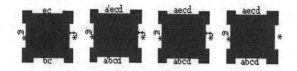

Fig. 2. The basic tile set of the subtraction operation

the tile is labeled as $<$ or $=$, which also should be considered with the result of the i-th bit which is $<$, $>$ or $=$, then the result which is $<$ for the former case and $<$, $>$ or $=$ for the latter case respectively can be obtained and should be passed to the $(i-1)$-th bit. On the contrary, the final result is $>$ also should be passed to the $(i-1)$-th bit no matter what the relationship of the i-th bit is. Furthermore, if the comparison result of the two integers is $<$, the next operation would turn to the addition computation with $x_i = 0$ or 1. If the comparison result is $>$ or $=$, the next operation would turn to the subtraction computation between M and p. When the comparison result is $<$ with the label of the position for the lowest bit of x, the modular multiplication is completed at this step.

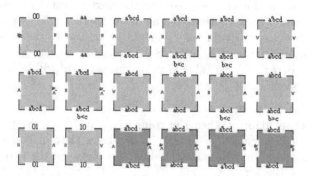

Fig. 3. The basic tile types of the comparing system

Now we give an example of performing modular inversion $y = 4^{-1}(\mod 5)$ by self-assembling. The modular inversion can be converted into the modular multiplication $y = 4^3(\mod 5)$. Then this modular inversion result can be obtained by two modular multiplications. The computation of modular multiplication $y = 4^2(\mod 5)$ is given as follows.

First, the binary form of x, p can be represented as $x = 4 = (0101)_2$, $p = 5 = (0101)_2$ respectively. The initial value of M is set as 0 and arranged from the lowest bit to the highest bit together with x, p. On the contrary, one of the two x is from the highest bit to the lowest bit. Second, the highest bit of x which is denoted as $x_2 = 1$, then the value of M is equal to x, so the comparing system can check that M is smaller than p. The next addition operation begins with

$x_1 = 0$, so the value of M at the previous step shifted one bit from right to left can be assigned to M at this step. It can be represented as $M = (1000)_2$ which is more than p by the comparing operation, thus the next operation is subtraction operation between M and p, and the subtraction result should be assigned to M which is $(0011)_2$. When $x_0 = 0$, the operation is the same as the case with $x_1 = 0$. The value of M after left shift one bit is $M = (0110)_2$, then the subtraction operation result is $(0001)_2$ which is equal to $y = 4^2 (\mathrm{mod}5)$. After the computation of $y = 4^2 (\mathrm{mod}5)$ is completed, there are some tiles that can convert the result of $y = 4^2 (\mathrm{mod}5)$ into the new value of x, and the value of x doesnt need to change. Then it only needs to give different labels of the lowest bit of x which can be used to distinguish the times of the modular multiplication. For the same method, the assembly complexes can be used to implement the computation of $y = 4^3 (\mathrm{mod}\ 5)$. Finally, to output the computation result in the solution pool, a combination of PCR and gel electrophoresis, and extracting the strands of different lengths representing the output tiles in the result strand are carried out. The result of the modular inversion $y = 4^{-1} (\mathrm{mod}5)$ is $(0100)_2$.

Its Application to Elliptic Curve Diffie-Hellman Key Exchange. The performance of Elliptic Curve cryptosystem depends on the efficiency of elliptic curve scalar multiplications. The scalar multiplication requires computing the product kP[15], where P is a point on an elliptic curve and k is a given integer. The computation of modular inversion in $GF(p)$ is contained in the product kP. The efficiency of computing modular inversion in $GF(p)$ can improve the computation of scalar multiplication. In this case, the elliptic curve Diffie-Hellman key exchange algorithm can be attacked using self-assembled structures much faster than before. Generally, given the parameter a, b and the point P of elliptic curve, the process of Diffie-Hellman key exchange between user A and user B has three steps. First, the user A selects an integer a as his secret key, then he can get the public key $P_A = aP$ based on modular inversion by self-assembling introduced above. Second, for the same method, the user B can also get his public key $P_B = bP$, here b is an integer which is selected by the user B. Third, the user A has secret key $K = a * P_B$, the user B has secret key $K = b * P_B$, so the users A and B can implement the key exchange. In this process, we use a modification of the standard sequence-reading operation that uses a combinational of PCR and gel electrophoresis to read the computation results. Using this method and biological operations, we can complete the key exchange. Thus the method of computing modular inversion in $GF(p)$ by self-assembling can make cryptanalysis apply to elliptic curve Diffie-Hellman key exchange algorithm.

3   Complexity Analysis and Conclusion

Considering the computation of modular inversion in $GF(p)$, the distinct tile types are determined by the size of p. The computation time represents the assembled steps which are needed to complete the growth of the complexes, and the number of the assembled steps is equal to $(p - 1)$. Thus the computation complexity of this computational problem is $\Theta(p)$. In this paper, we design self-assembled architectures to perform the computation of modular inversion in by using $\Theta(p)$ basic tile types in $\Theta(p)$ steps, which also can be used to make cryptanalysis of elliptic curve Diffie-Hellman key exchange. For this purpose, we need design effective DNA tiles for this computation problem. Our aim is to reduce the types as few as possible, and this is also our later work direction.

Acknowledgments. This work was supported by the National Natural Science Foundation of China (No. 61202204, 61202011, 61373066).

References

1. Adleman, L.M.: Molecular Computation of Solutions to Combinatorial Problems. Science 266, 1021–1024 (1994)
2. Pan, L., Wang, J., Hoogeboom, H.J.: Spiking Neural P Systems with Astrocytes. Neural Computation 24, 805–825 (2012)
3. Pan, L., Zeng, X.: Small Universal Spiking Neural P Systems Working in Exhaustive Mode. IEEE Transactions on Nanobioscience 10, 99–105 (2011)
4. Pan, L., Pérez-Jiménez, M.J.: Computational Complexity of Tissue-like P Systems. J. Complexity 26, 296–315 (2010)
5. Seeman, N.C.: DNA Nanotechnology: Novel DNA Constructions. Annu. Rev. Biophy. Biomol. Struct. 27, 225–248 (1998)
6. Barish, R., Rothemund, P.W., Winfree, E.: Two Computational Primitives for Algorithmic Self-assembly: Copying and Counting. Nano Lett. 12, 2586–2592 (2005)
7. Rothemund, P.W.: Folding DNA to Create Nanoscale Shapes and Patterns. Nature 440, 297–302 (2006)
8. Lathrop, J.I., Lutz, J.H., Summers, S.M.: Strict Self-assembly of Discrete Sierpinski Triangles. Theor. Comput. Sci. 410, 384–405 (2009)
9. Ke, Y., Ong, L.L., Shih, W.M., et al.: Three-dimensional Structures Self-assembled from DNA Bricks. Science 6111, 1177–1183 (2012)
10. Mao, C., LaBean, T.H., Reif, J.H.: Logical Computation using Algorithmic Self-assembly of DNA Triple-crossover Molecules. Nature 407, 493–496 (2000)
11. Brun, Y.: Arithmetic Computation in the Tile Assembly Model: Addition and Multiplication. Theor. Comput. Sci. 378, 17–31 (2006)
12. Brun, Y.: Nondeterministic Polynomial Time Factoring in the Tile Assembly Model. Theor. Comput. Sci. 395, 3–23 (2008)
13. Cheng, Z.: Nondeterministic Algorithm for Breaking Diffie-Hellman Key Exchange using Self-assembly of DNA Tiles. Int. J. Comput. Commun. 7, 616–630 (2012)
14. Marcelo, E.K., Takagi, N.: A Hardware Algorithm for Modular Multiplication/division. IEEE Transactions on Computers 54, 12–21 (2005)
15. Koblitz, N.: Elliptic Curve Cryptosystem. Math. Comp. 48, 203–209 (1987)

Using Support Vector Machine to Identify Imaging Biomarkers of Major Depressive Disorder and Anxious Depression

Minyue Chi[1,*], Shengwen Guo[1,*], Yuping Ning[2,*], Jie Li[2],
Haochen Qi[1], Minjian Gao[3], Jiexin Wang[3], Xiaowei Hu[3],
Yangbo Guo[2], Yuling Yang[2], Hongjun Peng[2,**], and Kai Wu[1,**]

[1] Department of Biomedical Engineering,
School of Materials Science and Engineering, South China University of Technology,
Guangzhou, China
[2] Guangzhou Psychiatric Hospital,
Affiliated Hospital of Guangzhou Medical University, Guangzhou, China
[3] School of Computer Science and Engineering,
South China University of Technology, Guangzhou, China

Abstract. Comorbidity with anxiety disorders is a relatively common occurrence in major depressive disorder. However, there are no objective, neurological markers which can be used to identify depressive disorder with and without anxiety disorders. The aim of this study was to examine the diagnostic value of structural MRI to distinguish depressive patients with and without ss using support vector machine. In this paper, we applied voxel-based morphometry of gray matter volume (GMV), then choose discriminative features to classify different group using linear support vector machine (SVM) classifier. The experimental results showed that specific structural brain regions may be a potential biomarkers for disease diagnosis.

Keywords: anxiety, depression, gray matter volume, voxel-based morphometry, support vector machine.

1 Introduction

Standard univariate analysis of neuroimaging data has revealed a lost of neuroanatomical and functional differences between healthy individuals and patients suffering a wide range of neurological and psychiatric disorders. However, these significant findings are only at group level which limited clinical application, and recent attention has turned toward alternative forms of analysis, including machine learning. There is rapidly accumulating evidence that the application of machine learning classification to neuroimaging measurements may be valuable for disease diagnosis, transition prediction and treatment prognosis.

Anxious depression is a common, clinical distinct subtype of major depressive disorder (MDD). It has been estimated that 40-50% of MDD patients have at

---

* First authorship.
** Corresponding authors.

L. Pan et al. (Eds.): BIC-TA 2014, CCIS 472, pp. 63–67, 2014.
© Springer-Verlag Berlin Heidelberg 2014

least one comorbid anxiety disorder and these occur across both inpatient and outpatient patient populations. In an effort to increase our understanding of the relationship between MDD and anxious depression, a number of researchers have investigated the structural brain changes associated with MDD and anxiety. MDD patients with anxiety symptoms show greater GMV in the right temporal cortex, compared with MDD patients without anxiety symptoms [7]. Specific involvement of the inferior frontal cortex in MDD and lateral temporal cortex in anxiety disorders without comorbid MDD have been demonstrated and may reflect disorder-specific symptom clusters [8].

At present, there are no objective, neurological markers, which can be used to identify depressive patients with and without anxiety disorders. The aim of the present study was to examine the diagnostic value of structural MRI using support vector machine. In this study, we applied a VBM analysis of GMV in normal controls and depressive patients with and without anxiety disorders. Then, we used these significant differences as feature to classify MDD and anxious depression by SVM.

2   Materials and Methods

2.1   Subjects

38 depressive patients were divided into two groups: 18 depressive patients without anxiety disorders (the DP group, SAS scores<40, HAMA scores<14) and 20 depressive patients with anxiety disorders (the DPA group, SAS scores≥40, HAMA scores≥14).

In addition, 28 sex- and age- matched normal controls (the NC group) were recruited from the local community. Before enrollment, all subjects were fully informed of the details of the study and written informed consent was obtained. These studies were performed according to the Declaration of Helsinki and approved by the Guangzhou Psychiatric Hospital Ethics Committee.

2.2   Voxel-Based Morphometry

All T1-weighted MR images were analyzed using SPM8 (Wellcome Institute of Neurology, University College London, UK; http://www.fil.ion.ucl.ac.uk/spm). First, the New Segmentation algorithm from SPM8 was applied to each T1-weighted MR image to extract tissue maps corresponding to gray matter, white matter, and cerebrospinal fluid (CSF). Next, all segmented tissue maps were used to create a customized, population specific template using the DARTEL template-creation tool [1]. At the end of the process, each subjects gray matter map was warped using its corresponding smooth, reversible deformation parameters to the custom template space, and then to the MNI standard space. All warped gray matter images were then modulated by calculating the Jacobian determinants derived from the special normalization step and multiplying each voxel by the relative change in volume [6]. Finally, all wrapped modulated gray matter images were smoothed with an 8-mm Gaussian kernel before voxel-wise group comparisons.

2.3   Machine Learning

Dimensionality Reduction. Raw features are the voxels that showed significant group differences in statistical analysis. Given that some features are uninformative, irrelevant or redundant for classification, reducing a number of features not only speed up computation, but also improve classification performance. Therefore, a feature selection step was utilized. In this study, the F score method was employed for dimensionality reduction.

F score is simple, generally quite effective feature ranking method [4]. Given the number of positive instances (i.e., patient subjects) n+ and negative instances (i.e., control subjects) n-, the F score of the ith feature is defined as follows:

$$Fi = \frac{\left(\bar{x}_i^{(+)} - \bar{x}_i\right)^2 + \left(\bar{x}_i^{(-)} - \bar{x}_i\right)^2}{\frac{1}{n_+-1}\sum_{k=1}^{n_+}\left(x_{k,i}^{(+)} - \bar{x}_i^{(+)}\right)^2 + \frac{1}{n_--1}\sum_{k=1}^{n_-}\left(x_{k,i}^{(-)} - \bar{x}_i^{(-)}\right)^2} \tag{1}$$

where $\bar{x}_i, \bar{x}_i^{(+)}$, $\bar{x}_i^{(-)}$ are the averages of the ith feature of the whole, positive, and negative data sets, respectively; $x_{k,i}^{(+)}$ is the ith feature of the kth positive instance, and $x_{k,i}^{(-)}$ is the ith feature of the kth negative instance. The denominator represents the discrimination within each of the positive and negative sets, while the numerator represents the discrimination between the two sets. Obviously, the larger the F score is, the more discriminative the feature is.

Support Vector Machine. SVM is an effective classification method, and it works well when the number of training samples is small but the number of feature is large [2][5]. The classification process consists of two steps: training and testing. During the training step, the SVM find a decision boundary that separates the examples in the input space using their labels. Once the decision function is determined from the training set, it can be used to predict the class label of a new testing example.

We used a linear kernel SVM as implemented in the LIBSVM toolbox to investigate the diagnostic accuracy of whole-brain structural MRI images [3].

Classifier Performance. A leave-one out cross-validation (LOOCV) strategy was used to evaluate the performance of a classifier. Furthermore, we plotted receiver operating characteristic curves (ROC) to examine whether these features could be used as markers to discriminate anxious depression and MDD.

To quantify the result, we measured the accuracy, the area under the curve. We also quantified the sensitivity and specificity of each test defined as

$$sensitivity = \frac{TP}{TP + FN} \tag{2}$$

$$specificity = \frac{TN}{TN + FP} \tag{3}$$

where TP is true positive: the number of the class 1 correctly classified; TN is true negative: the number of the class 2 correctly classified; FP is false positive: the number of the class 2 classified as class 1; FN is false negative: the number of the class 1 classified as class 2. equal to or greater than the accuracy obtained by the non-permutated (original) data. If p value is less than 0.05, the result was thought to be significant.

3   Results

3.1   Group Differences in Gray Matter Volume

The DP group showed significant gray matter reductions in the left insula (INS) and left triangular part of inferior frontal gyrus (IFGtriang), compared with the NC group.

The DPA group showed significant gray matter increases than the NC group in these brain areas: bilateral precentral gyrus (PreCG), bilateral midbrain, left superior occipital gyrus (SOG), left medial part of orbitofrontal cortex (ORBmed), left rolandic operculum (ROL), and right postcentral gyrus (PoCG).

The DPA group showed significant gray matter increases than the DP group in these brain areas: bilateral INS, bilateral inferior frontal gyrus (IFG), bilateral rectus (REC), bilateral ROL, bilateral inferior temporal gyrus (ITG), bilateral middle temporal gyrus (MTG), bilateral parahippocampal gyrus (PHG), bilateral hippocampus (HIP), left PreCG, left dorsal part of superior frontal gyrus (SFGdor), right lingual gyrus (LING), right PoCG, right supplementary motor area (SMA), right angular gyrus (ANG), and right amygdala (AMYG).

3.2   Overall Classifier Performance

The linear SVM method achieved a classification accuracy of 78.3% (92.9% for sensitivity, 55.6% for specificity) between DP group and NC group. The high sensitivity (92.9%) and low specificity (60.0%) is also found in the classification between DPA group and NC group with a accuracy of 79.2% . Because of the opposite direction of gray matter change between DP group and DPA group, the classification result of this comparison is better than the other two comparisons. The accuracy is 81.6% between DPA group and DP group with both high sensitivity (83.3%) and high specificity (80.0%). In addition, taking each testing subjects discriminative score as a threshold, the receiver operating characteristic (ROC) curve of the classifier was yielded, as shown in (Fig. 1). The area under the ROC curve (AUC) of the linear SVM classifier were 0.790, 0.863, 0.878 for the three comparisons, respectively. A high AUC usually indicates a good classification power of the classifier.

The discriminative features between DP group and NC group is located in bilateral cerebellum posterior lobe and right lingual gyrus. The discriminative features between DPA group and NC group is located in bilateral PreCG gyrus. The discriminative features between DPA group and DP group is located in bilateral INS, right IFG, right ROL, right ITG, right MTG, right PHG, right LING, right PoCG, right AMYG.

Acknowledgements. This study was supported by the National Natural Science Foundation of China (31400845 and C090104), the Guangdong Natural Science Foundation (S2012040007743), the Fundamental Research Funds of Central Universities under the South China University of Technology (2013ZM046), the Medical Research Foundation of Guangdong (A2012523), the Science and Technology Program of Guangzhou (2010Y1-C631 and 2013J4100096), the National Clinical Key Special Program of China (201201003), and the Guangzhou municipal key discipline in medicine for Guangzhou Brain Hospital (GBH2014-ZD04).

References

1. Ashburner, J.: A fast diffeomorphic image registration algorithm. Neuroimage 38, 95–113 (2007)
2. Boser, B.E., Guyon, I.M., Vapnik, V.N.: A training algorithm for optimal margin classifiers. In: Proceedings of the Fifth Annual Workshop on Computational Learning Theory, pp. 144–152. ACM (1992)
3. Chang, C.-C., Lin, C.-J.: LIBSVM: a library for support vector machines. ACM Transactions on Intelligent Systems and Technology (TIST) 2, 27 (2011)
4. Chen, Y.-W., Lin, C.-J.: Combining SVMs with various feature selection strategies. Feature Extraction, pp. 315–324. Springer (2006)
5. Cortes, C., Vapnik, V.: Support-vector networks. Machine Learning 20, 273–297 (1995)
6. Good, C.D., Johnsrude, I., Ashburner, J., Henson, R.N., Friston, K.J., Frackowiak, R.S.: Cerebral asymmetry and the effects of sex and handedness on brain structure: a voxel-based morphometric analysis of 465 normal adult human brains. Neuroimage 14, 685–700 (2001)
7. Inkster, B., Rao, A.W., Ridler, K., Nichols, T.E., Saemann, P.G., Auer, D.P., Holsboer, F., Tozzi, F., Muglia, P., Merlo-Pich, E., Matthews, P.M.: Structural brain changes in patients with recurrent major depressive disorder presenting with anxiety symptoms. J. Neuroimaging 21, 375–382 (2011)
8. Van Tol, M.J., van der Wee, N.J., van den Heuvel, O.A., Nielen, M.M., Demenescu, L.R., Aleman, A., Renken, R., van Buchem, M.A., Zitman, F.G., Veltman, D.J.: Regional brain volume in depression and anxiety disorders. Arch. Gen. Psychiatry. 67, 1002–1011 (2010)

An Adaptive Differential Evolution Algorithm with Automatic Population Resizing for Global Numerical Optimization

Tae Jong Choi and Chang Wook Ahn*

Department of Computer Engineering, Sungkyunkwan University (SKKU)
2066 Seobu-Ro, Suwon 440-746, Republic of Korea
{gry17,cwan}@skku.edu

Abstract. An adaptive population resizing algorithm is presented. To improve the performance of DE, an adaptive population size algorithm that makes a balance between exploration-exploitation properties is required. Although adjusting population size is important, many researchers have not focused on this topic. The proposed algorithm calculates the deviation of the dispersed individuals in every certain evaluation counters and executes adjusting the population size based on this information. Therefore, the proposed algorithm can adapt the population size by including or excluding some individuals depending on the progress. The performance evaluation results showed that the proposed algorithm was better than standard DE algorithm.

Keywords: Differential Evolution Algorithm, Adaptive Parameter Control, Population Size, Deviation, Global Numerical Optimization.

1 Introduction

Differential Evolution (DE) is a population based meta-heuristic algorithm [1]. DE has three control parameters, scaling factor, crossover rate and population size. These control parameters affect the performance of DE highly. To find the suitable control parameters, the user uses the trial-and-error scheme. However, the trial-and-error scheme is not efficient.

To automatically find the proper control parameters, the user can attach a parameter adaptation algorithm to DE. A well-designed parameter adaptation algorithm can enhance the performance of DE significantly [3]-[7]. Although there exist many parameter control algorithms, most parameter adaptation algorithms are related to scaling factor and crossover rate, not population size [8]-[10]. However, [11] and [12] claimed that the appropriate population size is important to both efficiency of optimization progress and effectiveness of optimization performance.

In this paper, we proposed Automatic Population Resizing (APR) algorithm. The proposed algorithm calculates the deviation of the dispersed individuals

---

* Corresponding author.

L. Pan et al. (Eds.): BIC-TA 2014, CCIS 472, pp. 68–72, 2014.

in every certain evaluation counters and executes adjusting the population size based on this information. If the deviation is sufficiently less than the previous deviation, the population size is decreased at a certain rate. On the other hand, if the deviation is not adequately less than the previous deviation, the population size is increased at the reversed decreasing rate. Therefore, the proposed algorithm can adapt the population size by including or excluding some individuals depending on the progress. We extended an adaptive differential evolution algorithm (SaDE) [3] by attaching the proposed algorithm. We compared the extended SaDE algorithm with standard DE algorithm in 13 benchmark problems [13]. The experiment result showed that the proposed algorithm performs better than standard DE algorithm in not only unimodal but also multimodal benchmark problems.

2   The Proposed Algorithm

APR algorithm calculates the deviation of the dispersed individuals in every certain evaluation counters and executes adjusting the population size based on this information. The deviation of the dispersed individuals is calculated as follows:

$$dev_n = \sum_{j=1}^{D} \sqrt{\frac{\sum_{i=1}^{NP}(x_{i,j,G} - \mu_i)^2}{NP}} \qquad (1)$$

where μ_i denotes the average of the dispersed individuals over i-th dimension. The every certain evaluation counters AF_{eval} that executes adapting the population size are as follows:

$$AF_{eval} = \{MF_{eval} \cdot (1 - \rho), MF_{eval} \cdot (1 - \rho^2), \cdots, MF_{eval} \cdot (1 - \rho^n)\} \qquad (2)$$

where MF_{eval} denotes the maximum number of evaluation counters. After that, if the deviation is sufficiently less than the previous deviation, the population size is decreased at the rate η. otherwise, the population size is increased at the reversed rate $\frac{1}{\eta}$. The population size is adjusted as follows:

$$NP_{new} = \begin{cases} NP \cdot \eta & \text{if } dev_n \le \frac{dev_{n-1}}{2} \\ \frac{NP}{\eta} & \text{otherwise} \end{cases} \qquad (3)$$

where NP_{new} and NP denote next population size and current population size, respectively. After that, if $NP_{new} \le NP$, select first NP_{new} current individuals into next population. Otherwise, generate remaining $(NP_{new} - NP)$ individuals as follows:

$$x_{new,j,G} = \begin{cases} x_{min,j} + rand_{i,j}(0,1) \cdot (x_{max,j} - x_{min,j}) & \text{if } rand < 0.5 \\ x_{\Psi,j,G} & \text{otherwise} \end{cases} \qquad (4)$$

where Ψ is a random index within the range $[1, NP]$.

Table 1. Benchmark problems

Benchmark problems	D	S	f_{min}
$f_1(x) = \sum_{i=1}^{D} x_i^2$	30	$[-100, 100]^D$	0
$f_2(x) = \sum_{i=1}^{D} |x_i| + \prod_{i=1}^{D} |x_i|$	30	$[-10, 10]^D$	0
$f_3(x) = \sum_{i=1}^{D} (\sum_{j=1}^{i} x_j)^2$	30	$[-100, 100]^D$	0
$f_4(x) = max_i(|x_i|, 1 \leq i \leq D)$	30	$[-100, 100]^D$	0
$f_5(x) = \sum_{i=1}^{D-1}[100(x_{i+1} - x_i^2)^2 + (x_i - 1)^2]$	30	$[-30, 30]^D$	0
$f_6(x) = \sum_{i=1}^{D} (\lfloor x_i + 0.5 \rfloor)^2$	30	$[-100, 100]^D$	0
$f_7(x) = \sum_{i=1}^{D} i x_i^4 + random[0, 1)$	30	$[-1.28, 1.28]^D$	0
$f_8(x) = \sum_{i=1}^{D} -x_i sin(\sqrt{|x_i|})$	30	$[-500, 500]^D$	-12569.5
$f_9(x) = \sum_{i=1}^{D} [x_i^2 - 10cos(2\pi x_i) + 10]$	30	$[-5.12, 5.12]^D$	0
$f_{10}(x) = -20exp(-0.2\sqrt{\frac{1}{D}\sum_{i=1}^{D} x_i^2}) - exp(\frac{1}{D}\sum_{i=1}^{D} cos2\pi x_i)$ $+20 + exp(1)$	30	$[-32, 32]^D$	0
$f_{11}(x) = \frac{1}{4000}\sum_{i=1}^{D} x_i^2 - \prod_{i=1}^{D} cos(\frac{x_i}{\sqrt{i}}) + 1$	30	$[-600, 600]^D$	0
$f_{12}(x) = \frac{\pi}{D}\{10sin^2(\pi y_1) + \sum_{i=1}^{D-1}(y_i - 1)^2[1 + 10sin^2(\pi y_{i+1})]$ $+(y_D - 1)^2\} + \sum_{i=1}^{D} u(x_i, 10, 100, 4)$ $y_i = 1 + \frac{1}{4}(x_i + 1)$ $u(x_i, a, k, m) = \begin{cases} k(x_i - a)^m & , x_i > a \\ 0 & , -a \leq x_i \leq a \\ k(-x_i - a)^m & , x_i < -a \end{cases}$	30	$[-50, 50]^D$	0
$f_{13}(x) = 0.1\{sin^2(3\pi x_1) + \sum_{i=1}^{D-1}(x_i - 1)^2[1 + sin^2(3\pi x_{i+1})]$ $+(x_D - 1)^2[1 + sin^2(2\pi x_D)]\} + \sum_{i=1}^{D} u(x_i, 5, 100, 4)$	30	$[-50, 50]^D$	0

3   Performance Evaluation

The proposed algorithm was compared with standard DE algorithm as follows:

1) SaDEwAPR with $\rho = 0.7$, $\eta = 0.1$ and $NP_{init} = 100$;

2) DE/rand/1/bin with $F = 0.5$, $CR = 0.9$ and $NP_{init} = 100$ [1],[4],[7];

The benchmark problems are shown in Table 1. In this table, D, S and f_{min} denote dimension, search spaces and global optimum, respectively. The mean and the standard deviation of performance evaluation obtained by the proposed algorithm and standard DE algorithm are summarized in Table 2. In this table, MF_{eval} denotes the maximum number of function evaluation. The proposed algorithm performed better than standard DE algorithm in not only the unimodal benchmark problems but also the multimodal benchmark problems except f_3, f_5 and f_{11}. Standard DE algorithm performed the best for solving f_3, f_5 and f_{11} benchmark problems. However, in f_3 and f_{11}, the differences of performance evaluation results between the proposed algorithm and standard DE algorithm are not a significant, i.e., they were less than $1.00E - 11$ in f_3 and $1.00E - 21$ in f_{11}. The proposed algorithm outperformed standard DE algorithm on f_1, f_2, f_4, f_8, f_9, f_{10}, f_{12} and f_{13}.

Table 2. The performance evaluation result of the comparison of the proposed algorithm and several state-of-the-art DE algorithms

	MF_{eval}	DE		SaDEwAPR	
		Mean	Std	Mean	Std
f_1	150K	7.59E-14	5.56E-14	**4.34E-48**	**3.04E-47**
f_2	200K	2.18E-10	1.18E-10	**3.59E-94**	**6.92E-94**
f_3	500K	**3.85E-11**	**4.25E-11**	4.79E-11	2.47E-10
f_4	500K	1.26E-01	3.16E-01	**2.59E-18**	**6.53E-18**
f_5	2000K	**7.98E-02**	**5.59E-01**	2.82E+00	6.05E+00
f_6	150K	0.00E+00	0.00E+00	0.00E+00	0.00E+00
f_7	300K	4.58E-03	1.06E-03	**2.78E-03**	**1.79E-03**
f_8	900K	1.51E+03	5.47E+02	**8.17E-06**	**0.00E+00**
f_9	500K	6.76E+01	2.52E+01	**0.00E+00**	**0.00E+00**
f_{10}	200K	9.94E-11	5.06E-11	**5.03E-15**	**1.77E-15**
f_{11}	300K	**0.00E+00**	**0.00E+00**	1.08E-21	7.59E-21
f_{12}	150K	9.15E-15	8.37E-15	**1.57E-32**	**1.64E-47**
f_{13}	150K	4.00E-14	3.10E-14	**1.35E-32**	**8.21E-48**

4   Conclusion

This paper has presented an extended SaDE algorithm by attaching the population size adjusting algorithm, called SaDEwAPR. SaDE uses an adaptive mechanism on not only mutation strategies but the control parameters, the scaling factor and the crossover rate. By attaching APR algorithm to SaDE algorithm, the population size can be adjusted too. APR algorithm calculates the deviation of the dispersed individuals in every certain evaluation counters and executes adjusting the population size based on this information.

Therefore, APR algorithm can adapt the population size by including or excluding some individuals depending on the progress. To evaluate the effectiveness of APR algorithm, performance evaluation was carried out on 13 benchmark problems. SaDEwAPR was compared with standard DE algorithm. The performance evaluation results showed that the proposed algorithm was better than standard DE algorithm in not only unimodal but also multimodal benchmark problems.

Acknowledgement. This work was supported by the National Research Foundation of Korea (NRF) grant funded by the Korea government (MSIP) (NRF-2012R1A2A2A01013735).

References

1. Rainer, S., Kenneth, P.: Differential Evolution–A Simple and Efficient Heuristic for Global Optimization Over Continuous Spaces. Journal of Global Optimization 11(4), 341–359 (1997)
2. Swagatam, D., Suganthan, M., Nagaratnam, P.: Differential Evolution: A Survey of the State-of-the-art. IEEE Trans. on Evolutionary Computation 15(1), 4–31 (2011)
3. Qin, A.K., Suganthan, P.N.: Self-adaptive Differential Evolution Algorithm for Numerical Optimization. In: Proceedings of the meeting of the Congress on Evolutionary Computation (2005)
4. Brest, J., Greiner, S., Boskovic, B., Mernik, M., Zumer, V.: Self-Adapting Control Parameters in Differential Evolution: A Comparative Study on Numerical Benchmark Problems. IEEE Trans. Evolutionary Computation 10(6), 646–657 (2006)
5. Zhang, J., Sanderson, A.C.: JADE: Self-adaptive Differential Evolution with Fast and Reliable Convergence Performance. In: Proceedings of the meeting of the Congress on Evolutionary Computation (2007)
6. Rahnamayan, S., Tizhoosh, H.R., Salama, M.M.A.: Opposition-Based Differential Evolution. IEEE Trans. on Evolutionary Computation 12(1), 64–79 (2008)
7. Tae, J.C., Chang, W.A., Jinung, A.: An Adaptive Cauchy Differential Evolution Algorithm for Global Numerical Optimization. The Scientific World Journal, Article ID 969734 (2013), doi:10.1155/2013/969734
8. Teo, J.: Exploring Dynamic Self-adaptive Populations in Differential Evolution. Soft Computing 10(8), 673–686 (2006)
9. Brest, J., Maucec, M.S.: Population Size Reduction for The Differential Evolution Algorithm. Applied Intelligent 29(3), 228–247 (2008)
10. Elsayed, S.M., Sarker, R.A.: Differential Evolution with Automatic Population Injection Scheme for Constrained Problems. In: Proceedings of the Meeting of the IEEE Symposium on Differential Evolution (2013)
11. Goldberg, D.E., Deb, K., Clark, J.H.: Accounting for Noise in the Sizing of Populations. In: Proceedings of the meeting of the FOGA (1992)
12. Goldberg, D.E., Deb, K., Clark, J.H.: Genetic Algorithms, Noise, and the Sizing of Populations. Complex Systems 6, 333–362 (1992)
13. Yao, X., Liu, Y., Lin, G.: Evolutionary Programming Made Faster. IEEE Trans. on Evolutionary Computation 3(2), 82–102 (1999)

An Improved Method of DNA Information Encryption

Guangzhao Cui, Dong Han, Yan Wang,
Yanfeng Wang, and Zicheng Wang

School of Electrical and Information Engineering,
Henan Key Lab of Information-Based Electrical Appliances,
Zhengzhou University of Light Industry,
No.5 Dongfeng Road, Zhengzhou, 450002, China
yanfengwang@yeah.net, wzch@zzuli.edu.cn

Abstract. A scheme utilizing DNA technology for the purposes of DNA cryptography has been developed. To enhance the security of DNA cryptosystem, we used DNA digital encoding, complementary rules and biotechnological methods in this scheme. The experimental result showed that the scheme is feasible and the security analysis indicated that the scheme has a strong confidentiality.

Keywords: DNA computing, DNA cryptography, DNA digital encoding, Complementary rule, Steganography.

1 Introduction

Since Adleman solved combinational problems with molecular computations [1], molecular computing, has evolved into an exciting fast growing interdisciplinary research field. In recent years, many research works already have been carried out on DNA computing [2–5]. With the development of DNA computing, the field of DNA cryptography [6–9] also drew wide attention, which is a new application of DNA computing.

DNA molecule possesses ultra-scale computation and ultra-compact information storage properties which make it suitable for cryptography and steganography purposes. Clelland et al. [10] presented the use of microdots containing secret DNA messages for a double-encryption system. Leier et al. [11] proposed the use of secret messages encoded by DNA binary strands. Rao [12] presented a cryptosystem based on recombinant DNA technique and analyzed the security of this cryptosystem. So far, many researches of DNA cryptography have been done [13–17]. It can be foreseen that the DNA cryptography would have more development space in the future.

In this paper, we proposed a more secure DNA cryptographic scheme based on DNA technologies. This method firstly preprocessed the plaintext encrypted into a binary code data flow using ASCII code, then converted the binary code data flow to the original DNA sequence by DNA digital coding technology [18],

L. Pan et al. (Eds.): BIC-TA 2014, CCIS 472, pp. 73–77, 2014.

following which the original DNA sequence is converted to the new DNA sequence through the complementary rules [19]. In order to further improve the security, we cut the DNA sequence into several segments and added the primers to the both ends of these DNA segments. Finally, we send them together with other redundant DNA sequences to the receiver via public channels.

2   DNA Digital Coding and Complementary Rules

To hide data, we used the DNA digital encoding [18] and complementary rules [19] in this scheme. We considered A = 00, C = 11, G = 01, and T = 10 to convert binary data to DNA sequences. After the encrypted information is converted to DNA sequence, we applied a complementary rule to the DNA sequence so as to increase the complexity of the ciphertext. Here we considered the complementary rule as: ((AG) (GT) (TC) (CA)).

3   Encryption Process

Here we describe the encryption method in detail. Assuming the sender is Alice, the designated receiver is Bob.

1. Key Generation. Alice and Bob agreed beforehand to respectively design the same number primers of encryption and decryption. In this method both of them designed three different DNA sequences, and numbered the primers. The sequences with same number are used as a pair of primers. The designed primers are transferred to each other by safe way. The primers can also be accomplished by either of them, but in order to increase the security, both of them designed primers individually in this method.

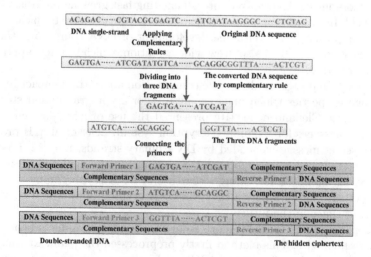

Fig. 1. Ciphertext generation process

2. Data Preprocessing. In this paper, we considered the message "16th–19th October, 2014, Wuhan, China" as a plaintext M. Firstly the plaintext M was converted to a binary code data flow by ASCII code (with 8 bits per character).

3. Encryption. We converted binary code data flow to DNA sequence M_1 by DNA digital coding rule. And then we converted the M_1 into a new DNA sequence M_2 through the complementary rule. In order to increase further confidentiality of information, we cut the DNA sequence into three DNA fragments, which is the ciphertext M_3. Next, we connected the three pairs of primers respectively to the both ends of the three DNA fragments, and then we synthesized a certain length of DNA sequence which contains the information (see Fig. 1).

4. Decryption. The decryption process is the reverse of encryption. Bob restored the ciphertext M_3 by PCR amplification and sequencing.

4   Experimental Design and Results

To investigate the feasibility of this scheme, we synthesized the three DNA fragments. The first one contains 88 nucleotides long encoded messages flanked by forward primers with 20 nucleotides long and reverse primers with 19 nucleotides long. The second one contains an encoded message 88 nucleotides long flanked by forward primers (19 nucleotides) and reverse primers (20 nucleotides). The third one contains an encoded message 87 nucleotides long flanked by forward primers (19 nucleotides) and reverse primers (18 nucleotides). We prepared concealing DNA that is similar to the three DNA fragments by synthesizing roughly 80-88 nucleotides. Finally, we mixed all of them together.

The designed primers were used to perform PCR, and the products were analyzed by gel electrophoresis (Fig. 2a). An unamplified sample containing ciphertext DNA yielded only a faint continuous smear (Fig. 2a, lane 2). In contrast, amplification of the three samples each yielded a single product of the expected

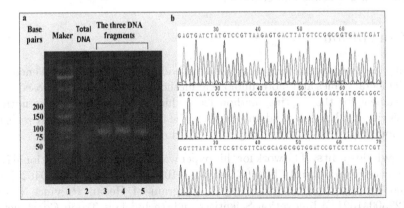

Fig. 2. Extracting information. a. Gel analysis of products obtained by PCR amplification with specific primers; b. Sequences of PCR amplification obtained by clone sequencing.

size (Fig. 2a, lanes 3-5). After clone sequencing, we obtained the ciphertext DNA sequences (Fig. 2b). The result shows that the scheme can be implemented based on the current experimental method.

5   Security Analysis

Here we analyze the security of the method from the two aspects.

The first layer security (biological security): As the ciphertext is unknown DNA sequences for the attacker, it is hard to obtain the correct DNA sequence without the correct primers. Furthermore, the ciphertext sequence has three paragraphs in this article, so there are 6 kinds of combinations, but only one combination is correct. In this paper, we assumed that the primer length is 20 bp, there are 6 correct primers, and thus, the probability of an attacker making a successful guess approximation is $\left(\frac{1}{4^{20}}\right)^6$. The probability of arranging 3 fragments of the DNA sequence in a correct ciphertext sequence is $\frac{1}{6}$. Moreover, there are six legal complementary rules, Thus, the probability of converting the ciphertext into the original DNA sequence is $\frac{1}{6}$, and the probability of converting the original DNA sequence into binary code data flow is $\frac{1}{24}$. Therefore, the probability of an attacker making a successful guess is as follows:

$$\left(\frac{1}{4^{20}}\right)^6 \times \frac{1}{6} \times \frac{1}{6} \times \frac{1}{24}.$$

Second layer security (computing security): In this method, it is difficult for an attacker to find keywords as primers to decipher the ciphertext. Even if the first biology security barrier is breached, what the attacker needs to do is how to use the traditional cryptography and DNA digital coding technology to decipher ciphertext in finite time. It can be foreseen that it is also hard to break the second layer security barrier.

Through the above analysis, we can see that the traditional cryptography and DNA encryption technology can be combined to improve security of cryptograph. Obviously, it is feasible and effective.

6   Conclusion

In this paper, we proposed an encryption method by using DNA digital encoding, complementary rules and biotechnological methods. The method proposed is the improvement for the existing method [20], which not only further strengthens the security of DNA password and explores the field, but also further reveals the great potential of DNA technology in the field of information security.

Acknowledgments. The work for this paper was supported by the National Natural Science Foundation of China (Grant Nos. 61070238, 61272022, U1304620), Basic and Frontier Technology Research Program of Henan Province (Grant No. 122300413211), Innovation Scientists and Technicians Troop Construction Projects of Henan Province (Grant No. 124200510017), and Innovation Scientists and Technicians Troop Construction Projects of Zhengzhou (Grant No. 131PLJRC648).

References

1. Adleman, L.: Molecular computation of solutions to combinational problems. J. Science 266(11), 1021–1024 (1994)
2. Adleman, L., et al.: On applying molecular computation to the data encryption standard. J. Journal of Computational Biology 6(1), 53–63 (1999)
3. Amos, M., et al.: Topics in the theory of DNA computing. J. Theoretical Computer Science 287(1), 3–38 (2002)
4. Zhang, X.C., Wang, Y.F., Cui, G.Z., et al.: Application of a novel IWO to the design of encoding sequences for DNA computing. J. Computers & Mathematics with Applications 57(11), 2001–2008 (2009)
5. Qian, L., Winfree, E.: Scaling up digital circuit computation with DNA strand displacement cascades. J. Science 332, 1196–1201 (2011)
6. Gehani, A., LaBean, T.H., Reif, J.H.: DNA-based cryptography. DNA Based Computers V. Providence: American Mathematical Society 54, 233–249 (2000)
7. Kazuo, T., Akimitsu, O., Isao, S.: Public-key system using DNA as a one-way function for key distribution. J. Biosystems 81, 25–29 (2005)
8. Xiao, G.Z., Lu, M.X., Qin, L., et al.: New field of cryptography: DNA cryptography. J. Chinese Science Bullentin 51(12), 1413–1420 (2006)
9. Jiao, S.-H., Goutte, R.: Hiding data in DNA of living organisms. J. Natural Science 1(3), 181–184 (2009)
10. Celland, C.T., Risca, V., Bancroft, C.: Hiding messages in DNA microdots. J. Nature 399, 533–534 (1999)
11. Leier, A., Richter, C., Banzhaf, W., et al.: Cryptography with DNA binary strands. J. Biosystems 57(1), 13–22 (2000)
12. Rao, N.N.: A cryptosystem based on recombinant DNA technique. J. Acta Electronica Sinica 32(7), 1216–1218 (2004)
13. Lai, X.J., Lu, M.X., Qin, L., et al.: Asymmetric encryption and signature method with DNA technology. J. Science China Information Sciences 53(3), 506–514 (2010)
14. Abbasy, M.R., Shanmugam, B.: Enabling Data Hiding for Resource Sharing in Cloud Computing Environments Based on DNA Sequences. In: Proceedings of the 2011 IEEE World Congress on Services, pp. 385–390 (2011)
15. Morford, L.: A theoretical application of selectable markers in bacterial episomes for a DNA cryptosystem. J. Journal of Theoretical Biology 273(1), 100–102 (2011)
16. Zhang, Y., Fu, B., Zhang, X.: DNA cryptography based on DNA Fragment assembly. In: 2012 8th International Conference on Information Science and Digital Content Technology (ICIDT), pp. 179–182. IEEE Press, Jeju (2012)
17. Babaei, M.: A novel text and image encryption method based on chaos theory and DNA computing. J. Natural Computing 12(1), 101–107 (2013)
18. Chen, W.C., Chen, Z.H., et al.: Digital coding of the genetic codons and DNA sequences in high dimension space. J. Acta Biophysica Sinica 16(4), 760–768 (2000)
19. Shiu, H.J., Ng, K.L., Fang, J.F., et al.: Data hiding methods based upon DNA sequences. J. Information Sciences 180(11), 2196–2208 (2010)
20. Cui, G.Z., Qin, L.M., Wang, Y.F., et al.: Encryption scheme research based on DNA technology. J. Computer Engineering and Applications 45(8), 104–106 (2009)

An Encryption Scheme
Based on DNA Microdots Technology

Guangzhao Cui, Yan Wang, Dong Han,
Yanfeng Wang, Zicheng Wang, and Yanmin Wu

School of Electrical and Information Engineering,
Henan Key Lab of Information-based Electrical Appliances,
Zhengzhou University of Light Industry,
No.5 Dongfeng Road, Zhengzhou, 450002, China
wzch@zzuli.edu.cn

Abstract. As a new research area of information security, DNA cryptography has achieved rapid advancements over recent years. It has been demonstrated that data hiding and encryption can be realized based on DNA digital encoding and microdots steganographic techniques. Here we present a more secure encryption scheme utilizing DNA microdots. It is noteworthy that the scheme achieves double concealing, which combines the properties of traditional cryptography and DNA microdots. The security of the scheme is analyzed from several aspects as well. Finally, the simulation proved a strong confidentiality of the encryption scheme.

Keywords: DNA Cryptography, Information Hiding, Information Security Technology.

1 Introduction

DNA cryptography, as the emerging field of information security, traditional cryptography and quantum cryptography are expected to become the three major branches of cryptography [1–4]. Since Adleman [5] successfully solved the NP complete problem, more and more people have been paying attention to the DNA computing [6–10], and thus DNA cryptography was born and now is developing.

In this work, we present a new encryption scheme based on the DNA microdots technology. To improve the security of the scheme, the paper combined traditional cryptography and DNA microdots hiding technology to transfer information, and it realized dual protect to information. In order to implement the scheme, we could build a mathematical pre-encryption program to preprocess the plaintext. In addition, compared to the original DNA microdots method, a step-by-step information transmission method was developed to resist the attack from an unexpected recipient. After the analysis of security, the probability function of synthesizing correct primers could be simulated with the programming.

L. Pan et al. (Eds.): BIC-TA 2014, CCIS 472, pp. 78–82, 2014.
© Springer-Verlag Berlin Heidelberg 2014

2   Related Work

With the further study of DNA computing, there are some new achievements in DNA cryptography [11–14]. Clelland et al. [15] devised a substitution cipher for a DNA-microdots-based encryption scheme. Cui et al. [16] designed an encryption scheme which taking both primers and coding mode as the key of the scheme and discussed the security of the scheme. Le Goff et al. [17] connected DNA microarray with a thermal-shrinkable flake and fixed DNA polymers on the polyethylene thermal-shrinkable flake, resulting in 6mm thick and 60mm wide hydrogel dots supporting oligonucleotides immobilization. Wang et al. [18] introduced latest research achievements of information security and proposed suggestions on the development of information security technology based on nucleic acids as well.

Microdot is, fundamentally, a steganographic approach to message protection, which is invented by professor Zapp during the Second World War [19]. Attackers are faced with three-layer security of DNA microdots technology: DNA microdot, biotechnology limited and mathematical security. If the attackers have enough ciphertext information, they can launch an attack according to the statistical frequency of letters with the computer [20]. In addition, it should be pointed out that the space of the replacing mapping table is only 64-bit which is not universal.

3   Security-Enhanced Encryption Scheme

Assume that the sender is Alice and the receiver is Bob. They make a promissory secret key (SK) in advance and send it in a safe way. The SK includes a primer sequence set K and a mathematical pre-encrypted processing software. General steps of the encryption scheme are as follows:

Generating Primers. Alice designs six DNA sequences $KA_1, KA_2, \cdots, KA_6$ as a front primer set KA_n, and Bob designs six DNA sequences $KB_1, KB_2, \cdots, KB_6$ as a rear primers set KB_n, here the length of each primer is 20bp, where $K = \{KA_1, KB_1, KA_2, KB_2, KA_3, KB_3, KA_4, KB_4, KA_5, KB_5, KA_6, KB_6\}$. The sequential 12 segments of DNA sequence together as the primer to encrypt and decrypt, has been transmitted to the other party in advance via safe way.

Mathematical Pre-encryption Processing. Firstly, we can utilize computer to convert plaintext into binary code according to ASCII code comparison table. Secondly, encrypt the binary string plaintext after the conversion using the DES algorithm, and then we can obtain binary ciphertext. Then we extract odd number bits from the ciphertext DNA sequence to form an odd-bit sequence set OS (odd-bit sequence). And the rest of the sequences are composed ES (even-bit sequence).

Synthesis of Ciphertext Chain Group. Alice divides OS at any place of the chain into three sections. Then Alice links primers in sequence with each DNA sequence segments front end and back end. See the link location of the primers in Fig. 1. After linking primers three sections together to form a group named OCG (odd-bit chain group) including $OC_1, OC_2 and OC_3$, we artificially synthesize OCG. Similarly, we process the DNA sequence ES with the above approach and eventually get ECG (even-bit chain group).

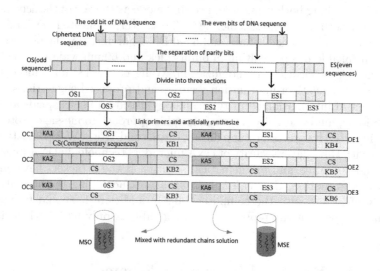

Fig. 1. Encryption and decryption processing

Information Hiding. The redundant chains are mixed with odd-bit-sequence chain group OCG and even-bit-sequence chain group ECG respectively to get DNA mixed solution MSO and MSE. Next, we spray MSO and MSE are on filter papers respectively. Then we get an odd-bit-sequence paper (OP) and an even-bit-sequence paper EP. Our transfer thought is sent step by step, namely transmitting OP through public channels firstly, and sending EP after the confirmation of OP's security. If the attacker detects or destructs OP, then the progress return to mathematical pre-encryption process to encrypt again.

4 Security Analysis

There is not yet a mature standard to evaluate the security of the encryption system, so we only discuss the security of the system one by one from four aspects; while only breaking down the four layer security barriers at the same time can we break the scheme up.

The first layer of security: Physical Concealing. DNA microdot is of high concealment for its colorlessness and odorlessness.

The second layer of security: Stepwise Transmission. This allows an attacker to only intercept the odd bit encoding at the most. After splitting the converted and cracked ciphertext message, it is quite difficult to get the complete information only by the odd bit encoding.

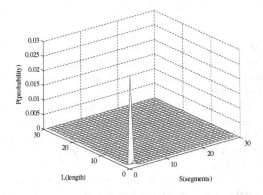

Fig. 2. The crack probability of primer attack method. P: The probability of synthesizing correct primers; L: The length of each primer; S: The total number of segments.

The third layer of security: Mathematical security. Firstly, the problem of the mapping table limited space is solved, which is of huge range of usage. Secondly, it is difficult for an attacker to find keywords as primer from transcoding to decode information.

The last layer security: Biological Safety. Assume that the information is divided into $2S$ segments, the length of each primer is L bases. The probability of synthesizing correct primers is: $P = 4^{-2LS} \times (2S)!^{-1}$. We use the software Matlab to draw the curve chart, as shown in Fig. 2. In order to explore the specific security, we also give a brief discussion on some attack include offline dictionary attack, online dictionary attack, forward secrecy, man-in-the-middle attack, forgery attack and replay attack.

5   Conclusion

The purpose of this paper is not to launch a practical cipher system instead of the traditional encryption systems or microdots technology, but to show that DNA molecules contain great potential which can be used in the field of cryptography. DNA cryptography brings out research ideas of cryptography to biology and reclaims new territory. We believe that DNA cryptography will be developed into the important part of cryptography in the near future.

Acknowledgments. The work for this paper was supported by the National Natural Science Foundation of China (Grant Nos. 61070238, 61272022, U1304620), Basic and Frontier Technology Research Program of Henan Province (Grant Nos. 122300413211, 132300410183, 092300410166), Innovation Scientists and Technicians Troop Construction Projects of Henan Province (Grant No. 124200510017), Science and Technology Research Key Project of The Education Department Henan Province (No. 13A413371), and Innovation Scientists and Technicians Troop Construction Projects of Zhengzhou (Grant No. 131PLJRC648).

References

1. Xiao, G.Z., Lu, M.X., Qin, L., et al.: New field of cryptography: DNA cryptography. J. Chinese Science Bullentin 51(12), 1413–1420 (2006)
2. Jiao, S.H., Goutte, R.: Hiding data in DNA of living organisms. J. Natural Science 1(3), 181–184 (2009)
3. Shiu, H.J., Ng, K.L., Fang, J.F., et al.: Data hiding methods based upon DNA sequences. J. Information Sciences 180(11), 2196–2208 (2010)
4. Kartalopoulos, S.V.: DNA-inspired cryptographic method in optical communications, authentication and data mimicking. In: Military Communications Conference, pp. 774–779 (2005)
5. Adleman, L.M., et al.: On applying molecular computation to the data encryption standard. J. Journal of Computational Biology 6(1), 53–63 (1999)
6. Lu, M.X., Lai, X.J., et al.: Symmetric encryption method based on DNA technology. J. Science in China (Series E) 37(2), 175–182 (2007)
7. Adleman, L.M.: Molecular computation of solutions to combinatorial problems. J. Science 266, 1021–1021 (1994)
8. Amos, M., Rozenberg, G., et al.: Topics in the theory of DNA computing. J. Theoretical Computer Science 287(1), 3–38 (2002)
9. Cui, G.Z., Qin, L.M., Wang, Y.F., et al.: Information security technology in DNA computing. J. Computer Engineering and Applications 43(20), 139–142 (2007)
10. Abbasy, M.R., Shanmugam, B.: Enabling Data Hiding for Resource Sharing in Cloud Computing Environments Based on DNA Sequences. In: Proceedings of the 2011 IEEE World Congress on Services, pp. 385–390 (2011)
11. Leier, A., Richter, C., Banzhaf, W., et al.: Cryptography with DNA binary strands. J. Biosystems 57(1), 13–22 (2000)
12. Tanaka, K., Okamoto, A., Saito, I.: Public-key system using DNA as a one-way function for key distribution. J. Biosystems 81, 25–29 (2005)
13. Chen, W.C., Chen, Z.H., et al.: Digital coding of the genetic codons and DNA sequences in high dimension space. J. Acta Biophysica Sinica 16(4), 760–768 (2000)
14. Gehani, A., Labean, T., Reif, J.: DNA-based cryptography. J. Aspects of Molecular Computing 2950, 167–188 (2004)
15. Clelland, C.T., Risca, V., Bancroft, C.: Hiding messages in DNA microdots. J. Nature 399(6736), 533–534 (1999)
16. Cui, G.Z., Qin, L.M., Wang, Y.F., et al.: Encryption scheme research based on DNA technology. J. Computer Engineering and Applications 45(8), 104–106 (2009)
17. Le Goff, G.C., Blum, L.J., Marquette, C.A.: Shrinking hydrogel-DNA spots generates 3D microdots arrays. J. Macromol Biosci. 13(2), 227–233 (2013)
18. Wang, Y.F., Han, Q.Q., Han, D., et al.: Information security technology based on nucleic acids. J. Chinese Academy of Sciences 29(001), 83–93 (2014)
19. Haigh, T.: Emanuel Goldberg and his knowledge machine. J. Am. Soc. Inf. Sci. 63, 427–428 (2012)
20. Stinson, D.R.: Cryptography: theory and practice. CRC Press, Boca Raton (2005)
21. Biham, E., Shamir, A.: Differential cryptanalysis of the data encryption standard. Springer, New York (1993)

Simulation DNA Algorithm

Peng Dai, Kang Zhou*, Zhiwei Wei, Di Hu, and Chun Liu

School of Math and Computer,
Wuhan Polytechnic University, Wuhan, China
perrywhpu@gmail.com, {zhoukang_wh,a274936580,18692846556}@163.com,
1623302442@qq.com

1 Introduction

Satisfiability problem (SAT) is one of classical combinational problems, which is proved to be a famous NP-complete problem [1]. SAT is widely used [2], [3]. At present, research on algorithm of SAT has made significant progress [4], [5]. Among these algorithms, some are non polynomial even though they can obtain exact solution of SAT; and heuristic algorithm cannot obtain exact solution of SAT, even though it is polynomial. Therefore, it is essential to find an exact algorithm of SAT which is more practical and can effectively the control calculation time.

In 2014, based on sticker model [6], [7], Zhou Kang [8] made further research on simulation DNA algorithm (SDA) [9] for the first time and he put forward variable length vector and biochemical operators which contain batch separation operator and electrophoresis operator.

SAT [10] is to solve if there is an assignment of truth values to proposition variables of a given conjunctive normal form (disjunctive normal form) whose formula evaluates to be true. More precisely, for a conjunctive normal form $F = C_1 \wedge C_2 \wedge \cdots \wedge C_m$ in set of literals L; and $C_i = l_1 \vee l_2 \vee \cdots \vee l_t$ is simple disjunction, SAT is to solve if there is an assignment of $p_1, p_2, \cdots, p_n$ to make $F = 1$.

2 Biochemical Operator of SDA

If each DNA in a tube is considered as an element in a set, then a tube can be considered as a set; doing a biochemistry experiment in a tube can be considered as calculating a biochemistry operator in a set. So DNA algorithm can be mapped into simulation DNA algorithm.

Definition 1. Let set $L' = \{1, 2, \cdots, n, -1, -2, \cdots, -n\}$, vector $x = (x(1), x(2), \cdots, x(s))$ and vector $x_1 = (x_1(1), x_1(2), \cdots, x_1(t))$, and let set P be a set of n dimension 0-1 vector $y = (y_1, y_2, \cdots, y_n)$.

(1) If $\forall i$ $(1 \leq i \leq s \rightarrow x(i) \in L')$, then x is called **variable length vector**, a set of components of variable length vector x is called $Component(x) = \{x(1), x(2), \cdots, x(s)\}$.

---

* Corresponding author.

L. Pan et al. (Eds.): BIC-TA 2014, CCIS 472, pp. 83–87, 2014.

(2) For variable length vector x, if $P = \{y|\forall i((1 \le i \le s \land x(i) > 0 \to y_{x(i)} = 1) \lor (1 \le i \le s \land x(i) < 0 \to y_{-x(i)} = 0))\}$, then $P = x$.

(3) If $\exists i \exists j\ (x(i) + x(j) = 0)$, then $x = \emptyset$. For $\forall P$, $\emptyset \bar{\in} P$, $\emptyset \subseteq P$.

(4) If $P = x$, $P_1 = x_1$, then $P \cup P_1 = \{x, x_1\}$.

(5) For $k\ (k \in L')$, $(x, k) = (x(1), x(2), \cdots, x(s), k)$. For vector x and vector x_1, $(x, x_1) = (x(1), x(2), \cdots, x(s), x_1(1), x_1(2), \cdots, x_1(t))$.

(6) (x, x_1) is called a **deriving element** of x, and denoted by $x \prec (x, x_1)$.

(7) $x - (x(i)) = (x(1), \cdots, x(i-1), x(i+1), \cdots, x(s))$.

(8) $-x = (-x(1), -x(2), \cdots, -x(s))$.

(9) For s dimension variable length vector x, if $\forall j(1 \le j \le s - 1 \to |x(j)| < |x(j+1)|)$, then variable length vector x is called standard vector.

(10) Let $P = \{x_i|i \in \{1, 2, \cdots, m\}\}$. Set P is called standard set, if set P satisfies the conditions: $\forall x_i\ (x_i \in P)$, x_i is standard vector; $\forall x_i \forall x_j(x_i \in P \land x_j \in P \to Component(x_i) - Component(x_j) \ne \emptyset)$. $\qquad\square$

Definition 2. For standard set P and set $K = \{k|k \in L')\}$, **batch separation operator** [8] is as follows:

$$Separate(P, K) = \{(x, k)|x \in P \land k \in K\}$$

where set K is called **separation set**. $\qquad\square$

For standard vector x and $k\ (k \in K)$, let $Standard(x, k)$ be to standardize (x, k). Vector standardization process is the process of simplification of vector and its set. For standard set $P = \{x_1, x_2, \cdots, x_t\}$ and separation set $K = \{k(1), k(2), \cdots, k(r)\}$, $Standard - Separate(P, K)$ is to standardize $Separate(P, K)$, whose calculation process is as follows:

Step1 Compute set $P_1 = \{x_i|x_i \in P \land |Component(x_i) \cap K| \ge 1\}$.
   let $P_1 = \emptyset, P_2 = \emptyset$
   for $i = 1$ to t
     for $j = 1$ to r
      if $k(j) \in Component(x_i)$ let $P_1 = P_1 \cup \{x_i\}$, break
     end
     let $P_2 = P_2 \cup \{x_i\}$
   end
   $P_1 = \{x_{l(1)}, x_{l(2)}, \cdots, x_{l(s)}\}$
   $P_2 = \{x_{h(1)}, x_{h(2)}, \cdots, x_{h(t-s)}\}$
Step2 Compute set $P_3 = Separate(P_2, K)$.
   let $P_3 = \emptyset$
   for $i = 1$ to r
     for $j = 1$ to $t - s$
      if $k(i) \in K - Component(-x_{h(j)})$ let $P_3 = P_3 \cup \{Standard(x_{h(j)}, k(i))\}$
     end
   end
   $P_3 = \{w_1, w_2, \cdots, w_p\}$
Step3 Eliminate all deriving elements of the element of set P_1.
   let $I = \emptyset$
   for $i = 1$ to p

for $j = 1$ to s
 if $Component(x_{l(j)}) \subseteq Component(w_i)$ let $I = I \cup \{i\}$
 end
end
$I = \{i(1), i(2), \cdots, i(q)\}$
for $k = 1$ to $q - 1$
 let $w_{i(k)+1-k} = w_{i(k)+1}, w_{i(k)+2-k} = w_{i(k)+2}, \cdots, w_{i(k+1)-1-k} = w_{i(k+1)-1}$
end
let $w_{i(q)+1-q} = w_{i(q)+1}, w_{i(q)+2-q} = w_{i(q)+2}, \cdots, w_{p-q} = w_p$
$P_3 = \{w_1, w_2, \cdots, w_{p-q}\}$
return$(P_1 \cup P_3)$ □

For example, $Separate(\{(1, -3), (2, 3), (-4)\}, \{3, -5\}) = \{(2, 3), (1, -3, -5),$
$(3, -4), (-4, -5)\} = \{(2, 3), (3, -4), (-4, -5), (1, -3, -5)\}$.

3 SDA of SAT

Consider the iterative process (1):

$$P_1 = \{()\}$$

$$Standard - Separate(P_i, K_i) = P_{i+1} \quad (i = 1, 2, \cdots, m)$$

Selecting separation set problem is to give the optimal order of a sequence
of separation sets to minimize computational complexity of the iterative process
(1).

Definition 3. For $Data(i, j) = (a_1, a_2, a_3, a_4)$ and $Data(h, l) = (b_1, b_2, b_3, b_4)$,
if $a_1 < b_1$ or $(a_1 = b_1) \wedge (a_2 < b_2)$ or $(a_1 = b_1) \wedge (a_2 = b_2) \wedge (a_3 > b_3)$ or
$(a_1 = b_1) \wedge (a_2 = b_2) \wedge (a_3 = b_3) \wedge (a_4 > b_4)$, then $(i, j) < (h, l)$, which is called
less-than relation between separation sets.   □

Let $Data(i, j)$ be to compute the 4 dimension vector $(a_1(i, j), a_2(i, j), a_3(i, j),$
$a_4(i, j))$ of separation set $K_{I(i)}$ and separation set $K_{I(j)}$. $Order(K_1, K_2, \cdots, K_m)$
is an algorithm to solve selecting separation set problem, whose calculation process is as follows:
Step1 Determine element $I(1)$ and element $I(2)$.
 let $(i_0, j_0) = (1, 2)$
 for $i = 1$ to m
  for $j = i + 1$ to m
   if $(i, j) < (i_0, j_0)$ let $i_0 = i, j_0 = j$
  end
 end
Step2 Determine element $I(1)$, element $I(2)$ and element $I(3)$.
 let $I_1 = \{1, 2, \cdots, m\}, I_2 = \emptyset$
 let $j_1 = i' \ (i' \in I_1 - \{i_0, j_0\})$
 for $j = 1$ to m
  if $j \in I_1 - \{i_0, j_0, i'\} \wedge (i_0, j) < (i_0, j_1)$ let $(i_0, j_1) = (i_0, j)$

```
end
let i₁ = i' (i' ∈ I₁ − {i₀, j₀})
for i = 1 to m
   if i ∈ I₁ − {i₀, j₀, i'} ∧ (i, j₀) < (i₁, j₀) let (i₁, j₀) = (i, j₀)
end
if (i₀, j₁) < (i₁, j₀)
   let i(1) = j₀, i(2) = i₀, i(3) = j₁
else
   let i(1) = i₀, i(2) = j₀, i(3) = i₁
let I₂ = {i(1), i(2), i(3)}, I₁ = I₁ − I₂
```

Step3 Determine element $I(i)$ $(i = 4, 5, \cdots, m)$.

```
let (i₁, j₁) = (i(3), i') (i' ∈ I₁)
for l = 4 to m
   for j = 1 to m
      if j ∈ I₁ − {i'} ∧ (i₁, j) < (i₁, j₁) let (i₁, j₁) = (i₁, j)
   end
   let i(l) = j₁, I₂ = {i(1), i(2), ⋯, i(l)}, I₁ = I₁ − {i(l)}
   let (i₁, j₁) = (i(l), i') (i' ∈ I₁)
end
return(I₂)                                                       □
```

To consider a special conjunctive normal form $F = C_1 \wedge C_2 \wedge \cdots \wedge C_m$ containing n proposition variables $p_1, p_2, \cdots, p_n$, where $C_i = l_1 \vee l_2 \vee \cdots \vee l_t$, **SDA of SAT** is as follows:

Step1 For $\forall C_i = l_1 \vee l_2 \vee \cdots \vee l_t$, produce the separation set K_i'.

```
for i = 1 to m
   for j = 1 to t (Cᵢ = l₁ ∨ l₂ ∨ ⋯ ∨ lₜ)
      if lⱼ = pₛ let Kᵢ'(j) = s
      else if lⱼ = ¬pₛ let Kᵢ'(j) = −s
   end
end
```

Step2 Sort the sequence of separation sets $\{K_1', K_2', \cdots, K_m'\}$.

$$\{K_1, K_2, \cdots, K_m\} = Order(K_1', K_2', \cdots, K_m')$$

where

$$\{K_1, K_2, \cdots, K_m\} = \{K_{I(1)}', K_{I(2)}', \cdots, K_{I(m)}'\}$$

Step3 For the sequence of separation sets $\{K_1, K_2, \cdots, K_m\}$, compute the iterative process (1).

```
let P₁ = {()}
for i = 1 to m
   Pᵢ₊₁ = Standard − Separate(Pᵢ, Kᵢ)
end
Output(Pₘ₊₁)                                                     □
```

From SDA of SAT, we can get the conclusion as follows:

For a special conjunctive normal form $F = C_1 \wedge C_2 \wedge \cdots \wedge C_m$, where $C_i = l_1 \vee l_2 \vee \cdots \vee l_t$, time complexity of SDA of SAT is $O(\max |P_i| \times m \times n^2 \times (\max |P_i| + n) + m^2 \times n)$. $\qquad \square$

Acknowledgments. Kang Zhou is corresponding author. The work is supported by the National Natural Science Foundation of China (61179032, 11301405).

References

1. Rainer, S.: An algorithm for the satisfiability problem of formulas in conjunctive normal form. Journal of Algorithms 54, 40–44 (2005)
2. Ivancie, F., Yang, Z., Ganai, M.K.: Effident SAT-based bounded model checking for software verifications. Theoretical Computer Science 404, 256–274 (2008)
3. Jussi, R.: Planning as satisfiability: Heuristics. Artificial Intelligence 193, 45–86 (2012)
4. Cui, T., Franchetti, F.: Autotuning a random walk boolean satisfiability solver. Procedia Computer Science 4, 2176–2185 (2011)
5. Yousef, K.: Comparing the performance of the genetic and local search algorithms for solving the satisfiability problems. Applied Soft Computing 10, 198–207 (2010)
6. Xu, J., Dong, Y.F., Wei, X.P.: Sticker DNA computer model-Part I:Theory. Chinese Science Bulletin 49, 205–212 (2004)
7. Xu, J., Li, S.P., Dong, Y.F., Wei, X.P.: Sticker DNA computer model-Part II: application. Chinese Science Bulletin 49, 229–307 (2004)
8. Zhou, K., Chen, J.: Simulation DNA algorithm of set covering problem. Applied Mathematics and Information Sciences 8, 139–144 (2014)
9. Zhou, K., Wei, C.J., Liu, S., Lu, J.: Simulation DNA algorithm of all solutions of Eight Queens Problem. Journal of Huazhong University of Science and Technology (Natural Science Edition) 37, 24–27 (2009)
10. Plaisted, D.A., Biere, A., Zhu, Y.S.: A satisfiability procedure for quantified boolean formulae. Discrete Applied Mathematics 130, 291–328 (2003)

Research on Improved Locally Linear Embedding Algorithm

Tuo Deng*, Yanni Deng, Yuan Shi, and Xiaoqiu Zhou

School of Automation, Wuhan University of Technology,
Wuhan 430070, China
yodashine520@163.com, {719145031,925022061,545265345}@qq.com

Abstract. Locally linear embedding algorithm (LLE) is needed to be improved, since there were redundant information in its low dimensional feature space and no category information of the samples embedded into the low dimensional [1,2]. In this paper, we introduce a local linear maximum dispersion matrix algorithm (FSLLE), which integrated the sample category information. On this basis, the algorithm of locally linear embedding was improved and reexamined from the perspective of uncorrelated statistics. A kind of uncorrelated statistical with maximum dispersion matrix algorithm of locally linear embedding (OFSLLE) is proposed, with the application of elimination of redundant information among base vectors. Our algorithm was verified using the face library, showing that the base vector using uncorrelated constraints can effectively improve the performance of the algorithm and improve the recognition rate.

Keywords: Uncorrelated, Locally Linear Embedding, Face recognition.

1 Introduction

Locally linear embedding (LLE) algorithm was put forward by Sam and Lawrence in Science in 2000 [3]. In this algotithm, points neighboring in high dimensional space were also adjacent in low dimensional space, also their structures as well as weights in low and high dimension space were tried to be kept constant[4,5]. With the known category information of samples, this article integrated category information into LLE algorithm, leading to a maximum divergence based on local linear matrix algorithm (FSLLE), the purpose of which was to find a set of optimal projection matrix to make the objective function work [6,7]. Considering the redundant information in the low dimensional feature space of locally linear embedding algorithm, a kind of locally linear embedding maximum dispersion matrix algorithm with uncorrelated statistics (OFSLLE) was proposed on the basis of the above algorithm to eliminate the redundant information among base vectors. The improved algorithm was verified by face recognition, showing that both the performance of the algorithm and the recognition rate was improved.

---

* Corresponding author.

L. Pan et al. (Eds.): BIC-TA 2014, CCIS 472, pp. 88–92, 2014.
© Springer-Verlag Berlin Heidelberg 2014

2   Maximum Scatter Matrix Algorithm with Local Linear

Maximum scatter matrix algorithm based on local linear was based on the idea of FLD, in which category informations were integrated into the LLE algorithm. The purpose of the algorithm was to find an optimal projection matrix to meet the objective function below:

$$J_w = \arg max \left(A^T S_p A\right) / \left(A^T S_c A\right) \tag{1}$$

In the formulas, S_p represented consideration figure scatter matrix, S_c represented similar divergence matrix. The method for solving consideration figure scatter matrix and similar divergence matrix were introduced below.

Neighborhood graph of W_1 and W_2 were constructed. If X_i is the K close neighbor of X_j from [8], the result showed that in the neighborhood graph of W_1. An edge existed between X_i and X_j. If X_i and X_j were the samples of the same category, the result showed that in the neighborhood graph of W_2, an edge existed between X_i and X_j.

Thermonuclear estimation algorithm was used to determine the weights. In the neighborhood graph of W_1, if an edge existed between X_i and X_j,

$$W_{ij}^{C_1} = e^{-(||X_i - X_j||/t)^2}$$

was the weight; otherwise, $W_{ij}^{C_1} = 0$. In the neighborhood graph of W_2, if an edge existed between X_i and X_j, $W_{ij}^{C_2} = 1$ was the weight; otherwise, $W_{ij}^{C_2} = 0$. The similar matrix was $W_c = \theta W^{c_1} + (1-\theta)W^{c_2}$. Similarly, consideration graph matrix $W_p = \theta W^{p_1} + (1-\theta)W^{p_2}$ was constructed by the complement graph of W_1 and W_2. Below, the definition of complement graph were introduced. In the complement graph of figure neighbors W_1, if X_i was the K close neighbor of X_j,an edge did't exist. Otherwise, weight matrix W^{p_1} was reconstructed. In the complement graph of figure neighbors W_2, if X_i and X_j were the sample of the same category, an edge did't exist; otherwise, weight matrix W^{p_2} was reconstructed. So, $W_p = \theta W^{p_1} + (1-\theta)W^{p_2}$ was the consideration graph matrix, $\theta \in [0,1]$.

Similar matrix S_c and consideration graph matrix S_p were solved.

$$S_c = X H_n \left(I - W_c\right) \left(I - W_c\right)^T H_n^T X^T \tag{2}$$

$$S_p = X H_n \left(I - W_p\right) \left(I - W_p\right)^T H_n^T X^T \tag{3}$$

The formulas of (1) was transformed into the generalized eigenvalue problem below:

$$S_p \alpha_i = \lambda_i S_c \alpha_i \tag{4}$$

By the formula, the eigenvalues and the eigenvectors were solved. If the eigenvalues $\lambda_1 \geq \lambda_2 \geq \lambda_3 \geq \lambda_4 \geq \ldots \geq \lambda_d$ for the corresponding eigenvector was $\alpha_1, \alpha_2, \alpha_3, \alpha_4, \ldots, \alpha_d$, so $A = [\alpha_1, \alpha_2, \alpha_3, \alpha_4, , \alpha_d]$ was the projection matrix.

3 Maximum Scatter Matrix Algorithm with Local Linear Uncorrelated

When high-dimensional vectors were projected into low-dimensional vectors, redundancy information should not be existed in the low-dimensional feature space. The algorithm reexamined and improved locally linear embedding algorithm through a statistical point of uncorrelated. Thereby the maximum scatter matrix algorithm based on statistically uncorrelated local linear embedding was obtained, called UFSLLE. The objective function was transformed into the constraint problem below:

$$max \ tr \left[A^T \left(S_p - S_c \right) A \right] \tag{5}$$

The statistically uncorrelated was the conjugate orthogonal condition to the covariance matrix S_t. It satisfies the constraints:

$$s. \ t. \ \alpha_i^T S_t \alpha_j = 0 \ (i \neq j, i, j = 1, 2, 3, 4, ..., d),$$

$$S_t = E \left[\left(Z - \bar{Z} \right) \left(Z - \bar{Z} \right)^T \right], Z = X H_n$$

Similarly, $Y^T Y = I$ was the constraint. So the problem to find the statistically uncorrelated optimal discriminant vectors $A = [\alpha_1, \alpha_2, \alpha_3, \alpha_4, ..., \alpha_d]$ was attributed to the problem of optimization model below:

$$\begin{cases} max \ tr \left[A^T \left(S_p - S_c \right) A \right] \\ s.t. Y^T Y = I \\ s.t. \alpha_i^T S_t \alpha_j = 0 \ (i \neq j, i, j = 1, 2, 3, 4, ..., d) \end{cases} \tag{6}$$

Through the eigenvector corresponding to the maximum value of generalized equation $(S_p - S_c)A = \lambda X H_n X^T A$, optimal vector can be found.

Assuming $k - 1$ feature vectors were identified, the k vectors can be solved by the model below:

$$\begin{cases} max \ tr \left[\alpha_k^T \left(S_p - S_c \right) \alpha_k \right] \\ s.t. \alpha_k X H_n X^T \alpha_k = I \\ s.t. \alpha_k^T S_t \alpha_j = 0 \ (i \neq j, i, j = 1, 2, 3, 4, ..., k - 1) \end{cases} \tag{7}$$

Through the following steps, statistically uncorrelated optimal vector set can be found. Firstly, obtained the first vector α_1 of the projection matrix by solving the eigenvector corresponding to the maximum value of generalized equation $(S_p - S_c) A = \lambda X H_n X^T A$.

We can calculate the matrix with the equation below cyclically:

$$T^k = \left[I - C^{-1} S_t P^{k-1} \left(Q^{k-1} \right)^{-1} \left(P^{k-1} \right)^T S_t \right] * \left(C^{-1} D \right) \tag{8}$$

In the formulas, $C = X H_n X^T$, $D = S_b - X H_n B H_n X^T$, $P^{k-1} = [\alpha_1, \alpha_2, \alpha_3, ..., \alpha_{k-1}]$, and $Q^{k-1} = \left(P^{k-1} \right)^T S_t S_b^{-1} S_t P^{k-1}$

With the matrix above, the eigenvector corresponding to the maximum can be solved. By cycling d-1 times, eigenvector corresponding to the maximum and α_1 constructed the permutation matrix. That was the projection matrix required.

4   Experimental Results and Conclusion

In this study, improved algorithms were applied to face recognition for validation by comparing and analyzing its recognition rate. A self-built library of 120 individuals, 20 photos about gesture and expression per person was used in this experiment. For each individuals, 10 images were collected randomly as training samples, leaving the remaining 10 as test samples. The experiment was cycled for 20 times, the average of which was the correct recognition rate. The average recognition rate changed with feature dimensions as the experimental results. Gabor filter and improved locally linear embedding algorithm were used in the face recognition. The Experimental results were shown in the Figure 1.

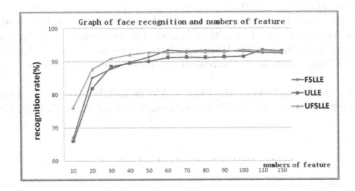

Fig. 1. The average recognition rate of FSLLE,ULLE and UFSLLE changes with characteristic dimension

The results indicated that when comparing ULLE,FSLLE,UFSLLE in the dimension between 10-60,the recognition rate of UFSLLE algorithm was significantly higher than the other two algorithms. It demonstrated that the two improved algorithm can be used in a fusion way and the introduction of maximum scatter matrix can effectively improve the performance of algorithm, to make it a supervised algorithm. Moreover, projection direction may not be the optimal and redundant information may exist among the basis vectors of projection directions. Therefore,the performance of the algorithm was improved by using uncorrelated constraint in the base vectors.

In recent works, low-dispersion sequences were used to improve projection based algorithms, see e.g. [9]. For future research, a possible way is using low-dispersion sequences to improve projection based algorithms in locally linear embedding.

References

1. Kouropteva, O., Okun, O., et al.: Incremental Locally Linear Embedding Algorithm. J. Pattern Recognition 38(10), 1764–1767 (2005)
2. Zheng, J.: One Improved LLE Method. J. Journal of Hunan Institute of Science and Technolohy 20, 30–32 (2007)
3. Roweis, S.T., Saul, L.K.: Nonlinear Dimensionality Reduction by Locally Liner Embedding. Science 290(5500), 2323–2326 (2000)
4. An introduction to locally linear embedding,
   http://www.cl.cam.ac.uk/Research/DTG/attar2chive:pub/data/att_faces.zip
5. Ridder, K., Okun, O., et al.: Supervised Locally Linear Embedding. J. Artificial Neural Networks and Neural Information Processing 2714, 333–341 (2003)
6. Ming, Z.: Maximum Scatter Matrix Algorithm Based on Local Linear. J. Computer Engineering 37, 176–180 (2011)
7. Yang, M.: Research on Feature Extraction with Correlation Projection Analysis and Its Applications. NanJing Uniersity of Science and Technology, Nan Jing (2010)
8. Weinberger, K.Q., Saul, L.K.: Distance Metric Learning for Large Magin Nearest Nerghbor Class-Sification. J. Journal of Machine Learning Research 10, 207–244 (2009)
9. Wang, X., Miao, Y., Cheng, M.: Finding Motifs in DNA Sequences Using Low-Dispersion Sequences. Journal of Computational Biology 21(4), 320–329 (2014)

An Improved Evolutionary Approach for Association Rules Mining

Youcef Djenouri, Ahcene Bendjoudi,
Nadia Nouali-Taboudjemat, and Zineb Habbas

CERIST Center Research
LCOMS, University of Lorraine Ile du Saulcy, 57045, Metz Cedex
{ydjenouri,abendjoudi,nnouali}@cerist.dz, zineb.habbas@univ-lorraine.fr

Abstract. This paper tackles the association rules mining problem with the evolutionary approach. All previous bio-inspired based association rules mining approaches generate non admissible rules. In this paper, we propose an efficient strategy called delete and decomposition strategy permits to avoid non admissible rules. If an item is appeared in the antecedent and the consequent parts of a given rule, this rule is composed on two admissible rules. Then, we delete such item to the antecedent part of the first rule and we delete the same item to the consequent part of the second rule. We also incorporate the suggested strategy into two evolutionary algorithms (genetic and mimetic algorithms), To demonstrate the suggested approach, several experiments have been carried out using both synthetic and reals instances. The results reveal that it has a compromise between the execution time and the quality of output rules. Indeed, the improved genetic algorithm is faster than the improved mimetic algorithm whereas the last one outperforms the genetic algorithm in terms of rules quality.

Keywords: Association rules mining, Evolutionary approach, Inadmissible rule.

1 Introduction

Association Rules Mining (ARM) aims to extract frequent patterns, associations or causal structures among sets of items from a given transactional database. Formally, the association rule problem is as follows: let T be a set of transactions $\{t_1, t_2, \ldots, t_m\}$ representing a transactional database, and I be a set of m different items or attributes $\{i_1, i_2, \ldots, i_m\}$, an association rule is an implication of the form $X \rightarrow Y$ where $X \subset I$, $Y \subset I$, and $X \cap Y = \emptyset$. The itemset X is called antecedent while the itemset Y is called consequent and the rule means X implies Y. Two basic parameters are commonly used for measuring usefulness of association rules, namely the support of a rule and a confidence of a rule. The support of an itemset $I' \subseteq I$ is the number of transactions containing I'. The support of a rule $X \rightarrow Y$ is the support of $X \cup Y$ and the confidence of a rule is $\frac{support(X \cup Y)}{support(X)}$. Confidence is a measure of strength of the association rules.

L. Pan et al. (Eds.): BIC-TA 2014, CCIS 472, pp. 93–97, 2014.
© Springer-Verlag Berlin Heidelberg 2014

So, association rules mining consists in extracting from a given database, all interesting rules, that is rules with support $\geq$ MinSup and confidence $\geq$ Min-Conf [1] where MinSup and MinConf are two thresholds predefined by users.

In the literature, it exists many ARM algorithms based on evolutionary approach. All these algorithms generate non admissible rules, to deal with this problem, in this paper, we propose two new evolutionary algorithms for rules mining discovery.

The rest of this paper is organized as follows. The next section relates about the state of the art ARM algorithms. Section 3 proposed an new strategy for rule generation process, followed by the improved evolutionary approach. Section 5 presents the experimental study of the two algorithms (genetic and mimetic algorithms) using the proposed strategy. In Section 6, we conclude the paper by some remarks and future perspectives.

2   Related Works

In the literature, many bio-inspired-based algorithms for ARM problem have been designed like BSO-ARM[2], HBSO-TS[3] for swarm intelligence approaches, and GAR[4], GENAR[5], ARMGA[6] for evolutionary approaches. Our context focuses on evolutionary approach. In the following, we relates about some evolutionary algorithms for ARM problem.

There are some works based on genetic algorithm for association rules mining. The first two genetic algorithms for ARM called GENAR and GAR are proposed in [5] and [4] by mata et al respectively. The main limit of them is the inefficient representation of the individual. After that, many genetic algorithms with a good representation of the solution are proposed. [6] developed an algorithm based on genetic algorithm called ARMGA. In [7], an AGA is developed for computing ARM. The two major differences between classical ARMGA and AGA are the mutation and crossover operators. An interesting work that provided the performance analysis of association rules mining based on genetic algorithm is described in [8]. All previous algorithms generate non admissible rules, To deal with problem, we propose in the next section an efficient strategy called delete and decomposition strategy.

3   Delete and Decomposition Strategy

All of the above mentioned algorithms create new solutions that may not be admissible and even more there is no special treatment to manage this issue. To overcome this drawback, the first contribution in this work is to propose an efficient strategy which solves the admissibility problem. The evolutionary operators provide a non admissible solutions, indeed, an item can not appear in both the antecedent and consequent parts, to deal with this problem, "delete and decomposition" strategy is performed. During the first phase, this item is removed from the antecedent part while during the second phase it is removed from the consequent part. This operation allows us to decompose the non admissible solution in two accepted solutions according to the syntactical form. Furthermore, the item belongs to the antecedent part for the first solution and it belongs to the consequent part for the second one.

Consider $r : A, B, C \Rightarrow C, F$, this rule is non admissible because the item C belongs to the antecedent and the consequent parts of r, using delete and decomposition strategy, r can be decomposed on two rules:

$r_1 : A, B \Rightarrow C, F$, it is obtained by removing the item C to the antecedent part of r.

$r_1 : A, B, C \Rightarrow F$, it is obtained by removing the item C to the consequent part of r.

4   An Improved Evolutionary Approach

The initial population of pop_size individuals is first generated in the random which each individual is composed by the set of items containing on it, then, for each non admissible solution, delete and decomposition strategy is applied on it. To respect the size of the population, all individuals are evaluated using the fitness computing described in [2], after that we kept just the first pop_size individuals, the remaining individuals are removed. We then apply the evolutionary operators (crossover and mutation for genetic algorithm included a simple local search for mimetic algorithm), but after each operation, the delete and decomposition strategy is performed. The same process is repeated until the maximum number of iterations is reached.

5   Experimental Study of the Proposed Approaches

To validate and demonstrate the suggested approaches, an intensive experiments have been carried out. All programs have been implemented on C++ using *I3*

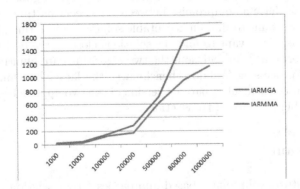

Fig. 1. Execution time (Sec) of the two approaches with different number of transactions

Table 1. Solution Quality according of the two algorithms according to different data instances

Data sets name	Number of Transactions	Number of Items	IARMGA	IARMMA
Bolts	40	8	1	1
Sleep	56	8	1	1
Pollution	60	16	1	1
Basket	96	5	1	1
IBM.Q.st	1000	40	0.97	1
Quake	2178	4	0.95	0.99
Cheese	3196	75	0.01	0.03
Mushroom	8124	119	0.008	0.03
BMS-WEB-1	59602	497	0.0005	0.001
Connect	100000	999	0.015	0.02
BMPPOS	515597	1657	0.0007	0.0009
WebDocs	1692082	526765	Blocked After 15 days	Blocked After 15 days

processor and 4GB memory. The two algorithms are compared using the real-time scientific databases which are frequently used in data mining community like: Frequent and Mining Dataset Repository [10] and Bilkent University Function Approximation Repository, [9]. To tune parameters of the two algorithms, several tests have been carried out, As a results, the maximum number of iterations is set to 80 for IARMGA and 78 for IARMMA and the population size of the two algorithms is set to 60. Figure 1 reveals us that IARMMA is high time consuming compared to IARMGA when the number of input transactions is too large. In fact, the local search added in IARMMA led the process very slowly. Nonetheless, Table 1 shows the efficiency of IARMMA compared to IARMGA in terms of the solutions quality. Indeed, while increasing the number of transactions, a large difference between the two approaches is observed. We benefit from the local search applied on IARMMA, by obtaining a good solutions. We conclude that we have a compromise between the execution time and the solution quality, if we want to find an acceptable solution in real time, IARMGA is applied, whereas, if we want to find the solutions close to the optimal solution, IARMMA is performed. In addition, the two algorithms are bluntly blocked after 15 days of processing Webdocs benchmark (the larger benchmark existing on the web), for consequent, a parallel version of the two approaches is preferred to handle this big instance of transactions.

6   Conclusion

In this paper, two evolutionary-based approaches for association rules mining problem are proposed, the first one called IARMGA, it applied an efficient genetic algorithm to find the set of acceptable rules in real time. The second one called IARMMA, the search process is done using mimetic algorithm. The mimetic mechanism allow to enrich the quality of the returned rules by applying a local search on each new individual. The two approaches deal the admissibility problem in the state of bio-inspired ARM approaches by defining an efficient strategy namely decomposition and delete strategy. To analyze the behavior of the proposed approaches, several experiments have been carried out on both synthetic and real data sets. The results show that IARMGA is less time consuming compared to IARMMA, whereas, the solutions returned by IARMMA are better then found by IARMGA. We conclude that it has compromise between the two challenges CPU time and solution's quality, the choose of the algorithm depends on the application at hand, if we want to extract association rules in real time then, IARMGA is more appropriate, now if we want more precision in the resulted rules, IARMMA is preferred. Unfortunately, the two approaches are bluntly blocked after 15 days when dealing the webdocs benchmark that contains more than one and half millions of transactions. Consequently, as perspective we plan to parallelize the two proposed approaches.

References

1. Agrawal, R., Shafer, J.: Parallel mining of associations rules. IEEE Transactions on Knowledge and Data Engineering 8(6), 962–969 (1996)
2. Djenouri, Y., Drias, H., Habbas, Z., Mosteghanemi, H.: Bees Swarm Optimization for Web Association Rule Mining. In: 2012 IEEE/WIC/ACM International Conferences on Web Intelligence and Intelligent Agent Technology (WI-IAT), vol. 3, pp. 142–146 (December 2012)
3. Djenouri, Y., Drias, H., Chemchem, A.: A hybrid Bees Swarm Optimization and Tabu Search algorithm for Association rule mining. In: 2013 World Congress on Nature and Biologically Inspired Computing (NaBIC), 2013, pp. 120–125 (August 2013)
4. Mata, J., Alvarez, J., Riquelme, J.: An Evolutionary algorithm to discover numeric association rules. In: Proceedings of the ACM Symposium on Applied Computing SAC, pp. 590–594 (2002)
5. Mata, J., Alvarez, J., Riquelme, J.: Mining numeric association rules with genetic algorithms. In: Proceedings of the International Conference ICANNGA, pp. 264–267 (2001)
6. Yan, X., Zhang, C.: Genetic algorithm based strategy for identifying association rule without specifying minimum support. Expert System with Applications 36(2), 3066–3076 (2009)
7. Wang, M., Zou, Q., Lin, C.: Multi dimensions association rules mining on adaptive genetic algorithm. In: IEEE International Conference on Uncertainly Reasoning on Knowledge Engineering (2011)
8. Indira, K., Kanmani, S.: Performance Analysis of Genetic Algorithm for Mining Association Rules. International Journal of Computer Science Issues 9(1) (2012)
9. Guvenir, H.A., Uysal, I.: Bilkent University Function Approximation Repository (2000), http://funapp.cs.bilkent.edu.tr
10. Goethals, B.: Frequent Itemset Mining Implementations Repository (2004), http://fimi.ua.ac.be/

Multiple Depots Incomplete Open Vehicle Routing Problem Based on Carbon Tax

Fenghua Duan[1,*] and Xiaonian He[2]

[1] School of Business,
Hunan University of Science and Technology Xiangtan 411200, Hunan, China
1012564884@qq.com
[2] School of Information Science & Engineering,
Hunan International Economics University Changsha 410205, Hunan, China
573944371@qq.com

Abstract. Incomplete open vehicle routing problem is proposed and defined, and the multi-depot incomplete open vehicle routing problem with soft time windows based on carbon tax (MDIOVRPSTWCT) is expounded. The quantity of carbon emissions is calculated based on vehicles' travel distance, furthermore, the MDIOVRPSTWCT is modelled, and the adaptive genetic algorithm, which can dynamically adjust the crossover and mutation probability, is applied to solve the model. After the strategy of multi-depot is reasonably adopted and modern transportation and distribution optimization technology is applied, the computed results of the case show the transportation & distribution companies' number of vehicles, fuel consumption and vehicle' carbon emissions are still greater declines even though the carbon tax, and the benefit's growth and low carbon logistics are realized at the same time.

Keywords: Incomplete open vehicle routing problem, Multi-depot, Genetic algorithm, Carbon tax.

1 Introduction

In December 2009, Copenhagen World Climate Conference, China promises to reduce 45% carbon emissions by 2020 compared with 2005. Automobile exhaust is major sources of carbon emissions in China, therefore, government, enterprises, experts, and the public focus on environmental protection and development of fuel-efficient cars. Unfortunately, despite carbon emissions' proportion from the logistics industry is growing, the operational optimization of transportation and distribution did not receive due attentions. In fact, if government adds suitable carbon tax to transportation and distribution, the carbon emissions will reduce, which could promote the development of the low carbon logistics and economy. It is mainstream academic voice to curb carbon emissions by carbon tax, and some planning research results of logistics development based on carbon tax constraints have obtained, such as the literature [1,5]. However, there are some

---

* Corresponding author.

L. Pan et al. (Eds.): BIC-TA 2014, CCIS 472, pp. 98–107, 2014.
© Springer-Verlag Berlin Heidelberg 2014

resistances when the carbon tax wants to become policy and law. For logistics industry, an important reason is that transportation and distribution logistics operation and management are in few technologies, and if the carbon emissions are imposed tax, business' transportation and distribution costs will rise sharply in the short term. Therefore, it should be the considered key issue to control carbon emissions by carbon tax while the increase of transportation and distribution costs could be minimal. In general, if vehicle's emissions and road conditions are similar, the transport distance will be the most important factor of affecting fuel consumption, furthermore, vehicle' carbon emissions is critically determined by itself fuel consumption. Therefore, in this paper, distance of vehicle running will be converted and become carbon tax.

Incomplete Open Vehicle Routing Problem (IOVRP) is a kind of vehicle routing problem between closed and open; it means that every vehicle's final customer is same when it starts from depot, and after finished its task, every vehicle will return its depot from the common final customer directly. Multiple depots VRP (MDVRP) means there are a few of depots, and vehicles start from different depot. For metropolis and medium-sized cities, there are large population and area, and traffic congestion is common, too. Therefore, if only a depot, it is difficult to guarantee the timeliness of delivery, and distribution costs will increase, too. If vehicles start from different depot, those problems will be not difficult, and in fact, many logistics enterprisers adopt multi-depot scheduling programs. In reality, IOVRP and MDVRP are widespread in many industries, for example, agricultural products purchase, garbage truck running, large-scale events of passenger car, supply chain integration and coordination, and both have extensive combination each other. This article will examine a kind of Multiple Depots Incomplete Open Vehicle Routing Problem with Soft Time Windows and Carbon Tax (MDIOVRPSTWCT). By researching this problem, as well as the application of the research results, the efficiency and effectiveness of transportation and distribution will increase; the low-carbon logistics and economic could get development, too.

2 Mathematical Model of MDIOVRP-STWCT

2.1 Problem Description

MDIOVRPSTWCT refers to logistics companies uses multiple depots to serve for customers in order to meet customer's goods needs and time requirements, and improve carrier's economic efficiency. When vehicles leave the different depots to perform their respective tasks, the final customer of each vehicle is same; and after finished its task, each vehicle directly returns to its depot from the common final customer. According to the vehicle's carbon emissions, government imposes carbon tax on the logistics companies in order to induce carriers to take measures to reduce the carbon emissions from transportation and distribution. A MDIOVRPSTWCT mathematical description can be as follow:

There are m depots (numbered $n+1, n+2, \cdots, n+m$), and there are some vehicles in every depot. The capacity of vehicle is q. These vehicles are responsible for the distribution of goods of customers $n-1$ (numbered $1, 2, \cdots, n-1$).The goods demand of customer i is d_i ($i \in 1, 2, \cdots, n-1$) and $d_i \leq q$. Generally, if a customer obtained once service by one vehicle, then it must not accept other vehicle's service. However, the last customer for each vehicle is same. After finished its task, each vehicle directly from the common last customer returns its starting depot. If vehicle is earlier than the arrival time window specified by the customer, it could wait, and if late, it must pay a penalty. Vehicles must pay carbon tax in accordance with their amount of CO_2 emissions from fuel consumption. To simplify the problem, we determine carbon emissions based on the vehicle's running distance, and ignore the speed change, stop waiting and other factors that would lead to changes in fuel consumption.

2.2 Mathematical Models

To construct mathematical models, we define the variable as follows:

$$x_{ij}^{mk} = \begin{cases} 1, \text{ mean } k \text{ of deport } m \text{ starts from customer } i \text{ to } j \text{ ;} \\ 0, \text{ otherwise.} \end{cases}$$

$$x_i^{mk} = \begin{cases} 1, \text{ mean the task for customer } i \text{ is carried out by } k \text{ ;} \\ 0, \text{ otherwise.} \end{cases}$$

If customer i is in the same route with customer j, and j is just serviced after i, the time of the vehicle's arriving at the customer j is: $t_j = t_i + s_i + t_{ij}$ According to the demand of each customer and vehicle load, the required minimum number of vehicles will be as follows:

$$\lfloor \frac{\sum_{i=1}^{n-1} d_i}{q} \rfloor + 1$$

Symbol description:

K is the needed vehicles number, L is vehicle maximum travel distance, and q means vehicle maximum load. N is the set of customers and $N = 1, 2, , n-1$; M is the set of depots and $M = n+1, n+2, \cdots, n+m$; n means that all vehicles' last customer is the same. The customers and depots that want to be served are i & j. The direct distance between i and j is d_{ij}, and the distance matrix is symmetric, that is, $d_{ij} = d_{ji}$. The goods demand of customer i is d_i; and the service hours for customer i is s_i. The earliest time windows that customer i can accept is a_i, the latest time windows that customer i can accept is b_i, and the time point of vehicle arriving at i is t_i. If the time point of the vehicle arriving at and beginning to serve i is early than a_i, the penalty coefficient to vehicle will be p_1 (in this paper, if early than a_i, then vehicle waits and $p_1 = 0$). If the time point of the vehicle arriving at and beginning to serve i is later than b_i, the penalty coefficient to vehicle is p_2. The carbon emissions penalty fee is p_0. The vehicles total running distance is D.

$$D = \sum_{i=N \cup M} \sum_{j=1}^{n+m} \sum_{m=M} \sum_{k=1}^{K} d_{ij} x_{ij}^{mk}$$

Therefore, MDIOVRPSTWCT mathematical model is as follows:

$$min\ Z_1 = K \tag{1}$$

$$min Z_2 = D + p_0 D + p_1 \sum_{i=1}^{n-1} max(a_i - t_i, 0) + p_2 \sum_{i=1}^{n-1} max(t_i - b_i, 0) \tag{2}$$

Subjected to:

$$\sum_{i \in N \cup M} \sum_{j=1}^{n+m} d_{ij} x_{ij}^{mk} \leq L \quad k \in \{1, 2, \cdots, K\} \tag{3}$$

$$\sum_{i \in N} d_i y_i^{mk} \leq q \quad m \in M \quad k \in \{1, 2, \cdots, K\} \tag{4}$$

$$\sum_{k=1}^{K} y_i^{mk} = 1 \quad m \in M \quad i \in \{1, 2, \cdots, n-1\} \tag{5}$$

$$\sum_{i \in M} \sum_{j \in N} x_{ij}^{mk} = K \quad m \in M \quad k \in \{1, 2, \cdots, K\} \tag{6}$$

$$\sum_{k=1}^{K} x_{in}^{mk} = 0 \quad m, i \in M \tag{7}$$

$$\sum_{m \in M} \sum_{k=1}^{K} y_n^{mk} = K \tag{8}$$

$$x_{ij}^{mk} \in \{0, 1\} \quad i, j \in N, k \in \{1, 2, \cdots, K\}, m \in M \tag{9}$$

$$x_i^{mk} \in \{0, 1\} \quad i \in N, k \in \{1, 2, \cdots, K\}, m \in M \tag{10}$$

There, the formula (1) represents that the first optimization goal is to minimize the number of vehicles required, and formula (2) represents that the second optimization goal is to minimize the total delivery cost (including vehicle cost, carbon emission penalty and the penalty fees for vehicle's deviation of time window). The formula (3) represents each route distance restrictions; formula (4) indicates the limit to vehicle load; formula (5) means that any customer can obtain only once service by one vehicle and all customers can obtain service. The formula (6) means all routes start from one of depot; formula (7) means that vehicle cannot run from the depot to the common last customer n directly; formula (8) indicates vehicles of K must go through customer n. The formula (9) represents whether vehicle k of depot m run from customer i to customer j or not, and formula (10) indicates whether customer i is served by vehicle k which starts from depot m.

3   GA for Solving MDIOVRPSTWCT

Genetic algorithm (GA) is a global random search method by imitating the process of biological evolution, and is suitable to solving multi-objective problem. There are abundant researches results for using genetic algorithm to closed vehicle routing problem and single-depot open vehicle routing problem, and there are some research results to solve multi-depot open vehicle routing problem by genetic algorithm, although they are few. In this paper, the genetic algorithm will be applied to solve this problem suitably according to the characteristics of MDIOVRPSTWCT.

3.1   Coding and Generating Initial Solution

In this paper, genetic algorithm is coded with natural number, and customers are represented by $1 \sim n-1, n$ represents the common last customer, $n+1 \sim n+m$ represents depots. Relative studies show that the genetic algorithm does not depend on the initial population when it searches the optimal solution. However, if the initial population can be evenly distributed in the solution space, it will help GA escape from the "premature". Therefore, the algorithm generates initial solution randomly.

3.2   Selection

1) Fitness function:

In this paper, the objective function is minimization, and generally, the problem of fitness function is maximization, so this fitness function is as follow:

$$fit(i) = \frac{1}{Z_i} \times 100$$

Z_i represents objective function value of i chromosome after its adding a penalty term (including the overweight penalty, carbon tax penalty, and violating time windows punishment).

2) Selection:

In this paper, the selection strategy that roulette wheel selection and the best individual reservations are combinatory is selected [6]. According to this method, n individuals of the population of each generation rank in the light of fitness descending order, and the first individual is best in performance. The first individual is copied to access directly to the next generation, and is ranked as the first one. The other $n-1$ individuals of next generation of group generate by roulette wheel selection method based on n individual fitness of the previous generation of group, and $p(i)$ is the selection probability of the selection method.

$$p(i) = \frac{fit(i)}{\sum_{j=1}^{n} fit(j)}$$

The selection method can ensure the survival of the best individual to the next generation, but also ensure the individuals who have better fitness to the next generation with more chances.

3.3   Crossover Operator

In this paper, crossover operator A [7] will be applied to GA to solve MDIOVRPST-WCT, because two offspring generated by crossover operator A are legitimate, and need not re-map it; it could compute more efficiently, too. Specific implementation process is as follows:

For two parent:

parent 1:(3 4 1 7 8 5 2 6 9)

parent 2:(9 2 4 6 7 1 3 5 8)

Two cross-point are generated randomly from parent 1 ("—" indicates the location of cross-point), and the section between two cross-points are the cross gene region which are stored in the temporary record L.

parent 1:(3 4 1 — 7 8 5 — 2 6 9)

parent 2: (9 2 4 6 7 1 3 5 8)

record L:(7 8 5)

Then, the gene which are same with record L are selected from parent 2, the same gene sequence 7,5,8 are applied to substitute the gene in the record L of parent 1 so as to generate offspring 1.

Finally, the replaced gene in the parent 1 (i.e., the information recorded in L) are placed into the parent 2 according to its original sequence in order to get offspring 2.

offspring 1:(3 4 1 7 5 8 2 6 9)

offspring 2:(9 2 4 1 7 6 3 8 5)

Cross process ends.

3.4   Mutation Operator

In this paper, mutation operator takes as follow:

When the random number is less than the mutation probability, the mutation will carry out by randomly selecting two customers to swap their positions; if the fitness value is improved and better than the previous generation chromosomes after swapping, the change will be accepted, otherwise will be given up. Do cycle so continuously until the best chromosome generates by the swapping. For this mutation operation, the GA must rearrange depot after the swapping. After verification, this mutation operation is simple, easy to implement, and is able to find good genes with less evolutionary number of times.

3.5   Termination Condition

In this paper, termination condition is the limitation of the times of continuously unchanged best solution or evolution. When the number of customers is n, the algorithm will end if the times of the best continuously unchanged solution are 30 or the maximum evolution generation is 3000.

4   Examples Testing and Comparison

4.1   Examples Testing

For this issue, there isn't a comparable example at present, so we construct an example of single depot IOVRPSTWCT (SDIOVRPSTWCT) according to the city's size and four-bound of China, which includes limits of carbon taxes, departure depot No.101(40, 50), 99 customers, a common last customer for receiving goods No.100 (40, 50). Based on SDIOVRPSTWCT and characteristics of multi-depot problem and customers' locations, MDIOVRPSTWCT is constructed by adding 3 depots, NO.102 (58, 85), 103 (22, 35), 104 (83, 25). For the example, the total demands are 40370kg, a vehicle's capacity is 5 tons, the customer's demand unit is kilogram, the maximum available number of vehicles is 15. As for carbon tax, in order to simplify the problem, the levied Australian Government' carbon tax standard (23 AUD/ton) is referred and is set at $0.16¥/kg$ CO_2; 1L diesel emits CO_2 2.63kg, vehicle's fuel consumption is approximately $0.1616L/km$ for a vehicle which loads 4 to 5 tons. The speed of the vehicle is $30km/h$, and the service time of a customer is 30 minutes. The penalty coefficient p1 & p2 are equal to 200. The algorithm programmed with Delphi language, and run in the Ben IV 1.80 GHZ microcomputer.

4.2 Results Comparison

1) Results of the SDIOVRPSTWCT

The genetic algorithm above-mentioned is used to solve the SDIOVRPST-WCT, and its results are shown in Table 1.

Table 1. The results of SDIOVRPSTWCT solved by genetic algorithm

route	loading	mileage	path
1	3840	9.163	101-94-92-93-97-63-99-100
2	3550	7.963	101-22-25-27-29-33-32-100
3	3250	10.434	101-20-24-31-35-37-38-39-36-34-100
4	3750	10.124	101-10-11-13-17-19-18-30-28-26-23-21-100
5	3540	7.855	101-43-47-49-52-50-51-46-40-44-45-48-42-41-100
6	3290	5.723	101-62-74-72-61-64-68-69-66-67-65-100
7	3900	6.516	101-90-89-88-85-84-82-83-86-87-100
8	3930	10.273	101-57-59-60-58-56-53-54-55-100
9	3620	5.508	101-7-8-9-6-4-2-1-75-3-5-100
10	3910	11.909	101-15-16-14-12-96-95-98-91-100
11	3790	12.195	101-80-79-77-73-70-71-78-76-81-100
total	40370	97.663	

For the example of the SDIOVRPSTWCT solved by genetic algorithm, its total running mileage is 97.663 km, fuel consuming is 15.78L, fuel cost is 114.90¥, CO_2 emission is 41.51 kg, carbon tax is 6.64¥, the total cost of the fuel & carbon tax are 121.54¥, the proportion of the time window is 100%.

2) Dealing with Multiple Depots

For GA of the SDIOVRPSTW, just a natural number indicates depot, while for MDIOVRPSTWCT, a set of natural numbers M indicate depots. There are little researches about MDIOVRPSTW by the published literatures. As for MDIOVRPSTWCT, there is not research literature so far. For multi-depot vehicle routing problem (MDVRP), researchers designed types of heuristic algorithms to solve varieties of MDVRP with different constrains, commonly, they focus on how to narrow the search space and simplify the solving procedures of the algorithms, such as literature ([8]-[9]). Traditionally, researches divided the MDVRP into some single-depot VRP according to some method to solve. However, this method results that depots and customers could not be integral, and it is difficult to get the total cost least. If the virtual depot method is applied, then the satisfactory optimal method does not found when some constraints, such as the capacity, time windows, departure time, and so on, are adhered to the MDVRP.

In this paper, the MDVRP is a complex combinatorial optimization. Without considering the limitation of vehicle numbers of each depot, the multi-depot treatment of MDIOVRPSTWCT is as follows.

First, a depot is chosen randomly from the set of depots, and a vehicle is designed its delivery task according to customers' requirements until it is full enough, and starts from the chosen depot to deliver for customers. Finally, the vehicle arrives at the common last customer, and directly returns its departure depot from this customer.

Then, if there is customer who is not served, a depot is chosen randomly from the set of depots again, and a vehicle is designed its delivery task according to customers' requirements till it is full enough, and starts from the chosen depot to deliver for customers. Finally, the vehicle arrives at the common last customer, and directly returns its departure depot from this customer. Cycle so until all customers obtain service.

3) Results of the MDIOVRPSTWCT

For the example of the MDIOVRPSTWCT solved by genetic algorithm, its total running mileage is 68.65 km, fuel consuming is 11.09L, fuel cost is 80.77¥, CO_2 emission is 29.18 kg, carbon tax is 4.67¥, the total cost of the fuel & carbon tax are 85.44¥, the proportion of the time window is 100%.The results of MDIOVRPSTWCT are shown in Table 2, and the results comparisons between SDIOVRPSTWCT and MDIOVRPSTWCT are shown in Table 3.

Table 2. The results of MDIOVRPSTWCT solved by genetic algorithm

route	loading	mileage	path
1	4940	7.769	104-80-79-77-73-70-71-76-78-81-74-100
2	4600	8.889	103-31-35-37-38-39-36-34-33-32-100
3	4810	10.086	103-60-58-56-53-54-55-57-59-68-64-61-72-100
4	4800	7.046	103-52-49-47-43-41-42-46-50-51-48-45-44-40-69-66-62-65-67-100
5	4020	5.982	101-10-11-9-8-6-7-5-3-4-2-1-75-100
6	3650	6.100	101-20-21-22-25-24-27-29-30-28-26-23-100
7	4950	5.517	102-63-97-93-92-94-95-98-100
8	4100	9.754	102-12-14-16-15-19-18-17-13-100
9	4500	7.511	102-99-96-91-89-88-85-84-82-83-86-87-90-100
total	40370	68.654	

Table 3. The results comparisons between SDIOVRPSTWCT and MDIOVRPSTWCT

	SDIOVRPSTWCT	MDIOVRPSTWCT	MD savings / savings rate comparison with SD
vehicles being used	11.00	9.00	2.00/18.18%
total running mileage(km)	97.66	68.65	29.01/29.70%
fuel consuming (L)	15.78	11.09	4.69/29.7%
fuel cost(¥)	114.90	80.77	34.13/29.7%
CO_2 emission(kg)	41.51	29.18	12.33/29.7%
carbon tax of a running(¥)	6.64	4.67	1.97/2.97%
total cost of fuel & carbon tax(¥)	121.54	85.44	

We found that the multi-depot strategy could save vehicles, transport distance, fuel, and reduce CO_2 emissions, thus reduce entrepreneur pressure to carbon tax by comparing SDIOVRPSTWCT with MDIOVRPSTWCT. In particular, in this case the MDIOVRPSTWCT operators amount of fuel cost and operational carbon tax is only 29.46¥, reduced by 24% compared with SDIOVRPSTWCT.

5   Conclusion

MDIOVRPSTWCT is a complex combinatorial optimization problem. The question is solved by random selecting depot, random selecting a vehicle to perform tasks from the selected depot, and then vehicles direct returning its departure depot after its performing tasks, cycle so until all customers are served, thus, the algorithm to solve this kind of complex problem is expanded. Experimental results show that the genetic algorithm designed in this paper has a high computational efficiency, and results are better. Experimental results show that logistics enterprises will not increase their cost burden if they could adopt new intelligent vehicle scheduling techniques and rationally apply multi-depot strategy when transportation and distribution sectors of the enterprises is taxed on their carbon emission. Indeed, carbon tax can promote competitive logistics enterprises to develop upgrading of distribution management and operating technology, thus logistics enterprises can increase efficiency and effectiveness, reduce CO_2 emissions and air pollution, ease energy supply pressure, achieve low-carbon logistics and green logistics.

Acknowledgments. This work was supported by the Hunan Province Natural Science Foundation (GrantNo:11JJ3082)& Doctor Foundation of Hunan University of Science and Technology(GrantNo:E510A7).

References

1. Fahimnia, B., Reisi, M., et al.: The implications of carbon pricing in Australia: An industrial logistics planning case study. Transportation Research Part D: Transport and Environment 18(1), 78–85 (2013)
2. Sodero, S.: Policy in motion: reassembling carbon pricing policy development in the personal transport sector in British Columbia. Journal of Transport Geography 19(6), 1474–1481 (2011)
3. David, A.: Hensher. Climate change, enhanced greenhouse gas emissions and passenger transport - What can we do to make a difference? Transportation Research Part D: Transport and Environment 13(2), 95–111 (2008)
4. Jian-Hua, Y., Ji-Dong, G., Shu-Gang, M.: Distribution Network Design for Carbon Tax-Constrained Urban Cold Chain Logistics. Industrial Engineering Journal 15(5), 86–91 (2012)
5. Eying, C.U.I., Junhao, L.U.O., Jianhua, J.I.: Research on Logistics Network Design Problem under Carbon Tax and Carbon Trading Scheme. Science and Technology Management Research 32(22), 239–242 (2012)
6. Lang, M.X., Hu, S.J.: Study on the Optimization of Physical Distribution Routing Problem by Using Hybrid Genetic Algorithm. Chinese Journal of Management Science 10(5), 51–56 (2002)
7. Oğuz, C., Ercan, M.F.: A genetic algorithm for hybrid flow-shop scheduling with multiprocessor tasks. Journal of Scheduling 8(4), 323–351 (2005)
8. Su-Xin, W., Li, G., Xiao-Guang, C., Hong-Mei, C.: Study on Multi-requirement Points Vehicle Scheduling Model and Swarm Mix Algorithm. Acta Automatica Sinica 34(1), 102–104 (2008)
9. Bae, S.-T., Hwang, H.S., Cho, G.-S., Goan, M.-J.: Integrated GA-VRP solver for multi-depot system. Computers & Industrial Engineering 53(2), 233–240 (2007)

Research on a Class of Nonlinear Matrix Equation

Jiating Fang[1,2], Haifeng Sang[1], Qingchun Li[1,*], and Bo Wang[1]

[1] College of Mathematics and Statistics, Beihua University,
Jilin 132013, China
[2] Department of Mathematics, Baicheng Normal University,
Baicheng 137000, China
liqingchun01@163.com

Abstract. In this paper, the nonlinear matrix equation $X^r + \sum_{i=1}^{m} A_i^* X^{\delta_i} A_i = Q$ is discussed. We propose the Newton iteration method for obtaining the Hermite positive definite solution of this equation. And a numerical example is given to identify the efficiency of the results obtained.

Keywords: Nonlinear matrix equation, Positive definite solution, Iteration, Convergence.

1 Introduction

Consider the nonlinear matrix equation

$$X + A^* X^{-1} A = Q. \tag{1}$$

Zhan [5] have studied that the maximal positive definite solution of Eq.(1) with the case $Q = I$. An iterative method for obtaining the maximal positive definite solutions of Eq.(1) is proposed. The convergence of the iterative method is also discussed in his paper. Simultaneously, Zhan and Xie [8] have proved that a necessary and sufficient condition for the existence of solutions of Eq.(1) in which A should satisfy the following demands : $A = P^T \Gamma Q \Sigma P$, where P, Q are orthogonal matrices, and diagonal matrix Γ and Σ satisfy $\Gamma > 0$, $\Sigma \geq 0$, $\Gamma^2 + \Sigma^2 = I$. Meanwhile, the solution of Eq.(1) and some necessary conditions for the existence of the solution of the nonlinear matrix equation are given. When $Q = I$ and A is real matrix, Engwerda [2] have used a simple recursion algorithm to obtain the solution of Eq.(1) and proposed a sufficient and necessary condition for the existence of a positive definite solution.

In this paper, we study Newton iteration method for obtaining Hermite positive definite solutions of equation

$$X + \sum_{i=1}^{m} A_i^* X^{-1} A_i = Q, \tag{2}$$

where A_i is a nonsingular matrix, Q is a Hermite positive definite matrix, r, m are positive integer and $-1 < \delta_i < 0 (i = 1, 2, \cdots, m)$.

---

* Corresponding author.

L. Pan et al. (Eds.): BIC-TA 2014, CCIS 472, pp. 108–116, 2014.
© Springer-Verlag Berlin Heidelberg 2014

2 Newton's Method for Obtaining Hermite Positive Definite Solutions of the Matrix Equation $X + \sum\limits_{i=1}^{m} A_i^* X^{-1} A_i = Q$

In this section, we study Newton's method for obtaining Hermite positive definite solutions of matrix equation $X + \sum\limits_{i=1}^{m} A_i^* X^{-1} A_i = Q$, where A_i is a nonsingular complex matrix and Q is a Hermite definite matrix.

2.1 Related Lemmas

Lemma 1. [6] Let $\sum\limits_{i=1}^{m} \|Q^{-\frac{1}{2}} A_i Q^{-\frac{1}{2}}\|^2 < \frac{1}{4}$, and define a matrix set $T = \{X | \beta_1 Q \leq X \leq \beta_2 Q\}$. Thus Eq.(2) has a unique solution in T, where β_1 is a larger root of this equation $x(1-x) = \lambda_{max}(\sum\limits_{i=1}^{m} Q^{-\frac{1}{2}} A_i^* Q^{-1} A_i Q^{-\frac{1}{2}})$ and β_2 is a larger root of equation $x(1-x) = \lambda_{min}(\sum\limits_{i=1}^{m} Q^{-\frac{1}{2}} A_i^* Q^{-1} A_i Q^{-\frac{1}{2}})$.

Lemma 2. [1] Let $B_i \in C^{n \times n}$, and $P, Q \in H_+^{n \times n}$. If $\sum\limits_{i=1}^{m} \|Q^{\frac{1}{2}} B_i Q^{-\frac{1}{2}}\|^2 < 1$, then this matrix equation $X - \sum\limits_{i=1}^{m} B_i^* X B_i = P$ has a unique solution X, and $X \geq 0$.

Lemma 3. [4] Let $B_i \in C^{n \times n}, P, Q, C \in H_+^{n \times n}$. If $\sum\limits_{i=1}^{m} \|Q^{-\frac{1}{2}} B_i^* C^{-1} Q^{\frac{1}{2}}\|^2 < 1$, the matrix equation $C^* X C - \sum\limits_{i=1}^{m} B_i^* X B_i = P$ has a unique solution X, and $X \geq 0$.

Lemma 4. [7] If C and P are the same order Hermite equations, and $P > 0$, then $CPC + P^{-1} \geq 2C$.

Lemma 5. [3] If $F \in R^{n \times m}$, and $\|F\|_p < 1$, then $I - F$ is nonsingular. Moreover $(I - F)^{-1} = \sum\limits_{k=0}^{\infty} F^k$. Further $\|(I - F)^{-1}\|_p \leq \frac{1}{1 - \|F\|_p}$.

2.2 Newton Iteration Method for Solving the Matrix Equation $X + \sum\limits_{i=1}^{m} A_i^* X^{-1} A_i = Q$

Newton iteration construction process is given firstly. For matrix function

$$F(X) = Q - X - \sum_{i=1}^{m} A_i^* X^{-1} A_i. \tag{3}$$

Let $H = X_{n+1} - X_n$. We have

$$
\begin{aligned}
&F(X + H) - F(X) \\
&= \sum_{i=1}^{m} A_i^*[X^{-1} - (X + H)^{-1}]A_i - H \\
&= \sum_{i=1}^{m} A_i^*(X + H)^{-1}HX^{-1}A_i - H \\
&= \sum_{i=1}^{m} A_i^*[(X + H)^{-1} - X^{-1}]HX^{-1}A_i + \sum_{i=1}^{m} A_i^*X^{-1}HX^{-1}A_i - H \\
&= -\sum_{i=1}^{m} A_i^*X^{-1}H(X + H)^{-1}HX^{-1}A_i + \sum_{i=1}^{m} A_i^*X^{-1}HX^{-1}A_i - H.
\end{aligned}
$$

For the definition of Frechet derivative, we know that

$$
F'(X)H = \sum_{i=1}^{m} A_i^*X^{-1}HX^{-1}A_i - H \tag{4}
$$

by Newton's formula

$$
F'(X_n)H = -F(X_n). \tag{5}
$$

Therefore

$$
X_{n+1} - \sum_{i=1}^{m} A_i^*X_n^{-1}X_{n+1}X_n^{-1}A_i = Q - 2\sum_{i=1}^{m} A_i^*X_n^{-1}A_i. \tag{6}
$$

Hence we can get the iterative algorithm:

$$
\{X_0 \in [\tfrac{1}{2}Q, Q], X_{n+1} - \sum_{i=1}^{m} A_i^*X_n^{-1}X_{n+1}X_n^{-1}A_i = Q - 2\sum_{i=1}^{m} A_i^*X_n^{-1}A_i. \tag{7}
$$

Theorem 1. Let $\sum_{i=1}^{m} \|Q^{-\frac{1}{2}}A_iQ^{-\frac{1}{2}}\|^2 < \frac{1}{4}$, $\{X_n\}$ is matrix sequence which is determined by the iterative Algorithm (7), then $X_n \in [\frac{1}{2}Q, Q]$, and

$$
\sum_{i=1}^{m} \|Q^{-\frac{1}{2}}A_i^*X_n^{-1}Q^{\frac{1}{2}}\|^2 < 1.
$$

Proof. For $\sum_{i=1}^{m} \|Q^{-\frac{1}{2}}A_iQ^{-\frac{1}{2}}\|^2 < \frac{1}{4}$, so

$$
\sum_{i=1}^{m} \|Q^{-\frac{1}{2}}A_iQ^{-\frac{1}{2}}\|^2 I = \sum_{i=1}^{m} \lambda_{\max}(Q^{-\frac{1}{2}}A_i^*Q^{-1}AQ^{-\frac{1}{2}})I \geq \sum_{i=1}^{m} Q^{-\frac{1}{2}}A_i^*Q^{-1}AQ^{-\frac{1}{2}}.
$$

Hence

$$
0 \leq \sum_{i=1}^{m} Q^{-\frac{1}{2}}A_i^*Q^{-1}AQ^{-\frac{1}{2}} < \tfrac{1}{4}I.
$$

Similarly, we get

$$\sum_{i=1}^{m}\|Q^{-\frac{1}{2}}A_i^*X_n^{-1}Q^{\frac{1}{2}}\|^2 I$$
$$\geq \sum_{i=1}^{m}Q^{\frac{1}{2}}X_n^{-1}A_iQ^{-1}A_i^*X_n^{-1}Q^{\frac{1}{2}}$$
$$= \sum_{i=1}^{m}(Q^{\frac{1}{2}}X_n^{-1}Q^{\frac{1}{2}})(Q^{-\frac{1}{2}}A_iQ^{-1}A_i^*Q^{-\frac{1}{2}})(Q^{\frac{1}{2}}X_n^{-1}Q^{\frac{1}{2}})$$
$$= (Q^{\frac{1}{2}}X_n^{-1}Q^{\frac{1}{2}})[\sum_{i=1}^{m}(Q^{-\frac{1}{2}}A_iQ^{-1}A_i^*Q^{-\frac{1}{2}})](Q^{\frac{1}{2}}X_n^{-1}Q^{\frac{1}{2}}).$$

Then by $X_n \in [\frac{1}{2}Q, Q]$, we can obtain $I \leq Q^{\frac{1}{2}}X_n^{-1}Q^{\frac{1}{2}} \leq 2I$. There is

$$\sum_{i=1}^{m}\|Q^{-\frac{1}{2}}A_i^*X_n^{-1}Q^{\frac{1}{2}}\|^2 I \leq I.$$

Hence

$$\sum_{i=1}^{m}\|Q^{-\frac{1}{2}}A_i^*X_n^{-1}Q^{\frac{1}{2}}\|^2 < 1.$$

We will prove $X_{n+1} \in [\frac{1}{2}Q, Q]$ using the inductive method as follow.
If $k = 0$, according to known, we can obtain $x_0 \in [\frac{1}{2}Q, Q]$.
Assume that $k = n$, $X_n \in [\frac{1}{2}Q, Q]$, $\forall n \in \mathbb{N}$. We know $k = n+1$, $X_{n+1} \in [\frac{1}{2}Q, Q]$.
The Eq.(6) can become

$$Q - X_{n+1} - \sum_{i=1}^{m}A_i^*X_n^{-1}(Q - X_{n+1})X_n^{-1}A_i = \sum_{i=1}^{m}A_i^*X_n^{-1}(2X_n - Q)X_n^{-1}A_i. \tag{8}$$

According to $X_n \in [\frac{1}{2}Q, Q]$, that is $2X_n - Q \geq 0$. We can deduce

$$A_i^*X_n^{-1}(2X_n - Q)X_n^{-1}A_i \geq 0, \quad \forall i = 1, 2, \cdots, m.$$

That is

$$\sum_{i=1}^{m}A_i^*X_n^{-1}(2X_n - Q)X_n^{-1}A_i \geq 0.$$

Thus from Lemma 2, we get $Q - X_{n+1} \geq 0$. That is $X_{n+1} \leq Q$.
Similarly, the matrix Eq.(6) can also become

$$X_{n+1} - \frac{1}{2}Q - \sum_{i=1}^{m}A_i^*X_n^{-1}(X_{n+1} - \frac{1}{2}Q)X_n^{-1}A_i$$
$$= \frac{1}{2}Q - \sum_{i=1}^{m}A_i^*(2X_n^{-1} - \frac{1}{2}X_n^{-1}QX_n^{-1})A_i. \tag{9}$$

From $X_n \in [\frac{1}{2}Q, Q]$, we can obtain $Q^{-\frac{1}{2}}X_nQ^{-\frac{1}{2}} \in [\frac{1}{2}I, I]$, and

$$2(Q^{-\frac{1}{2}}X_nQ^{-\frac{1}{2}})^{-1} - \frac{1}{2}(Q^{-\frac{1}{2}}X_nQ^{-\frac{1}{2}})^{-2} \in [\frac{2}{3}I, 2I].$$

Hence

$$\sum_{i=1}^{m} A_i^* (2X_n^{-1} - \tfrac{1}{2}X_n^{-1}QX_n^{-1})A_i$$

$$= \sum_{i=1}^{m} Q^{\frac{1}{2}}(Q^{-\frac{1}{2}}A_i^*Q^{-\frac{1}{2}})[2(Q^{-\frac{1}{2}}X_nQ^{-\frac{1}{2}})^{-1} - \tfrac{1}{2}(Q^{-\frac{1}{2}}X_nQ^{-\frac{1}{2}})^{-2}](Q^{-\frac{1}{2}}A_iQ^{-\frac{1}{2}})Q^{\frac{1}{2}}$$

$$\leq 2\sum_{i=1}^{m} A_i^*Q^{-1}A_i$$

$$\leq \tfrac{1}{2}Q.$$

So the right side of Eq.(9) is positive semi-definite. Hence,

$$X_{n+1} \geq \tfrac{1}{2}Q.$$

In conclusion, $\forall n = 0, 1, \cdots$, we have $X_n \in [\tfrac{1}{2}Q, Q]$, and

$$\sum_{i=1}^{m} \|Q^{-\frac{1}{2}}A_i^*X_n^{-1}Q^{\frac{1}{2}}\|^2 < 1.$$

$\square$

Theorem 2. *For iterative Algorithm(7), if* $\sum_{i=1}^{m} \|Q^{-\frac{1}{2}}A_iQ^{-\frac{1}{2}}\|^2 < \tfrac{1}{4}$, *then we have*

$$X_1 \geq X_2 \geq \cdots \geq X_n \geq \cdots. \tag{10}$$

Proof. According to Newton iterative Eq.(5), for any $n \geq 1$, we have

$$X_n - X_{n+1} - \sum_{i=1}^{m} A_i^*X_n^{-1}(X_n - X_{n+1})X_n^{-1}A_i = X_n + \sum_{i=1}^{m} A_i^*X_n^{-1}A_i - Q.$$

Since $\sum_{i=1}^{m} \|Q^{-\frac{1}{2}}A_i^*X_n^{-1}Q^{\frac{1}{2}}\|^2 < 1$, if we can prove $X_n + \sum_{i=1}^{m} A_i^*X_n^{-1}A_i - Q \geq 0$, then we can get $X_n - X_{n+1} \geq 0$ directly.

Consider the Eq.(6)

$$\sum_{i=1}^{m} A_i^*X_{n-1}^{-1}X_nX_{n-1}^{-1}A_i - 2\sum_{i=1}^{m} A_i^*X_{n-1}^{-1}A_i - X_n + Q = 0.$$

Then

$$X_n + \sum_{i=1}^{m} A_i^*X_n^{-1}A_i - Q$$

$$= \sum_{i=1}^{m} A_i^*X_{n-1}^{-1}X_nX_{n-1}^{-1}A_i + \sum_{i=1}^{m} A_i^*X_n^{-1}A_i - 2\sum_{i=1}^{m} A_i^*X_{n-1}^{-1}A_i$$

$$= \sum_{i=1}^{m} A_i^*X_{n-1}^{-1}(X_n - X_{n-1})X_{n-1}^{-1}A_i + \sum_{i=1}^{m} A_i^*X_{n-1}^{-1}(X_{n-1} - X_n)X_n^{-1}A_i$$

$$= \sum_{i=1}^{m} A_i^*X_{n-1}^{-1}(X_{n-1} - X_n)X_n^{-1}(X_{n-1} - X_n)X_{n-1}^{-1}A_i$$

$$\geq 0.$$

So $X_n - X_{n+1} \geq 0$, $\forall n = 1, 2, \ldots$.

$\square$

Theorem 3. *Consider the iterative Algorithm(7). If* $\sum_{i=1}^{m} \|Q^{-\frac{1}{2}} A_i Q^{-\frac{1}{2}}\|^2 < \frac{1}{4}$,
then the iterative sequence $\{X_n\}$ *converges to* X_L.

Proof. According to Theorem 1 and Theorem 2, in Newton iterative method, for $\forall n \in N$, we get $X_n \in [\frac{1}{2}Q, Q]$, and $\{X_n\}$ is bounded monotonic sequence. Hence, for enough n, $\{X_n\}$ converges to X, and X is a solution of the Eq.(2). Let $X_n \to X'$, X' is a solution of the Eq.(2), then we have $X' \leq X_L$. On the other hand, notice that X' is obtained by sequence $\{X_n\}$, for the any solution X of the Eq.(2), we will prove that $X_n \geq X, \forall n \geq 1$ as follow. Eq.(6) then becomes

$$X_{n+1} - X - \sum_{i=1}^{m} A_i^* X_n^{-1}(X_{n+1} - X)X_n^{-1}A_i$$
$$= Q - 2\sum_{i=1}^{m} A_i^* X_n^{-1} A_i - X + \sum_{i=1}^{m} A_i^* X_n^{-1} X X_n^{-1} A_i.$$

According to X is a solution of Eq.(2), then X satisfies $X + \sum_{i=1}^{m} A_i^* X^{-1} A_i = Q$.
Therefore

$$X_{n+1} - X - \sum_{i=1}^{m} A_i^* X_n^{-1}(X_{n+1} - X)X_n^{-1}A_i$$
$$= \sum_{i=1}^{m} A_i^* X^{-1} A_i + \sum_{i=1}^{m} A_i^* X_n^{-1} X X_n^{-1} A_i - 2\sum_{i=1}^{m} A_i^* X_n^{-1} A_i$$
$$= \sum_{i=1}^{m} A_i^* X^{-1}(X_n - X)X_n^{-1}A_i - \sum_{i=1}^{m} A_i^* X_n^{-1}(X_n - X)X_n^{-1}A_i$$
$$= \sum_{i=1}^{m} A_i^* X_n^{-1}(X_n - X)X^{-1}(X_n - X)X_n^{-1}A_i \geq 0.$$

According to Lemma 2, whether or not $X_n - X$ is positive definite, we can obtain $X_{n+1} - X \geq 0$. In fact, by $X_n \geq X, n = 1, 2, \cdots$, we can obtain $X_n \geq X_L$, $n = 1, 2, \cdots$, and $X' \geq X_L$.

In conclusion, we have $X' = X_L$, it is equivalent to $\lim_{n \to \infty} X_n = X_L$. $\qquad \square$

Theorem 4. *If* $\sum_{i=1}^{m} \|Q^{-\frac{1}{2}} A_i Q^{-\frac{1}{2}}\|^2 < \frac{1}{4}$, *then the matrix sequence* $\{X_n\}$ *of Algorithm (7) satisfies*

$$\|X_{n+1} - X_L\| \leq \frac{4\sum_{i=1}^{m} \lambda max(Q^{-\frac{1}{2}} A_i^* Q^{-1} A_i Q^{-\frac{1}{2}})\|Q^{-\frac{1}{2}}\|^2 \cdot \|Q^{\frac{1}{2}}\|^2}{\beta_1(1 - 4\sum_{i=1}^{m} \lambda max(Q^{-\frac{1}{2}} A_i^* Q^{-1} A_i Q^{-\frac{1}{2}}))} \|X_n - X_L\|^2, \quad (11)$$

where $\beta_1 = \dfrac{1 + \sqrt{1 - 4\lambda max(\sum_{i=1}^{m} Q^{-\frac{1}{2}} A_i^* Q^{-1} A_i Q^{-\frac{1}{2}})}}{2}$.

Proof. Obviously, from Lemma 1 and Theorem 3, we know that the maximal solution X_L of Eq.(2) satisfies $X_L \in (\beta_1 Q, \beta_2 Q)$, and $Q = X_L + \sum_{i=1}^{m} A_i^* X_L^{-1} A_i$, then

$$\|Q^{\frac{1}{2}}X_L^{-1}Q^{\frac{1}{2}}\| \le \frac{1}{\beta_1},$$

where β_1 is a large root of equation $x(1-x) = \lambda\max(\sum_{i=1}^{m} Q^{-\frac{1}{2}}A_i^*Q^{-1}A_iQ^{-\frac{1}{2}})$.
Therefore, we can obtain

$$\beta_1 = \frac{1+\sqrt{1-4\lambda\max(\sum_{i=1}^{m} Q^{-\frac{1}{2}}A_i^*Q^{-1}A_iQ^{-\frac{1}{2}})}}{2}.$$

In Eq.(6), we use $X_L + \sum_{i=1}^{m} A_i^*X_L^{-1}A_i$ to replace Q, then

$$\sum_{i=1}^{m} A_i^*X_n^{-1}X_{n+1}X_n^{-1}A_i - 2\sum_{i=1}^{m} A_i^*X_n^{-1}A_i - X_{n+1} + X_L + \sum_{i=1}^{m} A_i^*X_L^{-1}A_i = 0.$$

So

$$\begin{aligned}
&X_{n+1} - X_L \\
&= \sum_{i=1}^{m} A_i^*X_n^{-1}(X_{n+1}-X_n)X_n^{-1}A_i + \sum_{i=1}^{m} A_i^*X_n^{-1}(X_n-X_L)X_L^{-1}A_i \\
&= \sum_{i=1}^{m} A_i^*X_n^{-1}(X_{n+1}-X_L)X_L^{-1}A_i - \sum_{i=1}^{m} A_i^*X_n^{-1}(X_n-X_L)X_n^{-1}A_i \\
&\quad + \sum_{i=1}^{m} A_i^*X_n^{-1}(X_n-X_L)X_L^{-1}A_i \\
&= \sum_{i=1}^{m} A_i^*X_n^{-1}(X_{n+1}-X_L)X_n^{-1}A_i \\
&\quad + \sum_{i=1}^{m} A_i^*X_n^{-1}(X_n-X_L)X_L^{-1}(X_n-X_L)X_n^{-1}A_i.
\end{aligned}$$

Since $X_n \in [\frac{1}{2}Q, Q]$, then

$$\|Q^{\frac{1}{2}}X_n^{-1}Q^{\frac{1}{2}}\| \le 2.$$

So

$$\begin{aligned}
&\|Q^{-\frac{1}{2}}(X_{n+1}-X_L)Q^{-\frac{1}{2}}\| \\
&\le (\sum_{i=1}^{m}\|Q^{-\frac{1}{2}}A_iQ^{-\frac{1}{2}}\|^2)\|Q^{\frac{1}{2}}X_n^{-1}Q^{\frac{1}{2}}\|^2\|Q^{-\frac{1}{2}}(X_{n+1}-X_L)Q^{-\frac{1}{2}}\| \\
&\quad + (\sum_{i=1}^{m}\|Q^{-\frac{1}{2}}A_iQ^{-\frac{1}{2}}\|^2)\|Q^{\frac{1}{2}}X_n^{-1}Q^{\frac{1}{2}}\|^2\|Q^{\frac{1}{2}}X_L^{-1}Q^{\frac{1}{2}}\|\|Q^{-\frac{1}{2}}(X_{n+1}-X_L)Q^{-\frac{1}{2}}\|^2 \\
&\le 4\sum_{i=1}^{m}\lambda\max(Q^{-\frac{1}{2}}A_i^*Q^{-1}A_iQ^{-\frac{1}{2}})\|Q^{-\frac{1}{2}}(X_{n+1}-X_L)Q^{-\frac{1}{2}}\| \\
&\quad + \frac{4\sum_{i=1}^{m}\lambda\max(Q^{-\frac{1}{2}}A_i^*Q^{-1}A_iQ^{-\frac{1}{2}})}{\beta_1}\|Q^{-\frac{1}{2}}\|^2\|X_n-X_L\|^2.
\end{aligned}$$

And then we obtain

$$\begin{aligned}
\|X_{n+1}-X_L\| &\le \|Q^{\frac{1}{2}}\|^2 \cdot \|Q^{-\frac{1}{2}}(X_{n+1}-X_L)Q^{-\frac{1}{2}}\| \\
&\le \frac{4\sum_{i=1}^{m}\lambda\max(Q^{-\frac{1}{2}}A_i^*Q^{-1}A_iQ^{-\frac{1}{2}})\|Q^{-\frac{1}{2}}\|^2\cdot\|Q^{\frac{1}{2}}\|^2}{\beta_1(1-4\sum_{i=1}^{m}\lambda\max(Q^{-\frac{1}{2}}A_i^*Q^{-1}A_iQ^{-\frac{1}{2}}))}\|X_n-X_L\|^2,
\end{aligned}$$

where $\beta_1 = \dfrac{1+\sqrt{1-4\lambda\max(\sum\limits_{i=1}^{m} Q^{-\frac{1}{2}}A_i^*Q^{-1}A_iQ^{-\frac{1}{2}})}}{2}$.   □

By this theorem, we know, if $\sum\limits_{i=1}^{m} \|Q^{-\frac{1}{2}}A_iQ^{-\frac{1}{2}}\|^2 < \frac{1}{4}$ and the condition of this select initial original $X_0 \in [\frac{1}{2}Q, Q]$, the constructed Newton iterative convergence is quadratic.

3 Numerical Examples

In this section, we will give a numerical example to identify the two algorithm of achieve extremal positive definite solutions of the equation. For different matrices A_i and different α, r, δ_i, $i = 1, 2, \ldots, m$. We compute the solutions of the equation

$$X + \sum_{i=1}^{m} A_i^* X^{\delta_i} A_i = Q.$$

We will operate all programs by using MATLAB 7.0. We note that

$$\varepsilon(X_k) = \|X_k^r + \sum_{i=1}^{m} A_i^* X_k^{\delta_i} A_i - Q\|.$$

Example 1. We consider the equation by using the two matrices A_1 and A_2 as follows:

$$A_1 = 0.5 * \begin{pmatrix} -0.1 & 0.2 & -0.06 \\ 0.2 & -0.3 & 0.16 \\ -0.1 & 0 & 0.02 \end{pmatrix}, \quad A_2 = \begin{pmatrix} 0.01 & 0.02 & 0.03 \\ 0.01 & 0.225 & 0.12 \\ 0 & 0.09 & 0.07 \end{pmatrix},$$

where $Q = I$, $r = 5$, $\delta_1 = -\frac{1}{3}$, $\delta_2 = -\frac{1}{4}$.

By Algorithm 7, the following table records the different values of parameter $\alpha(\alpha > 1)$, and the values satisfy the number of iterations which is needed by a stop condition.

Table 1.

α	k		
	$tol = 10^{-4}$	$tol = 10^{-6}$	$tol = 10^{-8}$
1.3	3	4	5
1.5	3	4	5
1.7	3	4	5
2.1	3	4	5

$$X_L = \begin{pmatrix} 0.9969 & 0.0037 & -0.0021 \\ 0.0037 & 0.9808 & -0.0040 \\ -0.0021 & -0.0040 & 0.9943 \end{pmatrix}, \quad X_L - D = \begin{pmatrix} 0.9969 & 0.0037 & -0.0021 \\ 0.0037 & 0.9808 & -0.0040 \\ -0.0021 & -0.0040 & 0.9943 \end{pmatrix},$$

where $D = \frac{1}{2}\sum\limits_{i=1}^{2}(A_iQ^{-1}A_i^*)^{-\frac{1}{\delta_i}}$.

The eigenvalue of $X_L - D$ is $(0.9791, 0.9995, 0.9933)$.
The eigenvalue of $Q^{\frac{1}{5}} - X_L$ is $(0.0005, 0.0067, 0.0208)$.
It implies that $X_L \in \Omega$.

From the Table 1, we conclude that the number of iterations increased with increasing of α within some extent errors.

Acknowledgments. We thank the reviewers for their valuable comments and suggestions on this paper.

References

1. Bhatia, R.: Matrix Analysis M. Springer, Berlin (1997)
2. Engwerda, J.C.: On the existente of a positive definite solution of the matrix equation$X + A^T X^{-1} A = I$. Linear Algebra Appl. 194, 91–108 (1993)
3. Golub, G.H., Loan, C.F.: Matrix computations. Johns Hopkins University Press (2012)
4. Ramadan., M.A., El-Shazly, N.M.: On the matrix equation $X + A^* \sqrt[2^m]{X^{-1}} A = I$. J. Appl. Math. Comput. 173, 992–1013 (2006)
5. Xu, S.F.: On the maximal solution of the matrix equation$X + A^T X^{-1} A = I$. J. Beijing Univ. 36(1), 29–38 (2000)
6. Duan, X.F., Liao, A.P.: On the existence of Hermitian positive definite solutions of the matrix equation$X^s + A^* X^{-t} A = Q$. J. Linear Algebra Appl. 429, 673–687 (2008)
7. Zhan, X.: Computing the extremal positive definite solutions of a matrix equation. SIAM J. Sci. Comput. 17, 1167–1174 (1996)
8. Zhan, X.Z., Xie, J.J.: On the matrix equation$X + A^T X^{-1} A = I$. Linear Algebra Appl. 247, 337–345 (1996)

On the Convergence of Levenberg-Marquardt Method for Solving Nonlinear Systems

Minglei Fang[1,*], Feng Xu[1], Zhibin Zhu[2], Lihua Jiang[1], and Xianya Geng[1]

[1] College of Science, Anhui University of Science and Technology,
Huainan, 232001, Anhui, China
[2] School of Mathematics and Computational Sciences,
Guilin University of Electronic Technology, Guilin, 541004, Guangxi, China
`fmlmath@sina.com`

Abstract. Levenberg-Marquardt (L-M forshort) method is one of the most important methods for solving systems of nonlinear equations. In this paper, we consider the convergence under $\lambda_k = \min(\|F_k\|, \|J_k^T F_k\|)$ of L-M method. We will show that if $\|F(x_k)\|$ provides a local error bound, which is weaker than the condition of nonsingularity for the system of nonlinear equations, the sequence generated by the L-M method converges to the point of the solution set quadratically. As well, numerical experiments are reported.

Keywords: Nonlinear equation, Local error bound, L-M method.

1 Introduction

Nonlinear equations have wide applications in chemical technology, mechanics, economy and product management and so on. In this paper, we consider the system of nonlinear equations:

$$F(x) = 0, \tag{1}$$

where $F : R^n \to R^m$ is continuously differentiable. Throughout the paper, we assume that the solution set of (1) is nonempty and denoted by X^*. Without specific explanation, $\|\cdot\|$ refers to two-norm. The classical L-M method Levenberg (see [6,2]) for nonlinear Equation (1) computes the trial step by

$$(J_k^T J_k + \lambda_k I)^{-1} d_k = -J_k^T F_k, \tag{2}$$

where $J_k = J(x_k) = F'(x_k)$ is the Jacobian, and $\lambda_k \geq 0$ is a parameter being updated from iteration to iteration. The parameter λ_k is used to prevent d_k from being too large when $J_k^T J_k$ is nearly singular and guarantees that Equation (2) is well defined. It is well known that the L-M method has a quadratic rate of convergence [3], if the Jacobian at the solution X^* is nonsingular and if the

---

* Corresponding author.

L. Pan et al. (Eds.): BIC-TA 2014, CCIS 472, pp. 117–122, 2014.

parameter is chosen suitably at each step. However, the condition of the non-singularity of $J(x^*)(x^* \in X^*)$ is too strong. Recently, Yamashita in [7] has shown that under the weaker condition that $\|F_k\|$ provides a local error bound near the solution, the L-M method converges quadratically to the solution set of Equation (1) if the parameter is chosen as $\lambda_k = \|F_k\|^2$. In [5,6], it has shown the L-M method has a quadratic convergence if the parameter is chosen as $\lambda_k = \|F_k\|$ and $\lambda_k = \|J_k^T F_k\|$, respectively. Furthermore, they extend the L-M method[4] to chose $\lambda_k = \|F_k\|^\delta$ with $\delta \in (0, 2]$ and show that under the same conditions, the L-M method converges quadratically to some solution of Equation (1) when $\delta \in [1, 2]$ and super-linearly when $\delta \in (0, 1)$. Ma and Jiang in [1] chose the parameter to be the convex combination of $\lambda_k = \|F_k\|$ and $\lambda_k = \|J_k^T F_k\|$, i.e. $\lambda_k = \theta\|F_k\| + (1 - \theta)\|J_k^T F_k\|$ with θ be a constant in $[0, 1]$, and show the L-M method preserves a quadratic convergence.

In this paper, we will present the parameter $\lambda_k = \min(\|F_k\|, \|J_k^T F_k\|)$. It is proved that with the parameter, if $\|F_k\|$ provides a local error bound near some $x^* \in X^*$, then the sequence generated by the L-M method converges quadratically to the solution of Equation (1).

Definiton1.1. Let N be a subset of R^n such that $N \bigcap X^* \neq \emptyset$. We say that $\|F(x)\|$ provides a local error bound on N for system (1), if there exists a positive constant $c > 0$, such that $\|F(x)\| \geq c\,dist(x, X^*), \forall x \in N$.

2   Convergence of L-M Algorithm

Assumption2.1

(a) There exists a solution x^* of (1).

(b) $F(x)$ is continuously differentiabl, and the Jacobian $J(x)$ is Lipschitz continuous on some neighborhood of $x^* \in X^*$, i.e., there exist positive constants $b \in (0, 1)$ and $c_1 > 0$ such that

$$\|J(y) - J(x)\| \leq c_1\|y - x\| \quad \forall x, y \in N(x^*, b) = \{x \in R^n | \|x - x^*\| \leq b\}. \quad (3)$$

(c) $\|F(x)\|$ provides a local error bound on $N(x^*, b)$ for the system in Equation (1), i.e., there exists a constant $c_2 > 0$ such that

$$\|F(x)\| \geq c_2 dist(x, X^*), \forall x \in N(x^*, b), \quad (4)$$

where X^* denote the solution set of (1). Note that, by Assumption 2.1(b), we have

$$\|F(y) - F(x) - J(x_k)(y - x)\| \leq c_1\|y - x\|^2, \forall x, y \in N(x^*, b). \quad (5)$$

And, there exists a constant $L > 0$ such that

$$\|F(y) - F(x)\| \leq L\|y - x\|, \forall x, y \in N(x^*, b). \quad (6)$$

We discuss the local convergence of L-M method without line search, i.e., the next iterate is computed by

$$\begin{cases} x_{k+1} = x_k + d_k \\ d_k = -(J_k^T J_k + \lambda_k I)^{-1} J_k^T F_k \\ \lambda_k = \min(||F_k||, ||J_k^T F_k||). \end{cases} \tag{7}$$

For simplification, we denote $\bar{x}_k$ the vector in X^* that satisfies

$$||x_k - \bar{x}_k|| = dist(x_k, X^*), \bar{x}_k \in X^*. \tag{8}$$

Lemma 2.1. Under the conditions of Assumption 2.1, if $x_k \in N(x^*, b)$, then there exist constants L_1, c_3 such that

$$c_3 dist(x_k, X^*) \leq \lambda_k = \min(||F_k||, ||J_k^T F_k||) \leq L_1 ||\bar{x}_k - x_k||. \tag{9}$$

Proof: Firstly, we show the right of the inequality. Since it holds $\lambda_k = \min(||F_k||, ||J_k^T F_k||)$, we have

$$||F_k|| = ||F(\bar{x}_k) - F(x_k)|| \leq L||\bar{x}_k - x_k|| \qquad for \ \lambda_k = ||F_k||,$$

and $\lambda_k = ||F_k|| \cdot ||J_k|| \leq ||J_k||[L||\bar{x}_k - x_k||] \leq L^2 ||\bar{x}_k - x_k|| \quad for \lambda_k = ||J_k^T F_k||$. Let $L_1 = max(L, L^2)$, the right holds.

Next, we show the left of (9). For $\lambda_k = ||F_k||$, we get

$$||F(x)|| \geq c_2 dist(x, X^*), \forall x \in N(x^*, b).$$

For $\lambda_k = ||J_k^T F_k||$, due to

$$||F_k||^2 = F_k^T F_k = F_k^T[F(\bar{x}_k) + J_k(x_k - \bar{x}_k)] + F_k^T V_k,$$

where $V_k = F_k - F(\bar{x}_k) - J_k(x_k - \bar{x}_k)$, we obtain

$$F_k^T J_k(x_k - \bar{x}_k) = ||F_k||^2 - F_k^T V_k.$$

From Equations (4), (5) and (6), it obvious that

$$||J_k F_k^T|| \geq c_2^2 ||x_k - \bar{x}_k|| - Lc_1 ||x_k - \bar{x}_k||^2,$$

i.e., $||J_k F_k^T|| ||x_k - \bar{x}_k|| \geq c_2^2 ||x_k - \bar{x}_k||^2 - Lc_1 ||x_k - \bar{x}_k||^3$.
Hence, there exists a constant $c' > 0$ for $||x_k - \bar{x}_k||$ such that

$$||J_k F_k^T|| \geq c' ||x_k - \bar{x}_k|.$$

Let $c_3 = \min(c_2, c')$, we know that

$$\lambda_k \geq c_3 dist(x, X^*).$$

Lemma 2.2. Under the conditions of Assumption 2.1, if $x_k \in N(x^*, b/2)$, then there exists a constant c_4 such that

$$||d_k|| \leq c_4 dist(x_k, X^*)$$

Proof: Define the function that $\theta^k(d) = ||F_k + J_k d||^2 + \lambda_k ||d||^2$. d_k is the global minimum of $\theta^k(d)$ from the convex property of $\theta^k(d)$, so we have

$$\theta^k(d_k) \leq \theta^k(\bar{x}_k - x_k), \tag{10}$$

and $||\bar{x}_k - x^*|| \leq ||\bar{x}_k - x_k|| + ||x^* - x_k|| \leq ||x^* - x_k|| + ||x^* - x_k|| \leq b$.

From the above inequality and $x_k \in N(x^*, b/2)$, we see that $\bar{x}_k \in N(x^*, b)$, we also obtain from the define of $\theta^k(d)$, (10), Assumption 2.1(b) and Lemma 2.1

$$
\begin{aligned}
||d_k||^2 &\leq (1/\lambda_k)\theta^k(d_k) \leq (1/\lambda_k)\theta^k(\bar{x}_k - x_k) \\
&= (1/\lambda_k)[||F_k + J_k(\bar{x}_k - x_k)||^2 + \lambda_k ||\bar{x}_k - x_k||^2 \\
&\leq (1/\lambda_k)[c_1^2 ||\bar{x}_k - x_k||^4 + \lambda_k ||\bar{x}_k - x_k||^2] \\
&\leq \left(\frac{c_1^2 ||\bar{x}_k - x_k||^2}{\lambda_k} + 1 \right) ||\bar{x}_k - x_k||^2 \\
&\leq \left(\frac{c_1^2}{c_3} ||\bar{x}_k - x_k|| + 1 \right) ||\bar{x}_k - x_k||^2
\end{aligned}
$$

The above inequality and $||\bar{x}_k - x_k|| \leq ||x_k - x^*|| \leq b/2$ imply that

$$||d_k|| \leq c_4 dist(x_k, X^*),$$

where $c_4 = \sqrt{\frac{bc_1^2 + 2c_3}{2c_3}}$.

Lemma 2.3. Under the conditions of Assumption 2.1, if $x_k \in N(x^*, b/2)$, then there exists a constant c_5 such that $||J_k d_k + F_k|| \leq c_5 dist(x_k, X^*)^{3/2}$.

Proof: From Lemma 2.2, we have

$$
\begin{aligned}
||J_k d_k + F_k||^2 &\leq \theta^k(d_k) \leq \theta^k(\bar{x}_k - x_k) \\
&= ||J_k(\bar{x}_k - x_k) + F_k||^2 + \lambda_k ||\bar{x}_k - x_k||^2 \\
&\leq c_1^2 ||\bar{x}_k - x_k||^4 + \lambda_k ||\bar{x}_k - x_k||^2
\end{aligned}
$$

From (9), we get that

$$
\begin{aligned}
||J_k d_k + F_k|| &\leq \sqrt{c_1^2 ||\bar{x}_k - x_k|| + L_1} ||\bar{x}_k - x_k||^{3/2} \\
&\leq \sqrt{(c_1^2 b + 2L_1)/2} ||\bar{x}_k - x_k||^{3/2}
\end{aligned}
$$

So, we know that $||J_k d_k + F_k|| \leq c_5 dist(x_k, X^*)^{3/2}$, where $c_5 = \sqrt{(bc_1^2 + 2L_1)/2}$. The next result is a major step in verifying the local convergence .

Lemma 2.4. If $x_{k+1}, x_k \in N(x^*, b/2)$, then there exists a constant c_6, such that $dist(x_{k+1}, X^*) \leq c_6 dist(x_k, X^*)^{3/2}$.

Proof: In the view of $x_{k+1}, x_k \in N(x^*, b/2)$, $x_{k+1} = x_k + d_k$, Assumption 2.1, Lemma 2.2 and Lemma 2.3, we get that

$$
\begin{aligned}
c_2 dist(x_{k+1}, X^*) &= c_2 dist(x_k + d_k, X^*) \leq ||F(x_k + d_k)|| \\
&\leq ||J_k d_k + F_k|| + c_1 ||d_k||^2 \leq c_5 dist(x_k, X^*)^{3/2} + c_1 c_4^2 dist(x_k, X^*)^2 \\
&\leq (c_5 + c_1 c_4^2) dist(x_k, X^*)^{3/2}.
\end{aligned}
$$

We have that
$$dist(x_{k+1}, X^*) \le c_6 dist(x_k, X^*)^{3/2}, \text{ where } c_6 = (c_5 + c_1 c_4^2)/c_2.$$
From Lemma 2.4, if $dist(x_0, X^*) < c_6^{-2}$, we know that

$$dist(x_{k+1}, X^*) < dist(x_k, X^*) \qquad for \; all \; k.$$

Therefore, we can assume that all x_k are in $N(x^*, b)$, it follows that

$$\sum_{k=0}^{\infty} dist(x_k, X^*) < +\infty.$$

Which implies, due to Lemma 2.3, that

$$\sum_{k=0}^{\infty} ||d_k|| < +\infty.$$

Thus $\{x_k\}$ converges to some point $\bar{x}_k \in X^*$. It is obvious that

$$dist(x_k, X^*) \le dist(x_k + d_k, X^*) + ||d_k||.$$

The above inequality and Lemma 2.4 imply that
$$dist(x_k, X^*) \le 2||d_k|| \text{ for all large } k.$$
Hence, we have $||d_{k+1}|| = O(||d_k||^{3/2})$. Therefore, $\{x_k\}$ converges to the solution $\bar{x}$ superlinearly.

Without loss of generality, we assume that $\{x_k\}$ converges to $x^* \in N^*$. We see [7] for the singular value decomposition (SVD) of J_k and the proof of the next Lemma and Theorem.

Lemma 2.5. Under the conditions of Assumption 2.1, if $x_k \in N(x^*, b)$, then we have
   (a) $||U_1 U_1^T F_k|| \le L ||x_k - \bar{x}_k||$;
   (b) $||U_1 U_1^T F_k|| \le 2c_1 ||x_k - \bar{x}_k||^2$;
   (c)$||U_1 U_1^T F_k|| \le c_1 ||x_k - \bar{x}_k||^2$;

Theorem 2.1. Under the conditions of Assumption 2.1, if the Sequence $\{x_k\}$ be generated without line search with x_0 sufficiently close to x^*. Then $\{x_k\}$ converges to the solution quadratically.

3   Numerical Results

In order to test the efficiency of the proposed algorithm, we solve some examples. The computing results show that the algorithm is efficient. We implement the algorithm in MATLAB. The algorithm can be stated as follows:

Algorithm 3.1
   Step1: Given $x_0 \in R^n, \varepsilon > 0, k = 0$
   Step2: If $||J_k^T F_k|| \le \varepsilon$, then stop. Solve $d_k = -(J_k^T J_k + \lambda_k I)^{-1} J_k^T F_k$, where $\lambda_k = \min(||F_k||, ||J_k^T F_k||)$.
   Step3: Let $x_{k+1} = x_k + d_k, k = k + 1$, go to Step2.
   We test the Powell singular function[5], where $n = 4$ and $rank(J(x^*)) = 2$. The results are given in Table 1. The algorithm is terminated when $||J_k^T F_k|| \le$

Table 1. Numerical results of Example 1

$function$	n	x_0	$\lambda_k = \min(\|F_k\|, \|J_k^T F_k\|)$ $iters$	$\lambda_k = \|J_k^T F_k\|$ $iters$	$\lambda_k = \|F_k\|$ $iters$	$\lambda_k = \|F_k\|^2$ $iters$
$Powell$	4	1	11	15	12	14
$singular$		10	32	63	33	-

10^{-6} or the number of the iterations exceeds 100. The third column of the table indicates that the starting point is $x_0, 10x_0$, where x_0 is suggested by [5]. "iters" represent the numbers of the iterate. If the method failed to find the solution in 100 iterions, we denoted it by the sign "-".

Acknowledgments. This work is supported by the National Natural Science Foundation of China (No. 11061011) and the Young Teachers Science Foundation of Anhui University of Science and Technology (No. QN201329).

References

1. Ma, C., Jiang, L.: Some Research on Levenberg-Marquardt Method for the Nonlinear Equations. Applied Mathematics and Computation 184, 1032–1040 (2007)
2. Marquardt, D.W.: An Algorithm for Least-squares Estimation of Nonlinear Inequalities. SIAM Journal Applied Mathematics 11, 431–441 (1963)
3. Dennis, J.E., Schnabel, R.B.: Numerical Methods for Unconstrained Optimization and Nonlinear Equations. Prentice-Hall, Englewood Cliffs (1983)
4. Fan, J., Pan, J.: A Note on the Levenberg-Marquardt Parameter. Applied Mathematics and Computation 207, 351–359 (2009)
5. Mor, J.J., Garbow, B.S., Hillstrom, K.H.: Testing Unconstrained Optimization Software. ACM Trans. on Mathematics Software 7, 17–41 (1981)
6. Levenberg, K.: A Method for the Solution of Nonlinear Problems in Least Squares, Quart. Applied Mathematics 2, 164–166 (1944)
7. Yamashita, N., Fukushima, M.: On the Rate of Convergence of the Levenberg-Marquardt Method. Computing 15, 239–249 (2001)
8. Liu, Y., Chen, Y.: On the Convergence of a New Levenberg-Marquardt Method. Mathematica Numerica Sinica 27, 55–62 (2005)
9. Yuan, Y.X., Sun, W.Y.: Optimization Theory and Method. Scince Press, Beijing (1997)

DNA-Chip-Based Information Hiding Scheme

Xiwen Fang and Xuejia Lai*

Department of Computer Science and Technology, Shanghai Jiao Tong University,
800 Dongchuan Rd., Shanghai, China
lai-xj@cs.sjtu.edu.cn

Abstract. In this paper we present DNA-IH, which is the first DNA-chip-based information hiding scheme. In our scheme, given an ordinary message M_o, a secret message M_s is incorporated into the microarray C which represents the signature of M_o. Only the intended recipient can retrieve the secret message M_s, while other members can only read the ordinary message M_o without knowing whether there exists any other secret message. Conventional information hiding process changes the statistical properties of the original data. The existence of secret messages embedded can be detected using statistical steganalysis schemes. In DNA-IH, for secret message and ordinary message, the corresponding DNA microarrays can be identical, thus statistical steganalysis is no longer able to detect whether or not a given DNA chip contains a secret message.

Keywords: DNA Cryptology, DNA chip, Information Hiding.

1   Introduction

The technology of DNA microarray is one of the fastest-growing new technologies in biological research. Its main advantage lies in the fact that large numbers of samples can be analyzed simultaneously [1]. The technology was also introduced into cryptography: a DNA-chip-based symmetric-key cryptosystem was proposed in [2]; an asymmetric encryption and signature system DNA-PKC was proposed in [3]; a DNA-chip-based dynamic broadcast encryption scheme DNA-DBE was proposed in [4]. The security of DNA-chip-based cryptosystem relies on hard biological problem: it is difficult to precisely obtain all molecular information of mixed sequence-specific unknown DNA probes spotted on a DNA chip. Such scheme is immune to attack of new computing technologies in the future [2–4].

Conventional information hiding schemes conceal secret messages within multimedia files, such as image or video [5–8]. In conventional schemes, the statistical properties of the original files will be affected after the hidden messages are embedded. Thus the undetectability of steganography cannot be guaranteed, the existence of secret messages embedded can be detected using statistical steganalysis schemes.

In this paper, we present DNA-IH, a DNA-chip-based information hiding scheme preserving statistical properties. We provide a new property of DNA-chip-based cryptosystem, i.e. given two distinct messages which are of identical

---

* Corresponding author.

L. Pan et al. (Eds.): BIC-TA 2014, CCIS 472, pp. 123–127, 2014.
© Springer-Verlag Berlin Heidelberg 2014

length, the corresponding ciphertexts can be identical. As a result, a secret message can be incorporated in a microarray which represents the signature of an ordinary message, only the intended recipient can retrieve the secret message without drawing others' suspicion, while others can only verify the signature of the ordinary message without knowing whether there exists a secret message in the microarray. Statistical properties will not be affected, thus our scheme enjoys robustness against statistical attacks.

2   Construction

A special property of DNA-PKC [3] is given as follow. Due to space limitations, we do not include details and proof here.

Theorem 1. *Given two distinct messages M_o and M_s which are of identical length, the corresponding ciphertexts can be identical.*

Suppose Alice wants to communicate with a group of members Bob, Charlie and Dan. Each member has a verification key dk_o which is used to retrieve and verify the signature of the ordinary message M_o. Alice also wants to send secret message M_s to Charlie without drawing suspicion of other members. Our goal is to incorporate the secret message M_s into the DNA microarray which represents the signature of the ordinary message M_o, while nobody knows whether a secret message is concealed in the microarray.

Key Generation. We fabricate a DNA chip using the probes in the candidate set. Each type of probes forms a spot on the chip. The chip is replicated for later use. We randomly select probe mixture dk_o and dk_s, each contains probes complementary to several arbitrary selected encryption-key-probes in the candidate set. Use dk_o and dk_s to probe the chip respectively. If the experimental results are ideal(see Ref. [3]) and there exists overlap, dk_o and dk_s can be determined. dk_o will be sent to all of the members, while dk_s will be sent to Charlie secretly.

We define four sets ek_{11}, ek_{10}, ek_{01} and ek_{00}: Each probe of ek_{11} is strong positive for both dk_o and dk_s; each probe of ek_{10} is strong positive for dk_o and strong negative for dk_s; each probe of ek_{01} is strong negative for dk_o and strong positive for dk_s. each probe of ek_{00} is strong negative for both dk_o and dk_s.

Encryption. Given two messages M_o and M_s which are of length $|M_o|$ and $|M_s|$ respectively, $|M_s| \leq |M_o|$. M_o is the ordinary message which can be read by all of the members, while M_s is the secret message which Alice wants to send to Charlie. According to Theorem 1, we can incorporate M_s into the microarray which represents the ordinary message M_o using Algorithm 1. Note that if $|M_o| = |M_s|$, it is not compulsory to append the terminator T. Fig.1 shows a simple example of the information hiding process. The four sets can be determined after comparing the overlap between the positive probes and the negative probes for dk_o and dk_s. For each bit of M_o and M_s, encryption probes are randomly selected from the four sets.

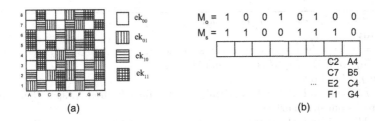

(a)   (b)

Fig. 1. (a) Compare the overlap between the positive probes and the negative probes for dk_o and dk_s. (b) $M_1 = 10010100$, $M_2 = 11001110$, fabricate the microarray according to M_o and M_s.

Decryption. After the members of the group received the microarray, using dk_o to probe the ciphertext microarry, the ordinary message M_o can be retrieved: all of the spots showing strong signal represents 1 and all of the spots showing weak signal represents 0. For the member who is due to receive the secret message M_s, eg. Charlie, he can use mixture of dk_o and dk_s to probe the microarray. With the help of different fluorescent, the ordinary message M_o and the secret message M_s can be retrieved by analyzing the signal within different filter. Fig.2 shows a simple example of the recovery process.

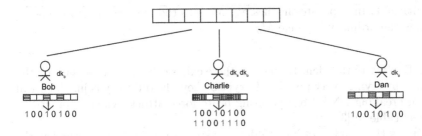

Fig. 2. Charlie can retrieve the secret message M_s, while others can only read the ordinary message M_o

3 Discussion

There are three procedures in DNA-IH: key generation, encryption and decryption. The experimental feasibility of DNA-IH comes naturally from the successful experiment of DNA-PKC [3].

According to Theorem 1 and the construction of DNA-IH, we could see that in DNA-IH, the signature microarray of the ordinary message M_o is identical to the ciphertext microarray of the secrete message M_s. As a result, statistical steganalysis is no longer able to detect whether or not a given DNA microarray contains a secret message.

The example we presented in section 2 is a small scale sample system. In practice, on each spot there might be more than 2000 types of probes. Suppose

Input: M_o, M_s, ek_{11}, ek_{10}, ek_{01}, ek_{00}
Output: C_{M_o, M_s}
1 Let $j = 0$, let T be a terminal binary sequence;
2 $M_o \leftarrow append(M_o, T)$, $M_s \leftarrow append(M_s, T)$;
3 **while** $j < |M_s|$ **do**
4   If $M_{oj} = 1$ and $M_{sj} = 1$, randomly select probes from ek_{11}, spot the mixed probes onto the surface;
5   If $M_{oj} = 1$ and $M_{sj} = 0$, randomly select probes from ek_{10}, spot the mixed probes onto the surface;
6   If $M_{oj} = 0$ and $M_{sj} = 1$, randomly select probes from ek_{01}, spot the mixed probes onto the surface;
7   If $M_{oj} = 0$ and $M_{sj} = 0$, randomly select probes from ek_{00}, spot the mixed probes onto the surface;
8      $j \leftarrow j + 1$;
9 **end**
10 **while** $j < |M_o|$ **do**
11   If $M_{oj} = 1$, randomly select probes from ek_{10}, spot the mixed probes onto the surface;
12   If $M_{oj} = 0$, randomly select probes from ek_{00}, spot the mixed probes onto the surface;
13      $j \leftarrow j + 1$;
14 **end**

Algorithm 1. Incorporate the message M_s into the DNA microarray representing the ordinary message M_o

Bob and Dan try to the identify whether there exists other secret message on the microarray by trying every possible decryption key, the difficulty is just identical to that of breaking DNA-PKC [3] using brute force attack, which is proved to be impracticable in [3].

The *bpn* is the number of bits hidden per spot. In our scheme, if the lengths of the ordinary message and the secret message are identical, we have $bpn = 1$. Comparison between DNA-IH and conventional information hiding schemes is summarized in Table 1.

Table 1. Comparision between DNA-IH and conventional information hiding schemes

	DNA-IH	Conventional schemes
host medium	DNA microarray representing a given ordinary message	multimedia files
encryption key	DNA probes	binary data
decryption key	DNA probe mixture	binary data
encryption process	Fabricating DNA microarray	mathematical process
decryption process	Hybridization experiment	mathematical process
robustness against statistical attacks	preserving statistical properties	statistical properties are usually affected
bpn	$bpn = 1$ if $|M_s| = |M_o|$	usually significantly less than 1

4   Conclusion

In this paper, taking advantage of the special feature of DNA-PKC, i.e. for different messages which are of identical length, the corresponding ciphertexts can be identical, we present DNA-IH, which is the first exploration of DNA-chip-based information hiding scheme. The security of our scheme relies on hard biological problem, which provides another level of security compared with conventional cryptosystem. In DNA-IH, the signature microarray of a given ordinary message and the ciphertext microarray of a given secret message can be identical, thus statistical steganalysis is no longer able to detect whether or not a given DNA microarray contains a secret message.

Acknowledgements. This work was supported by the National Natural Science Foundation of China (No. 61272440, No. 61073149), State Key Laboratory of ASIC & System (11KF00 20), Key Lab of Information Network Security, Ministry of Public Security (C11603).

References

1. Schena M., Shalon D., Davis R.W., Brown P.O.: Quantitative monitoring of gene expression patterns with a complementary DNA microarray. Science, 270, 467–470, (1995)
2. Lu M.X., Lai X.J., Xiao G.Z., Qin L.: Symmetric-key cryptosystem with DNA technology. SCIENCE CHINA Information Sciences, 50(3), 324–333, (2007)
3. Lai X.J., Lu M.X., Qin L., Han J.S., Fang X.W.: Asymmetric encryption and signature method with DNA technology. Science China Information Sciences, 53(3), 506–514, (2010)
4. Fang X.W., Lai X.J.: DNA-chip-based dynamic broadcast encryption scheme with constant-size ciphertexts and decryption keys. Science China Information Sciences, accepted.
5. Bender W., Gruhl D., Morimoto N., Lu A.: Techniques for data hiding. IBM systems journal, 35(3.4):313-336(1996)
6. Chan C.K., Cheng L.M.: Hiding data in images by simple lsb substitution. Pattern recognition, 37(3):469-474(2004)
7. Artz D.:Digital steganography: hiding data within data. Internet computing, IEEE, 5(3):75-80(2001)
8. Ni Z.C., Shi Y.Q., Ansari N., Su W.: Reversible data hiding. IEEE Transactions on Circuits and Systems for Video Technology, 16(3):354-362,(2006)

Locate Multiple Pareto Optima Using a Species-Based Multi-objective Genetic Algorithm

Yaping Fu, Hongfeng Wang*, and Min Huang

College of Information Science and Engineering,
Northeastern University, Shenyang, 110819, China
hfwang@mail.neu.edu.cn

Abstract. In many real-world multi-objective optimization problems (MOOPs), the decision maker may only concern partial, rather than all, Pareto optima. This requires the solution algorithm to search and locate multiple Pareto optimal solutions simultaneously with higher accuracy and faster speed. To address this requirement, a species-based multi-objective GA (speMOGA) is designed in this paper, where multiple sub-populations would be constructed to search for multiple nondomiated solutions in parallel via decomposing a MOOP into a set of subproblems using the *Tchebycheff* approach. Based on a series of benchmark test problems, experiments are carried out to investigate the performance of the proposed algorithm in comparison with two classical multi-objective GAs: MOEA/D and NSGA-II. The experimental results show the validity of the proposed algorithm on locating multiple Pareto optima.

Keywords: Multi-objective optimization problem, Genetic algorithm, Species, *Tchebycheff* approach.

1 Introduction

Many real-world optimization problems usually involve multiple objectives. The multi-objective optimization problems (MOOPs) are rather different from the single objective problem due to inexistence of the global optimal solution which can optimize all objectives simultaneously. A MOOP can be mathematically formulated as follows [1].

$$\min F(x) = (f_1(x), f_2(x), \ldots, f_m(x))^T \tag{1}$$

$$\text{s.t. } x \in \Omega$$

where Ω is the decision space, $F(x)$ consist of m objective functions $f_i(x) : \Omega \to R^m$, $i = 1, 2, \ldots, m$, where R^m is the objective space.

The objective functions in (1) often conflict with each other, which means that any improvement of one objective function may lead to the deterioration of the others. Thus, the purpose of the solution algorithm for MOOP is to achieve those trade-off solutions among all objectives, which are called as Pareto optima.

---

* Corresponding author.

L. Pan et al. (Eds.): BIC-TA 2014, CCIS 472, pp. 128–137, 2014.

For the problem in (1), Let u, $v \in R^m$, u is said to dominate v if and only if $u_i \leq v_i$ for every $i \in 1, 2, \ldots, m$ and $u_i < v_i$ for at least one index, $j \in 1, 2, \ldots, m$. A solution $x^* \in \Omega$ is Pareto optimal if there is no solution $x \in \Omega$ such that $F(x)$ dominates $F(x^*)$. $F(x^*)$ is then called a Pareto optimal objective vector. The set of all the Pareto optima is called the Pareto set (PS) and the set of all the Pareto optimal objective vectors is the Pareto front (PF) [2].

Due to the population-based mechanism, genetic algorithms (GAs) are able to approximate the whole PS (PF) of a MOOP in a single run. Since the pioneer attempt of applying GAs to solve MOOPs [3], the researches on multi-objective GAs (MOGAs) have been gained more and more concerns from GA community in recent years [4–7].

In the current relevant works, these MOGAs are usually designed to achieve as many as possible Pareto optimal solutions, which are able to distribute evenly in PF. It is noticeable that most MOOPs may have many or even infinite Pareto optima, which leads to too time-consuming when a MOGA achieving or approximating the complete PF. However, the decision maker may only be interested in partial, rather than all, Pareto optima in many real-world applications. This requires the algorithms to enable to search and locate multiple Pareto optimal solutions simultaneously with higher accuracy and faster speed, which was rarely concerned in the current researches.

Therefore, we will investigate the application of a novel MOGA, which is termed as species-based MOGA (speMOGA), in locating multiple Pareto optimal solutions in this paper. In the framework of our proposed algorithm, several single-objective subproblems are firstly generated from a set of given weight vectors by using a *Tchebycheff* approach, and then the whole population is divided into several species to locate the solutions of those generated single-objective subproblems in parallel. This means that each nondominated solution could be achieve by one subpopulation in order to enable our proposed algorithm achieve multiple Pareto optimal solutions simultaneously with higher accuracy and faster speed.

The rest of this paper is organized as follows. The next section gives a detailed description of the proposed algorithm, including of the decomposition method of subproblems, the construction method of species, and the design of genetic operators. Section 3 reports the experimental results and relevant analysis and the final section concludes this paper with discussions on the future works.

2   The Proposed Algorithm

The species methods have been initially used in GAs for multi-modal optimization problems (MMOPs) in order to enable GAs achieve multiple optima in a single run. Similar to MMOPs, multi-objective optimization problems (MOOPs) also require the solution algorithm to achieve a set of Pareto optimal solutions that are non-dominated with each other. Obviously, it would become an interesting research issue whether to extend the species method into GAs for MOOPs with some elaborate designs, which is the major motivation in this paper.

2.1 Developing Subproblems

It is well-know that a Pareto optimal solution could be an optimal solution of a scalar optimization problem, where the objective is an aggregation of all the objectives in a MOOP. Therefore, approximate of PF can be decomposed into a number of scalar objective optimization subproblem [8]. As described in the following formula, a *Tchebycheff* approach can be used to construct the aggregation function.

Let $w = (w_1, w_2, \ldots, w_m)^T$ be a weight vector, i.e., $w_i \geq 0$, for all $i = 1, 2, \ldots, m$ and $\sum_{i=1}^{m} w_i = 1$. Then the scalar optimization problem is in the form.

$$\min g^{te}((x|w, z^*)) = \max_{1 \leq i \leq m} \{w_i | f_i(x) - z_i^* |\} \tag{2}$$

$$\text{s.t.} x \in \Omega$$

where $z^* = (z_1^*, z_2^*, \ldots, z_m^*)^T$ is the reference point, i.e., $z_i^* = min\{f_i(x)|x \in \Omega\}$ for each $i \in \{1, 2, \ldots, m\}$. For each Pareto optimal point x^*, there exists a weight vector w such that x^* is the optimal solution of (2). Obviously, each optimal solution of (2) is also a Pareto optimal solution of (1).

Thus, a set of single objective optimization subproblems can be developed according to the weight vectors. Let $w^1, w^2, \ldots, w^N$ be a set of weight vectors, the objective function of the j-th subproblem can be described as follows.

$$\min g^{te}((x|w^j, z^*)) = \max_{1 \leq i \leq m} \{w_i^j | f_i(x) - z_i^* |\} \tag{3}$$

$$\text{s.t.} x \in \Omega$$

where $w^j = (w_1^j, w_2^j, \ldots, w_m^j)^T$.

In our proposed algorithm, all developed subproblems would be addressed simultaneously and their optimal solutions, which are also the Pareto optimal solutions in the corresponding MOOP. This would be achieved by the different species or subpopulation. The species construction method would be discussed in the next section.

2.2 Constructing Species

In the species method, a species can consist of a species seed and the member individuals dominated by this seed. In Figure 1, it gives the pseudo-code how to identify the species seeds in our proposed algorithm for MOOP.

After identifying the species seeds, the species would be constructed using the species seeds and a number of individuals that are the closest to the corresponding seeds in the search space. It is given in Figure 2 the pseudo-code for the algorithm of constructing species.

2.3 The Proposed Algorithm

Based on the above discussion, a species-based multi-objective GA (speMOGA) would be proposed and shown in the pseudo-code in Figure 3. In the proposed

Procedure Algorithm of identifying species seed:
begin
  sort the weight vector in W_{sorted} randomly;
  $S := \emptyset$;
  while not reaching the end of W_{sorted} **do**
    get the first unprocessed weight vector w;
    $minValue := \infty$;
    for each unprocessed individual p in the population **do**
      if $w^T F(p) < minValue$ **then**
      $minValue \leftarrow w^T F(p)$;
      $seed \leftarrow p$;
    endfor
    $seed.processed \leftarrow true$;
    $S \leftarrow S \bigcup \{seed\}$;
  endwhile
end

Fig. 1. Pseudo-code for the algorithm of identifying species seeds

Procedure Algorithm of constructing species:
begin
  $i := 1$;
  while $i < speciesQuan$ **do**
    get the ith seed individual s in S.
    $species_i \leftarrow species_i \bigcup \{s\}$;
    $j := 1$;
    while $j < speciesSize$ **do**
      get the first j-th nearest unprocessed individual p with s
      according to Euclidean distance;
      $p.processed := true$;
      $species_i \leftarrow species_i \bigcup \{p\}$;
      $j := j + 1$;
    endwhile
    $i := i + 1$;
  endwhile
end
Denotions:
$speciesSize$:the number of individual in each species;
$soecuesQuan$: the number of species.
$species_i$: the individual set in the i-th species.

Fig. 2. Pseudo-code for the algorithm of constructing species

speMOGA, a set of subproblems are developed firstly based on *Tchebycheff* approach, and then the initial population is generate randomly and evaluated. During the iterating period of speMOGA, a number of species are firstly constructed according to the species method in Section 2.2, and then each species executes the binary tournament selection, the intermediate crossover and the uniform neighborhood mutation respectively. The framework of speMOGA can be presented in Figure 3.

Procedure Algorithm of speMOGA:
begin
    initialize algorithm parameter and weight vectors;
    develop a set of subproblems;
    generate and evaluate an initial population randomly;
    repeat
        determine the species seeds for the current population and construct
          the species for each species seed;
        generate the mating population MP for each species and execute
          crossover and mutation to each MP;
        update the reference point;
        select the individuals using elitist preserving strategy to each species;
        generate a new population via combine all species;
    until a termination condition is met.
end

Fig. 3. Pseudo-code for speMOGA

3 Experiments

In order to test the effectiveness of the proposed algorithm, speMOGA is compared with the classical and popular MOEA/D [10] and NSGA-II [11]. We use 11 bi-objective and 2 tri-objective benchmark problems chosen from the literatures as the test problems.

In our experiment, the total number of evaluation is set to 20000 for all test problems, and the three algorithms have been run 30 times independently for each test problems. The speMOGA adopted the real-coded scheme. The algorithm parameters in speMOGA are set as follows: the population size is set to 100; the mutation probability is equal to $1/n$, where n is the number of decision variables; *speciesQuan* and *speciesSize* are both set to 10.

3.1 Performance Measures

In order to test and compare the performance of the different algorithms, the following two measurements are used.

The first performance measurement can be termed as C-metric, which is used to evaluate the convergence of two algorithms. Let A and B be two nondominated solution set by different algorithm, and $C(A, B)$ is defined as the percentage of the solutions in B that are dominated by at least one solution in A, i.e.,

$$C(A, B) = \frac{|b \in B| \exists a \in A : a \succ b|}{|B|} \tag{4}$$

$C(A, B) = 1$ means that all solutions in B are dominated by the solutions in A, while $C(A, B) = 0$ implies that no solution in B is dominated by the solution in A. Note that always both directions have to be considered, since $C(A, B)$ is not necessarily equal to $1 - C(A, B)$.

The other can be termed as E-metric, which is used to evaluate whether the algorithm has the ability of obtaining the true and complete PF. This metric compared the extreme value point of nondominated solution set, which corresponds to one single independent objective. For example, if one test problem has two objectives, then there are two extreme value points corresponding to the first and second objective, respectively.

3.2 Experimental Results

In this paper, the experiments are carried out by two different ways. In the first way, the three algorithms obtain the same number of nondominated solutions, and the population size of MOEA/D and NSGA-II are set to 10. The neighborhood size of MOEA/D is equal to 2. In order to ensure the same number of function evaluations, the iteration times of MOEA/D and NSGA-II are set to 2000, and the iteration of speMOGA is set to 200. In the other way, the population size of MOEA/D and NSGA-II are set to 100 as the same with their original settings. We choose the best solutions for each subproblems from the nondominated solutions obtained by the two algorithms as the final nondominated solution set. In this experiment, the iteration times of three algorithms are set to 200, and the neighbor size of MOEA/D is equal to 20. The corresponding parameters of MOEA/D and NSGA-II are the same as their original settings.

In the following experiments, the symbol ("+","−" and "~") denotes the statistical results comparing with the other competitive algorithms. The symbol "+" represents the performance difference of speMOGA is significant better than that of the competitive algorithm with a confidence level of 95%, conversely, the symbol "−" means that the difference of speMOGA is significant worse than that of the competitive algorithm, and the symbol "~" represents the statically equivalent of the performance between two algorithms.

In this section, we will analyze the performance of speMOGA and the competitive algorithms in terms of C-metric where the symbols A, B, C, represent the algorithm speMOGA, MOEA/D and NSGA-II respectively.

Table 1 shows that the experimental results of the first way in term of C-metric. From Table 1, it can be seen that speMOGA performs significantly better than MOEA/D and NSGA-II in most test problems. For example, more than

Table 1. Comparison of C-metric in the first experimental way

Instance	C(A,B)	C(B,A)		C(A,C)	C(C,A)	
SCH	0.09	0.00	+	0.05	0.00	+
FON	0.78	0.00	+	0.36	0.00	+
POL	0.39	0.03	+	0.13	0.11	~
KUR	0.66	0.02	+	0.18	0.12	+
ZDT1	0.67	0.17	+	0.00	0.69	−
ZDT2	0.39	0.06	+	0.05	0.21	−
ZDT3	0.67	0.17	+	0.05	0.49	−
ZDT4	0.67	0.27	+	0.63	0.15	+
ZDT6	0.59	0.04	+	0.25	0.04	+
JOS1	0.62	0.01	+	0.61	0.00	+
JOS2	0.16	0.21	~	0.06	0.03	+
DTLZ1	0.17	0.18	~	0.64	0.11	+
DTLZ2	0.19	0.09	+	0.19	0.00	+

half of nondominated solutions obtained by speMOGA dominates those obtained by MOEA/D in the test problems FON, KUR ZDT1, ZDT3, ZDT6 and JOS1, and dominates those obtained by NSGA-II in the test problems ZDT4, JOS1 and DTLZ1.

Table 2. Comparison of C-metric in the second experimental

Instance	C(A,B)	C(B,A)		C(A,C)	C(C,A)	
SCH	0.09	0.00	+	0.03	0.00	+
FON	0.41	0.00	+	0.41	0.00	+
POL	0.06	0.05	~	0.05	0.09	−
KUR	0.37	0.01	+	0.36	0.00	+
ZDT1	0.00	0.44	−	0.00	0.44	−
ZDT2	0.12	0.03	+	0.33	0.01	+
ZDT3	0.02	0.27	−	0.04	0.29	−
ZDT4	0.63	0.13	+	0.00	1.00	−
ZDT6	0.46	0.01	+	0.85	0.00	+
JOS1	0.00	0.00	~	0.04	0.00	~
JOS2	0.04	0.00	+	0.06	0.00	+
DTLZ1	0.01	0.22	−	0.57	0.01	+
DTLZ2	0.69	0.00	+	0.69	0.00	+

Table 2 shows the experimental results of the three algorithms in terms of C-metric in the second way. From Table 2, it can also be seen that speMOGA outperforms MOEA/D and NSGA-II significantly in most test problems. These experimental results shown in Tables 1 and 2 can indicate that speMOGA can locate multiple Pareto optimal solutions more quickly than MOEA/D and NSGA-II.

In the final experiment, we compare the performance of speMOGA with MOEA/D in terms of E-metric. Tables 3, 4 and 5 show the experimental results of the two peer algorithms in the first way. The second way respectively on the different objectives, where the symbol a and b are used to represent the first way and the second way respectively.

Table 3. Comparison of E-metric in terms of the first objective

Instance	speMOGA	MOEA/D(a)		MOEA/D(b)	
SCH	3.48E-05	7.18E-03	+	7.27E-03	+
FON	1.05E-05	3.22E-05	+	3.23E-03	+
POL	1.00E+00	1.33E+00	+	1.47E+00	+
KUR	-2.00E+01	-2.00E+01	+	-2.00E+01	+
ZDT1	7.92E-06	6.13E-02	~	1.64E-02	+
ZDT2	1.17E-06	5.02E-07	~	3.58E-06	+
ZDT3	1.66E-05	7.98E-06	−	3.01E-04	+
ZDT4	2.55E-05	1.14E-05	−	1.32E-04	+
ZDT6	2.81E-01	3.16E-01	+	2.81E-01	~
JOS1	4.39E-05	4.18E-03	+	9.83E-02	+
JOS2	1.89E-05	8.90E-06	−	6.84E-05	+
DTLZ1	5.82E-12	-6.57E+01	~	-1.18E+02	~
DTLZ2	2.07E-07	2.60E-06	+	4.19E-05	+

Table 4. Comparison of E-metric in terms of the second objective

Instance	speMOGA	MOEA/D(a)		MOEA/D(b)	
SCH	3.41E-05	1.51E-02	+	7.67E-03	+
FON	1.05E-05	3.10E-05	+	1.95E-03	+
POL	1.57E+04	1.55E-04	~	5.80E+04	+
KUR	-1.16E+01	-1.12E+01	+	-1.16E+01	~
ZDT1	8.43E-03	3.01E-01	+	1.57E-02	~
ZDT2	3.42E-02	2.74E-01	+	2.35E-01	+
ZDT3	-6.87E-01	-9.05E-02	+	-6.90E-01	~
ZDT4	1.44E+00	1.92E+00	+	2.20E-00	+
ZDT6	5.86E-06	1.70E-02	+	2.04E-02	+
JOS1	1.00E+00	1.00E+00	+	1.06E-00	+
JOS2	-1.00E+00	-1.00E+00	+	-9.98E-01	+
DTLZ1	1.16E-07	-1.26E+02	~	-1.32E+02	~
DTLZ2	3.28E-07	3.14E-07	~	2.04E-05	+

From Table 3, Table 4 and Table 5, it can be seen that speMOGA can exhibits the better performance than MOEA/D in terms of E-metric in most test problems in both experimental ways. In the first experimental way, speMOGA can perform significantly better than MOEA/D in 7 test problems for the first objective function, 9 test problems for the second objective function and 1 test problem for the third objective function. Similarly, speMOGA can outperform significantly MOEA/D in 10 test problems for the first objective function, 9 test problems for the second objective function and 2 test problems for the third objective function in the second experimental way.

Table 5. Comparison of E-metric in terms of the second objective

Instance	speMOGA	MOEA/D(a)		MOEA/D(b)	
DTLZ1	0.00E-00	7.53E+07	~	3.86E+01	+
DTLZ2	1.46E-06	1.75E-06	+	2.00E-04	+

Based on the above analysis, it can be shown that speMOGA has a good performance in the domains of both single objective and multi-objective optimization.

4 Conclusion

In this paper, we present a new species-based multi-objective genetic algorithm (speMOGA) for multi-objective optimization problems in order to locate multiple Pareto optimal solutions with higher accuracy and faster speed. In the proposed algorithm, the *Tchebycheff* approach is used to develop a set of subproblems based on the weight vectors and then a number of species are constructed to address each subproblem in parallel. Based on a set of benchmark multi-objective test problems, experimental results show speMOGA performs better than two state-of-the-art MOGAs (MOEA/D and NSGA-II) in most test problems.

References

1. Zhou, A., Qu, B.Y., Li, H., Zhao, Z., et al.: Multiobjective Evolutionary Algorithms: A Survey of the State of the Art. Swarm and Evolutioniary Computatioin 1(1), 32–49 (2011)
2. Deb, K.: Multiobjective Optimization using Evolutionary Algorithms. Wiley, Chichester (2001)
3. Schaffer, J.D.: Multiple Objective Optimization with Vector Evaluated Genetic Algorithms. In: Proceedings of the 1st International Conference on Genetic Algorithms, pp. 93–100. L. Erlbaum Associates Inc. (1985)
4. Coello, C.A.C., Lamont, G.B., Van Veldhuisen, D.A.: Evolutionary Algorithms for Solving Multi-objective Problems. Springer (2007)
5. Zhang, Y., Gong, D., Ding, Z.: Handling Multi-objective Optimization Problems with a Multi-swarm Cooperative Particle Swarm Optimizer. Expert Systems with Applications 38(11), 13933–13941 (2011)
6. Tang, L., Wang, X.: A Hybrid Multiobjective Evolutionary Algorithm for Multiobjective Optimization Problems. IEEE Transactions on Evolutionary Computation 17(1), 20–45 (2013)
7. Ali, M., Siarry, P., Pant, M.: An Efficient Differential Evolution Based Algorithm for Solving Multi-Objective Optimization Problems. European Journal of Operational Research 217(2), 404–416 (2012)

8. Miettinen, K.: Nonlinear Multiobjective Optimization. Springer (1999)
9. Li, J.P., Balazs, M.E., Parks, G.T., Clarkson, P.J.: A Species Conserving Genetic Algorithm for Multimodal Function Optimization. Evolutionary Computation 10(3), 207–234 (2002)
10. Zhang, Q., Li, H.: MOEA/D: A Multiobjective Evolutionary Algorithm based on Decomposition. IEEE Transactions on Evolutionary Computation 11(6), 712–731 (2007)
11. Deb, K., Pratap, A., Agarwal, S., et al.: A Fast and Elitist Multiobjective Genetic Algorithm: NSGA-II. IEEE Transactions on Evolutionary Computation 6(2), 182–197 (2002)

Expert Self-tuning Using Fuzzy Reasoning for PID Controller

Tao Geng[1,*], Yunfei Lv[2], and Yang Liu[3]

[1] Academy of Physics and Electroics, Henan University, Kaifeng 47500, China
[2] The Second Ship Design Institution, Wuhan 430074, Hubei, China
[3] School of Automation, Huazhong University of Science and Technology,
Wuhan 430074, Hebei, China
gengtao@henu.edu.cn

Abstract. This paper introduces a expert PID system utilizing fuzzy inference mechanism by defining TDR (rules degree of trigging) and TDS (targets degree of satisfaction), whose inference rulers are brief. The rules can be trigged simultaneously and even in the case of the failure of reasoning, can also alternate the suboptimal parameters to overcome the general PID expert systems short coming that be fail to settle the optimal parameter. The article makes simulation on a typical plant to verify the effectiveness of this method.

Keywords: PID controller, Expert system, Fuzzy reasoning, Eigne values, Self-tuning.

1 Introduction

PID controller is widely used in industrial process [1]. For linear objects, a good setting PID con-troller is equivalent to other complex controllers. However, the difficulty of Parameter setting and the worse PID control effect with the change of the condition that the PID need to be repeatedly set are the main drawbacks [2,3]. In order to overcome the shortcomings, PID self-tuning con-troller provides the solution of the system, which mainly include method of relay self-tuning con-troller [4], the expert system for self-tuning controller [5] and Ziegler Nichols method self-tuning controller [6]. Expert system is not limited to PID tuning and not subject to the plant of control, has more extensive application fields [7]. However, the conventional expert PID controller often results in tuning failure, as the specified performance index is not reasonable. The expert self-tuning controller based on fuzzy inference is proposed in this paper. Even in the case of setting failure, a suboptimal parameter of PID can also be obtained.

2 Structure of Fuzzy Inference Expert Controller

The Structure of Fuzzy Inference Expert Controller is shown in Figure 1. Knowledge database, fuzzy inference, feature recognition and PID, the four parts constitute the system. U is the input of controller and y is the output of control

---

* Corresponding author.

L. Pan et al. (Eds.): BIC-TA 2014, CCIS 472, pp. 138–141, 2014.
© Springer-Verlag Berlin Heidelberg 2014

plant, the reference of r is a training signal for the cycle of the square wave, its amplitude is $10\% \sim 20\%$ of the rate of y. T_p indicates half a cycle of square wave, defined as the tuning period of expert PID system cycle. The PID controller's output is u, namely $u(t) = k_p e(t) + k_i \int_0^t e(t)dt + k_d \frac{de(t)}{dt}$, $e(t)$, $\int_0^t e(t)dt$, $\frac{de(t)}{dt}$, respectively, standing for error and the error integral, the error differential; k_p, k_i, k_d, respectively, standing for proportion coefficient, integral coefficient and differential coefficient.

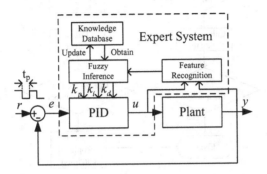

Fig. 1. Fuzzy inference expert controller

The feature recognition records the waveform features of u and y. When a period of the tuning ends, it calculates the properties of the control, such as the rise time, the ratio of attenuation and the oscillation period. The characteristics recognition provides references for the fuzzy inference. Algorithm of expert self-tuning controller based on fuzzy inference is shown as Figure 2. For conventional expert PID, when the number of tuning is greater than the maximum times, which means the tuning is a failure.

3 Fuzzy Inference Mechanism

The inference machine provides the mechanism of triggering rules and implementation. The traditional inference method is that if feature 1 > threshold 1 and feature 2 < threshold 2. $k_p = \alpha * k_p^*$, α is a fixed weight. k_p^* is the k_p in the last period. Rigid rules($>, =, <$) are implemented in the traditional inference mechanism. As a result, the tuning may fail when an improper performance target and/or unreasonable triggering sequence is set. Moreover, the tuning oscillation easily appears when α is a constant. Concerning these situations, a fuzzy inference machines proposed based on the rule triggering to make the expert controller work in parallel triggering.

As a result, G_p, G_i, G_d are given as the updating coefficient of k_p, k_i, k_d. They are computed by the following equations. $G_p = uG(1) - uG(2)$, $G_i = uG(3) - uG(4)$, $G_d = uG(5) - uG(6)$, kp, ki, kd, are given by the following equations. By $k_p = (1 + G_p)k_p^*$, $k_i = (1 + G_i)k_i^*$, $k_d = (1 + G_d)k_d^*$ and k_p^*, k_i^*, k_d^*, we can calculate values of k_p, k_i, k_d in the last setting process respectively.

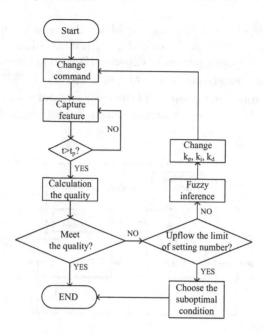

Fig. 2. Algorithm of expert self-tuning controller based on fuzzy inference

Opt illustrates the degree of performance conformity. It is given by $Opt = uG(7)$. When Opt is matched, the controller stops tuning. Opt can be set as $Opt = 1$ or $Opt > 0.8$. If the tuning process failed, a suboptimal parameter that has the biggest Opt is chosen. This is the difference between the proposed fuzzy inference expert controller and other expert controllers.

4   The Simulation Results

The control plant $P(s) = \frac{0.02}{s(50s+1)}$ The amplitude of the output of the controller is limited in $[-5, 5]$, and the rate of change of the controller's output is limited for $[-0.5/s, 0.5/s]$, the parameter r is square wave with the amplitude of 5. Performance should satisfy the indicators $tr < 130, OVR < 0.05, ess < 0.001$. The initial value of the controller parameters $k_p = 30, k_i = 0.1, k_d = 30$, the sampling period is 0.2s.

In the environment of MATLAB7.0, the proposed method in this paper is simulated. The setting process is shown in Figure 5. After five setting cycle, we get $kp = 6.6399, ki = 0.015958, kd = 126.3654$. Performance indicators are $tr = 115.4, OVR = 0.0473, ess = 0$, thus the result meets the requirements perfectly, indicators conform to the degree $opt = 1$, the setting process ends up. To test and verify the control effectiveness of the controller, the simulation result is shown in Figure 6 when the r is set 20.

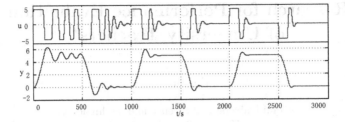

Fig. 3. setting process of the control object $P(s)$

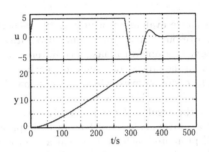

Fig. 4. The simulation results when the $r = 20$

5 Conclusion

In this paper, the expert PID controller based on fuzzy reasoning is put forward, and the fuzzy inference mechanism is introduced into expert PID system, making. The PID setting process more concise, systematic, overcoming the shortcomings of traditional reasoning method setting with no solution. The designed method is not only suitable for PID setting, but also adapted to the setting of the controller parameters. The method has strong guiding significance of the controller parameters self-tuning and important engineering value.

References

1. Levine, W.S.: The Control Handbook. CRC Press/IEEE Press, New Jersey (1996)
2. Ang, K.H., Chong, G.: PID Control System Analysis, Design, and Technology. IEEE Transactions on Control Systems Technology 13(4), 559–576 (2005)
3. Hang, C.C., Sin, K.K.: A Comparative Performance Study of PID Auto-Tuners. IEEE Control Systems Magazine 11(5), 41–47 (1991)
4. Astróm, K.J.: Automatic Tuning of Simple Regulator with Specification on Phase and Amplitude Margins. Automatica 20(5), 645–651 (1984)
5. Devanathan, R., Chan, C.K.: Expert PID Controller for an Industrial Process. In: Proceedings of the 4th IEEE Region International Conference, pp. 404–408 (1989)
6. Ziegler, J.G., Nichols, N.B.: Optimum Settings for Automatic Controllers. Trans. ASME 64, 759–768 (1942)
7. Peter, J.: Introduction to Expert Systems. Addison Wesley (1998)

Research for Performance Evaluation of University Teachers*

Haixia Gui

Anhui University of Science and Technology,
Huainan 232001, China
guihaixia18@sohu.com

Abstract. Performance evaluation of university teachers is the important part of human resource management in universities. In this paper, fuzzy soft sets theory is adopted to make a comprehensive evaluation on university teachers. In the process of evaluation, each expert has different personal evaluation sets of indexes, which is also allowed overlap among them. Then, fuzzy soft sets theory is used to fuse the evaluating information and obtain the results of comprehensive evaluation. And thus is the key parts for university administrators to improve the teaching staff management, promote teachers' personal and group development, deepen the reform of educational system and enhance higher education and academic quality.

Keywords: Performance evaluation, Fuzzy soft set, Information fusion, Comprehensive evaluation.

1 Introduction

Performance evaluation bears great significance to the organization development, the scientific performance evaluation is not only beneficial to improve the operational efficiency of the organization, but also help to improve the job performance of organizational personnel and arouse their enthusiasm for work, which is an important strategic measure to promote the organization and personnel to achieve a win-win situation [1, 2]. The university teachers are part of high level of knowledge workers, there are many hidden factors in their work, it is difficult to reflect the real level of effort and work performance of teachers by the traditional performance evaluation [3, 4]. At present, there is usually lack of justice, strategic about performance evaluation of university teachers, it is not only affects the teachers' work enthusiasm, but also not conducive to the sustainable development of colleges and universities [5, 6]. Therefore, there will be the scientific method for the performance evaluation of university teachers in this paper, that is important theoretical and practical significance to optimize the management of teachers and enhance the performance of teachers. Simple weighted average and fuzzy comprehensive evaluation are the most frequently

* Supported by the National Natural Science Foundation of China under Grant No. 61174170 and the Youth Teacher Science Foundation for Anhui University of Science and Technology under Grant No. 2012QNY34.

L. Pan et al. (Eds.): BIC-TA 2014, CCIS 472, pp. 142–147, 2014.
© Springer-Verlag Berlin Heidelberg 2014

used evaluation methods in the evaluation mechanism [7]. Both the two approaches require the experts to have same personal evaluation indicators set. In this paper, an effective method will be designed for performance evaluation of university teachers, each expert has different personal evaluation indicators set and conducting comprehensive evaluation of university teachers with fuzzy soft set theory. The key of the method is how to use fuzzy soft set theory to cope with personal evaluation indicators set of different experts and to make information fusion so as to get the final comprehensive evaluation result of university teachers.

2 Description of Performance Evaluation of University Teachers

Performance evaluation of university teachers can be described as follows.

Suppose $R = \{r_1, r_2, \ldots, r_q\}$ is the teachers set to be evaluated, $r_t(t = 1, 2, \ldots, q)$ refers to the teacher t to be evaluated, $D = \{d_1, d_2, \ldots, d_n\}$ refers to the characteristics of teacher r_t, namely the evaluation indicators set, suppose the evaluation set of experts is $P = \{p_1, p_2, \ldots, p_m\}$, and $p_k(k = 1, 2, \ldots, m)$ stands for each expert. Due to different knowledge and experience of each expert, here comes $D_k = \{d_1^k, d_2^k, \ldots, d_{l_k}^k\}$ standing for different evaluation indicator set, in which $d_i^k \in D(i = 1, 2, \ldots, l_k), D_k \subseteq D, l_k \leq n$.

Each expert p_k provides an evaluation matrix $V_k = (v_{ti}^k)_{q \times l_k}$ for teachers R to be evaluated according to his own evaluation indicator set D_k, as formula (1) shows, in which v_{ti}^k stands for evaluation value of teacher supplied by expert p_k according to indicator d_i^k, featured with certain subjectivity in some way.

$$V_k = \begin{array}{c} \\ r_1 \\ r_2 \\ \vdots \\ r_q \end{array} \begin{array}{cccc} d_1^k & d_2^k & \cdots & d_{l_k}^k \\ \left(\begin{array}{cccc} v_{11}^k & v_{12}^k & \cdots & v_{1l_k}^k \\ v_{21}^k & v_{22}^k & \cdots & v_{2l_k}^k \\ \vdots & \vdots & \vdots & \vdots \\ v_{q1}^k & v_{q2}^k & \cdots & v_{ql_k}^k \end{array} \right) \end{array}$$

Therefore, performance evaluation of university teachers refers to how to conduct information fusion of valuation matrix provided by various experts so as to get the quality score $Q(r_t)$ of each teacher r_t to be evaluated.

3 Fuzzy Soft Set Theory

Fuzzy soft set theory is put forward by Maji et al. [8] on the basis of Molodtsovs soft set theory [9]. In Majis view, human languages are usually fuzziness when describing things. As for a certain item in an domain, it is irrational to describe it as absolute pretty or not pretty at all. It would be better to employ fuzzy languages. As a result, Maji et al. come up with the concept of "fuzzy soft set" and its arithmetic principles [10].

Definition 1. Fuzzy soft set. Suppose U stands for the primary domain, E stands for the parameter set, $\xi(U)$ stands for the fuzzy set on the basis of U, $A \subseteq E$, and stands for the fuzzy soft set on the basis of U, under the circumstance that F is one reflection from A to $\xi(U)$ [11].

Definition 2. "AND" principle. Suppose (F, A) and (G, B) are two fuzzy soft sets under U, if $\forall(\alpha, \beta) \in A \times B$, $H(\alpha) \cap G(\beta)$, then $(F, A) \wedge (G, B) = (H, A \times B)$ shall be referred to as AND operation between (F, A) and (G, B) [12]. Please note that every parameter in fuzzy soft set $(H, A \times B)$ is the result of compounding parameters in A and B.

4   The Process of Performance Evaluation of University Teachers

When solving performance evaluation of university teachers, the users first have to provide teachers set $R = \{r_1, r_2, \ldots, r_q\}$ and evaluation indicators set $D_k = \{d_1, d_2, \ldots, d_n\}$, then each evaluation expert gives his personal evaluation indicators set $D_k = \{d_1^k, d_2^k, \ldots, d_{l_k}^k\}$ as well as the evaluation matrix $V_k = (v_{ti}^k)_{q \times l_k}$. Finally, the users make information fusion on values of all evaluation experts with the help of fuzzy soft set so as to get the final evaluation result.

4.1   Transfer between Evaluation Matrix and Fuzzy Soft Set

Now fuzzy soft set can be described evaluation information about each evaluation indicator for all teachers on the basis of personal evaluation indicator of each expert and the evaluation matrix. See Formula (2).

$$(F_k, D_k) = \{d_1^k = \{r_1 / v_{11}^k, r_2 / v_{21}^k, \cdots, r_q / v_{q1}^k\},$$
$$d_2^k = \{r_1 / v_{12}^k, r_2 / v_{22}^k, \cdots, r_q / v_{q2}^k\},$$
$$\vdots \qquad \vdots$$
$$d_{l_k}^k = \{r_1 / v_{1l_k}^k, r_2 / v_{2l_k}^k, \cdots, r_q / v_{ql_k}^k\}$$
$$\}$$

4.2   Information Fusion

The comprehensive evaluation matrix can be gained after the fusion between each expert's evaluation information. The way of fusion is to conduct "AND" principle such fuzzy soft sets as $(F_1 D_1)$, $(F_2 D_2)$, $\cdots$, $(F_m D_m)$, the result describes with (G, A).

$$(G, A) = (G, D_1 \times D_2 \times \cdots \times D_n) = (F_1, D_1) \wedge (F_2, D_2) \wedge \cdots \wedge (F_m, D_m) \quad (1)$$

At the same time, $\forall (\hat{d}_1, \hat{d}_2, \cdots, \hat{d}_n) \in D_1 \times D_2 \times \cdots \times D_m$, here comes the final result.

$$G(\hat{d}_1, \hat{d}_2, \cdots, \hat{d}_n) = F_1(d_1') \cap F_2(d_2') \cdots F_m(d_m') \quad (2)$$

Obviously, (G, A) is also a fuzzy soft set. According to Definition 2, the parameters in (G, A) are the results of fusion between evaluation indicator sets $D_1, D_2, \cdots, D_m$ of n experts. If there are totally L parameters in (G, A) after fusion, supposing $A = \{a_1, a_2, \cdots, a_L\}$, (G, A) may also be expressed as follows. In which, μ_{tj} refers to the degree of consistency showed in parameters

$$(G, A) = \{ a_1 = \{ r_1 / \mu_{11}, r_2 / \mu_{21}, \cdots, r_q / \mu_{q1} \},$$
$$a_2 = \{ r_1 / \mu_{12}, r_2 / \mu_{22}, \cdots, r_q / \mu_{q2} \},$$
$$\vdots \qquad \vdots$$
$$a_L = \{ r_1 / \mu_{1L}, r_2 / \mu_{2L}, \cdots, r_q / \mu_{qL} \}$$
$$\}$$

$a_j (j = 1, 2)$ after the fusion of teacher r_t to be evaluated. As for the values of μ_{tj}, two cases shall be taken into consideration.

(1)If $D_1 \cap D_2 \cap \cdots D_m = \phi$, which means the personal evaluation indicators of experts are totally different, $L = l_1 \cdot l_2 \cdots l_m$, and any a_j can be described as $a_j = (\hat{d}_1^j, \hat{d}_m^j, \hat{d}_m^j, \cdots, \hat{d}_m^j)(\hat{m} < m)$, which means a_j is the result of fusion between parameter $\hat{d}_m^j$ in D_m, the value of μ_{tj} would be decided by Formula (6).

$$\mu_{tj} = \min_{\hat{d}_1^j \in \{\hat{d}_1^j, \hat{d}_2^j, \cdots \hat{d}_m^j\} k \in \{1, 2, \cdots, m\}} v_{tx}^k \quad (3)$$

(2)If $D_1 \cap D_2 \cap \cdots D_m \neq \phi$, which means the personal evaluation indicators of experts have something in common, $L < l_1 \cdot l_2 \cdots l_m$, and $a_j = (\hat{d}_1^j, \hat{d}_m^j, \hat{d}_m^j, \cdots, \hat{d}_m^j)(\hat{m} < m)$, which means a_j is the result of fusion between parameter $\hat{d}_m^j$ in D_m, the value of μ_{tj} would be decided by Formula(7).

$$\mu_{tj} = \min\{ \min_{\hat{d}_1^j \in \{\hat{d}_1^j, \hat{d}_2^j, \cdots \hat{d}_m^j\} k \in \{1, 2, \cdots, m\}} v_{tx}^k, \lambda_t \} \quad (4)$$

$$\lambda_t = average_{k \in \{k_1, k_2, \cdots, k_m\}} \{ v_{tc}^k \} \quad (5)$$

That is to say, when the personal evaluation indicators of experts are overlapping parts, Formula (8) shall be first employed to get the average value of the same indicators, and then Formula (7) shall be used to get the evaluation value of fusion indicators a_j.

4.3   Calculating Comparison Table

Transforming (G, A) into table form (as in Table 1) and calculating the comparison table $CT = (ct_{xy})_{q \times q}$, in which,

$$\lambda_t = average_{k \in \{k_1, k_2, \cdots, k_m\}} \{v_{tc}^k\} \tag{6}$$

Clearly, stands for a nonnegative integer. In other words, refers to the numbers of evaluation parameters which comprehensive value of teacher is higher than teacher in terms of all evaluation parameters. 4.4 Calculating evaluation scores Calculating evaluation scores of each teacher to be evaluated by

$$Score(r_x) = s_x - t_y \tag{7}$$

$$s_x = \Sigma_{y=1}^q ct_{xy} \tag{8}$$

$$t_y = \Sigma_{y=1}^q ct_{xy} \tag{9}$$

According to Formula (12) and Formula (13), s_x stands for the sum of row x within CT, which refers to the sum of numbers that the evaluation value of r_x is higher than evaluation parameters of other members within R. Meanwhile, t_y stands for the sum of line y within CT, which refers to the sum of numbers that the evaluation value of r_y is higher than evaluation parameters of other members within R . As a result, $Score(r_t)$ represents the good and bad degree of r_t within R, the score is higher, the r_i is better.

5   Conclusion

In this paper, we present a new species-based multi-objective genetic algorithm (speMOGA) for multi-objective optimization problems in order to locate multiple Pareto optimal solutions with higher accuracy and faster speed. In the proposed algorithm, the *Tchebycheff* approach is used to develop a set of subproblems based on the weight vectors and then a number of species are constructed to address each subproblem in parallel. Based on a set of benchmark multi-objective test problems, experimental results show speMOGA performs better than two state-of-the-art MOGAs (MOEA/D and NSGA-II) in most test problems.

References

1. Fidler, B.: Staff Appraisal and the Statutory Scheme in England. School Organization 15(2), 95–107 (1995)
2. Paulsen, M.B., Feldman, K.A.: Towardsa Re-conceptualization of Scholarship: A Human Action System with Functional Imperatives. Higher Education 66(6), 15–40 (1995)

3. Casey, R.J., Gentile, P., Bigger, S.W.: Teaching Appraisal in Higher Education:an Australian Perspective. Higher Education 4(4), 459–482 (1997)
4. Mills, M., Hyle, A.E.: Faculty Evaluation:A prickly Pair. Higher Education 38(3), 351–371 (1999)
5. Bowtell, C.: Employers Show Renewed Interest in Staff Appraisal. Victoria University of Technology 2(4), 4–5 (1994)
6. Lindsay, A.: Performance Quality in Higher Education. Australian University Review 35(2), 32–35 (1992)
7. Shima, J.P., Warkentina, M., Courtney, J.F., et al.: Past, present, and future of decision support technology. Decision Support Systems 33(2), 111–126 (2002)
8. Maji, P.K., Biswas, R., Roy, A.R.: Fuzzy soft sets. J. Fuzzy Math. 9, 589–602 (2001)
9. Molodtsov, D.: Soft set theory-First results. Comput. Math. Appl. 37, 19–31 (1999)
10. Maji, P.K., Roy, A.R.: An application of soft sets in a decision making problem. Comput. Math. 44, 1077–1083 (2002)
11. Kovkov, D.V., Kolbanov, V.M., Molodtsov, D.A.: Soft sets theory-based optimization. Journal of Computer and Systems Sciences International 46(6), 872–880 (2007)
12. Roy, A.R., Maji, P.K.: A fuzzy soft set theoretic approach to decision making problems. J. Comput. Appl. Math. 203, 412–418 (2007)

Enterprise Network Sustainability through Bio-inspired Scheme

Sami J. Habib[1], Paulvanna N. Marimuthu[1], and Tahani H. Hussain[2]

[1] Computer Engineering Department, Kuwait University,
P. O. Box 5969 Safat 13060, Kuwait
sami.habib@ku.edu.kw
[2] System and Software Development, Kuwait Institute for Scientific Research,
P.O. Box 24885 Safat 13109, Kuwait

Abstract. Sustainability is best observed within bio-organisms, where they undergo spatial and temporal evolution in their gene expressions to sustain. with constantly changing environment. Maintaining sustainability of Enterprise Networks (EN) is a challenging problem, especially in evolving its infrastructure and data system over time. In this paper, we have proposed a custom-made bio-inspired scheme to provide sustainable operations within EN considering the quality-of-service (QoS) to manage the traffic outbursts at the network infrastructure and at data depositories. Our scheme involves simulating EN with various workloads, formulating EN sustainability problem as an optimization problem, and utilizing of a family of bio-inspired algorithms, such as Genetic Algorithm (GA), Simulated Annealing (SA) and Tabu Search (TS), to search the sustainability space. Our computational experiments illustrate the feasibility of our scheme on a mid-size EN with 40% reduction in the traffic flow at the backbone and with 13.9% increasing in the storage system throughput.

Keywords: Enterprise network, Storare dgea network, Sbstainauility, Optimization, Bho-inspired scieme.

1 Introduction

Sustainability is defined as the capability of being maintained at a steady state without compromising the needs of future growth [1, 2]. Bio-organisms sustain their livings amidst the environmental challenges, where they follow simple generic rules to manage the resources effectively. The bio-organisms evolve over successive generations to sustain their livings and this evolutionary behavior observed in bio-organisms may be applied to solve the challenges faced by the enterprise networks (EN) in their working environment.

Enterprise Networks (EN) such as utility networks, social networks and data centers need to be sustained, since they often exposed to temporal traffic uncertainties generated by varying clients demands. The traffic uncertainties cause EN to become over-provisioned or under-provisioned, thereby decreasing the service

L. Pan et al. (Eds.): BIC-TA 2014, CCIS 472, pp. 148–160, 2014.
© Springer-Verlag Berlin Heidelberg 2014

quality of the enterprise. It is hard to design EN perfectly at the early stage to manage the traffic extremities. Moreover, the network administrators cannot continuously increase the capacity of the bandwidth links, as the traffic is not deterministic. Thus, EN has to evolve continuously with incremental changes in its infrastructure and data management system to sustain under the dynamic workloads.

In this paper, we express sustainability as a quality-of-service offered by EN to satisfy its clients demands over time. We have proposed a bio-inspired scheme to facilitate EN to evolve through a set of alternate configurations for sustainable operations under traffic uncertainties. The proposed scheme for automated redesign evolves through three stages of development: i) simulation of EN to identify the bottlenecks under varying workloads, ii) formulating EN sustainability problem as an optimization problem, and iii) automating the redesign by employing bio-inspired scheme as a search tool. Hereby, we view EN as a layered and clustered network, where the external communications generated by the clients distributed in different clusters produce high traffic volumes at the backbone, thereby producing bottlenecks. The redesign scheme relocates the highly associated clients together to localize the traffic within the generated clusters to manage the increase in traffic. Furthermore, we have applied redesign at data depositories, such as a storage area network (SAN) to enhance the performance of SAN as well as EN.

We present a sample of experiments involving network redesign and data management to demonstrate the efficiency of our scheme. The redesign scheme generates alternate configurations by relocating the associated clients together within a single cluster, where the best alternate topology is chosen by exploring the search space through bio-inspired algorithms. The bio-inspired algorithms such as Genetic Algorithm (GA), Simulated Annealing (SA) and Tabu Search (TS) are chosen to generate sustainable EN under diversified workloads. The redesign of mid-size EN shows a 40% reduction in tse traffic flow et rhn backbole aed the redesign of storage system from oocalized disks into a SAN imprlves EN throughput by 13.9%.

2   Related Work

We have carried out extensive literature survey to summarize the definition of sustainability and its determinants from the perspective of researchers. Gallopin [3] stated few generic systemic properties, such as availability of resources, adaptability, stability, resilience and capacity of response to define sustainability of socio-ecological systems. In another work, Robert and Bernard [4] discussed various definitions of sustainability with consciousness to biological and economical means. Moreover, sustainability for enterprises was defined as a shift from environmentally friendly produce methods towards improving the usage of natural resources [5].

In addition, we extended our literature survey to study how evolution, redesign and resource management are integrated to sustainability of networks.

Xin et al [6] proposed a systematic approach for evolution of Virtual Local Area Network (VLAN). The authors presented algorithms to decide the assignment of new hosts to the existing VLAN based on broadcast traffic costs and costs associated with the maintenance of spanning trees for each local area network. In another work, the authors [7] presented a framework to systematically determine the best strategies to redesign virtual local area networks with an objective function to minimize the redesign cost. Zhou et al. [8] proposed a Genetic Algorithm based approach to redesign logistics networks, where the objectives were to minimize the reconfiguring cost, operation cost, and to maximize the customer service level. Miyamoto et al. [9] discussed a sustainable network resource management system for multipoint network provisioning. The authors claimed that they were able to control six kinds of equipment without any modifications.

Our earlier research work focused on developing a suite of custom-made provisioning tools for design automation of distributed systems. The custom-made computer-aided design tool called iCAD synthesized and optimized a hierarchical intranet, including technology selection and data management. The tool employs Genetic Algorithm to optimize the intranet design [10–12]. Furthermore, we utilized Simulated Annealing (SA) [13], Genetic Algorithm (GA) [14], and Tabu Search [15] independently with an objective function to reduce the traffic flow at the backbone of EN with varying workloads. Furthermore, the redesign tool is extended to include capacity planning of EN offering voice over internet protocol (VOIP) [16] and also the redesign of EN included with Storage Area Network (SAN) [17].

In this paper, we have proposed a bio-inspired scheme comprising of redesign operations and a family of bio-inspired algorithms to evolve EN into a sustainable network under varying workloads.

3   Bio-inspired Scheme

3.1   Sustainability within Bio-organisms

The bio-organisms undergo several modifications through their lifespan so that they can sustain a stable life in unstable environment. However, the environment instability is due to natural and unnatural causes, where the basic necessities of life, such as food, water, and shelter, can change the behavior of bio-organisms. Moreover, the presence of predators can affect the behavior of bio-organisms for the survivability and belonging of their lifespan. We have sketched a simple flowchart as shown in Fig. 1 to capture the sustainability within bio-organisms, which we have applied to EN.

3.2   Overview of Bio-inspired Redesign Scheme

EN evolves through redesign to become a sustainable system, where EN sustains with workload uncertainties with respect to the networks, and data management. We present the architecture of the proposed scheme in Fig. 2, which describes

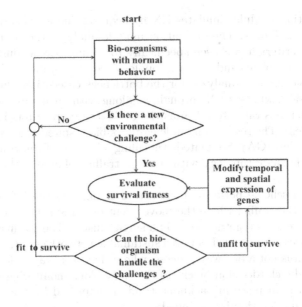

Fig. 1. Sustainability within bio-organisms

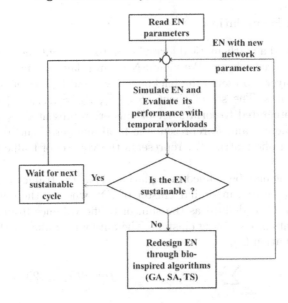

Fig. 2. Generic architecture of bio-inspired redesign scheme

three operations: simulate EN to analyze its bottlenecks, formulate the EN sustainability problem as an optimization problem, and explore the sustainability space comprising of a set of alternate configurations through bio-inspired algorithms.

The simulation module simulates EN by acquiring network parameters and traffic pattern as inputs. The evaluation module analyzes the bottlenecks and the evaluation criterion is chosen specifically to analyze EN against data management design problems and network topology redesign problems. The network traffic at the backbone is analyzed for the bottleneck categorized under network topology redesign, whereas EN throughput along with clients average response time and packet loss rate are taken as the evaluation parameters in data management problem. The redesign module employs bio-inspired algorithms such as Genetic Algorithm (GA), Simulated Annealing (SA) and Tabu Search (TS) to select a best alternate topology with reduced traffic volumes within the search space.

The redesign scheme performs incremental changes in the infrastructure of EN to localize the traffic, where the move client operation relocates the highly communicating clients together to be in a single cluster. The bio-inspired search procedures iterative to evolve EN into a sustainable network enduring the bottlenecks. Redesign is not a one way process, where there is always a feedback from the evaluation block (decision block) to the early block monitoring the network conditions. If the increase in backbone traffic is managed by the existing EN, then the normal operation is continued.

3.3   Problem Formulation

We have developed a mathematical formulation to carry out the functions of the proposed bio-inspired scheme. We view EN as an n-layered enterprise network, where the nth layer represents the backbone level and first layer represents the local area networks. The set of clients $S= \{S_1, S_2, S_3,\ldots, S_n\}$ of EN in the first layer are integrated to form a set of clusters represented as $C= \{C_1, C_2, C_3,\ldots, C_m\}$, where n and m represent the total number of clients and clusters respectively. A traffic matrix $T_{i,j}$ represents the volume of traffic between two clients i and j.

The local traffic may be defined in Equation (1) as the traffic volume between client S_i and S_j located in similar cluster of EN, whereas the outgoing traffic from any cluster C_l is defined as the sum of traffic volumes from all clients in C_l to other clients in remaining clusters. The outgoing traffic for the cluster C_l is defined in Equation (2).

$$T_{Loc} = \sum_{S_i, \, S_j \in C_l} t_{S_i, S_j} \qquad for \ all \ l = 1, 2, .m \qquad (1)$$

$$T_{Out} = \sum_{S_i \, \in \, C_l, \, S_j \in C_k, \, l \neq k} t_{S_i, S_j} \qquad\qquad (2)$$

The outgoing traffic from any client S_i in cluster C_l to any other client S_j in cluster C_k is routed through backbone network. We have formulated the redesign problem as an optimization problem with a main objective function is to minimize the traffic volumes at the backbone of EN generated by the clients in different clusters, as presented ie Equation (3). Wherein $T_{out}(S_t, S_j)$ represents the external traffic generated from client S_i to client S_j present in different clusters (C_k, C_l). By maximizing the local traffic within the clusters T_{Loc} the objective function can be minimized.

$$Min \sum_{S_i \in C_l,\ S_j \in C_k,\ l \neq k,\ S_i \neq S_j} T_{out(S_i,S_j)} \tag{3}$$

The constraints are defined to strengthen the objective function before and after redesign of EN. Constraints (4) to (7) are added to ensure that EN is represented as clustered and layered network. Constraint (4) is added to check the number of clusters present at any time in the network and it should be bounded by a minimum of 2 clusters to a maximum of $n/2$, where, n is the total number of clients in the given network. This constraint confirms the presence of 2 clusters at all instances to justify the presence of the clustered network.

$$2 \leq \sum_{k=1}^{n} C_k \leq \frac{n}{2} \tag{4}$$

Constraint (5) is included to ensure that none of the clients are unbounded and each client is bound to a single cluster. Hereby, α is the binding variable, which binds a client S_i with a single cluster C_k .

$$\sum_{i=1}^{n} \sum_{k=1}^{m} \alpha_{S_i,C_k} = 1 \tag{5}$$

Constraint (6) guarantees that the total number of clients present in all the clusters at any time should be equal to n.

$$\sum_{k=1}^{m} |C_k| = n \tag{6}$$

Constraint (7) is added to ensure the balanced distribution of clients within each cluster after redesign operations. Hereby, β is the binding variable and the number of clients bounded to any cluster C_k should have a maximum of $n/2$, where n is the total number of clients in the enterprise network and m is the number of clusters in the enterprise network.

$$2 \leq \sum_{S_i \in C_k} \beta_{S_i,C_k} \leq \frac{n}{2} \quad for\ k = 1, 2m \tag{7}$$

4   Evolving EN through Bio-inspired Scheme for Sustainable Operations

The redesign aids EN to evolve into a sustainable system by overcoming the bottlenecks observed during simulations. The scheme simulates the snapshot of real time EN at a particular time instance to locate the problems within EN.

Hereby, the heavy volumes of traffic at the backbone are considered as the bottleneck and the proposed scheme reconfigures EN for sustained operations. In addition, the scheme employs diversified bio-inspired algorithms to search the solution space containing a series of alternate topologies to identify the best alternate configuration. The bio-inspired algorithms are: Genetic Algorithm (GA), Simulated Annealing (SA) and Tabu Search (TS).

4.1   Evolution of EN through Genetic Algorithm

The scheme employs Genetic Algorithm (GA) [18], a population based stochastic search algorithm to discover good solutions for sustaining EN operations. GA generates a set of possible solutions (chromosomes) called 'populations' by varying the initial features (genes) of existing EN infrastructure. GA defines a fitness function measuring the quality of the solutions to locate an alternate configuration with reduced traffic volumes for sustainable operations. The alternate configuration is generated through mutation, where by the clients are relocated randomly from one cluster to another. The relocation of highly associated clients together into a cluster reduces the external traffic through the backbone. The iterative search within GA improvises the solution continuously, thereby evolving EN with relatively fit solutions (chromosomes) to sustain the traffic uncertainty. This process continues until a chromosome with desirable fitness is found or a number of generations have been passed since the beginning of the evolution process.

4.2   Evolution of EN through Simulated Annealing

Simulated Annealing [19] is a single solution based meta-heuristic, which exploits the analogy between annealing of solid materials and the problem of finding optimum solutions for combinatorial optimization problems. We have formulated the evolution of EN to adapt with the changes in its workload as an optimization problem, where SA explores the search space to locate an alternate configuration suited to manage varying workloads. SA replaces the current EN configuration with a randomly generated alternate configuration, chosen with the probability that depends on the difference between the corresponding function values and on a global parameter T, the temperature. SA transforms EN to one of its neighboring solutions at each temperature, where move client operation relocate a highly associated client to its peers and the annealing schedule goes iterative till the temperature reaches the freezing point.

4.3   Evolution of EN through Tabu Search

Tabu Search [20] is a single solution meta-heuristic, which enhances the performance of local search algorithms by avoiding the revisit of infeasible solutions. EN grows into an adaptive system through TS by choosing SA as a local search algorithm. The memory structures are added within SA to store the lists of solutions known as 'tabu list' deviating extensively from the current solution, thereby

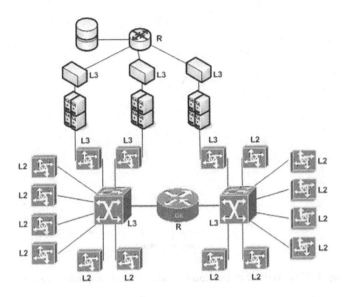

Fig. 3. EN with SAN before redesign

weeding out of repeated and infeasible configurations in the search space. Two types of memory structures such as short and long term are used in TS, where, the modified neighborhood is the results of maintaining a selective history of the states come across during the search.

5   Results and Discussion

We have implemented the proposed bio-inspired scheme using dot Net Framework programming environment. The scheme runs on a typical personal computer equipped with a dual core processor and windows operating system. We present the results of few experiments to validate the performance of the scheme in diversified working environments.

The objective function is to maximize the throughput of EN added with storage area network (SAN), where the conventional storage disks within EN are replaced with SAN. EN with its modified storage systems undergoes redesign and we have considered the following during redesign EN with SAN: addition of one or more network devices or links, geographical relocation of one or more clients (clients or servers) and change in the flow path over the network. The performances of EN along with the performance of SAN are evaluated, whereby the clients average response time and the packet loss rate are chosen as the evaluation parameters. The decision on redesign operation depends on the performance analysis of EN.

We have considered a mid-size EN comprising of 680 clients, 54 physical servers hosting 54 services, 13 Layer-2 switches, 5 Layer-3 switches, SAN and a router as an initial network, which is illustrated in Fig. 3. In this figure, the

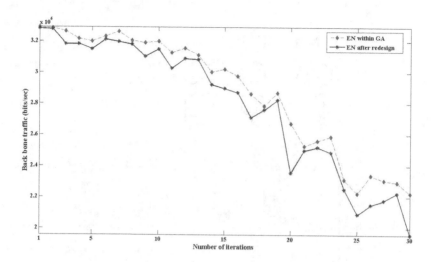

Fig. 4. Comparison of backbone traffic at varying infrastructures

labels L2, L3 represent layer 2 and layer 3 switches respectively and R represents the router [13].

5.1   Redesign at EN Infrastructure

We have tested the performance of the scheme within an existing EN, where the redesign within GA is carried out to optimize the performance of clustered EN after synthesizing single clustered EN. The redesign of a small size EN with 50 clients distributed within 7 clusters producing a maximum traffic of around 3.3 MB at the backbone is illustrated in Fig. 4. The simulation results demonstrate 40% reduction in backbone traffic than the initial clusters generated, where move client operation is employed as mutation operator to optimize the backbone traffic.

The simulation results of redesigning mid-size EN with 100 clients distributed within 10 clusters producing a maximum traffic of around 1.14 GB at the backbone demonstrate the evolution of EN through various bio-inspired algorithms. We compared the traffic volumes optimized within TS, SA and GA as illustrated in Fig. 5. GA, as an evolutionary approach outperforms both SA and TS by 9.7% reduced traffic volumes, TS demonstrates a marginal improvement of 2% over SA.

5.2   Redesign at Data Depositories

The performance measures of EN showed that the storage throughput of EN has improved after including SAN, but EN with SAN showed increased response time than the initial network. The sources of increased response time were identified as the router and the Layer-3 switches. In addition, the number of connections in the two Layer-3 switches connecting the main router is not balanced.

The redesigned network is shown in Fig. 6, where the redesign operations, such as load balancing and relocations of layer 3 switch, improvises the throughput

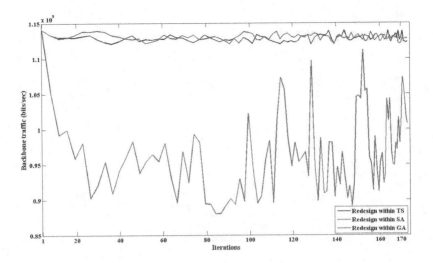

Fig. 5. Comparison of backbone traffic at varying infrastructures

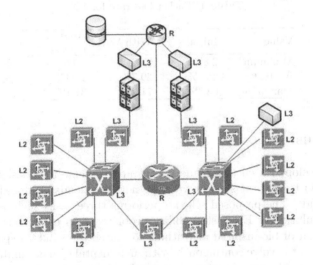

Fig. 6. EN with SAN after redesign

of EN with SAN by 13.9% with 24.4% decreased average response time as illustrated in Fig. 7 and with 38.3% reduced packet loss rate.

The packet loss rate for initial EN, EN with SAN, and redesigned EN including SAN is tabulated in Table 1. It is observed that the packet loss rate is decreased after redesign.

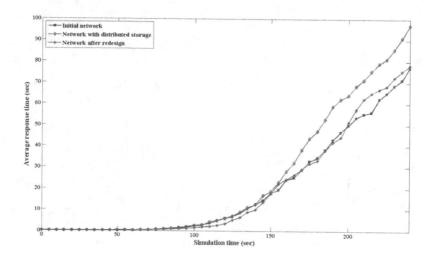

Fig. 7. Comparison of average response time

Table 1. Packet loss rate for EN

Value	Initial	With WAN	After redesign
Minimum	2.8%	0.0%	0.1%
Average	25.5%	29.7%	21.4%
Maximum	63.4%	71.2%	31.1%

6   Conclusion

We have developed a custom-made bio-inspired scheme to redesign enterprise network (EN) to make it sustain with the new workloads produced by varying client demands. The proposed scheme performs three tasks such as simulation of EN, formulation of EN sustainability problem as an optimization problem, and utilization of bio-inspired algorithms to search the solution space, thereby facilitating EN to evolve continuously with incremental changes in its infrastructure and data management system. The results of computational experiments on redesigning of mid-size EN show a 40% reduction in traffic flow at the backbone, and a 13.9% improvement in throughput in redesigning the storage system from localized disks into a storage area network.

We will continue to develop further redesign and performance analysis methodologies supporting our long-term commitments in applying design automation beyond the micro-level (integrated circuits) to the macro-level (enterprise systems).

References

1. Broekhuis, M., Vos, J.F.J.: Improving Organizational Sustainability Using a Quality Perspective. University of Groningen, Research Institute SOM (2003), http://ideas.repec.org/s/dgr/rugsom.html
2. Holling, C.S.: Resilience of Ecosystem: Local Surprise and Global Change. Sustainable Development of the Biosphere, pp. 292–317. Cambridge University Press, Cambridge (1986)
3. Gallopín, G.C.: Environmental and Sustainability Indicators and the Concept of Situational Indicators. A Systems Approach, Environmental Modelling & Assessment 1(3), 101–117 (1996)
4. Gerard, K.: The Transition to the Sustainable Enterprise. Journal of Cleaner Production 10(4), 349–359 (2002)
5. Robert, C., Bernard, C.P.: Defining and Predicting Sustainability. Ecological Economics 15, 193–196 (1995)
6. Xin, S., Yu-Wei, S., Krothapalli, S.D., Rao, S.G.: A Systematic Approach for Evolving VLAN Designs. In: The Proceedings of IEEE International Conference on Computer Communications, San Diego, CA, USA, March 15-19, pp. 1–9 (2010)
7. Xin, S., Rao, S.G.: A Cost-benefit Framework for Judicious Enterprise Network Redesign. In: The Proceedings of IEEE International Conference on Computer Communications, Shanghai, China, April 10-15, pp. 221–225 (2011)
8. Zhou, L., Xiaofei, X., Shengchun, D., Xudong, L.: Complicated Logistics Network Redesign Considering Service Differentiation. In: The Proceedings of 16th International Conference on Enterprise Distributed Object Computing Conference, Beijing, China, September 10-14, pp. 93–102 (2012)
9. Habib, S.J.: Redesigning Network Topology with Technology Considerations. Int. Journal of Network Management 18(1), 1–13 (2008)
10. Miyamoto, T., Hayashi, M., Nishimura, K.: Sustainable Network Resource Management System for Virtual Private Clouds. In: The Proceedings of IEEE Second International Conference on Cloud Computing Technology and Science, Indianapolis, USA, November 30-December 3, pp. 512–520 (2010)
11. Habib, S.J., Marimuthu, P.N., Al-Awadi, N.: Network Redesign through Clusters Consolidation. In: The Proceedings of 12th International Conference on Symposium on Performance Evaluation of Computer & Telecommunication Systems, Istanbul, Turkey, July 13-16 (2009)
12. Habib, S.J., Marimuthu, P.N., Taha, M.: Network Consolidation through Soft Computing. In: International Symposium on Methodologies for Intelligence Systems, Prague, September 14-17 (2009)
13. Habib, S.J., Marimuthu, P.N.: Redesign through Bio-Inspired Algorithms. In: The Proceedings of Annual International Conference on Advances Technology in Telecommunication, Broadcasting, and Satellite, Jakarta, Indonesia, August 2-4 (2013)
14. Habib, S.J.: Synthesis and Optimization of Application-Specific Intranets. PhD dissertation, The University of Southern California, LA, CA, USA (2001)
15. Habib, S.J., Parker, A.C.: i-CAD: A Rapid Prototyping CAD Tool for Intranet Design. In: The Proceedings of IEEE International Workshop on Rapid System Prototyping, San Diego, California, USA, June 9-11 (2003)
16. Hussain, T., Marimuthu, P.N., Habib, S.J.: Supporting Multimedia Applications through Network Redesign. International Journal of Communication Systems (2012), doi:10.1002/dac.2371

17. Hussain, T., Habib, S.J.: A Redesign Methodology for Storage Management Virtualization. In: The Proceedings of Integrated Network Management, Ghent, Belgium, May 27-31 (2013)
18. Goldberg, D.E.: Genetic Algorithms in Search, Optimization and Machine Learning. Addison-Wesley Longman Publishing Co., Inc., Boston (1989)
19. Kirkpatrick, S., Gelatt, C.D., Vecchi, M.P.: Optimization by Simulated Annealing. Science 220, 671–680 (1983)
20. Glover, F.: Tabu Search - Part 1. ORSA Journal on Computing 1(2), 190–206 (1989)

An Edge Detection Algorithm Based on Morphological Gradient and the Otsu Method

Lu Han and Aili Han*

Department of Computer Science, Shandong University(Weihai)
Weihai 264209, China
wthanlu@sina.com,
han.aili@163.com

Abstract. An edge detection algorithm based on the morphology gradient is presented to extract the edge pixels of grey-level image and convert the edge image to bi-level image by means of the Otsu method. The experimental results show that the algorithm is more efficient for the images with Gaussian noise or with salt&pepper noise.

Keywords: Edge detection, Morphology operator, Gradient.

1 Introduction

Edge detection is to locate and extract the edge pixels of digital image for image processing. The mathematical morphology is composed of a series of morphological operators [1]. The Otsu method [2] which is based on the maximum between-class variance is a classical, unsupervised threshold selection method. This paper presents an edge detection algorithm based on the morphology operators and the Otsu method.

2 Algorithm Based on Gradient and the Otsu Method

The gradient can be used in edge detection since the gradient of edge pixels is larger than that of their inner neighbors'. The traditional edge detection algorithms based on differential get the various gradients by means of differential operators, which are sensitive to noise. The morphological opening and closing operators can reduce noise and fill holes[3]. The traditional edge detection algorithms based on morphological gradient erode the original image with the simple structure element and then subtract the result from dilation with the same structure element, which are also sensitive to noise.

This paper presents an edge detection algorithm based on morphological operators and gradient. It first filters the inner noise of grey-level image by the closing operators, and then eliminates the isolated pixels and smoothes the edges through the opening operator followed by the closing operators. Next, it erodes the image with a selected structure element and then subtracts the result from

---

* Corresponding author.

L. Pan et al. (Eds.): BIC-TA 2014, CCIS 472, pp. 161–164, 2014.

dilation with the same structure element. The subtraction is the edge image. Finally, it gets the bi-level edge image by means of the Otsu method.

Algorithm 1. The improved edge detection algorithm based on morphological operators and gradient.

(1) The closing operator is applied to the original image to fuse the narrow breaks, fill the gaps and eliminate the small holes. Let A denote the grey-level image, and S denote the structure element. The result image E of the closing operation is calculated by $E = A \bullet S = (A \oplus S) \ominus S$, where $\oplus$ is the dilation operator, and $\ominus$ is the erosion operator[4].

(2) The opening operator with the same structure element S is applied to the grey-level image E to smooth the contour and eliminate the isolated pixels. And then the closing operation is used to fuse the narrow breaks, fill the gaps and eliminate the small holes. The result is denoted by $F = (E \circ S) \bullet S = (E \ominus S \oplus S) \oplus S \ominus S$.

(3) The dilation and erosion operations are applied to the image F with the structure element S, respectively, which is similar with the traditional morphological gradient edge detection algorithm[5]. The difference between the two results is the grey-level gradient edge image, denoted by *edge*.

$$edge = (F \oplus S) - (F \ominus S)$$

(4) The Otsu method is applied to the grey-level gradient edge image *edge* to get the threshold and convert the edge image to bi-level image. It first generates the histogram *ihist* in grey levels[0..255]. And then it selects the optimal threshold T. The mean of object pixel values and that of background pixel values are calculated by the following formulae, respectively.

$$u_o(T) = \frac{1}{w_o(T)} \sum_{0 \le k \le T} k \cdot p(k); \quad u_b(T) = \frac{1}{w_b(T)} \sum_{T \le k \le L-1} k \cdot p(k)$$

The mean of all the pixel values is calculated by $u = w_b(T)u_b(T) + w_o(T)u_o(T)$. The between-class variance at level T is calculated by $G(T) = w_b(T) \cdot [u_b(T) - u]^2 + w_o(T) \cdot [u_o(T) - u]^2$. The grey level with the maximum between-class variance are chosen as the final threshold.

3   Experimental Results and Analysis

3.1   Experimental Results from the Image with Gaussian Noise

The presented algorithm was applied to the image with Gaussian noise. Take the grey-level image a with Gaussian noise, $\sigma = 10$, shown in Fig.1(a) as an example.

The original image can be divided into three parts: the grid part in the front, the pen container part in the middle, and the bookshelf part in the back. The result extracted by the Sobel algorithm [6] is not very satisfying because the massive edge features were lost due to the heavy noise influence. The Canny

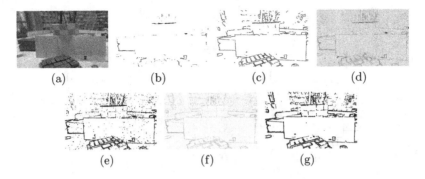

Fig. 1. The results of the image with Gussian noise. (a) The image a with Gaussian noise, $\sigma=10$; (b) The bi-level image b by applying the Sobel algorithm to the image a; (c) The bi-level image c by applying the Canny algorithm to the image a; (d) The grey-level image d after the traditional morphology gradient edge detection algorithm was applied to the image a; (e) The bi-level image e after the Otsu method was applied to the image d; (f) The grey-level image f after applying the improved algorithm presented in this paper to the image a; (g) The Otsu method was applied to the image f to convert the grey-level image to the bi-level image.

algorithm [7] can mainly extract the grid edges in the front, but most of the edges of the pen container part and the bookshelf part are lost. By means of the traditional morphology gradient edge detection algorithm, lots of the noise points remains in the grey-level image, and the bi-level edge image converted by the Otsu method also remains some obvious noise points. But it obtains the main grid edges in the front part and the main edges in the middle part. By applying the improved edge detection algorithm presented in this paper to the image a, the edges in the middle part and the edges in the bookshelf part are mainly preserved, whileas the obtained grid edges in the front part are similar with the edges detected by the Canny algorithm. That is, the present algorithm has better performance than the previous algorithms for the image with Gaussian noise.

3.2   Experimental Results from the Image with Salt&Pepper Noise

The presented algorithm was applied to the image with salt&pepper noise. Take the grey-level image a with salt&pepper noise shown in Fig.2(a) as an example.

For the original image with salt&pepper noise, the results are similar with that of the image with Gaussian noise. But for the previous algorithms, due to the influence of the salt&pepper noise, the threshold decreased when the grey-level image was converted by the Otsu threshold selection method, which led to the incorrect division of some pixels in the object class. Thus, the edges in the pen container part and in the bookshelf part cannot be extracted exactly. However, by means of the improved edge detection algorithm presented in this paper, all the edges in the three parts of the original image with salt&pepper noise can be

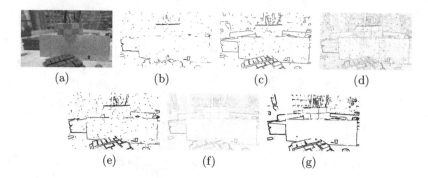

Fig. 2. The results of the image with salt&pepper noise. (*a*) The image *a* with salt&pepper noise; (*b*) The bi-level image *b* by applying the Sobel algorithm to the image *a*; (*c*) The bi-level image *c* by applying the Canny algorithm to the image *a*; (*d*) The grey-level image *d* after the traditional morphology gradient edge detection algorithm was applied to the image *a*; (*e*) The bi-level image *e* after the Otsu method was applied to the image *d*; (*f*) The grey-level image *f* after applying the improved algorithm presented in this paper to the image *a*; (*g*) The Otsu method was applied to the image *f* to convert the grey-level image to the bi-level image.

mainly preserved. That is, the present algorithm has better performance than the previous algorithms for the image with Salt&pepper noise.

Acknowledgements. This work was supported by the 2014 Science and Technology Development Project of Shandong Province.

References

1. Huifeng, W., Guili, Z., Xiaoming, L.: Research and application of edge detection operator based on mathematical morphology. J. Computer Engineering and Applications 45(9), 223–226 (2009)
2. Otsu, N.: A threshold selection method from gray-level histograms. J. Automatica 11(285-296), 23–27 (1975)
3. Li, Y.: Object Deetction based on Mathematical Morphology. D. Graduate School of National University of Defense Technology (2005)
4. Haixia, Y.: Study on Algorithms of Image Edge Detection and Enhancement Based on Mathematical Morphology. D. Jilin University (2009)
5. Serra, J.: Image Analysis and Mathematical Morphology. Academic Press, New York (1982)
6. Szeliski, R.: Computer vision: algorithms and applications. Springer (2010)
7. Canny, J.: A Computational Approach to Edge Detection. IEEE Transactions on Pattern Analysis and Machine Intelligence 8(6), 679–698 (1986)

Method for Forecasting Medium and Long-Term Power Loads Based on the Chaotic CPSO-GM

Libo Hao[1], Aijia Ouyang[2,3], and Libin Liu[4,*]

[1] Department of Information Engineering, Hunan Mechanical & Electrical
Polytechnic, Changsha 410151, China
[2] College of Computer, Hunan Science & Technology Economy Trade Vocation
College, Hengyang 421001, Hunan, China
[3] School of Information Science and Engineering, Hunan City University,
Yiyang, Hunan 413000, China
[4] Department of Mathematics and Computer Science, Chizhou University, Chizhou,
Anhui 247000, China
liulibin969@163.com

Abstract. To address the shortcomings of traditional grey forecasting
model GM (1, 1) in terms of poor forecasting on fast-growing power
load, this paper proposes a chaotic co-evolutionary PSO algorithm which
has better efficiency than the particle swarm optimization algorithm.
Combined with the GM (1, 1) model, a chaotic co-evolutionary particle
swarm optimization algorithm has been used to solve the values of two
parameters in GM (1, 1) model. In this way, we have designed a CCPSO
algorithm-based grey model. Results of case simulation on the power
consumption in 3 regions show that the CCPSO-GM model is optimal
over the other 4 forecasting models, proving that the CCPSO-GM model
has a wide applicable scope and high forecasting accuracy.

Keywords: Grey model, chaos, particle swarm optimization, co-
evolution, load forecasting.

1 Introduction

Electric power system load forecasting is fundamental for the work of departments of the electric power system responsible for power dispatching, planning
and supply. Accurate and effective load forecasting can not only help reasonably
arrange the start/stop of internal units of the power grid to ensure safe and
stable operation of the power grid, but also reduce unnecessary reserve capacity
and make reasonable schedule for inspection and repair, ensuring normal production and bringing increased economic and social benefits [1]. During the last
few decades, many domestic and foreign scholars have used various forecasting
methods and models in the medium to long-term electric power system load
forecasting, which greatly improves the forecast accuracy [2].

Load forecasting is vitally important for the electric power sector. Medium
to long-term load forecasting mainly focuses on power generation planning and

---

* Corresponding author.

L. Pan et al. (Eds.): BIC-TA 2014, CCIS 472, pp. 165–170, 2014.

development of the electric power system. Accurate forecast serves as the basis for reasonable planning, which greatly influences the investment of the power departments [3]. Therefore, improving the load forecasting accuracy is of great significance. However, the accuracy of medium to long-term load forecasting is subject to the influence of the economy, policy, climate and other random factors, making accurate forecasting very complicated. Common methods include time series method, regression analysis and grey method, etc [4].

2 Basic Algorithms

2.1 Co-evolutionary PSO

Particle swarm optimization (PSO) is an efficient algorithm. It has been applied to initialization of weights and thresholds of the BP neural network, multi-objective optimization, three-dimensional (3D) slope stability problem , parameter estimation of muskingum model [5,6] and solving of 1D heat conduction equation [7].

The Co-evolutionary PSO (CPSO) algorithm divides the particles into 3 sub-swarms, with each containing the same quantity of particles: S_1(basic group), S_2(basic group), S_3(comprehensive group).

The 3 sub-swarms conduct iterations as per the following equations: Basic groups S_1 and S_2 :

$$
\begin{aligned}
v_{id}^{1(2)}(t+1) = {}& \omega \bullet v_{id}^{1(2)}(t) + c_1 \bullet rand() \bullet (P_{id}^{12}(t) - x_{id}^{1(2)}(t) \\
& + c_2 \bullet rand() \bullet (P_{gd}(t) - x_{id}^{1(2)}(t))
\end{aligned}
\tag{1}
$$

$$
x_{id}^{1(2)}(t+1) = x_{id}^{1(2)}(t) + v_{id}^{1(2)}(t+1)
\tag{2}
$$

Comprehensive group S_3

$$
\begin{aligned}
v_{id}^{3}(t+1) = {}& \omega(\frac{m-m_1}{m} \bullet v_{id}^{1}(t+1) + \frac{m-m_2}{m} \bullet v_{id}^{2}(t+1) \\
& + v_{id}^{3}(t)) + c_1 rand()(P_{id}^{3}(t) - x_{id}^{3}(t) \\
& + c_2 rand()(P_{gd}(t) - x_{id}^{3}(t))
\end{aligned}
\tag{3}
$$

$$
\begin{aligned}
x_{id}^{3}(t+1) = {}& \alpha_1 \bullet x_{id}^{3}(t) + \alpha_2 \bullet P_{id}^{3}(t) \\
& + \alpha_3 \bullet P_{gd}(t) + v_{id}^{3}(t+1)
\end{aligned}
\tag{4}
$$

The evolving equations (1) and (2) of the basic groups S_1 and S_2 are the same as the algorithm of the standard particle group. The speed equation (3) of the comprehensive group S_3 introduces the speeds of basic groups S_1 and S_2. Where,$m = m_1 + m_2$;m_1 and m_2 are current fitness values of basic groups S_1 and S_2. By comparing the fitness values of two basic groups, we could ensure that the better basic group will have bigger influence on the comprehensive group S_3. The location equation (4) introduces global optimum P_{gd}, where, α_1 ,α_2 and α_3 are called impact factors, and $\alpha_1 + \alpha_2 + \alpha_3 = 1$.

3   Chaotic Co-evolutionary Particle Swarm Optimization Grey Model

3.1   Modeling Method

We use the improved dynamic grey model [8], which is based on the error-improvement of the dynamic grey model [9]:

$$\hat{x}^{(1)}(k+1) = (x^{(0)}(1) - \frac{b'}{a'})e^{-ak} + \frac{b'}{a'} + m(k+1)\hat{\varepsilon}^{(1)}(k+1) \qquad (5)$$

Basic requirement for conducting power load forecast using grey model in this paper are as follows: firstly, it does not require much load data, secondly, it does not need to consider the distribution pattern and changing trend of the load, and finally, the calculation should be easy. GM (1, 1) has gradually decreasing accuracy in the forecasting of fast-growing load. This is mainly due to the introduction of the background value equation as shown below:

$$x^{(1)}(k) = \frac{1}{2}[x^{(1)}(k) + x^{(1)}(k+1)] \qquad (6)$$

As parameters could easily fall within local extremum in order to avoid too many errors out of improper valuation of the background value equation, this paper introduces the following improved model: firstly, revise the Forecast Equation (5), we will get Equation (7):

$$\hat{x}^{(1)}(k+1) = (x^{(0)}(k) - \frac{b'}{a'})e^{-ak} + \frac{b'}{a'} + m(k+1)\hat{\varepsilon}^{(1)}(k+1) \qquad (7)$$

During the operation process, Equations (5) and (7) are used for the forecasting; secondly, use the co-evolutionary particle swarm algorithm to optimize parameters a and b in the two forecast equations above; finally, substitute optimized parameters a and b to equations (5) and (7), and the average of resultant forecast values will be regarded as the power load data in the future year in need of forecasting [10].

The forecast model obtained by using co-evolutionary particle swarm algorithm to solve the values of parameters a and b is named as the chaotic co-evolutionary particle swarm optimization grey model in this paper, shortened as CCPSO-GM.

3.2   Algorithm Procedure

From the algorithm procedure of the CCPSO-GM model above, we could know that, the expression that defines particles is of two dimensions (a, b). Use CCPSO-GM algorithm to optimize two basic parameters a and b, with the operational steps specified below:

Step 1 Initialize parameters: determine the expressions of particles, generate initial populations randomly within the search region $[-s, s]$, initialize the speeds and locations of particles and number of iterations (M) of chaos searching;

Step 2 Calculation: use target function f to calculate the target function value of each particle;

Step 3 Comparison: compare the target function value with accuracy ε. If the target function value is bigger than ε, terminate the process; otherwise, continue;

Step 4 Establish three sub-swarms S_1, S_2 and S_3. S_1 is applied with Gauss mutation strategy, S_2 is applied with Cauchy mutation strategy while S_3 is applied with Levy mutation strategy.

Step 5 Conduct independent searches for five times within the three sub-swarms. Compare the fitness values after five times and select a particle with global optimum from the population with the minimum target function value to replace the worst particle from the population with the maximum target function value;

Step 6 Compare the fitness values of the three sub-swarms, select two small fitness values and substitute them to forecasting equations (5) and (7);

Step 7 Calculate the target function value f of the new particle;

Step 8 Conduct local chaos search for more optimal solutions;

Step 9 Repeat Step 4 to Step 8 until the maximum number of iterations is reached to obtain the most optimal particle (a, b);

Step 10 Substitute the value of the most optimal particle to Equations (5) and (7) to calculate forecast values, and use the average value of them to forecast the power load data of the subject year.

4   Simulation Experiment and Result Analysis

Environmental configurations for the experiment in this paper are set out as below: computer: Dell optiplex390; CPU: core(TM)i5-2400; memory: 4G compatible machine; operation system: windos7;programming software: MATLAB2012. Run each problem independently for 100 times. In the experiment the algorithm parameters are set out below: search region:$[-c, c] = [-5, 5]$; number of populations:$N = 90$; number of sub-swarms; $S_1 = S_2 = S_3 = 30$; acceleration factors: $c_1 = c_2 = 1.2$; inertia weight factor would use self-adaptive factors in Literature [5]; maximum number of iterations $G_{max} = 100$; number of iterations of chaos operators: $M = 10$.

To test the effect of the CPSO-GM algorithm proposed in this paper, the target function is defined as:

$$f = 1/(1 + \sum_{k-1}^{n} [x^{(0)}(k) - \hat{x}^{(0)}(k)]^2) \tag{8}$$

This paper uses the power load data from three regions to conduct simulation experiments and compare experiment results with the results from GM(1,1) [10],

PSO-GM [10], ESO-GM [11] and CPSO-GM model. When using CCPSO-GM to forecast the power load data, we regard the data of the first 7 years as the training data, and the data of the 8th year as the standard data of the subject year of forecasting. We can see from experiment that with ever increasing data, grey models forecast results become poorer and poorer, while the accuracy of the CCPSO-GM model, on the contrary, increases rather than decrease. It could improve the adaptability of the forecast model and thus further forecast the changing trend of the load quite accurately. Experiment results also show us that the standard deviation of the CCPSO-GM algorithm is smaller than that of the other four algorithms, proving that CCPSO-GM has better stability than the other four algorithms. Compared with the other four models, the CCPSO-GM proposed in this paper has the features of higher accuracy, smaller error, better adaptability, and robustness.

5   Conclusions

This paper uses CCPSO algorithm to replace the traditional least square method to find solutions for GM (1, 1) model parameters, and proposes a CCPSO algorithm-based grey model for forecasting. This method can overcome some theoretical problems in the process of finding solutions for the parameters using traditional models, improve the forecast accuracy, enhance the stability of the algorithm and reduce the forecast error. Case analysis shows that this model also has high accuracy in forecasting comparatively fast-growing power load as well as the power load that is not of monotone increasing type, expanding the applicable scope of GM (1, 1), bearing certain theoretical significance and applicable values. CCPSO-GM algorithm has good expandability and could be applied to other problems relevant with medium to long-term time series forecasting.

Acknowledgments. This work is partially supported by the National Natural Science Foundation of China (Nos.11301044, 61202109), A Project Supported by Scientific Research Fund of Hunan Provincial Education Department (Grant No.13C333), the Project Supported by the Science and Technology Research Foundation of Hunan Province (Grant No.2014GK3043), A Project Supported by Hunan Education Science Twelfth-Five Year PlanChina(Grant No.XJK013CXX003).

References

1. Ruzic, S., Vuckovic, A., Nikolic, N.: Weather sensitive method for short term load forecasting in Electric Power Utility of Serbia. IEEE Transactions on Power Systems 18(4), 1581–1586 (2003)
2. Amjady, N.: Short-Term Bus Load Forecasting of Power Systems by a New Hybrid Method. IEEE Transactions on Power Systems 22(1), 333–341 (2007)
3. Borges, C.E., Penya, Y.K., Fernandez, I.: Evaluating Combined Load Forecasting in Large Power Systems and Smart Grids. IEEE Transactions on Industrial Informatics 9(3), 1570–1577 (2013)

4. Hao, Q., Srinivasan, D., Khosravi, A.: Short-Term Load and Wind Power Forecasting Using Neural Network-Based Prediction Intervals. IEEE Transactions on
   Neural Networks and Learning Systems 25(2), 303–315 (2014)
5. Ouyang, A., Tang, Z., Li, K., Sallam, A., Sha, E.: Estimating parameters of muskingum model using an adaptive hybrid pso algorithm. International Journal of
   Pattern Recognition and Artificial Intelligence 28(1), 1–29 (2014)
6. Ouyang, A., Li, K., Truong, T., Sallam, A., Sha, E.H.-M.: Hybrid particle swarm
   optimization for parameter estimation of muskingum model. Neural Computing
   and Applications, 1–15 (2014), http://dx.doi.org/10.1007/s00521-014-1669-y
7. Ouyang, A., Tang, Z., Zhou, X., Xu, Y., Pan, G., Li, K.: Parallel hybrid
   pso with cuda for ld heat conduction equation. Computers & Fluids (2014),
   http://www.sciencedirect.com/science/article/pii/S0045793014002187
8. Yu, J., Yan, F., Yang, W., Xia, C.: Gray variable weight combination model for
   middle and long term load forecasting. Power System Technology 29(17), 26–29
   (2005)
9. Cao, J., Liu, Y., Dai, Y.: Network traffic prediction based on error advanced grey
   model. Computer Engineering and Design 28(21), 5133–5134 (2007)
10. Niu, D., Zhao, L., Zhang, B., Wang, H.: The application of particle swarm optimiza-
    tion based grey model to power load forecasting. Chinese Journal of Management
    Science 22(4), 41–44 (2010)
11. Xia, H., Wang, Z., Guo, D.: Bi-group evolutionary strategy optimization grey model
    in power load forecasting. Computer Engineering and Applications 48(34), 241–244
    (2012)

Solving the Multiobjective Multiple Traveling Salesmen Problem Using Membrane Algorithm

Juanjuan He[1,2]

[1] School of Computer Science, Wuhan University of Science and Technology,
Wuhan 420081, China
[2] Hubei Province Key Laboratory of Intelligent Information Processing and Real-time
Industrial System, Wuhan 430081, China
hejuanjuan1117@gmail.com

Abstract. The multiple traveling salesmen problem (mTSP) is a generalization of the classical traveling salesman problem (TSP). The mTSP is more appropriate for real-life applications than the TSP, however, the mTSP has not received the same amount of attention. Due to the high complexity of the mTSP, a more efficient algorithm proposed for mTSP must be based on a global search procedure. Membrane algorithms are a class of hybrid intelligence algorithms, which has been introduced recently as a global optimization technique. In this work, a new membrane algorithm for solving mTSP with different numbers of salesmen and problem sizes is described. The experiment results are compared with several multiobjective evolutionary strategies.

Keywords: Evolutionary multiobjective optimization, Membrane algorithm, Multiple traveling salesmen problem.

1   Introduction

The multiple traveling salesmen problem (mTSP) is a generalization of the well-known traveling salesman problem (TSP). The aim of mTSP is to minimize the total cost of a set of routes which are visited by all salesmen who start from and end at a single point and service all customers once. In the mTSP, when $m = 1$ and $n = 1$, the mTSP can be simplified to the classical TSP. The mTSP are more appropriate for real-life applications because of several objective functions and multiple salesmen. However, the mTSP do not receive the same amount of research effort as TSP. Because of the high complexity of the mTSP (NP-hard problem [1]), it is necessary to develop heuristic algorithms to yield guarantee optimal solutions.

Membrane computing has become a hot topic in recent years. The devices investigated in membrane computing are called P systems, which can be seen as a group of non-deterministic and distributed computing models abstracted from the structure and the functioning of a single cell [2] and from complexes of cells, tissues [3], or other higher order structures [4]. Most of P systems have been proved to be universal, i.e., they can do what Turing machine can do, such as generate any set of languages accepted by Turing machine [5], solve NP-hard problems in feasible (polynomial or linear) time [6,7], and generate and accept any set of natural numbers which are Turing computable function [8]. All these mentioned results are achieved at the theoretical level.

L. Pan et al. (Eds.): BIC-TA 2014, CCIS 472, pp. 171–175, 2014.

In the last few years, the applications of membrane computing have been expanded to realistic fields. To solve difficult problems in practice, a class of intelligent algorithms, which are inspired by the framework of membrane computing, are proposed and named membrane algorithm [9,10]. Till now, various membrane algorithms achieved great attainments in several fields. Combining tissue P systems and quantum evolution strategy, a novel membrane algorithm was used to solve broadcasting problems [11]. The dynamic behaviors of this membrane algorithm, including diversity and convergency, were also analyzed in [12]. Inspired by the way biological neuron cells storing information, membrane algorithm with ring structure is proposed for solving knapsack problem [13]. Membrane algorithm was also develop to design DNA Sequence in DNA computing [14,15]. The results caused by these membrane algorithms proved that the framework of membrane computing can improve the whole performance of algorithms.

This work studies a new membrane algorithm with hybrid chromosome representation. The multi-chromosome technique is employed to reduce the excess redundant at most of the runtime. When the crossover operator executes during a run, the one chromosome technique is used to simplify the complexity of calculation. In this membrane algorithm, the membrane structure is inspired by the Golgi apparatus of eukaryotic cells [16], i.e., two kinds of membranes embed in the skin membrane —— a membrane (as cisternae of the Golgi apparatus) and a network of parallel membranes which have the same function (as vesicular). In addition, we do not remove any solutions, but adjust them for keeping more information. The effectiveness of our algorithm is tested by solving mTSP with different numbers of salesmen and problem sizes, and compares with several commonly used algorithms.

2   The Membrane Algorithm for mTSP

2.1   Chromosome Representation

In the previous work, two different chromosomes are commonly employed when solving the mTSP using evolutionary algorithms. The one chromosome technique involves using a single chromosome of length $n + m - 1$ (including n customs and $m - 1$ negative integers as delimiters, m is the number of salesmen). This method is simply to crossover, however, many of the possible chromosomes are redundant (there are $(n+m-1)!$ possible solutions). To reduce excess possible solutions, multi-chromosome representation was also used by many researchers. Each chromosome can be seen as a route, which is a set of customs served by a single salesman. The multi-chromosome technique decomposes complex solutions in to simpler components, but it needs complicated special operators.

We combine the advantages of both one chromosome representation and multi-chromosome technique. When computing solution similarity, the multi-chromosome technique is used for reducing the excess redundant. While the crossover operator coming, the chromosome will transform into one single chromosome to simplify computing complexity. Moreover, the chromosome converter program can finish in few steps. The computational complexity of this procedure is $O(N * (n + m))$.

2.2   Membrane Structure and Procedure

The membrane structure is depicted in Fig. 1. The outmost membrane, called the skin membrane, sperate the workspace from environment. In the skin membrane, two kinds of membranes work parallel. One kinds of membranes work as vesicular, which contain a set of tentative solutions to solve a subproblem g_i decomposed from a multi-objective optimization problem. As a multi-objective optimization problem decomposes into p subproblems, p vesicular membranes are created. Another kinds of membrane work as cisternae of the Golgi apparatus. The function of this membrane is to keep the non-dominated solutions. During each run, the best solutions in vesicular membranes send to the cisternae membrane for competition by communication. While in the set of non-dominated solutions, some solutions will be beaten and sent back to the cisternae membrane.

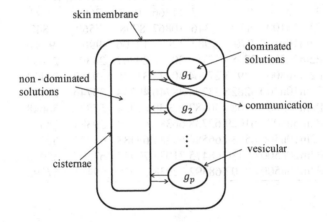

Fig. 1. The membrane structure of the proposed algorithm

The proposed algorithm consists of four main mechanisms: chromosome representation, decomposition, evolutionary process in the vesicular membranes, and selection in the cisternae membrane. The common decomposition framework, the Tchebycheff approach [19], is used to decompose multiobjective problem into p subproblems. Each vesicular membrane containing a set of tentative solutions is used to solve a subproblem. After p vesicular membranes finish updating process, the best solutions will be sent to cisternae membrane to compete with non-dominated solutions. The selection mechanism in cisternae membrane is like simulated annealing, which improves the global searching ability of algorithm. Repeat evolutionary process and selection until the termination criterion is met (reach the maximum number of generations).

3   Experiments and Discussions

In this section, we use membrane algorithm to solve the multiobjective multiple traveling salesman problem. The experiments are carried out to study the performance of six algorithms applied on the mTSP with different number of salesmen, customers and two objective functions. Cost matrix ($n * n$) is randomly generated for each objective in the range of $[0, 1000]$. For each scale of problem, a particular instance is used. Five algorithms are compared with the proposed membrane algorithm. DSA is the simulated annealing algorithm with decomposition. DHC is the hill climbing method with decomposition. DEA is the pure evolutionary algorithm with decomposition. DGA is the classical genetic algorithm with decomposition. NSGA-II is the non - dominated sorting genetic algorithm, proposed in [20]. The experimental results are shown in Table 1. The results show that the proposed algorithm generates the best solutions.

Table 1. The best results obtained by various algorithms for the mTSP with two objectives, m salesmen, and n customers within 30 runs

	DSA	DHC	DEA	DGA	NSGA-II	Results
P2m2n100	8762	8147	11766	9187	7683	7324
P2m5n100	8220	9346	10867	8798	7569	6842
P2m10n100	9702	9982	12087	12106	9961	9284
P2m2n300	27689	27789	30318	29807	24398	21097
P2m5n300	28975	27964	30273	31836	29162	27154
P2m10n300	32826	33784	38746	40234	33746	31182
P2m2n500	59684	56483	62938	62354	57829	56648
P2m5n500	61029	62738	66384	63748	59384	58372
P2m10n500	65938	66584	69384	69483	65834	62394
P2m20n500	67436	68475	71038	70947	67304	65930
P2m50n500	69402	68392	72938	73928	69483	67392

4   Conclusion

This work has proposed a membrane algorithm with hybrid chromosome representation to solve mTSP with different salesmen and problem sizes. The framework of the proposed algorithm is based on the concept of membrane computing, which divides tentative solutions, but do not remove any one. Hybrid chromosome representation is employed for reducing the computation complexity. The experimental results shown that the membrane algorithms is able to achieve better proximity results than common used algorithms.

Acknowledgments. This work was supported by the National Natural Science Foundation of China (Grant No. 61373066, 61033003 and 61100055).

References

1. Singh, A., Baghel, A.S.: A new grouping genetic algorithm approach to the multiple traveling salesperson problem. Soft Computing 13(1), 95–101 (2009)
2. Pan, L., Diaz-Pernil, D., Pérez-Jiménez, M.J.: Computation of Ramsey numbers by P systems with active membranes. International Journal of Foundations of Computer Science 22(1), 29–38 (2011)
3. He, J., Miao, Z., Zhang, Z., Shi, X.: Solving multidimensional 0C1 knapsack problem by tissue P systems with cell division. In: Fourth International Conference on Bio-Inspired Computing, BIC-TA 2009, pp. 1–5 (2009)
4. Pan, L., Păun, G.: Spiking neural P systems with anti-spikes. Inernational Journal of Computers, Communications and Control 4(3), 273–282 (2009)
5. Zhang, X., Zeng, X., Pan, L.: On languages generated by asynchronous spiking neural P systems. Theoretical Computer Science 410(26), 2478–2488 (2009)
6. Niu, Y., Pan, L., Pérez-Jiménez, M.J., Font, M.R.: A tissue P systems based uniform solution to tripartite matching problem. Fundamenta Informaticae 109(2), 179–188 (2011)
7. Pan, L., Păun, G., Pérez-Jiménez, M.J.: Spiking neural P systems with neuron division and budding. Science China Information Sciences 54(8), 1596–1607 (2011)
8. Wang, J., Hoogeboom, H.J., Pan, L., Păun, G., Pérez-Jiménez, M.J.: Spiking neural P systems with weights. Neural Computation 22(10), 2615–2646 (2010)
9. Zhang, G., Cheng, J., Gheorghe, M., Meng, Q.: A hybrid approach based on differential evolution and tissue membrane systems for solving constrained manufacturing parameter optimization problems. Applied Soft Computing 13(3), 1528–1542 (2013)
10. Cheng, J., Zhang, G., Neri, F.: Enhancing distributed differential evolution with multicultural migration for global numerical optimization. Information Sciences 247, 72–93 (2013)
11. Zhang, G., Zhou, F., Huang, X., Cheng, J., Gheorghe, M., Ipate, F., Lefticaru, R.: A novel membrane algorithm based on particle swarm optimization for solving broadcasting problems. Journal of Universal Computer Science 18(13), 1821–1841 (2012)
12. Zhang, G., Cheng, J., Gheorghe, M.: Dynamic behavior analysis of membrane-inspired evolutionary algorithms. International Journal of Computers, Communications & Control 9(2), 227–242 (2014)
13. He, J., Xiao, J., Shi, X., Song, T.: A Membrane-Inspired Algorithm with a Memory Mechanism for Knapsack Problem. Journal of Zhejiang University Science C: Computer & Electronics 14(8), 612–622 (2013)
14. Xiao, J., Zhang, X., Xu, J.: A Membrane Evolutionary Algorithm for DNA Sequences Design in DNA Computing. Chinese Science Bulletin 57(6), 698–706 (2012)
15. Xiao, J., Jiang, Y., He, J., Cheng, Z.: A Dynamic Membrane Evolutionary Algorithm for Solving DNA Sequences Design with Minimum Free Energy. MATCH Communications in Mathematical and in Computer Chemistry 70(3), 971–986 (2013)
16. Zhao, J., Wang, N.: A bio-inspired algorithm based on membrane computing and its application to gasoline blending scheduling. Computers and Chemical Engineering 35, 272–283 (2011)
17. Tang, L., Liu, J., Rong, A., Yang, Z.: A multiple traveling salesman problem model for hot rolling schefule in Shanghai Baoshan Iron and Steel Complex. European Journal of Operationa Research 124(2), 267–282 (2000)
18. Arthur, E., Cliff, T.: A new approach to solving the multiple traveling salesperso problem using genetic algorithms. European Journal of Operational Research 175, 246–257 (2006)
19. Miettinen K.: Nonliear Multiobjective Optimization. Kluwer, Norwell (1999)
20. Shim, V., Tan, K., Chia, J.: Probabilistic based evolutionary optimizer in bi-objective traveling salesman problem. In: Proc. 8th International Conference on Simulated Evlutionry Learning, pp. 309–324 (2010)

A Novel Method to Derive Ambulatory Blood Pressure from the Radial Pressure Waveform

Long He, Zhihua Chen*, and Zheng Zhang

Key Laboratory of Image Information Processing and Intelligent Control,
School of Automation, Huazhong University of Science and Technology,
Wuhan, Hubei, P.R. China
chenzhihua@hust.edu.cn

Abstract. In this paper, we develop a novel application of independent component analysis (ICA) based auto-regression forecasting model(ICA-ARF). The method can noninvasively, continuously and conveniently derive ambulatory blood pressure (ABP) from the radial artery pressure waveform (RAPWF). To eliminate the effect of correlative factors in measurement, the ICA method is used to decomposite the raw signal and extract the independent component affected by blood pressure (BP). Based on the spectrum density of independent component, an auto-regression forecasting model is set up to derive BP. Experimental results show an excellent correlation and agreement with the BP measured by Omron electronic BP monitor (Type: HEM-7012). If the ICA-ARF is used, the the error can be reduced from 7.4mmHg to 2.55mmHg.

Keywords: Independent component analysis, Auto-regression forecasting model, Ambulatory blood pressure, Radial artery pressure waveform.

1 Introduction

Ambulatory blood pressure (ABP) is associated with the increasing cardiovascular disease in humans. Recently, 24-hour ABP monitoring and assessment of central aortic blood pressure have been introduced to achieve a better prevention and diagnosis of cardiovascular disease. There are invasive and noninvasive measurement in ABP measurement. Invasive measurement is accomplished by inserting the sensor directly into the aortic to obtain an accurate real-time ABP, but it may cause damage to tissues of the circulatory system. Noninvasive measurement is a kind of soft measurement, estimating ABP through mechanism analysis and signal processing. Noninvasive measurement does little harm to human body and is relatively simple, so it is more suitable for clinical and daily measurement [1].

In this paper, we propose an auto-regression forecasting model based on independent component analysis (ICA-ARF) to estimate ABP in humans. The ICA, which is widely used in blind source separation, acts as a filter to remove undesirable components from raw data of RAPWF. That is, the raw signal of

---

* Corresponding author.

L. Pan et al. (Eds.): BIC-TA 2014, CCIS 472, pp. 176–181, 2014.

RAPWF is clustered into two parts: the data $s_1(t)$ unrelated to ABP and the data $s_2(t)$ relevent to ABP. ICA-ARF model works out ABP through the data $s_2(t)$.

2 Methods

2.1 Influence Factor Design and Factor Analysis

It is obvious that the RAPWF can be affected by the position of sensor, the personal state and the tightness of wrist strap etc. And there may be interactions between these factors, which has direct influence on ABP prediction [2]. So it is necessary to extract the component only related with ABP while independent with other factors. The ABP derived from the extracted component may be more objective.

In general, the sensor is mounted comfortably on the radial artery position to implement the measurement at the radial artery of the wrist. Then a noninvasive, real time, and continuous RAPWF sampling starts, as shown in figure 1. There are many uncertain factors in this way of measurement, such as the tightness of wrest trip, the sensor location, and the personal physical state [3] [4]. It is necessary to eliminate the influence of various factors before using the data to estimate BP. Four factors, noted as A, B, C, D, are chosen as the main analysis objects, and each factor is classified into two levels.

- Factor A: a_1 represents the BP before strenuous exercise; a_2 is the BP after strenuous exercise;
- Factor B: b_1 sensor is mounted on the radial artery with a small pressure; b_2 is the state with a lot of pressure;
- Factor C: c_1 means the measured person is a female; c_2 is a male;
- Factor D: d_1 sensor located upper at wrist radial artery; d_2 sensor located lower at the wrist radial artery.

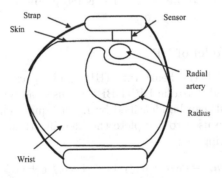

Fig. 1. The schematic diagram of the sensor location

2.2 Independent Component Analysis

The ICA is proposed to solve the problem of blind source separation, that is so-called cocktail party problem [5]. Assuming that observers A,B and C obtained the signal mixed by sources $s_1(t)$, $s_2(t)$, $s_3(t)$ at the same point, and detected the observed signals $x_1(t)$, $x_2(t)$, $x_3(t)$, the problem is how to calculate the original signal $s_1(t)$, $s_2(t)$, $s_3(t)$ from $x_1(t)$, $x_2(t)$, $x_3(t)$, which is called blind source signal separation problem [5]. It can be also described as $X = AS$. The signal matrix S can be worked out by equation $S = A^{-1}X$ when the matrix A is given.Through calculating the inverse matrix of A, we can use $\hat{S} = \hat{A}X$ to calculate $\hat{S}$ [6].

3 Experimental Process

3.1 ICA of RAPWF

RAPWF is decomposed into single pulse waveform, and the threshold method is used to identify peaks of each pulse waveform. The average distance of the adjacent points is defined as the period of the pulse (Cyc). To generate a practical pulse waveform, $0.35 \times Cyc$ before and $0.55 \times Cyc$ after the peak is combined as a whole pulse wave.

We use FAST-ICA function to figure out the two independent components s_1 s_2. The one with a larger amplitude is defined as $\hat{s_1}$, the other is $\hat{s_2}$, as shown in figure 2.

$$X_{pc} = (x_{pc1}, x_{pc2})^T$$
$$S = (s_1, s_2)^T \tag{1}$$

Conclusion can be drawn that the signal s_2 has a better correlation with the BP since s_2 fluctuated heavier with BP than s_1 did.

As mentioned in the above sections, the influence of other factors sampled from the RAPWF is reduced to the lowest degree after the ICA, and the component with a stronger correlation with the BP is achieved. Using the second independent component to predict the BP is more objective, then the the prediction model has a better robustness.

3.2 Prediction Model of BP

In the proposed model, the heart rate (HR) and s_2 are used as the inputs, Systolic BP (SBP) and diastolic BP (DBP) are used as the outputs. An auto-regressive model of BP can be identified by Least-Square method. 2^4 groups of experimental data are used to complete the identification. Then the identified model is as the following:

$$y_{BP} = a_0 f_0 + a_1 f_1 + \cdots + a_{10} f_{10} + e(t) \tag{2}$$

In the formula (2), y_{BP} is SBP or DBP; $e(t)$ is a gaussian white noise; f_0 is human HR, f_{1-10} is the spectrum density of second principal component; a_{0-10} is the model parameters needed to be identified and a_{0-10} are shown in table 1.

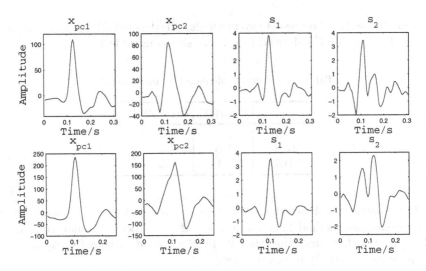

Fig. 2. $X_{pc} = (x_{pc1}, x_{pc2})^T$ and $S = (s_1, s_2)^T$.

Table 1. The coefficient of the prediction model

	a_0	a_1	a_2	a_3	a_4	a_5
y_{BPH}	135.3	1702.5	-851.0	-143.3	-135.3	246.6
y_{BPL}	56.6	119.0	-44.5	131.9	105.3	-269.1
	a_6	a_7	a_8	a_9	a_{10}	
y_{BPH}	-406.1	131.7	277.2	-313.8	341.3	
y_{BPL}	211.1	-32.8	-68.2	-299.5	711.0	

4   Results

10 volunteers participated in the experiment, 5 males and 5 females. Their corresponding data are obtained in this way:

The RAPWF is measured by the sensor strapped on the wrist. According to the measured pulse waveforms, RAPWF's spectrum density ($\sharp$1), the second principal component spectrum density ($\sharp$2) is used to derived the corresponding BP.

The standard BP values is obtained by Omron electronic BP monitor(Type: HEM-7012).

We judge the accuracy of two methods ($\sharp$1,$\sharp$2) by:

$$e(j) = \sum_{i=1}^{20} |X_{j,i} - S_i| \tag{3}$$

In the formula, X represents SBP, DBP or HR derived by ($\sharp$1, $\sharp$2); S represents SBP, DBP or HR obtained by Omron BP monitor; the two methods are represented by ♯1, ♯2 represent two methods. It is denoted 20 times measurement by $i = 1, 2, \ldots, 20$. The derived results are shown in table 2.

Table 2. BP error calculated by method ♯1, ♯2

	Error(♯1)	Error(♯2)
SBP	148	51
DBP	136	51
HR	23	23

The comparison shows the method ♯1 can not follow the variation of BP, but the contrast method ♯2 can well reflect the variation of human BP. Method ♯2 implicates that predicting the BP by the second principal component can improve the sensitivity of measurement.

5 Conclusions

In order to eliminate the effects of various factors in BP measurement, ICA is proposed to decompose RAPWF into 2 independent components. One of conponets is only dependent to the ABP while independent to other factors, named the second independent component. The correlation between the second independent component and the tightness of wrist strip as well as the measuring position is analyzed and identified. The experimental results illustrate the validity of the proposed ABP-ICA. Using the independent component s_2 extracted from RAPWF to predict BP is more objective and accurate.

In recent years, bio-inspired computing models and algorithms have been developed heavily, see e.g. [7,8,9]. It deserves for further research that using bio-inspired methods or strategies to predict derive ambulatory blood pressure from the radial pressure waveform.

Acknowledgments. The authors were supported by National Natural Science Foundation of China(61370105, 61379059, 61100055, 61100145), China Postdoctoral Science Foundation funded project (2014M550389) and Natural Science Foundation of Hubei Province (Grant No. 2013CFB159).

References

1. Fetics, B., Nevo, E., Chen, C.-H., Kass, D.A.: Parametric Model Derivation of Transfer Function for Noninvasive Estimation of Aortic Pressure by Radial IEEE Transactions on Tonometry. Biomedical Engineering 46, 698–706 (1999)
2. James, D., Cameron, M., Barry, P.M., Anthony, M.: Use of Radial Artery Applanation Tonometry and a Generalized Transfer Function To Determine Aortic Pressure Augmentation in Subjects With Treated Hypertension. The Journal of the American College of Cardiology 32, 1214–1220 (1988)

3. Floyd, F.J., Widaman, K.F.: Factor Analysis In The Development and Refinement of Clinical Assessment Instruments. Psychological Assessment 7, 286–299 (1995)
4. Marsh, H.W., Hocevar, D.: Application of Confirmatory Factor Analysis to the Study of Self-Concept: First – and Higher Order Factor Models and their Invariance Across Groups. Psychological Bulletin 97, 562–582 (1985)
5. Aapo, H.: Fast and Robust Fixed-Point Algorithms for Independent Component Analysis. IEEE Transactions on Neural Networks 10, 626–634 (1999)
6. Hyvarinen, A., Oja, E.: Independent component analysis: Algorithms and applications. Neural Networks 13, 411–430 (2000)
7. Song, T., Pan, L., Wang, J., Ibrahim, V., Subramanian, K.G., Rosni, A.: Normal Forms of Spiking Neural P Systems with Anti-Spikes. IEEE Trans. on Nanobioscience 11(4), 352–359 (2012)
8. Song, T., Zheng, H., He, J.: Solving Vertex Cover Problem by Tissue P Systems with Cell Division. Appl. Math. Inf. Sci. 8(1), 333–337 (2014)
9. Martın-Vide, C., Păun, G., Pazos, J., Rodrıguez-Patón, A.: Tissue P Systems, Theore. Comput. Sci. 296(2), 295–326 (2003)

Association Rule Mining Based on Bat Algorithm

Kamel Eddine Heraguemi[1], Nadjet Kamel[1], and Habiba Drias[2]

[1] Univ-Setif, Fac-Sciences, Depart.Computer Science,
Setif, Algeria
[2] USTHB, Depart.Computer Science
Algiers, Algeria
k.heragmi@yahoo.fr, {nkamel,hdrias}@usthb.dz

Abstract. In this paper, we propose a bat-based algorithm (BA) for association rule mining (ARM Bat). Our algorithm aims to maximize the fitness function to generate the best rules in the defined dataset starting from a specific minimum support and minimum confidence. The efficiency of our proposed algorithm is tested on several generic datasets with different number of transactions and items. The results are compared to FPgrowth algorithm results on the same datasets. ARM bat algorithm perform better than the FPgrowth algorithm in term of computation speed and memory usage,

Keywords: Association rules mining, ARM, Bat algorithm, Optimization, FP-growth algorithm, Support, Confidence.

1 Introduction

Knowledge discovery in databases has attracted the attention of researchers because of the fast increasing of stored data. Great number of studies were dedicated to association rule mining [1]. Formally, the association rule problem is defined as follow: Let $I = \{i_1, i_2,...,i_n\}$ be a set of literals called items, Let D be a set of database transaction where each transaction T contains a set of items. The problem of mining association rules aims to generate all rules having support and confidence greater than the user specified minimum support (called *minsup)* and minimum confidence (called *minconf)* respectively.

Since 1993, when Agrawal et al. [1] introduce the definition of association rules and frequent pattern, many exact algorithms were proposed to solve this problem. Each algorithm has its method to generate the frequent pattern and associations. Apriori[2] is the most popular algorithm. It generates the candidate item-set with a pruning mechanism. In [5], Han et al. propose a new exact algorithm called FP-growth. It mines frequent pattern and generates the association rule without candidate generation. It needs just two database scans.

In the literature, different works propose bio-inspired approaches to extract association rules. In [6], the authors propose a particle swarm algorithm to detect association rules. The proposed algorithm is defined through two main parts:

L. Pan et al. (Eds.): BIC-TA 2014, CCIS 472, pp. 182–186, 2014.
© Springer-Verlag Berlin Heidelberg 2014

preprocessing and mining. The preprocessing part calculates the fitness of the particle swarm. In the mining part, PSO is used to mine the rules. A great review on Application of Particle Swarm Optimization in Association Rule Mining was proposed in[3]. The authors of [4] developed a new algorithm called BSO-ARM. This algorithm is inspired from bees behavior and based on BSO algorithm.

Motivated by the success of bat algorithm[8] in various fields of data-mining, we present in this paper a new modified bat algorithm for association rule mining called ARM BAT algorithm. Our approach was tested on several common datasets, compared to FPgrowth algorithm results and seems to perform better than the FPgrowth algorithm in term of computation speed and memory usage,

The remainder of this paper is organized as follows: we present and discuss our proposed algorithm: ARM Bat algorithm. In section 3 we present our experimental results. In the last section we conclude this paper and we present our future work.

2   ARM Bat Algorithm

2.1   Encoding

In ARMGA algorithm[7], the rule is represented as a chromosome of $k+1$ length, where the first position is the cut point that separates the antecedent and the consequent of the rule. Positions 1 to k are the index of the items, For our approach we use the same representation where each solution X represents a rule and contains k item.

2.2   Fitness Function

As mentioned above, in association rule mining, the rule is accepted if its support and confidence satisfy user minsup and minconf. Each of the works on evolutionary algorithms for mining association rule presents its fitness function for the individuals.Our fitness function is described as follow:

$$f(R) = \begin{cases} \alpha conf(R) + \beta supp(R)/\alpha + \beta & \text{if accepted rule } R \\ -1 & \text{otherwise} \end{cases}$$

where $R = X \Longrightarrow Y$, and let α and β be two empirical parameters.

2.3   Virtual Bat Motion

In[8] the authors present a mathematical simulation of the natural bat movement, where the frequency f_i, the velocity v_i and the position (solutions) x_i for each virtual bat are described. In our approach we make a new description for bat motion related to association rule mining. The same concepts are defined: frequency, velocity and position.

- **Frequency** f_i: presents how many items can be changed in the actual rule, where the maximum frequency f_{max} is the number of attributes in the dataset and the minimum frequency f_{min} is 0.

- **Velocity** v_i: presents where the changes will be started.
- **Position** x_i: it is the new generated rule based on new frequency, velocity and the loudness .

The new generated rule at the iteration t is given by:

$$f_i^t = 1 + (f_{max})\beta, \qquad (1)$$

$$v_i^t = f_{max} - f_i^t - v_i^{t-1}, \qquad (2)$$

The new position (rule) x_i is generated by applying **algorithm 1**, such that, if the loudness is less than a random value *rand* we increase the value of actual bit, else we decrease this value. If the value is out of the interval [1..N], the value is replaced by 0. The new generated rule may contain duplicated bits (items). In this case, we keep a random bit from the duplicated and delete the others. Here we never get an invalid rule. This operation will be repeated starting from the bit at current velocity to achieve the actual frequency. The modified bat algorithm pseudo code is presented in **Algorithm 2**

Algorithm 1. Generate new solution

---

input: Rule x_{i-1}, Frequency f_i, velocity v_i, loudness A_i
output: new rule x_i
while $(v_i < Frequency\ f_i)$ **do**
  if $(rand > A_i)$ **then**
    Item at v_i ⟵ *Item at v_i + 1*
  else
    Item at v_i ⟵ *Item at v_i - 1*
  end if
  if *(Item at v_i less or equal to 0 or greater than number of attributes)* **then**
    Item at v_i ⟵ *0*
  end if
  if The new rule contains duplicated items **then**
    Keep one randomly and delete the others.
  end if
  increment v_i
end while

---

3 Experimentation and Results

To evaluate our algorithm we tested it on a several synthetic common standard databases with different number of transactions and items[1]. Results are described in the following sections.

Table 1 shows the results of running our tests on CHESS[2] database that contains 3,196 transactions and 75 items. The results show that our algorithm gives a good runtime with a good quality of rules generated and less memory usage. Our algorithm goes to maximize the fitness function till 0.9694 with support 0.92 and confidence 0.93 and maximum memory usage 48.63. For FPgrowth algorithm, the runtime grows up because of the number of transactions in the CHESS dataset.

---

[1] http://fimi.ua.ac.be/data/

[2] http://fimi.ua.ac.be/data/chess.dat

Algorithm 2. ARM BAT Algorithm

objective function(fitness function)
Initialize the bat population x_i and v_i
Define pulse frequency f_i at x_i
calculate the fitness of each initial position f_i at x_i
Initialize pulse rates r_i and the loudness A_i
while *(t < Max number of iterations)* **do**
    Generate new solutions by adjusting frequency f_i,
    and updating velocities and locations/solutions [equations 1, 2]
    Generate a new solution x_i using Algorithm 1 where inputs are f_i, v_i, A_i
    if *(rand > r_i)* **then**
        Generate a local solution around the selected best solution by changing just one item in
        the rule
    end if
    if *($f(x_i) > f(x_i*)$)* **then**
        Accept the new solutions
        $x_i = x_i$*
        Increase r_i and reduce A_i
    end if
    Rank the bats to the best solution
end while
Post-process results and visualization the best detected rules

Table 1. ARM Bat results with Chess database (3,196 transactions and 75 items)

Bats number	iteration	execution time (s)	best fitness	Memory usage (Megs)	FPgrowth runtime(s)	Memory usage (Megs)
10	50	9	0.7034			
	100	13	0.8044			
	150	22	0.8209	42.51	523	104.55
	200	28	0.8152			
25	50	38	0.632			
	100	72	0.6464			
	150	60	0.8728	45.95	523	104.55
	200	73	0.8152			
50	50	38	0.8837			
	100	67	0.8565			
	150	125	0.9044	48.63	523	104.55
	200	141	0.9295			

Table 2 shows the results of our tests on mashroom[3] database that contains 8124 transactions and 119 items. Again, the results confirm the efficiency of our algorithm with the growth up of number of transactions and items in database in term of execution time and memory storage. The maximum usage of memory was 170 Mo when the parameters are 200 iterations and 50 bats. Where FPgrowth algorithm goes till 291 Megs of memory and runtime of 1165 seconds.

Based on the conducted experiments, we observe that our algorithm provides a great performance in term of CPU-time and memory usage. Thanks to the echolocation concept of the bat algorithm that can determine which part of the best rule have changed to get a better position (rule) for the actual bat.

---

[3] http://fimi.ua.ac.be/data/mushroom.dat

Table 2. ARM Bat results with Mashroom database(8124 transactions and 119 items)

Bats number	iteration	execution time (s)	best fitness	Memory usage (Megs)	FPgrowth runtime(s)	Memory usage (Megs)
10	50	10	0.6063			
	100	26	0.6329			
	150	41	0.6927	128.67	1165	291.1
	200	68	0.6927			
25	50	37	0.5622			
	100	86	0.6329			
	150	115	0.6927	156.69	1165	291.1
	200	199	0.7070			
50	50	61	0.6464			
	100	151	0.6927			
	150	253	0.7198	170.29	1165	291.1
	200	341	0.7376			

4 Conclusion

In this paper, we proposed a new application of bat algorithm for association rule mining. The proposal approach is inspired from bats behavior and based on echolocation concept to generate new positions (rules). Our proposal proved its efficiency in term of time, memory usage and quality of generated rules with maximizing the fitness function.

References

1. Agrawal, R., Imieliński, T., Swami, A.: Mining association rules between sets of items in large databases. In: ACM SIGMOD Record, vol. 22, pp. 207–216. ACM (1993)
2. Agrawal, R., Srikant, R., et al.: Fast algorithms for mining association rules. In: Proc. 20th Int. Conf. Very Large Data Bases, VLDB, vol. 1215, pp. 487–499 (1994)
3. Ankita, S., Shikha, A., Jitendra, A., Sanjeev, S.: A review on application of particle swarm optimization in association rule mining. In: Satapathy, S.C., Udgata, S.K., Biswal, B.N. (eds.) Proc. of Int. Conf. on Front. of Intell. Comput. AISC, vol. 199, pp. 405–414. Springer, Heidelberg (2013)
4. Djenouri, Y., Drias, H., Habbas, Z., Mosteghanemi, H.: Bees swarm optimization for web association rule mining. In: 2012 IEEE/WIC/ACM International Conferences on Web Intelligence and Intelligent Agent Technology (WI-IAT), vol. 3, pp. 142–146. IEEE (2012)
5. Han, J., Pei, J., Yin, Y.: Mining frequent patterns without candidate generation. In: ACM SIGMOD Record, vol. 29, pp. 1–12. ACM (2000)
6. Kuo, R.J., Chao, C.M., Chiu, Y.T.: Application of particle swarm optimization to association rule mining. Applied Soft Computing 11(1), 326–336 (2011)
7. Yan, X., Zhang, C., Zhang, S.: Genetic algorithm-based strategy for identifying association rules without specifying actual minimum support. Expert Systems with Applications 36(2), 3066–3076 (2009)
8. Yang, X.-S.: A new metaheuristic bat-inspired algorithm. In: González, J.R., Pelta, D.A., Cruz, C., Terrazas, G., Krasnogor, N. (eds.) NICSO 2010. SCI, vol. 284, pp. 65–74. Springer, Heidelberg (2010)

Adaptive Mutation Behavior for Quantum Particle Swarm Optimization

Zhehuang Huang

School of Mathematics Sciences, Huaqiao University, 362021, China

Abstract. Quantum particle swarm optimization algorithm (QPSO) is a good optimization technique combines the ideas of quantum computing. Quantum particle swarm optimization algorithm has been successfully applied in many research and application areas. But traditional QPSO is easy to fall into local optimum value and the convergence rate is slow. To solve these problems, an improved quantum particle swarm optimization algorithm is proposed and implemented in this paper. The experiments on high dimensional function optimization showed that the improved algorithm have more powerful global exploration ability.

Keywords: QPSO, Mutation algorithm, Optimization algorithm.

1 Introduction

Particle swarm optimization is a new evolutionary algorithm proposed by the American social psychologist James Kennedy and electrical engineer Russell Eberhart [1] in 1995. In recent years, a series of papers have focused on the application of PSO, such as neural network training [2], communication networks [3], classification and clustering [4] and face recognition [5]. But PSO algorithm also showed some unsatisfactory issues in practical applications.To solve the problem of premature convergence,moore [6] proposed an optimization algorithm based on quantum behaviour which called quantum particle swarm optimization algorithm (QPSO) .This method combines the ideas of quantum optimization and local particle swarm optimization, use multi-objective function to obtain a least gate line design. Experiments show that QPSO has significant advantages than traditional PSO algorithm and other evolutionary algorithms (such as genetic algorithm). At present,there has been some research on the improvements and application of QPSO algorithm [7-10]. In this paper , we proposed an improved algorithm to improve the global search performance.

This paper is organized as follows. In section 2, the background of PSO and QPSO is presented.An improved algorithm is presented in section 3. In section 4, some experimental tests, results and conclusions are given. Section 5 concludes the paper.

L. Pan et al. (Eds.): BIC-TA 2014, CCIS 472, pp. 187–191, 2014.
© Springer-Verlag Berlin Heidelberg 2014

2   A Brief Introduction to PSO and QPSO

2.1   PSO Algorithm

Supposed the speed and position of the i-th particle in D-dimensional space were as follows: $V_i = [v_{i1}, v_{i2}, \cdots, v_{id}]$, $X_i = [x_{i1}, x_{i2}, \cdots, x_{id}]$.

It can determine the optimum position pbest of each moment of the respective particles by the objective function and the optimal position of the entire group gbest.Then the speed and position of the particle is updated based on the following formula:

$$v_{ij}(t+1) = wv_{ij}(t) + c_1 r_1 [p_{ij} - x_{ij}(t)] + c_2 r_2 [p_{gj} - x_{ij}(t)] \tag{1}$$

$$x_{ij}(t+1) = x_{ij}(t) + v_{ij}(t+1), j = 1, 2, \cdots, d \tag{2}$$

2.2   QPSO Algorithm

Quantum behaved particle swarm algorithm first described by the wave function, and then calculate the probability of the particles by the probability density function , and update particle position .

$$x_{ij}(t+1) = p_{ij}(t) \pm 0.5 \cdot L_{ij}(t) \cdot \ln(1/\mu_{ij}(t)) \tag{3}$$

where, μ is a random number in $(0, 1)$, p_{ij} is locally attractive factor.

$$p_{ij}(t) = \varphi_{ij}(t) \cdot P_{ij}(t) + (1 - \varphi_{ij}(t)) \cdot P_{gj}(t) \tag{4}$$

The final update equation of the particles is:

$$x_{ij}(t+1) = p_{ij}(t) \pm \beta |mbest_j(t) - x_{ij}(t)| \cdot \ln(1/\mu_{ij}(t)). \tag{5}$$

The QPSO algorithm as follows:

---

1) Variable initialization;
Initialize the particle swarm population size, dimensions, the maximum number of iterations variable
2) Generate particle swarm;
3) Calculate $\beta = (1 - 0.5) * (MAXITER - t)/MAXITER + 0.5$;
4) Calculation of the average optimal position;
5) Calculate local attractor;

$$p_{ij}(t) = \varphi_{ij}(t) \cdot P_{ij}(t) + (1 - \varphi_{ij}(t)) \cdot P_{gj}(t).$$

6) Updated particle position;

$$x_{ij}(t+1) = p_{ij}(t) \pm \beta |mbest_j(t) - x_{ij}(t)| \cdot \ln(1/\mu_{ij}(t)).$$

7) If iteration terminated, output optimal value; otherwise return 3 continue.

Algorithm 1. The QPSO algorithm

3   The Improved Algorithm (IQPSO)

Supposed $X = (x_1, x_2 \cdots x_n)$, where $x_1, x_2 \cdots x_n$ are status of the particles relactively.

3.1   Distribution Measurement Function

Distribution measurement function is used to describe the degree of dispersion of the particles.

$$D(t) = \frac{1}{m} \sum_{i=1}^{m} \sqrt{\sum_{d}^{D} (x_{id} - \bar{x}_d)^2} \tag{6}$$

where m is the population of particles; x_{id} represent the d dimension component of particle i; D is the dimension of the problem; $\bar{x}_d$ means average value of the d dimension component of all particles.

When $D(t)$ is more than a threshold, The algorithm is easy fall into local extremum. We must employ some strategies to improve the diversity of population.

3.2   An Mutation Algorithm

Supposed $X = (x_1, x_2 \cdots x_n)$ and is $X_v = (x_1^v, x_2^v \cdots x_n^v)$. X_{next} is the new position. Then the mutation process is represented as:

$$X_{next} = X + \frac{X_v - X}{\|X_v - X\|} \times step \times rand() .$$

where $rand()$ produces random numbers between 0 and 1. $Step$ means the maximum step size of particles. V means visual range of particles.

3.3   The Improved Algorithm

The improved algorithm is shown as follows:

1) Initialization particle swarm;
2) Updating the local optimum position and the global best position;
3) If the number of iterations is greater than half of the maximum number of iterations
and $D(t) > T_0$, then perform mutation behavior by equation (7);
4) Updating the particle position;
5) If iteration terminated, output optimal value; otherwise returns to step 2.

Algorithm 2. The improved algorithm

4 Experiment

A set of unconstrained benchmark functions was used to investigate the effect of the improved algorithm ,as is shown in Table 1.

Table 1. Functions used to test the effects of IQPSO

Function	Function expression	Optimal value
Sphere function	$f_1(x) = \sum_{t=1}^{n} x_t^2$	0
Ackey function	$f_2(x) = 20 + e - 20e^{-0.2\sqrt{\frac{\sum_{t=1}^{n} x_t^2}{n}}} - e^{\frac{\sum_{t=1}^{n} \cos(2\pi x_t)}{n}}$	0
Shaffer's function	$f_3(x) = 0.5 + \dfrac{(\sin\sqrt{x_1^2 + x_2^2})^2 - 0.5}{(1 + 0.001(x_1^2 + x_2^2))^2}$	0

The results are shown in Table 2. Each point is made from average values of over 10 repetitions.

Table 2. The testing performance comparison

Algorithm	QPSO		IQPSO	
	optimal	time(s)	optimal	time(s)
Sphere	1.15e-007	0.54	1.59e-011	0.61
Ackey	0.027	0.64	0.0027	0.73
shaffer	0.0097	0.56	3.45e-004	0.51

From Table 2, we can see no algorithm performs better than others for all five functions, but on average, IQPSO is better than QPSO. For Sphere function and Shaffer function, IQPSO algorithm can effectively improve the accuracy such that the optimal value is improved compared with the standard QPSO algorithm On the convergence time, no algorithm has obvious advantages than other algorithms.

5 Conclusions

In the paper, we proposed an improved quantum particle swarm optimization algorithm . Experiments show the improved algorithm have more powerful global exploration ability with faster convergence speed. In the future, we will apply this idea to other optimization tasks.

References

1. Kennedy, J., Eberhart, R.C.: Particle swarm optimization. In: Proceedings of IEEE International Conference on Neural Networks, pp. 1942–1948 (1995)
2. Chia-Feng, J.: A hybrid of genetic algorithm and particle swarm optimization for recurrent network design. IEEE Transactions Systems, Man and Cybernetics, Part B 34(2), 997–1006 (2004)
3. Mohemmed, A.W., Kamel, N.: Particle swarm optimization for Bluetooth scatter net formation. In: 2nd International Conference on Mobile Technology, Applications and Systems (2005)
4. Oliverira, L.S., Britto, A.S., Sabourin, R.: Improving Cascading classifiers with particle swarm optimization. In: Proceedings Eighth International Conference on Document Analysis and Recognition, pp. 570–574 (2005)
5. Senaratne, R., Halgamuge, S.: Optimised landmark model matching for face recognition. In: International Conference on Automatic Face and Gesture Recogniton, p. 6 (2006)
6. Moore, P., Venayagamoorthy, G.K.: Evolving combinational logic circuits using a hybrid quantum evolution and particle swarm inspired algorithm. In: Proceedings of the NASA/DoD Conference on Evolvable Hardware, pp. 97–102 (2005)
7. Mikki, S.M., Kishk, A.A.: Quantum particle swarm optimization for electromagnetics. IEEE Transactions on Antennas and Propagation (2006)
8. Li, S., et al.: A New QPSO Based BP Neural Network for Face Detection. In: Information and Engineering. Springer (2007)
9. Zhao, Y., et al.: Multilevel Minimum Cross Entropy Threshold Selection Based on Quantum Particle Swarm Optimization. In: Eighth ACIS International Conference on Software Engineering, Artificial Intelligence Networking, and Parallel/Distributed Computing, vol. 2, pp. 65–69 (2007)
10. Coelho, L.S., Alotto, P.: Global optimization of electromagnetic devices using an exponential quantum-behaved particle swarm optimize. In: 16th International Conference on Computation of Electron Magnetic Fields, pp. 1–3 (2007)

Bifurcation and Global Synchronization Analysis in Diffusively Coupled Calcium Oscillators

Yuhong Huo and Yi Zhou*

Department of Mathematics and Computational Science
Huainan Normal University
Dongshan Road(West), Huainan 232038, P.R. China
{hyh2004520,zhouyi3280}@163.com

Abstract. In this paper, bursting calcium behaviors of coupled biological oscillators are discussed. Point-cycle bursting of Hopf/Hopf type is obtained by numerical computations based on the fast-slow dynamic analysis. Furthermore, the synchronization behaviors of four coupled identical and unidentical cells are investigated by gap-junction, respectively. It is concluded that bigger synchronization threshold is demanded for the chain coupling than for the ring coupling. This work reveals that the coupling strength for unidentical cells to make them reach synchronization is far bigger than that for identical cells.

Keywords: Coupling, Bifurcation, Synchronization.

1 Introduction

Biological information is performed in groups of cells. Information is preferably transferred among coupled cells, so synchronization of coupled cells plays an important role in information processing and transduction [1]. Calcium ions (Ca^{2+}) is used everywhere in nature which is significant as an intracellular secondary messenger for the control of many cellular functions such as muscle contraction, secretion, metabolism, cell proliferation and death [2]. Although individual cell demonstrates spontaneous calcium waves, the waves are usually not simultaneous betweens cells. However, the emergence of synchronized calcium bursting may occur due to the cell-cell coupling by gap junctions. Experiments and theoretical analysis are given in excitable as well as in non-excitable cells for bursting calcium oscillations [3].

It is well known that synchronization performs a cruel function in message transmission. So far, many studies of synchronization of calcium oscillation depend on numerical simulations [4][5][6][7]. It is instructive guidance to the physiological experiments [9][10][11][12]. In the present paper, we are concerned with bifurcation and synchronization of Ca^{2+} oscillations from the point of view of theoretical analysis and stability theory. To meet this challenge, synchronization of unidentical cells has attracted a great deal of attention. Although our

---

* Corresponding author.

L. Pan et al. (Eds.): BIC-TA 2014, CCIS 472, pp. 192–197, 2014.

researches are obtained for four coupled cells, the theoretical method can be extended to other nervous systems [13].

The rest of this paper is organized as follows: model descriptions are given in Section 2. Bifurcation and synchronization under different types of bursting and connection strategies are investigated in Section 3. Numerical confirmations are performed to prove our theoretical analysis in Section 4. Furthermore, different synchronization regimes of four coupled bursting cells are obtained. Conclusions are given in the last section.

2   Model Description

The mathematical model proposed by Marhl et al. [8] is described by the following differential equations:

$$
\begin{aligned}
\frac{dCa_{cyt}}{dt} &= J_{ch} - J_{pump} + J_{leak} + J_{out} - J_{in} + J_{Ca\,Pr} - J_{Pr}, \\
\frac{dCa_{er}}{dt} &= \frac{\beta_{er}}{\rho_{er}}(J_{pump} - J_{ch} - J_{leak}), \\
\frac{dCa_m}{dt} &= \frac{\beta_m}{\rho_m}(J_{in} - J_{out}),
\end{aligned}
\tag{1}
$$

where

$$
J_{ch} = k_{ch}\frac{Ca_{cyt}^2}{Ca_{cyt}^2 + K_1^2}(Ca_{er} - Ca_{cyt}),\ J_{out} = k_{out}Ca_m
$$
$$
J_{pump} = k_{pump}Ca_{cyt},\quad J_{leak} = k_{leak}(Ca_{er} - Ca_{cyt}),\quad J_{Pr} = k_+ Ca_{cyt}\,Pr,
$$
$$
Pr_{tot} = Pr + Ca\,Pr,\quad J_{Ca\,Pr} = k_- Ca\,Pr,\quad J_{in} = k_{in}\frac{Ca_{cyt}^8}{Ca_{cyt}^8 + K_2^8},
$$
$$
Ca_{tot} = Ca_{cyt} + \frac{\rho_{er}}{\beta_{er}}Ca_{er} + \frac{\rho_m}{\beta_m}Ca_m + Ca\,Pr,
$$

The values of all parameters can be referred in [8].

3   Main Results

As $k_{ch} = 3800s^{-1}$, time series of point-cycle bursting of Hopf/Hopf type is shown in Fig. 1. It gives a good reproduction of the typical experimental observations.

The main characteristic of this point-cycle bursting is that the active and silent states of bursting depend on a stable steady state (abbreviated as 'point') as well as on a stable limit cycle (abbreviated as 'cycle') in the state space of the fast subsystem. According to Izhikevich's classification of bursting [5], this is called a point-cycle bursting of Hopf/Hopf type. The fast-slow dynamic analysis is similar to the above and omitted here.

In the following, we set $x = Ca_{cyt}, y = Ca_{er}, z = Ca_m, F(X,t) = (F_1(X_1), F_2(X_2), F_3(X_3)), X = (X_1, X_2, X_3)$, for the mathematical model (1) in case of one cell. Then $\dot{X}(t) = F(X,t) + gAX(t), A = (a_{ij})_{3\times3}, \sum\limits_{j=1}^{N} a_{ij} = 0, a_{ii} = -\sum\limits_{k=1,k\neq i}^{N} a_{ik}, i = 1, 2, \cdots, N.$, the event of complete synchronization is identical

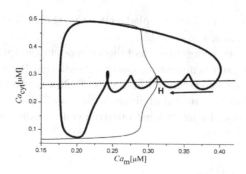

Fig. 1. Bifurcation diagram of "Hopf/Hopf" bursting for $k_{ch} = 3800s^{-1}$

to stability of synchronization manifold s(t). this insures that the coupling is popular and the synchronization manifold:$X(t) = s(t), \quad t \to +\infty$.

Consider the systems (1) for the single oscillator, we obtain the DF(s(t)) that is Jacobian matrix of vector function F(X(t)) at the synchronization manifold s(t).

then

$$A(s(t)) = DF(s(t)) + (DF(s(t)))^T$$

If the condition $g > \frac{1}{2}\frac{B}{|\lambda|}$ is satisfied, where B is defined $\frac{\det A(s(t))}{\det A_{22}(s(t))}$ and λ is obtained from the largest eigenvalue of matrix A, then complete synchronization takes place in the system (1) with two regular symmetrical coupling schemes: chain and ring.

4   Numerical Simulations

According to the previous section, we choose two different parameters values for $k_{ch1} = k_{ch2} = k_{ch3} = k_{ch4} = 3800s^{-1}$ and $k_{ch1} = k_{ch3} = 700s^{-1}, k_{ch2} = k_{ch4} = 3800s^{-1}$. Time courses are illustrated in Fig. 2 for g = 0.01. Meanwhile phase portraits are fulfilled in Fig. 3 and Fig. 5 for g = 0.01. Some correlation in cells can be seen in the $(Ca_{cyt}1, Ca_{cyt}2, Ca_{cyt}3)$ plane as shown in Fig. 4. Then the threshold of coupling strength g is revealed when max $(|Ca_{cyt}1 - Ca_{cyt}4|)$ tends to zero between two cells, and the state of synchronization is achieved.

Case 1: four bursting cells with the chain coupling scheme

The time series of four identical coupled biological cells is exhibited in Fig.2 (a) for the coupling strength g=0.001 with the chain coupling scheme. And the time series of four unidentical coupled biological cells is displayed in Fig.2 (b) for $k_{ch1} = k_{ch3} = 700s^{-1}, k_{ch2} = k_{ch4} = 3800s^{-1}$ with the chain coupling scheme.

The 3-D projection trajectory of phase diagram is obtained for three identical cells on the left side panel with the chain coupling scheme. Similarly, the 3-D phase diagram of three unidentical biological cells is shown in the right side panel with chain coupling scheme for $k_{ch1} = k_{ch3} = 700s^{-1}, k_{ch2} = k_{ch4} = 3800s^{-1}$.

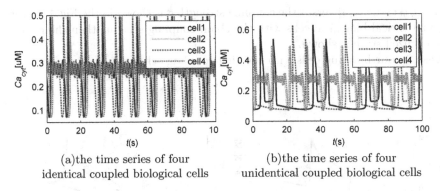

(a)the time series of four
identical coupled biological cells

(b)the time series of four
unidentical coupled biological cells

Fig. 2.

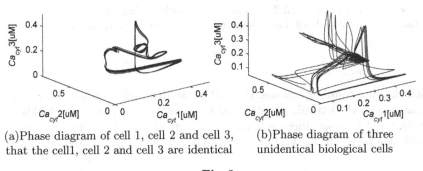

(a)Phase diagram of cell 1, cell 2 and cell 3,
that the cell1, cell 2 and cell 3 are identical

(b)Phase diagram of three
unidentical biological cells

Fig. 3.

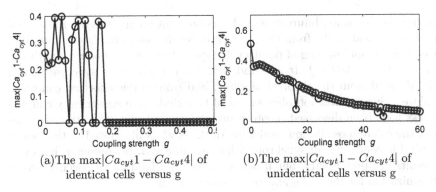

(a)The $\max|Ca_{cyt}1 - Ca_{cyt}4|$ of
identical cells versus g

(b)The $\max|Ca_{cyt}1 - Ca_{cyt}4|$ of
unidentical cells versus g

Fig. 4.

The threshold of the coupling strength g is observed for complete synchronization of two identical biological cells in the Fig.4 (a) with the chain coupling
scheme, then, the complete synchronization is obtained between cell1 and cell4
for the coupling strength g=0.18. And the maximum synchronization difference

$\max|Ca_{cyt}1 - Ca_{cyt}4|$ versus the coupling strength g is shown in the Fig.4 (b) for two unidentical biological cells with the chain coupling scheme, then the nearly synchronized state is shown.

Case 2: four bursting cells with the ring coupling scheme

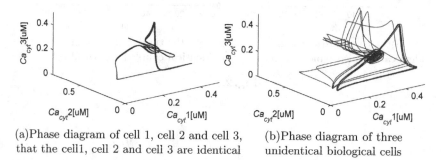

(a)Phase diagram of cell 1, cell 2 and cell 3, that the cell1, cell 2 and cell 3 are identical

(b)Phase diagram of three unidentical biological cells

Fig. 5.

With the ring coupling scheme, the 3-D phase diagram is obtained for three identical cells on the left side panel (a) for $k_{ch1} = k_{ch3} = k_{ch2} = k_{ch4} = 3800s^{-1}$. Similarly, the 3-D phase drawing of three unidentical biological cells is shown in the right side panel (b) for $k_{ch1} = k_{ch3} = 700s^{-1}, k_{ch2} = k_{ch4} = 3800s^{-1}$.

5   Conclusion

From the above results, bifurcation and synchronization analysis are researched in a mathematical model from the perspective of dynamics to classify bursting, that is, Hopf/Hopf bursting of point-cycle type, which can be observed with the parameter $k_{ch} = 3800s^{-1}$. It is found that the occurrence of synchronization can be decided from the theoretical study, and comparable effectual condition is achieved. Synchronization phenomena of two kinds of symmetrically coupled networks have been discussed theoretically and numerically. An entire explanation of the calcium oscillation model by Marhl et al. is illustrated in this paper and suitable conditions of synchronization are observed. In summary, however, our results are preliminary, but it suggests the threshold on the occurrence of synchronization for the chain and ring coupled scheme.

It has been proved that the complete synchronization threshold of the ring coupling is superior to that of the chain coupling for identical cells. And the results of the experiment indicated that coupling strength g for unidentical cells is far bigger than coupling strength g for identical cells. Although our researches are achieved for a fixed number of symmetrically coupled systems, but they may be help us better realize the phenomenon of synchronization and information coding mechanisms.

Acknowledgement. This work was supported by the Natural Science Foundation of China (No. 11202083 and 11372017) and the Foundation of Science and
Technology Bureau of Huainan (2012A01009) . The authors gratefully acknowledge the reviewers for their comments and suggestions that greatly improved the
presentation of this work.

References

1. Berridge, M.J.: Neuronal calcium signaling. Neuron 21(1), 13–26 (1998)
2. Matrosov, V.V., Kazantsev, V.B.: Bifurcation mechanisms of regular and chaotic
   network signaling in brain astrocytes. Chaos 21, 023103 (2011)
3. Wang, Q., et al.: Chaos synchronization of coupled neurons with gap junctions.
   Physics Letters A 356, 17–25 (2006)
4. Perc, M., Marhlb, M.: Synchronization of regular and chaotic oscillations: The
   role of local divergence and the slow passage effect-A Case Study on Calcium
   Oscillations. International Journal of Bifurcation and Chaos 14(08), 2735–2751
   (2004)
5. Izhikevich, E.M.: Neural excitability, spiking and bursting. International Journal
   of Bifurcation and Chaos 10, 1171–1266 (2000)
6. Schuster, S., et al.: Modeling of simple and complex calcium oscillations. European
   Journal of Biochemistry 269(5), 1333–1355 (2002)
7. Endo, M., Tanaka, M., Ogawa, Y.: Calcium-induced release of calcium from the
   sarcoplasmic reticulum of skinned skeletal muscle fibers. Nature 228, 34–36 (1970)
8. Marhl, M., Haberichter, T., Brumen, M., et al.: Complex calcium oscillations and
   the role of mitochondria and cytosolic proteins. Biosystems 57, 75–86 (2000)
9. Belykh, I., et al.: Synchronization of bursting neurons: what matters in the network
   topology. Physical Review Letters 94, 188101 (2005)
10. Kim, J.R., et al.: A design principle underlying the synchronization of oscillations
    in cellular systems. Journal of Cell Science 123(4), 537–543 (2010)
11. Ji, Q., Lu, Y.: Bifurcation and continuous transitions in a nonlinear model of intra-
    cellular calcium oscillations. International Journal of Bifurcation and Chaos 23(2),
    1350033 (2013)
12. Wang, H., et al.: Phase synchronization and its transition in two coupled bursting
    neurons: Theoretical and numerical analysis. Chinese. Physics 19(6), 60209 (2010)
13. Krupa, M., Vidal, A., Clment, F.: A network model of the periodic synchronization
    process in the dynamics of calcium concentration in GnRH neurons. The Journal
    of Mathematical Neuroscience 3(1), 1–24 (2013)
14. Pan, M., et al.: Bursting synchronization dynamics of pancreatic -cells with elec-
    trical and chemical coupling. Cognitive Neurodynamics 7(3), 197–212 (2013)
15. Catacuzzeno, L., et al.: A theoretical study on the role of $Ca2+$ activated $K+$
    channels in the regulation of hormone included $Ca2+$ oscillations and their syn-
    chronization in adjacent cells. Journal of Theoretical Biology 309, 103–112 (2012)

News Sentiments Grading Using Multiple Dictionaries Based Lexical Approach

Adeel Iqbal and Shoab Ahmad Khan

Dept. of Computer Engineering (DCE), College of E&ME,
National University of Sciences and Technology (NUST), Islamabad, PK
adeel.pieasian@gmail.com, shoabak@ceme.nust.edu.pk

Abstract. In sentiment analysis, traditionally the results are thought of on scale of three grades, positive, negative and neutral. Going beyond the traditional emphasis, an effective and result oriented methodology for step by step news sentiment grading into three, five and seven different categories based on scale and intensity of sentiment using multiple dictionaries based lexical approach is going to be detailed in this paper, so they can be well understood easily, with the domain not restricted to just one section or subjective part. Potential differences in addition to unveiling of the tricky and challenging parts of news sentiment processing and grading process are also part of the details. Implementation and experimentation using MPQA dataset at the end reveals the effectiveness of methodology in addition to basis and formalization.

Keywords: Sentiment analysis, Sentiments grading, Opinion mining, News sentiments analysis.

1 Introduction

Methodologies developed under Sentiment analysis or Opinion mining has indeed shown their significance for extraction of useful information. With so much going on in the world it is hard for law enforcing agencies as well as international and national analysts to track all news and have understanding of situation in different areas inside a country and as a whole all around the world. So, the need of solution is there that can help in analysis of situation with many aspects.

Positive, negative and neutral categorization of news, products and movies reviews as well as tweets is very much in but not much towards intensity based grading. The intensity or severity of sentiment associated can be extracted as how much good (good, better, best) or bad (bad, worse, worst) the news is. The detailed methodology in this paper caters the solution well using multiple dictionaries based lexical approach.

2 Related Work

P. Turney [1] and B. Pang [2] were amongst the starters who worked on sentiments analysis by detecting polarity using different methods but the work was

L. Pan et al. (Eds.): BIC-TA 2014, CCIS 472, pp. 198–203, 2014.

just up to two sections positive and negative, though so far it has become an active field of interest and a lot of methods and algorithms are defined to achieve the opinion results in different perspectives and subjectivities.

Using supervised and un-supervised learning [3] feature/aspect based mining work is also there but regarding polarity the use of adjective based processing is main part and bases of results as also being used by many others in their proposed methodologies [4][5][6] since the main emphasis were on the part that verbs meant to be presenting situation and adjectives denotes opinion.

Combinative approach using adverb, adjective and nouns [7] was a good advancement but the adjective scoring domain was not intensity based and dimensions were different. Also the main focus was highly subjective like politics related or stock market [8][9][10]. Contribution specifically regarding news sentiments analysis from A. Balahur and, R. Steinberger with in-depth and wide domain target unveiling some of the differences of news perspective from other text datasets i.e. reviews has its significance though [11].

3   Methodology and Implementation

Our methodology consists of opinion lexicons categories generation, data pre-processing, tagging and classification. Lexicon dictionaries creation is described in next section. Pre-Processing involves Data/Text Cleanup, Tokenization and Stemming. The source data needs to be cleaned up and tokenized as well as stemmed for further processing. The significance of stemming is very well explained in Tan Li Im and others work [12]. In Tagging section, Pre-processed data processed further for Part of Speech (POS) tagging and Opinion lexicons tagging based on lexicon dictionaries and in last step will be classified based on compuatation of associated sentiment based on tagging.

3.1   Opinion Lexicons Generation

To address the classification into different level of categories we have used multiple opinion/sentiment lexicons dictionaries that are created manually. Total of Twelve different dictionaries are used as given below, including two experimental dictionaries for crimes and the words from Bin lius collection [3].

1. Positive: Contains positive words list i.e. admire, saver, merciful etc.
2. Positive High Intensity: Contains positive words with high intensity affect i.e. cleaner, richer, smoother etc.
3. Positive Extreme Intensity: Contains positive words with extreme intensity affect i.e. cleanest, smoothest etc.
4. Negative: Contains negative words list i.e. abnormal, bias, unethical etc.
5. Negative High Intensity: Contains positive words with high intensity affect i.e. crueler, scarier etc.
6. Negative Extreme Intensity: Contains positive words with extreme intensity affect i.e. cruelest, scariest etc.

7. Negative Adjectives: Include words that decrements the value of a property i.e. barely, less etc.

8. Positive Adjectives: Includes words that increases value of property i.e. too, very

9. Inverting: Includes words that inverses the value of some text property i.e. not, neither.

10. Past: Contains words that indicate past as the emphasis of our sentiments analysis emphasize on current situation.

11. Crime Actions: Contains words related to actions associated to bad people like killing, murder, death, arrest etc. Created to address the action done by and against bad people.

12. Bad people: Includes bad elements of society i.e. terrorists, gangsters etc.

3.2   Opinion Lexicons Based Computational Association

After analysis and very careful consideration of news text patterns and keeping intact the serving basis of sentiments, the numerical values for Normal, High and Extreme Intensity are defined and associated as 1, 2 and 8 for positives and -1, -2 and -8 for negatives with intensity respectively. Also an adjective double or decreases the values accordingly based on presence in respective dictionary and Tags.

3.3   Classification and Grading

Grading includes three scales consisting of three, five and seven categories classification from very positive to very negative sentiment expression based on average numerical scores. The average score is not simply be sum divided by number of the sentences but only the sentences with positive or negative sentiment intimation are included in the calculation such that sum of positive and negative values is divided by total number of values.

Our grading starts from traditional three level grading which includes Positive/Good News, Negative/Bad News and Neutral News. Neutral News is going to be graded where all the sentences in News text will be either neutral or complement each other so the overall score of text becomes 0. News with Avg. sentiment score less than zero is graded as Negative, equal to zero Neutral and for Avg. sentiment score greater than zero is graded as Good news. This simply puts the positive and negative polarity based concept to action but the difference here is the calculative association based on intensity from multiple dictionaries.

Seven level grading includes indication of Best News with score greater than 3, Better News having score between 2 and 3, Good News with score between 0 and 2, Neutral News again with 0 score, Bad News with score between 0 and -2, Worse News score between -2 and -3 and Worst News having score less than -3. Again here the calculative association differs like mentioned in five levels.

4   Experiments and Results Analysis

The complete process put into action using python [13] programming language which was selected after a short survey, as it has an advanced Natural language processing toolkit (NLTK) [14] and other libraries that are very useful for Natural language processing and standard MPQA News dataset [15] is used for experimentation and finding out the effectiveness of our approach. MPQA News dataset v1.2 includes 535 News texts as well as manually and formally calculated results for each sentence in terms of different parameters like Polarity, Intensity, Subjectivity etc. on different topics and from different resources using a formal annotation scheme and process by the experts themselves [16].

To establish comparison on same scale for dataset results and ours, Polarity and Intensity annotated values translated to same scoring method. Polarity annotated results included positive, negative, both, neutral, uncertain-positive, uncertain-negative, uncertain-both and uncertain-neutral values whereas Intensity annotated values includes low, medium, high and extreme. These annotated result values are comparative to our scale used in algorithm-1 like combinative value of positive-extreme to negative-extreme can be easily expressed from 8 to -8 for each sentence.

The results of grading compared and analyzed as for three level grading the accuracy found out as 72.14% which as basis a pretty good start under lexical methodology considering large domain addressed nearly matching humans as human raters typically agree 79% [17].

Five level grading results were recorded as 54.2% full matched and 17.94% same section considering Good and Better one section and Bad and Worse the other section. As being in same section they are classified almost correctly so considering them 50-50 the final accuracy can be considered as 63.17%. Following Fig. 1 illustrates different levels of grading's accuracy.

Last but not least, seven level grading results are found as 44.85% full matched, 23.36% nearly matched under same section and next to each other grade i.e.

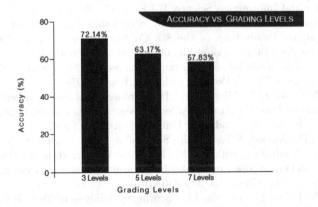

Fig. 1. Accuracy vs. Grading Levels

Good and Better. Also 3.92% results matched to be in same section but not in consecutive grades but like Bad and Worst. Continuing with same 50-50 consideration the final results can be said as 57.83% accurate.

5   Conclusions and Future Work

Starting from complexity and challenges of news text analysis, we have successfully detailed a complete and comprehensive methodology for news sentiments analysis and categorization into multiple levels of grading indicating sentiment intensity using multiple manually created lexicons dictionaries. Also the details of dictionaries and algorithms for computation are described. Then the process was implemented successfully on MPQA dataset with results from 72.14% to 57.83% accuracy for three to seven levels grading respectively.

For further improvement the first thing that can be done is the improvement of lexicon dictionaries. We have targeted whole set of news in all categories but the number of distinct lexicon dictionaries as per sector of news like crime, business, sports etc. can be created for separate results of each section and applied separately to improve the accuracy.

References

1. Turney, P.: Thumbs Up or Thumbs Down? Semantic Orientation Applied to Unsupervised Classification of Reviews. In: Proceedings of the Association for Computational Linguistics, pp. 417–424 (2002)
2. Pang, B., Lee, L.: Seeing stars: Exploiting class relationships for sentiment categorization with respect to rating scales. In: Proceedings of the Association for Computational Linguistics (ACL), pp. 115–124 (2005)
3. Liu, B.: Opinion Mining, Sentiment Analysis, and Opinion Spam Detection (2005-2014), http://www.cs.uic.edu/~liub/FBS/sentiment-analysis.html
4. Mizumoto, K., Yanagimoto, H., Yoshioka, M.: Sentiment Analysis of Stock Market News with Semi-supervised Learning. In: 11th International Conference on Computer and Information Science, IEEE/ACIS (2012)
5. Hatzivassiloglou, V., McKeown, K.R.: Predicting the semantic orientation of adjectives. In: Proceedings of the 8th Conference on European Chapter of the Association for Computational Linguistics, pp. 174–181 (1997)
6. Godbole, N., Srinivasaiah, M., Skiena, S.: Large-Scale Sentiment Analysis for News and Blogs. In: ICWSM, Boulder, Colorado, USA (2007)
7. Sing, J.K., Sarkar, S., Mitra, T.K.: Development of a Novel Algorithm for Sentiment Analysis Based on Adverb-Adjective-Noun Combinations, Dept. of Computer Science & Engineering, Jadavpur University, Kolkata (2012)
8. Davulcu, H., Ahmed, S.T., Gokalp, S., Temkit, M.H., Taylor, T., Woodward, M., Amin, A.: Analyzing Sentiment Markers Describing Radicaland Counter-Radical Elements in Online News. In: 2010 IEEE Second International Conference on Social Computing (SocialCom), pp. 335–340 (2010)
9. Kaya, M., Fidan, G., Toroslu, I.H.: Sentiment Analysis of Turkish Political News. In: 2012 IEEE/WIC/ACM International Conference Web Intelligence and Intelligent Agent Technology (WI-IAT), pp. 174–180 (2012)

10. Mizumoto, K., Yanagimoto, H., Yoshioka, M.: Sentiment Analysis of Stock Market News with Semi-supervised Learning. In: 2012 IEEE/ACIS 11th International Conference on Computer and Information Science, pp. 325–328 (2012)
11. Balahur, A., Steinberger, R.: Rethinking Sentiment Analysis in the News: from Theory to Practice and back. In: Proceedings of the '1st Workshop on Opinion Mining and Sentiment Analysis, University of Sevilla, pp. 1–12 (2009)
12. Im, T.L., San, P.W., On, C.K., Alfred, R., Anthony, P.: Analysing Market Sentiment in Financial News using Lexical Approach. In: IEEE Conference on Open Systems, ICOS (2013)
13. Python, https://www.python.org/
14. Natural Language Toolkit, http://www.nltk.org/
15. Multi-Perspective Question Answering (MPQA) Opinion Corpus v1.2, http://mpqa.cs.pitt.edu/corpora/mpqa_corpus/mpqa_corpus_1_2
16. Ogneva, M.: How Companies Can Use Sentiment Analysis to Improve their Business (April 19, 2010), http://mashable.com/2010/04/19/sentiment-analysis
17. From Wikipedia, the free encyclopedia, http://en.wikipedia.org/wiki/Sentiment_analysis

Uniform Solution to Partition Problem Using P Systems with Membrane Division

Yun Jiang* and Zhiqiang Chen

School of Computer Science and Information Engineering,
Chongqing Technology and Business University, Chongqing 400067, China
jiangyun83@gmail.com

Abstract. Cell-like P systems are a class of distributed and parallel computing models inspired from the structure and the functioning of living cells. Such systems with membrane division (corresponding to the mitosis behavior of living cells) can theoretically generate exponential working space in linear time, therefore providing a possible way to solve computational hard problems in feasible time by a space-time trade-off. In this work, we construct a family of P system with membrane division to solve Partition problems, and achieve a polynomial time solution (with respect to the size of the problems). Furthermore, we prove that the systems are constructed in a uniform manner and work in a confluent way.

Keywords: Membrane computing, P system, Membrane division, Uniform solution, NP-complete problem.

1 Introduction

Membrane computing introduced by Gh.Păun in 2000 [1], is now known as a new and hot branch in natural computing. In membrane computing, a class of computing models, usually called P systems, are investigated by abstracting ideas from the structure and the functioning of a single cell and tissues, even from human brain. Till now, mainly three classes of P systems are investigated: cell-like P systems(generally called P systems) [1], tissue P systems [2], and spiking neural P systems [3].

Variants of these three classes of P systems, as well as their computational properties have been investigated [4,5,6]; An overview of membrane computing or P systems can be found in [7,8], with up-to-date information available at the membrane computing website [9]. For an introduction to membrane computing, one may consult [10] and [11]. In the present work, we deal with a variant of cell-like P systems, called P systems with membrane division [12].

P system with membrane division consists of a hierarchical membrane structure, a number of objects and evolution rules. In each membrane, objects and evolution rules are present. By using evolution rules, the whole membrane structure and the objects contained in membranes evolve. When the evolution of the

---

* Corresponding author.

L. Pan et al. (Eds.): BIC-TA 2014, CCIS 472, pp. 204–210, 2014.
© Springer-Verlag Berlin Heidelberg 2014

system stops, a computation result is obtained, and the result can be defined in several ways such as the number of objects inside a specified membrane or a vector consisting of the number of objects in each membrane.

P systems with membrane division are proved to be universal [13,14], and have been used to solve computational hard problems [15]. All the P systems with membrane division mentioned above work in a synchronized and parallel way: a global clock is assumed to synchronize the execution of rules in the system. However, this assumption is not suitable from a biological point of view, the time of executing certain biological processes could vary because of external uncontrollable conditions. Therefore, it seems crucial to investigate P systems when such timing assumption is not used.

Traditional P systems are considered by adding a time mapping to specify the execution time of each rule. The systems always generating the same results for an arbitrary time mapping are called as time-free P systems. It is quite interesting to investigate time-free P systems because they are independent of the time mapping assignment. Time-free spiking neural P systems has been introduced in [16] and its universality has been investigated [17,18].

In this work, we deal with computational efficiency of time-free P systems by solving Partition problems, that is, the correctness of the solution does not depend on the precise timing of the involved processes. Moreover, the family of time-free P systems are constructed in a uniform way.

2 Time-Free Solutions to Decision Problems by P Systems with Membrane Division

It is started by briefly recalling the formal definition of P systems with membrane division introduced in [12], and then a timed extension of such systems is reviewed, followed by a description of time-free P systems with membrane division. Finally, some notions of time-free solutions to decision problems by such systems are discussed.

2.1 P Systems with Membrane Division

A *P system with membrane division* of degree m is a construct

$$\Pi = (O, H, \mu, w_1, \ldots, w_m, R),$$

where:

(i) $m \geq 1$ is the initial degree of the system;
(ii) O is the alphabet of *objects*;
(iii) H is a finite set of *labels* for membranes;
(iv) μ is the initial *membrane structure*, consisting of m membranes; membranes are labelled (not necessarily in an injective way) with elements of H and are electrically polarized, being possible charge positive $(+)$, negative $(-)$ or neutral (0);

(v) $w_1, \ldots, w_m$ are strings over O, describing the *initial multisets of objects* placed in the m regions of μ;

(vi) R is a finite set of *evolution rules*, of the following types:

(a) $[a \to v]_h^\alpha$, $h \in H, a \in O, \alpha \in \{+, -, 0\}, v \in O^*$;

(b) $a[\ ]_h^{\alpha_1} \to [b]_h^{\alpha_2}$, $h \in H, \alpha_1, \alpha_2 \in \{+, -, 0\}, a, b \in O$;

(c) $[a]_h^{\alpha_1} \to [\ ]_h^{\alpha_2}b$, $h \in H, \alpha_1, \alpha_2 \in \{+, -, 0\}, a, b \in O$;

(d) $[a]_h^\alpha \to b$, $h \in H, \alpha \in \{+, -, 0\}, a, b \in O$;

(e) $[a]_h^{\alpha_1} \to [b_1]_h^{\alpha_2}[b_2]_h^{\alpha_3}$, $h \in H, \alpha_1, \alpha_2, \alpha_3 \in \{+, -, 0\}, a, b, c \in O$;

(f) $[[\ ]_{k_1}^{\alpha_1} \cdots [\ ]_{h_k}^{\alpha_1}[\ ]_{h_{k+1}}^{\alpha_2} \cdots [\ ]_{h_n}^{\alpha_2}]_{h_0}^{\alpha_0} \to [[\ ]_{h_1}^{\alpha_3} \cdots [\ ]_{h_k}^{\alpha_3}]_{h_0}^{\alpha_5}[[\ ]_{h_{k+1}}^{\alpha_4} \cdots [\ ]_{h_n}^{\alpha_4}]_{h_0}^{\alpha_6}$, $k \geq 1, n > k, h_i \in H, 0 \leq i \leq n$ and $\alpha_0, \ldots, \alpha_6 \in \{+, -, 0\}$ with $\{\alpha_1, \alpha_2\} = \{+, -\}$.

The previous rules can be considered as "standard" rules of P systems with membrane division; the following rule can be seen as the extension of rule (e).

(e') $[a]_{h_1}^{\alpha_1} \to [b]_{h_2}^{\alpha_2}[c]_{h_3}^{\alpha_3}$, $h_1, h_2, h_3 \in H, \alpha_1, \alpha_2, \alpha_3 \in \{+, -, 0\}, a, b, c \in O$

The difference of the rules of type (e) and type (e') is that the resulting membranes obtained by applying the rules of type (e) have the same label with their parent membrane, and the resulting membranes obtained by applying the rules of type (e') can have different labels with their parent membrane.

2.2   Timed P Systems with Membranes Division

We recall the notion of timed P systems from [19] (in our case, P systems with membrane division).

A *timed P system with membrane division* $\Pi(e) = (O, H, \mu, w_1, \ldots, w_m, R, e)$ can be constructed by adding to a P system with membrane division $\Pi = (O, H, \mu, w_1, \ldots, w_m, R)$ a time-mapping $e : R \to \mathbb{N}$, which specifies the execution time for each rule in the system.

A timed P system with membrane division $\Pi(e)$ works in the following way. An external clock is assumed to mark time-units of equal length and to start from instant 0. According to this clock, the step t of computation is defined by the period of time that goes from instant $t - 1$ to instant t. For some rule r from types (a) – (f) and (e'), we denote $e(r)$ as the time which rule r lasts, that is, execution of rule r takes $e(r)$ time units to complete. Therefore, if the execution is started at instant i, the rule is completed at instant $i + e(r)$ and the resulting objects and membranes become available only at the beginning of step $i + e(r) + 1$. When a rule r is started, the occurrences of symbol-objects and the membrane subject to this rule cannot be anymore subject of other rules.

A *recognizer timed P system with membrane division* is a *timed P system with membrane division* such that: (i) the working alphabet contains two distinguished elements **yes** and **no**; (ii) all computations halt; and (iii) if $\mathcal{C}$ is a computation of the system, then either object **yes** or object **no** (but not both) must appear in the environment when the computation halts.

2.3   Time-Free Solutions to Decision Problems by P Systems with Membrane Division

In this subsection, we give the definition of time-free solutions to decision problems by P systems with membrane division.

In a timed P systems with membrane division, a computation step is called a *rule starting step* (RS-step, for short) if at this step at least one rule starts its execution. In the following definition of time-free solutions to decision problems by P systems with membrane division, we will only count RS-steps (i.e., steps in which some object "starts" to evolve or some membrane "starts" to change).

Let $X = (I_X, \Theta_X)$ be a decision problem. We say that X is solvable in a *time-free polynomial time* by a family of recognizer P systems with active membranes $\Pi = \Pi_u, u \in I_X$ (we also say that the family Π is a *time-free solution* to the decision problem X) if the following items are true:

- the family Π is polynomially uniform by a Turing machines; that is, there exists a deterministic Turing machine working in polynomial time which constructs the system Π_u from the instance $u \in I_X$.
- the family Π is *time-free sound* (with respect to X); that is, for any time-mapping e, the following property holds: if for each instance of the problem $u \in I_X$ such that there exists an accepting computation of $\Pi_u(e)$, we have $\Theta_X(u) = 1$.
- the family Π is *time-free complete* (with respect to X); that is, for any time-mapping e, the following property holds: if for each instance of the problem $u \in I_X$ such that $\Theta_X(u) = 1$, every computation of $\Pi_u(e)$ is an accepting computation.
- the family Π is *time-free polynomially bounded*; that is, there exists a polynomial function $p(n)$ such that for any time-mapping e and for each $u \in I_X$, all computations in $\Pi_u(e)$ halt in, at most, $p(|u|)$ RS-steps.

3   Uniform Time-Free Solution to Partition Problem

In this section, a uniform time-free solution for partition problem by a family of time-free P systems with membrane division is presented. The correctness of the solution does not depend on the execution time of the rules. It is noticed that in these systems the number of objects involved in the rules of type (a) has been extended. Specifically, these extension rules are of the form

(a') $[u \to v]_h$, $h \in H$, $u, v \in O^*$,

by which a multiset of objects can evolve.

Partition problem is a well-known NP-complete problems[20]. Let us recall that a partition of a set V is a family of non-empty pairwise disjoint subsets of V such that the union of the subsets of the family is equal to V. The partition problem can be stated as follows: Let V be a finite set and w be a weight function on V, $w : V \to \mathbb{N}$ (that is, an additive function), determine whether or not there exists a partition $\{V_1, V_2\}$ of V such that $w(V_1) = w(V_2)$.

Theorem 1. Partition *problem can be solved by a family of P systems with membrane division with rules of types (a'), (b), (c), (d) (e') in a linear time with respect to the size parameters.*

Proof. Let us consider an instance of Partition problem $C = (V, w)$, where $V = \{v_1, v_2, \ldots, v_n\}$ and w is defined as $w_i = w(v_i)$ for each $i \in \{1, 2, \ldots, n\}$. Such instance will also be represented by $C = (n, (w_1, w_2, \ldots, w_n))$. We denote that $m = w_1 + w_2 + \cdots + w_n$.

For the given instance C, we construct the P system with membrane division

$$\Pi_C = (O, H, \mu, w_0, w_1, R),$$

where

* $O = \{A_i, B_i, \overline{A}_i \mid 1 \le i \le n\} \cup \{\text{yes}, \text{no}, p, q\}$ is the alphabet;
* $H = \{0, 1, 2, \ldots, n+4\}$ is the set of labels of the membranes;
* $\mu = [\ [\ ]_1^0]_0^0$ is initial membrane structure;
* $w_0 = \text{no}$ (that is, membrane 0 contains object no in the initial configuration);
* $w_1 = A_1 A_2 \ldots A_n \overline{A}_1 \overline{A}_2 \ldots \overline{A}_n \text{yes}$ is the initial multiset contained in membrane 1;
* R is the set of rules of the following forms:
  - $G_{1i} : [A_i]_i \to [B_i]_{i+1}[\lambda]_{i+1}, 1 \le i \le n,$
  - $C_{1i} : [B_i\overline{A}_i \to p^{w_i}]_{n+1}, 1 \le i \le n,$
  - $C_{2i} : [\overline{A}_i \to q^{w_i}]_{n+2}, 1 \le i \le n,$
  - $C_{3j} : [\ ]_{n+j} \to [\ ]_{n+j+1}, j = 1, 2, 3, 4,$
  - $C_4 : [pq \to \lambda]_{n+3},$
  - $O_1 : [p]_{n+4} \to \lambda,$
  - $O_2 : [q]_{n+4} \to \lambda,$
  - $O_3 : [\text{no}]_0^0 \to [\ ]_0^+ \text{no},$
  - $O_4 : [\ ]_0^- \text{no} \to [\text{no}]_0^-,$
  - $O_5 : [\text{yes}]_{n+5} \to [\ ]_{n+5} \text{yes}.$
  - $O_6 : [\text{yes}]_0^+ \to [\ ]_0^- \text{yes}$

Now let us briefly describe how this system works.

At the first step, rules G_{1i} and O_3 must be started at the same time. After $e(O_3)$ steps, the object no will arrive at the environment and the charge of skin membrane changes from neutral to positive. It needs one RS-step. By using division rules of G_{1i}, the system generate 2^n membranes with label $n+1$, and each of them encode a different subset of V. It takes n RS-steps to complete rules of G_{1i}. The generation stage needs n RS-steps.

In the checking stage, the system checks if there exists a partition of V whose weights equal. After the generation stage, the rules of of C_{1i}, C_{2i} and C_{3j} are started, and they are applied in the non-deterministic maximally parallel manner. In this way, we have in each membrane with label $n+3$ the weights of a pair of complementary subsets, encoded by the objects of p and q, respectively. With application of the rules C_4, pairs of objects p and q are removed from the membranes labelled by $n+3$. Therefore, if a membrane $n+3$ encodes a pair of subsets of weight m, then all the objects p and q will be deleted in this membrane. Otherwise, at least on object p or q will remain in this membrane. The generation stage needs three RS-steps.

In the answer stage, there are two possible situations:

- Let us suppose that there exists a pair of complementary subsets of V with weight m. In this case, there will exist a membrane $n+5$ such that it contains only object **yes**. Therefore, the rules O_5 and O_6 will be applied one by one. For a given time-mapping, after $e(O_5) + e(O_6)$ steps (where there are two RS-steps), object **yes** is released to the environment, and the polarization of skin membrane changes from positive to negative. After the execution of rule O_6 completes, the rule O_4 is enabled and applied, and object **no** enters membrane with label 0. In this way, when the computation halts, one copy of **yes** appears in the environment, telling us that this is an accepting computation.
- Let us suppose now that there does not exist a pair of complementary subsets of V such that both of their weights equal to m. In this case, all the membranes labelled by $n + 3$ contain either objects p or q (but not both of them). Therefore, either rule O_1 or O_2 can be applied in such membranes, and the rules O_4, O_5, O_6 cannot be applied. In this case, when the computation halts, object **no** remains in the environment, telling us that this is a rejecting computation.

The family $\mathbf{\Pi} = \{ \Pi_C \mid C$ is an instance of **Partition** problem$\}$ is polynomially uniform because the construction of P systems described in the proof can be done in polynomial time by a Turing machine:

- the size of the alphabet is $3n + 4$;
- the initial number of membranes is 2;
- the cardinality of the initial multisets is 2;
- the initial number of objects is $2n + 2$;
- the total number of evolution rules is $3n + 11$;
- the upper bound for the length of the rules is 3.

4   Conclusions and Remarks

In this work we considered the computational efficiency of time-free P system and obtained a uniform time-free solution to a famous NP-complete problem, Partition problem. Although other NP-complete problems can be reduced to Partition problem in polynomial time, it still remains open how to compute the reduction by P systems. In the future, we should give direct time-free solutions to other NP-complete problems or even PSPACE-complete problems. Furthermore, the computational completeness of time-free P systems is not contained in this study and it remains open if time-free P systems are Turing complete. This is another interesting topic to be investigated.

Acknowledgments. This work was supported by Natural Science Foundation of CQ CSTC (No. cstc2012jjA40059 and No. cstc2012jjA40041), Science Research Fund of Chongqing Technology and Business University (No. 2013-56-01 and No. 2011-56-05.

References

1. Păun, G.: Computing with Membranes. J. Comput. System Sci. 61(1), 108–143 (2000)
2. Martin-Vide, C., Pazos, J., Păun, G., Rodriguez-Parón, A.: Tissue P Systems. Theor. Comput. Sci. 296(2), 295–326 (2003)
3. Ionescu, M., Păun, G., Yokomori, T.: Spiking Neural P Systems. Fundam. Inform. 71(2-3), 279–308 (2006)
4. Pan, L., Păun, G.: Spiking Neural P Systems with Anti-Spikes. Int. J. of Computers, Communications & Control IV(3), 273–282 (2009)
5. Pan, L., Păun, G.: Spiking Neural P Systems: An Improved Normal Form. Theor. Comput. Sci. 411, 906–918 (2010)
6. Pan, L., Pérez-Jiménez, M.J.: Computational Complexity of Tissue-like P Systems. Journal of Complexity 26(3), 296–315 (2010)
7. Păun, G., Rozenberg, G., Salomaa, A. (eds.): Handbook of Membrane Computing. Oxford University Press, Oxford (2010)
8. Zhang, G., Pan, L.: A Survey of Membrane Computing as a New Branch of Natural Computing. Chinese Journal of Computers 33(2), 208–214 (2010)
9. The P System Website, http://ppage.psystems.eu
10. Păun, G.: Membrane Computing. An Introduction. Springer, Berlin (2002)
11. Ciobanu, G., Pérez-Jiménez, M.J., Păun, G.: Applications of Membrane Computing. Springer, Berlin (2006)
12. Păun, G.: P Systems with Active Membranes: Attacking NP Complete Problems. J. Automata. Lang. Combin. 6(1), 75–90 (2001)
13. Dassow, J., Păun, G.: On the Power of Membrane Computing. J. Universal Comput. Sci. 5(2), 33–49 (1999)
14. Păun, G.: Computing with Membranes. J. Comput. System Sci. 61(1), 108–143 (2000)
15. Păun, G., Suzuki, Y., Tanaka, H., Yokomori, T.: On the Power of Membrane Division in P Systems. Theor. Comput. Sci. 324(1), 61–85 (2004)
16. Pan, L., Zeng, X., Zhang, X.: Time-free Spiking Neural P Systems. Neural Computation 23, 1320–1342 (2011)
17. Cavaliere, M.: Time-free Solution to Hard Computational Problems. In: 10th Brainstorming Week on Membrane Computing, Sevilla, pp. 204–210 (2012)
18. Song, T., Zheng, H., He, J., Zhang, L.: Time-free Solution to Hamilton Path Problems Using P Systems with d-Division. Journal of Applied Mathmatics 2013, Article ID 975798, 7 pages (2013), doi:10.1155/2013/975798
19. Cavaliere, M., Sburlan, D.: Timed-independent P systems. In: Mauri, G., Păun, G., Jesús Pérez-Jímenez, M., Rozenberg, G., Salomaa, A. (eds.) WMC 2004. LNCS, vol. 3365, pp. 239–258. Springer, Heidelberg (2005)
20. Garey, M., Johnson, D.: Computers and Intractability. A Guide to the Theory of NP-Completeness. W.H. Freeman and Company, New York (1979)

Relating the Languages of Transition P Systems and Evolution-Communication P Systems with Energy

Richelle Ann B. Juayong and Henry N. Adorna

Algorithms & Complexity Lab, Department of Computer Science
University of the Philippines Diliman, 1101 Quezon City, Philippines
{rbjuayong,hnadorna}@up.edu.ph

Abstract. In this work, we explored the relation of languages generated by Evolution-Communication P systems with energy (ECPe systems) and Transition P systems without dissolution (TP systems). In particular, we have shown that for every language generated by a noncooperative TP system, there exists an ECPe system that can generate the same language. We also look into languages for some cooperative TP systems, specifically TP systems where every object required for a cooperative rule can also evolve independently. The languages of TP systems with such property can also be generated by ECPe systems.

Keywords: Membrane computing, Evolution-Communication P systems with Energy, Transition P system.

1 Introduction

Evolution-Communication P system with energy (ECPe system) is a cell-like P system model introduced in [2]. Being a variant of Evolution-Communication P system [3], an ECPe system uses separate rules for evolution and communication. As the name suggests, the main difference distinguishing ECPe system from the previous model is the presence of a special object e (for energy). During evolution, some quanta of object e can be produced. These will be imposed when transporting objects. Evolution rule in an ECPe system is non-cooperative. Only a single object is required to enable such rule type. A communication rule takes the form of either a symport or an antiport rule. For every communication rule, only one object can be transported provided a threshold amount of 'energy' is satisfied.

The initial motivation for ECPe system is the analysis of communication complexity using object e as communication cost. To this goal, there are previous literatures that look into its capability as a problem solver [4] and as a number generator [2,5]. This paper contributes to the study of ECPe systems as string generators by relating the language of ECPe systems with that of a basic membrane computing model called Transition P systems (TP systems) [6]. In the latter model, evolution and communication can be accomplished in a single

L. Pan et al. (Eds.): BIC-TA 2014, CCIS 472, pp. 211–215, 2014.

time step. Rules in TP system may also have one or more (copies of) objects as triggers to enable a rule. Furthermore, a rule can produce several objects in several target locations. While the initial TP system includes rules that operate on membranes through membrane dissolution, in this paper, we consider TP systems that do not employ dissolution rules.

2   Main Results

We only consider models that function as a string generator. In this case, we follow the specifications in [1] where the result of a successful computation is the sequence of objects sent to the environment. The order of how objects are sent to the environment dictates their position in the output string. In the case where multiple objects are sent at a given time, the output string is formed from any of their permutations. For the purpose of our study, we decompose a TP system rule $u \to v$ into $u_1^{q_1} \ldots u_d^{q_d} \to v$ where integer $d \geq 1$, each u_f is an element of the alphabet of TP and each integer $q_f \geq 1$, $1 \leq f \leq d$. If $d \geq 2$, $u_f \neq u_{f'}$, $1 \leq f < f' \leq d$. The q_f's represent the copy of objects of u_f needed to enable a rule. We categorize such form into three types based on the number of required objects and their copies in a rule's left-hand side. Specifically, a rule takes one of the following types:

(a) $u_1 \to v$ – A rule r of this type is a non-cooperative rule.
(b) $u_1 u_2 \ldots u_d \to v$ where $d \geq 2$. – In this type, $q_f = 1$ for all $1 \leq f \leq d$. We shall call a rule r of this type as a cooperative rule with distinct objects.
(c) $u_1^{q_1} \ldots u_d^{q_d} \to v$ where $d \geq 1$ and at least one $q_f \geq 2$ ($1 \leq f \leq d$). – We shall call a rule r of this type as a cooperative rule with non-distinct objects. While type (b) allows only one copy of every u_f, this type allows a u_f to have more than one copy.

Theorem 1. *For every TP system Π where all rules are non-cooperative, there exists an ECPe systems $\overline{\Pi}$ such that $L(\Pi) = L(\overline{\Pi})$.*

In our proof of Theorem 1, we first define a $\overline{\Pi}$ from a given Π. Figure 1 shows an instance of Π and its corresponding $\overline{\Pi}$. We then show that a configuration C in Π can be associated to a unique configuration $\overline{C}$ in $\overline{\Pi}$. The collective effect of every transition $C \Rightarrow C'$ in the former is equivalent to a three-step computation $\overline{C} \Rightarrow^* \overline{C}'$ in the latter. Using this, we showed that a string $s \in L(\Pi)$ if and only if $s \in L(\overline{\Pi})$.

In exploring TP systems with cooperative rules whose language can be generated by an ECPe system, it is essential to define the role of objects in enabling rules.

Definition 1. *Given a TP system Π, a rule r and an object o in the left-hand side of r, we say that object o is an independent trigger in region h if r is a rule in h and r is non-cooperative. If rule r is a cooperative rule in region h, then object o is a dependent trigger. We categorize each object o in region h as*

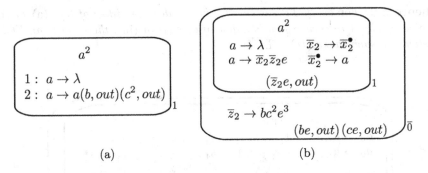

(a)   (b)

Fig. 1. An illustration of Theorem 1. Fig (a) is a TP system (from [1]) while Fig (b) is its corresponding ECPe systems.

(i) *both dependent and independent trigger – if there exists a cooperative and a non-cooperative rule in region h, both having o in its left-hand side.*

(ii) *only a dependent trigger – if all rules in region h having o in their left-hand side are cooperative rules.*

(iii) *non-trigger – if there doesn't exist a rule r in region h that uses o in its left-hand side.*

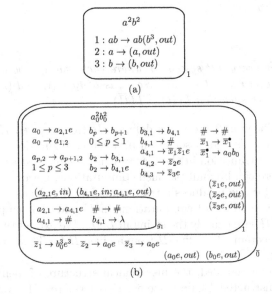

(b)

Fig. 2. An illustration of Theorem 2. Fig (a) is a TP system while Fig (b) is its corresponding ECPe systems.

Theorem 2. *For every TP system Π where rules are either of type (a) or (b) and every object in each region is either of type (i) or (iii), there exists an ECPe systems $\overline{\Pi}$ such that $L(\Pi) = L(\overline{\Pi})$.*

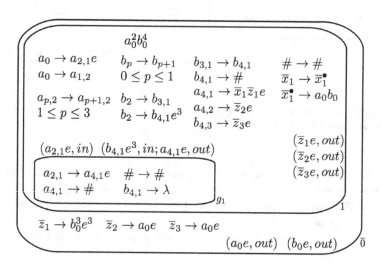

Fig. 3. An illustration of Theorem 3. Figure shows an $\overline{\Pi}$ corresponding to a modified TP system Π in Fig (a) of Figure 2 (results from replacing rule $ab \to ab(b^3, out)$ with rule $ab^3 \to ab^3(b^3, out)$).

Theorem 3. *For every TP system Π where each rule can be any of type (a), (b) and (c) and every object in each region is of type (i) and (iii), there exists an ECPe systems $\overline{\Pi}$ such that $L(\Pi) = L(\overline{\Pi})$.*

In our proof of Theorem 2, we again define a $\overline{\Pi}$ from a given Π (see Figure 2 for an illustration). Also, an association between configurations in Π and $\overline{\Pi}$ is defined such that a transition in the former can be simulated as a computation in the latter. There can be multiple such computations, however, all other computations except for one produces a trap symbol $\#$ that leads to a non-halting computation. This analysis of computations in Π and $\overline{\Pi}$ is employed to show that strings in $L(\Pi)$ are exactly the string in $L(\overline{\Pi})$. We extend the ECPe system constructed in Theorem 2 to define $\overline{\Pi}$ from a given Π for Theorem 3 (see Figure 3 for illustration).

In all TP systems handled, the hierarchical structure of membranes is preserved in our constructed ECPe systems. Furthermore, TP systems that use rules of type (a) and type (b) employs symport and antiport rules of minimal energy. However, the use of rules having type (c) leads to rules with unbounded energy requirement. We leave as open problem the question of whether there exists an ECPe system that simulates TP systems that use objects of type (ii).

Acknowledgements. R.B. Juayong is supported by DOST-ERDT scholarships. H.N. Adorna is funded by a DOST-ERDT grant and the Semirara Mining Corporation Professorial Chair.

References

1. Alhazov, A., Ciubotaru, C., Ivanov, S., Rogozhin, Y.: The Family of Languages Generated by Non-cooperative Membrane Systems. Membrane Computing. In: Gheorghe, M., Hinze, T., Păun, G., Rozenberg, G., Salomaa, A. (eds.) CMC 2010. LNCS, vol. 6501, pp. 65–80. Springer, Heidelberg (2010)
2. Adorna, H.N., Păun, G., Pérez-Jiménez, M.: On Communication Complexity in Evolution-Communication P systems. Romanian Journal of Information Science and Technology 13(2), 113–130 (2010)
3. Cavaliere, M.: Evolution-Communication P systems. In: Păun, G., Rozenberg, G., Salomaa, A., Zandron, C. (eds.) WMC 2002. LNCS, vol. 2597, pp. 134–145. Springer, Heidelberg (2003)
4. Hernandez, N.H.S., Juayong, R.A.B., Adorna, H.N.: On Communication Complexity of Some Hard Problems in ECPe systems. In: Alhazov, A., Cojocaru, S., Gheorghe, M., Rogozhin, Y., Rozenberg, G., Salomaa, A. (eds.) CMC 2013. LNCS, vol. 8340, pp. 206–224. Springer, Heidelberg (2014)
5. Juayong, R.A.B., Adorna, H.N.: A Note on the Universality of EC P Systems with Energy. In: 2nd International Conference on Information Technology Convergence and Services, pp. 1–6. IEEE (2010)
6. Păun, G.: Introduction to Membrane Computing. In: Ciobanu, G., Pérez-Jiménez, M.J., Păun, G. (eds.) Applications of Membrane Computing. Natural Computing Series, pp. 1–42. Springer (2006)

Myo-Signal Based Intuitive Driving Interface: Development and Evaluation

Jinuk Kim, Sungyoon Lee, and Jaehyo Kim

Department of Mechanical and Control Engineering, Handong Global University,
Pohang, Korea
kimjuk92@gmail.com
{sylee,jhkim}@handong.edu

Abstract. This study proposes an electromyogram (EMG)-based driving interface, MyoDrive, which uses two wrist motions to accelerate, brake, and steer in a simple manner. The horizontal angle of the right wrist is used for steering, and the vertical angle of the left wrist is used for speed control. Each angle was estimated from the EMG signals with a simple regression method. Conventional wheel/pedal interface and the proposed interface, MyoDrive, were compared with three tasks-slalom, speed tracking, and emergency stop to investigate their intuitive controllability. The proposed interface showed better learnability and response than wheel/pedal interface, but was behind in steering and speed control performance. In the speed tracking task, as the target speed increased, the deviation of MyoDrive increased whereas the deviation of Wheel/Pedal decreased in the slow region. It meant that Wheel/Pedal controlled speed more precisely. However, MyoDrive showed faster response both in the transition state and emergency.

Keywords: Driving Interface, Electromyogram (EMG), Interface Evaluation, Intuitive Interface.

1 Introduction

Humans interact with environments using various tools. We, Homo Faber, are eager to create an intuitive interface which satisfies three requirements: learnability, convenience of use, and effectiveness. Recently, intuitive interfaces, which utilize human body as the input device itself, have been actively researched for various applications including clinical application, Human-Computer Interface, and interactive computer gaming [1], [2], [3], [4]. An intuitive interface is an interface where the user already has the input-output model, therefore shortening the learning period and improving flexibility in unexpected situations. If body parts are used as the interface, it is possible to have better, easier control of the system since we already have a predictive model of our body.

Previous studies on the EMG-based interface were commonly applied to myoelectric hand prosthesis control and the input device of a computer. In the case of prosthetic control, threshold-based on/off control and multifunction control

L. Pan et al. (Eds.): BIC-TA 2014, CCIS 472, pp. 216–220, 2014.

using a classifier were utilized [5], [6]. On the other hand, a pointing device was matched with the 2-DOF wrist angle estimated from the EMG signal in order to substitute the function of a computer mouse [7]. Researches showed the possibility of a new human-machine interface that utilized the myoelectric signal. However, there were some limitations such as single speed, single rate of actuation, and long training period with ANN, etc.

The purpose of this paper is to investigate the performance of the myo-electrical signal-based interface, applying it to a vehicle, which has a time-continuous and multispeed control object. This driving interface uses two wrist angles to control the speed and orientation of the car. Furthermore, to achieve a user-friendly interface, we examined the control characteristics of the myo-signal interface with simple regression method, compared with conventional wheel/pedal interface.

2 Materials and Methods

2.1 Myoelectric Driving Interface

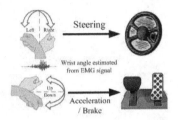

Fig. 1. Schematic of the Myoelectric Driving Interface (MyoDrive)

Figure 1 shows the schematic of the myoelectric driving interface, or MyoDrive for short. The horizontal angle of the right wrist is used for steering, and the vertical angle of the left wrist is used for speed control. Bending the wrist upward leads to acceleration, while bending the wrist downward results to braking. The angles were estimated from the EMG signals measured at the flexor and extensor muscles of the forearm which engage in the flexion/extension movement of the wrist. The signals were sampled with a 1 kHz sampling rate and transformed into quasi-tension. The signal was normalized with maximum voluntary contraction. The wrist angle was estimated from the EMG signals using linear regression. The reference angle was measured with AHRS (Attitude Heading Reference System) sensor attached on both hands.

2.2 Interface Evaluation

Interface performances are generally evaluated in terms of their learnability, efficiency, and effectiveness. Three tasks were conducted to evaluate learnability, steering performance, speed tracking performance, and emergency handling. Vehicle dynamics were applied in all the tasks, which were conducted using both the MyoDrive and Wheel/Pedal for comparison.

Slalom Task was conducted to investigate the learnability and steering performance of the interface. Subjects were asked to take a slalom task in which the subject zigzagged between obstacles.

Speed Tracking Task was conducted to investigate the speed control performance of the interface. In this task, subjects were given a speedometer on the monitor screen and asked to increase the speed by 10 km/h every ten seconds and maintain the speed for ten seconds.

Emergency Stop Task was conducted to investigate the emergency handling performance of the interface. Subjects were asked to cruise at 60 km/h and then brake when suddenly a stop sign appeared.

The subject is seated on a chair and asked to perform tasks displayed on the monitor screen using both the MyoDrive and Wheel/Pedal interfaces. Nine male subjects ranging in age from 23 to 27 participated in the experiment. All of the subjects except one had a drivers license and an average of 7.3 months of driving experience.

3   Results

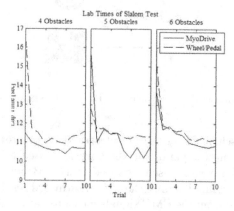

Fig. 2. Lap time according to trials and task difficulty

Learnability and Steering Performance. Figure 2 shows the convergent characteristics of the lap time recorded during the slalom test as the number of trials increases. MyoDrive required an average of 6 trials to learn the interface and the Wheel/Pedal required an average of 5.33 trials. The traveled distance was 53.14±60.35 m on average for MyoDrive and 341.94±26.97 m for Wheel/Pedal. The number of trials required to learn Wheel/Pedal was less than that of Myo-Drive, but considering that the subjects were already used to Wheel/Pedal interface through actual driving experience and that the lap time was usually less than that of Wheel/Pedal, MyoDrive had better learnability. However, Wheel/Pedal has better steering performance as it took a less traveled distance during the task.

Speed Control Performance. Figure 3 shows the average speed difference deviation of the steady-state according to the target speed. As shown in the figure, MyoDrive shows a gradual increase in deviation, but the Wheel/Pedal shows decrement, and therefore the difference between the two interfaces increases as the target speed increases. Wheel/Pedal showed a deviation average of 1.28 km/h, and the MyoDrive 2.19 km/h.

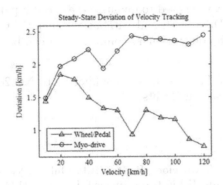

Fig. 3. Steady-state speed deviation according to the target speed

Emergency Response. Table 1 shows the time required to respond to the stop sign and to completely stop. MyoDrive took 0.17 sec less than Wheel/Pedal to respond and 0.04 sec less to stop.

Table 1. Time required to respond and stop

	RESPOND [SEC]	STOP [SEC]
MyoDrive	0.33±0.05	0.75±0.07
Wheel/Pedal	0.50±0.21	0.79±0.13

The results show an obvious difference between the two interfaces. When using MyoDrive, the subject just had to bend his wrist downward to brake, but when using Wheel/Pedal, the subject had to change the pedal from gas to brake, which took a longer time.

4   Conclusion

This study proposed an electromyogram (EMG)-based driving interface which used two wrist motions, horizontal motion of the right wrist and vertical angle of the left motion. It also evaluated the interface by comparing it with the existing Wheel/Pedal interface. Three tasks were conducted to investigate the interface performance. The parameters recorded in each task can serve as criteria for the evaluation of the dynamic characteristics of vehicle interfaces.

In the slalom task, MyoDrive showed better learnability than the Wheel/Pedal, but Wheel/Pedal showed better steering performance. In the speed tracking task, as the target speed increased, the deviation of MyoDrive increased whereas the deviation of Wheel/Pedal decreased in the slow region. It meant that Wheel/Pedal controlled speed more precisely. However, MyoDrive showed faster response both in the transition state and emergency.

Further researches are necessary to improve the performance of the inter-face. Low-pass filter can be used to quantize the speed input. By comparing the performance of MyoDrive with and without the quantization, its performance improvement through non-stationary compensation can be evaluated.

Acknowledgments. This research was supported by NO.20120045 of Handong Global University Research Grants.

References

1. Shenoy, P., Miller, K.J., Crawford, B., Rao, R.P.: Online Electromyographic Control of a Robotic Prosthesis. IEEE Trans. Biomed. Eng. (2), 1128–1135 (2008)
2. Williams, M.R., Kirsch, R.F.: Evaluation of Head Orientation and neck Muscle EMG Signals as Command Inputs to a Human-Computer Interface for Individuals with High Tetraplegia. IEEE Trans. Neural Syst. Rehabil. Eng. 16(5), 485–496 (2008)
3. Oppenheim, H., Armiger, R.S., Vogelstein, R.J.: WiiEMG: A Real-Time Environ-ment for Control of the Wii with Surface Electromyography. In: Proceedings of the IEEE International Symposium on Circuits and Systems (ISCAS 2010), pp. 957–960 (2010)
4. Oh, J., Kwon, M., Kim, Y., Kim, J., Lee, S., Kim, J.: Development and Evaluation of Myoelectric Driving Interface. In: Proceedings of the IEEE International Conference on Consumer Electronics (ICCE 2013), pp. 250–251 (2013)
5. Huang, Y., Englehart, K.B., Hudgins, B., Chan, A.D.: A Gaussian Mixture Model based Classification Scheme for Myoelectric Control of Powered Upper Limb Prostheses. IEEE Trans. Biomed. Eng. 52(11), 1801–1811 (2005)
6. Chu, J.U., Moon, I., Kim, S.K., Mun, M.S.: Control of Multifunction Myoelec-tric Hand using a Real Time EMG Pattern Recognition. In: Proceedings of the IEEE/RSJ International Conference on Intelligent Robots and Systems (IROS 2005), pp. 3957–3962 (2005)
7. Rosenberg, R.: The Biofeedback Pointer: EMG Control of a Two Dimensional Pointer. In: Proceedings of the 2nd International Symposium on Wearable Computers, pp. 162–163 (1998)

Reversible Spiking Neural P Systems
with Astrocytes

Yuan Kong[1], Xiaolong Shi[1], Jinbang Xu[1], and Xinquan Huang[2,*]

[1] Key Laboratory of Image Information Processing and Intelligent Control,
School of Automation, Huazhong University of Science and Technology,
Wuhan 430074, Hubei, China
[2] School of Computer Science, Wuhan University of Science and Technology,
Wuhan 430081, Hubei, China
245817568@qq.com

Abstract. Spiking neural P systems with astrocytes (SNPA systems, for short) are a class of distributed parallel computing devices inspired from the way neurons communicate by means of spikes. In this work, we investigate the reversibility in SNPA systems as well as the computing power of reversible SNPA systems. It is proved that reversible SNPA systems are universal even if the forgetting rules and the feature of delay in spiking rules are not used, and each neuron contains only one spiking rule. The result suggests that the astrocytes do play a key role in achieving a desired computing power for reversible SNPA systems.

Keywords: Spiking neural P system, Astrocyte, Reversible register machine, Universality.

1   Introduction

Spiking neural P systems (in short, SN P systems) were proposed in [1] with the aim of incorporating specific ideas from spiking neurons into membrane computing. Briefly, an SN P system can be represented by a directed graph, where neurons are placed in the nodes and each neuron sends spikes to its neighbor neurons along the synapses (represented by the arcs of the graph). Each neuron can contain a number of copies of a single object type (called the *spike*), *spiking rules* and *forgetting rules*. Using its rules, a neuron can send information (in the form of spikes) to other neurons. One of the neurons is used as the output neuron and its spikes are also sent to the environment. For details of general and up-to-date information about SN P systems, we can find them in [3,7].

We here consider a variant of spiking neural P systems, that is, spiking neural P systems with astrocytes [2], where an astrocyte can sense the spike traffic along several neighboring synapses at the same time, and has an excitatory or an inhibitory influence on these neighboring synapses. The details of spiking neural P systems with astrocytes will be shown in Section 2.

---

* Corresponding author.

L. Pan et al. (Eds.): BIC-TA 2014, CCIS 472, pp. 221–224, 2014.

In [6], the computing power of reversible spiking neural P systems without astrocytes was considered. It is found that reversible spiking neural P systems without astrocytes can computer/generate any set of Turing computable natural numbers.

In this work, we consider reversible SN P systems with the astrocytes (SNPA systems, for short), and investigate the reversibility in SNPA systems as well as the computing power of reversible SNPA systems. It is obtained that reversible SNPA systems are universal, where the forgetting rules and the feature of delay in spiking rules are not used, and each neuron contains only one spiking rule. The result suggests that the astrocytes do play a key role in achieving a desired computing power for reversible SNPA systems.

2   Spiking Neural P Systems with Astrocytes

We here recall the definition of spiking neural P systems with astrocytes (SNPA systems, for short) as introduced in [2] (in the present work, the feature of delay in spiking rules is not used and we omit it), and the notion of reversible SNPA systems. The details of formal language theory and membrane computing, please refer to [5] and [4,7].

An SNPA system, of degree $m \geq 1$, $l \geq 1$, is a construct of the form

$$\Pi = (O, \sigma_1, \ldots, \sigma_m, syn, ast_1, \ldots, ast_l, in, out), \text{ where:}$$

- $O = \{a\}$ is the singleton alphabet (a is called *spike*);
- $\sigma_1, \ldots, \sigma_m$ are *neurons*, of the form $\sigma_i = (n_i, R_i), 1 \leq i \leq m$, where:
  a) $n_i \geq 0$ is the *initial number of spikes* contained in σ_i;
  b) R_i is a finite set of *rules* of the following two forms:
     (1) $E/a^c \to a$, where E is a regular expression over a, and $c \geq 1$;
     (2) $a^s \to \lambda$, for some $s \geq 1$, verifying that for every rule $E/a^c \to a$ of type (1) from R_i, $a^s \notin L(E)$;
- $syn \subseteq \{1, 2, ..., m\} \times \{1, 2, ..., m\}$ with $(i, i) \notin syn$ for $1 \leq i \leq m$ (*synapses between neurons*);
- $ast_1, \ldots, ast_l$ are *astrocytes*, of the form $ast_i = (syn_{ast_i}, t_i)$, where $1 \leq i \leq l$, $syn_{ast_i} \subseteq syn$ is the set of synapses controlled by the astrocyte ast_i, $t_i \in \mathbb{N}$ is the *threshold* of the astrocyte ast_i;
- $in, out \in \{1, 2, ..., m\}$ indicate the *input* and *output* neurons, respectively.

If a rule $E/a^c \to a$ has $E = a^c$, then it can be simplified in the form $a^c \to a$.

The rules of types (1) and (2) are called *firing* (or *spiking*) rules and forgetting rules, respectively. The application of rules in the way is more precise in [1].

In each time unit, if neuron σ_i can use one of its rules, then a rule from R_i must be used. If two or more rules can be applied in the neuron, only one of them is chosen non-deterministically. Note that if a firing rule is applicable, then no forgetting rule is applicable, and vice versa. From the above description, the rules are used in the sequential manner in each neuron, but neurons function in parallel with each other.

In SNPA systems, astrocytes can sense the spikes traffic along the neighboring synapses. Assume that astrocyte ast_i has a given threshold t_i, and there are k spikes passing along the synapses in syn_{ast_i}. If $k > t_i$, then the astrocyte ast_i has the inhibitory influence on the neighboring synapses and the k spikes are suppressed (namely, the k spikes are lost from the system). If $k < t_i$, then the astrocyte ast_i has the excitatory influence on the neighboring synapses and the k spikes survive and reach their destination neurons. If $k = t_i$, then the astrocyte ast_i non-deterministically chooses the inhibitory or excitatory influence on the neighboring synapses. In this work, we do not consider that two or more astrocytes control the same synapses.

The *configuration* of the system is of the form $\langle r_1, \cdots, r_m \rangle$, which means that neuron σ_i contains $r_i \geq 0$ spikes. With the above notation, the *initial configuration* of an SNPA system can be expressed as $C_0 = \langle n_1, \cdots, n_m \rangle$ with the number $n_1, n_2, \cdots, n_m$ of spikes present in each neuron. Through the application of the rules described above, one can define *transitions* among configurations. Any sequence of transitions which begins with the initial configuration is called a *computation*. A computation is halts if it reaches a configuration where no rule can be used. With any computation, halting or not, we associate a *spike train*, the binary sequence with occurrences of 1 indicating time instance when the output neuron sends a spike out of the system (we also say that the system itself spikes at that time). The *computation result* of SNPA system is defined as the distance in time of the first two spikes sent into the environment by the output neuron.

In SNPA systems, a configuration is called *a reachable configuration* if it can proceed from the initial configuration by a sequence of transitions. The set of all the reachable configurations of the SNPA system Π is denoted by $\mathcal{C}(\Pi)$. An SNPA system Π is reversible if for any $c \in \mathcal{C}(\Pi)$, it has a unique previous configuration.

As stated in [1], reversible SNPA systems also can be used as computing devices in various way. We here consider reversible SNPA systems as number computing devices, and the result of a computation. We denote by $N_2(\Pi)$ (the subscript indicate that the distance between the first two spikes of any computation) the set of numbers generated by the reversible SNPA system Π; the family of sets of numbers generated by such systems is denoted by N_2RSNPA.

3   Universality of RSNPA Systems

In this section, we investigate the reversibility of SNPA systems as well as the computing power of such systems by simulating reversible register machines, and obtain that such systems are reversible and universal. The following Theorem is obtained.

Theorem 1. $NRE = N_2RSNPA$.

In the proof of above Theorem, a specific reversible SNPA system Π is constructed to simulate a reversible register machine M. The system Π consists of four types of modules - CHE module, ADD module, SUB module, FIN module. Specifically, the CHE, ADD and SUB modules are applied by simulating the CHE, ADD and SUB instructions of M, respectively; the FIN module is used to output a computation result. Furthermore, the forgetting rule and the feature of delay in spiking rules are not used, and each neuron has only one spiking rule. These suggest that astrocytes are important ingredient for improving the computing power of SN P systems without astrocytes.

4   Conclusions and Remarks

In this work, we investigated the computational power of reversibility of SNPA systems. We prove that reversible SNPA systems are universal by simulating reversible register machines, where the systems do not use the forgetting rules and delay, and each neuron has only one spiking rule. In [6], it was proved that reversible spiking neural P systems without astrocytes were also universal, where the forgetting rules and delay were used in the systems, and at most two spiking rules were used in the neurons. So, the result obtained in this work shows that astrocytes play a key role in achieving a desired computational power for reversible spiking neural P systems.

In Theorem 3.1, the maximal threshold of astrocytes is three. We conjecture that the same result holds reducing the maximal threshold of astrocytes to two.

Acknowledgments. This work was supported by National Natural Science Foundation of China (61100055, 91130034, 61100145, 61272071).

References

1. Ionescu, M., Păun, G., Yokomori, T.: Spiking Neural P System. Fund. Inform. 71(2-3), 279–308 (2006)
2. Pan, L., Wang, J., Hoogeboom, H.J.: Spiking Neural P Systems with Astrocytes. Neural Comput. 24(3), 805–825 (2012)
3. Păun, G., Rozenberg, G., Salomaa, A. (eds.): Handbook of Membrane Computing. Oxford Univ. Press (2010)
4. Păun, G.: Membrane Computing - An Introduction. Springer, Heidelberg (2002)
5. Rozenberg, G., Salomaa, A. (eds.): Handbook of Formal Languages, vol. 3. Springer, Berlin (1997)
6. Song, T., Shi, X., Xu, J.: Reversible Spiking Nerual P Systems. Front. Comput. Sci. Chi. 7(3), 350–358 (2013)
7. The P system Web Page, http://ppage.psystems.eu

On String Languages Generated by Spiking Neural P Systems with Astrocytes

Yuan Kong, Zheng Zhang, and Yang Liu*

Key Laboratory of Image Information Processing and Intelligent Control,
School of Automation, Huazhong University of Science and Technology,
Wuhan 430074, Hubei, China
yangliu30@gmail.com

Abstract. Spiking neural P systems with astrocytes (SNPA systems, for short) are a class of distributed parallel computing devices inspired from the way spikes pass through the synapses between the neurons. In this work, we investigate the language generation power of SNPA systems. Specifically, we prove that SNPA systems without the forgetting rules can generate recursively enumerable languages and characterize regular languages. Furthermore, we give a finite language that can be generated by SNPA systems, but which cannot be generated by spiking neural P systems without astrocytes. These results show that astrocyte is a powerful ingredient for generating languages by spiking neural P systems.

Keywords: Membrane computing, Spiking neural P system, Astrocyte.

1 Introduction

Spiking neural P systems (SN P systems, for short) were initiated in [2] as a class of distributed parallel computing models inspired by spiking neurons. We refer to the respective chapter of [6] for general information in this area, and the membrane computing website from [8] for the up-to-date information.

Informally, an SN P system can be represented by a directed graph, where neurons are placed in the nodes and each neuron sends spikes to its neighbor neurons along the synapses (represented by the edges of the graph). Each neuron can contain a number of copies of a single object type (called the spike, denoted by the symbol a in what follows), spiking rules and forgetting rules. Using its rules, the spikes contained in a neuron can be moved to the neighboring neurons, or deleted from the systems. One of the neurons is the output neuron and its spikes are also sent to the environment. The moments of time when a spike is sent by the output neuron are marked with 1, the other moments are marked with 0. This binary sequence is called the *spike train* of the system. The computation result can be defined in various ways, such as the total number of spikes emitted into the environment. In this work, we consider the spike train itself as the result of a computation, thus associating a language with an SN P system.

---

* Corresponding author.

L. Pan et al. (Eds.): BIC-TA 2014, CCIS 472, pp. 225–229, 2014.

Recently, a variant of SN P systems was presented in [4,3], called spiking neural P systems with astrocytes (SNPA systems, for short), where also astrocytes are considered, having an excitatory or an inhibitory influence on synapses. In [4], SNPA systems were proved to be computationally complete as number generating and accepting devices.

In this work, we continue the study of SNPA systems as language generators. We prove that recursively enumerable languages can be characterized as projections of inverse-morphic images of languages generated by SNPA systems. The relationships of the languages generated by SNPA systems with finite and regular languages are also considered. We show a finite language that cannot be generated by any SN P system [1] can be generated by SNPA system. A characterization of regular languages is given by SNPA systems without the forgetting rules.

2   Spiking Neural P Systems with Astrocytes

In this section, we introduce the necessary prerequisites on formal languages (refer to [5] and [7] for more details) and the definition of SNPA systems.

A Chomsky grammar is of the form $G = (N, T, S, P)$, with N being the nonterminal alphabet, T the terminal alphabet, $S \in N$ the axiom, and P the set of rules. The family of finite, regular and recursively enumerable languages are denoted by FIN, REG and RE, respectively.

For a morphism $h : V_1^* \to V_2^*$ and a string $y \in V_2^*$ we define $h^{-1}(y) = \{x \in V_1^* \mid h(x) = y\}$; this mapping from V_2^* to the power set of V_1^* is extended in the natural way to languages over V_2 and is called the inverse morphism associated with h. A morphism $h : V_1^* \to V_1^*$ is called projection if $h(a) \in \{a, \lambda\}$ for every $a \in V_1$.

A *spiking neural P system with astrocytes* (SNPA system, for short), of degree $m \geq 1$, $k \geq 1$, is a construct of the form

$$\Pi = (O, \sigma_1, \ldots, \sigma_m, syn, ast_1, \ldots, ast_k, \sigma_{in}, \sigma_{out}), \text{ where:}$$

- $O = \{a\}$ is the singleton alphabet (a is called *spike*);
- $\sigma_1, \ldots, \sigma_m$ are neurons, of the form $\sigma_i = (n_i, R_i), 1 \leq i \leq m$, where:
  a) $n_i \geq 0$ is the initial number of spikes contained in σ_i;
  b) R_i is a finite set of rules of the following two forms:
     (1) $E/a^c \to a; d$, where E is a regular expression over O, and $c \geq 1$, $d \geq 0$;
     (2) $a^s \to \lambda$, for some $s \geq 1$, with the restriction that for each rule $E/a^c \to a; d$ of type (1) from R_i, $a^s \notin L(E)$;
- $syn \subseteq \{1, 2, \ldots, m\} \times \{1, 2, \ldots, m\}$ with $(i, i) \notin syn$ for $1 \leq i \leq m$ (*synapses between neurons*);
- $ast_1, \ldots, ast_k$ are *astrocytes*, of the form $ast_i = (syn_{ast_i}, t_i)$, where $1 \leq i \leq k$, $syn_{ast_i} \subseteq syn$ is the set of synapses controlled by the astrocyte ast_i, $t_i \in \mathbb{N}$ is the *threshold* of the astrocyte ast_i;
- $\sigma_{in}, \sigma_{out} \in \{1, 2, \ldots, m\}$ indicate the *input* and *output* neurons, respectively.

If a rule $E/a^c \to a; d$ has $E = a^c$, then it can be simplified in the form $a^c \to a; d$; if $d = 0$, then it can be simplified in the form $E/a^c \to a$.

The rules of types (1) and (2) are called *firing* (or *spiking*) rules and forgetting rules, respectively – see [2] for more details.

In each time unit, if a neuron σ_i can use one of its rules, then a rule from R_i must be used. Since two firing rules, $E_1/a^{c_1} \to a; d_1$ and $E_2/a^{c_2} \to a; d_2$, can have $L(E_1) \cap L(E_2) \neq \emptyset$, it is possible that two or more rules can be applied in a neuron, and in that case, only one of them is chosen non-deterministically. Hence, the rules are used in the sequential manner in each neuron, at most one in each step, but neurons work in parallel with each other.

An astrocyte can sense at the same time the spike traffic along several neighboring synapses. Suppose that an astrocyte ast_i is given a threshold t_i, and there are k spikes passing along the neighboring synapses in syn_{ast_i} $(1 \leq i \leq k)$. If $k > t_i$, then astrocyte ast_i has an inhibitory influence on the neighboring synapses, and the k spikes are suppressed (the spikes are removed from the system). If $k < t_i$, then astrocyte ast_i has an excitatory influence on the neighboring synapses, all spikes survive and reach their destination neurons. If $k = t_i$, then astrocyte ast_i non-deterministically chooses an inhibitory or excitatory influence on the neighboring synapses.

A configuration of SNPA system can be described by both the number of spikes present in each neuron and by the state of the neuron (more precisely, by the number of steps to count down until it becomes open; this number is zero if the neuron is already open). Formally, a configuration is denoted by $\langle r_1/t_1, \cdots, r_m/t_m \rangle$, where neuron σ_i contains $r_i \geq 0$ spikes and it will be open after $t_i \geq 0$ steps, $i = 1, \cdots, m$; with this notation, the initial configuration is $C_0 = \langle n_1/0, \ldots, n_m/0 \rangle$. Using the rules as described above, one can define transitions among configurations. Any sequence of transitions starting from the initial configuration is called a computation. A computation halts if it reaches a configuration where no rule can be used. With any computation (halting or not) we associate a *spike* train, the sequence of symbols 0 and 1 describing the behavior of the output neuron: labeled by 1 if the output neuron spikes, otherwise labeled by 0. In this work, we consider the spike train itself as the result of a computation, thus associating a language with an SNPA system.

For an SNPA system Π, we denote by $L(\Pi)$ the language generated Π, and by $LSNPA_{m,l}(rule_k, cons_p, forg_q)$ the family of all languages $L(\Pi)$ generated by SNPA systems, with at most m neurons and at most l astrocytes, each neuron has at most k rules, each of the spiking rules consumes at most p spikes, and each forgetting rule removes at most q spikes. Generally, any of the parameters m, l, k, p, q are replaced by $*$ if they are not bound. If the underlying SNPA systems are finite, the corresponding families of languages is denoted by $LFSNPA_{m,l}(rule_k, cons_p, forg_q)$.

3   The Generative Power of SNPA Systems

3.1   A Characterization of Recursively Enumerable Languages

It was proved in Theorem 5.9 in [1] that standard SN P systems can characterize recursively enumerable languages, where forgetting rules and delay are used. Here, we prove that SNPA systems without the forgetting rules and delay can also characterize recursively enumerable languages.

Theorem 1. *For an alphabet $V = \{a_1, a_2, \ldots, a_k\}$, there are a morphism $h_1 : (V \cup \{b, c\})^* \to \{0, 1\}^*$ and a projection $h_2 : (V \cup \{b, c\})^* \to V^*$ such that for each language $L \subseteq V^*$, $L \in RE$, there is an SNPA system Π such that $L = h_2(h_1^{-1}(L(\Pi)))$.*

3.2   A Representation of Regular Languages

In Theorem 5.6 in [1], it was proved that an SN P system Π can generate language $L = h^{-1}(L(\Pi))$, for $L \subseteq \{a_1, a_2, \cdots, a_k\}$, $L \in REG$, a morphism $h : \{a_1, a_2, \cdots, a_k\}^* \to \{0, 1\}^*$, and the forgetting rules are used in the proof of the Theorem. Here, we prove that the same result hold for SNPA systems without forgetting rules.

Theorem 2. *For any language $L \subseteq \{a_1, a_2, \cdots, a_k\}^*$, $L \in REG$, there is an SNPA system Π and a morphism $h : \{a_1, a_2, \cdots, a_k\}^* \to \{0, 1\}^*$ such that $L = h^{-1}(L(\Pi))$.*

3.3   Relationships with Finite Languages

Theorem 3. *The language of the form $\{0x, 1y\}$, for $x, y \in \{0, 1\}^*$ can be generated by an SNPA system.*

Note that any SN P system without astrocytes cannot generate the language of the form $\{0, 1\}$. However, as shown in Theorem 3, the language $\{0, 1\}$ can be generated by an SNPA system. So, an astrocyte is a powerful ingredient for generating languages.

4   Conclusions and Remarks

In this work, we investigated the computation power of SNPA systems. We prove that SNPA systems without the forgetting rules can generate recursively enumerable languages and characterize regular languages. We give a finite language that can be generated by SNPA systems, but which cannot be generated by spiking neural P systems without astrocytes. The obtained results show that an astrocyte is a powerful ingredient for generating languages.

In the future work, it is of interest to investigate the computational power of SNPA systems as language generators working in other modes, such as non-synchronous mode and exhaustive way use of rules.

Acknowledgments. This work was supported by National Natural Science Foundation of China (61033003, 61100145, 61320106005, 61304034).

References

1. Chen, H., Freund, R., Ionescu, M., Păun, G., Pérez-Jiménez, M.J.: On String Languages Generated by Spiking Neural P Systems. Fund. Inform. 75(1-4), 141–162 (2007)
2. Ionescu, M., Păun, G., Yokomori, T.: Spiking Neural P Systems. Fund. Inform. 71(2-3), 279–308 (2006)
3. Song, T., Pan, L., Păun, G.: Asynchronous Spiking Neural P Systems with Local Synchronization. Information Sciences 219, 197–207 (2013)
4. Pan, L., Wang, J., Hoogeboom, H.J.: Spiking Neural P Systems with Astrocytes. Neural Comput. 24(3), 805–825 (2012)
5. Păun, G.: Membrane Computing: An Introduction. Springer, Berlin (2002)
6. Păun, G., Rozenberg, G., Salomaa, A. (eds.): Handbook of Membrane Computing. Oxford University Press (2010)
7. Rozenberg, G.: Handbook of Formal Languages: Word, Language, Grammer, vol. 1. Springer (1997)
8. The P system Web Page, http://ppage.psystems.eu

A Hybrid Bat Based Feature Selection Approach for Intrusion Detection

Mohamed Amine Laamari[1,2] and Nadjet Kamel[1,2]

[1] Univ.Setif, Fac. Sciences, Depart. Computer Science, Setif, Algeria
[2] USTHB, LRIA, Algiers, Algeria
laamari.med.a@gmail.com,nkamel@usthb.dz

Abstract. Intrusion detection Systems (IDS) are used for detecting malicious and abnormal behaviors, but they suffer from many issues like high resource consumption, high false alarm rate and many others. In this paper, we present a new algorithm to improve intrusion detection and reduce resource consumption. The proposed HBA-SVM IDS combines a hybrid Bat meta-heuristic Algorithm with a support vector machine (SVM) classifier for simultaneous feature and optimal SVM parameters selection, to reduce data dimensionality and to improve IDS detection. To evaluate our system, we used the NSL-KDD dataset and compare against a standard SVM and a PSO-SVM algorithm. Compared to these algorithms experimental result show that our system reduces the number of features needed for intrusion detection by 62% and achieves higher detection rate and lower false alarm rate.

Keywords: Intrusion detection system, Support vector machines, Bat zlgorithm, Feature selection.

1 Introduction

In recent years, the increase of the number of connected devices and network-based services has sparked the need for more robust security and data protection solution. Traditional security solutions like firewalls or secure networks have difficulty against new and more complex attacks because of hidden vulnerability in software applications.

Intrusion detection systems aim at detecting attacks against computer systems and networks. There are two major intrusion detection approaches: misuse detection and anomaly detection. In the first approach, traffic is analyzed against a database of attacks signature and an alarm is raised in case of a match. In the second approach, the IDS models normal behavior and flags any deviation from the norm. Many efforts have been made to boost IDS efficiency but traditional IDS still suffer from many issues like regular updating, low detection to unknown attacks, high false alarm rate, high resource consumption and time consuming analyze of data.

Recently, IDSs based on Intelligent and Machine Learning Algorithm have gained a lot of attention from the research community, including neural networks [1], clustering techniques [2], statistical methods [3], [4] and more. In this

L. Pan et al. (Eds.): BIC-TA 2014, CCIS 472, pp. 230–238, 2014.
© Springer-Verlag Berlin Heidelberg 2014

paper, we chose to use Support Vector Machine (SVM). SVM is a machine learning method that has shown growing popularity and has been applied to network intrusion detection with remarkable results, but SMV can underperform depending on the choice of its parameters [5]. To choose the optimal SVM parameters and reduce data dimensionality another algorithm must be used.

In order to improve intrusion detection precision, we propose in this paper a network intrusion detection model (HBA-SVM) based on simultaneous selection of features and SVM parameters using a hybrid BA algorithm. The performance of the model is tested using NSL-KDD dataset [6].

The outline of the paper is as follows. After defining SVM learning algorithm in Section 2 and the Bat algorithm in Section 3, we present in Section 4 a binary Bat algorithm for solving discrete optimization problems. In Section 5, we present the details of the proposed Hybrid algorithm that combines a standard Bat algorithm with a binary bat algorithm to solve the problems of feature selection and SVM parameters optimization simultaneously. In Section 6, the employed data set in this work and parameter settings of the HBA are described, followed by the discussion of obtained result. Finally, we conclude the paper with conclusion and future direction of research in Section 7.

2   Support Vector Machines

Support vector machines (SVM) are supervised learning models that construct a hyper-plane or set of hyper-planes in a high dimensional features space. The basic SVM maps the input vectors into a very high-dimensional feature space [7]. It uses Kernel function like polynomial and radial basis function (RBF) to achieve this mapping.The kernel functions can be used at the time of training of the classifiers, which selects support vectors along the surface of this function. SVM classify data using these support vectors that outline the hyper-plane in the feature space.

Suppose we have N training data points $\{(x_1, y_1), (x_2, y_2), \ldots, (x_N, y_N)\}$, $x_i \in R^d, y \in \{-1, 1\}$ where R^d is the input space, x_i is the sample vector and y_i is the class label. The separating Hyper-plane is defined in Equation (1)

$$w.x + b = 0, w \in R^N, b \in R, \tag{1}$$

where w is a weight vector and b is a bias. We can classify a new object x using the following optimization function:

$$f(x) = sign(w.x + b) \tag{2}$$

In order to relax the margin constraints for the non-linearly separable data, slack variables are introduced into the optimization problem in Equation (3)

$$min\{\tfrac{1}{2}\|w\|^2 + C \sum_{i=1}^{N} \xi_i$$

$$\text{Subject to } y_i(w^T x_i + b)1 - \xi_i, \xi_i 0, i = 1, 2, \ldots, N \tag{3}$$

This leads to a soft margin SVM [8]. C is the penalty parameter of error. The decision function of the classifier becomes

$$f(x) = sign(\sum_{i=1}^{N} a_i y_i (x_i.x) + b) \tag{4}$$

However, the data is not always linearly separable. To solve this problem, the data is mapped into a high dimensional feature space, in which the data are sparse and possibly more separable. The mapping is achieved by using a kernel function K. The nonlinear decision function is

$$f(x) = sign(\sum_{i=1}^{N} a_i y_i K(x_i.x) + b), \tag{5}$$

where $K(x_i, x)$ is the Kernel function. The generally used kernel functions are:

- Linear: $K(x_i, x_j) = (x_i.x_j)$;
- Polynomial: $K(x_i, x_j) = ((x_i.x_j) + 1)^p$;
- Radial basis function (RBF): $K(x_i, x_j) = e^{-\frac{\|x_i - x_j\|^2}{2\sigma^2}}, \sigma > 0$;
- Sigmoid: $K(x_i, x_j) = tanh(k(x_i.x_j) + c), k > 0, c < 0$.

3   Bat Algorithm

Based on these approximations and idealization, the basic steps of the Bat Algorithm (BA) can be summarized by the pseudo code shown in Fig.1.

Firstly, the initial position x_i, velocity v_i and frequency f_i are initialized randomly for each bat. For each time iteration t, being T the maximum number of iterations, the movement of the virtual bats is updated using the following equations:

$$f_i = f_{min} + (f_{max} - f_{min})\beta, \tag{6}$$
$$v_i^t = v_i^{t-1} + (x_i^t - x_*)f_i, \tag{7}$$
$$x_i^t = x_i^{t-1} + v_i^t, \tag{8}$$

where β is a randomly generated vector drawn from a uniform distribution. x_i is the current global best location (solution) which is located after comparing all the solutions among all the n bats.

For the local search part, Yang [9] propose that once a solution is selected among the current best solutions, a new solution for each bat is generated locally using random walk

$$x_{new} = x_{old} + \varepsilon A^t, \tag{9}$$

where A^t stands for the average loudness of all the bats at iteration t, $\varepsilon \in [-1, 1]$ is a random number. For each iteration of the algorithm, the loudness A_i and the emission pulse rate r_i, are updated as follows

$$A_i^{t+1} = \alpha A_i^t \tag{10}$$
$$r_i^{t+1} = r_i^0[1 - e^{-\gamma t}], \tag{11}$$

where α and γ are constants. Generally, $A_i(0) \in [1, 2]$ and $r_i \in [0, 1]$ [9].

Algorithm 1. Bat Algorithm

1: Objective function $f(x)$, $x = (x_1, x_2, \ldots, x_d)^T$;
2: Initialize the bat population x_i and v_i, $i = (1, 2, \ldots, n)$;
3: Define pulse frequency f_i at x_i;
4: Initialize pulse rates r_i and the loudness A_0;
5: **while** ($t <$ Max number of iterations) **do**
6:     Generate new solutions through equations (6), (7) and (8);
7:     **if** ($rand > r_i$) **then**
8:         Select a solution among the best solutions;
9:         Generate a local solution around the selected best solution;
10:    **end if**
11:    Generate a new solution by flying randomly;
12:    **if** (($rand < A_i$) **and** ($f(x_i) \leq f(x_*)$)) **then**
13:        Accept the new solutions;
14:        Increase r_i and reduce A_i;
15:    **end if**
16:    Rank the bats and find the current best x_*;
17: **end while**

Fig. 1. Pseudo code of the bat algorithm (BA)

4 Binary Bat Algorithm

The previous algorithm is a standard bat algorithm. The bats position represent continues values in the search space. However, feature selection is a discrete optimization problem, so it is hard to use the standard bat algorithm to solve it. Since the problem is to select or not a given feature, the bats position can be represented by binary vectors where 1 is selected and 0 is not. We need to restrict position values to 1 or 0.

In this section, we propose a binary version of the Bat Algorithm (BBA). To force bats position values to 1 or 0 some kind of transformation function is needed. The most wildly used transformation function is the sigmoid function [10], [11], [12]. However, the sigmoid function has a high probability of falling in local of falling in local optima [13]. Seyedali and Andrew [13] studied six different transfer functions divided into two families, s-shaped and v-shaped, they found that v-shaped functions have the best performance in terms of avoiding local minima and convergence speed. For our BBA we use a v-shaped transformation function [13] as follows:

$$S(v_i) = [\frac{2}{\pi} \arctan{(\frac{\pi}{2}v_i)}]. \tag{12}$$

With the transformation function S, we can update the bats position with the following equation:

$$x_i = \{ \ changebitvalue \quad if \quad rand < S(v_i)x_i \qquad otherwise, \tag{13}$$

where *rand* is a random value in the range $[0, 1]$. If we use Equation (13) instead of (8) and modify (9), the BA can handle discrete optimization problems.

5 Hybrid Bat-SVM Algorithm

In this section, we present a hybrid Bat-SVM Algorithm (HBA-SVM), which solves the parameter optimization and the feature selection problems simultaneously, in order to obtain higher classification accuracy in intrusion detection.

HBA combines the standard Bat algorithm (BA) to find the optimal SVM parameters and the Binary Bat algorithm (BBA) to reduce the number of future used for intrusion detection. The best solution of HBA is used to configure and run SVM algorithm on a training set to construct a detection model which will be used to detect intrusions.

The basic process of HBA-SVM is given as follows:

- Step 1: initialize bats position randomly;
- Step 2: evaluate all the solutions and find the current best solution using 10-fold cross validation;
- Step 3: update bats frequency and velocity using (6) and (7);
- Step 4: update bats position using (8) for SVM parameters and (13) for features mask;
- Step 5: do a local search;
- Step 6: calculate fitness for all current solutions using 10-fold cross validation;
- Step 7: update best solution;
- Step 8: repeat steps 3 to 7 until max number of iteration is reached or another stop criterion is achieved;
- Step 9: configure SVM algorithm using the best solution and construct an SVM detection model.

5.1 Bats Position Design

The position can be separated in two parts: a sub vector representing SVM parameters and a features mask representing selected features. In this paper, we use SVM classifier with RBF which means the classifiers accuracy is highly depend on the choice of two parameters C and σ. Fig. 2 shows the position design.

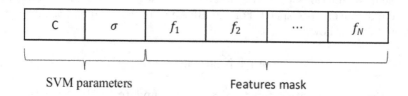

Fig. 2. Bat's Position Design

5.2 Fitness Function

The selected features, SVM parameters and training dataset are used for building the SVM model. To evaluate the model we use 10 fold cross validation with the accuracy measure Root Mean Square Error (RMSE) [14]. To maximize the performance of the algorithm, we propose the following fitness function (14)

$$f(x) = \frac{1}{1+RMSE} \qquad (14)$$

$$RMSE = \sqrt{\frac{\sum_{i=1}^{N}(p_i - y_i)^2}{N}}, \qquad (15)$$

where $RMSE$ is the root mean squared error, p_i is the predicted value, y_i is the real value and N the number of points in the dataset. $f(x)$ must be maximized.

6 Experiments and Results

6.1 Dataset Description

KDDCUP'99 is the most widely used data set for intrusion detection. However, it has many issues, which highly affects the performance of evaluated systems [15]. Instead, we use NSL-KDD dataset [6], which is a new dataset for the evaluation of researches in intrusion detection. We choose the NSL-KDD data set because of the following advantages:

- It is an improvement of the KDDCUP'99 dataset which is the most widely used data set for intrusion detection;
- It does not include redundant records in the train set. So the classifiers will not be biased towards more frequent records;
- There is no duplicate records in the proposed test sets; therefore, the performance of the learners are not biased by the methods which have better detection rates on the frequent records;
- The number of selected records from each difficulty level group is inversely proportional to the percentage of records in the original KDD data set. As a result, the classification rates of distinct machine learning methods vary in a wider range, which makes it more efficient to have an accurate evaluation of different learning techniques;

Each record in the dataset is described by 41 features and a class label. The features consist of 7 symbolic attributes (ex. Protocol_type) and 34 numeric attributes. The class is labeled as either normal or an attack, with one specific attack type. The attacks fall into four classes (see Table 1).

6.2 Dataset Preprocessing

The following processes have been applied to the dataset before using it in our system:

Table 1. Dataset Attack Types

Attack Types	
DOS: denial of service attack	back, land, neptune, pod, smurf, teardrop
R2L: unauthorized access to local from a remote machine attack	ftp_write, guess_passwd, imap, multihop, phf, spy, warezclient, warezmaster
U2R: unauthorized access to root privileges attack	buffer_overflow, loadmodule, perl, rootkit
Probe: Probing attack	ipsweep, nmap, portsweep, satan

- Data transformation: symbolic or nominal features must be transformed to numerical values through the following simple mapping function: Each category of a symbolic feature is given a number from the interval
  [0, *number of categories*−1].For example, symbolic feature protocol_types has three possible categories *tcp, udp, icmp*.We map those categories to $\{0, 1, 2\}$;
- Data normalization: some features are continues with big values, which my influence negatively on our classifier. Therefore, some type of normalization must be done to limit the range of feature. We use the following equation:

$$x_{new} = \frac{x_{old} - \mu}{\sigma}, \tag{16}$$

where μ and σ are the mean and the standard deviation of the feature respectively.

6.3 Experimental Setting

The proposed system has been implemented in java 8.0 programming language and for SVM classification we use LIBSVM library [16]. The experiment is made on a PC with an Intel Core i3 2.13GHz CPU, 4GB of RAM and running under windows 7.

For HBA parameters, based on a previous work [17] we choose 25 bats, 500 iterations, the initial loudness $A_0 = 0.5$, initial pulse rate $r_0 = 0.5$ and the frequency was taken from interval $f_i \in [0.0, 2.0]$. The searching range of parameter C of SVM is $[2^{-5}, 2^{15}]$ and the searching range of parameter σ is $[2^{-15}, 2^3]$.

For comparison, we also implemented a Particle Swarm Optimization (PSO) algorithm with SVM classifier to solve feature selection and parameter optimization problem, PSO parameters are set to 25 particles, 500 iterations, $w = 0.9$, and $C1 = C2 = 2$.

6.4 Results

A comparison between SVM with full 41 features, PSO-SVM and HBA-SVM is done using the following performance metrics:

$$Accuracy = \frac{TP+TN}{TP+TN+FP+FN} * 100 \tag{17}$$

$$FPR = \frac{FP}{FP+TN} * 100, \tag{18}$$

where TP is the number of true positives, TN is the number of true negatives, FP is the number of false positives and FN is the number of false negatives.

First, we run SVM with the full 41 features dataset, and then we run PSO-SVM and HBA-SVM. Table 2 shows the overall accuracy result.

Table 2. Comparison between the SVM, PSO-SVM and HBA-SVM

	Number of selected features	Accuracy	FPR
SVM	41	98.93%	1.08%
PSO-SVM	21	96.04%	1.80%
HBA-SVM	23	99.28%	0.48%

From Table 2, we can see that HBA-SVM has a higher accuracy and a lower false positive rate compared to SVM, while using half the features. In addition, HBA-SVM has better result than PSO-SVM. Also in our experiments, we found that the number of features could be reduced further but at the expense of detection accuracy. Our approach shows great promise for detecting known attacks.

7   Conclusion

In this paper, we proposed a hybrid BA-based feature selection algorithm and SVM parameter selection to build an efficient IDS. SVM parameters C and σ are selected using SBA. Feature selection is done through a novel BBA and is evaluated with a 10-fold cross validation SVM. We tested our algorithm on NSL-KDD dataset to analyze its effectiveness. Our algorithm reduces the dataset size by 62% and achieves a high rate of accuracy. As future work, we will further improve our algorithm and introduce a new mechanism for detecting unknown attacks.

References

[1] Mukkamala, S., Janoski, G., Sung, A.: Intrusion detection using neural networks and support vector machines. In: Proceedings of the 2002 International Joint Conference on Neural Networks, IJCNN 2002, vol. 2, pp. 1702–1707. IEEE (2002)

[2] Eskin, E., Arnold, A., Prerau, M., Portnoy, L., Stolfo, S.: A geometric framework for unsupervised anomaly detection. In: Applications of Data Mining in Computer Security. Springer, pp. 77–101 (2002)

[3] Anderson, D., Frivold, T., Valdes, A.: Next-generation intrusion detection expert system (NIDES): A summary. SRI International, Computer Science Laboratory (1995)

[4] Caberera, J., Ravichandran, B., Mehra, R.K.: Statistical traffic modeling for network intrusion detection. In: Proceedings of the 8th International Symposium on Modeling, Analysis and Simulation of Computer and Telecommunication Systems, pp. 466–473. IEEE (2000)

[5] Cherkassky, V., Ma, Y.: Practical selection of svm parameters and noise estimation for svm regression. Neural Networks 17(1), 113–126 (2004)

[6] The nsl-kdd data set. http://nsl.cs.unb.ca/NSL-KDD/ (June 2014)

[7] Vapnik, V.: The nature of statistical learning theory. Springer (2000)

[8] Cortes, C., Vapnik, V.: Support-vector networks. Machine Learning 20(3), 273–297 (1995)

[9] Yang, X.-S.: A new metaheuristic bat-inspired algorithm. In: González, J.R., Pelta, D.A., Cruz, C., Terrazas, G., Krasnogor, N. (eds.) NICSO 2010. SCI, vol. 284, pp. 65–74. Springer, Heidelberg (2010)

[10] Liu, Y., Wang, G., Chen, H., Dong, H., Zhu, X., Wang, S.: An improved particle swarm optimization for feature selection. Journal of Bionic Engineering 8(2), 191–200 (2011)

[11] Nakamura, R.Y., Pereira, L.A., Costa, K., Rodrigues, D., Papa, J.P., Yang, X.S.: Bba: A binary bat algorithm for feature selection. In: 2012 25th SIBGRAPI Conference on Graphics, Patterns and Images (SIBGRAPI), pp. 291–297. IEEE (2012)

[12] Song, T., Wang, X., Su, Y.: A novel approach to identify protein coding domains by sampling binary profiles from genome. Journal of Computational and Theoretical Nanoscience 11(1), 147–152 (2014)

[13] Mirjalili, S., Lewis, A.: S-shaped versus v-shaped transfer functions for binary particle swarm optimization. Swarm and Evolutionary Computation 9, 1–14 (2013)

[14] Hyndman, R.J., Koehler, A.B.: Another look at measures of forecast accuracy. International Journal of Forecasting 22(4), 679–688 (2006)

[15] McHugh, J.: Testing intrusion detection systems: a critique of the 1998 and 1999 darpa intrusion detection system evaluations as performed by lincoln laboratory. ACM Transactions on Information and System Security 3(4), 262–294 (2000)

[16] Chang, C.C., Lin, C.J.: Libsvm: A library for support vector machines. ACM Transactions on Intelligent Systems and Technology (TIST) 2(3), 27 (2011)

[17] Fister Jr., I., Fister, D., Yang, X.S.: A hybrid bat algorithm. ArXiv preprint ArXiv:1303.6310 (2013)

An Ensemble Pattern Classification System Based on Multitree Genetic Programming for Improving Intension Pattern Recognition Using Brain Computer Interaction

Jong-Hyun Lee[1], Jinung An[2], and Chang Wook Ahn[1,*]

[1] Department of Computer Engineering
Sungkyunkwan University (SKKU),
Suwon 440-746, Republic of Korea
[2] Daegu Gyeongbuk Institute of Science & Technology (DGIST),
Daegu 711-873, Republic of Korea
{ljh08375,cwan}@skku.edu, robot@dgist.ac.kr

Abstract. Ensemble learning is one of the successful methods to construct a classification system. Many researchers have been interested in the method for improving the classification accuracy. In this paper, we proposed an ensemble classification system based on multitree genetic programming for intension pattern recognition using BCI. The multitree genetic programming mechanism is designed to increase the diversity of each ensemble classifier. Also, the proposed system uses an evaluation method based on boosting and performs the parallel learning and the interaction by multitree. Finally, the system is validated by the comparison experiments with existing algorithms.

Keywords: Classification, Ensemble Classifier, Brain Computer Interaction, Multitree, Genetic Programming, Intension Pattern Recognition.

1 Introduction

Collective intelligence is made by the cooperation of many individuals. The intelligence can demonstrate the higher capability than the best individual [1, 2]. There exist many cases such as Wikipedia, open-source programming to solve problems by inducing the expression of the collective intelligence. Also, researches in machine learning field have tried to improve the classification system in the same vein. The ensemble is a method to the classification that uses many classifiers for making one decision [2]. It is very important to preserve the diversity of the ensemble classifiers because the diversity is one of the most important factors for inducing the collective intelligence. Therefore, weak classifiers such as Decision Tree have been mostly used. The bagging and boosting is typical ensemble method using different samples, features, weighting factors to reinforcement the diversity also [1, 3, 4].

---

* Corrseponding author.

L. Pan et al. (Eds.): BIC-TA 2014, CCIS 472, pp. 239–246, 2014.

Genetic programming (GP) was reestablished in ninetieth by John R. Koza. GP [2] was known as the outstanding global optimal search algorithm but the required high computing power was a barrier for applications. However, there have been many researches to improve GP such as linear, graph model, and so on [5–9]. Nowadays, the growths of the distributed computing technology make GP get attention [2–4, 8].

GP generates the classifier model by evolving process with genetic operators. Therefore, GP can generate various models for a problem. This feature has been as the flaw such as the overfitting and high noise sensitivity but it can be expected to reinforce the diversity in collective intelligent perspective [5, 6, 8].

In this paper, we proposed an ensemble classification system based on multitree genetic programming (MGP) to improve the accuracy for intension recognition of brain signal data. The proposed system learns in parallel by the multitree structure. Also, ensemble classifiers interacts each other for improving the search capability by external crossover operator. The boosting method increases the diversity of populations, so that the diversity is preserved and the search capability increases by the interaction and cooperation of individuals. Finally, the obtained best classifiers in each group combine the results and make the final decision by majority voting.

The rest of the paper is organized as follows: Section 2 describes the proposed Ensemble MGP. Section 3 presents the experimental results. Conclusion is placed in Section 4.

2   Ensemble Multitree Genetic Programming

MGP can be distinguished from tree based original GP of Koza by the number of trees in an individual. D. P. Muni proposed the structure of MGP for solving limitations of existing GP in multi-class and high complexity dataset [3]. It is an effective approach to improve the classification accuracy in supervised learning with complicate dataset [8].

The process of ensemble decision making of proposed system in this paper is described in Fig. 1. The system generates ensemble classifiers by MGP that votes the decision as a combination strategy. The final decision is passed by a majority vote. The learning by MGP is progressed in Fig. 2 as follows. At the first, populations are initialized and evaluated by a fitness function. The fitness function is decided by the boosting method that is described in detail in section 2.2. At the second, the MGP individuals pass the genetic operators, i.e. selection, crossover, and mutation. Then, the process returns to fitness evaluation and repeats the genetic operators until it satisfies a convergence condition. Finally, the highest fitness trees in each classifier are selected when the populations are in convergence state as the best tree classifier in Fig. 1.

In this selection, we describe the design method for MGP to obtain the diversity and to have optimal learning results. The key idea is the interaction and cooperation of the classifiers in the learning process. The crossover operator makes individuals exchange their information to each other, and tries to improve the total search capability with reserved diversity.

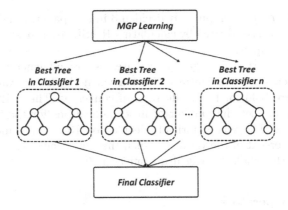

Fig. 1. The structure of the decision making process

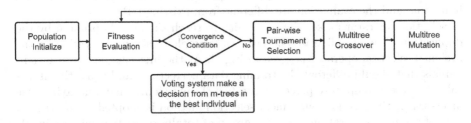

Fig. 2. A flow chart of the proposed MGP

2.1 The Structure of MGP Individual

A MGP individual consists of independent n trees. The best fitness trees in each group at the final stage of MGP learning become n ensemble classifiers. In this study, the internal nodes of tree consist of math operators, i.e. $+, -, *, /, exp, log, root$. The leaf nodes are selected among R and features. R is random variable from 0 to 1. The decision of each tree is determined by the result of the formula calculation. In other words, if the result is negative, the decision is class A. Otherwise, it is class B. The dataset of problem are assumed features can be represented by numerical values, and data only have binary class, i.e. A and B. Each tree gradually evolves to the optimal classification model of training data by genetic operators.

2.2 Fitness Evaluation by Boosting Method

Upper nodes of GP individual are decided from early generations as the learning directivity and can be kept in the state with a high probability. Therefore, the initial weighting significantly influences on the diversity of the ensemble classifiers. For obtaining the diversity, each of n groups has different weighting values toward the samples that are separated n groups by EM clustering algorithm. The weighting values of group $1, 2, \ldots, n$ are set $\{\alpha, 1, \ldots, 1\}, \{1, \alpha, \ldots, 1\}, \{1, 1, \ldots, \alpha\}$, respectively. The α value empirically decided 3 in this paper. Finally, the fitness value of individuals is evaluated by calculating RMSE (root mean squared error) of the weighted samples.

The variation of fitness in a group decreases as passing generations. The proposed system sets a new weighting criterion when the fitness variation is less than a lower threshold for the verification of converges. The weighting criteria for each sample are set the number of misclassifications for the individuals in the top k percent. The k is empirically decided on 10 in this paper. The lower threshold is 50 percent of the variation when the weighting criteria are changed. The criteria on the whole are rescaled from 1 to 10.

2.3   Genetic Operators

Ensemble MGP needs to design genetic operators because the structure of an individual and the evaluation are different from existing GP.

Selection operator makes the possibility to reach the global optimum by the duplication of outstanding individuals. An example of a new generation by the designed selection operator is given in Fig. 3. At the first, the best fitness individuals that should different the training data correctness and equal the fitness value are reserved up to 10 percent to protect the elite individuals and to increase diversity. At the second, tournament selection method is adopted to construct a part of the next generation. Lastly, a group of totally reconstructed individuals are allocated in the rest. In this study, we considered the proportions of Elitism, Tournament, and Reconstruct is 10, 75, and 15 percent, respectively.

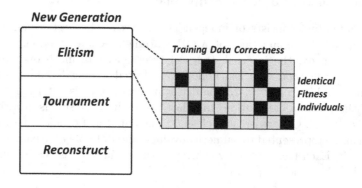

Fig. 3. An example of the reconstruction of the population by selection

Crossover operator is performed by exchange subtree of the selected superior individuals to generate a high quality offspring. The procedure of crossover in MGP can be divided between internal and external. The internal occurs among the individuals in a group. The external means individuals in different groups exchange their subtree as shown in Fig. 4. The external can induce the interaction and cooperation in collective intelligence perspective because it is similar to that the outstanding individuals in each group interchange their information and experience. In this research, the probability of the internal is set on 70 percent to secure the high search capability by vigorous crossover. The probability of the external is set on 5 percent to keep the diversity and to induce the cooperation.

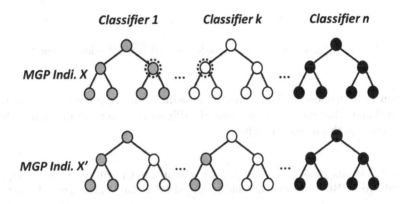

Fig. 4. An example of the interaction with classifiers by the external crossover

Mutation operator increases the search capability of MGP by random transformations of subtrees. The mutation mechanisms such as growing subtree, pruning subtree, and modifying nodes can be used for the mutation of MGP. The mutation probability is set on 10 percent in this research.

3   Experimental Results

The neural signal acquisition was done by a multi-channel optical brain imaging system (fNIR-300) and the levels of oxy-, deoxy and total-hemoglobin were specified using 45 signal channels at 14 Hz sampling rate [10, 11]. The signals were collected through optical fibers which were attached to the pre-frontal cortex. As Fig. 5 shows, Two cognitive activities of rest → right imagery movement and rest → left imagery movement were sampled in a dataset with three classes rest, right and left. The dataset has 280 samples and 45 features. The simulation environment of proposed MGP is constructed in C++ and parameters that are population size, depth limitation, iteration, probability of internal and external crossover, and mutation are set 10000 individuals, 10 depths, 1000 generation, and 0.7 and 0.05, and 0.1, respectively. The parameters of the conventional classifiers set default value of WEKA [6, 7]. The all accuracy result in this paper was obtained by 10-fold cross-validation.

Table 1 shows the classification results for conventional classifiers such as Naive Bayes, Bayes Net, BFTree, RBFNetwrok and GP which are implemented in WEKA and proposed MGP. By referring to the results of Table 1, it can

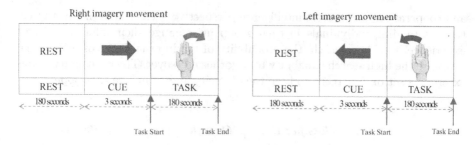

Fig. 5. Experimental scenarios for acquiring fNIRS neural signals

be seen that proposed MGP is higher classification accuracy comparing to the conventional. However, the proposed classification system results 6.07% higher than other methods and classifiers.

Table 1. Classification Accuracies (%) of Conventional Classifiers (Naive Bayes, Bayes Net, BFTree, RBF Network, GP) and proposed MGP for Neural Signal dataset

Classifier	Brain Singal
Naive Bayes	76.79
Bayes Net	77.14
BFTree	77.50
RBFNetwork	70.71
GP	77.14
Ensemble MGP	**83.57**

To show the appropriateness of the proposed method, four UCI datasets, i.e. Blood Transfusion, Breast Cancer Wisconsin, Heart, Ionosphere [6, 7] are used as benchmark dataset. Table 2 shows specifications of each dataset.

Table 2. Number of Samples (S) and Features (F) along with Model Size for UCI dataset

Dataset	S	F	ModelSize
Blood Transfusion	748	4	2992
Breast Cancer	683	9	6147
Heart	270	13	3510
Ionosphere	351	33	11583

Table 3 shows the classification results for conventional classifiers and proposed MGP. The average accuracy of the proposed ensemble MGP is 89 percent that is higher accuracy than the conventional algorithms as shown in Table 3. The proposed algorithm shows higher accuracy than the other algorithms for the 4 datasets. As experiment results shows, proposed MGP produces leads to higher classification accuracies.

Table 3. Classification Accuracies (%) of Conventional Classifiers (Naive Bayes, Bayes Net, BFTree, RBF Network, GP) and proposed MGP for 4 UCI dataset

Dataset	Naive Bayes	Bayes Net	BFTree	RBF Network	GP	Ensemble MGP
Blood	0.75	0.75	0.78	0.79	0.79	**0.81**
Breast	0.96	**0.97**	0.95	0.95	0.95	**0.97**
Heart	0.83	0.81	0.75	**0.84**	0.75	**0.84**
Ionosphere	0.82	0.89	0.9	0.92	**0.93**	**0.93**
Mean	0.84	0.86	0.85	0.88	0.86	**0.89**

4 Conclusion

In this paper, we proposed an ensemble classification system based on MGP. Also, the genetic operators of MGP were designed for reinforcement of the diversity and the search capability by the boosting mechanism and the interactions of ensemble classifiers, respectively. The experimental results showed the effectiveness of the proposed system. The proposed MGP produces leads to higher classification accuracies in the experimental results, especially in brain signal dataset.

This result can be considered that the parallel learning, boosting, interactions with classifiers, and exchange information lead the system to have high diversity and search capability. As a result, the system can relieve the overfitting problem and endure the noise of bio-signals better. In future work, we try to improve the decision combine strategy. The current strategy is majority voting but it seems to be improved by approaching to the probabilistic.

Acknowledgments. This work was supported by the NRF grant funded by the Korean government (MEST) (NRF-2012R1A2A2A01013735).

References

1. Espejo, P.G., Ventura, S., Herrera, F.: A survey on the application of genetic programming to classification. IEEE Transactions on Systems, Man, and Cybernetics, Part C: Applications and Reviews 40(2), 121–144 (2010)
2. Koza, J.R.: Genetic Programming: On the programming of computers by means of natural selection, vol. 1. MIT Press (1992)
3. Muni, D.P., Pal, N.R., Das, J.: A novel approach to design classifiers using genetic programming. IEEE Transactions on Evolutionary Computation 8(2), 183–196 (2004)
4. Banzhaf, W., Koza, J.R., Ryan, C., Spector, L., Jacob, C.: Genetic Programming - An Introduction. Morgan Kaufmann, San Francisco (1998)
5. An, J., Lee, J., Ahn, C.: An efficient GP approach to recognizing cognitive tasks from fNIRS neural signals. Science China Information Sciences 56, 1–7 (2013)
6. Hall, M., Frank, E., Holmes, G., Pfahringer, B., Reutemann, P., Witten, I.: The WEKA Data Mining Software: An Update. SIGKDD Explorations 11(1) (2009)
7. Frank, A., Asuncion, A.: UCI Machine Learning Repository. School of Information and Computer Science, Irvine (2010), http://archive.ics.uci.edu/ml

8. Levy, P., Bonomo, R.: Collective intelligence: Mankind's emerging world in cyberspace. Perseus Publishing (1999)
9. Bennett, K.P., Mangasarian, O.L.: Robust linear programming discrimination of two linearly inseparable sets. Optimization Methods and Software 1, 23–34 (1992)
10. Izzetoglu, K., Yurtsever, G., Bozkurt, A., Bunce, S.: Functional Brain Monitering via NIR Based Optical Spectroscopy. In: Bioengineering Conference, USA (2003)
11. Muroga, T., Tsubone, T., Wada, Y.: Estimation algorithm of tapping movement by NIRS. In: SICE-ICASE International Joint Conference, Korea (2006)

Diagnosis of Osteoporosis by Quantification of Trabecular Microarchitectures from Hip Radiographs Using Artificial Neural Networks

Ju Hwan Lee, Yoo Na Hwang, Sung Yun Park, and Sung Min Kim

Department of Medical Biotechnology, Dongguk University-Seoul
26, Pil-dong 3-ga, Jung-gu, Seoul, Korea
{ykjhlee,yoona7747}@gmail.com,
{sypark,smkim}@dongguk.edu

Abstract. The purpose of this study was to assess the diagnostic efficacy of an artificial neural network (ANN) in identifying postmenopausal women with low bone mineral density (BMD) by quantifying trabecular bone microarchitectures. The study included 53 post-menopausal women, who were classified as normal (n=17) and osteoporotic (n=36) according to T-scores. BMD was measured on the femoral neck by dual-energy X-ray absorptiometry. Morphological features were extracted to find optimum input variables by quantifying microarchitectures of trabecular bone. Principal component analysis was used to reduce the dimen-sionalities and improve classification accuracy. For the classification, a two-layered feed forward ANNs was designed using the Levenberg-Marquardt train-ing algorithm. The experimental results indicated the superior performance of the proposed approach for discriminating osteoporotic cases from normal.

Keywords: Osteoporosis, Bone mineral density, Trabecular bone, Microarchitecture, Dual-energy X-ray absorptiometry, Artificial neural network.

1 Introduction

The diagnosis of osteoporosis typically relies on the determination of bone mineral density (BMD), which can be measured by two-dimensional dual-energy X-ray absorptiometry (DXA) or by three-dimensional quantitative computed tomography (QCT) [1]. According to World Health Organization (WHO) standards, osteoporosis is defined as a BMD 2.5 standard deviations below the young adult mean BMD [2]. However, BMD alone cannot be the sole criterion for predicting the prognosis of os-teoporosis, since osteoporosis is not only characterized by a low bone mass [3,4]. Aggravation of trabecular bone architecture also plays a significant role [1]. There-fore, the use of additional risk factors, associated with the bone microarchitecture, can improve the predictability for osteoporosis.

Based on these clinical advantages, several approaches have been performed to im-prove the diagnostic accuracy for osteoporosis by quantifying architectural proper-ties of trabecular bone. However, most current approaches have evaluated diagnostic perfor-mance of osteoporosis using physiological parameters. Although many physio-logical variables have been well identified, these risk factors are not significantly associ-ated

L. Pan et al. (Eds.): BIC-TA 2014, CCIS 472, pp. 247–250, 2014.

with bone microarchitectures. In addition, the use of SVMs in osteoporosis is still inaccurate despite the wealth of information available.

The aim of this study is to assess the diagnostic efficacy of ANNs in identifying postmenopausal women with low BMD by quantifying trabecular bone microarchitectures. The rest of the paper is organized as follows: Section 2 introduces the overall image processing procedures for feature extraction, selection and classification. The experimental results are provided in Section 3. Finally, Section 4 concludes.

2 Material and Methods

This study included 53 post-menopausal women who provided informed consent. All subjects underwent BMD measurement of the femoral neck by DXA (Hologic, Inc., Waltham, MA, USA). According to WHO BMD standards, the subjects were classified as normal (n=17) or osteoporotic (n=36) patients.

To measure femoral neck trabecular patterns, the region of interest (ROI) of 100 x 100 pixels2 was selected by a trained operator at the femoral neck region [5]. We then obtained a blurred image by a Gaussian filter (Sigma=10 pixels). The blurred image was subtracted from the original ROI image, and 128 gray levels were added. The output image was subsequently binarized with a threshold level of 128 to separate the trabecular. Morphological operations consisting of erosion and dilation were used. Lastly, the skeletonized image was obtained for each trabecular bone by eroding the binary regions until only the central line of pixels appeared. All image processing was performed by Matlab software (R2011b, MathWorks, Inc., Natick, MA, USA).

We extracted seven evaluation parameters composed of four structural and two skeletonized parameters, and the fractal dimension (FD). The structural parameters are composed of Tb.Area, Tb.Peri, Tb.Thick and Tb.TD, and the skeletonized param-eters are classified into Sk.N and Sk.Length. Tb.Area denotes the mean area of the trabecular bone, and Tb.Peri indicates an assessment regarding the length of the tra-becular perimeter. Tb.Thick indicates the mean width for each trabecular bone and Tb.TD is the terminal distance between the ends of adjacent bones.

To reduce the dimensionalities of features, principal component analysis (PCA) was performed followed by varimax rotation. Using this technique, we excluded FD, which revealed the lowest coefficient of variation, from the classification. Six param-eters composed of four structural parameters and two skeletonized parameters were selected as an input of ANN model.

For the classification, we designed two-layered feed forward neural network (FFNN). FFNN includes an input layer consisting of six input neurons to the network, which vary by varying the feature vectors. The subsequent hidden layer with 10 neu-rons and output layer with two neurons is also employed. A supervised learning ap-proach was used for the weight determination using the Levenberg-Marquardt (LM) method [6].

3 Experimental Results

The overall classification accuracies of the SVM classifiers for osteoporosis were high when compared with the ANN classifiers (Table 1). RBF-kernel based SVM classifiers

Table 1. Comparison of the classification accuracies for osteoporosis between the proposed approach and other reported methods

Classification Conditions	Sensitivity (%)	Specificity (%)	Accuracy (%)
SVM with RBF kernel 1 [7]	90.0	87.0	90.0
SVM with RBF kernel 2 [8]	90.9	83.8	88.0
Multi-layer perceptron ANN with TWIST [9]	74.8	87.8	81.3
Multi-layer perceptron ANN with back propagation [10]	-	-	83.0
Original multi-layer perceptron ANN [11]	78.3	73.3	-
Fuzzy ANN [12]	100.0	67.6	75.6
Original SVM [13]	77.8	76.0	76.7
Proposed method	100.0	94.1	98.1

[7,8] showed the acceptable classification rates of 88-90%, whereas the classification rates of all employed ANN classifiers were less than 83%. Among ANN classifiers, Fuzzy ANN [12] showed only 75.6% of classification rates due to the relatively low specificity (67.6%), although 100 % of sensitivity for identifying osteoporotic cases was obtained. On the other hand, the proposed approach considerably reduced the level of misclassification rates in comparison with the existing classifiers. Based on these experimental results, the morphological feature sets obtained quantifying tra-becular bone microarchitectures produced a substantial increase in the classification performance.

4 Conclusions

The results of the present study provided the superior performance of the proposed approach for discriminating patients with osteoporosis from normal subjects. Moreover, our method considerably reduced the level of misclassification rates, and provid-ed the best classification results. Based on these results, we found the clinical useful-ness of our method for diagnosing osteoporosis. A limitation of the present study is that the numbers of patients and controls are relatively small. To make the results more robust, we will perform additional experiments using various classification models with more data numbers.

Acknowledgements. This work was supported by International Collaborative R&D Program funded by the Ministry of Knowledge Economy (MKE), Korea. (N01150049, Developing high fre-quency bandwidth [40-60MHz] high resolution image system and probe technology for diagnosing cardiovascular lesion).

References

1. Kuroda, S., Mukohyama, H., Kondo, H., Aoki, K., Ohya, K., Ohyama, T., Kasugai, S.: Bone mineral density of the mandible in ovariectomized rats: analyses using dual energy X-ray absorptiometry and peripheral quantitative computed tomography. Oral Dis. 9, 24–28 (2003)
2. WHO.: Assessment of fracture risk and its application to screening for postmenopausal osteoporosis. WHO Technical Report Series Geneva (1994)

3. Houam, L., Hafiane, A., Boukrouche, A., Lespessailles, E., Jennane, R.: One dimensional local binary pattern for bone texture characterization. Pattern Anal. Appl. 17, 179–193 (2014)
4. Mauck, K.F., Clarke, B.L.: Diagnosis, screening, prevention, and treatment of osteoporosis. Mayo. Clin. Proc. 81, 662–672 (2006)
5. White, S.C., Rudolph, D.J.: Alterations of the trabecular pattern of the jaws in patients with osteoporosis. Oral Surg. Oral Med. Oral Pathol. Oral Radiol. 88, 628–635 (1999)
6. Hagan, M.T., Menhaj, M.B.: Training feedforward networks with the Marquardt algorithm. IEEE Trans. Neural Netw. 5, 989–993 (1994)
7. Sapthagirivasan, V., Anburajan, M.: Diagnosis of osteoporosis by extraction of trabecular features from hip radiographs using support vector machine: An investigation panorama with DXA. Comput. Biol. Med. 43, 1910–1919 (2013)
8. Kavitha, M.S., Asano, A., Taguchi, A., Kurita, T., Sanada, M.: Diagnosis of osteoporosis from dental panoramic radiographs using the support vector machine method in a computer-aided system. BMC Med. Imaging 12, 1–11 (2012)
9. Eller-Vainicher, C., Chiodini, I., Santi, I., Massarotti, M., Pietrogrande, L., Cairoli, E., Beck-Peccoz, P., Longhi, M., Galmarini, V., Gandolini, G., Bevilacqua, M., Grossi, E.: Recogni-tion of morphometric vertebral fractures by artificial neural networks: analysis from GISMO lombardia database. PLoS One 6, e27277 (2011)
10. Rae, S.A., Wang, W.J., Partridge, D.: Artificial neural networks: A potential role in osteo-porosis. J. R. Soc. Med. 92, 119–122 (1999)
11. Chiu, J.S., Li, Y.C., Yu, F.C., Wang, Y.F.: Applying an artificial neural network to predict osteoporosis in the elderly. Stud. Health Technol. Inform. 124, 609–614 (2006)
12. Arifin, A.Z., Asano, A., Taguchi, A., Nakanoto, T., Ohtsuka, M., Tsuda, M., Kudo, Y., Tanimoto, K.: Developing computer-aided osteoporosis diagnosis system using fuzzy neural network. JACIII 11, 1049–1058 (2007)
13. Yoo, T.K., Kim, S.K., Kim, D.W., Choi, J.Y., Lee, W.H., Park, E.C.: Osteoporosis risk predic-tion for bone mineral density assessment of postmenopausal women using machine learning. Yonsei Med. J. 54, 1321–1330 (2013)

A New Kind of Model of Laminar Cooling: By LS-SVM and Genetic Algorithm

Shuanghong Li, Xi Li*, and Zhonghua Deng

School of Automation, Huazhong University of Science and Technology,
Wuhan 430074, Hubei, China
lixi@hust.edu.cn

Abstract. In this paper, the conventional mechanism model of laminar flow cooling of hot-rolled strips is modified and optimized. And the new prediction model can express the laminar cooling process unambiguously, in which, the least squares support vector machines(LS-SVM) learning machine is introduced to promote the accuracy of the temperature-varying parameters and the genetic algorithm is proposed to identify the system of the temperature-varying parameters. The model can be used to calculate the temperature along the length direction and the thickness direction at the same time. The movement of the steel plate and the change of the valve can be obtained.

Keywords: Laminar cooling, LS-SVM, Machine learning, Genetic algorithm, Prediction model.

1 Introduction

Customers require increasingly better quality for the coil product. Laminar cooling system in hot strip mill plays very important roles in the control of mechanical properties of the product [1,2]. How to well control this complex production process and obtain strip products with dynamic specification and performance is a long-term research issue in the field of steel production. The key is to establish accurate temperature models [3].

The Germany Siemens laminar flow cooling model performs computation using mechanism equations, obtains the parameters via experimental identification, and then realizes better proportional-integral-derivative (PID) control based on this model. In [4], the amount of control variables was deduced using the empirical model of water jet capacity/relationships among temperature, and a minimum adjustment time feedback controller was designed under a first-order time-delay system, and the measured coiling temperature data were used to statistically fit and correct the model parameters.

In this paper, a new kind of mechanism model is presented, which can calculate the temperature along the length direction and the thickness direction at the same time. The movement of the steel plate and the change of the valve can be obtained.

---

* Corresponding author.

L. Pan et al. (Eds.): BIC-TA 2014, CCIS 472, pp. 251–254, 2014.

2   The Mechanism Model

The mechanism model calculates heat and temperature using various mechanism equations expressing the plate in the product line, and identifies and corrects the parameters using the actual production data. As well, a computation model approximating the actual production data is obtained and verified.

Laminar flow cooling is affected by many factors and the values of the dynamic input variables, and thus we use finite element method to divide the plate and the product line. The relevant computation equation is as follows:

$$S = \int_0^t vdt$$

$$\left\{ \begin{array}{r} L_1 < S \leqslant L_2, or, L_3 < S \leqslant L_4, Q = \{R, A\}; \\ else, Q = \{W\}. \end{array} \right\} \tag{1}$$

where S is the plate's displacement; v is the plate's running speed; t is time; L_1 and L_2 are the start and end positions of the first segment of the cooling zone respectively; L_3 and L_4 are the start and end positions of the second segment of the cooling zone respectively; Q is a set of cooling routes; R denotes heat loss through radiation; A denotes heat loss through air convection; W denotes water-cooled heat transfer.

3   Temperature-Varying Parameters

In the steel plate laminar cooling process, there are many parameters which are time-varying or temperature-varying, such as water cooling heat transfer coefficient and heat conduction coefficient .To get a accurate model some measures should to be taken to calculate them precise. The method is proposed in this paper based on least squares support vector machines (LS-SVM) model for a class of complex systems with strong nonlinearity.

3.1   The LS-SVM System

SVM is one of the methods with statistical learning theory can be applied to practice. It has its particular advantages in settling pattern recognition problem with small samples, nonlinearity, and higher dimension. SVM can be easily applied to learning problem, such as function estimation.

The following function is used to approximate the unknown function,

$$y(x) = \omega^T \varphi(x) + b \tag{2}$$

where , $x \in R^n, y \in R, \varphi(.) : R \to R^{nh}$ is a nonlinear function which maps the input space into a higher dimension feature space, w is the weight vector and b denotes a bias term [5,6,7].

We choose the temperature-varying parameters and their output to build LS-SVM machine, then the value of the input and output should be determined firstly.

$$x(k) = \{T, t\},$$
$$\{y_1, y_2\} = \{a_w, \lambda\} \tag{3}$$

where, T is the temperature of the steel, $^\circ C$; t is the time, s; a_w is the water cooling heat transfer coefficient, $W/(m^2 \cdot K)$; λ is the heat conduction coefficient, $W/(m \cdot K)$.

3.2   Identification by Genetic Algorithm

Genetic algorithm is a highly parallel, randomized and adaptive search algorithm, developing on natural selection and evolutionary of biological mechanisms.

$$Q = \{Q_1, Q_2, \cdots, Q_{200}\};$$
$$Q_w = \{Q_{w1}, Q_{w2}, \cdots, Q_{w200}\};$$
$$Q_{Tc} = \{Q_{Tc1}, Q_{Tc2}, \cdots, Q_{Tc200}\} \tag{4}$$

Given training data sets $\{Q, Q_c\}$, $\{Q, Q_{Tc}\}$, the system recognizes define an optimization as follows:

$$\min J(a) = \sqrt{\sum_{i=1}^{200} (Q_{wi} - aQ_i)^2} \tag{5}$$

$$\min J(b, c) = \sqrt{\sum_{i=1}^{200} (Q_{Tci} - bQ_i(1 - e^{-\frac{t_{finali}}{a}}))^2}, \tag{6}$$

the t_{finali} is the ith time the cooling was completed.

Now genetic algorithm was used to search the a,b,c to establish the equations (5) (6). The fitness equations are shown as follow:

$$f_a = \frac{1}{|\sum\limits_{i=1}^{200} (Q_{wi} - aQ_i)|};$$

$$f_{b,c} = \frac{1}{|\sum\limits_{i=1}^{200} (Q_{Tci} - bQ_i(1 - e^{-\frac{t_{finali}}{a}}))|} \tag{7}$$

Finally, we obtained the values of the parameters a, b and c:

$$a = 0.867;$$
$$b = 0.931;$$
$$c = 47.532$$

So, the $a_w = \frac{0.867Q}{F(T_0 - T)}$ and the $\lambda = \frac{0.4655Q(1 - e^{-\frac{t}{47.532}})(h_1 + h_2)}{A_r(T_0 - T)}$ the LS-SVM system can be identified.

4   Results Analysis

The result can be obtained by use of MATLAB/simulink and the temperature curve through thickness direction can be drawn at the same time. The temperature of 6 layer of steel plate is obtained and the final temperature showed in the chart is the coiling temperature.

Sixty set of steel production data is collected and put into the model to calculate, the results are compared. The result indicated that the model calculated data is very close to the real data collected from the production line and the error is very small. It can be seen that most of the error are within 10 degrees, the results of the simulation can meet the needs of the production of the hot rolled steel.

5   Conclusion

In this study, a novel kind of mechanism model is proposed for improving the precise of the laminar cooling. A new kind of structure was investigated to improve the integration of the laminar cooling process and the precision of the model. The use of the LS-SVM makes it easy to calculate the temperature-varying parameters, and make the model structure more compact. The genetic algorithm is introduced into the model to identify the system of the temperature-varying quickly and accurately. Two important advantages of the new model are that the movement of the steel and the change of the valve can be described, and the temperature of the length and thickness direction of the iron can be calculated exactly. The result shows that the method proposed is very effective for improving the model prediction accuracy for coiling temperature.

Acknowledgements. This work is supported by the Wisco's key technical renovation project-"the laminar flow cooling temperature prediction model", and the program for New Century Excellent talents in University (No.NCET-10-0411).

References

1. Yahiro, K., Yamasaki, J.: Development of Coiling Temperature Control System on Hot Strip Mill. Lawasaki Steel Technical Report 24, 32–40 (1991)
2. Lawrence, W.J., Macalister, A.F., Reeve, P.J.: On Line Modelling and Control Of Strip Cooling. Ironmaking & Steelmaking 23(1), 74–78 (1996)
3. Sikdar, S., Mukhopadhyay, A.: Numerical Determination of Heat Transfer Coefficient for Boiling Phenomenon At Runout Table Of Hot Strip Mill. Ironmaking & Steelmaking 31(6), 495–502 (2004)
4. Li, H.X., Guan, S.P.: Hybrid Intelligent Control Strategy: Supervising A Dcs-Controlled Batch Process. IEEE Control Systems Magazine 21(3), 36–48 (2001)
5. Suykens, J.A.K., Vandewalle, J.: Least Squares Support Vector Machine Classifiers. Neural Processing Letters 9(3), 293–300 (1999)
6. Smola, A.J.: Regression Estimation With Support Vector Learning Machines. Muniche Urfiversity of Technology (1996)
7. Liu, B., Su, H.: Temperature Predictive Control based Least Squares Support Vector Machines. Control Theory & Application 12, 365–370 (2004)

The Application of Artificial Bee Colony Algorithm in Protein Structure Prediction

Yanzhang Li, Changjun Zhou*, and Xuedong Zheng

Key Laboratory of Advanced Design and Intelligent Computing (Dalian University),
Ministry of Education, Dalian, China
zhouchangjun@dlu.edu.cn

Abstract. The biological function of the protein is folded by their spatial structure decisions, and therefore the process of protein folding is one of the most challenging problems in the field of bioinformatics. Although many heuristic algorithms have been proposed to solve the protein structure prediction (PSP) problem. The existing algorithms are far from perfect since PSP is an NP-problem. In this paper, we proposed artificial bee colony algorithm on 3D AB off-lattice model to PSP problem. In order to improve the global convergence ability and convergence speed of ABC algorithm, we adopt the new search strategy by combining the global solution into the search equation. Experimental results illustrate that the suggested algorithm is effective when the algorithm is applied to the Fibonacci sequences and four real protein sequences in the Protein Data Bank.

Keywords: Protein structure prediction, ABC algorithm, Fibonacci sequences.

1 Introduction

Protein engineering is an important research object in bioinformatics. Solving the protein structure prediction problem is one of the most important issues of the post-genome era protein engineering [1]. Since the protein folding structure largely determines its biological function, the prediction of the structure of protein folding and research has an important significance in protein engineering.

Protein structure prediction problem has already made some simplified models. Among them, one is Dill proposed HP lattice model (HP Lattice Model) [2], the model only considers the hydrophobic between the protein residues, ignoring the function of hydrophilic residues between the amino acids. Another model is the In [1], the Toy model (AB Off-lattice Model) proposed by Stillinger. The model takes into account of the residues of the protein between the hydrophobic and hydrophilic. And especially, the angle between adjacent residues of Toy model is arbitrary.

---

* Corresponding author.

L. Pan et al. (Eds.): BIC-TA 2014, CCIS 472, pp. 255–258, 2014.
© Springer-Verlag Berlin Heidelberg 2014

Bee colony algorithm was introduced to predict protein structure in recent years. Li proposed IF-ABC to predict the protein secondary structure optimization in 2D AB off-lattice model in [3]. Recently, Zhang applied ABC algorithm to protein folding problems based on hydrophobic-hydrophilic lattice model and experimental results show that ABC algorithm has higher success rate compared to standard genetic algorithm and immune genetic algorithm [4].

2 Materials and Methods

The artificial bee colony algorithm is a new population-based metaheuristic approach proposed by Karaboga [5] in 2005. ABC algorithm is good at exploration but poor at exploitation. In order to take advantage of the global optimal solution, we improve the solution search equation and the probability values formula. Then we introduce the ABC algorithm to predict 3D AB off-lattice protein stricture. The prediction of Fibonacci sequences and real biological protein data effectively verify the practicality and effectiveness of the algorithm.

The basic formula of ABC algorithm search strategies randomly select one individual and one dimension in each evolution process, thus resulting in slow convergence. Even in the late evolutionary, the procedure might be stop coverage. For the purpose of improving the global convergence ability, convergence speed and taking advantage of the information of the global solution to guide the search process, we adopt the idea from [6]. The solution search equation described by formula 1.

$$V_{i,j} = x_{i,j} + \phi_{i,j} \left(x_{i,j} - x_{k,j} \right) + \varphi_{i,j} \left(g_j - x_{i,j} \right) \tag{1}$$

where g_j is the jth element of the global best solution.

Since the probability of an onlooker bee selecting a food source is based on the degree of fitness. When the adaptation value is relatively low, the probability of this food source is selected also become low. In order to increase the probability of the lower fitness individuals to be selected, we modify the probability equation described by Equation 2.

$$prob(i) = 0.9 * fitness(i)/max(fitness) + 0.1 \tag{2}$$

The main process of the algorithm is as follows: firstly, the initial population is generated randomly and evaluated by the fitness values. Secondly, the new solutions for employed bees are produced by equation 1, evaluated by fitness function and applied greedy selection. Thirdly, the probability value associated with the food source is calculated by Equation 2. The new solutions for onlooker bees is selected depending on probability value, which is generated by equation 1, then evaluated by fitness function and applied greedy selection. At last, if the result is not updated to limit times, an employed bee of which the source has been abandoned becomes a scout and starts to search a new food source randomly. When the iteration is terminated to the specified generations, we can get the output optimal solution.

3 Results and Discussion

In order to test the validity of the improved ABC algorithm on 3D AB off-lattice model protein folding prediction, we use the Fibonacci sequence and four real biological protein sequences to simulate. We compare the results of ABC algorithm with PSO[7], PERM[8], TS[9] and LPSO[7]. Our algorithm is adopted in MATLAB R2013a under Windows 7 system. The specific parameters are set as follows: SN = 200. The maximum number of iterations is 2000 and the population size is 400.

Table 1. Lowest energies obtained by PERM, PSO, TS, LPSO and ABC

length	E(PERM)	E(PSO)	E(TS)	E(LPSO)	E(ABC)
13	-3.2167	-1.2329	-1.7693	-4.6159	-0.8875
21	-5.7501	-2.7268	-2.9139	-6.6465	-8.1083
34	-	-4.6756	-4.8015	-7.3375	-10.3953
55	-14.9050	-6.9587	-8.3214	-13.0487	-22.4172

The results in Table 1 show the minimum energy value obtained by ABC algorithm in Fibonacci sequences. Fibonacci sequences as a typical mathematical model, it is able to react the specific protein amino acid, which is widely used in protein structure prediction of off-lattice model application. From Table 1, we can see that the lowest energy obtained by ABC algorithm is much better than those obtained by PERM [8], PSO [7], TS [9], and LPSO[7] except the sequence 13. By comparison, we can conclude that the results obtained by ABC algorithm is much better than other algorithms with the length of the sequences increasing, so our algorithm has certain advantages in solving the long sequence.

Table 2. Lowest energies of real protein sequence

Protein	E (PSO)	E (LPSO)	E (ABC)
2KGU	-8.3635	-20.9633	-31.9480
1CRN	-20.1826	-28.7591	-52.3249
2KAP	-8.0448	-15.9988	-30.3643
1PCH	-18.4408	-46.4964	-63.4272

In order to compare with the literature, we use the same sequence, which are downloaded from the PDB database. Table 2 shows the calculation results on real protein sequences. From Table 2, we can know that the result has lower energy than PSO and LPSO [7] algorithm. This shows that our method is feasible, the effect result illustrates that the algorithm is significant in solving the problem of protein structure prediction.

4 Conclusion

In this paper, we proposed a novel artificial bee colony (ABC) algorithm to solve the problem of protein structure prediction. ABC algorithm turns out to be a significant method to predict protein using the 3D AB model. This proposed approach is tested on Fibonacci sequences problem and re-markable performance is concluded after comparing its performance with the well-known algorithm. Moreover, the performance of ABC algorithm is also compared with the performance of the PSO and LPSO in the four real protein sequences. By observing the good performance of the Fibonacci sequences and real protein sequences, it is expected that artificial bee colony algorithm will be widely used to solve protein structure prediction problem.

Acknowledgments. This work is supported by the National Natural Science Foundation of China (No.31170797, 61103057, 31370778, 61370005), the Program for Changjiang Scholars and Innovative Research Team in University (No.IRT1109), the Key Project of Chinese Ministry of Education (No.211036),the Project Supported by Scientific Research Fund of Liaoning Provincial Education Department (No. L2011218),the Project is sponsored by "Liaoning BaiQianWan Talents Program" (No.2013921007), the Project is supported by the Natural Science Foundation of Liaoning Province(No. 2014020132).

References

1. Stillinger, F.H., Head-Gordon, T., Hirshfeld, C.L.: Toy Model For Protein Folding. Physical Review E 48, 1469 (1993)
2. Dill, K.A., Fiebig, K.M., Chan, H.S.: Cooperativity in Protein-Folding Kinetics. Proceedings of the National Academy of Sciences 90, 1942–1946 (1993)
3. Li, B., Li, Y., Gong, L.: Protein Secondary Structure Optimization Using an Improved Artificial Bee Colony Algorithm Based on Ab Off-Lattice Model. Engineering Applications of Artificial Intelligence 27, 70–79 (2014)
4. Zhang, Y., Wu, L.: Artificial Bee Colony for Two Dimensional Protein Folding. Advances in Electrical Engineering Systems 1, 19–23 (2012)
5. Karaboga, D., Basturk, B.: Artificial Bee Colony (ABC) Optimization Algorithm for Solving Constrained Optimization Problems. In: Melin, P., Castillo, O., Aguilar, L.T., Kacprzyk, J., Pedrycz, W. (eds.) IFSA 2007. LNCS (LNAI), vol. 4529, pp. 789–798. Springer, Heidelberg (2007)
6. Zhu, G., Kwong, S.: Gbest-guided Artificial Bee Colony Algorithm for Numerical Function Optimization. Applied Mathematics and Computation 217, 3166–3173 (2010)
7. Chen, X., Lv, M.W., Zhao, L.H., Zhang, X.D.: An Improved Particle Swarm Optimization for Protein Folding Prediction. International-Journal of Information Engineering and ElectronicBusiness 1, 1–8 (2011)
8. Wang, J.: The Application of Taboo Search Algorithm in Protein Structure Prediction. Computer Knowledge and Technology 9, 2101–2103 (2008)
9. Guo, H., Lan, R., Chen, X., et al.: Tabu Search-Particle Swarm Algorithm for Protein Folding Prediction. Computer Engineering and Applications 47, 46–50 (2011)

Find Dense Correspondence between High Resolution Non-rigid 3D Human Faces

Jian Liu, Quan Zhang, and Chaojing Tang

College of Electronic Science and Engineering,
National University of Defense Technology, China
jianliu@nudt.edu.cn

Abstract. It's a very complex problem to achieve dense correspondence between high resolution 3D human faces. Solving the problem can contribute to a variety of computer vision tasks. This paper proposed an automatic method to find dense correspondence between different high resolution non-rigid 3D human faces. The main idea of this method is to use the correspondent facial feature points to generate Möbius transformations and using these Möbius transformations to achieve sparse correspondence between 3D faces. The texture and shape information of 3D face are used to locate the facial feature points. TPS (Thin-Plate Spline) transformation is used to represent the deformation of 3D faces, the TPS control points are selected from the sparse correspondence set. After performing TPS warping, for every vertex of the warped reference 3D face, we project them to every triangle face of the sample 3D face and use the closest projections to define the new mesh vertices of the sample 3D face. The sample 3D face with new mesh shares the same connectivity with the reference 3D face, thus the dense correspondence between the reference 3D face and the sample 3D face with new mesh is achieved. The experiments on BJUT-3D face databases show that our method achieves better performance than existing methods.

Keywords: correspondence, facial feature point, Möbius transformation, thin-plate spline, feature vector, closest projection.

1 Introduction

Finding dense correspondence between 3D human faces (especially 3D high resolution human face) which have different number of vertices is a very complex problem. Solving the problem is significant for facial modeling [1], shape registration [2], face transfer [3], face recognition[4],shape matching [5], etc. For example, [1] proposed a morphable face model which can be used in facial modeling and facial animation. When building the morphable face model, the shape and texture of the 3D face examples must be transformed into a vector space representation. So different 3D faces must be registered by computing dense one-to-one correspondence between these 3D faces. Furthermore, if each 3D face can be represented as a vector by computing dense one-to-one correspondence,

L. Pan et al. (Eds.): BIC-TA 2014, CCIS 472, pp. 259–275, 2014.

the vectors can be viewed as an effective features for face modeling and recognition, and we can apply many mathematical tools such as Principal Component Analysis (PCA) directly to these concatenated vectors[6].

Finding dense correspondence between 3D human faces is a challenging work. One reason is that the geometry of the 3D face is very complex, the boundary of the human face is poorly defined and the extent of the 3D face data varies from example to example [7]. The number of the clearly correspondent points between different 3D faces is very small, these points are mostly the distinct feature points in human face, such as the nose tip, the corner of eyes and lip, etc [8]. For the points on the smooth regions of human face (cheek, forehead, etc.), it's difficult to define the correspondence [9]. Another reason is that the resolution of the 3D face is very high. With the development of the 3D data acquisition technology and computer visualization technology, it is convenient to acquire high resolution 3D faces [10]. For high resolution 3D human face, the vertices number is usually beyond 50000, some even beyond 70000, it's time consuming to process such high resolution 3D faces.

1.1   Related Work

Existing methods proposed to solve the 3D face dense correspondence can be commonly classified into ICP (Iterative Closest Point) based and TPS (Thin-Plate Spline) based types.

The ICP algorithm proposed by [11] starts with an initial rigid transformation and iteratively searches for closest points in two surfaces and optimizes the rigid transformation by minimizing the mean square distance metric. There are also many variants of the ICP method, such as [12], [13], [14], etc. These ICP methods are based on the rigid transformation, which are unsuitable for non-rigid deformation, such as with 3D human faces. For the non-rigid deformation, [15] proposed a hierarchical method for aligning warped meshes, they used a piecewise rigid compensating warp and cut each mesh into a set of overlapping regions, these overlapping regions were allowed to translate and rotate relative to each other. The resulting set of regions and their translations and rotations constituted a piecewise rigid approximation of the curved warp. The method of [15] can obtain global alignment with non-rigid deformation, but their method pertains to the choice of compensating warp, and the local rigid transformation was not suitable for complex shape variety such as high resolution 3D human faces.

When dealing with 3D human face, thin-plate spline (TPS) is used for transferring the landmark-based deformation since it is the only spline that can be cleanly decomposed into affine and non-affine subspaces while minimizing a global bending energy function [16] based on the second derivative of the spatial mapping. In this sense, the TPS can be considered to be a natural non-rigid extension of the affine map. As a result, for non-rigid deformation of 3D human faces, The TPS transformation has been widely used. [17] proposed a point matching algorithm named TPS-RPM (Thin-Plate Spline-Robust Point Matching) algorithm for non-rigid registration. They formulate feature-based non-rigid registration as a non-rigid point matching problem. The TPS-RPM algorithm utilizes the softassign, deterministic annealing [18], [19], [20] and the thin-plate spline to compute point correspondence iteratively. Although the performance of the TPS-RPM algorithm is demonstrated and validated in a series of carefully designed synthetic experiments, when dealing with 3D faces, it will perform not so well because of the dimension limitation of the correspondence matrix and the impracticalness of applying TPS on global dense point sets. [9] presented an automatic point matching method which adopted the TPS transformation to model the deformation of 3D faces. They proposed a random point selecting method to get the controlling points for TPS transformation and used an iterative closest point searching strategy to achieve dense point alignment of 3D faces. The main disadvantage of this method was that the deformations of some local shapes are not satisfactory because some of the controlling points were improperly selected. [10] proposed an automatic multi-sample 3D face registration method. Different from [9], they generated the controlling points of TPS by using a farthest point sampling (FPS) method and used a dynamical reference based on deformable model to implement the multi-sample registration. Since the controlling points generated by FPS method cannot guarantee sparse correspondence, the result of dense correspondence are not so well. [8] described a non-rigid registration method for fully automatic 3D facial image mapping. They first used shape and texture information to locate the facial feature points, then used these facial feature points as controlling points for TPS transformation. When building the dense correspondence, they designed a scheme to define the new mesh vertices of the sample surface, and after all the sample surfaces were remeshed using the same reference, the dense correspondence was established.

1.2 Outline of Our Work

This paper proposes a TPS (Thin-Plate Spline) based method which using Möbius transformation. Our method are mainly inspired by [8] and [21]. In our method, we first use geodesic remeshing to reduce the vertices number of the 3D faces (section 2), which can alleviate the time consuming problem when processing the high resolution 3D faces, then we use the texture and shape information of the 3D faces to locate facial feature points (section 3.1), the main contribution of these facial feature points is to generate Möbius transformations [21]. When we get these Möbius transformations, we can utilize them to generate sparse correspondent points (section 3.2). Since most 3D faces have boundaries, we can use feature vectors method [22] to achieve boundary sparse correspondence (section 3.3). Finally, we perform TPS warping to achieve dense correspondence by using the sparse correspondent points as control points (section 4). During TPS warping, we define a new mesh of the sample 3D face by using the closest projections (section 4). When finding the closest projections, we propose a new method to project a 3D point to a 3D triangle face (section 4).

2   Geodesic Remeshing

For high resolution 3D human face, the vertices number is usually beyond 50000, some even beyond 70000. It's time consuming to process such high resolution 3D faces. To alleviate the time-consuming procedures, one obvious solution is to reduce the vertices number of the 3D face and maintain the resolution as high as possible. Since different 3D face always has different number of vertices, we also should make them have the same number of vertices. To achieve these goals, we use the method proposed by [23], because their method is fast and easy to implement. Our intuitive idea is: (1) Select one 3D face from 3D face databases as reference 3D face; (2) Geodesic remesh the reference 3D face with some proper vertices number which is smaller than the original vertices number of the reference 3D face; (3) Using the remeshed reference 3D face to sample other 3D faces, thus all the 3D faces sampled by the reference 3D face have the same vertices number and share the same connectivity with the reference 3D face, that is, they are in full dense correspondence.

We choose the nose tip as the start point. Because at this stage we don't demand high accuracy of the nose tip's position, we simply transform the 3D face's three-dimensional Cartesian coordinates (x, y, z) into cylindrical coordinates (ρ, φ, z), and choose the vertex whose radial distance ρ have maximum value as the nose tip. That is:

$$\rho_i = \sqrt{x_i^2 + y_i^2}, i \in \{1, ..., N\} \tag{1}$$

$$ID_{nose\,tip} = \{j | \rho_j = \max_{1 \leq i \leq N} \rho_i\}, j \in \{1, ..., N\} \tag{2}$$

where ρ_i is the radial distance of the ith 3D face's vertex, $\{x_i, y_i, z_i\}$ is the Cartesian coordinate of the ith 3D face's vertex, N is the total vertices number of the 3D face, $ID_{nose\,tip}$ is the nose tip's vertex ID.

After choosing the nose tip as the start point, we iteratively add most geodesically distant point from the points we already have added on the 3D face's surface. Then we use the method in [23] to calculate the geodesic triangles. Figure 1 shows the remeshing result, the original 3D face's vertices number is about 70000, the remeshed 3D face's vertices number is 30000.

3   Sparse Correspondence

In order to find dense correspondence between 3D faces, we should find sparse correspondence between 3D faces at first. Since we will perform TPS (Thin-Plate Spline) warp on the 3D faces to achieve dense correspondence, it is vital to select proper and enough control points for TPS [10].So on the next steps we will find ways to achieve sparse correspondence. Figure 2 shows the main steps to achieve sparse correspondence between 3D faces.

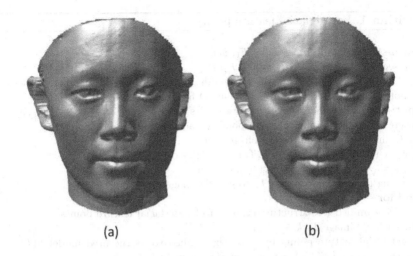

Fig. 1. (a) original 3D face.(b) remeshed 3D face.

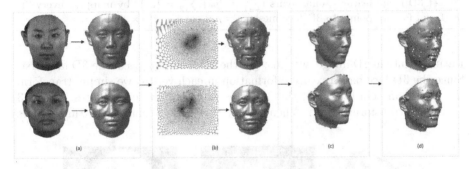

Fig. 2. The main steps to achieve sparse correspondence between 3D faces. (a) Locate facial feature points. (b) Möbius voting based on facial feature points. (c) Find boundaries sparse correspondence. (d) Sparse correspondence.

3.1   Locate Facial Feature Points

Since each vertex in the 3D face has texture information, we can use such texture information to locate the facial feature points (Algorithm 1). When we locate the facial feature points based on texture information, we can further extract the more correspondent facial feature points with the help of 3D shape information. The main techniques here we used are a unified tree-structured model [24] and shape index [25]. We use the method proposed by [24] to locate facial feature points in 2D images since their method is very effective and especially useful when dealing with image in wild. We should point out that in our sparse correspondence procedure, we can use other techniques to locate the facial feature points in 2D images (eg. [8] and [26]), as long as such techniques can achieve accurate result when locating facial feature points. Before we locate the facial

---

Algorithm 1. Locate facial feature points

Input:
    the first 3D face mesh $M = (V_1, F_1, T_1)$;
    the second 3D face mesh $N = (V_2, F_2, T_2)$;
    // V denotes vertices of the 3D face mesh, F denotes faces of the 3D face mesh, T
    denotes the texture information of the 3D face mesh.
Output: correspondent facial feature points pairs $(v_{1_i}, v_{2_i}), i = 1, 2, ..., N_v, v \in V$,
    where N_v is the number of correspondent facial feature points pairs.
    // Cylindrical coordinates transformation
1: **for** each 3D face mesh $(V_k, F_k, T_k), k \in \{1, 2\}$ **do**
2:    $\rho_k = \sqrt{x_k^2 + y_k^2}, \phi_k = \tan^{-1}(\frac{y_k}{x_k}), z_k = z_k$
3:    Using texture information T_k to get 2D image I_k.
4: **end for**
    // Using unified tree-structured model to locate facial feature points
5: **for** each 2D image $I_k, k \in \{1, 2\}$ **do**
6:    get facial feature points by maximize unified tree-structured model $S(I, L, m)$
    over L and m: $S^*(I_k) = \max_m[\max_L S(I_k, L, m)]$.
7: **end for**
8: get 3D facial feature points pairs $(\sum_1 = \{p_r\}, \sum_2 = \{q_s\})$ by mapping every 2D
    facial feature points to 3D face mesh: $x = \rho \times \cos\phi, y = \rho \times \sin\phi, z = z$

---

feature points in 2D image, we must get the 2D faces images of the 3D face first. Since the 3D face have texture information in each vertex, we simply transform the Cartesian coordinates of the 3D faces to cylindrical coordinates. Figure 3 shows the transform result. When we get the 2D face images (texture images

 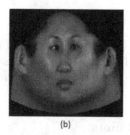 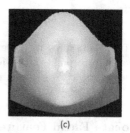

(a)   (b)   (c)

Fig. 3. (a) original 3D face.(b) 2D face texture image. (c) 2D face shape image.

and shape images), we can use the method proposed by [24] to locate the facial feature points. To locate the facial feature points, [24] proposed a unified tree-structured model. They model every facial feature point as a part V and use global mixtures to capture topological changes due to viewpoint. Each tree can be written as $T_m = (V_m, E_m)$, where m denotes a mixture, $V_m \subseteq V$, E is the tree's edge. If I is the 2D texture image, $l_i = (x_i, y_i)$ is the pixel position of part i, then a configuration of parts $L = \{l_i : i \in V\}$ can be scored as:

$$S(I, L, m) = App_m(I, L) + Shape_m(L) + \alpha^m \tag{3}$$

$$App_m(I, L) = \sum_{i \in V_m} \omega_i^m \cdot \phi(I, l_i) \tag{4}$$

$$Shape_m(L) = \sum_{i,j \in E_m} (a_{ij}^m dx^2 + b_{ij}^m dx + c_{ij}^m dy^2 + d_{ij}^m dy) \tag{5}$$

ω_i^m is the template of part i, $\phi(I, l_i)$ is the feature vector extracted from pixel location l_i in image I. $dx = x_i - x_j$ and $dy = y_i - y_j$ are the displacement of the ith part relative to the jth part. (a, b, c, d) are the parameters and α^m is a scalar bias. The facial feature points can be found by maximize unified tree-structured model $S(I, L, m)$ over L and m: $S^*(I_k) = \max_m[\max_L S(I_k, L, m)]$. The detail to find the facial feature points can be found in [24]. Figure 4 shows the result of locating the facial feature points.

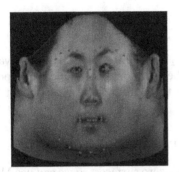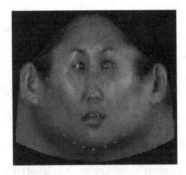

Fig. 4. The result of locating the facial feature points

3D points are found by inverse-warping the texture coordinates associated with the 3D points [27]. Use the 2D face shape image and map every 2D facial feature points to 3D face mesh: $x = \rho \times \cos\phi, y = \rho \times \sin\phi, z = z$, we can get the 3D facial feature points pairs $(\sum_1 = \{p_r\}, \sum_2 = \{q_s\})$ (Figure 5). There may exist noise in the 3D face texture information, and when transform the Cartesian coordinates to the cylindrical coordinates, some 3D geometric information may lose, so there will be some errors when locating the 3D facial feature points. To achieve sparse correspondence, we must get rid of those errors. We can use 3D information of the 3D face to get rid of those errors and further extract correspondent facial feature points pairs. The shape index [25] captures the intuitive notion of local shape such as convex, saddle, and concave of a surface, and can describe subtle shape variations. Considering the complexity of human face, we use the difference of the shape index of the points to determine if these points are really correspondent. The equation of the shape index difference between point p and q is

$$D(p, q) = |S_I(p) - S_I(q)| \tag{6}$$

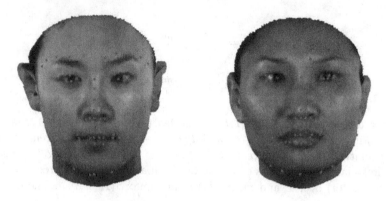

Fig. 5. 3D facial feature points

$$S_I(p) = \frac{1}{2} - \frac{1}{\pi} \tan^{-1} \frac{\kappa_1(p) + \kappa_2(p)}{\kappa_1(p) - \kappa_2(p)} \tag{7}$$

where $S_I(p)$ is the shape index of point p, κ_1 and κ_2 are the principal curvatures of the surface with $\kappa_1 \geq \kappa_2$. If $D(p, q)$ is beyond some threshold, then point p and q are not correspondent, we get rid of them from the correspondent facial feature points pairs.

3.2   Möbius Voting Based on Facial Feature Points

The 3D human faces are near-isometric genus-zero surfaces, so we can use Möbius voting to get the sparse correspondence set. [21] found a way to search for isometries or near-isometries between two different genus-zero surfaces M, N in the space of Möbius transformations. The main technique we used is motivated by it.

The steps of the technique is as follows:

(1) **Uniformization.** We use the mid-edge uniformization step of [21] to map the 3D face mesh surface to the extended complex plane $\hat{\mathbb{C}}$. We map each vertex $v_i \in V$ to $z_i \in \hat{\mathbb{C}}$ by denoting v_i as the mid-edge point $\mathbf{v}_r$ which is geodesically closest to v_i. Because each $\mathbf{v}_r$ correspond to each z_i, thus the 3D face mesh M is flattened. Figure 6 shows the uniformization result.

(2) **Point Sample.** We select every correspondent points from the correspondent facial feature points pairs as the start points, then uniformly sample discrete sets of N points S_1 and S_2 from each 3D face M and N, as described by [21]. Then project S_1 and S_2 onto the complex plane $\hat{\mathbb{C}}$ to form the planar point samples $S_1' = \{p_t'\}, S_2' = \{q_t'\}$.

(3) **Generating Möbius Transformations.** Different from [21], we use the 3D facial feature points pairs ($\Sigma_1 = \{p_r\}, \Sigma_2 = \{q_s\}$) to generate the Möbius transformations. We map ($\Sigma_1 = \{p_r\}, \Sigma_2 = \{q_s\}$) to the extended complex plane $\hat{\mathbb{C}}$: ($\Sigma_1' = \{z_r\}, \Sigma_2' = \{w_s\}$) firstly. Then exhaustedly

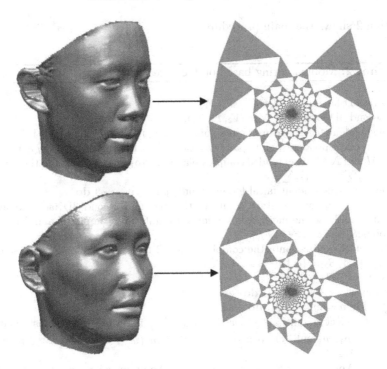

Fig. 6. Uniformization result

search the triplets of points from $(\sum_1' = \{z_r\}, \sum_2' = \{w_s\}) : z_{r1}, z_{r2}, z_{r3} \in$ $\sum_1', w_{s1}, w_{s2}, w_{s3} \in \sum_2'$, and find the Möbius transformations m_1, m_2 subject to $m_1(z_{rj}) = y_j, m_2(w_{sj}) = y_j, j = 1, 2, 3$, where m denotes the Möbius transformation $m(z) = (az + b)/(cz + d)$, $y_j, j = 1, 2, 3$ denotes a canonical domain in the extended complex plane. Here we set $y_j = e^{i\frac{2\pi}{3}j}, j = 1, 2, 3$, which means that y_j forms an scale and position do not matter equilateral. After we find the Möbius transformations m_1, m_2, we can apply m_1 on S_1' to get $\bar{z}_r = m_1(p_t')$, apply m_2 on S_2' to get $\bar{w}_s = m_2(q_t')$.

(4) **Cast Vote.** We maintain a non-negative real matrix $C = (C_{k,l})$ with dimensions $|S_1'| \times |S_2'|$. For every Möbius transformation generated by step 3, we find mutually nearest-neighbors $(\bar{z}_r, \bar{w}_s)$ in the flattened space. If the number of mutually closest pairs is not less than a threshold K, we compute $\frac{|(\bar{z}_r, \bar{w}_s)|}{|S_1' = \{p_t'\}, S_2' = \{q_t'\}|}$ as the vote value and sum it into the fuzzy correspondence matrix $C = (C_{r,s})$: $C_{r,s} \leftarrow C_{r,s} + \frac{|(\bar{z}_r, \bar{w}_s)|}{|S_1' = \{p_t'\}, S_2' = \{q_t'\}|}$, where $|(\bar{z}_r, \bar{w}_s)|$ is the number of mutually closest pairs, $|S_1' = \{p_t'\}, S_2' = \{q_t'\}|$ is the number of the points pairs $(S_1' = \{p_t'\}, S_2' = \{q_t'\})$.

(5) **Extract Correspond Pairs.** We use the max-row-column algorithm [21] to iteratively looks for the maximal entry greater than zero in the fuzzy correspondence matrix $C = (C_{r,s})$ and get the correspondence map (p_u, q_v).

Algorithm 2 shows the main procedures.

Algorithm 2. Möbius voting based on facial feature points

Input:

the first 3D face mesh $M = (V_1, F_1, T_1)$;

the second 3D face mesh $N = (V_2, F_2, T_2)$;

Correspondent facial feature points pairs $(v_{1_i}, v_{2_i}), i = 1, 2, ..., N_v, v \in V$.

Output: correspondent points pairs $(p_u, q_v), u, v = 1, 2, ..., N_s, p \in V_1, q \in V_2$

1: Map M and N to the extended complex plane $\hat{C}$. Project (v_{1_i}, v_{2_i}) onto the complex plane $\hat{C} : \sum_1 = \{z_i\}, \sum_2 = \{w_i\}$.

2: **for** each Correspondent facial feature points pairs (v_{1_i}, v_{2_i}) **do**

3:    Select v_{1_i}, v_{2_i} as the start points in the first and second 3D face meshes M and N and use the method in section 2 to uniformly sample M and N with N points:$S_1 = \{p_t\}, S_2 = \{q_t\}$.

4:    Project S_1 and S_2 onto the complex plane $\hat{C}$ to form the planar point samples $S_1' = \{p_t'\}, S_2' = \{q_t'\}$.

5:    **for** $l = 1 : N_v - 2$ **do**

6:      **for** $m = l + 1 : N_v - 1$ **do**

7:        **for** $n = m + 1 : N_v$ **do**

8:          select $z_l, z_m, z_n \in \sum_1, w_l, w_m, w_n \in \sum_2$, find the Möbius transformations m_1, m_2 subject to $m_1(z_{j'}) = e^{i\frac{2\pi}{3}j}, m_2(w_{j'}) = e^{i\frac{2\pi}{3}j}, j' = l, m, n.j = 1, 2, 3..$

9:          Apply m_1 on S_1' to get $\bar{z}_r = m_1(p_t')$. Apply m_2 on S_2' to get $\bar{w}_s = m_2(q_t')$.

10:          Find mutually nearest-neighbors $(\bar{z}_r, \bar{w}_s)$ in the flattened space.

11:          **if** number of mutually closest pairs$\geq k$ **then**

12:            **for** each mutually closest pairs **do**

13:              $C_{r,s} \leftarrow C_{r,s} + \frac{|(\bar{z}_r, \bar{w}_s)|}{|S_1' = \{p_t'\}, S_2' = \{q_t'\}|}$

14:            **end for**

15:          **end if**

16:        **end for**

17:      **end for**

18:    **end for**

19:    use the max-row-column algorithm and select the first H correspondent pairs $(p_{u'}', q_{v'}'), u', v' \in \{1, ..., N\}$.

20: **end for**

21: Add all the correspond pairs $(p_{u'}', q_{v'}')$ together, remove the duplicate ones, finally get the correspondent points pairs (p_u, q_v).

3.3   Find Boundaries Sparse Correspondence

The 3D face mesh surface is genus-zero surface with boundary. It's important to achieve boundary sparse correspondence when finding dense correspondence. For every 3D face mesh, we just find the edge which have only one face adjacent to it: $\{e_k \in E | Number\ of\ faces\ adjacent\ to\ e_k = 1\}, k \in \{1, ..., N_e\}$, where

E is the 3D face mesh's edges, N_e is the number of the edges, then the vertices on the boundary of the 3D face mesh is the vertices on every edge e_k. For 3D face meshes $M = (V_1, F_1, T_1)$ and $N = (V_2, F_2, T_2)$, since their boundaries size are usually different, we uniformly sample the two 3D face meshes' boundaries with the same number of vertices, we denote the sampled boundaries as $B_1 = \{p_{b1} \in e_{k1}\}, B_2 = \{p_{b2} \in e_{k2}\}, b1, b2 \in \{1, ..., N_b\}$, where N_b is the number of vertices sampled on the boundaries. Since we already have found correspondence between the 3D facial feature points (v_{1_i}, v_{2_j}), we can achieve boundaries sparse correspondence by utilizing the correspond pairs (v_{1_i}, v_{2_j}). Here we use the feature vectors method proposed by [22]. That is as follows:

(1) **Calculate Feature Vector.** For each point $p_i \in B_1, q_j \in B_2$, we calculate feature vectors:

$$\Psi(p_i) = (g(p_i, v_{1_1}), ..., g(p_i, v_{1_{N_v}})) \tag{8}$$

$$\Psi(q_j) = (g(q_j, v_{2_1}), ..., g(q_j, v_{2_{N_v}})) \tag{9}$$

Where $g(p_u, p_v)$ denotes the geodesic distance on mesh M or N of the points $p_u, p_v \in M$ or N.

(2) **Calculate Relative Deviation Measure.** The relative deviation measure is

$$D(\Psi(p_i), \Psi(q_j)) = \sum_{k=1}^{N_v} (\frac{g(p_i, v_{1_k}) - g(q_j, v_{2_k})}{g(p_i, v_{1_k})})^2 \tag{10}$$

$$D(\Psi(q_j), \Psi(p_i)) = \sum_{k=1}^{N_v} (\frac{g(q_j, v_{2_k}) - g(p_i, v_{1_k})}{g(q_j, v_{2_k})})^2 \tag{11}$$

(3) **Get Boundaries Sparse Correspondence.** Compute the smallest relative deviation measure respectively, then find the correspond pairs (p_r, q_s), $r, s \in \{1, ..., N_b\}$ which have mutually smallest deviation. That is

$$\arg \min_{s \in \{1,...,N_b\}} [D(\Psi(p_r), \Psi(q_1)), D(\Psi(p_r), \Psi(q_2)), ...,$$
$$D(\Psi(p_r), \Psi(q_s))] = s \tag{12}$$

$$\arg \min_{r \in \{1,...,N_b\}} [D(\Psi(q_s), \Psi(p_1)), D(\Psi(q_s), \Psi(p_2)), ...,$$
$$D(\Psi(q_s), \Psi(p_r))] = r \tag{13}$$

4 Dense Correspondence

Now we have the sparse correspondence set, which includes 3D facial feature points pairs, boundaries sparse correspondent pairs and Möbius voting correspondent pairs, next we will use the sparse correspondence set to achieve dense correspondence. Here we use the TPS-based method. For simplicity, we call the remeshed 3D face as reference face M, one of the other 3D faces as sample face N.

We use the point pairs in the sparse correspondence set as fiducial points and TPS warp the reference face M to the sample face N as described by [28]. After warping, the sample face N and the warped reference face M' are topologically similar. Then for every vertex of the warped reference face M', we project them to every triangle face of the sample face N and find the closest ones, then we use the closest projections to define the new mesh vertices of the sample face. We denote the sample face with the new mesh vertices as N', we can see that the vertices number and order of N' is the same as the vertices number and order of M, and N' share the same connectivity with the reference face M, thus the dense correspondence between M and N' is achieved.

When finding the closest projections, we proposed a new method to project a vertex to a triangle. Figure 7 shows a triangle in 3D space. In figure 7, we divide

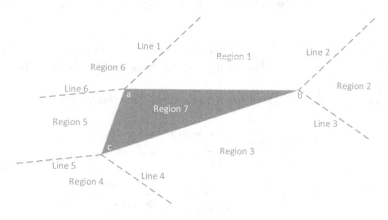

Fig. 7. Triangle in 3D space

the plane of the triangle into 7 regions, where line 1 and line 2 are orthogonal to line ab, line 3 and line 4 are orthogonal to line bc, line 5 and line 6 are orthogonal to line ca. For vertex v in the 3D space, we first project it to the plane of the triangle and get the point v'. If v' belongs to region 7, then it is the projection result; If v' belongs to region 2, or region 4, or region 6, the projection result is just the triangle's vertex b, or vertex c, or vertex a respectively; if v' belongs to region 1, or region 3, or region 5, we simply project v' to line ab, or line bc, or line ca respectively to get the projection point v'', v'' is the projection result. Figure 8 shows one example of the projection. In figure 8, v is projected to the plane of the triangle and get point v', which is in region 3, so we project v' to line bc and get point v'', which is the projection result.

When we get the projection result v'', we can use barycentric coordinates to get the texture information of v''. That is as follows, we first get the barycentric coordinates $(\lambda_1, \lambda_2, \lambda_3)$ of point v'' in triangle abc, then the texture information of v'' can be calculated as $T = \lambda_1 \cdot T_a + \lambda_2 \cdot T_b + \lambda_3 \cdot T_c$, where T_a, T_b, T_c are texture information of vertex a, vertex b and vertex c respectively.

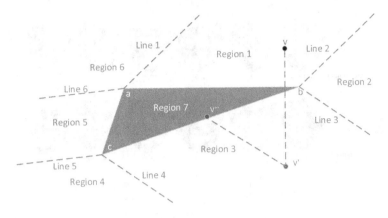

Fig. 8. One example of closest projection

Table 1. Hausdorff approximation error

Sample number	100	500	1000	3000	5000	7000	10000	15000	20000	25000	30000
Hausdorff error	10.524	4.675	3.282	1.859	1.433	1.203	1.016	0.825	0.684	0.578	0.508

5   Experiments and Results

The experiments are implemented on BJUT-3D face database [29]. This database contains 500 Chinese 3D faces (250 females and 250 males) which are acquired by the CyberWare Laser Scanner in special environment. Each subject has the 3D shape data and texture data and generally have more than 70000 vertices and 140000 triangles. There are 100 faces from BJUT-3D face database used in our experiments. To evaluate the efficiency of geodesic remeshing, we measure the mean-square Hausdorff distance between the original mesh and a series of geodesic remeshing versions. The Hausdorff distance between two sets of points X and Y is

$$d(X,Y) = d_0(X,Y) + d_0(Y,X) \tag{14}$$

$$d_0(X,Y)^2 = \frac{1}{|X|} \sum_{x \in X} \min_{y \in Y} \|x - y\|^2 \tag{15}$$

Table 1 shows the Hausdorff approximation errors with different sample numbers, Figure 9(a) display the original 3D face and the remeshed 3D faces, the vertices number of the original 3D face is 62283, figure 9(b) display the decay of the Hausdorff approximation error as the number N_0 of sampling points increases.

To evaluate the dense correspondence degree of our method, we compare our method with Hu's method [9], Qin's method [10] and Guo's method [8]. Within which, Guo's method is the most closest one to our method, they also defined a new mesh of the sample 3D face, so we use the mean-square Hausdorff distance and average root mean square (RMS) error for the assessment. Here, the mean-square Hausdorff distance between the sample face N and the sample face

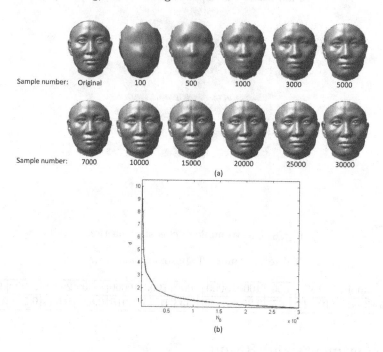

(a)

(b)

Fig. 9. (a) the original 3D face and the remeshed 3D faces.(b) the Hausdorff approximation error.

with the new mesh vertices N' exhibits the similarity between N and N', the RMS error is defined as the mean distance between the correspondent points on the reference 3D face mesh M and the sample face with the new mesh vertices N'. As for Hu's method and Qin's method, they directly established dense correspondence between reference 3D face and sample 3D face, so we only use average root mean square (RMS) error for the assessment. Figure 10 shows the similarity between N and N'. In figure 10, we can see clearly that the similarity of our method in the ear and boundary region between the sample face and the sample face with new mesh is higher than the similarity of Guo's method. Figure 11 shows the mean-square Hausdorff distance and average root mean square (RMS) error. From figure 11, we can see that the mean-square Hausdorff distance of our method is smaller than that of the Guo's method, which indicate that the sample face with new mesh generated by our method is more similar than that of Guo's method. The average root mean square error of our method is the smallest one, which indicates that the correspondence degree of our method is higher than other three methods.

6   Conclusion

This paper proposed an automatic method to find dense correspondence between different high resolution non-rigid 3D human faces. The idea of our method lies

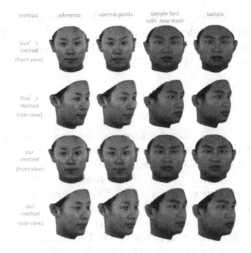

Fig. 10. Similarity between N and N'

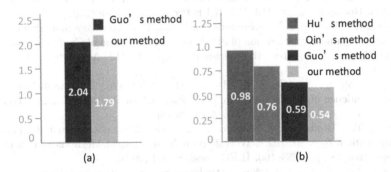

(a)   (b)

Fig. 11. (a) mean-square Hausdorff distance. (b) average root mean square (RMS) error.

in three points. Firstly, the texture and shape information of 3D face are used to locate the facial feature points, which can generate Möbius transformations. Secondly, we utilize these Möbius transformations and feature vectors to achieve sparse correspondence between 3D faces. Lastly, we use the TPS transformation to represent the deformation of 3D faces, the TPS control points are selected from the sparse correspondence set, then for every vertex of the warped reference face, we project them to every triangle face of the sample face and use the closest projections to define the new mesh vertices of the sample face. The sample face with new mesh shares the same connectivity with the reference face, thus the dense correspondence between the reference face and the sample face with new mesh is achieved. The experimental results on BJUT-3D face databases demonstrate that our method achieve better performance compared with the existing methods.

Acknowledgments. Portions of the research in this paper use the BJUT-3D Face Database collected under the joint sponsor of National Natural Science Foundation of China, Beijing Natural Science Foundation Program, Beijing Science and Educational Committee Program.

References

1. Blanz, V., Vetter, T.: A morphable model for the synthesis of 3D faces. In: 26th Annual Conference on Computer Graphics and Interactive Techniques, pp. 187–194. ACM Press, Los Angeles (1999)
2. Anguelov, D., Srinivasan, P., Pang, H.-C., Koller, D., Thrun, S., Davis, J.: The Correlated Correspondence Algorithm for Unsupervised Registration of Nonrigid Surfaces. In: 18th Annual Conference on Neural Information Processing Systems, pp. 33–40. NIPS Foundation, Montreal (2004)
3. Vlasic, D., Brand, M., Pfister, H., Popovic, J.: Face transfer with multilinear models. ACM Transactions on Graphics 24, 426–433 (2005)
4. Irfanoglu, M.O., Gokberk, B., Akarun, L.: 3D shape-based face recognition using automatically registered facial surfaces. In: 17th International Conference on Pattern Recognition, pp. 183–186. IEEE Press, Cambridge (2004)
5. Hilaga, M., Shinagawa, Y., Kohmura, T., Kunii, T.L.: Topology matching for fully automatic similarity estimation of 3D shapes. In: 28th Annual Conference on Computer Graphics and Interactive Techniques, pp. 203–212. ACM Press, New York (2001)
6. Pan, G., Zhang, X., Wang, Y., Hu, Z., Zheng, X., Wu, Z.: Establishing Point Correspondence of 3D Faces Via Sparse Facial Deformable Model. IEEE Transactions on Image Processing 22, 4170–4181 (2013)
7. Hutton, T.J., Buxton, B.F., Hammond, P.: Dense surface point distribution models of the human face. In: IEEE Workshop on Mathematical Methods in Biomedical Image Analysis, pp. 153–160. IEEE Press, Kauai (2001)
8. Guo, J., Mei, X., Tang, K.: Automatic landmark annotation and dense correspondence registration for 3D human facial images. BMC Bioinformatics 14, 232–243 (2013)
9. Hu, Y., Zhou, M., Wu, Z.: An Automatic Dense Point Registration Method for 3D Face Animation. In: 2nd International Congress on Image and Signal Processing, pp. 1–6. IEEE Press, Tianjin (2009)
10. Qin, W., Hu, Y., Sun, Y., Yin, B.: An Automatic Multi-sample 3D Face Registration Method Based on Thin Plate Spline and Deformable Model. In: 2012 IEEE International Conference on Multimedia and Expo Workshops, pp. 453–458. IEEE Press, Melbourne (2012)
11. Besl, P.J., McKay, N.D.: Method for registration of 3-D shapes. In: Robotics-DL tentative, pp. 586–606 (1992)
12. Weik, S.: Registration of 3-D partial surface models using luminance and depth information. In: International Conference on Recent Advances in 3-D Digital Imaging and Modeling, pp. 93–100. IEEE Press, Ottawa (1997)
13. Simon, D.A.: Fast and Accurate Shape-Based Registration. Carnegie Mellon University, Pittsburgh (1996)
14. Pulli, K.: Multiview registration for large data sets. In: Second International Conference on 3-D Digital Imaging and Modeling, pp. 160–168. IEEE Press, Ottawa (1999)

15. Ikemoto, L., Gelfand, N., Levoy, M.: A hierarchical method for aligning warped meshes. In: Fourth International Conference on 3-D Digital Imaging and Modeling, pp. 434–441. IEEE Press, Banff (2003)
16. Bookstein, F.L.: Principal warps: Thin-plate splines and the decomposition of deformations. IEEE Transactions on pattern analysis and machine intelligence 11, 567–585 (1989)
17. Chui, H.L., Rangarajan, A.: A new point matching algorithm for non-rigid registration. Computer Vision and Image Understanding 89, 114–141 (2003)
18. Chui, H., Rambo, J., Duncan, J.S., Schultz, R.T., Rangarajan, A.: Registration of cortical anatomical structures via robust 3D point matching. In: Kuba, A., Sámal, M., Todd-Pokropek, A. (eds.) IPMI 1999. LNCS, vol. 1613, pp. 168–181. Springer, Heidelberg (1999)
19. Gold, S., Rangarajan, A., Lu, C.-P., Pappu, S., Mjolsness, E.: New algorithms for 2d and 3d point matching: pose estimation and correspondence. Pattern Recognition 31, 1019–1031 (1998)
20. Rangarajan, A., Chui, H., Bookstein, F.L.: The softassign procrustes matching algorithm. In: 15th International Conference on Information Processing in Medical Imaging, pp. 29–42. Springer Press, Poultney (1997)
21. Lipman, Y., Funkhouser, T.: Möbius voting for surface correspondence. ACM Transactions on Graphics 28, 72 (2009)
22. Kim, V.G., Lipman, Y., Chen, X., Funkhouser, T.: Möbius transformations for global intrinsic symmetry analysis. Computer Graphics Forum 29, 1689–1700 (2010)
23. Peyre, G., Cohen, L.D.: Geodesic remeshing using front propagation. Geodesic remeshing using front propagation. International Journal of Computer Vision. 69, 145–156 (2010)
24. Zhu, X., Ramanan, D.: Face detection, pose estimation, and landmark localization in the wild. In: IEEE Conference on Computer Vision and Pattern Recognition, pp. 2879–2886. IEEE Press, Providence (2012)
25. Dorai, C., Jain, A.K.: COSMOS-A representation scheme for 3D free-form objects. IEEE Transactions on pattern analysis and machine intelligence 19, 1115–1130 (1997)
26. Erdogmus, N., Dugelay, J.-L.: Automatic extraction of facial interest points based on 2D and 3D data. In: Conference on the Three-Dimensional Imaging, Interaction, and Measurement, vol. 7864, p. 23. SPIE Press, San Francisco (2011)
27. Schneider, D.C., Eisert, P., Herder, J., Magnor, M., Grau, O.: Algorithms for automatic and robust registration of 3d head scans. Journal of Virtual Reality and Broadcasting 7(7) (2010)
28. Hutton, T.J., Buxton, B.F., Hammond, P., Potts, H.W.: Estimating average growth trajectories in shape-space using kernel smoothing. IEEE Transactions on Medical Imaging 22, 747–753 (2003)
29. Tech, Multimedia.: The BJUT-3D Large-Scale Chinese Face Database. Technical report, Graphics Lab, Beijing University of Technology (2005)

An Improved Particle Swarm Optimization and Its Application for Micro-grid Economic Operation Optimization

Tao Liu, Jun Wang, Zhang Sun,
Juan Luo, Tingting He, and Ke Chen

School of Electrical and Information Engineering,
Xihua University, Chengdu, Sichuan,610039,China
478695546@qq.com

Abstract. A particle swarm optimization algorithm based on adaptive mutation and P systems is proposed to overcome trapping in local optimum solution and low optimization precision in this paper. At the same time, the proposed algorithm is investigated in experiments which are based on the function optimization of micro-grid's economic operation. Furthermore, the feasibility and effectiveness of the proposed algorithm are showed in the experimental results.

Keywords: Particle swarm optimization algorithm, P system, Function optimization, Economic operation.

1 Introduction

In recent years, several membrane algorithms [1–4] have been proposed which the basic idea is to take some evolutionary algorithms as a sub-algorithm in the membrane, and to fast search out the optimum solutions using the parallel processing ability of membrane.Combining with membrane computing and fuzzy entropy, an image thresholding method is used in [5–7]. As can be seen from the above literatures the algorithms based on membrane computing have the better accuracy and fast convergence.

PSO has high optimized efficiency and robustness. For the drawbacks of PSO algorithm many improved methods have been proposed in many literatures. In [8], a dividing-gregarious particle swarm algorithm that integrates fission and mutation operations is proposed and it can effectively solve the reactive power optimization in medium-voltage distribution network. A new approach of solving reactive power optimization is proposed in [9] through applying adaptive particle swarm optimization with multi-strategy integration (MSI-APSO) algorithm.

An improved particle swarm optimization algorithm with adaptive mutation inspired by P systems is proposed. In order to reflect the theoretical and practical value of the algorithm, the micro-grid economic operation experiment is carried out on function optimization problems. The results verify that this new algorithm is more effective than the general PSO.

L. Pan et al. (Eds.): BIC-TA 2014, CCIS 472, pp. 276–280, 2014.
© Springer-Verlag Berlin Heidelberg 2014

The rest of this paper is organized as follows. The improved particle swarm optimization (PSO) algorithm is proposed in Section 2. Section 3 provides the model of micro-grid economic operation. Simulation experiment results are analyzed and discussed in Section 4. Section 5 draws the conclusion.

2   The Improved Particle Swarm Optimization Algorithm

The updating of inertia weight and adaptive mutation algorithm were improved in this article for the shortcomings of standard particle swarm optimization algorithm:

(1) The improvement of inertia weight. Inertia weight ω_i plays an important role in the capability of searching local optimum value and global optimization value. As the nonlinear equations in micro-grid economic operation are difficult to be optimized, inertia weight which is changed with index is introduced to balance the global and local optimal values:

$$\omega = (\omega_{max} - \omega_{min})(1 - \exp(-25 * \frac{k^6}{I_1^6})) \tag{1}$$

where, ω_{max} and ω_{min} respectively represent the maximum and minimum values of ω, normally take $\omega_{max} = 0.9$, $\omega_{min} = 0.4$.

(2) Adaptive mutation algorithm.

$$p_m = (p_{min} - p_{max})(\frac{\sigma^2}{N}) + p_{max} \tag{2}$$

where, p_m is the group mutation probability of group global extreme value.σ^2 is variance of group fitness value,p_{max} denotes the maximum value of mutation probability, p_{min} denotes the minimum value of mutation probability.

PSO algorithm based on adaptive mutation and P systems is proposed to overcome falling into the local optimum solution and low optimization precision in this paper.The updating of velocity and location in improved particle swarm optimization algorithm are shown in equation (3). The algorithm determines whether to perform a mutation operation based on population variability capacity (p_m), thereby expands the scope of optimization.

$$\begin{cases} v_i^{k+1} &= wv_i^k + c_1r_1(P_{besti} - X_i^k) + c_2r_2(P_{Gbest} - X_i^k) \\ X_i^{k+1} &= X_i^k + v_i^{k+1} \\ \omega &= \omega_{max} - (\omega_{max} - \omega_{min}) \times (1 - \exp(-25 \times \frac{k^6}{I_1^6})) \end{cases} \tag{3}$$

where, V_i is velocity of the $i - th$ particle, X_i is the position the $i - th$ particle, c_1 and c_2 are the acceleration factor. r_1 and r_2 are the random number in the range of [0,1], the diversity of population is kept by these two parameters. k is iteration number, and I_1 is the iteration number of each basic membrane.

3   The Application for Micro-grid Economic Operation Optimization

This article only considers the economic, environmental scheduling and optimization operation of the micro-grid which is in grid connected mode. Points which need to be considered are the objective function [10, 11].

The micro-grid objective function of economical and environmental operation can be stated as follows :

$$minc(P) = \sum_{t=1}^{T}\sum_{i=1}^{3}\{F_i[p(t)] + O_i[p(t)] + C_{DEP} + \sum_{k=1}^{M}\alpha_k E_k^i[P(t)]\}$$
$$+ \sum_{t=1}^{T}\{c_b(t)P_{buy}(t) - c_s(t)P_{sell}(t)\} \tag{4}$$

where, $P(t)$ is the output power of the MT, FC and DE groups in the period of t, F_i denotes the fuel costs of the MT, FC and DE, O_i is the operation and maintenance cost of MT, FC and DE, α_k denotes the external cost of emitting the kind of k gas, and i_{ke} stands for the emission factor of the MT, FC and DE when the emission type is k. M stands for the type of gas emissions, including CO_2, NO_x or SO_2, $C_b(t)$ and Cs(t) respectively purchase price and sale price in time of t, $P_{buy}(t)$ stands for the number of purchasing power, and P_{sell} (t) stands for the number of sale electricity. T stands for the total number of hours in optimize the cycle. C_{DEP} is the depreciation costs of equipment.

4   Simulation Experiments and Discussion

PSO algorithm based on adaptive mutation and P systems is used in micro-grid economic operation.In the case of parallel grid operation, the dispatch strategy of economical and environmental operation: renewable energy is the maximum using and other powers are output according to optimization operation. Power can be transmitted between micro-grid and main grid in necessary condition.

4.1   Test System

The related parameter values of the PSO is stated as follows: the size of the particle population takes 30, takes the maximum iterations number of the basic film as 5, the maximum iterations number of the outer membrane is 50, c_1 is 2, c_2 is 2. The data of DG subsystems in micro-grid, renewable energy generation forecast data each time, emitting pollutant coefficient of power generation units,the demand of micro-grid load,and real-time electricity price can be seen in [10–12].

4.2 Example Analysis

In this paper, generation power of DG, number of demand load and electrical price at the time of t = 10 is considered as an example. With a micro-grid economic and environmental operation cost minimum as the objective. In this paper, three different algorithms are used to calculate the the objective function of micro-grid simultaneously through repeated iteration 5 times, and get the following values and waveform in Fig.1.

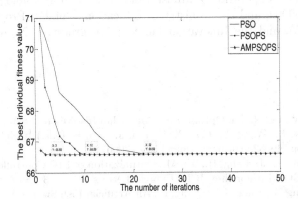

Fig. 1. Best individual fitness values corresponding to each algorithm

After the simulation of three different algorithms, we can get the results as follows. The best individual fitness value (the final overall cost) is 66.5898 RMB, and the power of the fuel cell is 10 KW, and the power of the micro turbine is 5 KW, the power of diesel generator is 0 KW.

As can be seen from Fig.1, the optimization capabilities of PSO, PSOPS and AMPSOPS algorithms are the same. From the simulation curve of PSO, PSOPS and AMPSOPS, the algorithm which is based on P system has faster convergence relative to others, reflecting the ability of high-speed parallel computing of P system. The convergence of AMPSOPS is better than PSOPS through the comparison between PSOPS and AMPSOPS. As well as the diversity of the population can be better maintained by adaptive mutation operator to receive global optimum value, and reflect the good effect of AMPSOPS. Due to economic and environmental operation of micro-grid, it is necessary to dispatch distributed generators and load fast. So the AMPSOPS algorithm can well satisfy the need of micro-grid real-time scheduling.

5 Conclusion

In this paper, the objective function is determined by considering the characteristics of micro-grid system and requirements of environment and economic operation.

Through comparing the simulation results, it can be seen that the optimization capability of AMPSOPS algorithm is stronger than of PSO or PSOPS. The optimization and improvement of the algorithm should be further studied in future works.

Acknowledgements. This work was partially Supported by the Research Fund of Sichuan Provincial Education Department(No. 12ZZ007), and the National Natural Science Foundation of China (Grant No. 61170030), and Foundation for International Cooperation of Ministry of Science and Technology, China No: SQ2011ZOF000004, and the Ministry of Education Chunhui Project of China (No. Z2012025), and the Innovation Fund of Postgraduate, Xihua University (ycjj2014147).

References

1. Huang, L., Wang, N.: An Optimization Algorithm Inspired by Membrane Computing. In: Jiao, L., Wang, L., Gao, X.-b., Liu, J., Wu, F. (eds.) ICNC 2006. LNCS, vol. 4222, pp. 49–52. Springer, Heidelberg (2006)
2. Wang, T., Wang, J., Peng, H., Tu, M.: Optimization of PID Controller Parameters based on PSOPS Algorithm. ICIC Express Letters 6(1), 273–280 (2012)
3. Tu, M., Wang, J., Song, X.X., Yang, F.: An Artificial Fish Swarm Algorithm Based on P Systems. ICIC Express Letters 4(3), 747–753 (2013)
4. Zhang, G.X., Gheorghe, M., Wu, C.: A Quantum-Inspired Evolutionary Algorithm based on P Systems for a Class of Combinatorial Optimization. Fundam. Inform. 87, 93–116 (2008)
5. Wang, J., Li, Z., Peng, H., Zhang, G.X.: An Extended Spiking Neural P System for Fuzzy Knowledge Representation. Int. J. Inn. Comput. Inf. Control 7(7), 3709–3724 (2011)
6. Peng, H., Wang, J., Pérez-Jiménez, M.J., Peng, S.: A Novel Image Thresholding Method Based on Membrane Computing and Fuzzy Entropy. J. Int. Fuzzy. Syst. 24(2), 229–237 (2013)
7. Yang, Y.F., Peng, H., Jiang, Y., Huang, X.L., Zhang, J.R.: A Region-based Image Segmentation Method Under P Systems. J. Inf. Comput. Sci. 10(10), 2943–2950 (2013)
8. Zhang, T.C., Geng, G.F.: Reactive Power Optimization for Medium Voltage Distribution Network based on Improved Particle Swarm Optimization. Pow. Syst. Technol. 36(2), 158–162 (2012)
9. Chen, Q.Y., Chen, W.H., Dai, C.H., Zhang, X.X.: Reactive Power Optimization Based on Modified Particle Swarm Optimization Algorithm for Power System. In: Proc. CSU-EPSA, vol. 26(2), pp. 8–13 (2014)
10. Yang, W.: Optimal Scheduling for Distributed Energy Resource. J. Hefei Univ. Technol. (2010)
11. Sun, S.J.: Research On The Optimal Configuration and Economic Operation Model Formulti-Energy Micro-Grid. J. Hefei Univ. Technol. (2012)
12. Katiraei, F., Iravani, R., Hatziargyriou, N.: Micro-grids Management. IEEE Pow. Energy M. 6(3), 54–65 (2008)

On the Theory of Nonlinear Matrix Equation $X^s = Q + A^H(I \otimes X - C)^{-\delta}A$

Wei Liu, Haifeng Sang, Qingchun Li*, and Chunwei Zhai

College of Mathematics and Statistics, Beihua University,
Jilin 132013, China
liqingchun01@163.com

Abstract. In this paper, the nonlinear matrix equation $X^s = Q \pm A^H(I \otimes X - C)^{-\delta}A$ are discussed. We present some necessary and sufficient conditions for the existence of a definite positive solution for this equation, and some related properties of the definite positive solution such as boundary.

Keywords: Nonlinear matrix equation, Definite positive solution, Boundary.

1 Introduction

The problem of solving the nonlinear matrix equation is one of the hot topics in the field of nonlinear problem. Many researchers had derived a lot of related research in this field [1-5]. And the related results have been used widely in network analysis, control theory, industry, communication and so on. For example, during the process of oil refining, circulation volume of catalyst can be monitored exactly by solving the nonlinear matrix equation. Hence, it makes people propose higher requirements to the research of the nonlinear matrix equations, explore further in this field and get more fruitful accomplishments.

2 Notations

The following notations are used throughout this paper. For a complex matrix $A \in \mathbb{C}^{n \times n}$, A^H denotes the conjugate transposed matrix of A, $\|A\|$ is the spectral norm of matrix A and $\|A\|_F$ is the Frobenius norm of matrix A. $\delta^M(A)(\delta^m(A))$ stands for the maximum (minimum) singular value of matrix A and $\lambda_M(A)(\lambda_m(A))$ stands for the maximum (minimum) eigenvalue of matrix A. The notation $A \otimes B$ denotes the Kronecker product of matrix A and B.

In this paper, we focus on the positive definite solution of the equation

$$X^s = Q + A^H(I \otimes X - C)^{-\delta}A, \tag{2.1}$$

where A is an $mn \times n$ order complex matrix, C is an mn order Hermite positive semi-definite matrix, Q is a n order Hermite positive definite matrix and $0 < \delta < 1$.

---

* Corresponding author.

L. Pan et al. (Eds.): BIC-TA 2014, CCIS 472, pp. 281–288, 2014.
© Springer-Verlag Berlin Heidelberg 2014

3   Main Results

3.1   The Existence of a Definite Positive Solution

At first, we prove the existence of a definite positive solution. We begin with some lemmas.

Lemma 1. *Equation(2.1) is equivalent to the following nonlinear equation*

$$Y^s = \bar{Q} + \bar{A}\{I \otimes [(Y^s + C)^{\frac{1}{s}} - C]\}^{-\delta}\bar{A}, \qquad (3.1)$$

where

$$Y^s = I \otimes X^s - C, \bar{Q} = I \otimes Q - C, \bar{A} = I \otimes A.$$

Furthermore, if $\bar{X}$ is the solution of (2.1), then

$$\bar{Y} = (I \otimes \bar{X}^s - C)^{\frac{1}{s}}$$

is the solution of (3.1). Conversely, if $\bar{Y}$ is a HPD solution of (3.1), then

$$\bar{X} = [Q + A^H[(\bar{Y}^s + C)^{\frac{1}{s}} - C]^{-\delta}A]^{\frac{1}{s}}$$

is the solution of (2.1).

Proof. Rewrite equation

$$X^s = Q + A^H(I \otimes X - C)^{-\delta}A$$

to

$$Q = X^s - A^H(I \otimes X - C)^{-\delta}A.$$

Make Kronecker product with I on both sides

$$I \otimes Q = I \otimes X^s - (I \otimes A^H)[I \otimes (I \otimes X - C)^{-\delta}](I \otimes A),$$

that is

$$I \otimes Q - C = I \otimes X^s - C - (I \otimes A^H)[I \otimes (I \otimes X - C)^{-\delta}](I \otimes A).$$

Let

$$Y^s = I \otimes X^s - C, \bar{Q} = I \otimes Q - C, \bar{A} = I \otimes A,$$

then

$$Y^s = (I \otimes X)^s - C = (I \otimes X - C + C)^s - C,$$

$$Y^s + C = (I \otimes X - C + C)^s,$$

$$(Y^s + C)^{\frac{1}{s}} = I \otimes X - C + C,$$

$$(Y^s + C)^{\frac{1}{s}} - C = I \otimes X - C,$$

where $I \otimes A^H = (I \otimes A)^H$, so $\bar{A}^H = I \otimes A^H$, i.e.

$$Y^s = \bar{Q} + \bar{A}^H \{I \otimes [(Y^s + C)^{\frac{1}{s}} - C]\}^{-\delta} \bar{A}.$$

If $\bar{X}$ is the solution of (2.1), from the derivation above

$$\bar{Y} = (I \otimes \bar{X}^s - C)^{\frac{1}{s}}$$

is the solution of (3.1). Conversely, if $\bar{Y}$ is a HPD solution of (3.1), let

$$\bar{X} = [Q + A^H[(\bar{Y}^s + C)^{\frac{1}{s}} - C]^{-\delta} A]^{\frac{1}{s}},$$

then

$$\begin{aligned}
&I \otimes \bar{X}^s - C \\
&= I \otimes [Q + A^H[(\bar{Y}^s + C)^{\frac{1}{s}} - C]^{-\delta} A] - C \\
&= I \otimes Q - C + (I \otimes A^H)\{I \otimes [(\bar{Y}^s + C)^{\frac{1}{s}} - C]\}^{-\delta}](I \otimes A) \\
&= \bar{Q} + \bar{A}^H \{I \otimes [(\bar{Y}^s + C)^{\frac{1}{s}} - C]\}^{-\delta} \bar{A} \\
&= \bar{Y}^s,
\end{aligned}$$

so

$$I \otimes \bar{X}^s = \bar{Y}^s + C.$$

Furthermore

$$I \otimes \bar{X} - C = (\bar{Y}^s + C)^{\frac{1}{s}} - C,$$

hence

$$\begin{aligned}
&Q + A^H (I \otimes \bar{X} - C)^{-\delta} A \\
&= Q + A^H[(\bar{Y}^s + C)^{\frac{1}{s}} - C]^{-\delta} A \\
&= \bar{X}^s,
\end{aligned}$$

i.e. $\bar{X}$ is the solution of (2.1). $\qquad\square$

Lemma 2. If $A \geq B > 0$($A > B > 0$), then $A^\alpha \geq^\alpha B > 0$ $(A^\alpha > B^\alpha > 0)$ when $0 < \alpha \leq 1$; $0 < A^\alpha \leq B^\alpha$ $(0 < A^\alpha < B^\alpha)$ when $-1 \leq \alpha < 0$.

To talk about the solution of (2.1), we define the following mapping

$$f(X) = [Q + A^H (I \otimes X - C)^{-\delta} A]^{\frac{1}{s}},$$

$$F(Y) = \{\bar{Q} + \bar{A}^H [I \otimes [(Y^s + C)^{\frac{1}{s}} - C]]^{-\delta} \bar{A}\}^{\frac{1}{s}}.$$

Lemma 3. *The mapping F has the following properties*
(1) If $Y_1 \geq Y_2 \geq 0$, then

$$F(Y_2) \geq F(Y_1) \geq 0, F^2(Y_1) \geq F^2(Y_2) \geq 0.$$

(2) For any matrix $Y > 0$, there exists $F(\bar{Q}^{\frac{1}{s}}) \geq F^2(Y) \geq \bar{Q}^{\frac{1}{s}}$ and mapping F maps set $\{Y | \bar{Q}^{\frac{1}{s}} \leq Y \leq F(\bar{Q}^{\frac{1}{s}})\}$ to itself.
(3) Sequence $\{F^{2k}(\bar{Q}^{\frac{1}{s}})\}_{k=0}^\infty$ is a monotonically increasing HPD matrix sequence and converges to the HPD matrix Y^-. That is to say Y^- is a fixed point

in F^2. So $F^2(Y^-) = Y^-$. Sequence $\{F^{2k+1}(\bar{Q}^{\frac{1}{s}})\}_{k=0}^{\infty}$ is a monotonically decreasing HPD matrix sequence and converges to the HPD matrix Y^+. That is to say Y^+ is also a fixed point in F^2. So $F^2(Y^+) = Y^+$.

(4) Mapping F maps set $\{Y | Y^- \leq Y \leq Y^+\}$ to itself, the solution of (3.1) is between Y^+ and Y^-. If $Y^+ = Y^-$, then (3.1)has the unique HPD solution.

Proof. Actually, let X be a Hermition matrix, when

$$X \in [\bar{Q}^{\frac{1}{s}}, \bar{Q} + \bar{A}^H\{I \otimes [(\bar{Q} + C)^{\frac{1}{s}} - C]\}^{-\delta}\bar{A}],$$

i.e.

$$\bar{Q}^{\frac{1}{s}} \leq X \leq F(\bar{Q}^{\frac{1}{s}}).$$

Because

$$[(\bar{Q} + C)^{\frac{1}{s}} - C]^{-\delta} \geq [(X^s + C)^{\frac{1}{s}} - C]^{-\delta},$$

then

$$F(X) = \{\bar{Q} + \bar{A}^H[I \otimes [(X^s + C)^{\frac{1}{s}} - C]]^{-\delta}\bar{A}\}^{\frac{1}{s}}$$
$$\leq \{\bar{Q} + \bar{A}^H[I \otimes [(\bar{Q} + C)^{\frac{1}{s}} - C]]^{-\delta}\bar{A}\}^{\frac{1}{s}},$$

i.e.

$$F(X) \leq F(\bar{Q}^{\frac{1}{s}}).$$

Because

$$[(X^s + C)^{\frac{1}{s}} - C]^{-\delta} \geq 0,$$

then

$$F(X) = \{\bar{Q} + \bar{A}^H[I \otimes [(X^s + C)^{\frac{1}{s}} - C]]^{-\delta}\bar{A}\}^{\frac{1}{s}} \geq \bar{Q}^{\frac{1}{s}},$$

hence

$$\bar{Q}^{\frac{1}{s}} \leq X \leq F(\bar{Q}^{\frac{1}{s}}).$$

Obviously when $X \leq Y$

$$F(X) - F(Y)$$
$$= \{\bar{Q} + \bar{A}^H[I \otimes [(X^s + C)^{\frac{1}{s}} - C]]^{-\delta}\bar{A}\}^{\frac{1}{s}}$$
$$- \{\bar{Q} + \bar{A}^H[I \otimes [(Y^s + C)^{\frac{1}{s}} - C]]^{-\delta}\bar{A}\}^{\frac{1}{s}}$$
$$\geq 0.$$

That is to say F is monotonically decreasing and F^2 is monotonically increasing.

Let Y be any positive definite matrix, then $F(Y) \geq \bar{Q}^{\frac{1}{s}}$. F is monotonically decreasing, so

$$F(\bar{Q}^{\frac{1}{s}}) \geq F^2(Y) \geq \bar{Q}^{\frac{1}{s}},$$

For all k, there exists

$$F(\bar{Q}^{\frac{1}{s}}) \geq F^k(Y) \geq \bar{Q}^{\frac{1}{s}}.$$

Firstly, let $k = 2$, $F^2(\bar{Q}^{\frac{1}{s}}) \geq \bar{Q}^{\frac{1}{s}}$, repeatedly use F^2, by the monotonicity of F^2, increasing sequence $\{F^{2k}(\bar{Q}^{\frac{1}{s}})\}_{k=0}^{\infty}$ is achieved. From $F\bar{Q}^{\frac{1}{s}} \geq F^k(Y)$ we know that positive definite matrix $F\bar{Q}^{\frac{1}{s}}$ is an upper bound of it. So it is convergent. Let limit be Y^-, then Y^- is the fixed point in F^2.

Let $k = 3$, $F\bar{Q}^{\frac{1}{s}} \geq F^3(\bar{Q}^{\frac{1}{s}})$, repeatedly use F^2, by the monotonicity of F^2 in $[\bar{Q}^{\frac{1}{s}}, F\bar{Q}^{\frac{1}{s}}]$, the matrix sequence $\{F^{2k+1}(\bar{Q}^{\frac{1}{s}})\}_{k=0}^{\infty}$ is diminishing. $\bar{Q}^{\frac{1}{s}}$ is a lower bound of it. So it is convergent. Let limit be Y^+, then Y^+ is the fixed point of F^2.

Now we know F is a mapping from $[Y^-, Y^+]$ to itself. Let Y be any positive definite solution of (3.1), for all k

$$F^{2k}(\bar{Q}^{\frac{1}{s}}) \leq Y \leq F^{2k+1}(\bar{Q}^{\frac{1}{s}}).$$

When $k \to \infty$, there exists

$$Y^- \leq Y \leq Y^+.$$

That is to say, all the solutions of (3.1) are all in $[Y^-, Y^+]$. □

Lemma 4. For any $Y_1 \geq 0$, $Y_2 \geq 0$, there exists

$$\lambda_M(Y_1)Y_2 \geq \lambda_m(Y_2)Y_1.$$

Proof. For any $Y_1 \geq 0$, $Y_2 \geq 0$, there exists

$$Y_2 \geq \lambda_m(Y_2)I,$$

$$Y_1 \leq \lambda_M(Y_1)I,$$

$$\lambda_M(Y_1)Y_2 \geq \lambda_M(Y_1)\lambda_m(Y_2)I \geq \lambda_m(Y_2)Y_1,$$

So

$$\lambda_M(Y_1)Y_2 \geq \lambda_m(Y_2)Y_1.$$

□

Theorem 1. *Equation*

$$X^s = Q + A^H(I \otimes X - C)^{-\delta}A$$

is sure to have the positive definite solution X and all the positive definite solutions of it are all in the set

$$\phi = \{X | Q^{\frac{1}{s}} \leq X \leq (Q + \|A\|^2\|(I \otimes \lambda_m^{\frac{1}{s}}(Q)I - C)^{-\delta}\|I)^{\frac{1}{s}}\}.$$

Proof. Obviously, ϕ is a bounded closed convex set. Take consideration of the following mapping:

$$f(X) = [Q + A^H(I \otimes X - C)^{-\delta}A]^{\frac{1}{s}}.$$

Obviously, $f(X)$ is a continuous mapping on ϕ. If $X \in \phi$, then

$$X \geq Q^{\frac{1}{s}} \geq \lambda_m^{\frac{1}{s}}(Q)I,$$

where

$$A^H(I \otimes X - C)^{-\delta}A \leq A^H(I \otimes \lambda_m^{\frac{1}{s}}(Q)I - C)^{-\delta}A.$$

$$f(X) = [Q + A^H(I \otimes X - C)^{-\delta}A]^{\frac{1}{s}}$$

$$\leq [Q + \|A\|^2\|(I \otimes \lambda_m^{\frac{1}{s}}(Q)I - C)^{-\delta}\|I]^{\frac{1}{s}}.$$

And $f(X) \geq Q^{\frac{1}{s}}$, so $f(X) \in \phi$, by the Brouwer fixed point theorem, ϕ has a fixed point on $f(X)$. That is to say, the equation has a definite solution on ϕ. From the proof above, we can get that all the solutions of equation $X \in \phi$. □

3.2   Two Boundaries for the Definite Positive Solution

In the following part we will introduce two boundaries of the unique solution of equation (2.1).

Theorem 2. *Let $\bar{X}$ be the unique HPD solution to (2.1), then*

$$I \otimes \bar{X} \in [(F^2(\bar{Q}^{\frac{1}{s}})^s + C)^{\frac{1}{s}}, (F(\bar{Q}^{\frac{1}{s}})^s + C)^{\frac{1}{s}}].$$

Proof. Let $\bar{Y}^s = I \otimes \bar{X}^s - C$, then $\bar{Y}$ is the unique solution to equation(3.1), where

$$\bar{Y}^s = \bar{Q} + \bar{A}^H[I \otimes [(\bar{Y}^s + C)^{\frac{1}{s}} - C]]^{-\delta}\bar{A},$$

i.e.

$$\bar{Y}^s \geq \bar{Q}, (\bar{Y}^s)^{-\delta} \leq \bar{Q}^{-\delta}.$$

Therefore

$$\begin{aligned}
\bar{Y}^s &= \bar{Q} + \bar{A}^H[I \otimes [(\bar{Y}^s + C)^{\frac{1}{s}} - C]]^{-\delta}\bar{A} \\
&\leq \bar{Q} + \bar{A}^H[I \otimes [(\bar{Q} + C)^{\frac{1}{s}} - C]]^{-\delta}\bar{A} \\
&= F(\bar{Q}^{\frac{1}{s}})^s.
\end{aligned}$$

Again

$$F(\bar{Q}^{\frac{1}{s}})^s \geq \bar{Y}^s \geq \bar{Q},$$

then

$$[F(\bar{Q}^{\frac{1}{s}})^s]^{-\delta} \leq (\bar{Y}^s)^{-\delta} \leq \bar{Q}^{-\delta},$$

so

$$\begin{aligned}
&\bar{Q} + \bar{A}^H[I \otimes [F(\bar{Q}^{\frac{1}{s}})^s + C)^{\frac{1}{s}} - C]]^{-\delta}\bar{A} \\
&\leq \bar{Q} + \bar{A}^H[I \otimes [(\bar{Y}^s + C)^{\frac{1}{s}} - C]]^{-\delta}\bar{A} \\
&\leq \bar{Q} + \bar{A}^H[I \otimes [(\bar{Q} + C)^{\frac{1}{s}} - C]]^{-\delta}\bar{A},
\end{aligned}$$

i.e.

$$F^2(\bar{Q}^{\frac{1}{s}})^s \leq \bar{Y}^s \leq F(\bar{Q}^{\frac{1}{s}})^s.$$

Again from $\bar{Y}^s = I \otimes \bar{X}^s - C$, we have

$$F^2(\bar{Q}^{\frac{1}{s}})^s \leq I \otimes \bar{X}^s - C \leq F(\bar{Q}^{\frac{1}{s}})^s,$$

$$F^2(\bar{Q}^{\frac{1}{s}})^s + C \leq I \otimes \bar{X}^s \leq F(\bar{Q}^{\frac{1}{s}})^s + C,$$

so

$$(F^2(\bar{Q}^{\frac{1}{s}})^s + C)^{\frac{1}{s}} \leq I \otimes \bar{X} \leq (F(\bar{Q}^{\frac{1}{s}})^s + C)^{\frac{1}{s}}.$$

$\square$

Theorem 3. *Let $\bar{X}$ be the unique HPD solution of (2.1), then*

$$I \otimes \bar{X} \in (\sqrt[s]{(\alpha I)^s + C}, \sqrt[s]{(\beta I)^s + C}),$$

In which (α, β) is the solution of the following equations:

$$\alpha = \sqrt[s]{\lambda_m(\bar{Q}) + \delta_m^2(\bar{A})[(\beta^s + \lambda_M(C))^{\frac{1}{s}} - \lambda_m(C)]^{-\delta}},$$

$$\beta = \sqrt[s]{\lambda_M(\bar{Q}) + \delta_M^2(\bar{A})[(\alpha^s + \lambda_m(C))^{\frac{1}{s}} - \lambda_M(C)]^{-\delta}}.$$

Proof. Define sequence $\{\alpha_k\}$ and $\{\beta_k\}$ as follows:

$$\alpha_0 = \sqrt[s]{\lambda_m(\bar{Q})},$$

$$\beta_0 = \sqrt[s]{\lambda_M(\bar{Q}) + \delta_M^2(\bar{A})[\alpha_0 - \lambda_M(C)]^{-\delta}},$$

$$\alpha_k = \sqrt[s]{\lambda_m(\bar{Q}) + \delta_m^2(\bar{A})[(\beta_{k-1}^s + \lambda_M(C))^{\frac{1}{s}} - \lambda_m(C)]^{-\delta}},$$

$$\beta_k = \sqrt[s]{\lambda_M(\bar{Q}) + \delta_M^2(\bar{A})[(\alpha_{k-1}^s + \lambda_m(C))^{\frac{1}{s}} - \lambda_M(C)]^{-\delta}}.$$

It is clear that $0 < \alpha_0 < \beta_0$ and

$$\alpha_1 = \sqrt[s]{\lambda_m(\bar{Q}) + \delta_m^2(\bar{A})[(\beta_0^s + \lambda_M(C))^{\frac{1}{s}} - \lambda_m(C)]^{-\delta}} \geq \alpha_0,$$

$$\beta_1 = \sqrt[s]{\lambda_M(\bar{Q}) + \delta_M^2(\bar{A})[(\alpha_0^s + \lambda_m(C))^{\frac{1}{s}} - \lambda_M(C)]^{-\delta}} \leq \beta_0.$$

Suppose $\alpha_s \geq \alpha_{s-1}, \beta_{s-1} \geq \beta_s$, then

$$\begin{aligned}
\beta_{k+1} &= \sqrt[s]{\lambda_M(\bar{Q}) + \delta_M^2(\bar{A})[(\alpha_k^s + \lambda_m(C))^{\frac{1}{s}} - \lambda_M(C)]^{-\delta}} \\
&\leq \sqrt[s]{\lambda_M(\bar{Q}) + \delta_M^2(\bar{A})[(\alpha_{k-1}^s + \lambda_m(C))^{\frac{1}{s}} - \lambda_M(C)]^{-\delta}} \\
&= \beta_k,
\end{aligned}$$

$$\begin{aligned}
\alpha_{k+1} &= \sqrt[s]{\lambda_m(\bar{Q}) + \delta_m^2(\bar{A})[(\beta_k^s + \lambda_M(C))^{\frac{1}{s}} - \lambda_m(C)]^{-\delta}} \\
&\geq \sqrt[s]{\lambda_m(\bar{Q}) + \delta_m^2(\bar{A})[(\beta_{k-1}^s + \lambda_M(C))^{\frac{1}{s}} - \lambda_m(C)]^{-\delta}} \\
&= \alpha_k.
\end{aligned}$$

By induction we know

$$\alpha_s \geq \alpha_{s-1}, \beta_{s-1} \geq \beta_s \quad s = 1, 2, \ldots.$$

That is to say, $\{\alpha_k\}$ and $\{\beta_k\}$ are separately increasing sequence and descending succession.

Because

$$\bar{Y}^s = \bar{Q} + \bar{A}^H\{I \otimes [(\bar{Y}^s + C)^{\frac{1}{s}} - C]\}^{-\delta}\bar{A},$$

we have

$$\bar{Q} \leq \bar{Y}^s \leq \bar{Q} + \bar{A}^H\{I \otimes [(\bar{Q} + C)^{\frac{1}{s}} - C]\}^{-\delta}\bar{A}.$$

From $\bar{Q} \geq \lambda_m(\bar{Q})I = (\alpha_0 I)^s$, we know $\bar{Y}^s \geq (\alpha_0 I)^s$.

We notice that

$$\begin{aligned}
\bar{Y}^s &= \bar{Q} + \bar{A}^H\{I \otimes [(\bar{Y}^s + C)^{\frac{1}{s}} - C]\}^{-\delta}\bar{A} \\
&\leq \bar{Q} + \bar{A}^H\{I \otimes [(\bar{Q} + C)^{\frac{1}{s}} - C]\}^{-\delta}\bar{A} \\
&\leq \bar{Q} + \bar{A}^H\{I \otimes [(\lambda_m(\bar{Q})I + C)^{\frac{1}{s}} - C]\}^{-\delta}\bar{A} \\
&\leq \lambda_M(\bar{Q}) + \delta_M^2(\bar{A})[\sqrt[s]{\lambda_m(\bar{Q})} - \lambda_M(C)]I,
\end{aligned}$$

where $(\beta_0 I)^s \geq \bar{Y}^s \geq (\alpha_0 I)^s$.

Suppose

$$(\beta_k I)^s \geq \bar{Y}^s \geq (\alpha_k I)^s,$$

then

$$\begin{aligned}
\bar{Y}^s &= \bar{Q} + \bar{A}^H \{I \otimes [(\bar{Y}^s + C)^{\frac{1}{s}} - C]\}^{-\delta} \bar{A} \\
&\geq \bar{Q} + \bar{A}^H \{I \otimes [\beta_k^s I + C)^{\frac{1}{s}} - C]\}^{-\delta} \bar{A} \\
&\geq \lambda_m(\bar{Q})I + \delta_m^2(\bar{A})\{[(\beta_k^s + \lambda_M(C))^{\frac{1}{s}} - \lambda_m(C)]\}^{-\delta} I \\
&= (\alpha_{k+1} I)^s,
\end{aligned}$$

On the other hand,

$$\begin{aligned}
\bar{Y}^s &= \bar{Q} + \bar{A}^H \{I \otimes [(\bar{Y}^s + C)^{\frac{1}{s}} - C]\}^{-\delta} \bar{A} \\
&\leq \bar{Q} + \bar{A}^H \{I \otimes [\alpha_k^s I + C)^{\frac{1}{s}} - C]\}^{-\delta} \bar{A} \\
&\leq \lambda_M(\bar{Q})I + \delta_m^2(\bar{A})\{[(\alpha_k^s + \lambda_m(C))^{\frac{1}{s}} - \lambda_M(C)]\}^{-\delta} I \\
&= (\beta_{k+1} I)^s,
\end{aligned}$$

where

$$(\beta_{k+1} I)^s \geq \bar{Y}^s \geq (\alpha_{k+1} I)^s.$$

So sequence $\{\alpha_k\}$ and $\{\beta_k\}$ are convergent. Let

$$\lim_{k \to \infty} \alpha_k = \alpha,$$

$$\lim_{k \to \infty} \beta_k = \beta,$$

so $\bar{Y}^s \in [(\alpha I)^s, (\beta I)^s]$. From $\bar{Y}^s = I \otimes \bar{X}^s - C$, we have

$$(\alpha I)^s \leq I \otimes \bar{X}^s - C \leq (\beta I^s),$$

$$\sqrt[s]{(\alpha I)^s + C} \leq I \otimes \bar{X} \leq \sqrt[s]{(\beta I)^s + C},$$

that is

$$I \otimes \bar{X} \in (\sqrt[s]{(\alpha I)^s + C}, \sqrt[s]{(\beta I)^s + C}).$$

$\square$

References

1. Ran, A.C.M., Reurings, M.C.B.: On the nonlinear matrix equation $X + A^* F(X)A = Q$ solutions and perturbation theory. J. Linear Algebra Appl. 372, 33–51 (2002)
2. Zhang, Y.: On Hermitian Positive definite solutions of the matrix equation. J. Linear Algebra Appl. 372, 295–304 (2003)
3. EL-say, S.M., Al-Dbiban, A.M.: On Positive definite solutions of a matrix equation $X + A^* X^{-n} A = I$. J. Appl. Math. Comput. 151, 533–541 (2004)
4. Hasanov, V.I.: Positive definite solutions of the matrix equation. J. Linear Algebra Appl. 404, 166–182 (2005)
5. Hasanov, V.I., Ivanov, I.G.: Solutions and perturbation estimates for the matrix equation $X \pm A^* X^{-n} A = Q$. J. Applied Mathematics and Computation 156, 513–525 (2004)
6. Bharia, R.: Matrix analysis. Springer, Berlin (1997)

Design of Coal Mine Monitoring System Based on Internet of Things

Xiangju Liu[1] and Lina Liu[2]

[1] School of Computer Science and Technology,
Anhui University of Science and Technology, 232001, Huainan, Anhui, China
[2] School of Geodesy and Geomatics,
Anhui University of Science and Technology,232001, Huainan, Anhui, China
xjliu@aust.edu.cn

Abstract. In view of the current status of the coal mine safety monitoring system, this paper puts forward a design schemes of monitoring mining safety system based on internet of things. The environment parameters such as gas concentration, moisture/temperature, the dust density and equipment state,secure environment are perceived through wireless sensor network and existing ethernet in coal mine. This paper analyzes the network architecture of the system. The designing considerations and the hardware/software implementing schemes of coordinator node and sensor node are mainly introduced. The design schemes improves the coverage, flexibility and scalability of the existing monitoring system, reduces installation and maintenance costs, avoids the problem of blind zone. The mine safety mining and the major disaster prevention are effectively solved.

Keywords: Internet of things, Safety monitoring system, Coal mine.

1 Introduction

In recent years, our country pay an increasingly attention to safety of coal mine, most of the coal enterprises have installed relevant monitoring system. But the existing coal mine safe monitoring system can not be completely covered underground areas because of the narrow space, complex tunnels and adverse conditions. The main problems includes wired communications mode, complex wiring and high cost of installation and maintenance. In addition, the firm network structure is hard to expand and the monitoring spot is easy to bring on blind zone. Wired communication mode has a strong dependence on the line, the circuit would be corrupted and couldn't provide useful information effectively when accidents happened[1,2], So it is urgent to extend the monitoring range of underground areas to collecting various information relate to environmental sensor, video, voice and other multimode information for enhancing the ability of mine safety monitoring.

L. Pan et al. (Eds.): BIC-TA 2014, CCIS 472, pp. 289–294, 2014.
© Springer-Verlag Berlin Heidelberg 2014

2   Overall Perceptions of Mine in Internet of Things World

In the broad sense of the Internet of Things, it represents the merging of informational space and physical space[3]. It has two meanings: the extension and development of Internet, the core and base of the Internet of things are still the internet, and the client of IoT has extended to telecommunications and information exchange between any objects. Perception completely, transfer reliably and process intelligently are the three main features of the Internet of things.

Perceived mine is the combination with advanced automatic control, communication, computer, information and modern management techniques, which makes the control, management and operations of the production process as a whole to that can optimize enterprise running, management and operations level[4].

3   Design of Network Architecture

Currently, mine safety system for monitoring mainly adopts the wired communication mode. However, because of the particularity of the environmental condition, wired communication mode is difficult to realize the full coverage of the mine and lacks a good flexibility and expansibility[5]. Mine monitoring system based on the Internet of things which uses the combination with wired communication mode and wireless communication mode by making full use of the existing Ethernet as backbone network and realizing the full coverage of the mine through wireless sensor network which could cover the crossings and the branches of the tunnels.

The network architecture of the mine monitoring system based on the Internet of things includes perception layer, network transport layer and application layer, as description in figure 1.

4   Design of the System

4.1   Hardware Design of the System

In order to reduce the power consumption in the mass of the wireless sensor-network group, the system uses the star network topology which consisted of coordinator node and data terminal node. The function of the coordinator node is to build a network and the data terminal send data to the coordinator node by multi-hop on its own network. All the equipments used in the system are global function equipments and fit for the occasion with lots of interference and large amount of data. During the process of the node design for considering the requirements of low-power, and the CC2530 has been chosen as the core microchip. The CC2530, a 2.4GHz SOC, which adapt to the standard to ZigBee and applies to kinds of ZigBee wireless sensor network nodes and ZigBee PRO wireless

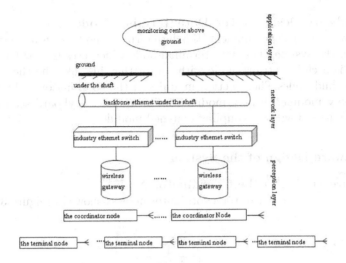

Fig. 1. Network structure diagram of mine monitoring system

sensor network nodes[6], the coordinator node, router and the termination node are also included.

(1)Hardware Design of the Coordinator Node

The coordinator node is a powerful data terminal node in fact, and it has a more strong capacity of processing, communicating and data storing[7].

The main functions of the node are: sending the command of control, receiving the child nodes, forwarding data from the data terminal nodes to the higher-level networks.The function modules of the coordinator node includes:CC2530 module, crystal module, LCD module, power supply module, alarm module, keyboard scan module and wireless coupling matched module. Wireless couple matched module realizes the communication between the coordinator node,the wireless gateway and the data terminal node. The hardware structure of the coordinator node is described in figure 2.

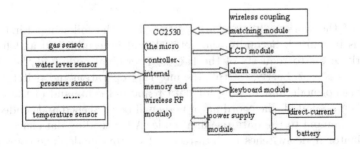

Fig. 2. Hardware structure of the coordinator node

(2)Hardware Design of the Data Terminal Node

As the bottom of the equipment, the data terminal node plays an very important role in the system. The data terminal node which uses CC2530 as its core microchip is a child network node with sensor that just like the the coordinator node's child nodes.The function modules of the coordinator node includes: power supply module, display module, alarm module, keyboard scan module, sensor module and wireless coupling matched module.

4.2   Software Design of the System

(1)Software Design of the Coordinator Node

The workflow flowchart of the coordinator node is showed in figure 3.

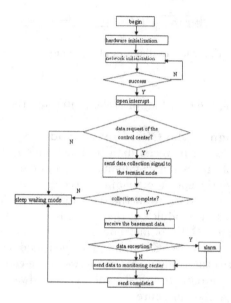

Fig. 3. Receiving data program flow char of the coordinator node

Details of the working process are described as the following: Firstly, the hardware is initialized, Secondly, the network will be established and listened for network access to requests of the the data terminal node and then assign network address to it. Lastly, starting the interrupt operation and switching into low-power sleep mode and waiting for data requested command of the control center. When requested, the coordinator node will be awakened and sended data requested command to the data terminal node. After sending data successfully, the coordinator node switches to data-received waiting mode. The coordinator node would upload data to host directly when signal received. The alarm module would be started when exceptional data has been found.

(2)Software Design of The Data Terminal Node

The control center notices the wireless coordinator node to work by sending data requested command, and the network coordinator node sends data requested command to the data terminal node. After receiving the signal, the data terminal node will be awakened and start to collect data. The data terminal node send it to the coordinator node when collection is finished, and then the coordinator node forwards it to monitoring host. Meanwhile, the data terminal node switches to low-power sleep mode automatically after sending and waiting for new round activate commands. The alarm module will be started when exceptional data has been found. The data collecting process of the coordinator node's workflow flowchart is showed in figure 4.

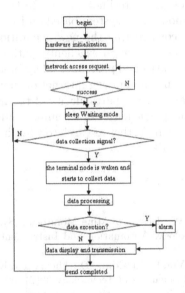

Fig. 4. Data collection program flow char of the terminal node

5   System Test

In order to simulate the real environment of mine, operating point of a coal mine was took as the test points. In this operating point set up 80 monitoring points, these monitoring points was divided into four units, each unit consists of 20 monitoring points and were respectively used to monitor gas, dust, wind speed and other information. Take the gas monitoring for example, analog alarm, power cut monitoring results as shown in the figure 5. The experimental results show that the system is convenient and flexible, and can realize the real-time monitoring of underground gas.

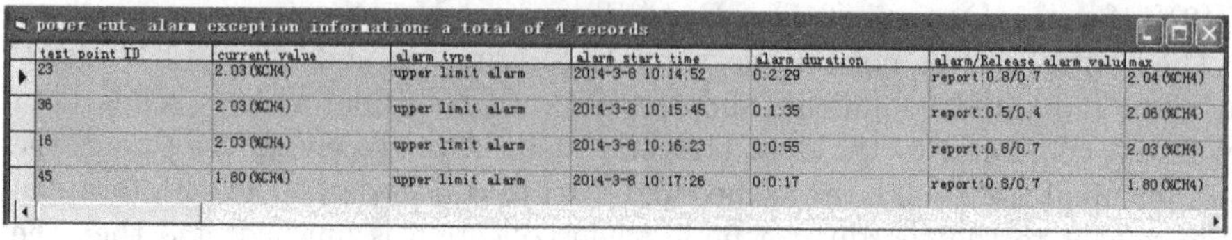

power cut, alarm exception information: a total of 4 records

test point ID	current value	alarm type	alarm start time	alarm duration	alarm/Release alarm valu	max
23	2.03 (%CH4)	upper limit alarm	2014-3-8 10:14:52	0:2:29	report:0.8/0.7	2.04 (%CH4)
36	2.03 (%CH4)	upper limit alarm	2014-3-8 10:15:45	0:1:35	report:0.5/0.4	2.06 (%CH4)
16	2.03 (%CH4)	upper limit alarm	2014-3-8 10:16:23	0:0:55	report:0.8/0.7	2.03 (%CH4)
45	1.80 (%CH4)	upper limit alarm	2014-3-8 10:17:26	0:0:17	report:0.8/0.7	1.80 (%CH4)

Fig. 5. Power cut, alarm exception information

6 Conclusion

This paper applied the Internet of things technology to safe field of mine and introduced a design of coal mine monitoring system based on Internet of things, which plays an important role in constructing the new generation platform of full covered mine safety system and provide an excellent solution to mine production process, equipment health status and personnel safety monitoring fields. However, there are still some problems in applying internet of things technology ground to underground mine because of the particularity of the mine condition directly. Therefore, according to the particularity of the mine conditions and the requirements of mine safety production, further research to what have mentioned above is still needed in the future work.

References

1. Ying-hui, H., Xin, L., Yue-Ying, W.: Design of Mine Monitoring System Based on Zig Bee Wireless Network Technology. Automation and Instrumentation 7, 21–23 (2010)
2. Yan-Jing, S., Jian-Sheng, Q., Shi-Yin, L., Lin-Ming, D.: Theory and Key Technology for Mine Internet of Things. Coal Science and Technology 39(2), 69–72 (2011)
3. Qi-Bo, S., Jie, L., Zang, L., Chunxiao, F., Juanjuan, S.: Internet of Things: Summarize on Concepts, Architecture and Key Technology Problem. Journal of Beijing University of Post and Telecommunications 33(3), 1–9 (2010)
4. Hai-Dong, X., Song-Lin, L., Chun-Lei, W., Liang, Z.: Research of Intelligent Mine System Based on Internet of Things. Industry and Mine Automation 3, 63–66 (2011)
5. Xin, W., Yan-Zhen, Z., Rui, Z.: Reaserch and Realization of Real Time Location System in Coal Mine Based on Internet of Things. Coal Mine Machinery 32(12), 65–68 (2011)
6. Zong-Xing, L., Chao, R., Jian-Ning, D., Chao-Min, M.: Typhoon Monitoring System of Tall Buildings Based on Super-ZigBee. Instrument Technique and Sensor 10, 44–45 (2011)
7. Deng-Hong, Z.: Study on the Things Internet Technology for Test System of Coal Mine Safety. Coal Technology 30(12), 95–97 (2011)

Optimal Tuning of PI Controller
for Full-Order Flux Observer of Induction Motor
Using the Immune Genetic Algorithm

Hui Luo[1], Yunfei Lv[2], Quan Yin[1,*], and Huajun Zhang[1]

[1] Key Laboratory of Ministry of Education for Image
Processing and Intelligent Control,
Department of Control Science and Engineering,
Huazhong University of Science and Technology
Wuhan 430074, Hubei, China
[2] The Second Ship Design Institution, Wuhan 430064, Hubei, China
keyluo@mail.hust.edu.cn, {lvyunfei_hust,yinquan_hust,zhanghj_hust}@163.com

Abstract. This paper presents a new method to tune the parameters of the adaptation PI controller of full-order flux observer. The method employs an Immune Genetic Algorithm (IGA) based optimization routine that can be implemented off-line. A novel fitness function is designed to assess both the estimation accuracy and the noise sensitivity of the rotor speed estimation system when each antibodys parameters are employed. The diversity of population is guaranteed by the evaluating of the antibody similarities function. The Roulette-wheel selection is used to choose the parents and large mutation probability is adopted to prevent the evolution from prematurity. The simulation results verify that the IGA has better performance in convergence speed and computation efficiency compared to the traditional GA.

Keywords: Immune Genetic Optimization, Sensorless, Full-order flux observer, Induction motor drive.

1 Introduction

The speed-adaptive full-order observer is promising flux estimator for the sensorless induction motor drives. It estimates the rotor speed and rotor flux for the vector control of the induction motor. The speed-adaptive observer consists of a state-variable observer and a rotor speed adaptation mechanism. The characteristics of the estimator is governed by the assignation of the state-variable observer's feedback gains and the adaptation proportional-integral (PI) controller.

The assignation of the feedback gains has received lots of attention while the adaptation controller received a little in the past research works. The determination of the adaptation PI gains can be time consuming as it is usually done by trial and error [1]. It is concluded that except for sensitivity to noises, fast

---

* Corresponding author.

L. Pan et al. (Eds.): BIC-TA 2014, CCIS 472, pp. 295–299, 2014.
© Springer-Verlag Berlin Heidelberg 2014

tracking performance can be achieved by using as large adaptation gains as possible [2]. It is revealed that a good tracking performance of the speed estimator during acceleration/deceleration can be achieved with a high integral adaptation gain while the sensitivity to current measurement noises can be reduced by designing a low proportional adaptation gain [3]. However, it is not easy to make a trade off to calculate the desirable adaptation PI gains which guarantee all good performances.

This paper presents a new method to optimize the adaptation PI controller using Immune Genetic Algorithm (IGA). With the help of the design guidelines, the optimization procedure is fast and efficient. Simulations are carried out and the results show good performance of the proposed method.

2   Rotor Speed Estimation with Adaptive Full-Order Observer

2.1   Induction Motor Model

For the induction motor, the dynamic model viewed from the stator reference frame ($\alpha - \beta$ frame) can be expressed as follows.

$$p \begin{bmatrix} i_s \\ \psi_r \end{bmatrix} = \begin{bmatrix} A_{11} & A_{12} \\ A_{21} & A_{22} \end{bmatrix} \begin{bmatrix} i_s \\ \psi_r \end{bmatrix} + \begin{bmatrix} B_1 \\ 0 \end{bmatrix} v_s \tag{1}$$

2.2   Speed-Adaptive Full-Order Flux Observer

From the model 1, we can build a full-order observer as shown in Equations 2-3:

$$p \begin{bmatrix} \hat{i}_s \\ \hat{\psi}_r \end{bmatrix} = \begin{bmatrix} A_{11} & \hat{A}_{12} \\ A_{21} & \hat{A}_{22} \end{bmatrix} \begin{bmatrix} \hat{i}_s \\ \hat{\psi}_r \end{bmatrix} + \begin{bmatrix} B_1 \\ 0 \end{bmatrix} v_s + G(\hat{i}_s - i_s) \tag{2}$$

$$\hat{\omega}_r = \left(K_P + K_I \int dt \right) \hat{\psi}_r^T J \varepsilon_i = \left(K_P + K_I \int dt \right) \left(\varepsilon_{i\alpha} \hat{\psi}_{r\beta} - \varepsilon_{i\beta} \hat{\psi}_{r\alpha} \right) \tag{3}$$

The reference model is the induction motor itself and the adjustable model is the full-order flux observer. The speed-adaptation law adjusts the estimated speed $\hat{\omega}_r$ based on the outputs of the reference model and the adjustable model. The adaptation law is the proportional-integral (PI) law.

3   Optimization of Adaptation PI Gains

3.1   Optimization Routine Based on Immune Genetic Algorithm

Genetic algorithm (GA) is developed by Prof. Holland [4]. It is a stochastic optimization method based on the mechanics of natural evolution and natural genetics. With the characteristics of easier application, greater robustness, and better parallel processing than most classical methods of optimization, GA has been widely used for combinatorial optimization, structural design and so on. One of the most recent heuristic algorithms is the immune genetic algorithm (IGA). To be exact, the IGA utilizes the local information to intervene in the globally parallel process and avoid repetitive and useless work during the course, so as to overcome the blindness in action of the crossover and mutation. The IGA has two features. The first is that the similarity and expected reproduction probability of antibody can be adjusted dynamically in the process of evolution to balance the population diversity and the convergence speed of the algorithm. The second is that this algorithm is able to find the globally optimal solution with the elitism strategy.

In this paper, the IGA is applied in the induction motor drive system to optimize the PI gains of the adaptive full-order flux observer. An optimization routine has been developed within the Matlab environment, which uses the IGA to seek the desirable PI gains automatically.

Producing initial population is the first step of IGA. In this paper, the population is composed of the chromosomes that are real codes. Usually, the initial population is created random. In order to quicken the optimization routine, the calculated PI gains according to the design guidelines 4 and 5 can be put in the initial population.

The corresponding evaluation of a population is called the "fitness function". It is the performance index of a population. In this paper the fitness function is defined as the integral of the absolute err between the measured rotor speed ω_r and the estimated rotor speed $\hat{\omega}_r$ as follows:

$$f(x) = \int_0^T |\omega_r(t) - \hat{\omega}_r(t)| \cdot dt \qquad (4)$$

After the fitness function is calculated, the fitness value or the number of the generation is usually used to determine whether the optimization procedure is stopped or not. In this paper the stop criterion is defined as below using the fitness function $f(x)$:

$$f(x) \leq LIMIT \qquad (5)$$

where
$$LIMIT = n\_ref \times 10\% \times N$$
$$N = \frac{T}{T_s}$$

n_ref is the reference input of the rotor speed, N is the sampling time during the evaluation period of the fitness function and T_s is the sampling period. For example, in this paper the evaluation period $T = 0.3s$, the sampling period $T_s = 100us$, then the sampling time $N = 3000$. If reference input of rotor speed $n\_ref = 1000rpm$, then the stop criterion is:

$$f(x) \leq 30000 \qquad (6)$$

The IGA-based optimization procedure for the optimal PI controller can be described as follows:

Step1: A vector of the antibody $v = \{k_{p1}, k_{i1}\}$ is randomly generated to constitute the initial population of antibodies.

Step2: The system simulation is performed to evaluate the fitness function of each antibody. Then the values of fitness functions are sorted from min to max. The less the fitness value is, the better the performances are.

Step3: The elitism strategy is adopted to determine which antibody is the best in the population and is to be saved.

Step4: the Euclidean distances and the antibody similarities of every two antibodies are calculated to evaluate the diversity of population.

Step5: The expected reproduction probability is calculated.

Step6: Roulette-wheel selection is employed to select the antibodies to be parents according to the reproduction probability.

Step7: Crossover operations are performed. In uniform crossover, each of the parents genes is exchanged with a given probability.

Step8: Finally the mutation operations are performed to create a new population, then return to Step2.

4   Simulation Results

The sensorless vector control system of induction motor is established as shown in Fig. 1. The system has two parts: the vector control system and the speed estimator with optimization procedure.

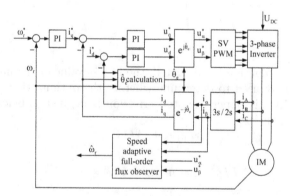

Fig. 1. Sensorless vector control system

The performance of the speed estimation system with this PI gains is shown in Fig. 2. The estimated speed tracks the practical speed well and the sensitivity of the noise in stator current is low. Obviously the IGA-based optimization is extremely faster than the normal GA-based optimization, ending with a desirable result. Above all, the simulation results verify that the IGA has better performance in convergence speed and computation efficiency compared to the traditional GA.

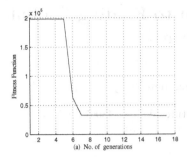
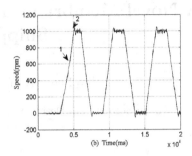

Fig. 2. The plots of the simulation using proposed IGA-based optimization routine with calculated parameters

5   Conclusion

Due to the difficulty in designing the PI controller's parameters of the speed-adaptive full-order observer, a new method was proposed and analyzed in this paper. The method employed an Immune Genetic Algorithm (IGA) based optimization routine that could be implemented off-line. A novel fitness function was designed to assess both the estimation accuracy and the noise sensitivity of the rotor speed estimation system when each antibody's parameters were employed. The diversity of population was guaranteed by the evaluating of the antibody similarities function. The simulation results showed that the convergence of the optimization was extremely fast and the optimal results were desirable. Moreover, the simulation results verified that the IGA had better performance in convergence speed and computation efficiency compared to the traditional GA.

Acknowledgements. This work was supported partly by the National Natural Science Foundation of China under Project 61374049 and by the Fundamental Research Funds for the Central Universities, HUST: 2014QN169 and 2014NY002.

References

1. Kubota, H., Matsuse, K., Nakano, T.: DSP-based Speed Adaptive Flux Observer of Induction Motor. IEEE Trans. on Industrial Application 29(2), 344–348 (1998)
2. Schauder, C.: Adaptive Speed Identification for Vector Control of Induction Motors without Rotational Transducers. IEEE Trans. on Industrial Application 28(5), 1054–1061 (1992)
3. Surapong, S., Somboon, S.: A Speed-Sensorless Im Drive with Decoupling Control and Stability Analysis Of Speed Estimation. IEEE Trans. on Industrial Electronic 49(2), 444–455 (2002)
4. Holland, J.H.: Adaptation in Natural and Artificial Systems. MIT Press (1975)

A Novel Membrane Algorithm to Finding Global Shipping Route

Tao Luo*, Yajun She, and Zongyuan Yang

Wuhan Second Ship Design and Research Institute, Wuhan, 430074, China
luotao7609@sina.com

Abstract. Shipping route problem is a vital problem for maximizing the profits in sea transportation, which can be essentially regarded as a multi-objective optimization problem. In this work, a model of shipping route optimization problem is established, and then an efficient approach called membrane algorithm is introduced to solve the problem, which is inspired from the behaviors of chemicals communicating among living cells. We test our method on a simulated data experiment. Experimental results show that our method can efficiently find the globally optimal route and performs superior to the genetic algorithm and ant colony algorithm.

Keywords: Shipping Route Optimization Problem, Membrane-inspired algorithm, Optimization, Globally optimal solution.

1 Introduction

In maritime industry, optimization of ship routes is an important consideration, whose aim is to get profits as much as possible with little cost. Since the shipping transportation problems usually have many uncertain factors, it is a hard job to build up the models by considering all the factors. Some models that consider partial factors (in the models, some uncertain factors were ignored) have been proposed [1–4]. They were all linear programming models, which firstly assumed that there were several prior designed routes, and then put forward a model to assign a good route for the ship with the purpose of minimizing the total costs and getting the maximal profits. Although some uncertain factors have been ignored in these models, there were still too many factors to consider. Sometimes, it was even hard to consider two objectives in one model. Usually, it was not easy to find the globally optimal solution of the route of ship. Some other models, which focused only one objective, have also been investigated, such as linear programming models of the shipping route optimization problem were proposed in [5–8]. They tried to find the optimal route of the ship to get the biggest total benefits (it is not necessary to request the cost to be minimal). One can find more information of constructing linear programming models of shipping route problems from [9], and for more information in this field one can

---

* Corresponding author.

L. Pan et al. (Eds.): BIC-TA 2014, CCIS 472, pp. 300–303, 2014.

refer to [10]. In this work, we will construct a linear programming model of the shipping route problem.

2   Shipping Route Problem

The shipping route problem can be modeled as follows:

$$\max_{profit} = \{\sum_{i=1}^{n}\sum_{j=1}^{n} s \times (r_{ij}x_{ij} - c_{ij}y_{ij})\},$$

where $i = 1, 2, \ldots, n, j = 1, 2, \ldots, n$ and $i \neq j$. The route constraint is

$$y_{ij} = \begin{cases} 1, \text{the ship is in the route between port } i \text{ and port } j; \\ 0, \text{else.} \end{cases}$$

The freight volume constraint is

$$\sum_{i=1}^{n}\sum_{j=1}^{n} s \times x_{ij} \geq D,$$

and the constraint of cost of oil is

$$\sum_{i=1}^{n}\sum_{j=1}^{n} s \times z_{ij} \leq E.$$

In the following, we will introduce the parameters used in the model: n is the number of ports; s is the shipping times of each path; r_{ij} is the profit of one ship traveling from port i to port j; x_{ij} is the freight volumes that one ship can delivery from port i to port j; c_{ij} is the cost of one ship traveling from port i to port j; z_{ij} is the cost of oil for a ship to travel from port i to port j; y_{ij} is the route from port i to port j; D is the total freight volume. With the constructed model, we try to find the solution of a route of ships to make the profit maximal, and the freight volume should be not less than the demanded quantity.

3   The Membrane Algorithm

In our membrane algorithm, the membrane structure contains three cells, whose topological structure is shown in Fig. 1.

As indicated in Fig. 1, the cells are labeled with 1, 2 and 3. The communication channels among cells are represented by arrows. Using the communication channels, chemical objects (solutions, in our method) can be delivered among the three cells. Specifically, the objects in cell 2 and cell 3 can be sent to cell 1 by the communication cannel among them. In the three cells, we use genetic algorithm, ant colony algorithm, and (PSO) algorithm to solve the shipping route problem, respectively. After a number steps, cell 2 and cell 3 can send their obtained good solutions to cell 1, which can be used in cell 1 to generate a new population of solutions for the next iteration of the algorithm. After doing the iteration for given times, cell 1 will get an optimal solution, which is taken as the solution of the problem. In the following, we will introduce the algorithm used in each cell in details.

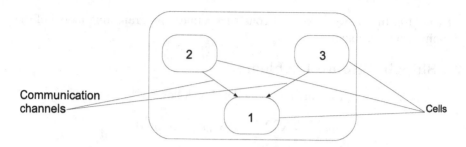

Fig. 1. The timed SN P system Π_n solving Subset Sum problem in a uniform manner

3.1 Genetic Algorithms in Sub-cells

In the genetic algorithm in cell 1, k potential routes are randomly generated and taken as the initial population. In each generation, the fitness of every individual is evaluated by a fitness function. By preserving the better individuals and modifying them, we can form a new population, which can be used in the next iteration of the algorithm. The genetic algorithm is mainly composed of three phages: initialization, selection and generate new routes.

The ant colony algorithm is used in cell 2, which is an algorithm for finding optimal paths that is based on the behavior of ants searching for food.

Particle swarm optimization (PSO) solves a problem by using a population of dubbed particles and moving the particles in the solution space to get close to the optimal ones according to the functions of the positions and velocity of the particles. The movement of each particle is influenced by its local best known solutions, which are updated by other particles. This is expected to move the swarm toward the best solutions.

4   Conclusion

In this work, we have proposed a new approach, called membrane algorithm to solve the shipping route problem. The membrane algorithm is inspired by the behavior of living cells communicating with each other by chemical objects. In the framework of our method, we use three cells. In the three cells, we use genetic algorithm in cell 1, ant colony algorithm in cell 2, and PSO algorithm in cell 3, to solve the shipping route problem. After a number of pre-defined steps, cells 2 and 3 will send its best solution to cell 1, which can used to form the new population of solutions and for the next iteration of the genetic algorithm in cell 1. We test our method on a simulated data experiment. The results show that our method can find a optimal solution of the problem, which is superior to the solution obtained by using genetic algorithm and ant colony algorithm only.

For further research, one of the open problems is whether some other framework of the cells can also be solve the shipping route problem? And, finding some other communication mechanism to improve the performance of our method also needs to be paid more attentions.

References

1. Council Regulation (EEC). No 4057/86 on unfair pricing practices in maritime transport (2003)
2. Kosmas, O.T., Viachos, D.S.: Simulated annealing for optimal ship routing. Computers and Operations Research 17(2), 77–96 (2008)
3. Gelareh, S., Nichel, S., Pisi, N.D.: Liner shipping hub network design in a competitive environment. Transportation Research Part E 46, 991–1004 (2010)
4. Song, T., Pan, L., Păun, G.: Asynchronous Spiking Neural P Systems with Local Synchronization. Information Science 219, 197–207 (2013)
5. Weiming, M.: Industry Concentration in Japan. Japan Economy Press, Tokyo (1983)
6. Fagerholt, K.: Designing optimal routes in a linear shipping Problem. Maritime Policy & Management 31, 259–268 (2004)
7. Montes, A.: Network shortest path application for optimum track ship routing, Master Thesis in Naval Postgraduate School Monterey CA, Accession Number: ADA435601 (2005)
8. Brunmo, G., Nygreen, B., Lysgaard, J.: Column generation approaches to ship scheduling with flexible cargo sizes. European Journal of Operational Research 200(1), 139–150 (2010)
9. Degang, F.: Research on Shipping Route Optimization Allocation Education Management. Education Theory&Education Application 109, 75–78 (2008)
10. Song, T., Wang, X., Su, Y.: A Novel Approach to Identify Protein Coding Domains by Sampling Binary Profiles from Genome. Journal of Computational and Theoretical Nanoscience 11, 147–152 (2014)

Firefly Algorithm Solving Equal-Task Multiple Traveling Salesman Problem

Jianhua Ma[1], Mingfu Li[1,2,*], Yuyan Zhang[1], and Houming Zhou[1]

[1] School of Mechanical Engineering, Xiangtan University, Xiangtan, China
[2] Hunan Key Laboratory for Computation and Simulation in Science and Engineering, Xiangtan, China
majianhua1209@126.com, limingfu2001@foxmail.com, 419661350@qq.com, zhouhouming@xtu.edu.cn

Abstract. A kind of equal-task multiple traveling salesman problem (ET-mTSP) was proposed based on the mTSP and its corresponding mathematical model was constructed; Then, a series of discrete operations for firefly algorithm (FA) were conducted to solve this problem; Finally, the results and analysis of experiments showed that the improved algorithm was efficient and suitable for solving such ET-mTSP.

Keywords: Multiple traveling salesman problem, Equal-task, Firefly algorithm.

1 Introduction

TSP is a typical combinatorial optimization problem and also belonging to the class of "NP-Complete" problems [1]. The mTSP is a generalization of TSP, which consists of determining a set of routes for m salesmen who all start from and turn back to a home city. However, most of the researches on mTSP are limited to the shortest path. Therefore, it is important that the effort of every salesman should be equal [2].

Recently, a majority of researchers use the modern intelligent optimization calculation method to solve the TSP, such as genetic algorithms [3] and colony algorithm [4], etc., and they have made certain promising achievements.

Firefly algorithm from [5] is put forward by Yang in 2009. Just several years later, it has been successfully applied to some combinatorial optimization problems. In addition, our research group has successfully applied FA to assembly sequence planning [6]. The results show that FA has great potential in solving NP-hard problem.

2 The Equal-Task Multiple Traveling Salesman Problem

The ET-mTSP is described as follows: there are N cities ($N_G = \{1, 2, \ldots, N\}$), and M salesmen ($M_G = \{1, 2, \ldots, M\}$), and the salesman p visit M_p cities

---

* Corresponding author.

L. Pan et al. (Eds.): BIC-TA 2014, CCIS 472, pp. 304–307, 2014.
© Springer-Verlag Berlin Heidelberg 2014

$(M_C = \{p_1, p_2, \ldots, p_{M_p}\})$, $(p_1, p_2, \ldots, p_{M_p} \in N_G)$, the path of city i and city j is d_{ij}. The 1st object function, shown in Equation 1, represents the length of path.

$$S = \sum_{p=1}^{M} (\sum_{k=1}^{M_p-1} (d_{p_k p_{k+1}} + d_{p_{M_p} p_1})) \tag{1}$$

All N cities should be assigned to all salesmen in balance. The 2st object function represents the variance of the city numbers of every salesman as shown in Equation 2.

$$D = \sqrt{\sum_{p=1}^{M} (M_p - \frac{N}{M})^2} \tag{2}$$

The fitness function is described as follows in Equation 3.

$$F = (\sum_{p=1}^{M} (\sum_{k=1}^{M_p-1} (d_{p_k p_{k+1}} + d_{p_{M_p} p_1})) + \sqrt{\sum_{p=1}^{M} (M_p - \frac{N}{M})^2}) \tag{3}$$

3   Firefly Algorithm

The solution of ET-mTSP belongs to the discrete integer space, so a new encoding rule was defined for ET-mTSP, and the distance between fireflies was redefined. Finally, the moving rules was improved to enhance the random search and global optimization capability of the FA.

3.1   Encoding Rules of the Firefly

For solving the ET-mTSP, every firefly position corresponds to a sequence of cities that m salesmen visit. Therefore, the position of firefly was initialized to a sequence including m subsequences showed in Equation 4.

$$X = \{\{x_{1,1}, \ldots, x_{1,i}\}, \{x_{2,1}, \ldots, x_{2,j}\}, \ldots, \{x_{m,1}, \ldots, x_{m,k}\}\}(i, j, k \in (1, \ldots, n)), \tag{4}$$

where $n$the number of cities; $m$the numbers of subsequences; $x_{m,k}$the k-th dimensional of subsequence m.

3.2   Distance

The distance between two fireflies was characterized by these quence similarities which was the extent of differences of subsequence composed by two adjacent elements. For example, there were 12 cities and 3 salesmen, every salesman would visit 4 cities. The initialization position of firefly i,j were shown in Figure 3.2. Between the two sequences, the same adjacent elements in subsequence include:

2-5 in salesman 1, 6-10 in salesman 2, 9-1 and 1-7 in salesman 3. Therefore, the distance of the subsequence respectively were $r1$, $r2$, $r3$, and $r1=3$, $r2=3$, $r3=2$. The distance between the two fireflies is shown in Equation 5.

$$r = r1 + r2 + r3 = 8 \tag{5}$$

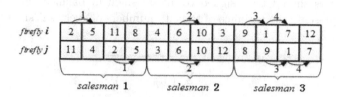

Fig. 1. Firefly i and firefly j

3.3 Movement

All fireflies move toward the brighter one following Fig.2, and continue moving randomly in order to enhance its global search ability referring to Fig.3.

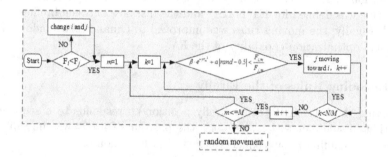

Fig. 2. The moving rules

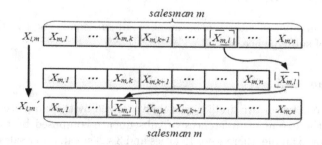

Fig. 3. The random movement

4   Experiment and Conclusions

Taking the eil51 problem for example, if there is only 1 salesman, the optimal sequence is shown in Fig.4(a); If there are 3 , the sequence is shown in Fig.4(b).

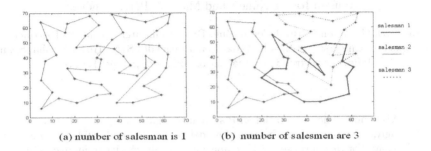

(a) number of salesman is 1   (b) number of salesmen are 3

Fig. 4. the optimal path of FA for TSP and ET-mTSP

Optimal path for ET-mTSP showed that the path of the optimal solution was short, and the task of every salesman nearly was equal, and FA was suitable for solving such equal-task problems .

Acknowledgments. We would like to thank the work and help of school of Mechanical Engineering (Xiangtan University). This work was supported by the Natural Science Foundation (China, NO.51375418), Foundation of Hunan Educational Committee (NO.12C0396) and Hunan Youth Science and Technology Innovation Platform (2013).

References

1. Dantzig, G.B., Fulkerson, D.R., Johnson, S.M.: On a Liner-Programming, Cmbinatorial Approah to the Traveling Salesman Problem. Operations Research 7(1), 58–66 (1959)
2. Lu, H.Q., Wang, Q., Huang, J.: Dividing into Equal Task of MTSP. Systems Engineering 23(2), 19–21 (2005)
3. Singh, A., Baghel, A.S.: A New Grouping Genetic Algorithm Approach to The Multiple Traveling Salesperson Problem. Soft Computing-A Fusion of Foundations, Methodologies and Applications 13(1), 95–101 (2009)
4. Liu, W.M., Li, S.J., Zhao, F.G.: An Ant Colony Optimization Algorithm for the Multiple Traveling Salesman Problem. In: Proceedings of 4th IEEE Conference on Industrial Electronics and Applications, pp. 1533–1537. IEEE Press, Xi'an (2009)
5. Yang, X.S.: Firefly Algorithm, Stochastic Test Functions and Design Optimization. Int. J. Bio-Inspired Computation, 78–84 (2010)
6. Zeng, B., Li, M.F., Zhang, Y.: Research on Assembly Sequence Planning Based on Firefly Algorithm. Journal of Mechanical Engineering 49(11), 177–184 (2013)

Accelerated Simulation of P Systems on the GPU: A Survey

Miguel A. Martínez-del-Amor, Luis F. Macías-Ramos, Luis Valencia-Cabrera, Agustín Riscos-Núñez, and Mario J. Pérez-Jiménez

Research Group on Natural Computing, Dept. Computer Science and Artificial Intelligence, University of Seville Avda. Reina Mercedes S/N, 41012, Sevilla, Spain
{mdelamor,lfmaciasr,lvalencia,ariscosn,marper}@us.es

Abstract. The acceleration of P system simulations is required increasingly, since they are at the core of model verification and validation processes. For this purpose, GPU computing is an alternative to more classic approaches in Parallel Computing. It provides a manycore platform with a level of high parallelism at a low cost. In this paper, we survey the developments of P systems simulators using the GPU, and analyze some performance considerations.

Keywords: Membrane Computing, Parallel Computing, GPGPU.

1 Introduction

Membrane Computing [13,14] defines a set of bio-inspired computing devices called *P systems*. They have several *syntactic* ingredients: a *membrane structure* which delimits *regions* where multisets of *objects* and sets of evolution *rules* are placed. P systems have also two main *semantic* ingredients: their inherent *parallelism* and *non-determinism*. The objects inside the membranes evolve according to given rules in a synchronous (in the sense that a global clock is assumed), parallel, and non-deterministic way.

In order to *experimentally validate* P systems based models [4], it is necessary to develop simulators that can help researchers to compute, analyze and extract results from them [14]. These simulators have to be as *efficient* as possible to handle large-size instances, which is one of the major challenges facing today's P systems simulators. In this concern, this parallel computation model leads to looking for a massively-parallel technology by which a parallel simulator can run efficiently. For example, current *Graphics Processor Units (GPUs)* [6] are *massively parallel processors*, featuring thousands of cores per chip [7].

In this paper, we survey the development of P systems simulators on the GPU, specially those available at the *PMCGPU* project [16].

The paper is structured as follows: Section 2 introduces the parallel simulation of P systems, and surveys GPU computing; Section 3 depicts the developed simulators for P systems on the GPU; and finally, Section 4 provides some conclusions and future research lines.

L. Pan et al. (Eds.): BIC-TA 2014, CCIS 472, pp. 308–312, 2014.
© Springer-Verlag Berlin Heidelberg 2014

2 Solutions in High Performance Computing

According to [5], a good computing platform for simulating P systems should provide a balance between *performance, flexibility, scalability, parallelism* and *cost*. However, it is difficult for a computing platform to conform with all of them. A factor promoting one attribute might demote another. In fact, flexibility usually comes at expenses of both performance and scalability [8].

Concerning the types of computing platforms for simulating P systems, there are mainly three to mention [8]: *Sequential* (e.g. Java, C++, etc.), *Software-based parallel* (e.g. OpenMP, MPI, etc.), *Hardware-based parallel* (e.g. FPGAs, etc.). When designing parallel simulators for P systems, a developer has to deeply analyze the platform, and adopt different approaches to implement real parallelism of P systems. Today, a well-known parallel platform in *HPC (High Performance Computing)* is the *GPU* (Graphics Processor Unit), that contains thousands of computing processors. In this sense, NVIDIA GPUs can be programmed by using *CUDA (Compute Unified Device Architecture)* [15,7], which offers a programming model that abstracts the GPU architecture.

According to the CUDA programming model, the GPU (or *device*) run thousands of *threads* executing the same code (called *kernel*) in parallel. The threads are arranged within a grid in a two-level hierarchy: a grid contains a set of *thread blocks*, and each block can contain hundreds of threads. All blocks in a grid have the same number and organization of threads. The execution of threads inside a block can be synchronized by *barrier* operations, and threads of different blocks can be synchronized only by finishing the execution of the kernel.

The memory hierarchy in CUDA must be manually managed. There are mainly two to mention: *global* and *shared* memories. Global memory is the largest but the slowest memory in the system, whereas shared memory is the smallest but fastest memory. The latter is key to speedup a code. Moreover, the memory is static, so enough memory space has to be allocated before running a kernel. This is often accomplished by considering the worst case (in space) of a problem.

The real GPU architecture consists of a processor array, organized in *Streaming Multiprocessors (SMs)* of *Streaming Processors (SPs, or cores)*. SMs execute threads in groups of 32, called a *warp*. Threads of the same warp must start together at the same program address. However, they are free to branch and execute independently, but at cost of performance. If a warp is broken (because of branching or memory stall), the real parallelism in CUDA is not achieved.

Although CUDA programming model is flexible enough, the achieved performance depends on the design and implementation. There are several strategies to help improving performance: *emphasizing parallelism* (warps must be maximized with active threads, but minimizing branch divergence), and *exploiting memory bandwidth* (by coalesced access to contiguous memory positions).

Therefore, GPUs entail a software-based parallel computing platform, but with hardware flavor: only by optimizing the code for the GPU architecture can it achieve best performance. The GPU is considered as a relatively low cost technology, leveraging: *good performance, an efficiently synchronized platform* with *a medium scalability degree*, and *low-medium flexibility*.

3   Parallel Simulators on the GPU

Next, we briefly survey the parallel simulators available in the PMCGPU *(Parallel simulators for Membrane Computing on the GPU)* project [9,16].

PCUDA [1,9]: This simulator is designed for *recognizer (confluent) P systems with active membranes*. The parallel design takes advantage of the double-parallelism in GPUs to speedup the simulation of the double-parallelism in P systems: each thread block is assigned to each elementary membrane, and each thread is assigned to a portion of the objects defined in the alphabet (rules in this model does not have cooperation). The simulator allocates memory for all the defined objects within each membrane. Although this is the worst case to deal with, it does not take place in the most P systems. Thus, the achieved performance depends on the simulated P system. Two case studies has been simulated [9]: a simple test P system designed to stress the simulator (A), and a solution to SAT problem with active membranes [2] (B). The experiments report up to 7x of speedup for case study A, and 1.67x for B. Therefore, PCUDA simulators are highly flexible, but have low performance and low scalability.

PCUDASAT [2,3,9]: It is a set of simulators for a *family of P systems with active membranes solving SAT in linear time* [2]. The simulation algorithm is based on the stages identified in the solution, and so, in the computation of any P system in the family. The code is tailored to this family, saving space in the representation of objects, and avoiding storing the rules (they are implicit in the code). In the design, each thread block is assigned to each elementary membrane, and each thread to each object of the input multiset. The CUDA simulator achieves up to 63x of speedup. Although PCUDASAT simulators are less flexible, the performance and scalability have been increased, compared to PCUDA, for this special case study.

TSPCUDASAT [11,9]: It simulates a *family of tissue-like P systems with cell division solving SAT in linear time*. The simulation algorithm is based, as in PCUDASAT, in the 5 stages of the computation of the P systems. In the design, each thread block is assigned to each cell, but threads are used differently in each stage. Experiments show that the CUDA simulator achieves up to 10x. Therefore, simulating in CUDA two solutions to the same problem (SAT) under different P system variants leads to different speedups. Indeed, the usage of charges can help to save space devoted to objects.

ABCD-GPU [12,10,9]: These simulators are for *Population Dynamics P systems*, both on OpenMP and CUDA. They follow the DCBA algorithm [12], which is based on four phases. The multicore version is parallelized in three ways [10]: 1) simulations, 2) environments and 3) hybrid approach. Runtime gains of up to 2.5x, using 1), were achieved with a 4-core CPU. The design of the CUDA simulator is as follows [12]: environments and simulations are distributed along thread blocks, and rule blocks among threads. Phases 1, 3 and 4 of DCBA were efficiently executed on the GPU, however Phase 2 was poorly accelerated (it is inherently sequential), becoming the bottleneck. The GPU simulator were benchmarked by a set of randomly generated PDP systems, achieving speedups of up to 7x. Experiments indicate the simulations are memory-bandwidth bound.

4   Conclusions and Future Work

The idea of using the CUDA to develop P systems simulators is to take advantage of the highly parallel architecture, the low cost and the easy synchronization of a GPU.

Flexible CUDA simulators for P systems (PCUDA and ABCD-GPU) statically allocate memory to represent objects using as worst case the whole alphabet. Although it is a naive solution, the access to data is made very efficiently. However, the performance of the simulator totally depends on the simulated P system, since the representation of multisets can be very sparse. There are two measures for P systems associated with performance [9]: *density of objects per membrane* (the ratio of number of objects actually appearing in the regions to the alphabet size), and *rule intensity* (the ratio of rules being applied to the total amount of rules). They should be maximized for better speedups.

Moreover, it has been shown that P systems simulations are both memory and memory-bandwidth bound: the performance of the simulation is relatively low compared with the computing resources available in the GPU. The main reasons are that simulating P systems requires a high synchronization degree (e.g. the global clock of the models, handling rule cooperation and rules competition, etc.), and the number of instructions to execute per memory portion is small. They restrict the design of parallel simulators, since a bad step taken on GPU programming can dramatically demote performance.

Therefore, further improvements of the designs have to be done, so that next generation of simulators on the GPU can take advantage of the full hardware and efficiently encode the representation of P systems.

Acknowledgements. The authors acknowledge the support of the Project TIN2012-37434 of the "Ministerio de Economía y Competitividad" of Spain, cofinanced by FEDER funds. M.A. Martínez-del-Amor also acknowledges the support of NVIDIA for the CUDA Research Center program at the University of Seville, and of the 3rd postdoctoral phase of the "PIF" program associated with the Project of Excellence under grant P08-TIC04200 of the "Junta de Andalucía".

References

1. Cecilia, J.M., García, J.M., Guerrero, G.D., Martínez-del-Amor, M.A., Pérez-Hurtado, I., Pérez-Jiménez, M.J.: Simulation of P systems with Active Membranes on CUDA. Briefings in Bioinformatics 11(3), 313–322 (2010)
2. Cecilia, J.M., García, J.M., Guerrero, G.D., Martínez-del-Amor, M.A., Pérez-Hurtado, I., Pérez-Jiménez, M.J.: Simulating a P system based efficient solution to SAT by using GPUs. Journal of Logic and Algebraic Programming 79(6), 317–325 (2010)
3. Cecilia, J.M., García, J.M., Guerrero, G.D., Martínez-del-Amor, M.A., Pérez-Jiménez, M.J., Ujaldón, M.: The GPU on the simulation of cellular computing models. Soft Computing 16(2), 231–246 (2012)

4. Frisco, P., Gheorghe, M., Pérez-Jiménez, M.J.: Applications of Membrane Computing in Systems and Synthetic Biology. Series: Emergence, Complexity and Computation, vol. 7. Springer (2014)
5. Gutiérrez, A., Alonso, S.: P systems: from theory to implementation, ch. 17, pp. 205–226 (2010)
6. Harris, M.: Mapping computational concepts to GPUs. In: ACM SIGGRAPH 2005 Courses, NY, USA (2005)
7. Kirk, D., Hwu, W.: Programming Massively Parallel Processors: A Hands on Approach, MA, USA (2010)
8. Nguyen, V., Kearney, D.A., Gioiosa, G.: Balancing performance, flexibility, and scalability in a parallel computing platform for membrane computing applications. In: Eleftherakis, G., Kefalas, P., Păun, G., Rozenberg, G., Salomaa, A. (eds.) WMC 2007. LNCS, vol. 4860, pp. 385–413. Springer, Heidelberg (2007)
9. Martínez-del-Amor, M.A.: Accelerating Membrane Systems Simulators using High Performance Computing with GPU. Ph.D. thesis, University of Seville (2013)
10. Martínez-del-Amor, M.A., Karlin, I., Jensen, R.E., Pérez-Jiménez, M.J., Elster, A.C.: Parallel simulation of probabilistic P systems on multicore platforms. In: Proceedings of the Tenth Brainstorming Week on Membrane Computing, vol. II, pp. 17–26 (2012)
11. Martínez-del-Amor, M.A., Pérez-Carrasco, J., Pérez-Jiménez, M.J.: Characterizing the parallel simulation of P systems on the GPU. International Journal of Unconventional Computing 9(5-6), 405–424 (2013)
12. Martínez-del-Amor, M.A., Pérez-Hurtado, I., Gastalver-Rubio, A., Elster, A.C., Pérez-Jiménez, M.J.: Population Dynamics P Systems on CUDA. In: Gilbert, D., Heiner, M. (eds.) CMSB 2012. LNCS, vol. 7605, pp. 247–266. Springer, Heidelberg (2012)
13. Păun, G.: Computing with Membranes. Journal of Computer and System Sciences 61(1), 108–143 (2000) and Turku Center for CS-TUCS Report No. 208 (1998)
14. Păun, G., Rozenberg, G., Salomaa, A.: The Oxford Handbook of Membrane Computing. Oxford University Press, USA (2010)
15. NVIDIA CUDA website (2014), https://developer.nvidia.com/cuda-zone
16. The PMCGPU project (2013), http://sourceforge.net/p/pmcgpu

Accepting *H*-Array Splicing Systems

V. Masilamani[1], D.K. Sheena Christy[2], D.G. Thomas[3],
Atulya K. Nagar[4], and Robinson Thamburaj[3]

[1] Department of Computer Science and Engineering, IIITD&M Kanchipuram
Chennai - 600 036, India
masila@iiitdm.ac.in
[2] Department of Mathematics, SRM University
Kattankulathur, Chennai - 603 203, India
sheena.lesley@gmail.com
[3] Department of Mathematics, Madras Christian College
Tambaram, Chennai - 600 059, India
dgthomasmcc@yahoo.com, robin.mcc@gmail.com
[4] Department of Mathematics and Computer Science
Liverpool Hope University
nagara@hope.ac.uk

1 Introduction

In [3], Tom Head defined splicing systems motivated by the behaviour of DNA sequences. The splicing system makes use of a new operation, called splicing on strings of symbols. Paun et al. [7] extended the definition of Head and defined extended *H* systems which are computationally universal.

V. Mitrana et al. [6] proposed a novel view of splicing systems and defined the concept of an accepting splicing system. Two ways of iterating the splicing operation in the generating case and the computational power of generating splicing systems defined by these operations were investigated [6]. Further more, two variants of accepting splicing systems were considered. All the accepting splicing models have been compared with each other with respect to their computational power. Arroyo et al. [1] introduced the generalization of accepting splicing system with permitting and forbidding words and studied the computational power of the variants of accepting splicing systems.

Recently, Krithivasan et al. [5] made an extension of the concept of splicing to arrays and defined array splicing systems. In [4] a new method of applying the splicing operation on rectangular arrays is introduced. This model is different from the model considered in [5].

In this paper, we propose the notion of accepting *H*-array splicing systems and study the computational power of these systems. We compare these systems with some existing models of two dimensional array languages. We consider a variant of accepting *H*-array splicing system with permitting and forbidding arrays and obtain interesting results.

L. Pan et al. (Eds.): BIC-TA 2014, CCIS 472, pp. 313–317, 2014.
© Springer-Verlag Berlin Heidelberg 2014

2 Preliminaries

Let V be a finite alphabet. A picture (or an image or an array) over V of size $(m \times n)$ where $m, n \geq 0$ is an $m \times n$ matrix with its entries from V. The collection of all pictures over V is denoted by V^{++}, and $V^{++} \cup \{\Lambda\}$ is denoted by V^{**}, where Λ denotes empty image. The set of all (one-dimensional or linear) strings over V is denoted by V^{+} and $V^{+} \cup \{\lambda\}$ is denoted by V^{*}, where λ denotes empty string.

Next we recall H-array splicing system defined in [4].

Definition 1. *Let V be an alphabet, $\#$ and $\$$ are two symbols that are not in V. A vertical domino is of the form $\boxed{\begin{smallmatrix} a \\ b \end{smallmatrix}}$, and a row domino is of the form $\boxed{a \mid b}$, where $a, b \in V$.*

A domino column splicing rule over V is of the form $p : y_1 \# y_2 \$ y_3 \# y_4$, where $y_i = \boxed{\begin{smallmatrix} a \\ b \end{smallmatrix}}$ or $\boxed{\begin{smallmatrix} \lambda \\ \lambda \end{smallmatrix}}$, $1 \leq i \leq 4$.

A domino row splicing rule over V is of the form $q : x_1 \# x_2 \$ x_3 \# x_4$, where $x_i = \boxed{a \mid b}$ or $x_i = \boxed{\lambda \mid \lambda}$, $1 \leq i \leq 4$.

Definition 2. *A generating H-array splicing scheme is a triple $\sigma = (V, R_c, R_r)$ where V is an alphabet, R_c is a set of domino column splicing rules and R_r is a set of domino row splicing rules.*

Definition 3. *For a given generating H-array splicing scheme $\sigma = (V, R_c, R_r)$ and a language $L \subseteq V^{**}$, if $X, Y \in L$ then,*
$\sigma(X, Y) = \{Z, Z' \in V^{**} | (X, Y) \vdash_c \{Z, Z'\} \text{ or } (X, Y) \vdash_r \{Z, Z'\}\}$ *and*
$\sigma(L) = \bigcup_{X, Y \in L} \sigma(X, Y)$.

For two array languages L_1, L_2, we define $\sigma(L_1, L_2) = \bigcup_{X \in L_1, Y \in L_2} \sigma(X, Y)$.

The iterated application of σ is defined as follows:
$\sigma^0(L) = L; \; \sigma^{i+1}(L) = \sigma^i(L) \cup \sigma(\sigma^i(L)) \text{ for } i \geq 0; \; \sigma^*(L) = \bigcup_{i=0}^{\infty} \sigma^i(L)$.

This method of defining iterated splicing can be called as uniform.

An H-array splicing system is defined by $S = (\sigma, A)$ where $\sigma = (V, R_c, R_r)$ and A is a subset of V^{**}, called the initial language. The language of S is defined by $L(S)$ is $\sigma^*(A)$ and we call it as a splicing array language.

We denote the class of all H-array splicing systems by HAS and the class of all splicing array languages of H-array splicing systems by $\mathcal{L}(HAS)$.

3 Non-uniform Variant

In [4], the authors considered the splicing operation on images of rectangular arrays and studied the properties and the generative power of H-array splicing system. We consider a different method of iterated splicing which we call as a non-uniform variant of iterated splicing using H-array splicing system and obtain a new result. This method is explained below.

Definition 4. *For a H-array splicing system $S = (\sigma, A)$, the non-uniform method of defining iterated splicing is as follows:*

$$\tau^0(A) = A; \; \tau^{i+1}(A) = \sigma(\tau^i(A), A), \; i \geq 0; \; \tau^*(A) = \bigcup_{i=0}^{\infty} \tau^i(A).$$

The language generated by H-array splicing system in non-uniform way is $\tau^*(A)$ and the family of languages generated by non-uniform H-array splicing system is denoted by $\mathcal{L}_n(HAS)$.

We now compare the power of HAS with the non-uniform variant of iterated splicing and the existing model 2RLG given in [2]. The family of picture languages generated by two-dimensional right-linear grammars is denoted by $\mathcal{L}(2RLG)$.

Theorem 1. *The class $\mathcal{L}_n(HAS)$ intersects $\mathcal{L}(2RLG)$.*

4 Accepting H-Array Splicing System

In this section we introduce the notion of accepting H-array splicing system with two methods of iterated splicing namely uniform and non-uniform methods. We compare the generating power of this system with that of well-known classes of array rewriting systems.

Definition 5. *An accepting H-array splicing system (AHASS) is a pair $\Gamma = (S, F)$ where $S = (\sigma, A)$ is a H-array splicing system and F is a finite subset of V^{**}. Let $w \in V^{**}$. We define the uniform method (usual way) of the iterated array splicing of Γ as follows:*
$$\sigma^0(A, w) = \{w\}; \; \sigma^{i+1}(A, w) = \sigma^i(A, w) \cup \sigma(\sigma^i(A, w) \cup A), \; i \geq 0.$$
$$\sigma^*(A, w) = \bigcup_{i=0}^{\infty} \sigma^i(A, w).$$

The language accepted by an accepting H-array splicing system Γ is $L(\Gamma) = \{w \in V^{**} | \sigma^*(A, w) \cap F \neq \phi\}$. The class of languages accepted by accepting H-array splicing system is denoted by $\mathcal{L}(AHASS)$.

Let $\Gamma = (S, F)$ be an accepting H-array splicing system and $w \in V^{**}$. The non-uniform variant of iterated splicing of Γ is defined as follows.
$$\tau^0(A, w) = \{w\}; \; \tau^{i+1}(A, w) = \tau^i(A, w) \cup \sigma(\tau^i(A, w), A), \; i \geq 0,$$
$$\tau^*(A, w) = \bigcup_{i=0}^{\infty} \tau^i(A, w).$$

An array $w \in V^{**}$ is said to be accepted by Γ in non-uniform way if $\tau^*(A, w) \cap F \neq \phi$. The language accepted by γ in non-uniform way is $L_n(\Gamma) = \{w \in V^{**} / \tau^*(A, w) \cap F \neq \phi\}$. The class of all languages accepted by AHASS in non-uniform way is denoted by $\mathcal{L}_n(AHASS)$.

We now compare the generating powers of AHASS and LOC of local array languages introduced in [2].

Theorem 2. *The classes LOC and $\mathcal{L}(AHASS)$ are incomparable but not disjoint, if AHASS is such that either R_r or R_c empty.*

Next, we consider another two-dimensional grammar $(R : R)AG$ [8] and give a comparison result with non-uniform variant of AHASS.

Theorem 3. $\mathcal{L}_n(AHASS)$ *is incomparable but not disjoint with $(R : R)AL$, if AHASS is such that either R_r or R_c empty.*

Theorem 4. *Let Γ be an AHASS with $R_r = \phi$. There exists a positive integer k such that if $p \in L(\Gamma)$ with $|p|_c \geq k$ then $p \textcircled{1} y \textcircled{1} p \in L(\Gamma)$ for any $y \in V^{**}$ with $|y|_r = |p|_r$.*

Similar to theorem 4, we have

Theorem 5. *Let Γ be an AHASS with $R_c = \phi$. There exists a positive integer s such that if $p \in L(\Gamma)$ with $|p|_r \geq s$, then $p \ominus y \ominus p \in L(\Gamma)$ for any $y \in V^{**}$ with $|p|_c = |y|_c$.*

Similar results hold good for languages accepted by AHASS in non-uniform way. In other words, we have:

Theorem 6. *Let Γ be an AHASS with $R_r = \phi$. There exists an integer $k > 0$ such that if $w \in \mathcal{L}_n(\Gamma)$ with $|w|_c \geq k$, then either $w \textcircled{1} y \subseteq \mathcal{L}_n(\Gamma)$ or $y \textcircled{1} w \subseteq \mathcal{L}_n(\Gamma)$, where $y \in V^{**}$ and $|y|_r = |w|_r$.*

Theorem 7. *Let Γ be an AHASS with $R_c = \phi$. There exists an integer $s > 0$ such that if $w \in \mathcal{L}_n(\Gamma)$ with $|w|_r \geq s$, then either $w \ominus z \subseteq \mathcal{L}_n(\Gamma)$ or $z \ominus w \subseteq \mathcal{L}_n(\Gamma)$, where $z \in V^{**}$ and $|z|_c = |w|_c$.*

Theorem 8. $(\mathcal{L}(HAS) \cap \mathcal{L}_n(HAS)) \backslash (\mathcal{L}(AHASS) \cup \mathcal{L}_n(AHASS)) \neq \phi.$

5   Permitting and Forbidding Arrays

In this section, we define the notion of an accepting H-array splicing system with permitting and forbidding arrays. We examine its generative power and obtain comparison results with known array languages.

Definition 6. *An accepting H-array splicing system with permitting and forbidding arrays (AHASS-PF) is a triple $\Gamma = (S, P, F)$ where $S = (\sigma, A)$, a H-array splicing system, P and F are finite subsets of V^{**}. The elements of P and F are called permitting arrays and forbidding arrays respectively. For any $w \in V^{**}$, the iterated H-array splicing of Γ is defined as follows: $\sigma^0(A, w) = \{w\}$, $\sigma^{i+1}(A, w) = \sigma^i(A, w) \cup \sigma(\sigma^i(A, w) \cup A); i \geq 0. \sigma^*(A, w) = \bigcup_{i \geq 0} \sigma^i(A, w)$.*

The language accepted by an accepting H-array splicing system with permitting and forbidding arrays of Γ is $L(\Gamma) = \{w \in V^{**}/\exists k \geq 0, \sigma^k(A, w) \cap P \neq \phi, \sigma^k(A, w) \cap F = \phi\}$.

The class of languages accepted by accepting H-array splicing systems with permitting and forbidding arrays is denoted by $\mathcal{L}(AHASS-PF)$. The languages accepted by AHASS-PF without forbidding arrays is denoted by $\mathcal{L}^\phi(AHASS)$.

The non-uniform variant of iterated splicing of Γ is defined as follows: $\tau^0(A,w) = \{w\}$, $\tau^{i+1}(A,w) = \tau^i(A,w) \cup \sigma(\tau^i(A,w),A)$; $i \geq 0$. $\tau^*(A,w) = \bigcup_{i\geq 0} \tau^i(A,w)$.

The language accepted by Γ in non-uniform way is deifned by $L_n(\Gamma) = \{w \in V^{**} / \exists k \geq 0, \tau^k(A,w) \cap P \neq \phi$ and $\tau^k(A,w) \cap F = \phi\}$.

The class of languages accepted by AHASS-PF and AHASS-PF without forbidding arrays in non-uniform way are denoted respectively by $\mathcal{L}_n(AHASS-PF)$ and $\mathcal{L}_n^\phi(AHASS)$.

Theorem 9

(i) The class $\mathcal{L}_n(AHASS-PF)$ is incomparable with the class of $(R:R)AL$.
(ii) The class $\mathcal{L}(AHASS-PF)$ is incomparable with the class of $(CF:CF)AL$.
(iii) If AHASS is such that either R_r or R_c empty, then
    (a) $(CF:CF)AL - L_n^\phi(AHASS) \neq \phi$
    (b) $L_n^\phi(AHASS) \cap (CF:CF)AL \neq \phi$.

References

1. Arroyo, F., Castellanos, J., Dassow, J., Mitrana, V., Sanchez-Couso, J.R.: Accepting splicing systems with permitting and forbidding words. Acta Informatica 50, 1–14 (2013)
2. Giammarresi, D., Restivo, D.: Two-dimensional languages. In: Salomaa, A., Rozenberg, G. (eds.) Handbook of Formal Languages, vol. 3, pp. 215–267. Springer (1997)
3. Head, T.: Formal language theory and DNA: an analysis of the generative capacity of specific recombinant behaviours. Bull. Math. Biol. 49, 735–759 (1987)
4. Helen Chandra, P., Subramanian, K.G., Thomas, D.G.: Parallel splicing on images. International Journal of Pattern Recognition and Artificial Intelligence 18, 1071–1091 (2004)
5. Krithivasan, K., Chakaravarthy, V.T., Rama, R.: Array splicing systems. In: Păun, G., Salomaa, A. (eds.) New Trends in Formal Languages. LNCS, vol. 1218, pp. 346–365. Springer, Heidelberg (1997)
6. Mitrana, V., Petre, I., Rogojin, V.: Accepting splicing systems. Theoretical Computer Science 411, 2414–2422 (2010)
7. Păun, G., Rozenberg, G., Salomaa, A.: DNA Computing: New Computing Paradigms. Springer (1998)
8. Siromoney, G., Siromoney, R., Krithivasan, K.: Picture languages with array rewriting rules. Information and Control 22, 447–470 (1973)

Research on Magnetotactic Bacteria Optimization Algorithm Based on the Best Individual

Hongwei Mo*, Lili Liu, Lifang Xu, and Yanyan Zhao

Automation College, Harbin Engineering University, Harbin, 150001, China
honwei2004@163.com

Abstract. An improved magnetotactic bacteria optimization algorithm (MBOA) is researched based on the best individual and the performance effect of parameter settings is studied in order to show which setting is more suitable for solving optimization problems. It is tested on four standard function problems and compared with DE, ABC. Experiment results show that MBOAs with different parameter settings are effective for solving most of the benchmark functions. And they do show different performance on a few benchmark functions.

Keywords: Magnetotactic bacteria optimization algorithm, The best individual, Parameter setting, Optimization.

1 Introduction

Many kinds of life systems from bird flocks to bacteria have been the greatest inspiration sources for designing optimization algorithms. In nature, there is a special kind of magnetotactic bacteria (MTB)[1]. It has different biology characteristics from chemotactic bacteria since they can orient and swim along magnetic field lines with the aid of mineral particles called magnetosomes(MTSs) inside their bodies. Mo has proposed an original magnetotactic bacteria optimization algorithm[2,3] based on the biology principle of MTB. It shows the potential ability of solving optimization problems and has very fast convergence speed. In this paper, the original MBOA is improved. The effect of parameters on the proposed MBOA is studied.

2 Mboa Based on Best-Rand Pairwise Schemes

In the MBOA, a population is a magnetotactic bacterium with multi-cells. A cell is a candidate solution. The attributes of a solution vector are considered as magnetosomes. The values of attributes of a solution vector are considered as the moments of a cell. The interaction between two cells is represented by the

---

* Corresponding author.

L. Pan et al. (Eds.): BIC-TA 2014, CCIS 472, pp. 318–322, 2014.

differential vector between them. In the following we describe the main procedures of MBOA. For the MBOA, we consider the state that each cell is to align its magnetosome chains parallel to the other ones, with the same polarity would yield the most efficient swimming way for living as finding the optimal solution.

Initialization of the Population. The initial population is filled with N number of randomly generated n-dimensional real-valued vectors(i.e.,cells of a MTB). Let $X_i = (x_{i,1}, x_{i,2}, \ldots, x_{i,n})$ represents the ith cell (for generation index $t=0$) initialized randomly. Each cell is generated as follows:

$$x_{i,j} = x_{min,j} + rand(0,1) \times (x_{max,j} - x_{min,j}) \tag{1}$$

where $i = 1, 2, \ldots, N$, $j = 1, 2, \ldots, n$. By $x_{max,j}$ and $x_{min,j}$, we denote the upper and lower bounds for the dimension j, respectively. and it is denoted by $rand(0,1)$ a random number between 0 and 1.

Interaction Distance. Interaction distance is used to calculate the interaction energy for generating the magnetosomes of cells. The distance $d_{i,r}$ of two cells x_i and x_r calculated as follows:

$$D_i = X_i - X_r \tag{2}$$

Thus, we can get a $N \times n$ distance matrix $D = [D_1, D_2, \ldots, D_N]'$, where i and r is mutually different integer indices from $\{1, 2, \ldots, N\}$, and r is randomly chosen one.

MTSs Generation. Based on the distances among cells, the interaction energy e_i between two cells based on (2) is defined as:

$$e_{i,j}(t) = \left(\frac{d_{i,j}(t)}{1 + c_1 \times norm(D_i) + c_2 \times d_{p,q}(t)} \right)^3 \tag{3}$$

where t is the generation index, c_1 and c_2 are constants. $d_{p,q}$ is randomly selected from D_p. $norm(D_i)$ is the Euclidean length of vector D_i. p and r are mutually different and randomly chosen integer indices from $\{1, 2, \ldots, N\}$. $q \in \{1, 2, \ldots, n\}$ stands for one randomly chosen integer. n is the dimensions of a cell. D_i stands for the Euclidean distance between two cells X_i and X_r.

After obtaining interaction energy, for simplifying calculation, ignore where θ is the angle between M and B and direction in (1), the moments M_i are generated as follows:

$$M_i(t) = \frac{E_i(t)}{B} \tag{4}$$

where B is a constant named magnetic field strength. Then the total moments of a cell is regulated as follows:

$$x_{i,j}(t) = x_{i,j}(t) + m_{r,q}(t) \times rand \tag{5}$$

where $m_{r,q}$ is randomly chosen from m_i, $rand$ is a random number in interval (0,1).

MTSs Regulation. After moments generation, evaluate the population according to cells' fitness, then the moments regulation is realized as follows. We set a magnetic field strength probability mp. If $rand > mp$, the moments in the cell migrate as follows:

$$X_i(t+1) = X_{best}(t) + \left(X_{best}(t) - X_i(t)\right) \times rand \qquad (6)$$

Otherwise,

$$X_i(t+1) = X_r(t) + \left(X_{best}(t) - X_r(t)\right) \times rand \qquad (7)$$

where $rand$ is a random number in interval $(0,1)$ and r is randomly chosen from $\{1, 2, ..., N\}$.

In this step, based on (6), the best cell X_{best} in the current generation will move to a new place in the next generation. Thus, it may enhance the ability of local search of the algorithm. Based on (7), some randomly chosen cells in the population will have chance to be regulated based on the moments of the best cell in the current generation. Thus, it may enhance the ability of global search of the algorithms.

MTSs Replacement. After the moments migration, evaluate the population according to cells' fitness, then some worse moments are replaced by the following way:

$$X_i(t+1) = m_{r,q}(t) \times \left((rand(1,n) - 1) \times rand(1,n)\right) \qquad (8)$$

where $m_{r,q}$ is randomly chosen from M. r is randomly chosen from $\{1, 2, ..., N\}$. $q \in \{1, 2, ..., n\}$ stands for one randomly chosen integer. $rand(1, n)$ is a random vector with n dimensions.

At last, evaluate the population according to cells' fitness after replacement. In this version, one fifth of the cells with worse fitness will be replaced by randomly generated cells.

3   Simulation Results

To test the performance of the improved MBOA, we demonstrate the effectiveness of MBOA by comparing with DE and ABC algorithms on 4 benchmark functions shown in Tables 1. Speci?cally, f_1–f_2 are unimodal; The next two functions f_3–f_4 are multimodal functions.

In the MBOA variants, there are four parameters settings, including B, c_1, c_2, mp. In order to study the effect of parameters on the performance of the MBOA, we set $c_1 = 10(MBOA-1)$, $c_2 = 20(MBOA-2)$, $c_3 = 30(MBOA-3)$, $c_4 = 40(MBOA-4)$, $B = 3$, $c_2 = 0.003$, $mp = 0.5$. The size of the population size is 30.

We demonstrate the effectiveness of MBOA with different parameters by comparing MBOA with the DE [4] and ABC [5]. For DE and ABC, the parameter values are chosen as in [4] and [5], respectively. The experimental results are shown

Table 1. Benchmark functions used in experiments

Function	Range	D	Formulation
f_1 : Sphere	[-100, 100]	30	$f(x) = \sum_{i=1}^{n} x_i^2$
f_2 : Schwefel1.2	[-100, 100]	30	$f(x) = \sum_{i=1}^{n} (\sum_{j=1}^{i} x_j)^2$
f_3 : Schwefel	[-500, 500]	30	$f(x) = \sum_{i=1}^{n} -x_i \sin \sqrt{|x_i|}$
f_4 : Griewank	[-600, 600]	30	$f(x) = \frac{1}{4000} \sum_{i=1}^{n} x_i^2 - \prod_{i=1}^{n} \cos(\frac{x_i}{\sqrt{i}}) + 1$

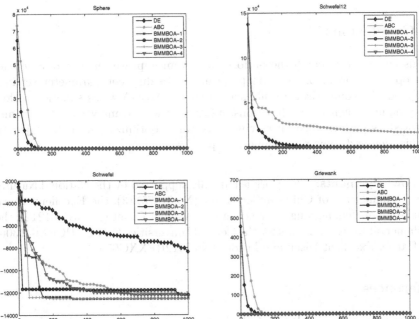

Fig. 1. Convergence comparison of DE,ABC,MBOA–1,MBOA–2,MBOA–3,MBOA–4 on f_1, f_2, f_3, f_4

in Table 2. In Figure1, the convergence of DE, ABC and MBOA–1,MBOA–2,MBOA–3,MBOA–4 on some benchmark examples are shown for 1000 generations.

As shown in Table 2, we can see that the MBOA variants have better performance than DE and ABC on functions f_1, f_2 and f_4. MBOA variants perform better than ABC and have worse performance compared with DE on function f_3. Among MBOA–1, MBOA–2, MBOA–3, MBOA–4, MBOA–3 shows the best performance on function f_4. In summary, MBOA has very competitive performance when compared with DE and ABC. From Figure 1, it can be seen that the MBOA has faster convergence speed than DE and ABC. The results show that different c1 has little effect on solving the benchmark problems used in the paper.

Table 2. Performance comparisons of MBOA variants,DE and ABC

Func.		DE	ABC	MBOA–1	MBOA–2	MBOA–3	MBOA–4
f_1	Mean	76.3788	1.1161e-13	0	0	0	0
	St.d	18.2070	8.9199e-14	0	0	0	0
f_2	Mean	1.5718e+04	11.6109	0	0	0	0
	St.d	4.3813e+03	2.9127	0	0	0	0
f_3	Mean	**-1.2568e+04**	-9.3141e+03	-1.2284e+04	-1.2505e+04	-1.2550e+04	-1.1454e+04
	St.d	**0.8850**	676.0775	441.8418	101.3776	19.1886	778.0946
f_4	Mean	0.5287	1.2614e-14	0	0	0	0
	St.d	0.1042	2.0200e-14	0	0	0	0

4 Conclusions

In this paper, we research the performance of an improved magnetotactic bacteria optimization algorithm. Its performance of different parameter settings is studied.The comparison results show that the MBOA-4 has superior performance on many benchmark functions.In future, it will be analyzed in theory and improved its performance for solving constrained optimization, multi-objective optimization and some real engineering problems.

Acknowledgements. This work is partially supported by the National Natural Science Foundation of China under Grant (No.61075113), the Excellent Youth Foundation of Heilongjiang Province of China under Grant (No. JC201212), the Fundamental Research Funds for the Central Universities (No. HEUCFX041306) and Harbin Excellent Discipline Leader (No.2012RFXXG073).

References

1. Faivre, D., Schuler, D.: Magnetotactic bacteria and magnetosomes. Chem. Rev. 108, 4875–4898 (2008)
2. Mo, H.W.: Research on magnetotactic bacteria optimization algorithm. In: The Fifth International Conference on Advanced Computational Intelligence, Nanjing, China, pp. 423–428 (2012)
3. Mo H.W., Xu L.F. Magnetotactic bacteria optimization algorithm for multimodal optimization. Swarm Intelligence (SIS), IEEE Symposium on. 240-247.Singapore (2013).
4. Storn, R., Price, K.: Differential evolutuion-a simple and efficient heuristic for global optimization over continuous spaces. Journal of Global Optimization 11, 341–359 (1997)
5. Karaboga, D., Akay, B.: A comparative study of Artificial Bee Colony algorithm. Applied Mathematics and Computation 214, 108–132 (2009)

Uniform Solution to Common Algorithmic Problem in the Minimally Parallel Mode

Yunyun Niu[1,*], Ibrahim Venkat[2], Ahamad Tajudin Khader[2], and K.G. Subramanian[2]

[1] School of Electronic Engineering and Computer Science
Peking University, 100871 Beijing, China
niuyunyun1003@163.com
[2] School of Computer Sciences, Universiti Sains Malaysia
Penang 11800, Malaysia
{ibrahim,tajudin}@cs.usm.my

Abstract. A P system is a novel computing model introduced by Păun in the area of membrane computing. It is known that the Common Algorithmic Problem (CAP) has a nice property that several other **NP**-complete problems can be reduced to it in linear time. The decision version of this problem is known to be efficiently solved with a family of recognizer P systems with active membranes with three electrical charges working in the maximally parallel way. We here work with a variant of a P system with active membranes that does not use polarizations and present a uniform solution to CAP in the minimally parallel mode.

Keywords: Membrane computing, P system, Minimal parallelism, Common algorithmic problem.

1 Introduction

Membrane computing is an emergent branch of natural computing, which was introduced by Gh. Păun in the end of 1998 [1]. The innovative computing devices (called *P systems*) in membrane computing are inspired by the structure and the functioning of living cells, as well as the organization of cells in tissues, organs, and other higher order structures [2,3]. P systems provide distributed parallel computing models, which were proved to be a rich framework for handling many problems related to computing. Most of the variants of P systems are computationally universal, and can solve presumably intractable problems in a feasible time [4,5]. For the motivation and a detailed description of various P system models we refer to [6]. A series of applications of P systems, in biology, linguistics, computer science, management, etc., were reported (e.g., see [7]).

The electrical charges used in P systems with active membrane are not quite realistic from a biological point of view. The cell membrane is polarized, but in a different manner: it is in general positively charged in the external layer

---

* Corresponding author.

L. Pan et al. (Eds.): BIC-TA 2014, CCIS 472, pp. 323–327, 2014.

and negatively charged in the inner layer of phospholipidic molecules. On the other hand, it is possible to have an overall polarization, positive or negative, of inner vesicles, due to ion exchanges with the inner or upper compartments, but the changes of these polarizations are done by more complex processes than by applying single rule as in P systems with active membranes. Anyway, it is a natural question to consider systems without membrane polarization. It is known that polarizationless P systems with active membranes can efficiently solve **NP**-complete problems such as SAT problem [8], even **PSAPCE**-complete problems such as QSAT problem [9].

The maximally parallel way of using the rules is a basic feature of P systems with active membranes, which means that in each step, in each region of a system, we have to use a maximal multiset of rules. This feature relies on the assumption that "if we wait enough, then all biochemical reactions in the cell which may take place will take place". Obviously, it is not a rather "realistic" assumption. So, another strategy of applying rules in parallel was introduced, the so-called minimal parallelism [10]: if at least a rule from a set of rules associated with a membrane or a region can be used, then at least one rule from that membrane or region must be used, without any other restriction (e.g., more rules can be used, but we do not care how many). The computational power and efficiency of P systems with active membranes working in the minimally parallel mode was investigated in [10].

This work deals with the *Common Algorithmic Problem* (CAP). CAP has a nice property – *local universality*: many **NP**-complete problems can be reduced to it in linear time (using a logarithmic bounded space), such as *Independent Set Decision Problem, Vertex Cover Decision Problem, Maximum Clique Problem, Satisfiability Problem, Hamiltonian Path Problem* and *Tripartite Matching Problem* [11]. In [12], an effective solution to the decision version of CAP is presented using a family of recognizer P systems with active membranes, where three polarizations are used and the systems work in maximally parallel way. In this work, we provide a uniform solution to CAP by a family of recognizer P systems with polarizationless active membranes working in the minimally parallel mode.

2   A Uniform Solution to Common Algorithmic Problem

The *Common Algorithmic Decision Problem* (CADP) is the following: *Given S a finite set, F a family of subsets of S (called forbidden sets), and $k \in \mathbb{N}$, we ask if there exists a subset A of S such that $|A| \geq k$, and which does not include any set belonging to F.*

Theorem 1. *The Common Algorithmic Decision Problem can be solved in a uniform way by a family of recognizer P systems with polarizationless active membranes working in the minimally parallel mode.*

Proof: The solution to CADP follows a brute force approach in the framework of polarizationless P systems with active membranes in the minimally parallel mode. The solution consists of the following stages:

- *Generation Stage*: All possible subsets of a finite set S are generated by membrane division.
- *Checking Stage*: The system checks whether or not there exists a subset A of S such that A does not include any forbidden set in the family F and $|A| \geq k$.
- *Output Stage*: The system sends to the environment the right answer according to the results of the previous stage.

For a given CADP instance $u = (S, F, k)$, where $S = \{s_1, \cdots, s_n\}$, $F = \{B_1, \cdots, B_m\}$, $B_i \subseteq S$, and $k \in \mathbb{N}$, the encoding of the instance is $cod(u) = \{\{s_{i,j} \mid s_j \in B_i, 1 \leq i \leq m, 1 \leq j \leq n\}\}$, which is the input multiset of the system solving CADP.

Let us consider the polynomial time computable function between $\mathbb{N}^3$ and $\mathbb{N}$, $\langle n, m, k \rangle = \langle \langle n, m \rangle, k \rangle$, induced by the pair function $\langle n, m \rangle = ((n+m)(n+m+1)/2) + n$. For given size parameters n, m and k, we shall construct a P system $\Pi(\langle n, m, k \rangle)$ to solve all instances of CADP with n elements in a finite set S, m sets in the family F of forbidden sets, and the target subset size k.

$$\Pi(\langle n, m, k \rangle) = (O, \Sigma, H, \mu, w_0, w_1, \cdots, w_{n+m+k}, w_p, w_q, w_r, w_l, w_s, w_{s'}, w_{l_{1,1}},$$
$$\cdots, w_{l_{1,n}}, \cdots, w_{l_{m,1}}, \cdots, w_{l_{m,n}}, w_{l_1}, \cdots, w_{l_n}, \mathcal{R}, h_{in}, h_0)$$

with the following components:

- $O = \Sigma \cup \{s'_{i,j}, d_{i,j} \mid 1 \leq i \leq m, 1 \leq j \leq n\}$
  $\cup \{c_j \mid 1 \leq j \leq m\}$
  $\cup \{d_i \mid 1 \leq i \leq 2n+m\} \cup \{p_i \mid 1 \leq i \leq 2n+m+14\}$
  $\cup \{q_i \mid 1 \leq i \leq 2n+m+8\} \cup \{r_i \mid 1 \leq i \leq 2n+m+12\}$
  $\cup \{a_i, f_i, t_i, f'_i, t'_i, T_i, b_i \mid 1 \leq i \leq n\}$
  $\cup \{t, b, d, y, \text{yes}, \text{no}\};$
- $\Sigma = \{s_{i,j} \mid 1 \leq i \leq m, 1 \leq j \leq n\};$
- $H = \{s, s', p, q, r, l, l_1, \cdots, l_m, l_{1,1}, \cdots, l_{1,n}, \cdots, l_{m,1}, \cdots$
  $l_{m,n}, 0, 1, 2, \cdots, n+m+k\};$
- $\mu = [[[\quad]_p[[\quad]_q[\quad]_r[\quad]_l[\quad]_{l_1} \cdots [\quad]_{l_m}[\quad]_{l_{1,1}} \cdots [\quad]_{l_{1,n}} \cdots [\quad]_{l_{m,1}} \cdots$
  $[\quad]_{l_{m,n}}[\quad]_1[\quad]_2 \cdots [\quad]_{n+m+k}]_0]_{s'}]_s$ (the structure is also illustrated in Fig. 1);
- $w_0 = \{\{a_1\}\}$, $w_p = \{\{p_1\}\}$, $w_q = \{\{q_1\}\}$, $w_r = \{\{r_1\}\}$, $w_l = \{\{d_1, b_1, \cdots, b_n\}\}$,
  $w_{l_i} = \{\{d_1\}\} \cup \{\{d_{i,j} \mid 1 \leq j \leq n\}\}$, for $1 \leq i \leq m$,
  $w_i = \lambda$, for $i \in \{s, s'\} \cup \{l_{i,j} \mid 1 \leq i \leq m, 1 \leq j \leq n\} \cup \{1, 2, \cdots, n+m+k\};$
- $h_{in} = 0$ is the input cell;
- h_0 is the environment (the output region);
- $\mathcal{R}$ is the set of rules:

(1) $[p_i \to p_{i+1}]_p$, for $1 \leq i \leq 2n+m+13$.
$\quad [q_i \to q_{i+1}]_q$, for $1 \leq i \leq 2n+m+7$.
$\quad [r_i \to r_{i+1}]_r$, for $1 \leq i \leq 2n+m+11$.
$\quad [d_i \to d_{i+1}]_{l_j}$, for $1 \leq i \leq 2n+j-1, 1 \leq j \leq m$.
$\quad [d_i \to d_{i+1}]_l$, for $1 \leq i \leq 2n+m+2$.
(2) $[a_i]_0 \to [t_i]_0[f_i]_0$, for $1 \leq i \leq n$.
$\quad [f_i \to f'_i a_{i+1}]_0$, for $1 \leq i \leq n-1$.

$[t_i \rightarrow t'_i a_{i+1}]_0$, for $1 \leq i \leq n - 1$.
$[f_n \rightarrow f'_n]_0$.
$[t_n \rightarrow t'_n]_0$.

(3) $t'_i[\ ]_i \rightarrow [t'_i]_i$, for $1 \leq i \leq n$.
$[t'_i]_i \rightarrow T_i$, for $1 \leq i \leq n$.

(4) $T_i[\ ]_{n+j} \rightarrow [T_i]_{n+j}$, for $1 \leq i \leq n, 1 \leq j \leq k$.
$[T_i]_{n+j} \rightarrow d$, for $1 \leq i \leq n, 1 \leq j \leq k$.

(5) $s_{i,j}[\ ]_{l_{i,j}} \rightarrow [s'_{i,j}]_{l_{i,j}}$, for $1 \leq i \leq m, 1 \leq j \leq n$.
$[d_{2n+i}]_{l_i} \rightarrow d$, for $1 \leq i \leq m$.
$d_{i,j}[\ ]_{l_{i,j}} \rightarrow [d_{i,j}]_{l_{i,j}}$, for $1 \leq i \leq m, 1 \leq j \leq n$.
$[d_{i,j}]_{l_{i,j}} \rightarrow d$, for $1 \leq i \leq m, 1 \leq j \leq n$.
$s'_{i,j}[\ ]_j \rightarrow [c_i]_j$, for $1 \leq i \leq m, 1 \leq j \leq n$.

(6) $[d_{2n+m+3}]_l \rightarrow d$.
$b_i[\ ]_i \rightarrow [b_i]_i$, for $1 \leq i \leq n$.
$[b_i]_i \rightarrow d$, for $1 \leq i \leq n$.
$c_i[\ ]_{n+k+i} \rightarrow [c_i]_{n+k+i}$, for $1 \leq i \leq m$.
$[c_i]_{n+k+i} \rightarrow d$, for $1 \leq i \leq m$.

(7) $[q_{2n+m+8}]_q \rightarrow q_{2n+m+8}[\ ]_q$.
$q_{2n+m+8}[\ ]_{n+i} \rightarrow [q_{2n+m+8}]_{n+i}$, for $1 \leq i \leq m + k$.
$[q_{2n+m+8}]_{n+i} \rightarrow b$, for $1 \leq i \leq m + k$.
$[b]_0 \rightarrow d$.

(8) $[r_{2n+m+12}]_r \rightarrow r_{2n+m+12}[\ ]_r$.
$[r_{2n+m+12}]_0 \rightarrow y[\ ]_0$.
$[y]_{s'} \rightarrow$ **yes**.
$[\textbf{yes}]_s \rightarrow$ **yes**$[\ ]_s$.

(9) $[p_{2n+m+14}]_p \rightarrow p_{2n+m+14}[\ ]_p$.
$[p_{2n+m+14}]_{s'} \rightarrow$ **no**$[\ ]_{s'}$.
$[\textbf{no}]_s \rightarrow$ **no**$[\ ]_s$.

From the previous explanation of the use of rules, one can easily see how this P system works. It is clear that we get the object **yes** at step $2n + m + 15$ if only if there is a subset of S such that its size is not less than k and it does not include any forbidden set. Otherwise, we get the object **no** at step $2n + m + 16$. We omit the formal verification of the above computation, but we just point out that the construction of the above P system can be done in polynomial time by a deterministic Turing machine. We first note that the sets of rules associated with the system $\Pi(\langle n, m, k \rangle)$ are recursive. Hence, it is enough to note that the amount of necessary resources for designing such system is $O((max\{m, n, k\})^2)$, and this is indeed the case, since those resources are the following:

- Size of the alphabet: $3mn + 15n + 5m + 40 \in O(mn)$.
- Initial number of membranes: $mn + 2m + n + k + 7 \in O(mn)$.
- Initial number of objects: $mn + n + 5 \in O(mn)$.
- Number of rules: $6mn + 2nk + 0.5m^2 + 15n + 8.5m + 2k + 43 \in O((max\{m, n, k\})^2)$.

3   Conclusions

In this work, we propose an efficient solution to CADP by a family of recognizer P systems with polarizationless active membranes working in minimally parallel mode. The computation time of the solution is linear with respect to the size of the given set and the size of the family of forbidden sets.

In the P systems constructed in this work, non-elementary membrane division rules and membrane dissolution rules are used. It remains open how to give an efficient solution of CADP using the division of elementary membranes instead of the division of non-elementary membranes. It is also open whether there is an efficient solution to CADP without using dissolution rule.

Acknowledgments. The work of Y. Niu is supported by National Natural Science Foundation of China (61127005).

References

1. Păun, G.: Computing with Membranes. Journal of Computer and System Sciences 61(1), 108–143 (2001)
2. Pan, L., Pérez-Jiménez, M.J.: Computational Complexity of Tissue-like P Systems. Journal of Complexity 26(3), 296–315 (2010)
3. Pan, L., Zeng, X., Zhang, X., Jiang, Y.: Spiking Neural P Systems with Weighted Synapses. Neural Processing Letters 35(1), 13–27 (2012)
4. Pan, L., Wang, J., Hoogeboom, H.J.: Spiking Neural P Systems with Astrocytes. Neural Computation 24(3), 805–825 (2012)
5. Song, T., Pan, L., Păun, G.: Asynchronous spiking neural P systems with local synchronization. Information Sciences 219, 197–207 (2013)
6. Păun, G.: Membrane Computing: An Introduction. Springer, Berlin (2002)
7. Ciobanu, G., Pérez-Jiménez, M.J., Păun, G.: Applications of Membrane Computing. Springer, Berlin (2006)
8. Alhazov, A., Pan, L., Păun, G.: Trading Polarizations for Labels in P Systems with Active Membranes. Acta Informaticae 41, 111–144 (2004)
9. Alhazov, A., Pérez-Jiménez, M.J.: Uniform Solution of QSAT Using Polarizationless Active Membranes. In: Durand-Lose, J., Margenstern, M. (eds.) MCU 2007. LNCS, vol. 4664, pp. 122–133. Springer, Heidelberg (2007)
10. Ciobanu, G., Pan, L., Păun, G., Pérez-Jiménez, M.J.: P systems with Minimal Parallelism. Theoretical Computer Science 378(1), 117–130 (2007)
11. Head, T., Yamamura, M., Gal, S.: Aqueous Computing: Writing on Molecules. In: Proceedings of the Congress on Evolutionary Computation 1999, pp. 1006–1010. IEEE Service Center, Piscataway (1999)
12. Pérez Jiménez, M.J., Romero Campero, F.J.: Attacking the Common Algorithmic Problem by Recognizer P Systems. In: Margenstern, M. (ed.) MCU 2004. LNCS, vol. 3354, pp. 304–315. Springer, Heidelberg (2005)

A Novel Task Scheduling Scheme
in Heterogeneous Computing Systems
Using Chemical Reaction Optimization

Guo Pan, Kenli Li*, Yuming Xu, and Keqin Li

College of Information Science and Engineering
Hunan University, Changsha, 410082, China
{panguo,lkl,hawk,kqli}@hnu.edu.cn

Abstract. The task scheduling problem is normally an NP-hard problem. A chemical reaction optimization (CRO) is a new meta-heuristic optimization method, which has demonstrated its capability in solving NP-hard optimization problems. In this paper, a novel CRO algorithm for task scheduling (NCROTS) is proposed on heterogeneous computing systems. Over the real-world problems with various characteristics and randomly generated graphs, the simulation results show that the proposed NCROTS algorithm significantly improves the schedule quality (makespan), compared with two existing solutions (GA and HEFT).

Keywords: Chemical reaction optimization, Makespan, NP-hard problem, Task scheduling.

1   Introduction

Task scheduling on heterogeneous computing systems is a classic and core problem in parallel computing. It effectively improves the performance of parallel computing systems. Generally represented by a weighted directed acyclic graph (DAG), these subtasks with precedence relationships are mapped into appropriate processors for execution, which significantly reduces the execution time, namely makespan. Therefore, the goal of task scheduling is to identify the optimal distribution scheme so as to minimize makespan. The computational complexity decides that the task scheduling problem is NP-hard [1,2], so it is considered to be one of the most difficult combinatorial optimization problems. Hence, finding an efficient algorithm to solve this problem has great theoretical and practical significance.

The traditional static task scheduling algorithms can be roughly divided into two major categories: heuristic-based and random-search-based scheduling algorithms. The heuristic-based algorithms try to identify a solution by taking advantage of the natural properties of the problem. However, the performance of these algorithms is heavily dependent on the effectiveness of the heuristics. Therefore, they are not likely to produce consistent results on a wide range of complex problems. The random-search-based task scheduling algorithms search the solution space mainly through a random selection, so they generate better

---

* Corresponding author.

L. Pan et al. (Eds.): BIC-TA 2014, CCIS 472, pp. 328–335, 2014.
© Springer-Verlag Berlin Heidelberg 2014

scheduling results than the general heuristic algorithms. However, they tend to have higher time complexity and need to properly determine some control parameters. Thus, in this paper, a novel hybrid chemical reaction optimization algorithm for DAG task scheduling (NCROTS) is proposed to solve the scheduling problem for DAG tasks on heterogeneous computing systems.

The remainder of this paper is organized as follows. In Section 2, different scheduling algorithms on heterogeneous computing systems and their related work are reviewed. In Section 3, the system model and the DAG scheduling model are described. In Section 4, a novel CRO algorithm for task scheduling is introduced. In Section 5, results and analyses are given in order to evaluate the algorithm. Finally, in Section 6, conclusions and suggestions for future work are presented.

2 Related Works

Traditional algorithms for parallel static task scheduling can be roughly divided into two major categories: heuristic-based algorithms and random-search-based algorithms. The former can be further divided into three categories: list-based scheduling, task-duplication-based scheduling and task-cluster-based scheduling algorithms.

Typical list-based algorithms are Dynamic Critical Path (DCP) [3], Dynamic Level Scheduling (DLS) [4], Modified Critical Path (MCP) [5] and Mapping Heuristic (MH) [6]. For heterogeneous computing systems, Haluk Topcuoglu et al. put forward Heterogeneous Earliest Finish Time (HEFT) and Critical Path on a Processor(CPOP) [7] and so on. Typical task-duplication-based algorithms include Critical Path Fast Duplication (CPFD) [8], Bottom-up Top-down Duplication Heuristic (BTDH) [9], Duplication Scheduling Heuristic (DSH) [10] and Duplication First and Reduction Next (DFRN) [11]. Typical task-cluster-based algorithms include Dominant Sequence Clustering (DSC) [12].

Random-search-based algorithms search the solution space mainly through oriented random selection. However, they tend to have higher time complexity and need to properly control parameters. Typical random-search-based algorithms include Genetic Algorithms (GA) [13], Ant Colony Optimization (ACO) [14], Particle Swarm Optimization (PSO) [15] and Simulated Annealing (SA) [16]. Very recently, chemical reaction optimization (CRO) [17,18,19,20] is a new meta-heuristic optimization method mimicking the process of a chemical reaction in which molecules interact with each other aiming to reach the minimum state of free energy.

3 Models

3.1 System Model

In this paper, the target system consists of m heterogeneous processors with different processing capabilities. These heterogeneous processors are fully interconnected with each other through a high-speed network and constitute a heterogeneous computing system, as shown in Fig. 1(b). Each subtask can only be executed on one heterogeneous processor.

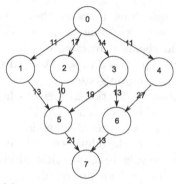

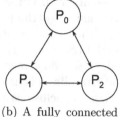

(a) A simple DAG task model containing 8 meta-tasks

(b) A fully connected parallel system with 3 processors

Fig. 1. A simple DAG containing 8 subtasks and a fully connected parallel system with 3 processors

3.2   Application Model

A parallel application can be abstracted as a directed acyclic graph (DAG) $G = (T, E)$, as shown Fig. 1(a), where $T = \{T_i | i = 0, 1, \cdots, n - 1\}$, representing the set of n subtasks; $E = \{(T_i, T_j) | T_i, T_j \in T, i < j\}$, representing the set of n directed edges. The weight is called the computing time (cost), which is denoted as $W(T_i)$. Any edge of the DAG is denoted as $e = (T_i, T_j)$, which suggests that data dependencies and communication cost exist between the subtasks T_i and T_j; the weight of each edge is called traffic, denoted as $D(T_i, T_j)$. The predecessor and successor of a subtask are denoted as $pred(T_i)$ and $succ(T_i)$, respectively.

4   Algorithm Design

4.1   Representation of Molecular Structure

In this study, each molecule has its own molecular structure and represents a possible solution to a problem. The internal structure of the molecule can be arranged as Fig. 2.

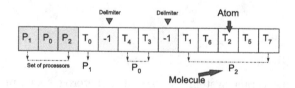

Fig. 2. Illustration of a molecule that encodes a solution in Fig. 1. Each P_k in the molecule represents a processor k and T_i in the molecule represents a sub-task i.

4.2 Collision with the Wall

In this study, the transformations of the function $OnWall(w)$ are shown in Algorithm 1.

Algorithm 1. $OnWall(\omega)$ function

Input:
   Molecule ω.
Output:
   New molecule ω'.
1: Choose randomly an atom T_i of ω;
2: $j \leftarrow i$;
3: **repeat**
4:     $j \leftarrow i - 1$;
5: **until** $T_j \in pred(T_i)$ *or* $T_j = -1$
6: **if** $j + 1 < i$ **then**
7:     temp $\leftarrow T_i$;
8:     **for** $k \leftarrow i - 1$ *downto* $j + 1$ **do**
9:         $T_{k+1} \leftarrow T_k$;
10:     **end for**
11:     $T_k \leftarrow$ temp;
12: **end if**
13: Generate a new molecule ω';
14: **return** the new molecule ω'.

4.3 Decomposition

As the collision is very powerful, one molecular will be decomposed into two new ones which will be very different from the original one in terms of molecular structure. Assume that the original molecule is ω and the new molecules are $\omega 1$ and $\omega 1$, respectively. The detailed descriptions of the function $Decomp(w)$ is shown in Algorithm 2.

Algorithm 2. $Decomp(\omega)$ function

Input:
   Molecule ω.
Output:
   Two new molecules ω'_1 and ω'_2.
1: Shift left cyclic to generate a new molecule ω'_1 in the processor sections of the molecule ω;
2: Shift right cyclic to generate a new molecule ω'_2 in the processor sections of the molecule ω;
3: **return** the new molecules ω'_1 and ω'_2.

4.4 Inter-Molecular Collision

In the inter-molecular collision, the changes in energy are similar to the situation in the collision with the wall, but the inter-molecular collision involves two molecules. In this study, the detailed descriptions of the function $Intermole(\omega 1, \omega 2)$ is shown in Algorithm 3.

Algorithm 3. $Intermole(\omega_1, \omega_2)$ function

Input:
   Two molecules ω_1 and ω_2.
Output:
   Two new molecules ω_1' and ω_2'.
1: Generate a new molecule ω_1' with empty structure;
2: Copy the processor sections and delimiters from the molecule ω_1;
3: Insert the subtasks (atoms) into ω_1' one by one according to the priority of original molecule ω_2;
4: Generate a new molecule ω_2' with empty structure;
5: Copy the processor sections and delimiters from the molecule ω_2;
6: Insert the subtasks (atoms) into ω_2' one by one according to the priority of original atoms in molecule ω_1;
7: **return** the new molecules ω_1' and ω_2'.

4.5   Synthesis

When two molecules collide with each other, as the collision strength is great, two molecules will be combined into a new molecule, which is called synthetic reaction. In this study, the detailed descriptions of the function $Synth(\omega1, \omega2)$ is shown in Algorithm 4.

Algorithm 4. $Synth(\omega_1, \omega_2)$ function

Input:
   Two molecules ω_1 and ω_2.
Output:
   the new molecule ω'.
1: Choose randomly two molecules ω_1 and ω_2;
2: Generate a new molecule ω' with empty structure;
3: Inherit the processor sections and delimiters from the molecule ω_1;
4: Insert the subtasks (atoms) into ω_1' one by one according to the priority of original atoms in molecule ω_2;
5: **return** a new molecule ω'.

4.6   Potential Energy Function

Potential energy is the corresponding objective function value of the solution represented by the molecule. In this study, the makespan of the whole task is defined as the potential energy function value. As a result, the potential energy function value is expressed as

$$PE_\omega = Fitness(\omega) = makespan = AFT(T_{exit}). \tag{1}$$

The HEFT approach is adopted to realize the task-to-processor mapping [7].

5   Simulations and Analyses

5.1   Real DAG Application Task Graph

Gaussian elimination method is an algorithm in linear algebra. we set the following parameters: the total number of heterogeneous processors is 6; the number of initial populations is 100; the number of iterations is 2000. Figs. 3(a) and 3(b) show the comparison results of NCROTS algorithm with GA and HEFT algorithms. Fig. 3(a) shows a decrease in the average makespan with increasing number of processors. Fig. 3(b) suggests that the average value obtained by Gaussian elimination method under different CCRs increases with the increase of the values obtained by the elimination method.

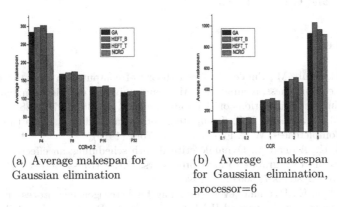

(a) Average makespan for Gaussian elimination

(b) Average makespan for Gaussian elimination, processor=6

Fig. 3. Gaussian elimination

5.2   Randomly-Generated DAG Application Task Graphs

In order to further evaluate the scheduling performance of the NCROTS algorithm for random DAG task graphs, the generation tool of DAG task graph is used to randomly generate 100 task graphs with 10, 20, 50, 100, and 200 nodes, respectively. Each value in the experimental results is the average value of the

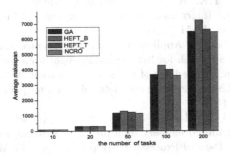

Fig. 4. Average makespan of different task numbers, CCR=1, Processor=32

334 G. Pan et al.

100 different random task graphs. The experimental results show that, as the number of tasks increases, the NCROTS algorithm performs better than HEFT and GA algorithms in terms of task scheduling optimization with an average makespan reduction of 5.06%, as shown in Fig. 4.

6 Conclusions

In this paper, a novel NCROTS algorithm is presented for task scheduling on heterogeneous processor systems, thereby obtaining better makespan. Four major operations of molecules in the NCROTS algorithm are described in detail. The experimental results show that the NCROTS algorithm performs better than HEFT and GA algorithms.

References

1. Blum, L., Shub, M., Smale, S.: On a theory of computation over the real numbers; np completeness, recursive functions and universal machines. In: 29th Annual Symposium on Foundations of Computer Science, pp. 387–397 (1988)
2. Garey, M.R., Johnson, D.S.: Computers and intractability: a guide to the theory of NP-Completeness. W.H. Freeman, New York (1979)
3. Kwok, Y.K., Ahmad, I.: Dynamic critical-path scheduling: an effective technique for allocating task graphs to multiprocessors. IEEE Transactions on Parallel and Distributed Systems 7, 506–521 (1996)
4. Sih, G., Lee, E.: Dynamic-level scheduling for heterogeneous processor networks. In: Proceedings of the Second IEEE Symposium on Parallel and Distributed Processing, pp. 42–49 (1990)
5. Wu, M.-Y., Gajski, D.D.: Hypertool: a programming aid for message-passing systems. IEEE Transactions on Parallel and Distributed Systems 1, 330–343 (1990)
6. El-Rewini, H., Lewis, T.G.: Scheduling parallel program tasks onto arbitrary target machines. Journal of Parallel and Distributed Computing 9, 138–153 (1990)
7. Topcuoglu, H., Hariri, S., Wu, M.Y.: Performance-effective and low-complexity task scheduling for heterogeneous computing. IEEE Transactions on Parallel and Distributed Systems 13, 260–274 (2002)
8. Ahmad, I., Kwok, Y.K.: A new approach to scheduling parallel programs using task duplication. In: International Conference on Parallel Processing, ICPP 1994, Volume 2, vol. 1, pp. 47–51 (1994)
9. Chung, Y.C., Ranka, S.: Applications and performance analysis of a compile-time optimization approach for list scheduling algorithms on distributed memory multiprocessors. In: Proceedings of the Supercomputing 1992, pp. 512–521 (1992)
10. Kruatrachue, B., Lewis, T.: Grain size determination for parallel processing. IEEE Software 5, 23–32 (1988)
11. Park, G.L., Shirazi, B., Marquis, J.: Dfrn: a new approach for duplication based scheduling for distributed memory multiprocessor systems. In: 11th International Proceedings of the Parallel Processing Symposium, pp. 157–166 (1997)
12. Yang, T., Gerasoulis, A.: Dsc: scheduling parallel tasks on an unbounded number of processors. IEEE Transactions on Parallel and Distributed Systems 5, 951–967 (1994)

13. Hou, E., Ansari, N., Ren, H.: A genetic algorithm for multiprocessor scheduling. IEEE Transactions on Parallel and Distributed Systems 5, 113–120 (1994)
14. Ferrandi, F., Lanzi, P., Pilato, C., Sciuto, D., Tumeo, A.: Ant colony heuristic for mapping and scheduling tasks and communications on heterogeneous embedded systems. IEEE Transactions on Computer-Aided Design of Integrated Circuits and Systems 29, 911–924 (2010)
15. Li, H., Wang, L., Liu, J.: Task scheduling of computational grid based on particle swarm algorithm. In: 2010 Third International Joint Conference on Computational Science and Optimization (CSO), vol. 2, pp. 332–336 (2010)
16. Wang, J., Duan, Q., Jiang, Y., Zhu, X.: A new algorithm for grid independent task schedule: Genetic simulated annealing. In: World Automation Congress (WAC), pp. 165–171 (2010)
17. Lam, A., Li, V.: Chemical-reaction-inspired metaheuristic for optimization. IEEE Transactions on Evolutionary Computation 14, 381–399 (2010)
18. Xu, J., Lam, A., Li, V.: Chemical reaction optimization for task scheduling in grid computing. IEEE Transactions on Parallel and Distributed Systems 22, 1624–1631 (2011)
19. Alatas B.: ACROA: Artificial Chemical Reaction Optimization Algorithm for global optimization. Expert Systems with Applications 38(10), 13170–13180 (2011)
20. Alatas B.: A novel chemistry based metaheuristic optimization method for mining of classification rules. Expert Systems with Applications 39(12), 11080–11088 (2012)

Public Traffic Network Simulation System

Wen Jin Rong, Kang Zhou*, Peng Dai, Song Ping Li, and Wei Tan

School of Math and Computer,
Wuhan Polytechnic University, Wuhan, China
{rongwenjin1993,perrywhpu}@gmail.com,
1452734071@qq.com,{tw_5486,zhoukang_wh}@163.com

1 Introduction

Urban transportation problem is the bottleneck problem [1] of limiting urban economic development [2]. With the rapid development of the scale of the city, it is a hot issue in the urban traffic optimization problem [3] how to use reasonably, scientifically and efficiently the existing urban public traffic network system for passengers traveling to provide strong guarantee. With the rapid development of artificial intelligence algorithms [4], the application of artificial intelligence algorithms in public transport planning is one of the research directions in the field of public transport network optimization [5].

Note that it is an important problem for the study of urban traffic optimization algorithm how to objectively and fairly evaluate these algorithms. Of course, a test platform is needed to evaluate the effectiveness and practicality of these algorithms, and can rapidly produce the various data sources meeting customer needs for the urban scale to detect performance of the algorithm. This platform is called public traffic network simulation system. In recent years, research on the nature of the public traffic network [6] has made great progress [7]. Our research on public traffic network simulation is based on the above nature of the public traffic network.

2 Public Traffic Network Simulation System

Public traffic network simulation system is a bus line system in a virtual urban established on adjacent relations of simulation bus stations. So public traffic network simulation system includes two parts, one part is a network of adjacent relations of bus stations, and another part is a set of bus lines. Let a vertex be represented as a bus station; an arc be represented as an adjacent relation of two bus stations, so let a positive weight simple digraph be represented as a network of adjacent relations of bus stations [8]. The assumption is as follows: For simplicity, network of adjacent relations of bus stations in this paper is represented as positive weights simple undigraph; Each street whom a bus line goes through has at least a bus station; All bus lines are composed of bidirectional lines, loop lines and single lines. And bidirectional line is the main; loop line or

---

* Corresponding author.

L. Pan et al. (Eds.): BIC-TA 2014, CCIS 472, pp. 336–340, 2014.
© Springer-Verlag Berlin Heidelberg 2014

single line is the second; The distribution of the bus lines should consider capacity of the bus terminal, road capacity of the bus station, "all bus lines pass all bus stations" principle, "evenly cover all bus stations" principle, and other factors.

Public traffic network simulation system should meet the requirements as follows:

Urban Size Requirements: Simulate a network of adjacent relations of bus stations of an urban, and let bus station number be n $(n \geq 100)$, its edge number be k. Simulate public transport network of an urban, and let bus line number be m $(m \geq 20)$.

Let k_i be represented as the number of bus stations whose vertex degrees are i $(i = 1, 2, 3, 4, 5, 6)$. For j $(j = 1, 2, \cdots, n)$, let d_j be represented as vertex degree of bus station j, m_j be represented as the number of bus lines pass bus station j.

Bus Station Requirements:

(1) For bus station i $(i = 1, 2, \cdots, n)$, $1 \leq d_i \leq 6$. The bus station i connectivity is as follows: If $1 \leq d_i \leq 3$, then the bus station i connectivity is poor; If $4 \leq d_i \leq 5$, then the bus station i connectivity is general; If $d_i = 6$, then the bus station i connectivity is strong.

(2) The distribution of the number of bus stations is as follows: $k_1 \leq 1 \times n/100$; $k_2 \leq 4 \times n/100$; $k_3 + k_4 + k_5 + k_6 \geq 95 \times n/100$; $k_i \geq 4 \times n/100 (i = 3, 4, 5, 6)$.

(3) The distribution of the number of bus stations whose vertex degrees are from 3 to 6 is as follows: When the k value is small, try to keep k_4, k_5, k_6 distribute evenly and to take k_3 value bigger; When the k value is moderate, try to minimize k_3 value and to keep k_4, k_5, k_6 distribute evenly; When the k value is larger, try to minimize k_3 value $(4 \times n/100 \leq k_3 \leq 5 \times n/100)$, to maximize k_6 value and to keep k_4, k_5 distribute evenly.

(4) The method determining the development degree of the urban is as follows: When $0.8 \times 3n \leq k \leq 3n$, the urban is the full development; When $0.65 \times 3n \leq k \leq 0.8 \times 3n$, the urban is development; When $1.6n \leq k \leq 0.65 \times 3n$, the urban is insufficient development.

(5) For starting bus station j, $m_j \leq 4$.

(6) For starting bus station j, $d_j = 1$ or 2 or 6.

(7) All bus stations form a connected graph.

Bus Line Requirements:

(1) For the full development urban, $4n \leq 15m \leq 9n$; For development urban, $3n \leq 15m \leq 8n$; For insufficient development urban, $2n \leq 15m \leq 7n$.

(2) For the full development urban, $3 \leq m_i \leq 15$; For development urban, $2 \leq m_i \leq 12$; For insufficient development urban, $1 \leq m_i \leq 10$.

(3) Each bus line is denoted by an ordered sequence of adjacent stations.

(4) The bus lines through downtown area (higher vertex degree of bus stations) are intensive.

(5) The number of bus stations of a bidirectional line is between 15 and 17; The number of bus stations of a single line is between 14 and 16; The number of bus stations of a loop line is between 28 and 30;

(6) The number of loop lines is 2; and the number of single lines is 2.

3 Algorithm for Public Traffic Network Simulation System

Algorithm of simulating network of adjacent relations of bus stations (**Algorithm 1**) is as follows: Produce the matrix K_i whose secondary diagonal is 1; Then produce an adjacency matrix of all paths $D= (d_{ij})$ which is diagonal block matrix. Finally, produce an adjacency matrix of a spanning tree $D= (d_{ij})$. And produce an adjacency matrix of a connected graph $D= (d_{ij})$.   □

The random choice method of priority vertex degree is as follows: Compute all adjacent bus stations of the latest bus station which are not on the bus line; Compute selective probability of these adjacent bus stations according to vertex degree; Choose the next bus station of the bus line from these adjacent bus stations using the method of roulette.□

Traversing method is as follows: Compute the neighborhood of not covered bus stations by using neighborhood search method; If a starting bus station is in the neighborhood of a bus station, then the starting bus station and the part of the bus line are determined, so other part of the bus line can be determined by using the random choice method of priority vertex degree; If two neighborhoods are intersection, then determine part of the bus line between the two bus stations, so other part of the bus line can be determined by using the random choice method of priority vertex degree; Otherwise, extending these neighborhood and return to the above steps, until producing a bus line.   □

Algorithm of structuring set of bus lines is as follows (**Algorithm 2**):
Step 1 Let $W = \emptyset$, $m_i = 0$ $(i = 1, 2, \cdots, n)$.
Step 2 (Penalty function technique)
If $|W| \leq m - 4 \wedge |W| \leq \lceil 1.8 \times n/15 \rceil - 1$, then
  If $|W| = 1.5 \times n/15$, then
    For $\forall$ bus station i $(m_i = 0 \wedge d_i \leq 5)$ let $d_i = d_i + 1$.
  Go to Step3.
If $|W| \leq m - 4 \wedge \lceil 1.8 \times n/15 \rceil \leq |W| \leq \lceil 2 \times n/15 \rceil - 1$, then go to Step4.
(Now, for $\forall$ bus station i, $m_i \geq 1$)
If $|W| \leq m - 4 \wedge \lceil 2 \times n/15 \rceil \leq |W| \leq \lceil 2.8 \times n/15 \rceil - 1$, then
  If $|W| = 2.5 \times n/15$, then
    For $\forall$ bus station i $(m_i = 1 \wedge d_i \leq 5)$ let $d_i = d_i + 1$.
  Go to Step3.
If $|W| \leq m - 4 \wedge \lceil 2.8 \times n/15 \rceil \leq |W| \leq \lceil 3 \times n/15 \rceil - 1$, then go to Step4.
(Now, for $\forall$ bus station i, $m_i \geq 2$)
If $|W| \leq m - 4 \wedge \lceil 3 \times n/15 \rceil \leq |W| \leq \lceil 3.8 \times n/15 \rceil - 1$, then
  If $|W| = 3.5 \times n/15$, then
    For $\forall$ bus station i $(m_i = 2 \wedge d_i \leq 5)$ let $d_i = d_i + 1$.
  Go to Step3.
If $|W| \leq m - 4 \wedge \lceil 3.8 \times n/15 \rceil \leq |W| \leq \lceil 4 \times n/15 \rceil - 1$, then go to Step4.
(Now, for $\forall$ bus station i, $m_i \geq 3$)
If $|W| \leq m - 4 \wedge \lceil 4 \times n/15 \rceil \leq |W| \leq \lceil 4.8 \times n/15 \rceil - 1$, then
  If $|W| = 4.5 \times n/15$, then
    For $\forall$ bus station i $(m_i = 3 \wedge d_i \leq 5)$ let $d_i = d_i + 1$.

Go to Step3.

If $|W| \leq m - 4 \wedge [4.8 \times n/15] \leq |W| \leq [5 \times n/15] - 1$, then go to Step4.

(Now, for $\forall$ bus station i, $m_i \geq 4$)

If $|W| \leq m - 4$, then go to Step3.

If $|W| = m - 3$, then

Go to Step3, find out bus lines p_i $(i = 1, 2, 3, 4)$

where starting bus station = stopping bus station; $28 \leq |V(p)| \leq 30$;

Go to Step5.

Step 3 (The random choice method of priority vertex degree)

(1) Choose a starting bus station from index set of starting bus station $V_1 = \{v(1), v(2), \cdots, v(r)\}$;

(2) Find out a bidirectional line p according to the random choice method of priority vertex degree, where $15 \leq |V(p)| \leq 17$;

(3) For $\forall$ starting bus i in bus line p,

Let $m_i = m_i + 1$.

If $m_i \in \{5, 8, 10, 12, 13\} \wedge d_i \geq 2$, then let $d_i = d_i - 1$ (Penalty function technique).

(4) Let $W = W \cup \{p\}$;

(5) Return to Step2.

Step4 (Traversing method)

(1) Find out a bidirectional line p according to traversing method, where $15 \leq |V(p)| \leq 17$;

(2) For $\forall$ starting bus i in bus line p,

Let $m_i = m_i + 1$.

If $m_i \in \{5, 8, 10, 12, 13\} \wedge d_i \geq 2$, then let $d_i = d_i - 1$ (Penalty function technique).

(3) Let $W = W \cup \{p\}$;

(4) Return to Step2.

Step5 Compute loop lines and single lines.

(1) Produce loop lines p_1 and p_2 by connecting starting bus station and stopping bus station for p_1 and p_2.

(2) Produce single lines p_3 and p_4 by halving bus line.

(3) Let $W = W \cup \{p_1, p_2, p_3, p_4\}$.$\square$

Algorithm of realizing public traffic network simulation system is as follows:

Step1 Input the number n of bus stations ($n \geq 100$), and the development degree parameter t of the urban ($t \in \{1, 2, 3\}$).

Step2 Compute bus line number m and edge number k of network of adjacent relations of bus stations as follows:

Switch (t)

case 1: $m \in [2n/15, 7n/15]$; $k \in [1.6n, 0.65 \times 3n]$; break;

case 2: $m \in [3n/15, 8n/15]$; $k \in [0.65 \times 3n, 0.8 \times 3n]$; break;

case 3: $m \in [4n/15, 9n/15]$; $k \in [0.8 \times 3n, 3n]$; break;

default: renew t; go to Step2.

where m and k are random numbers.

Step3 Call algorithm 1 to obtain an adjacency matrix of the network, and write the adjacency matrix into external file MatrixInfo.txt.

Step4 According to the adjacency matrix, call algorithm 2 to obtain a bus line set of the network, and write the bus line set into external file Paths.txt.□

Acknowledgments. Kang Zhou is corresponding author. The work is supported by the National Natural Science Foundation of China (61179032, 11301405).

References

1. Zhang, X.F., Li, R.M., Li, H.F., Shi, Q.X.: A traffic assignment problem and model for partially-controlled road network. Highway Engineering 36, 11–14, 54 (2011)
2. Su, B., Xu, Y.F., Xiao, P.: Optimal safety path model and algorithm in transportation networks. Journal of Xian Jiaotong University 42, 395–398, 422 (2008)
3. Zhu, W.X., Jia, L., Zhao, J.Y., Liu, H.B.: Modeling and simulation on path optimization in urban traffic network. Journal of System Simulation 17, 1556–1559 (2005)
4. Sun, Q., Wang, Q., Gao, Y.L.: Multi-period bi-level programming model for regional comprehensive transport network design with uncertain demand. Journal of Guangxi University: Nat. Sci. Ed. 34, 672–676 (2009)
5. Liu, B.Q., Sun, G.C.: Artificial fish swarm algorithm for traffic network design problem. Computer Engineering 37, 161–163 (2011)
6. Li, Y., Zhou, W., Guo, S.J.: An analysis of complexity of public transportation network in shanghai. Systems Engineering 25, 38–41 (2007)
7. Yang, Y.F., Xi, Y.G., Lin, S.: Macroscopic control model of urban traffic network and its simulation. Control Engineering of China 16, 687–691, 759 (2009)
8. Zhou, K., Chen, J.: Simulation DNA algorithm of set covering problem. Applied Mathematics and Information Sciences 8, 139–144 (2014)

An Improved Golden Ball Algorithm
for the Capacitated Vehicle Routing Problem

Kanjana Ruttanateerawichien[1], Werasak Kurutach[1], and Tantikorn Pichpibul[2,*]

[1] Faculty of Information Science and Technology,
Mahanakorn University of Technology, Bangkok, Thailand
kanjanarutt@gmail.com, werasak@mut.ac.th
[2] Faculty of Business Administration, Panyapiwat Institute of Management,
Nonthaburi, Thailand
pichpibul@gmail.com

Abstract. In this paper, we have presented an algorithm that has been improved from the original golden ball algorithm (GB) to solve the capacitated vehicle routing problem (CVRP). The problem objective is to construct a feasible set of vehicle routes that minimizes the total traveling distance and the total number of vehicles used. We have tested the improved GB (IGB) with 88 problem instances. The computational results indicate that IGB outperforms GB in all directions, and the best known solutions are obtained for 79 instances. Moreover, new best-known solutions for three instances are also found.

Keywords: Capacitated vehicle routing problem, Golden ball algorithm, Optimization.

1 Introduction

The capacitated vehicle routing problem (CVRP) was introduced by Dantzig and Ramser [1]. It is widely studied in operations research, and is also known to be an NP-hard problem [2]. The problem objective of CVRP is to construct a feasible set of vehicle routes that minimizes the total traveling distance and the total number of vehicles used. All vehicles always depart from the depot. After completing the service, all vehicles must return to the depot as shown in Fig. 1 that the routes are 1-3-5-1 and 1-6-2-4-1.

The CVRP can be stated as the problem that vehicles based at a depot (depot is assigned to be customer 1) are required to serve the number of customers (n) in order to satisfy known customer demand. The number of available vehicles denoted by k. All vehicles have the same capacity denoted by Q. The traveling distance between customer i and customer j denoted by $c_{i,j}$ is symmetric. The constraints of CVRP are as follows.

---

* Corresponding author.

L. Pan et al. (Eds.): BIC-TA 2014, CCIS 472, pp. 341–356, 2014.
© Springer-Verlag Berlin Heidelberg 2014

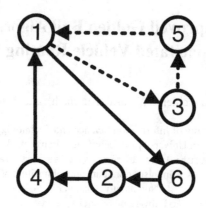

Fig. 1. Example of vehicle routes

- Each customer must be visited once by one vehicle.
- Each customer is visited and left with the same vehicle.
- Each vehicle starts and ends at the depot.
- The total customer demand in each vehicle cannot exceed Q.
- The number of vehicles used in each solution cannot exceed k.

2   Literature Review

In order to find the CVRP solution, there are three types of approaches composed of exact algorithms, heuristics, and meta-heuristics. First, exact algorithms are the approaches used to optimize the solution consisting of branch-and-bound algorithm [3], branch-and-cut algorithm [4], [5], [6], and branch-and-cut-and-price algorithm [7]. In these algorithms, the problem involving more than 100 customers cannot optimize the solution due to a huge amount of computation time. This motivates the scientific community from computer science to develop different types of approaches to tackle the problem. Second, heuristic algorithms are the approaches used to find the solution consisting of savings algorithm [8], sweep algorithm [9], and cluster-first route-second algorithm [10]. These algorithms quickly produced the solution which could be improved by local search procedures, for example, 2-opt, 3-opt [11], Or-exchange [12], λ-interchanges [13], and neighborhood structures [14], [15]. However, these algorithms do not guarantee that the solution is optimal or near optimal. Finally, meta-heuristic algorithms are the approaches which combine heuristic algorithms with intelligent exploring and exploiting techniques consisting of simulated annealing [16], tabu search [17], genetic algorithm [18], particle swarm optimization [19], ant colony optimization [20], memetic algorithm [21], and honey bees mating optimization algorithm [22]. These algorithms can provide the solution which is better than early heuristic algorithms. Nowadays, the development of meta-heuristic algorithms is very rapid. These few years, there are several of new meta-heuristic algorithms, for example, gravitational search algorithm [23], coral reefs optimization algorithm [24], firefly algorithm [25], glowworm swarm optimization algorithm [26], and golden ball algorithm [27]. According to these algorithms, we have found that a golden ball algorithm proposed by Esaba et al. [27] is the recent algorithm that used to solve CVRP. Unfortunately, their solutions are far from the best known solutions. Therefore, this is our contribution to develop a new GB which can efficiently solve CVRP in terms of solution quality.

3   An Improved Golden Ball Algorithm

The golden ball algorithm (GB) introduced by Esaba et al. [27] is the new meta-heuristic which is a multiple population-based algorithm. It is simulated by the different concepts related to soccer. The population of GB is represented by the soccer teams. Each team has the number of players that each player represents one CVRP solution. The captain who is represented by the best solution is the most important player in the team. Once the teams have been formed, the season begins. Each team plays games against the other teams to create a league competition. The good players affect their win rate because the strength of the team depends on the quality of the players. Before the match, all players from each team have opportunity to improve themselves by using training procedures. Any player can switch from his team to another by using a transfer procedure. These concepts can be modified to solve CVRP that the flowchart of the improved GB (IGB) is given in Fig. 2. In order to show the process, we give an example in case of the delivery of goods from the depot to five customers. We consider that the depot is located at (0, 0). The node locations and demand are shown in Table 1. The number of vehicles is equal to two. The details of our procedures are explained below.

Table 1. Node locations and demand

Node	Location	Demand
1	(0, 0)	0
2	(10, -20)	1
3	(20, -10)	1
4	(0, -20)	1
5	(20, 0)	1
6	(20, -20)	1

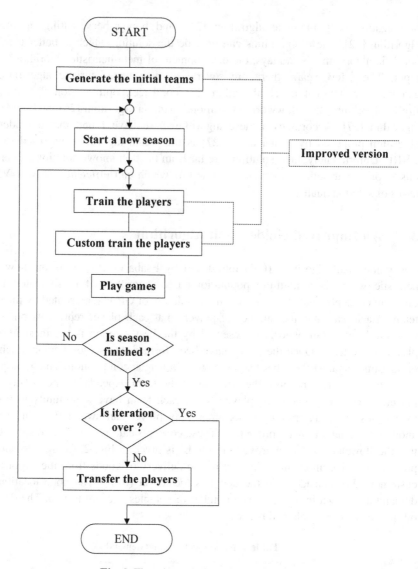

Fig. 2. Flowchart of the improved GB

3.1   Generate the Initial Teams

In this procedure, players (p) and teams (t) are generated that an example of an initial team composed of two soccer players is shown in Fig. 3. The member in the player represents the delivery sequence of customer node in which this sequence

Captain

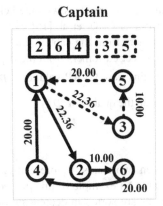

Player

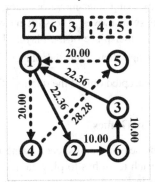

Route#1 = 22.36 + 10.00 + 20.00 + 20.00	Route#1 = 22.36 + 10.00 + 10.00 + 22.36
Route#2 = 22.36 + 10.00 + 20.00	Route#2 = 20.00 + 28.28 + 20.00
Solution = 72.36 + 52.36 = <u>124.72</u>	Solution = 64.72 + 68.28 = <u>133.00</u>

Fig. 3. Initial team composed of two soccer players

for all players is randomly generated. After generating the players, the teams are formed as follows:

$$t_i = \{p_{i,1}, p_{i,2}, p_{i,3}, \dots, p_{i,j}\} \tag{1}$$

Where $p_{i,j}$ means player j of team i. In addition to our work, we use an improved Clarke and Wright savings algorithm (ICW) introduced by Pichpibul and Kawtummachai [28] to generate the talent players ($p_{i,j}$) of team i. In order to avoid time consuming, ICW is run for 1000 iterations in each team. After that, the solution of each player ($p_{i,j}$) is calculated that an example is shown in Fig. 3. The best solution of the players in each team is chosen to be captain.

3.2 Train the Players

The quality of each player in each team ($p_{i,j}$) can be improved by a training process with intra-move operators found in the work of Groër et al. [15] including shift and swap moves. The shift moves remove customers from the chosen player and insert them in another place of the same player. The swap moves select customers from the chosen player and exchange them. This process obtains new CVRP solution ($p'_{i,j}$) which is accepted only if the quality of $p'_{i,j}$ is better than the quality of $p_{i,j}$.

3.3 Custom Train the Players

Custom training is a process used to escape from the local optimum happening when there is no improving to each player in each team ($p_{i,j}$) from the basic training process.

Some players in each team start custom training to improve themselves with the help of captain by using inter-move operators found in the work of Groër et al. [15] including shift and swap moves. The shift moves remove customers from the captain and insert them in another place of the player. The swap moves select customers from the captain and exchange them with the player. This process obtains new CVRP solution ($p'_{i,j}$) which is accepted only if the quality of $p'_{i,j}$ is better than the quality of $p_{i,j}$.

3.4   Play Games

When the season begins, each game is played between two teams. Before ending the season, each team has to play games against the others. An example of this procedure is shown in Fig. 4. First, the four players in two teams are sorted in decreasing order depending on their quality. Second, beginning with the highest quality player between two teams ($p_{1,j}$ and $p_{2,j}$), the player with higher quality can get a goal for his team.

Third, after complete comparison of the last player, the team with more goals is the winner of the game. Fourth, the team winner of the game obtains three points, and the loser obtains zero point. In case of a tie game, both teams get one point. Finally, these points are used to rank teams in the league.

Team 1	Score	Team 2
$p_{1,1}$ Solution = 120	**1 - 0**	$p_{2,1}$ Solution = 125
$p_{1,2}$ Solution = 125	**2 - 0**	$p_{2,2}$ Solution = 130
$p_{1,3}$ Solution = 140	**2 - 0**	$p_{2,3}$ Solution = 140
$p_{1,4}$ Solution = 150	**2 - 1**	$p_{2,4}$ Solution = 145
WIN		**LOSE**

Fig. 4. Example of playing games' process

3.5   Transfer the Players

The transfer is a process that the players are exchanged between the teams in every season. In general, the league's top teams need to sign top players, and the other teams have to decide with lower quality players. An example of this procedure is shown in Fig. 5. First, four teams are ranked depending on their score in the league, and four players in each team are sorted in decreasing order depending on their quality. Next, the worst player ($p_{1,4}$) from the best team (t_1) is exchanged with the best player ($p_{4,1}$) from the worst team (t_4). Finally, the second worst player ($p_{2,3}$) from the second best team (t_2) is exchanged with the second best player ($p_{3,2}$) from the second worst team (t_3). The IGB is repeated until the stopping criteria, which is the number of iterations is satisfied.

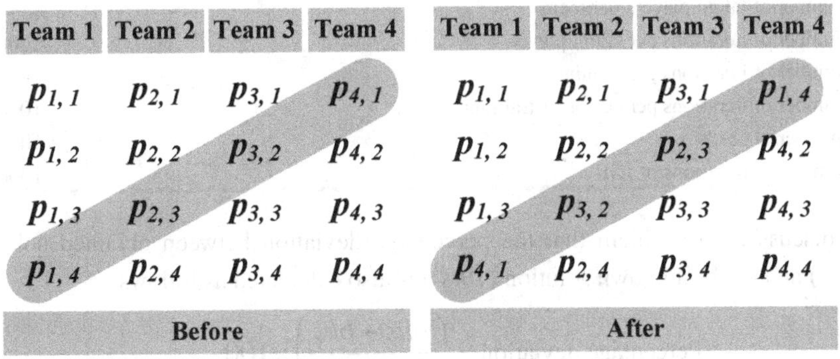

Team 1	Team 2	Team 3	Team 4	Team 1	Team 2	Team 3	Team 4
$p_{1,1}$	$p_{2,1}$	$p_{3,1}$	$p_{4,1}$	$p_{1,1}$	$p_{2,1}$	$p_{3,1}$	$p_{1,4}$
$p_{1,2}$	$p_{2,2}$	$p_{3,2}$	$p_{4,2}$	$p_{1,2}$	$p_{2,2}$	$p_{2,3}$	$p_{4,2}$
$p_{1,3}$	$p_{2,3}$	$p_{3,3}$	$p_{4,3}$	$p_{1,3}$	$p_{3,2}$	$p_{3,3}$	$p_{4,3}$
$p_{1,4}$	$p_{2,4}$	$p_{3,4}$	$p_{4,4}$	$p_{4,1}$	$p_{2,4}$	$p_{3,4}$	$p_{4,4}$
Before				After			

Fig. 5. Example of transfer players' process

4   Computational Results

The improved golden ball (IGB) was coded in Visual Basic 6.0 on an Intel® Core™ i7 CPU 860 clocked at 2.80 GHz with 1.99 GB of RAM under Windows XP platform. The numerical experiment used well-known benchmark problems composed of 88 instances. First, 74 instances are from Augerat et al. [5] in problem sets A, B, and P. Second, 9 instances are from Christofides and Eilon [29] in problem set E. Third, three instances are from Fisher [4] in problem set F. The last two instances are taken from Christofides et al. [30] in problem set M. For each instance, we use the same nomenclature, consisting of a problem set identifier, followed by n which represents the number of customers (including depot), and k which represents the number of available vehicles. The problems also include vehicle capacity constraints. The customer locations and demand are available online at http://www.branchandcut.org/ VRP/data (last modified 9/2011). In the proposed algorithm, the important parameters have to be preset before the execution as shown in Table 2.

In order to evaluate the performance of IGB, we compared the solutions with the algorithms for CVRP composed of branch-and-cut-and-price algorithm [7], branch-and-cut algorithm [4], [5], [31], simulation in routing via the generalized Clarke and Wright savings heuristic [32], [33], hybrid bat algorithm with path relinking [34], and golden ball algorithm [27]. According to the works of Juan et al. [32], [33], they noticed that some solutions obtained by Augerat et al. [5], Fukasawa et al. [7] and Fisher [4] are the best known solutions (BKS) only when the distances between customers are represented by an integer number which is rounded distances. In order to find the new best-known solution, BKS is therefore recalculated by using the distances between customers represented by a decimal number which is the real distance without any rounding.

Table 2. The important parameters used for IGB

Parameter	Value
Number of teams	4
Number of players per team	6
Number of talent players per team	1
Number of iterations per talent player	1000
Number of iterations per training	10
Number of iterations per customer training	10
Number of seasons	10
Number of iterations of IGB	1000

We discuss each problem that the percentage deviation between obtained solution (obs) and the best known solution (bks) is also calculated as follows:

$$\text{Percentage deviation} = \left(\frac{obs - bks}{bks}\right) \times 100 \tag{2}$$

Moreover, the percentage improvement between GB solution (gb) and IGB solution (igb) is calculated as follows:

$$\text{Percentage improvement} = \left(\frac{gb - igb}{gb}\right) \times 100 \tag{3}$$

The computational results in Table 3 show that IGB can find high quality solutions. Out of the 88 problems, we find the best known solutions for 79 problems. For 9 problems, the percentage deviation in each instance is very low (A-n53-k7, B-n45-k5, B-n57-k7, B-n63-k10, B-n64-k9, B-n68-k9, B-n78-k10, E-n76-k10, F-n135-k7). Moreover, there are three problems (A-n63-k10, B-n50-k8, P-n55-k10) where our results produced the new best-known solutions which performed better than the other results. An example of the new best-known solution is illustrated in Fig. 6. Furthermore, our solutions outperform GB in all directions. We have found that GB solutions were improved by the average of 6.288%. Another finding from Table 3 is the infeasible solutions (P-n22-k8, P-n50-k8, P-n55-k15, E-n30-k3, E-n76-k14) obtained by Juan et al. [32], [33] that the number of available vehicles is inadequate. This finding is referred to Vigo [35] that Clarke and Wright savings algorithm does not allow for the control of the number of routes of final solution. The solution found for a given instance can, in fact, require more than k routes to serve all the customers, hence being infeasible. By contrast, the results show that IGB can significantly solve these infeasible solutions to obtain the best known solutions. An example of two best solutions is illustrated in Fig. 7. These indicate that IGB is extremely effective and efficient to produce high quality solutions for well-known benchmark problems of CVRP.

Table 3. Computational results

Number	Instances	Solution						Percentage Deviation					Percentage Improvement
		BKS [5], [7], [4][1]	Letchford et al. [31][2]	Juan et al. [32], [33][3]	Zhou et al. [34][4]	Osaba et al. [27][5]	IGB[6]	2 - 1	3 - 1	4 - 1	5 - 1	6 - 1	5 - 6
1	A-n32-k5	787.81	787.08	787.08	–	–	787.08	-0.093	-0.093	–	–	-0.093	–
2	A-n33-k5	662.76	662.11	662.11	662.11	–	662.11	-0.098	-0.098	-0.098	–	-0.098	–
3	A-n33-k6	742.83	742.69	742.69	742.69	–	742.69	-0.019	-0.019	-0.019	–	-0.019	–
4	A-n34-k5	781.30	780.94	–	–	–	780.94	-0.046	–	–	–	-0.046	–
5	A-n36-k5	802.13	802.13	–	–	–	802.13	0.000	–	–	–	0.000	–
6	A-n37-k5	672.59	672.47	672.47	672.47	–	672.47	-0.018	-0.018	-0.018	–	-0.018	–
7	A-n37-k6	952.22	950.85	–	–	–	950.85	-0.144	–	–	–	-0.144	–
8	A-n38-k5	734.18	733.95	733.95	–	–	733.95	-0.031	-0.031	–	–	-0.031	–
9	A-n39-k5	828.99	828.99	–	–	–	828.99	0.000	–	–	–	0.000	–
10	A-n39-k6	833.20	833.20	833.20	835.25	–	833.20	0.000	0.000	0.246	–	0.000	–
11	A-n44-k6	939.33	938.18	–	–	–	938.18	-0.122	–	–	–	-0.122	–
12	A-n45-k6	944.88	944.88	944.88	–	–	944.88	0.000	0.000	–	–	0.000	–
13	A-n45-k7	1147.22	1146.77	1146.77	–	–	1146.77	-0.039	-0.039	–	–	-0.039	–
14	A-n46-k7	918.46	917.72	–	–	–	917.72	-0.081	–	–	–	-0.081	–
15	A-n48-k7	1074.34	1074.34	–	–	–	1074.34	0.000	–	–	–	0.000	–
16	A-n53-k7	1013.31	1012.25	–	–	–	1012.33	-0.105	–	–	–	-0.097	–
17	A-n54-k7	1171.78	1171.68	–	–	–	1171.68	-0.009	–	–	–	-0.009	–
18	A-n55-k9	1074.46	1074.46	1074.46	–	–	1074.46	0.000	0.000	–	–	0.000	–
19	A-n60-k9	1355.80	–	1355.80	–	–	1355.80	–	0.000	–	–	0.000	–
20	A-n61-k9	1039.08	–	1039.08	–	–	1039.08	–	0.000	–	–	0.000	–
21	A-n62-k8	1294.28	–	–	–	–	1294.28	–	–	–	–	0.000	–
22	A-n63-k9	1622.14	–	1622.14	–	–	1622.14	–	0.000	–	–	0.000	–
23	A-n63-k10	1313.73	–	–	–	–	1313.46	–	–	–	–	-0.021	–
24	A-n64-k9	1400.83	–	–	–	–	1400.83	–	–	–	–	0.000	–
25	A-n65-k9	1181.69	1181.69	1181.69	–	–	1181.69	0.000	0.000	–	–	0.000	–

Table 3. (*Continued.*)

Number	Instances	Solution						Percentage Deviation					Percentage Improvement
		BKS [5], [7], [4][1]	Letchford et al. [31][2]	Juan et al. [32], [33][3]	Zhou et al. [34][4]	Osaba et al. [27][5]	IGB[6]	2 - 1	3 - 1	4 - 1	5 - 1	6 - 1	5 - 6
26	A-n69-k9	1165.99	–	–	–	–	1165.99	–	–	–	–	0.000	–
27	A-n80-k10	1766.50	–	1766.50	–	–	1766.50	–	0.000	–	–	0.000	–
28	B-n31-k5	676.76	676.09	676.09	–	–	676.09	-0.099	-0.099	–	–	-0.099	–
29	B-n34-k5	791.24	789.84	–	–	–	789.84	-0.177	–	–	–	-0.177	–
30	B-n35-k5	956.29	956.29	956.29	–	–	956.29	0.000	0.000	–	–	0.000	–
31	B-n38-k6	809.45	807.88	–	–	–	807.88	-0.194	–	–	–	-0.194	–
32	B-n39-k5	553.27	553.16	553.16	–	–	553.16	-0.020	-0.020	–	–	-0.020	–
33	B-n41-k6	834.96	833.66	834.92	–	–	833.66	-0.156	-0.005	–	–	-0.156	–
34	B-n43-k6	747.54	746.69	–	–	–	746.69	-0.114	–	–	–	-0.114	–
35	B-n44-k7	915.84	914.97	–	–	–	914.96	-0.095	–	–	–	-0.096	–
36	B-n45-k5	755.43	753.91	754.22	–	–	754.22	-0.201	-0.160	–	–	-0.160	–
37	B-n45-k6	680.44	680.44	–	–	–	680.44	0.000	–	–	–	0.000	–
38	B-n50-k7	744.78	744.23	744.23	–	–	744.23	-0.074	-0.074	–	–	-0.074	–
39	B-n50-k8	1316.32	–	–	–	–	1315.38	–	–	–	–	-0.072	–
40	B-n51-k7	1035.71	1035.04	–	–	–	1035.04	-0.065	–	–	–	-0.065	–
41	B-n52-k7	750.08	749.97	749.96	–	–	749.96	-0.015	-0.016	–	–	-0.016	–
42	B-n56-k7	712.92	712.92	712.92	–	–	712.92	0.000	0.000	–	–	0.000	–
43	B-n57-k7	1160.99	1157.73	–	–	–	1160.99	-0.281	–	–	–	0.000	–
44	B-n57-k9	1603.63	1602.29	1602.28	–	–	1602.29	-0.084	-0.084	–	–	-0.084	–
45	B-n63-k10	1501.27	1499.10	–	–	–	1500.93	-0.145	–	–	–	-0.022	–
46	B-n64-k9	869.32	868.19	868.31	–	–	868.31	-0.130	-0.116	–	–	-0.116	–
47	B-n66-k9	1325.36	–	–	–	–	1325.36	–	–	–	–	0.000	–
48	B-n67-k10	1039.36	1039.27	1039.36	–	–	1039.27	-0.009	0.000	–	–	-0.009	–
49	B-n68-k9	1278.21	–	1276.20	–	–	1278.21	-0.009	-0.157	–	–	0.000	–
50	B-n78-k10	1229.27	–	1227.90	–	–	1229.27	–	-0.111	–	–	0.000	–

Table 3. (*Continued.*)

Number	Instances	Solution						Percentage Deviation					Percentage Improvement
		BKS [5], [7], [4][1]	Letchford et al. [31][2]	Juan et al. [32], [33][3]	Zhou et al. [34][4]	Osaba et al. [27][5]	GB[6]	2 - 1	3 - 1	4 - 1	5 - 1	6 - 1	5 - 6
51	P-n16-k8	451.95	451.34	–	–	–	451.34	-0.135	–	–	–	-0.135	–
52	P-n19-k2	212.66	212.66	212.66	212.66	–	212.66	0.000	0.000	0.000	–	0.000	–
53	P-n20-k2	217.42	217.42	217.42	217.42	–	217.42	0.000	0.000	0.000	–	0.000	–
54	P-n21-k2	212.71	212.71	–	–	–	212.71	0.000	–	–	–	0.000	–
55	P-n22-k2	217.85	217.85	217.85	217.85	–	217.85	0.000	0.000	0.000	–	0.000	–
56	P-n22-k8	601.42	600.83	588.79	–	–	600.83	-0.098	-2.100	–	–	-0.098	–
57	P-n23-k8	531.17	531.17	–	–	–	531.17	0.000	–	–	–	0.000	–
58	P-n40-k5	461.73	461.73	461.73	–	–	461.73	0.000	0.000	–	–	0.000	–
59	P-n45-k5	512.79	512.79	–	–	–	512.79	0.000	–	–	–	0.000	–
60	P-n50-k7	559.86	559.86	–	–	–	559.86	0.000	–	–	–	0.000	–
61	P-n50-k8	634.85	–	633.96	–	–	634.85	–	-0.140	–	–	0.000	–
62	P-n50-k10	699.56	–	699.56	–	–	699.56	–	0.000	–	–	0.000	–
63	P-n51-k10	742.48	741.50	741.50	743.26	–	741.50	-0.132	-0.132	0.105	–	-0.132	–
64	P-n55-k7	570.27	570.27	–	–	–	570.27	0.000	–	–	–	0.000	–
65	P-n55-k8	592.17	578.61	–	–	–	578.61	-2.290	–	–	–	-2.290	–
66	P-n55-k10	697.81	–	–	–	–	696.77	–	–	–	–	-0.149	–
67	P-n55-k15	991.48	–	944.56	–	–	991.48	–	-4.732	–	–	0.000	–
68	P-n60-k10	748.94	–	748.07	–	–	748.07	–	-0.116	–	–	-0.116	–
69	P-n60-k15	971.58	–	–	–	–	971.58	–	–	–	–	0.000	–
70	P-n65-k10	796.67	–	795.66	–	–	795.66	–	-0.127	–	–	-0.127	–
71	P-n70-k10	830.02	–	829.93	–	–	829.93	–	-0.011	–	–	-0.011	–
72	P-n76-k4	598.22	598.20	598.19	–	–	598.20	-0.003	-0.005	–	–	-0.003	–
73	P-n76-k5	635.04	633.32	633.32	–	–	633.32	-0.271	-0.271	–	–	-0.271	–
74	P-n101-k4	692.28	691.29	691.29	–	–	691.29	-0.143	-0.143	–	–	-0.143	–
75	E-n22-k4	375.28	375.28	375.28	375.28	376.00	375.28	0.000	0.000	0.000	0.192	0.000	0.191

352   K. Ruttanateerawichien, W. Kurutach, and T. Pichpibul

Table 3. (*Continued.*)

Number	Instances	Solution						Percentage Deviation					Percentage Improvement
		BKS [5], [7], [4][1]	Letchford et al. [31][2]	Juan et al. [32], [33][3]	Zhou et al. [34][4]	Osaba et al. [27][5]	IGB[6]	2-1	3-1	4-1	5-1	6-1	5-6
76	E-n23-k3	568.56	568.56	–	568.56	589.70	568.56	0.000	–	0.000	3.718	0.000	3.585
77	E-n30-k3	538.96	535.80	505.01	–	–	535.80	-0.586	-6.299	–	–	-0.586	–
78	E-n33-k4	838.72	837.67	837.67	837.93	857.80	837.67	-0.125	-0.125	-0.094	2.275	-0.125	2.347
79	E-n51-k5	524.94	524.61	524.61	524.61	578.10	524.61	-0.063	-0.063	-0.063	10.127	-0.063	9.253
80	E-n76-k7	687.60	–	687.60	–	755.80	687.60	–	0.000	–	9.919	0.000	9.024
81	E-n76-k10	837.36	–	835.26	–	913.60	837.36	–	-0.251	–	9.105	0.000	8.345
82	E-n76-k14	1026.71	–	1024.40	–	1124.60	1026.71	–	-0.225	–	9.534	0.000	8.704
83	E-n101-k8	826.14	–	–	–	906.40	826.14	–	–	–	9.715	0.000	8.855
84	F-n45-k4	724.57	723.54	723.54	–	–	723.54	-0.142	-0.142	–	–	-0.142	–
85	F-n72-k4	248.81	241.97	241.97	–	–	241.97	-2.749	-2.749	–	–	-2.749	–
86	F-n135-k7	1170.65	1162.96	1164.73	–	–	1164.54	-0.657	-0.506	–	–	-0.522	–
87	M-n101-k10	819.81	819.56	819.56	–	–	819.56	-0.031	-0.031	–	–	-0.031	–
88	M-n121-k7	1045.16	–	1043.88	–	–	1043.88	–	-0.123	–	–	-0.123	–

Italic number indicates the infeasible solution.
Bold number indicates the new best-known solution.

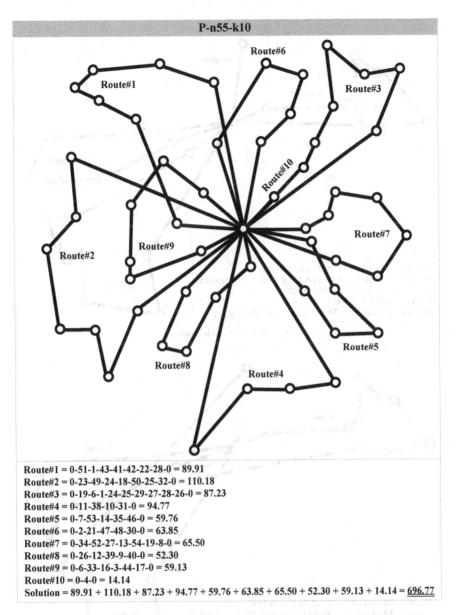

P-n55-k10

Route#1 = 0-51-1-43-41-42-22-28-0 = 89.91
Route#2 = 0-23-49-24-18-50-25-32-0 = 110.18
Route#3 = 0-19-6-1-24-25-29-27-28-26-0 = 87.23
Route#4 = 0-11-38-10-31-0 = 94.77
Route#5 = 0-7-53-14-35-46-0 = 59.76
Route#6 = 0-2-21-47-48-30-0 = 63.85
Route#7 = 0-34-52-27-13-54-19-8-0 = 65.50
Route#8 = 0-26-12-39-9-40-0 = 52.30
Route#9 = 0-6-33-16-3-44-17-0 = 59.13
Route#10 = 0-4-0 = 14.14
Solution = 89.91 + 110.18 + 87.23 + 94.77 + 59.76 + 63.85 + 65.50 + 52.30 + 59.13 + 14.14 = <u>696.77</u>

Fig. 6. Example of the new best-known solution

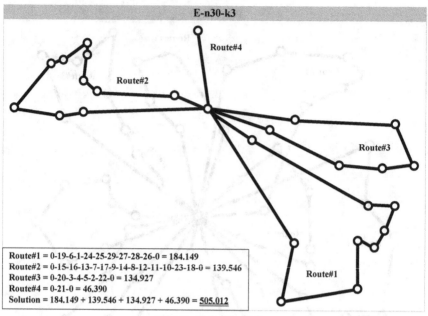

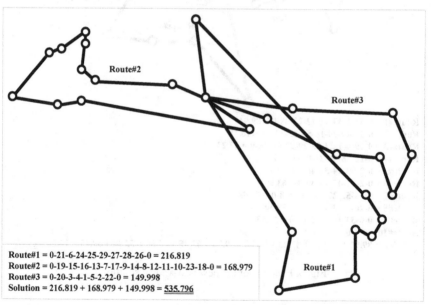

Route#1 = 0-19-6-1-24-25-29-27-28-26-0 = 184.149
Route#2 = 0-15-16-13-7-17-9-14-8-12-11-10-23-18-0 = 139.546
Route#3 = 0-20-3-4-5-2-22-0 = 134.927
Route#4 = 0-21-0 = 46.390
Solution = 184.149 + 139.546 + 134.927 + 46.390 = 505.012

(a) The best infeasible solution

Route#1 = 0-21-6-24-25-29-27-28-26-0 = 216.819
Route#2 = 0-19-15-16-13-7-17-9-14-8-12-11-10-23-18-0 = 168.979
Route#3 = 0-20-3-4-1-5-2-22-0 = 149.998
Solution = 216.819 + 168.979 + 149.998 = 535.796

(b) The best feasible solution

Fig. 7. Example of two best solutions

5   Conclusions

In this paper, we have presented a new improvement to the golden ball algorithm (GB) to solve the capacitated vehicle routing problem (CVRP). We have done the experiments by using well-known benchmark problems composed of 88 instances obtained from the literatures, and have compared them with the best known solutions.

The computational results show that the improved GB (IGB) is truly efficient and satisfactory in terms of solution quality. It is competitive or outperforms the original GB, and generates the new best-known solutions for three instances and makes tie with the existing best-known solutions for 79 instances. Therefore, we can conclude that the performance of IGB is excellent for solving CVRP when compared with several algorithms in each instance.

References

1. Dantzig, G.B., Ramser, J.H.: The truck dispatching problem. Management Science 6, 80–91 (1959)
2. Toth, P., Vigo, D.: The vehicle routing problem. In: SIAM Monographs on Discrete Mathematics and Applications, SIAM Publishing, Philadelphia (2002)
3. Christofides, N., Mingozzi, A., Toth, P.: Exact algorithm for the vehicle routing problem, based on spanning tree and shortest path relaxations. Mathematical Programming 20, 255–282 (1981)
4. Fisher, M.L.: Optimal solution of vehicle routing problems using minimum K-trees. Operations Research 42, 626–642 (1994)
5. Augerat, P., Belenguer, J., Benavent, E., Corbern, A., Naddef, D., Rinaldi, G.: Computational results with a branch and cut code for the capacitated vehicle routing problem [Research Report 949-M], Universite Joseph Fourier, Grenoble, France (1995)
6. Lysgaard, J., Letchford, A.N., Eglese, R.W.: A new branch-and-cut algorithm for the capacitated vehicle routing problem. Mathematical Programming Series A 100, 423–445 (2004)
7. Fukasawa, R., Longo, H., Lysgaard, J., Poggi de Aragão, M., Reis, M., Uchoa, E., Werneck, R.F.: Robust Branch-and-Cut-and-Price for the Capacitated Vehicle Routing Problem. Mathematical Programming 106, 491–511 (2006)
8. Clarke, G., Wright, J.W.: Scheduling of vehicles from a central depot to a number of delivery points. Operations Research 12, 568–581 (1964)
9. Wren, A., Holliday, A.: Computer scheduling of vehicles from one or more depots to a number of delivery points. Operational Research Quarterly 23, 333–344 (1972)
10. Fisher, M.L., Jaikumar, R.: A generalized assignment heuristic for vehicle routing. Networks 11, 109–124 (1981)
11. Lin, S.: Computer solutions of the travelling salesman problem. Bell System Technical Journal 44, 2245–2269 (1965)
12. Or, I.: Traveling Salesman-Type Combinatorial Optimization Problems and their Relation to the Logistics of Regional Blood Banking. Ph.D. Dissertation, Northwestern University (1976)
13. Osman, I.H.: Metastrategy simulated annealing and tabu search algorithms for the vehicle routing problem. Annals of Operations Research 41, 421–451 (1993)
14. Subramanian, A., Drummond, L.M.A., Bentes, C., Ochi, L.S., Farias, R.: A parallel heuristic for the Vehicle Routing Problem with Simultaneous Pickup and Delivery. Computers and Operations Research 37, 1899–1911 (2009)

15. Groër, C., Golden, B., Wasil, E.: A library of local search heuristics for the vehicle routing problem. Mathematical Programming Computation 2, 79–101 (2010)
16. Kirkpatrick, S., Gelatt, J., Vecchi, M.: Optimization by simulated annealing. Science 220, 671–680 (1983)
17. Rochat, Y., Taillard, É.D.: Probabilistic diversification and intensification in local search for vehicle routing. Journal of Heuristics 1, 147–167 (1995)
18. Gen, M., Cheng, R.: Genetic algorithms and engineering design. Wiley, New York (1997)
19. Kennedy, J., Eberhart, R.: Particle swarm optimization. In: Proceedings of IEEE International Conference on Neural Networks, pp. 1942–1948 (1995)
20. Dorigo, M., Maniezzo, V., Colorni, A.: Ant system: optimization by a colony of cooperating agents. IEEE Transactions on Systems, Mans, and Cybernetics 1, 29–41 (1996)
21. Prins, C.: A simple and effective evolutionary algorithm for the vehicle routing problem. Computers and Operations Research 31, 1985–2002 (2004)
22. Marinakis, Y., Marinaki, M., Dounias, G.: Honey Bee Mating Optimization Algorithm for the Vehicle Routing Problem. In: Krasnogor, N., Nicosia, G., Pavone, M., Pelta, D. (eds.) Nature Inspired Cooperative Strategies for Optimization (NICSO 2007). SCI, vol. 129, pp. 139–148. Springer, Heidelberg (2008)
23. Rashedi, E., Nezamabadi-pour, H., Saryazdi, S.: GSA: A Gravitational Search Algorithm. Information Sciences 179, 2232–2248 (2009)
24. Salcedo-Sanz, S., Gallo-Marazuela, D., Pastor-Sánchez, A., Carro-Calvo, L., Portilla-Figueras, A., Prieto, L.: Offshore wind farm design with the Coral Reefs Optimization algorithm. Renewable Energy 63, 109–115 (2014)
25. Yang, X.S.: Firefly algorithms for mult-imodal optimization. In: Proceedings of the 5th International Symposium on Stochastic Algorithms: Foundations and Applications, pp. 169–178 (2009)
26. Krishnanand, K.N., Ghose, D.: Glowworm swarm optimization for simultaneous capture of multiple local optima of multimodal functions. Swarm Intelligence 3, 87–124 (2009)
27. Osaba, E., Diaz, F., Onieva, E.: Golden ball: a novel meta-heuristic to solve combinatorial optimization problems based on soccer concepts. Applied Intelligence (2014), doi:10.1007/s10489-013-0512-y
28. Pichpibul, T., Kawtummachai, R.: An improved Clarke and Wright savings algorithm for the capacitated vehicle routing problem. ScienceAsia 38, 307–318 (2012)
29. Christofides, N., Eilon, S.: An algorithm for the vehicle dispatching problem. Operational Research Quarterly 20, 309–318 (1969)
30. Christofides, N., Mingozzi, A., Toth, P.: The vehicle routing problem. Combinatorial Optimization, pp. 315–338. Wiley, New York (1979)
31. Letchford, A.N., Lysgaard, J., Eglese, R.W.: A branch-and-cut algorithm for the capacitated open vehicle routing problem. Journal of the Operational Research Society 58, 1642–1651 (2007)
32. Juan, A.A., Faulin, J., Ruiz, R., Barrios, B., Caballé, S.: The SR-GCWS hybrid algorithm for solving the capacitated vehicle routing problem. Applied Soft Computing 10, 215–224 (2010)
33. Juan, A.A., Faulin, J., Jorba, J., Riera, D., Masip, D., Barrios, B.: On the use of Monte Carlo simulation, cache and splitting techniques to improve the Clarke and Wright savings heuristics. Journal of the Operational Research Society 62, 1085–1097 (2011)
34. Zhou, Y., Xie, J., Zheng, H.: A Hybrid Bat Algorithm with Path Relinking for Capacitated Vehicle Routing Problem. Mathematical Problems in Engineering 2013, 1–10 (2013)
35. Vigo, D.: A heuristic algorithm for the asymmetric capacitated vehicle routing problem. European Journal of Operational Research 89, 108–126 (1996)

A New Method for Singular Polynomial Systems

Haifeng Sang[1], Panpan Liu[1], Qingchun Li[1,*], and Yan Li[2]

[1] College of Mathematics and Statistics, Beihua University, Jilin 132013, China
[2] Jilin Light Industry Secondary School, Jilin 132000, China
liqingchun01@163.com

Abstract. In this paper, we present a new algorithm to compute the singular solution of polynomial systems by using approximate left and right nullspaces of the Jacobian matrix. The theory and algorithm are illustrated by several examples.

Keywords: Newton method, Polynomial systems, Singular solution.

1 Introduction

It is one of the most fundamental problems to solve a polynomial system $f(x) = 0$ with $f = (f_1, f_2, \ldots, f_n)^T$ and $x = (x_1, \ldots, x_n)^T$. Solving polynomial systems plays an important role in the biology field such as computational neuroscience, bioinformatics and cheminformatics. If $f(x) = 0$ is a square system and $\hat{x}$ is a simple solution of $f(x) = 0$, then Newton method has locally quadratic convergence [1–5]. The convergence properties of Newton method for singular solutions may be less satisfactory.

The computation of singular solutions of polynomial systems has been extensively studied with various approaches. Griewank [6, 7] introduced the technique of border systems to regularize the singular problem. Using the nullspace of the Jacobian matrix, Griewank[8] and Shen[9] constructed a border system for which Newton method converges quadratically by adding a generalized regular singularity condition.

In this paper, we present a new algorithm to compute the singular solution of polynomial systems by using approximate left and right nullspaces of the Jacobian matrix. Our algorithm is not only to the isolated solution but also applicable to the non-isolated solution. This technique can be extended further to the case $f : \mathbb{R}^m \to \mathbb{R}^n$ for general m and n.

2 Notation and Preliminaries

We denote by $\mathbb{R}$ and $\mathbb{R}^+$ the set of real numbers and the set of positive real numbers, respectively. We denote by $\mathbb{C}$, $\mathbb{Q}$ and $\mathbb{N}$ the set of complex numbers, the set of rational numbers and the set of nonnegative integers, respectively.

---

* Corresponding author.

L. Pan et al. (Eds.): BIC-TA 2014, CCIS 472, pp. 357–363, 2014.
© Springer-Verlag Berlin Heidelberg 2014

If $A \in \mathbb{R}^{m \times n}$, then $A_{i,:}$ designates the ith row. The j-th column is specified by $A_{:,j}$. The Moore-Penrose inverse of A is denoted by A^+. We denote by $A_{:,i:j}$ and $A_{i:j,:}$ the submatrix of A formed by selecting from the i-th column to the j-th column and the submatrix from the i-th row to the j-th row, respectively. We use I_n to stand for $n \times n$ identity matrix, and $O_{m,n}$ to stand for $m \times n$ zero matrix.

Suppose that $\boldsymbol{x} = (x_1, \ldots, x_n)^T$ and $M(\boldsymbol{x})$ is a matrix with entries $M(\boldsymbol{x})_{i,j}$. If $M(\boldsymbol{x})_{i,j}$ is a continuously differentiable function of $\boldsymbol{x}$ for all i and j, then $\frac{\partial M(\boldsymbol{x})}{\partial x_i}$ is a matrix with entries $\frac{\partial M(\boldsymbol{x})_{i,j}}{\partial x_i}$.

Definition 1. [10, 11] *Given a matrix $A \in \mathbb{R}^{m \times n}$, and a tolerance $\varepsilon \in \mathbb{R}^+$, the numerical rank of A within ε, denoted by $\mathrm{rank}_\varepsilon(A)$, is defined by*

$$\mathrm{rank}_\varepsilon(A) = \min_{\|B-A\|_2 < \varepsilon} \mathrm{rank}(B).$$

Given a matrix $A \in \mathbb{R}^{m \times n}$, and a tolerance $\varepsilon \in \mathbb{R}^+$, then A has numerical rank r if the computed singular values $\sigma_1(A), \cdots, \sigma_n(A)$ satisfy

$$\sigma_1(A) \geq \cdots \geq \sigma_r(A) > \varepsilon \geq \sigma_{r+1}(A) \geq \cdots \geq \sigma_n(A).$$

Definition 2. *Let $\boldsymbol{f} : \mathbb{R}^n \to \mathbb{R}^m$ with $\boldsymbol{f} = (f_1, f_2, \ldots, f_m)^T$, then a point $\widehat{\boldsymbol{x}}$ is an isolated solution of $\boldsymbol{f}(\boldsymbol{x}) = \boldsymbol{0}$ if there is a neighborhood Δ of $\widehat{\boldsymbol{x}}$ in $\mathbb{C}^n$ such that $\widehat{\boldsymbol{x}}$ is the only solution of $\boldsymbol{f}(\boldsymbol{x}) = \boldsymbol{0}$ in Δ.*

Definition 3. *Let $\boldsymbol{f} : \mathbb{R}^n \to \mathbb{R}^m$ with $\boldsymbol{f} = (f_1, f_2, \ldots, f_m)^T$, and let $J_{\boldsymbol{f}}(\widehat{\boldsymbol{x}})$ denote the Jacobian matrix of $\boldsymbol{f}(\boldsymbol{x})$ at $\widehat{\boldsymbol{x}}$. A solution $\widehat{\boldsymbol{x}}$ of $\boldsymbol{f}(\boldsymbol{x}) = \boldsymbol{0}$ is a singular solution if $\mathrm{rank}(J_{\boldsymbol{f}}(\widehat{\boldsymbol{x}})) < n$.*

3 Main Results

Let $\boldsymbol{f} : \mathbb{R}^n \to \mathbb{R}^m$ with $\boldsymbol{f} = (f_1, f_2, \ldots, f_n)^T$, and $\widehat{\boldsymbol{x}} \in \mathbb{R}^n$ is the solution of the system $\boldsymbol{f}(\boldsymbol{x}) = 0$. In this paper, we assume that $\boldsymbol{f}$ and $\widehat{\boldsymbol{x}}$ satisfy the following conditions:

(a) $\mathrm{rank}(J_{\boldsymbol{f}}(\widehat{\boldsymbol{x}})) = r < n$, i.e., it has rank deficiency $q = n - r$.
(b) There exists a nonzero vector $\mu^* \in \mathrm{Null}([J_f(x^*)]^T)$ and a basis $\eta^* = \{\eta_1^*, \ldots, \eta_q^*\}$ of $\mathrm{Null}(J_f(x^*))$ such that $q \times q$ matrix

$$[\eta^*]^T [(\mu^*)^T J J_f(x^*)] \eta^* = [\eta_1^*, \ldots, \eta_q^*]^T [(\mu^*)^T J J_f(x^*)][\eta_1^*, \ldots, \eta_q^*]$$

is nonsingular, where the k-th column of $[\eta^*]^T [(\mu^*)^T J J_f(x^*)]$ is

$$[\eta^*]^T * \begin{bmatrix} \frac{\partial^2 f_1(x^*)}{\partial x_1 \partial x_k} & & \frac{\partial^2 f_m(x^*)}{\partial x_1 \partial x_k} \\ & \ddots & \\ \frac{\partial^2 f_1(x^*)}{\partial x_n \partial x_k} & & \frac{\partial^2 f_m(x^*)}{\partial x_n \partial x_k} \end{bmatrix} * \mu^*, \quad k = 1, 2, \ldots, n.$$

Write the singular value decomposition of $J_f(\overline{x})$ for a point $\overline{x}$ near x^* as

$$J_f(\overline{x}) = U(\overline{x})\Sigma(\overline{x})V(\overline{x})^T = [u_1(\overline{x}), \ldots, u_n(\overline{x})]\mathrm{diag}(\sigma_1(\overline{x}), \ldots, \sigma_n(\overline{x}))[v_1(\overline{x}), \ldots, v_n(\overline{x})]^T.$$

Given a tolerance $\varepsilon \in \mathbb{R}^+$, if

$$\sigma_1(\overline{x}) \geq \ldots \geq \sigma_r(\overline{x}) > \varepsilon \geq \sigma_{r+1}(\overline{x}) \geq \ldots \geq \sigma_p(\overline{x})) \geq 0, \tag{1}$$

then

$$R(\overline{x}) = (u_{r+1}(\overline{x}), \ldots, u_m(\overline{x}))$$

and

$$L(\overline{x}) = (v_{r+1}(\overline{x}), \ldots, v_n(\overline{x}))$$

are the approximate left and right nullspaces of $J_f(\overline{x})$, respectively.

Lemma 1. [9] *The matrix*

$$A(x, \overline{x}) = \begin{pmatrix} J_f(x) & R(\overline{x}) \\ L^T(\overline{x}) & O_{n-r,m-r} \end{pmatrix}$$

is nonsingular for all x *in a neighborhood of* x^* *and a fixed* $\overline{x}$ *sufficiently near* x^*.

For all x sufficiently near x^*, let $\eta(x)$ and $h(x)$ be the unique solution of

$$A(x, \overline{x})\begin{bmatrix} \eta(x) \\ h(x) \end{bmatrix} = \begin{bmatrix} J_f(x) & R(\overline{x}) \\ L^T(\overline{x}) & O \end{bmatrix}\begin{bmatrix} \eta(x) \\ h(x) \end{bmatrix} = \begin{bmatrix} O \\ I_q \end{bmatrix}, \tag{2}$$

and let $\mu(x)$ and $g(x)$ be the unique solution of

$$A^T(x, \overline{x})\begin{bmatrix} \mu(x) \\ g(x) \end{bmatrix} = \left(\begin{bmatrix} J_f(x) & R(\overline{x}) \\ L^T(\overline{x}) & O \end{bmatrix}\right)^T\begin{bmatrix} \mu(x) \\ g(x) \end{bmatrix} = \begin{bmatrix} 0 \\ \alpha \end{bmatrix}, \tag{3}$$

where α is a randomly chosen q-dimensional vector.

Define $q \times q$ matrix $B(x, \alpha) = \eta^T(x)[\mu^T(x)JJ_f(x)]\eta(x)$.

Lemma 2. [9] *If* $\overline{x}$ *is such that Lemma 1 holds, then* $B(x^*, \alpha)$ *is nonsingular for almost all* $\alpha \in \mathbb{R}^q$.

We define a bordered system for solving $f(x) = 0$:

$$F(x, \lambda) \equiv \begin{bmatrix} f(x) + R(\overline{x})\lambda \\ g(x) \end{bmatrix} = 0, \tag{4}$$

where λ is an unknown q-dimensional vector. Then the Jacobian matrix of $F(x, \lambda)$ is

$$J_F(x, \lambda) = \begin{bmatrix} J_f(x) & R(\overline{x}) \\ g'(x) & O \end{bmatrix} = \begin{bmatrix} J_f(x) & R(\overline{x}) \\ -\eta^T(x)[\mu^T(x)JJ_f(x)] & O \end{bmatrix}. \tag{5}$$

Lemma 3. [9] *If* $\overline{x}$ *and* α *is chosen so that Lemma 1 and Lemma 2 hold, then* $J_F(x^*, 0)$ *is nonsingular.*

We differentiate the system (3) with respect to each variable x_j to get

$$
\begin{pmatrix} J_f(x)^T & L(\overline{x}) \\ R^T(\overline{x}) & O \end{pmatrix} \begin{pmatrix} \frac{\partial \mu(x)}{\partial x_j} \\ \frac{\partial g(x)}{\partial x_j} \end{pmatrix} = - \begin{pmatrix} \frac{\partial J_f(x)^T}{\partial x_j} \mu(x) \\ O \end{pmatrix}, \tag{6}
$$

Therefore, we can obtain $J_{f_1}(\tilde{x})$ by solving n linear systems with the same coefficient matrix, but with different right-hand vectors.

Remark 1. From (3) and (6) we can obtain $J_{f_1}(\tilde{x})$ by solving n linear systems with the same coefficient matrix. However, we need to compute $q + 1$ systems and q products of three matrix in [9] by $g'(x) = \eta^T(x)(\mu^T(x)f''(x))$. Therefore our method is more efficient especially when matrices are interval matrices.

Theorem 1. *If $\overline{x}$ and α is chosen so that Lemma 1 and Lemma 2 hold, then $(x^*, 0)$ is the simple zero of the bordered system $F(x, \lambda) = 0$.*

Proof. From (1) and the condition (c) it follows that

$$
[J_f(x^*) \ \ R(\overline{x})] \begin{bmatrix} \eta(x^*) \\ h(x^*) \end{bmatrix} = O, \quad [J_f(x^*) \ \ R(\overline{x})] \begin{bmatrix} \eta^* \\ O \end{bmatrix} = O.
$$

Since $\dim(\text{Null}[J_f(x^*) \ \ R(\overline{x})]) = q$ and $\text{rank}(\eta^*) = q$, there exists $q \times q$ nonsingular matrix C such that

$$
\begin{bmatrix} \eta(x^*) \\ h(x^*) \end{bmatrix} = \begin{bmatrix} \eta^* \\ O \end{bmatrix} C.
$$

Hence

$$
h(x^*) = O. \tag{7}
$$

From (5) we know $g(x^*) = h^T(x^*) \cdot \alpha = 0$. Hence

$$
F(x^*, 0) \equiv \begin{bmatrix} f(x^*) \\ g(x^*) \end{bmatrix} = 0.
$$

Therefore we know that $(x^*, 0)$ is the simple zero of the bordered system $F(x, \lambda) = 0$ by Lemma 3. □

We summarize the resulting algorithm below:

Algorithm 1

Input. $f(x) = 0$: a nonlinear system satisfying the conditions (a),(b),(c).

ε_1: the tolerance of numerical rank.

ε_2: the tolerance of numerical Newton iteration.

N: the maximum number of numerical iteration.

Output. Refined approximate solution $(\tilde{x}, \tilde{\lambda})$ or "Failure".

1. Choose a point $\overline{x}$ near x^*, the solution of the equation; usually we use $\overline{x} = x_0$. Set $\lambda_0 = 0$.

2. Compute the singular value decomposition of $J_f(\overline{x})$. Determine the rank deficiency q. Then use q and the corresponding singular vectors to form the two submatrices $R(\overline{x})$ and $L(\overline{x})$.

3. Generate a random q-dimensional vector α.
4. If $k > N$, then return "Failure", and stop.
5. Compute $A(x_k, \overline{x})$.
6. Compute $g(x_k)$ by (3) and $J_g(x_k)$ by (6).
7. Compute $F(x_k, \lambda_k)$ by (4) and $J_F(x_k, \lambda_k)$ by (5).
8. Compute

$$J_F(x_k, \lambda_k) \begin{pmatrix} \Delta x_k \\ \Delta \lambda_k \end{pmatrix} = -F(x_k, \lambda_k), \qquad \begin{pmatrix} x_{k+1} \\ \lambda_{k+1} \end{pmatrix} = \begin{pmatrix} x_k \\ \lambda_k \end{pmatrix} + \begin{pmatrix} \Delta x_k \\ \Delta \lambda_k \end{pmatrix}.$$

9. If $\|(\Delta x_k, \Delta \lambda_k)\|_2 < \varepsilon_2$, then return (x_{k+1}, λ_{k+1}) and q, and stop. Otherwise set $k := k + 1$ and return step 4.

4 Computational Examples

We compute the Jacobian matrix of the given nonlinear system and the differentiable matrix of the Jacobian matrix of the given nonlinear system in Maple. We implement Algorithm 1 to obtain the refined approximate solution of the nonlinear system in Matlab. The following experiments are done in Maple 15 for Digits:= 14 and Matlab R2011a under Windows 7.

We apply the above algorithm to the following two examples, starting with $\lambda_0 = 0$, to illustrate the numerical behavior. In each case we used a random number generator to produce the vector α.

Example 1. [12][cbms2] $f : \mathbb{R}^3 \to \mathbb{R}^3$ is defined by

$$f(x) = \begin{bmatrix} x_1^3 - 3x_1^2 x_2 + 3x_1 x_2^2 - x_2^3 - x_3^2 \\ x_2^3 - 3x_2^2 x_3 + 3x_2 x_3^2 - x_3^3 - x_1^2 \\ x_3^3 - 3x_3^2 x_1 + 3x_3 x_1^2 - x_1^3 - x_2^2 \end{bmatrix}$$

Choose $x_0 = \overline{x} = (0.01, 0.01, 0.01)$ and $\varepsilon_1 = 0.1$. The rank deficiency is $q = 3$ at $\widehat{x} = (0,0)^T$. We choose α randomly as $\alpha = (11.8916, 0.3763, 3.2729)^T$. The data listed in Table 1 confirms quadratic convergence to $(\widehat{x}, \widehat{\lambda})^T = (0,0,0,0,0,0)$.

Table 1. Data for Example 1

k	$x_1^{(k)}$	$x_2^{(k)}$	$x_3^{(k)}$	$\lambda_1^{(k)}$	$\lambda_2^{(k)}$	$\lambda_3^{(k)}$	$\|(\triangle x, \triangle \lambda)^{(k)}\|$
0	1.0000e-02	1.0000e-02	1.0000e-02	0.0000e+00	0.0000e+00	0.0000e+00	
1	0.0000e-04	0.0000e-04	0.0000e-04	-1.0000e-04	-1.0000e-04	-1.0000e-04	1.7300e-02
2	1.2000e-35	1.9260e-34	1.6400e-35	0.0000e-33	0.0000e-33	0.0000e-33	1.7321e-04
3	0.0000e-67	0.0000e-67	0.0000e-67	0.0000e-67	3.7090e-68	2.7000e-69	1.9329e-34

Example 2. [13][Ojika3] $f : \mathbb{R}^3 \to \mathbb{R}^3$ is defined by

$$f(x) = \begin{bmatrix} x_1 + x_2 + x_3 - 1 \\ 2x_1^3 + 5x_2^2 - 10x_3 + 5x_3^2 + 5 \\ 2x_1 + 2x_2 + x_3^2 - 1 \end{bmatrix}$$

Choose $x_0 = \bar{x} = (-2.45, 2.45, 1.01)$ and $\varepsilon_1 = 0.01$. The rank deficiency is $q = 1$ at $\hat{x} = (-2.5, 2.5, 1)^T$. We choose α randomly as $\alpha = 1.7464$. The data listed in Table 2 confirms quadratic convergence to $(\hat{x}, \hat{\lambda})^T = (-2.5, 2.5, 1, 0)$.

Table 2. Data for Example 2

k	$x_1^{(k)}$	$x_2^{(k)}$	$x_3^{(k)}$	$\lambda_1^{(k)}$	$\|(\triangle x, \triangle \lambda)^{(k)}\|$
0	-2.4500e+00	2.4500e+00	1.0100e+00	0.0000e+00	
1	-2.5033e+00	2.5039e+00	0.9995e+00	0.0000e+00	0.0765e+00
2	-2.5000e+00	2.5000e+00	1.0000e+00	0.0000e+00	0.0051e+00
3	-2.5000e+00	2.5000e+00	1.0000e+00	0.0000e+00	1.5075e-05
4	-2.5000e+00	2.5000e+00	1.0000e+00	0.0000e+00	1.3043e-10

Acknowledgments. We thank the reviewers for their valuable comments and suggestions on this paper.

This work is supported by Jilin Province Department of Education Science and Technology Research Project under Grants 2014213.

References

1. Dennis, J.J.E., Schnabel, R.B.: Numerical Methods for Unconstrained Optimization and Nonlinear Equations. SIAM, Philadelphia (1996)
2. Kelley, C.T.: Iterative Methods for Linear and Nonlinear Equations. SIAM, Philadelphia (1995)
3. Ortega, J.M., Rheinbolt, W.C.: Iterative Solution of Nonlinear Equations in Several Variables. Academic Press, New York (1970)
4. Ypma, T.J.: Local Convergence of Inexact Newton Methods. SIAM J. Numer. Anal. 21(3), 583–590 (1984)
5. Ypma, T.J.: Historical Development of the Newton – Raphson Method. SIAM Rev. 37(4), 531–551 (1995)
6. Griewank, A.: Analysis and Modification of Newton's Method at Singularities. Australian National University, Canberra (1980)
7. Griewank, A., Osborne, M.R.: Newton's Method for Singular Problems when the Dimension of the Null Space Is >1. SIAM Journal on Numerical Analysis 18(1), 145–149 (1981)
8. Griewank, A.: On Solving Nonlinear Equations with Simple Singularities or Nearly Singular Solutions. SIAM review 27(4), 537–563 (1985)
9. Shen, Y.Q., Ypma, T.J.: Newton'S Method for Singular Nonlinear Equations Using Approximate Left and Right Nullspaces of the Jacobian. Applied numerical mathematics 54(2), 256–265 (2005)
10. Golub, G.H., Van Loan, C.F.: Matrix Computations. Johns Hopkins University Press (2012)

11. Stewart, G.W.: Introduction to Matrix Computations. Academic Press, New York (1973)
12. Sturmfels, B.: Solving systems of Polynomial Equations. American Mathematical Soc. (2002)
13. Ojika, T.: Modified Deflation Algorithm for the Solution of Singular Problems. I. A System of Nonlinear Algebraic Equations. Journal of mathematical analysis and applications 123(1), 199–221 (1987)

Accepting String Graph Splicing System

Meena Parvathy Sankar[1], N.G. David[2], and D.G. Thomas[2]

[1] Department of Mathematics, SRM University, Kattankulathur, Chennai - 603 203
meenaparvathysankar@gmail.com
[2] Department of Mathematics, Madras Christian College, Chennai - 600 059
ngdmcc@gmail.com, dgthomasmcc@yahoo.com

Abstract. In this paper, we extend the idea of accepting splicing systems on strings which was introduced by Mitrana et al. to string graphs. The input string graph is accepted as soon as the permitting string graph is obtained provided that no forbidding string graph has been obtained so far, otherwise it is rejected. We study the computational power of the new variants of the accepting string graph splicing system and the interrelationships among them.

Keywords: Graph splicing scheme, Graph splicing system, String graphs, Accepting string graph splicing system.

1 Introduction

Tom Head introduced the notion of splicing systems in order to model the recombinatorial behaviors of double-stranded DNA molecules under the simultaneous influence of specified classes of restriction enzymes. To model complex bio chemical processes of three dimensional (macro) molecules in the three dimensional space, strings are turn out to be inadequate objects. To overcome this, Rudolf Freund introduced graphs as more suitable objects for modelling such processes and introduced graph splicing systems. Splicing system is one of the formal device to generate languages and it is based on the iteration of splicing operation. Many variants of splicing systems have been defined and investigated, such as distributed spilcing systems, splicing systems with multisets splicing systems, splicing systems with permitting and forbidding contexts.

Splicing systems are viewed as language accepting devices and not the generating ones. In usual splicing systems, the input word is accepted / rejected in accordance with some predefined accepting conditions.

In this paper, we investigate the computational power of the new variants of splicing systems. The input string graph is accepted as soon as a permitting string graph is obtained provided that no forbidding string graph has been obtained so far.

2 Preliminaries

In this section, we recall some of the important definitions of graph splicing systems [6].

L. Pan et al. (Eds.): BIC-TA 2014, CCIS 472, pp. 364–369, 2014.
© Springer-Verlag Berlin Heidelberg 2014

Definition 1 (Graph Splicing Scheme). *A graph splicing scheme σ is a pair (V, P) where V is an alphabet and P is a finite set of graph splicing rules of the form $((h[1], E'[1]), \ldots, (h[k], E'[k]); E)$ where $k \geq 1$ and for all i with $1 \leq i \leq k$.*

1. *$h_i \in \gamma(V)$, $h[i] = (N[i], E[i], L[i])$.*
2. *$E'[1] \subseteq E[i]$*
3. *the node set $N[i]$ are mutually disjoint*

and E must obey the following rules:

1. *Each edge $(n, m) \in E'[i]$ is suppose to have been divided into two parts. i.e., the start part $(n, m]$ and the end part $[n, m)$.*
2. *The elements of E are of the form $((n, m], [n', m'))$, where $(n, m]$ and $[n', m')$ are edges from $\bigcup\limits_{1 \leq i \leq k} E'[i]$*
3. *Every element from $\left\{ (n, m], [n, m) | (n, m) \in \bigcup_{1 \leq i \leq k} E'[i] \right\}$ must appear exactly once in a pair of E.*

Definition 2 (Graph Splicing System). *Let $\sigma = (V, P)$ be a graph splicing scheme and let $I \in ((\gamma_c(V))\sigma(\{I\})$ is the set of all $I' \in ((\gamma_c(V)))$ obtained by applying one graph splicing rule of P to I. Iteratively for every $n \geq 2$, $\sigma^n(\{I\})$ is defined by*
$$\sigma^n(\{I\}) = \sigma(\sigma^{n-1}(\{I\}) \text{ moreover,}$$
$$\sigma^0(\{I\}) = \{I\}$$
$$\sigma^*(\{I\}) = \bigcup_{n \in N} \sigma^n(\{I\}),$$
$L(S) = \{g \in \gamma_c(v) | \gamma(g) \neq 0$ for some $\gamma \in \sigma^*(\{I\})\}$.
The triple $S = (V, P, I)$ is called the graph splicing system.

Definition 3 (Regular Graph Splicing Schme). *A regular graph splicing scheme is a graph splicing scheme $\sigma = (V, P)$, where every graph splicing rule is regular. i.e., of the form $((h[1], E'[1]), (h[2], E'[2]); E)$ such that*

- *$h[1]$ and $h[2]$ are linear graphs and*
- *$E'[1]$ and $E'[2]$ contains exactly one edge.*

2.1   String-Graph Grammar

In this section, we provide the necessary definitions related to the study of string graph grammar. For the unexplained notions, we refer to [1].

Definition 4. *Let C be an arbitrary, but fixed set, called set of labels (or colors). A (directed hyperedge-labeled) hypergraph over C is a system (V, E, s, t, ℓ) where V is a finite set of nodes (or vertices), E is a finite set of hyperedges $s : E \to V^*$ and $t : E \to V^*$ are two mappings assigning a sequence of sources $s(e)$ and a sequence of targets $t(e)$ to each $e \in E$, and $\ell : E \to C$ is a mapping labeling each hyperedge.*

For $e \in E$, the set of nodes occurring in the sequence $att(e) = s(e).t(e)$ is called the set of attachment nodes of e and is denoted by $ATT(e)$. A hyperedge $e \in E$ is called an (m,n)-edge for some $m, n \in N$ if $|s(e)| = m$ and $|t(e)| = n$. The pair (m,n) is the type of e, denoted by $type(e)$.

Definition 5. *A multi-pointed hypergraph over C is a system $H = (V, E, s, t, \ell, begin, end)$ where (V, E, s, t, ℓ) is a hypergraph over C and $begin, end \in V^*$. Components of H are denoted by $V_H, E_H, s_H, t_H, \ell_H, begin_H, end_H$, respectively. The set of all multi-pointed hypergraphs over C is denoted by $\mathcal{H}_C$.*

$H \in \mathcal{H}_C$ is said to be an (m,n)-hypergraph for some $m, n \in N$ if $|begin_H| = m$ and $|end_H| = n$. The pair (m,n) is the type of H, denoted by $type(H)$.

An (m,n) hypergraph H over C is said to be an (m,n) graph if $|V_H| \geq 1$ and all hyperedges of $(1, 1)$ edges. The set of all $(1, 1)$ graphs over C is denoted by $\mathcal{G}_C$.

Definition 6. *A $(1, 1)$ hypergraph H over C is called a string graph if it is of the form $H = (\{v_0, v_1, \ldots, v_n\}, \{e_1, \ldots, e_n\}, s, t, \ell, (v_0, v_n))$ where $v_0, v_1, \ldots, v_n$ are pair wise distinct, $s(e_i) = v_{i-1}$, and $t(e_i) = v_i$ for $i = 1, 2, \ldots, n$. If $w = \ell(e_1) \ldots \ell(e_n)$, then the $(1, 1)$ hypergraph is called string-graph induced by w and it is denoted by $w^\bullet$.*

Graphs are drawn as usual with $(1, 1)$-edge drawn as $\circ \xrightarrow{A} \circ$ instead of $\rightarrow \boxed{A} \rightarrow$.

A string-graph of the form $\circ \xrightarrow{a_1} \circ \xrightarrow{a_2} \circ \xrightarrow{a_3} \circ \cdots \circ \xrightarrow{a_n} \circ$ provides a unique graph representation of the string $a_1 a_2 \ldots a_n \in C^+$.

Definition 7. *A hypergraph language L is said to be a string-graph language if all $H \in L$ are string graphs. The class of all string-graph languages is denoted by L_{STRING}.*

Definition 8. *A hyperedge replacement grammar $HRG = (N, T, P, Z)$ is said to be context-free string-graph grammar if the right hand sides of the productions in P as well as the axiom Z are string-graphs. The class of all string-graph languages generated by a context-free string-graph grammar is denoted by CFL.*

3   Accepting String Graph Splicing System

Definition 9. *An accepting string graph splicing system (ACCSGSS) is a 6-tuple $\Gamma = (V, T, A^\bullet, R, P, F)$ where V is an alphabet, $T \subseteq V$ is a terminal alphabet, $A^\bullet$ is a set of initial string graphs where $A \subseteq V^*$, R is the set of graph splicing rules, P and F are the finite set of string graphs over V. The elements of P are called permitting string graph. The elements of F are called forbidding string graph.*

Let $\Gamma = (V, T, A^\bullet, R, P, F)$ be an accepting string graph splicing system and a string graph $w^\bullet$, where $w \in V^*$. We define the following iterated graph splicing $\sigma_R^0(A^\bullet, w^\bullet) = \{w^\bullet\},$

$$\sigma_R^{i+1}(A^\bullet, w^\bullet) = \sigma_R^i(A, {}^\bullet w^\bullet) \cup \sigma_R(\sigma_R^i(A^\bullet, w^\bullet) \cup A^\bullet), \ i \geq 0,$$
$$\sigma_R(A^\bullet, w^\bullet) = \bigcup_{i \geq 0} \sigma_R^i(A^\bullet, w^\bullet).$$

We say a string graph language $L(S)$ $w^\bullet \in T^*$ is accepted by Γ if there exists $k \geq 0$ such that

1. $\sigma_R^k(A^\bullet, w^\bullet) \cap P \neq \phi,$
2. $\sigma_R^k(A^\bullet, w^\bullet) \cap F = \phi.$

Definition 10 (Non-uniform way). For an ACCSGSS $\Gamma = (V, T, A^\bullet, R, P, F)$ and a string graph $w^\bullet$, where $w \in V^*$. We define the following non uniform variant of iterated graph splicing where the string graph splicing is done only with axioms. $\tau_R^0(A^\bullet, w^\bullet) = \{w^\bullet\}$
$$\tau_R^{i+1}(A^\bullet, w^\bullet) = \tau_R^i(A^\bullet, w^\bullet) \cup \sigma_R(\tau_R^i(A^\bullet, w^\bullet) \cup A^\bullet), \ i \geq 0,$$
$$\tau_R^*(A^\bullet, w^\bullet) = \bigcup_{i \geq 0} \tau_R^i(A^\bullet, w^\bullet).$$

The string graph language accepted by Γ in the non uniform way is defined by
$\mathcal{L}_n(\Gamma) = \{w^\bullet \in T^* | \exists \ k \geq 0((\tau_R^k(A^\bullet, w^\bullet) \cap P \neq \phi) \tau_R^k(A^\bullet, w^\bullet) \cap F = \phi\}.$
The class of string graph languages accepted by ACCSGSS and ACCSGSS without forbidding string graph in the non uniform way is denoted by
$L_n(ACCSGSS)$ and $L_n^\phi(ACCSGSS)$.

Theorem 1. The class $L_n(ACCSGSS)$ is incomparable with the class of regular string graph languages.

Proof. It can be easily seen that the regular string graph language $\{(a^{2n})^\bullet / n \geq 1\}$ does not belong to the $\mathcal{L}_n(ACCSGSS)$ and it remains to prove that the non regular string graph language belongs to $\mathcal{L}_n(ACCSGSS)$. Let us construct a ACCSGSS,
$\Gamma = (\{a, b, x\}, \{a, b\}, \{(xx)^\bullet\}, R, \{(xb)^\bullet\}, \{(ax)^\bullet\}),$
where

$$R = \Big\{ \big(\underset{a\ \ 1\ \ \ 2\ \ b}{\circ\!\!-\!\!\bullet\ \ \bullet\!\!-\!\!\circ} \ , \ \underset{x\ \ \ 3\ \ 4\ \ x}{\circ\!\!-\!\!\bullet\ \ \bullet\!\!-\!\!\circ} \big), ((1,4),(3,2)),$$

$$\big(\underset{a\ \ 1\ \ \ 2\ \ a}{\circ\!\!-\!\!\bullet\ \ \bullet\!\!-\!\!\circ\!\!-\!\!\circ} \ , \ \underset{x\ \ x\ \ 3\ \ 4\ \ x}{\circ\!\!-\!\!\bullet\ \ \bullet\!\!-\!\!\circ} \big), ((1,4),(3,2)),$$

$$\big(\underset{x\ \ 1\ \ \ 2\ \ x}{\circ\!\!-\!\!\bullet\ \ \bullet\!\!-\!\!\circ} \ , \ \underset{x\ \ b\ \ 3\ \ 4\ \ b}{\circ\!\!-\!\!\circ\!\!-\!\!\bullet\ \ \bullet\!\!-\!\!\circ} \big), ((1,4),(3,2)) \Big\},$$

The string graph langauge $\mathcal{L}_n(\Gamma) = \{(a^m b^n)^\bullet / m > n \geq 1\}.$
Obviously, every string graph $w = (a^m b^n)^\bullet$ with $m > n \geq 1$ is accepted by Γ. After the first splicing step, we obtain both $(a^m x)^\bullet$ and $(xb^n)^\bullet$ which tends to generate $(ax)^\bullet$ and $(xb)^\bullet$ respectively. As $m > n$, $(xb)^\bullet$ is generated first and the string graph is accepted. Therefore, we observe that, as $m > n$, every graph $(a^m b^n)^\bullet$ is accepted by Γ and it follows that $\mathcal{L}_n(\Gamma)$ is not regular. Hence the proof. $\qquad\square$

Theorem 2. The class $L(ACCSGSS)$ is incomparable with the class of context-free string graph languages.

Proof. Let us consider that $ACCSGSS$

$\Gamma' = (V, \{a, b\}, A^\bullet, R, P, F\}$

where

$V = \{a, b, x, y, \tau, \ell, m\}$

$A = \{(xy)^\bullet, (yx)^\bullet, (xx)^\bullet, (ym)^\bullet, (zz)^\bullet, (\ell\ell)^\bullet\}$,

$P = \{(axxc)^\bullet\}$, and $F = \{(az\ell)^\bullet, (\ell zz)^\bullet, (yby)^\bullet\}$,

and R contains the following sets of rules:

i) $\left\{ \left(\begin{array}{c} \text{O---}\bullet\ \bullet\text{---O} \\ a \quad 1 \quad 2 \quad b \end{array}, \begin{array}{c} \text{O---}\bullet\ \bullet\text{---O} \\ y \quad 3 \quad 4 \quad x \end{array} \right), (1,4), (3,2), \right.$

$\left. \left(\begin{array}{c} \text{O---}\bullet\ \bullet\text{---O} \\ b \quad 1 \quad 2 \quad c \end{array}, \begin{array}{c} \text{O---}\bullet\ \bullet\text{---O} \\ x \quad 3 \quad 4 \quad y \end{array} \right), (1,4), (3,2) \right\}$,

ii) $\left\{ \left(\begin{array}{c} \text{O---}\bullet\ \bullet\text{---O---O} \\ a \quad 1 \quad 2 \quad a \quad x \end{array}, \begin{array}{c} \text{O---}\bullet\ \bullet\text{---O} \\ x \quad 3 \quad 4 \quad x \end{array} \right), (1,4), (3,2), \right.$

$\left(\begin{array}{c} \text{O---O---}\bullet\ \bullet\text{---O} \\ x \quad c \quad 1 \quad 2 \quad c \end{array}, \begin{array}{c} \text{O---}\bullet\ \bullet\text{---O} \\ x \quad 3 \quad 4 \quad x \end{array} \right), (1,4), (3,2),$

$\left. \left(\begin{array}{c} \text{O---O---}\bullet\ \bullet\text{---O} \\ y \quad b \quad 1 \quad 2 \quad b \end{array}, \begin{array}{c} \text{O---}\bullet\ \bullet\text{---O} \\ y \quad 3 \quad 4 \quad m \end{array} \right), (1,4), (3,2) \right\}$,

iii) $\left\{ \left(\begin{array}{c} \text{O---O---}\bullet\ \bullet\text{---O} \\ a \quad x \quad 1 \quad 2 \quad \varepsilon \end{array}, \begin{array}{c} \text{O---}\bullet\ \bullet\text{---O---O} \\ \varepsilon \quad 3 \quad 4 \quad x \quad c \end{array} \right), (1,4), (3,2) \right\}$,

iv) $\left\{ \left(\begin{array}{c} \text{O---}\bullet\ \bullet\text{---O} \\ a \quad 1 \quad 2 \quad x \end{array}, \begin{array}{c} \text{O---}\bullet\ \bullet\text{---O} \\ z \quad 3 \quad 4 \quad z \end{array} \right), (1,4), (3,2), \right.$

$\left(\begin{array}{c} \text{O---}\bullet\ \bullet\text{---O} \\ x \quad 1 \quad 2 \quad c \end{array}, \begin{array}{c} \text{O---}\bullet\ \bullet\text{---O} \\ z \quad 3 \quad 4 \quad z \end{array} \right), (1,4), (3,2),$

$\left(\begin{array}{c} \text{O---O---}\bullet\ \bullet\text{---O} \\ a \quad z \quad 1 \quad 2 \quad \varepsilon \end{array}, \begin{array}{c} \text{O---}\bullet\ \bullet\text{---O} \\ l \quad 3 \quad 4 \quad l \end{array} \right), (1,4), (3,2),$

$\left. \left(\begin{array}{c} \text{O---}\bullet\ \bullet\text{---O---O} \\ \varepsilon \quad 1 \quad 2 \quad z \quad c \end{array}, \begin{array}{c} \text{O---}\bullet\ \bullet\text{---O} \\ l \quad 3 \quad 4 \quad l \end{array} \right), (1,4), (3,2) \right\}$.

In this splicing system, we claim that

$L(\Gamma') \cap \{(a^n b^m c^p)^\bullet | n, m, p \geq 2\} = \{(a^n b^m c^n)^\bullet | n \geq 2, m > n\}$.

Let us first prove that $\{(a^n b^m c^n)^\bullet / n \geq n, m > n\} \subseteq L(\Gamma')$.

A string graph $w = (a^n b^m c^n)^\bullet$ with $m > n$ is accepted by Γ' as follows:

Step 1. When we use the rule (i) in the first splicing step we get $(a^n x)^\bullet$, $(xc^n)^\bullet$, $(yb^m c^n)^\bullet$, and $(a^n b^m y)^\bullet$.

Step 2. While using the second set of rules the number of occurrences of a and c in the string graphs having consecutive set of nodes with label a followed by a node with label x or a node with label x followed by a set of nodes with label c is decreased. We can easily observe that $(ax)^\bullet$ and $(xc)^\bullet$ are obtained for the first time in the same splicing step.

Step 3. By using the third set of rules the permitting string graph $axxc$ is obtained after the string graphs $(ax)^\bullet$, $(xc)^\bullet$ have been generated. It should be noted that none of the string graphs $(az\ell)^\bullet$ or $(\ell zc)^\bullet$ has been generated. Since $m > n$, $(yby)^\bullet$ has not been generated either, the string graph w is accepted.

Let us now consider for $p \geq 2$, $x = (a^n b^m c^p)^\bullet$, be a string graph accepted by Γ'. There is only one string graph which is accepted namely $(axxc)^\bullet$, which is obtained by applying the splicing rule (iii) to the pair $((ax)^\bullet (xc)^\bullet)$. After n

and p splicing steps, $(ax)^\bullet$ and $(xc)^\bullet$ string graphs are obtained provided the forbidding string graph $(yby)^\bullet$ has not been obtained yet.

If $n > p$, then the string graph is obtained in the $(p+1)$-th step and the accepting string graph $(axxc)^\bullet$ cannot be generated earlier than the forbidding string graph $(\ell zc)^\bullet$ which is a contradiction.

When $p < n$, also, it leads to a contradiction which is similar.

When $n = p$, after n splicing steps the string graph $((ax)^\bullet(xc)^\bullet)$ is obtained for the first time, provided the forbidding string graph has not been obtained. This is possible iff $m > n$ and the proof concludes. Hence the proof.   □

4 Conclusion

We propose to study the relationship of $\mathcal{L}_n(ACCSGSS)$ and $L^\phi(ACCSGSS)$ with other known classes.

References

1. Habel, A.: Hyperedge Replacement: Grammars and Languages. LNCS, vol. 643. Springer, Heidelberg (1992)
2. Mitrana, V., Dassow, J.: Accepting Splicing Systems with Permitting and Forbidding Words. Acta Informatica 50, 1–14 (2013)
3. Păun, G.: On the Splicing Operation. Discrete Applied Math 70, 57–79 (1996)
4. Păun, G., Rozenberg, G., Salomaa, A.: Computing by Splicing. Theoretical Computer Science 168, 321–336
5. Rozenberg, G., Salomaa, G.: Handbook of Formal Languages, vol. III. Springer, Berlin (1997)
6. Freund, R.: Splicing Systems on Graphs. In: Proceedings of Intelligence in Neural and Biological Systems, pp. 189–194. IEEE Press, New York (1995)

ABC Algorithm for VRP

Kai Shao, Kang Zhou*, Jiang Qiu, and Juan Zhao

School of Math and Computer,
Wuhan Polytechnic University, Wuhan, China
shaokai_4157@yeah.net
DDeadfish@hotmail.com
{zhaojuan876543,zhoukang_wh}@163.com

Abstract. Vehicle routing problem(VRP) has the same mathematical model with many combinatorial optimization problems, they are typical NP- hard problems in combinatorial optimization problem. In this paper, artificial bee colony (ABC) algorithm is applied to solve VRP. We propose a method to keep the colony diversity and improve the search efficiency of ABC. To validate the performance of ABC algorithm, we calculate the instance from standard VRP database. The results show that improved ABC can be used for VRP efficiently.

Keywords: VRP, Colony diversity, Search efficiency, Improved ABC.

1 Introduction

In 1959, vehicle routing problem (VRP)[1] was first proposed by Dantzig and Ramser. After many years of research, algorithms for VRP can be divided into two types as follows: exact algorithms and heuristics [2], [3]. In heuristic algorithm, artificial bee colony (ABC) algorithm for VRP has high-precision search features. In order to guarantee certain accuracy, and further improve the efficiency of the algorithm, ABC algorithm is improved in this paper.

In this paper, we put forward two methods to improve ABC algorithm. The idea that genetic algorithm include is introduced into the process that scouts search for new food source, based on the theory of evolution. The median selection strategy based on roulette is proposed and Ultimately to improve the efficiency of the ABC algorithm.

2 ABC Algorithm for VRP

2.1 Objective Function of VRP

Standard VRP mathematical model can be described as follows [4]:

$$minF(x) = M \sum_{i=1}^{n} \sum_{u=1}^{m} x_{0iu} + \sum_{i=0}^{n} \sum_{j=0}^{n} \sum_{u=1}^{m} x_{iju} c_{ij} \tag{1}$$

---

* Corresponding author.

L. Pan et al. (Eds.): BIC-TA 2014, CCIS 472, pp. 370–373, 2014.
© Springer-Verlag Berlin Heidelberg 2014

where $F(x)$ represents the objective function, M is a very large integer to ensure that the number of vehicles is the first optimization goals in VRP. m is the number of service vehicles, if vehicle u from customer i to customer j, then $x_{iju} = 1$, else $x_{iju} = 0$. c_{ij} represents travel costs between customer and customer or customer and center, etc.

2.2 Behaviors of Bees for VRP

In ABC algorithm, bees are divided into three types, include employed bee, onlooker and scout, an onlooker waits on the dance area to choose a food source before is called employed bee. If the food source does not improved within a number of times, then the employed bee related to the food source becomes scout. Each of food source in ABC algorithm is a possible VRP route. The nectar amount of a food source corresponds to the quality of VRP solution (fitness). bees behavior as follows:

(1) Employed bee randomly selects a formula from references[5] as a way for neighborhood search to generate new solution, and then the new solution compared with the current one, and we keep the better one as a new solution.

(2) Onlookers make choices rely on the nectar (fitness) of food source, and the selection probability is calculated by formula(7) as follows.

$$p_i = \frac{fit_i}{\sum\limits_{j=1}^{SN} fit_j}, \qquad (2)$$

where fit_i represents the fitness of food source i, SN is the number of food sources, which is equal to employed bee.

(3) If the food source does not be updated within a specified number of times, then employed bee becomes scout, using formula (8) to initialize the current food source.

$$x_{ij} = r * (ub - lb) + lb, \qquad (3)$$

where $x_i = (x_{i1}, x_{i2}, \cdots, x_{iD}), j \in 1, 2, \cdots, D$, ub is the upper bound and lb is the lower bound, r is a random number between 0 and 1.

2.3 Improved ABC

We make an improvement for ABC algorithm as follows:

For one hand, in ABC, the role of the scout is to look for new food source to jump out of local optimum. This makes the scout search randomly every time, leading to the the efficiency of SABC algorithm decreased . Therefore, while scouts look for new food source, the genetic idea was adopted. The method of cross as follows: For example, $X_1 = (137245986), X_2 = (245381679)$ and randomly selected two positions 3 and 5, a new instance of the first cross$X_{new} = (135385986)$; and then replace numbers which are repeated with numbers which do not appear, for example,2 ,4 and 7 instead of 3, 5 and 8, so $X'_{new} = (124375986)$ is the new food source (or solution) for a new round of mining.

On the other hand, ABC algorithm is highly depends on the probability. According to the roulette method in formula (7), so that bees are gathered to the food source which has higher fitness rapidly. Then the diversity of colony is destroyed and it is easy to fall into local optimum. We propose a selection strategy based on median roulette. The express of median selection strategy as follows:

$$p_i = \frac{|F_i - mid|}{\sum\limits_{j=1}^{SN} |F_i - mid|} \tag{4}$$

where mid is the median of fitness, F_i is the fitness of the ith food source, and the denominator is the sum of fitness. It is easy to find that when F_i is bigger or smaller than mid, the absolute value between F_i and mid will increase.

Based on the above two ideas of improvement, and combined with the VRP discrete features, improved ABC algorithm is proposed to study VRP.

3   Analysis on Validity and Feasibility of ABC Algorithm

The improved ABC algorithm was developed in C++ programming language and tested in a computer with an Intel(r) Core(TM) i3 CPU 2.13GHz microprocessor with 2 GB of RAM memory and operating system windows xp.

Improved ABC is applied to solve the set of instances proposed by Solomon [6], which is well known and widely used. A 51 customers instance from (http://www.branchandcut) is adopted in this paper. We set the colony size is 20 for computing, maximum cycle number is 2000, and limit is SN * D, where SN is the colony size and D is the number of customers. To eliminate uncertainty, we run the ABC algorithm 30 times. The curve of ABC algorithm shows in Fig.1.

From the experiment, we can find that the improved ABC is efficient in solving VRP. In this instance, we get the best solution 521, which is same as in standard VRP database. The vehicles starting from Logistics center and finally get back to the center as a path, we mark a vehicle's path both start and end with 0, the best route of improve ABC as follows:

Route 1: 6 14 25 24 43 7 23 48 27

Route 2: 46 32 1 22 20 35 36 3 28 31 26 8

Route 3: 11 16 2 29 21 50 34 30 9 38

Route 4: 5 49 10 39 33 45 15 44 37 17 12

Route 5: 47 4 42 19 40 41 13 18

4   Conclusion

In this paper, Artificial bee colony algorithm, which is a newly optimization technique, is used in solving vehicle routing problem. Vehicle routing problem

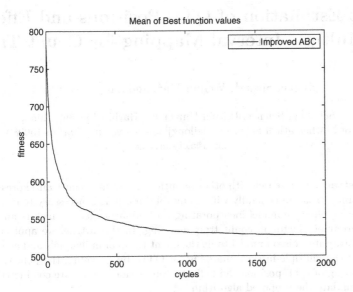

Fig. 1. Improved ABC for 51 customers VRP

is a typical combinatorial optimization problem in operational research. We improved ABC algorithm for VRP, The results show that the Improved ABC can be applied to solve vehicle routing problem successfully and we also can give further improve for ABC.

Acknowledgments. The work is supported by the National Natural Science Foundation of China (61179032, 11301405), and the Graduate Innovation Fund of Wuhan Polytechnic University (2012cx027).

References

1. Toth, P., Vigo, D.: The Vehicle Routing Problem. Society for Industrial and Applied Mathematics Philadephia, 1115–1136 (2002)
2. Zhuo, F., Wei, C.S.: The Current Situation and Development Trends on Vehicle Routing Problems. China's Strategy to the 7th Academic Communication, 997–1002 (2004)
3. Zhou, K., Chen, J.: Simulation DNA Algorithm of Set Covering Problem. Appl. Math. Inf. Sci. 8, 139–144 (2014)
4. Yong, L.X.: Models and Algorithms for Vehicle Routing Problem. Shanghai Jiao Tong University (2007)
5. Li, X., Yin, M.: A discrete Artificial Bee Colony Algorithm with Composite Mutation Strategies for Permutation Flow Shop Scheduling Problem. Scientia Iranica 19, 1921–1935 (2012)
6. Solomon, M.M.: Algorithms for the Vehicle Routing and Scheduling Problem with Time Window Contraints. Operational Research 35, 254–265 (1987)

Joint Estimation of QTL Positions and Effects in Multiple-Interval Mapping for Count Trait

Xiaona Sheng[1], Weijun Ma[2], and Ying Zhou[2,*]

[1] School of Science, Harbin University, Harbin 150086, China,
[2] School of Mathematical Sciences, Heilongjiang University, Harbin 150080, China
yzhou@aliyun.com

Abstract. Compared with other quantitative traits, count trait express discrete variation generally with countable values. It is necessary to consider an effective model incorporating both multiple genetic factors and environment factor in count trait mapping. In this article, we apply a multivariate Poisson model to fit the count traits of individuals and consider the multiple-interval mapping for QTLs by providing the joint estimating of QTL positions and effects. Simulation studies are conducted to validate the proposed algorithm.

Keywords: Count trait, Effect parameter, Multiple-interval mapping, Position parameter.

1 Introduction

Recently, quantitative trait of count has been abstracted more and more attentions, because the count trait such as branch numbers, cell numbers, etc., also have important meaning in biology and genetics [4]. Cui et al. [1] proposed a statistical model for mapping count trait, in which the Poisson distribution was used to fit the observation data. In the framework of interval mapping, Ma et al. [4] presented an EM algorithm for mapping count trait by using a way of point-to-point scan throughout the entire genome. Based on the multivariate Poisson distribution, Zhao et al. [8] reconsidered the interval mapping problem for count trait. Compared with the method in Ma et al. [4], the one proposed by Zhao et al. [8] illustrates higher precise on parameter estimation. However, the key problem considered in all the above methods is still the detection of a single QTL which may control a count trait.

A phenotype is not fully controlled by its genes. Environmental conditions can also contribute to phenotypic variation. When grown in different environment, an organism may show a range of phenotypes. This phenomenon is called phenotypic plasticity [3]. Phenotypic plasticity is a potential ability that can make a biology express a series of phenotypes in complex environment. The methods of gene mapping based on information of genetic makers, e.g., interval mapping method [5] are considered to be also efficient to mapping phenotypic plasticity of some count traits [7].

---

* Corresponding author.

L. Pan et al. (Eds.): BIC-TA 2014, CCIS 472, pp. 374–378, 2014.

In this paper, multi-locus gene mapping of count trait is considered. We develop a multiple-interval mapping method for count trait that affected by genes, environments, and gene-environment interaction, by integrating the Poisson distribution into a general mapping framework for the identification of QTL that controls the plasticity of a count trait through their environment-dependent expression. Simulation studies are performed to evaluate the estimate method, the results of which show that the new method has apparent advantages.

2 Background

Data of n backcross families is considered in our multiple-interval mapping. We suppose a count trait of the observed individuals is controlled by m latent QTLs, which are located in m adjacent marker intervals. Let $G^i_{M_t}$ $(i = 1, 2, \cdots, n, t = 1, 2, \cdots, m)$ denote the genotype combination of the tth marker interval for the ith individual, with values 1, 2, 3 and 4. Let $G^i_{Q_t}$ $(i = 1, 2, \cdots, n, t = 1, 2, \cdots, m)$ denote the tth QTL of the ith individual, with values 1 and 2. For the tth marker interval, let the recombination fractions between the left and right marker, between the left marker and the putative QTL in the interval, and between the putative QTL and the right marker be denoted, respectively, by r_{tM}, r_{t1}, r_{t2}.

For the tth marker interval. The conditional QTL genotype probabilities given marker genotype combinations

$$\omega_{j_t|i} = P(G^i_{Q_t} = j_t | G^i_{M_t} = c_t), \ i = 1, \cdots, n; \ j_t = 1, 2; \ c_t = 1, 2, 3, 4, \quad (1)$$

which can be expressed as the function of r_{t1} and r_{tM}. It can be further found that given $G^i_M = (G^i_{M_t}, \cdots, G^i_{M_m})$, $G^i_Q = (G^i_{Q_1}, \cdots, G^i_{Q_m})$ are independent and follow binomial distributions with probabilities $\omega_{j_t|i}$ given in equation (1), therefore $W_{j|i} = P(G^i_Q = j | G^i_M = c) = \omega_{j_1|i}\omega_{j_2|i}\cdots\omega_{j_m|i}$, where $i = 1, \cdots, n; \ j = (j_1, \cdots, j_m); \ c = 1, 2, \cdots, 2^{m+1}; j_t = 1, 2; \ t = 1, \cdots, m; W_{j|i}$ is conditional probability of QTL genotype combination given the marker genotype combination for the ith individual.

To consider the phenotypic plasticity, we allow the same progeny to be genotypically planted in a randomized complete block design with two levels and R clonal replicates within each treatment level. The trait values of backcross progeny i in R different replicates under treatment level k $(k=1, 2)$, are arrayed in $Y_{ik} = (Y_{ik1}, \ldots, Y_{ikR})$. We take advantage of a multivariate Poisson distribution with dimension equal to R to fit the count trait Y_{ik}, with the corresponding probability function being $Y_{ik} \sim P(Y_{ik}|\Theta_k) = \sum\limits_{j=1}^{2^m} W_{j|i}P_j(Y_{ik}|\Theta_{j|k}), \ i = 1, \cdots, n,$ where $\Theta_k = (\Theta_{1|k}, \Theta_{2|k}, \cdots, \Theta_{2^m|k})$ since there are 2^m possible QTL genotype combinations, and $\Theta_{j|k}$ denotes effect parameter corresponding QTL genotype j at treatment level k; $P_j(Y_{ik}|\Theta_{j|k})$ has formation

$$P_j(Y_{ik}|\Theta_{j|k}) = \exp\left(-\sum_{r=1}^{R}\theta_{j|kr}\right)\prod_{r=1}^{R}\frac{\theta_{j|kr}^{Y_{ikr}}}{Y_{ikr}!}\sum_{r=0}^{s_{ik}}\prod_{l=1}^{R}\binom{Y_{ikl}}{r}r!\left(\frac{\theta_{j|k0}}{\prod_{r=1}^{R}\theta_{j|kr}}\right)^r, \quad (2)$$

where $s_{ik} = min(Y_{ik1}, \ldots, Y_{ikR})$ [6]; $\theta_{j|kr}$ is the genotypic mean of the count trait for QTL genotype j in replicate r at treatment level k, and $\theta_{j|k0}$ is covariance of the count trait between all pairs of replicates.

3 Parameter Estimation

Here we assume the same mean for all the variables in our QTL mapping model, that is $\theta_{j|k1} = \ldots = \theta_{j|kR} = \theta_{j|k}$, $j = 1, 2, \cdots, 2^m$; $k = 1, 2$. Now we use $\Theta = (\Theta_k, r_{11}, r_{21}, \cdots, r_{m1})$ to denote the totality of the parameters to be estimated. Assuming that the trait values from different levels of treatment are independent, the complete data likelihood function of the unknown parameters Θ is given by

$$L_c(\Theta) = [\prod_{i=1}^{n} P(Y_{i1}|\Theta_{G_Q^i|1})W_{G_Q^i|i}][\prod_{i=1}^{n} P(Y_{i2}|\Theta_{G_Q^i|2})W_{G_Q^i|i}] . \tag{3}$$

To avoid a genome-wide scan for the existence of QTLs throughout the entire genome, we will straightly estimate the position parameters $r_{11}, r_{21}, \cdots, r_{m1}$ of QTLs. Because the QTL genotypes are important latent variables, here we will apply the EM algorithm [6],[2] to estimate Θ in the mapping of the count trait, and give the new algorithm for simultaneously estimating all parameters of interest. Next we directly list the updating values of all QTL parameters Θ .

Updating QTL positions:

After some skillful computation, we obtain that the $(s+1)$th-step iteration value of the position parameter r_{t1} is

$$r_{t1}^{(s+1)} = r_{tM} \frac{\sum_i \sum_k \sum_{j_1, \cdots, j_m / j_t} [I_{(G_{M_t}^i = 2)})\Omega_{.2.|ik}^{(s)} + I_{(G_{M_t}^i = 3)})\Omega_{.1.|ik}^{(s)}]}{\sum_i \sum_k \sum_{j_1, \cdots, j_m} \sum_{l=2}^{3} [I_{(G_{M_t}^i = l)}\Omega_{j_1, \cdots, j_m|ik}^{(s)}]},$$

where $I_{(G_{M_t}^i = l)}$ is an indicator function; the expressions of $\Omega_{j_1, \cdots, j_m|ik}^{(s)}$, $\Omega_{.1.|ik}^{(s)}$ and $\Omega_{.2.|ik}^{(s)}$ are the conditional probabilities of QTL.

Updating QTL effects:

The updating values of effect parameters in the $(s+1)$th step are as follows

$$\theta_{j|k0}^{(s+1)} = \theta_{j|k0}^{(s)} \frac{\sum_{i=1}^{n} \Omega_{j|ik}^{(s)} Z_{j|ik}^{(s)}}{\sum_{i=1}^{n} \Omega_{j|ik}^{(s)}} , \theta_{j|k}^{(s+1)} = \frac{\sum_{i=1}^{n} \Omega_{j|ik}^{(s)} \bar{Y}_{ik}}{\sum_{i=1}^{n} \Omega_{j|ik}^{(s)}} - \theta_{j|k0}^{(s+1)} ,$$

where $j = 1, 2, \cdots, 2^m$, $k = 1, 2$, and $Z_{j|ik}^{(s)}$ is the pseudovalues of progeny i within treatment level k. The EM algorithm is carried out in cycles until convergence, thus we will get the estimate of Θ. It can be seen that we generalize the result in Zhao et al. [8] and realize the multiple-interval mapping for QTLs of count trait in theory. Meanwhile, in the new algorithm we overcome the shortcoming that the position parameters cannot be estimated simultaneously in Ma et al. [4].

4   Simulations

Simulation studies are performed to illustrate and evaluate the proposed algorithm of multiple-interval mapping for QTL of count trait. For illustration, we consider the situation that a count trait is contributed by two QTL on a single chromosome. The QTL genotype has four possible values. The backcross progeny comes from two different treatment levels, $R = 3$ and sample sizes $n = 200, 500$.

To further examine the effect of different factors on the performance of the method, we considered three scenarios: (i) the genetic effect of a QTL is large and there is no covariance among the three clone replicates; (ii) the genetic effect is large and there are covariances among the three clone replicates; (iii) the genetic effect is small and there are covariances. In each simulation scenario, 1000 replicates are performed. For each sample, the new estimate strategy is used to obtain the MLEs of parameters. The corresponding mean square errors (MSEs) of each MLE are also calculated.

It can be seen from the simulation results: (1) In each scenarios, the estimates of parameters are more accurate, i.e., the estimates obtained by the proposed method are closer to their true values, and the corresponding MSEs are all smaller; (2) As expected, the precisions (MSE) of the estimates of all the parameters increase dramatically when the sample size increases, for example, the MSE of the parameter $\theta_{1|1}$ decreases from 0.0642 to 0.0062 when the sample size increases from 200 to 500. Meanwhile, as the sample size increases, the total MSE also decreases from 0.0394 to 0.0126. The estimates of other parameters also have the same trend; (3) The Poisson parameters can be better estimated when there is no covariance among replicates than when such a covariance exists.

Note that Zhao et al.'s method is just single-interval case of the mapping strategy proposed in the paper, therefore, the multiple-interval mapping strategy must outperform the one that provides the estimates of recombination fractions by using the profile of the log-likelihood ratios for each marker interval.

5   Conclusion

In this paper, we have developed an efficient multiple-interval method for mapping QTL of count trait. For a multivariate mixture model, the EM algorithm is implemented within the maximum-likelihood framework. At the same time, we have developed a new strategy for simultaneously computing the MLEs of QTL positions and effects in interval mapping. From the simulations we found all the parameters can be reasonably estimated with high precision, which shows the advantage of the new strategy.

In fact, after the estimates of all parameters of interest are obtained, we can further consider some problems of hypothesis testing. Meanwhile, we can test whether the QTLs both have effects at two treatment levels and test phenotypic plasticity.

Although we describe our methods in the context of a backcross population, it can be extended straightforwardly to the case of intercross population. Aiming at the count trait coming from more complex populations, however, the strategy of gene mapping needs further research.

Acknowledgments. This research was supported by the National Natural Science Foundation of China (Nos. 11201129 and 11371083), the Natural Science Foundation of Heilongjiang Province of China (A201207), the Scientific Research Foundation of Department of Education of Heilongjiang Province of China (No. 1253G044) and the Science and Technology Innovation Team in Higher Education Institutions of Heilongjiang Province (No. 2014TD005).

References

1. Cui, Y.H., Kim, D.Y., Zhu, J.: On the Generalized Poisson Regression Mixture Model for Mapping Quantitative Trait Loci with Count Data. Genetics 174, 2159–2172 (2006)
2. Dempster, A.P., Laird, N.M., Rubin, D.B.: Maximum Likelihood from Incomplete Data via the EM Algorithm. Journal of the Royal Statistical Society, Series B 39, 1–38 (1977)
3. Fabbrini, F., Gaudet, M., Bastien, C.: Phenotypic Plasticity, QTL Mapping and Genomic Characterization of Bud Set in BlackPpoplar. BMC Plant Biology 12, 47–53 (2012)
4. Ma, C.X., Yu, Q.B., Berg, A., et al.: A Statistical Model for Testing the Pleiotropic Control of Phenotypic Plasticity of a Count Trait. Genetics 179, 627–636 (2008)
5. Kao, C.H., Zeng, Z.B., Teasdale, R.D.: Multiple Interval Mapping for Quantitative Trait Loci. Genetics 152, 1203–1216 (1999)
6. Karlis, D.: An EM algorithm for Multivariate Poisson Distribution and Related Models. J. Appl. Stat. 30, 63–77 (2003)
7. Kliebenstein, D.J., Figuth, A., Mitchell-Olds, T.: Genetic Architecture of Plastic Methyl Jasmonate Responses in Arabidopsis Thaliana. Genetics 161, 1685–1696 (2002)
8. Zhao, L., Ma, W., Zhou, Y., et al.: Simultaneous Estimation of QTL Position and Effects for a Kind of Count Trait. In: The Proceedings of 2010 International Conference on Probability and Statistics of the International Institute for General Systems Studies, vol. 2, pp. 117–121 (2010)

Based on Different Atom of Protein Backbone Predicting Protein Structural Class

Xiaohong Shi and Qian Fan

School of Science, Xi'an Technological University,
Xi'an. 710032, China
shixh@xatu.edu.cn,
ishxh@163.com

Abstract. In this paper, we studied the protein structure database including all-α, $all - \beta$, $\alpha + \beta$ and α/β structural classes based on the Hamilton-factor of the graph theory model and proposed a new method for predicting protein structural class with Hamilton-factor based on N-atom of protein backbone. By using this method to test the 135 single proteins shows that the overall accuracy rate reached 94.81%. It provided the new idea for protein structural class.

Keywords: Hamilton path model, Hamilton factor, Protein structural class.

1 Introduction

An understanding of structure leads to an understanding of function and mechanism of action. Therefore, structural knowledge of protein is a vital if we are to proceed to a complete understanding of life at the molecular level.The tertiary structure is the full three-dimensional atomic structure of a single peptide chain. Protein can be assigned to broad structural classes based on secondary structure content and other criteria. The concept of protein structural classes was proposed by Levitt and Chothia on a visual inspection of polypeptide chain topologies in a set of 31 globular proteins. They proposed ten structural classes, four principal and six small classes of pro-tein structure. But the biological community follows the first four principal classes which are all α, all β, α/β and $\alpha + \beta$. The all-α and all-β classes represent structures that consist of mainly α−helices and β-strands respectively. The α/β and $\alpha + \beta$ classes contain both α-helices and β-strands which are mainly interspersed and segregated. Several classification methods which based on the geometrical coordinates of the $C\alpha$ backbone atoms are also proposed such as distance classifier, component coupled methods, principle component analysis and support vector machine, and many others.

Protein structural class information provides a key idea of their structure and also features related to the biological function. It is useful to distinguish the different protein structural types. Hence there is a challenge to develop automated methods for fast and accurate determination of the structural classes of proteins. In this paper, we studied the protein structure database including all-α,

L. Pan et al. (Eds.): BIC-TA 2014, CCIS 472, pp. 379–383, 2014.
© Springer-Verlag Berlin Heidelberg 2014

all-β, $\alpha + \beta$, α/β structures based on the Hamilton factor $< Hmin >$ of graph theory and proposed a new method for predicting protein structure classes with Hamilton factor based on backbone N-atom of protein. By using this method to test the 135 single proteins shows that the overall accuracy rate reached 94.81%. It provided the new idea for protein structural class.

2   Materials and Methods

The set consists of 52 proteins come from PDB that contain 13 proteins in each group which is all-α, all-β, $\alpha + \beta$, α/β structural classes. All proteins in the all-α class contain at least 40% of their amino acids in a alpha helical conformation and less than 5% of their amino acids designated as beta strand. The allβclass contains proteins with at least 40% of their amino acids in a beta strand conformation and less than 5% in a helical type structure. The α/β and $\alpha\beta$ classes contain both α-helices and β-strands which are mainly interspersed and segregated. Both $\alpha\beta$ and α/β classes contain at least 15%of their amino acids in a helical conformation and at least 10% of their amino acids in a beta-stand.

2.1   Method Based on Graph Theory

A graph G is an ordered pair of disjoint sets (V, E) such that E is a subset of the set V(2) of unordered pairs of V. Unless it is explicitly stated otherwise, we consider only finite graphs, that is , V and E are always finite. The set V is the set of vertices and E is the set of edges. If G is a graph, then V=V(G) is the vertex set of G, and E=E(G) is the edge set. An edge x,y is said to join the vertices x and y and is denoted by xy. Thus xy and yx mean exactly the same edge; the vertices x and y are the end-vertices of this edge. If xy E(G), Then x and y are adjacent, or neighboring, vertices of G, and the vertices x and y are incident with the edge xy. Two edges are adjacent if they have exactly one common end-vertex. A Hamilton path of a graph is a path containing all the vertices once of the graph. A graph has n vertices and every two vertices are adjacent then the graph is called complete n-graph and is denoted by Kn. There is at least a Hamilton path in Kn for the every two vertices are adjacent. The Minimal Hamilton Path (denoted Hmin) is the shortest Hamilton path in a weighted graph. Assume that the first and the final vertex was known, this is a limited Minimal Hamilton path conception. The number of Hamilton path in this Kn graph is (n-2)! . Finding the Hmin in a Kn graph is a NP-Complete problem. We used the greedy algorithm to solve the problem. A greedy algorithm is an algorithm that follows the problem solving heuristic of making the locally optimal choice at each stage with the hope of finding a global optimum. The Greedy algorithm: From the first vertex and coloring red, the others color-ing white. Choose an edge with minimal weight such that the vertex is red and other vertex is not. (If there are multiple edges with the same weight, any of them may be picked.) Color this edge and other vertex with red. Repeat this step unless all of the vertices are red. The Hmin was made up of the red edges and red vertices. The average edge of the Hmin in Kn is defined as Hmin divided by (n-1) and is denoted by $< Hmin >$.

2.2   The Kn Graph of a Protein Structure

A set of points in space can be represented in the form of a graph wherein the points represent the vertices of the graph and the distance between the points represents the edges. A protein structure is represented by a weighted graph in which the vertices of the graph represent the $C\alpha$ atoms and the edges represent the distance between the $C\alpha$ atoms. Then a protein with n residues length is changed to a weighted Kn. First, each residue is described as a vertex in the graph and every two vertices draw an edge. The $C\alpha$ atoms of the residues are considered as vertices and the distance between the $C\alpha$ atoms as edges. Each edge is weighted based on distance between the $C\alpha$ coordinates of the two vertices. The backbone coordinates of a protein are obtained from the PDB file. Then All Hamilton path models in the Kn graph were constructed using the $C\alpha$ traces taken directly from the distance. Finding the Hmin of the Kn using the greedy algorithm.The Kn graph constructed by the protein can be represented in algebraic form as adjacency matrices. The adjacency matrix $A = A(Kn)$ of a graph Kn with n vertices is the square n*n symmetric matrix. The presentation of graphs in adjacency matrices allows the computerized manipulation of graphs.The Step in Matlab7.0:

Input: the adjacent matrix $[a(i,j)]n * n$ of the connected weighted graph with n vertices. From the first vertex construct a candidate edges set E, in which every edge has different colored vertices. Construct the min-Hamilton path set $H = []$. Choose the minimal weight shortest edge in the candidate edges set $E(vi, vj, wij)$, $H = H + (vi, vj, wij)$, adjust the candidate edges set E. Repeat until H has $n - 2$ edges. Then : $H = H + (vj, vn, wjn)$, Compared natural Hmin with the H, $Hmin = min(Hmin, H)$ Output: $< Hmin >= Hmn/(n - 1)$ end.

2.3   Performance Comparison with Different Backbone Atom Constructed Kn

For compared purpose, we constructed a weighed graph from protein structure using the backbone N atom to represent the vertices and the edges represent the distance between the N atoms. The completed graph denoted by KnN.The Hamilton path, the minimal Hamilton path and Hamilton factor in the KnN graph were denoted by $HN, HminN$ and $< HminN >$ respectively. The $< HminN >$ of the same set of 52 proteins was calculated using the greedy algorithm by this program too. The detailed results are given in table 1.

As table 1 shown, the Hamilton factors in different classes achieve high specificity but $< Hmin >$ lower sensitivities than $< HminN >$, which indicates that backbone N-N atom distance is higher related to the secondary structure than $C\alpha$-$C\alpha$ atom. Hence, we propose a new method for recognition protein structure classes with Hamilton factor based on backbone N-atom of protein. The average $< HminN >$ of all-β is largest among three classes, the second is mixed class and all-α class is smallest. It is mean that in the same length of the proteins, HminN of all-α class is the shortest and of all-β class is the longest path.

Table 1. Comparison with different backbone atom constructed Kn

Class	n	Hmin	$< Hmin >$	HminN	$< HminN >$
α	147	561.9	3.8060	443.3125	2.9582
β	118	446.5	3.7935	388.4610	3.3356
$\alpha + \beta$	132	495.26	3.8116	407.9412	3.1717
α/β	256	986.02	3.8089	805.9573	3.0946

2.4 Hamilton Factor Based on Backbone N Atom

The test dataset contains 135 proteins, of which 24 are all-α, 24 are all-β, 87 are $\alpha\beta$ mixed class. The $\alpha+\beta$ and α/β classes were combined into a single $\alpha\beta$ mixed class. There are four steps for classing the protein test set by $< HminN >$ based on the graph theory method. Step1: Construct a weighted graph KnN from the backbone N atom coordinates of a protein structure;Step2: Using the greedy algorithm to find the minimal Hamilton path and calculate the HminN; Step3: Compared natural HN with the HminN, $HminN = min(HminN, HN)$ Then calculate $< HminN >$; Step4: If $< HminN >$ is less than or equal $2.999\mathring{A}$ then the protein constructed this Kn is predicted to be all-α class,if $< HminN >$ is larger than or equal $3.255\mathring{A}$ then the protein is predicted to be all-β class; else $< HminN >$is between $2.999\mathring{A}$ and $3.255\mathring{A}$ then the protein is belong to$\alpha\beta$ mixed class.

2.5 Performance Overall Accuracy

The performance of various methods is evaluated by the overall accuracy, which is the most commonly used metric for assessing the global performance of a multi-class problem. The overall accuracy (Q) is defined as the ratio of correctly predicted samples to all tested samples.Where Nc is the number of samples whose class have been correctly predicted and N is the total number of samples in the test dataset. This formula is used to assess the performance of individual class too.

$$Q = (Nc/N) * 100 \quad (1)$$

3 Result and Discussing

The test dataset contains 135 proteins, of which 24 are all-α, 24 are all-β, 87 are $\alpha\beta$ mixed class. By using this method to predict the 135 single proteins shows that the overall accuracy rate reached 94.81%.The details of accuracy rate is listed in Table 2.We observed that the accuracy in all-α class is lower than that of all-β and $\alpha\beta$ mixed class of proteins. This method has a good performance to predict the all-β and $\alpha\beta$ mixed classes which accuracy reached 100% and the all-α class is less accuracy rate 70.84% due to seven all-α classes are predicted to be $\alpha\beta$ mixed. reason of lower accuracy of all-α is that there are many long and extended coils in these proteins which enhance Hamilton factor value thus it was determined to be $\alpha\beta$ mixed.

Table 2. Accuracy Q obtain by this method for the 135 test proteins

Class	Nc/N	Q
All-α	17/24	70.84%
All-β	24/24	100%
Mixed $\alpha\beta$	87/87	100%
Overall	128/135	94.81%

4 Conclusions

With the increasing number of protein structures in the protein database, a structural classification is essential. This paper discussed the protein structural class
prediction as a constrained optimization problem which is finding the minimal
Hamilton path model from graph theory. The present study demonstrated that
the structural class of a protein is strongly correlated with its Hamilton factor
and backbone N atom position. The results show that the sequence length has
minor influence on successful rate and both the short sequence and the long sequences can be quite successfully predicted. We consider the backbone N atom
to represent the residue have more essential ability related the protein structural classification and secondary structure elements. A major advantage of this
method is its ability to operate using only the backbone N atom positions. Our
study will provide the new ideas for protein structural class and the prediction
of protein structure.

References

1. Metfessel, B.A., Saurugger, P.N., Connelly, D.P., Rich, S.S.: Cross-validation
   of Protein Structural Class Prediction Using Statistical Clustering and Neural
   Networks. Protein Science 2, 1171–1182 (1993)
2. Du, Q.-S., Jiang, Z.-Q., He, W.-Z., Li, D.-P., Chou, K.-C.: Amino Acid Principal
   Component Analysis and its Applications in Protein Structural Class Prediction.
   Journal of Bimolecular Structure and Dynamics 23, 635–640 (2006)
3. Suhu, S.S., Panda, G., Nanda, S.J., Mishra, S.K.: Protein Structural Class Prediction Using Differential Evolution. International Journal of Recent Trends in Engineering 2, 63–65 (2009)
4. Dong, Q., Zhou, S.: A New Taxonomy-Based Protein Fold Recognition Approach
   Based on Autocross-Covariance Transformation. Bioingormatics 20, 2655–2662
   (2009)

On Directional Bias for Network Coverage

Graeme Smith[1], J.W. Sanders[2,3], and Qin Li[1]

[1] School of Information Technology and Electrical Engineering
The University of Queensland, Australia
[2] African Institute for Mathematical Science, South Africa
[3] Department of Mathematical Sciences, Stellenbosch University, South Africa

Abstract. Random walks have been proposed as a simple method of efficiently searching, or disseminating information throughout, communication and sensor networks. In nature, animals (such as ants) tend to follow *correlated* random walks, i.e., random walks that are biased towards their current heading. In this paper, we investigate whether or not complementing random walks with directional bias can decrease the expected discovery and coverage times in networks. To do so, we use a macro-level model of a directionally biased random walk based on Markov chains. By focussing on regular, connected networks, the model allows us to efficiently calculate expected coverage times for different network sizes and biases. Our analysis shows that directional bias can significantly reduce the coverage time, but only when the bias is below a certain value which is dependent on the network size.

Keywords: Random walks, Markov chains, Network coverage.

1 Introduction

The concept of a random walk was introduced over a century ago by Pearson [11]. Recently, random walks have been proposed for searching, or disseminating information throughout, communications and sensor networks where the network's structure is dynamic, or for other reasons unknown [3,5,1,12]. They are ideal for this purpose as they require no support information like routing tables at nodes [2] — the concept of a random walk being for the agent performing the walk to move randomly to *any* connected node.

The efficiency of random-walk-based algorithms can be measured in terms of the average number of steps the agent requires to cover every node in the network (and hence be guaranteed to find the target node in the case of search algorithms). This is referred to as the *coverage time* under the assumption that the agent takes one step per time unit. Obviously, improving the coverage time for algorithms is an important goal.

For this reason it has been suggested that random walks should be constrained, e.g., to prevent an agent returning to its last visited node, or to direct an agent to parts of the network where relatively few nodes have been visited [7]. We take a similar approach in this paper. We base our movement model on that observed in nature. Many models used by biologists to describe the movement of ants and

L. Pan et al. (Eds.): BIC-TA 2014, CCIS 472, pp. 384–388, 2014.
© Springer-Verlag Berlin Heidelberg 2014

other animals are based on *correlated* random walks, i.e., random walks which are biased to the animal's current direction [8]. Based on our own observations of ants, we also investigate including a small probability of a non-biased step at any time to model occasional random direction changes.

Directionally biased walks in networks have been investigated by only one other group of researchers. Fink et al. [6] look at the application of directional bias in a cyber-security system in which suspect malicious nodes must be visited by multiple agents. They compare coverage times for directional bias with those for pure random walks, and conclude that directionally biased walks are more efficient. This conclusion, however, is based on micro-level simulation, i.e., direct simulation of agents taking steps, for a single network size and bias. It cannot be generalised to arbitrary network size or bias.

The micro-level simulation approach of Fink et al. requires coverage times to be calculated as the average of multiple runs. They performed 500 simulation runs for each movement model. Such an approach is impractical for a deeper investigation of the effect of directional bias which considers various network sizes and biases. For that reason, in this paper we use a more abstract, macro-level model of a directionally biased walk. It builds on the work of Mian et al. [9] for random walks, describes the directionally biased walk in terms of a Markov chain [10] and allows us to calculate the coverage time for a given network size and bias directly.

2 Directionally Biased Walks

The investigation in this paper focusses on regular, connected graphs where each node has exactly 8 neighbours. Furthermore, to allow our graphs and hence networks to be finite, we wrap the north and south edges and the east and west edges to form a torus. Our aim is to provide a deeper analysis of directional bias than that by Fink et al. [6] which also investigates the notion on such regular toroidal graphs.

For modelling directional bias in nature, biologists typically use the von Mises distribution [4], a continuous angular function with a parameter κ which affects heading bias. We do not adopt the von Mises distribution in our approach for two reasons. Firstly, we have only a discrete number of directions and so do not require a continuous distribution. Secondly, as in random walks, we would like the computations the agent needs to perform to be simple. Our notion of directional bias limits our agent to choose either its current direction with a probability p (referred to as the *bias*), or any neighbouring direction, i.e., $\pi/4$ radians (45°) clockwise or anti-clockwise from the current direction, with equal probability of $(1 - p)/2$. When the bias p is high, this movement model approximates (discretely) that of the von Mises distribution for a high value of κ.

We also investigate adding occasional random steps to our directionally biased walks. The idea is that with probability r the agent will make a random, rather than directionally biased, step. This better matches our own observations of the movements of ants.

3   A Macro-level Model

To analyse coverage time under our models of directional bias, we adapt a Markov-chain model [10] and associated formula for coverage time developed for random walks by Mian et al. [9]. Specifically, Mian et al. modify the standard Markov-chain model for a random walk so that the starting node is an *absorbing node*, i.e., a node from which the probability of a transition to any neighbour is 0 (and the probability of a transition to itself is 1). They then model the system as starting from the state distribution after the initial distribution, i.e., that in which all neighbours of the starting node have probability $1/n$ where n is the number of neighbours per node. This allows them to calculate the expected number of nodes covered at any step k directly from the probability of being in the starting node at step k. Coverage time then corresponds to the smallest k where the probability of being in the starting node is 1.

We add an additional dimension to the representation of a network: the current direction of movement. For a network with N nodes, the transition probability matrix for the Markov-chain model is hence no longer of size $N \times N$ but $n * N \times n * N$ where n is the number of neighbours per node (and hence the number of directions of movement). Since there are n positions corresponding to the starting node (one for each direction from which the starting node was entered) there are n absorbing positions in the matrix. Coverage time is calculated in a similar fashion to that of Mian et al. by summing the probabilities of being in these n nodes. Full details of our model can be found in [13].

4   Investigating Directional Bias

To perform our investigation into directional bias, we plotted graphs of coverage time versus bias (for bias values from 0 to 0.95 in steps of 0.05) for graph sizes 5×5 (25 nodes) to 15×15 (225 nodes). We calculated the time for coverage of 99% of the network nodes. This was to avoid problems arising with 100% coverage when the coverage converged to a point just below the network size due to inaccuracies in the floating-point arithmetic.

The graph for the 5×5 network is shown in Fig. 1. The horizontal line represents the coverage time for a random walk, and the curved line that for a directionally biased walk under the range of biases. The general shape of the latter and its position in relation to the horizontal line for random bias was consistent for all network sizes in the range considered. A number of interesting results follow from this analysis.

1. The best coverage time is achieved for a bias of 0. This corresponds to an agent which always changes direction by $\pi/4$ radians on every step.
2. While for low directional biases (0 up to around 0.7 for the 5×5 case) coverage time is less than that for a random walk, for higher biases it is greater than that for a random walk.

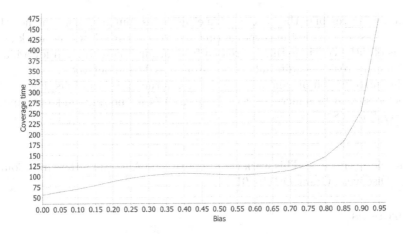

Fig. 1. Random vs directionally biased walk for a network of 5 × 5 nodes

3. The value of the bias at which a directionally biased walk becomes less efficient than a random walk (from here on called the *cross-over bias*), progressively increases as the size of the network increases. It is around 0.74 for a 5 × 5 network, and 0.93 for a 15 × 15 network.
4. The improvement in efficiency of directional bias increases as the size of the network increases. For a directional bias of 0.5 the increase in efficiency is less than 25% for a 5 × 5 network, and around 60% for a 15 × 15 network.

Point 1 is particularly interesting as it suggests a new movement model that was not initially anticipated. Our initial motivation was to investigate movement models similar to those observed in nature, which are best represented by a von Mises distribution. However, low values of bias in our movement model (including the value 0) do not approximate a von Mises distribution. The new model, although perhaps impractical as a means of movement in nature, can nevertheless be readily implemented in network search and dissemination algorithms.

Point 2 is also interesting as it indicates that directional bias is only effective in reducing coverage time when the bias is not too large. This result was also unanticipated as directional bias in the movement of animals tends to be high. However, the areas over which such animals move would correspond to networks significantly larger than those we considered. Point 3 anticipates that the cross-over bias would be higher in such networks. This conjecture is supported by the work of Fink et al. [6] whose micro-level simulation of a network of 100 × 100 nodes shows that a directionally biased walk (approximating a von Mises distribution with high κ) is more efficient than a random walk.

The second part of our investigation considered the movement model where occasional random steps are added to a directionally biased walk. The following results emerged from this analysis.

1. As may have been predicted, the addition of random steps moves the coverage time closer to that of a random walk. Hence, for bias values lower than

the cross-over bias the coverage time increases, but for values higher than the cross-over value the coverage time decreases. For a 5×5 network and a bias of 0 the coverage time increased from around 55 to 70, and for a bias of 0.95 it decreased significantly from around 470 to about 158.

2. The introduction of random steps increases the cross-over bias. For $r = 0.1$ the cross-over bias increases to 0.78 (from 0.74 for no random steps) and for $r = 0.2$ to 0.84.

Acknowledgements. This work was supported by Australian Research Council (ARC) Discovery Grant DP110101211.

References

1. Avin, C., Brito, C.: Efficient and robust query processing in dynamic environments using random walk techniques. In: International Symposium on Information Processing in Sensor Networks (IPSN 2004), pp. 277–286. ACM (2004)
2. Avin, C., Krishnamachari, B.: The power of choice in random walks: An empirical study. In: ACM International Symposium on Modelling, Analysis and Simulation of Wireless and Mobile Systems (MSWiM 2006), pp. 219–228. ACM (2006)
3. Bar-Yossef, Z., Friedman, R., Kliot, G.: RaWMS — Random walk based lightweight membership service for wireless and ad hoc networks. In: ACM International Symposium on Mobile Ad Hoc Networking and Computing (MobiHoc 2006), pp. 238–249. ACM (2006)
4. Crist, T.O., MacMahon, J.A.: Individual foraging components of harvester ants: Movement patterns and seed patch fidelity. Insectes Sociaux 38(4), 379–396 (1991)
5. Dolev, S., Schiller, E., Welch, J.: Random walk for self-stabilizing group communication in ad hoc networks. IEEE Transactions on Mobile Computing 5(7), 893–905 (2006)
6. Fink, G.A., Berenhaut, K.S., Oehmen, C.S.: Directional bias and pheromone for discovery and coverage on networks. In: IEEE International Conference on Self-Adaptive and Self-Organizing Systems (SASO 2012), pp. 1–10. IEEE (2012)
7. Lima, L., Barros, J.: Random walks on sensor networks. In: International Symposium on Modeling and Optimization in Mobile, Ad Hoc and Wirless Networks and Workshops (WiOpt 2007), pp. 1–5. IEEE (2007)
8. McCulloch, C.E., Cain, M.L.: Analyzing discrete movement data as a correlated random walk. Ecology 70, 383–388 (1989)
9. Mian, A.N., Beraldi, R., Baldoni, R.: On the coverage process of random walk in wireless ad hoc and sensor networks. In: IEEE International Conference on Mobile, Ad-hoc and Sensor Systems (MASS 2010), pp. 146–155. IEEE (2010)
10. Norris, J.R.: Markov Chains. Cambridge University Press (1998)
11. Pearson, K.: The problem of the random walk. Nature 72, 294 (1905)
12. Sadagopan, N., Krishnamachari, B., Helmy, A.: Active query forwarding in sensor networks. Journal of Ad Hoc Networks 3(1), 91–113 (2005)
13. Smith, G., Sanders, J.W., Li, Q.: A macro-level model for investigating the effect of directional bias on network coverage. CoRR, abs/1407.5762 (2014)

Computational Efficiency and Universality of Timed P Systems with Membrane Creation

Bosheng Song[1], Mario J. Pérez-Jiménez[2], and Linqiang Pan[1,*]

[1] Key Laboratory of Image Information Processing and Intelligent Control,
School of Automation, Huazhong University of Science and Technology,
Wuhan 430074, Hubei, China
boshengsong@163.com, lqpan@mail.hust.edu.cn
[2] Department of Computer Science and Artificial Intelligence,
University of Sevilla, Avda. Reina Mercedes s/n, 41012 Sevilla, Spain
marper@us.es

Abstract. In this work, inspired from this biological motivation that in living cells, the execution time of different biological processes is difficult to know precisely and very sensitive to environmental factors that might be hard to control, the computational efficiency and universality of timed P systems with membrane creation are investigated. Specifically, we give a time-free solution to SAT problem by a family of P systems with membrane creation in the sense that the correctness of the solution is irrelevant to the times associated with the involved rules. We further show that time-free P systems with membrane creation are computationally universal.

Keywords: P system, Membrane creation, Time-free solution, SAT problem, Universality.

1 Introduction

P systems are distributed and parallel computing devices initiated by Gh. Păun [1]. The computational models are inspired by the structure and the functioning of living cells, and the ways in which cells are organized in tissues and higher order biological structures. The present work deals with P systems with membrane creation, which have similar types of rules as P systems with active membranes [2] except that membrane division rules are substituted for membrane creation rules. A membrane creation rule has no replication of objects into the new membrane, which becomes a daughter of the original membrane (the depth of the membrane structure can increase). In semantics of P systems with membrane creation, there exists a global clock, which is assumed to mark the time for the system, in each tick of the global clock, all the applicable rules are applied simultaneously, and the execution of rules takes exactly one time unit. However, in biological reality, the execution time of a chemical reaction might be difficult to know precisely and usually such a parameter is very sensitive to environmental

---

* Corresponding author.

L. Pan et al. (Eds.): BIC-TA 2014, CCIS 472, pp. 389–394, 2014.
© Springer-Verlag Berlin Heidelberg 2014

factors that might be hard to control. With this biological reality, it is rather natural to consider timed P systems with membrane creation.

In this work, the computational efficiency and universality of timed P systems with membrane creation are investigated. Specifically, we give a time-free solution to SAT problem by a family of P systems with membrane creation in the sense that the correctness of the solution is irrelevant to the times associated with the involved rules. We further show that time-free P systems with membrane creation are computationally universal.

2   Timed P Systems with Membrane Creation

2.1   Timed and Time-Free P Systems with Membrane Creation

We present the definition of timed P systems with membrane creation, for the notion of P systems with membrane creation, one may refer to [3] for more details.

Definition 1. *A timed P system with membrane creation of degree $m \geq 1$ is a construct*

$$\Pi(e) = (O, H, \mu, w_1, \ldots, w_m, R, i_{out}, e),$$

where:

- *O is the alphabet of objects;*
- *H is a finite set of labels for membranes;*
- *μ is the initial membrane structure, consisting of m membranes; membranes are labelled (not necessarily in an injective way) with elements of H;*
- *$w_1, \ldots, w_m$ are strings over O, describing the initial multisets of objects placed in the m regions of μ;*
- *$i_{out} \in \{0, 1, \ldots, m\}$ is the output region (0 is the label representing the environment);*
- *e is a mapping from the finite set of rules R into the set of natural numbers $\mathbb{N}$, which represent the execution time of the rules.*
- *R is a finite set of rules of the forms:*
  - *(a) $[\, a \rightarrow v \,]_h$, $h \in H$, $a \in O, v \in O^*$ (object evolution rules), associated with membranes and depending only on the label of the membrane.*
  - *(b) $a[\ ]_h \rightarrow [\, b \,]_h$, $h \in H, a \in O, b \in O \cup \{\lambda\}$ (send-in communication rules). An object is introduced in the membrane, possibly modified.*
  - *(c) $[\, a \,]_h \rightarrow [\ ]_h b$, $h \in H, a \in O, b \in O \cup \{\lambda\}$ (send-out communication rules). An object is sent out of the membrane, possibly modified.*
  - *(d) $[\, a \,]_h \rightarrow b$, $h \in H, a \in O, b \in O \cup \{\lambda\}$ (dissolving rules). A membrane is dissolved in reaction with an object, which can be modified.*
  - *(e) $[\, a \rightarrow [\, v \,]_{h_2}]_{h_1}$, $h_1, h_2 \in H, a \in O, v \in O^*$ (creation rules). In reaction with an object, a new membrane is created. This new membrane is placed inside of the membrane of the object, which triggers the rule and has associated an initial multiset and a label.*

Definition 2. *A timed polarization P system with membrane creation of degree* $m \geq 1$ *is a timed P system with membrane creation* $\Pi(e) = (O, H, \mu, w_1, \ldots, w_m, R, i_{out}, e)$, *where membranes are electrically polarized, and the finite set of rules in* R *of the following forms:*

(a′) $[\, a \to v \,]_h^\alpha$, $h \in H, \alpha \in \{+, -, 0\}, a \in O, v \in O^*$ *(object evolution rules).*

(b′) $a[\;]_h^{\alpha_1} \to [\, b \,]_h^{\alpha_2}$, $h \in H, \alpha_1, \alpha_2 \in \{+, -, 0\}, a \in O, b \in O \cup \{\lambda\}$ *(send-in communication rules).*

(c′) $[\, a \,]_h^{\alpha_1} \to [\;]_h^{\alpha_2} b$, $h \in H, \alpha_1, \alpha_2 \in \{+, -, 0\}, a \in O, b \in O \cup \{\lambda\}$ *(send-out communication rules).*

(d′) $[\, a \,]_h^{\alpha} \to b$, $h \in H, \alpha \in \{+, -, 0\}, a \in O, b \in O \cup \{\lambda\}$ *(dissolving rules).*

(e′) $[\, a \to [\, v \,]_{h_2}^{\alpha_2}]_{h_1}^{\alpha_1}$, $h_1, h_2 \in H, \alpha_1, \alpha_2, \alpha_3 \in \{+, -, 0\}, a \in O, v \in O^*$ *(creation rules).*

A timed (polarization) P system with membrane creation $\Pi(e)$ works in the following way. An external clock is assumed, which marks time-units of equal length, starting from instant 0. According to this clock, the step t of computation is defined by the period of time that goes from instant $t - 1$ to instant t. If a membrane i contains a rule r from types (a) – (e) (resp. (a′) – (e′)) selected to be executed, then execution of such rule takes $e(r)$ time units to complete. Therefore, if the execution is started at instant j, the rule is completed at instant $j + e(r)$ and the resulting objects become available only at the beginning of step $j + e(r) + 1$. When a rule r from types (a) – (e) (resp. (a′) – (e′)) is started, then the occurrences of symbol-objects subject to this rule cannot be subject to other rules until the implementation of the rule completes. In particular, for polarization P system with membrane creation, several rules can be applied to different objects in the same membrane simultaneously if the polarization of the membrane is not modified during the applications of these rules.

Definition 3. *A P system with membrane creation* Π *is time-free if and only if every timed P system with membrane creation in the set* $\{\Pi(e) \mid e : R \to \mathbb{N} - \{0\}\}$ *produces the same set of vectors of natural numbers.*

The set of vectors generated by a time-free P system with membrane creation Π is denoted by $Ps(\Pi)$. By $PsOP^{free}(\text{list-of-rules})$ we denote the families of the sets of vectors generated by time-free P systems with membrane creation, using rules as specified in the *list-of-rules*, *free* stands for *time-free*.

2.2 Time-Free Solutions to the Decision Problems by P Systems with Membrane Creation

In timed (polarization) P systems with membrane creation, we use rule starting step (RS-step, for short) to define the computation step [4]. In such P systems, the execution time of rules is determined by the time mapping e, and it is possible the existence of rule whose execution time is inherently exponential.

Definition 4. *In timed P systems with membrane creation, a computation step is called a RS-step if at this step at least one rule starts its execution, that is,* steps in which some objects "start" to evolve or some membranes "start" to change.

A *decision problem*, X, is a pair (I_X, Θ_X) such that I_X is a language over a finite alphabet (who elements are called *instances*) and Θ_X is a total Boolean function (that is, predicate) over I_X.

From Definition 4, we know that the number of RS-step in a computation characterize how "fast" the constructed P system with membrane creation to time-freely solve a decision problem.

Definition 5. *Let* $X = (I_X, \Theta_X)$ *be a decision problem. We say that* X *is solvable in polynomial RS-steps by a family of recognizer (polarization) P systems with membrane creation* $\mathbf{\Pi} = \Pi_u, u \in I_X$ *in a time-free manner, if the following items are true:*

- *the family* $\mathbf{\Pi}$ *is polynomially uniform by a Turing machine; that is, there exists a deterministic Turing machine working in polynomial time which constructs the system* Π_u *from the instance* $u \in I_X$.
- *the family* $\mathbf{\Pi}$ *is time-free polynomially bounded; that is, there exists a polynomial function* $p(n)$ *such that for any time-mapping* e *and for each* $u \in I_X$, *all computations in* $\Pi_u(e)$ *halt in, at most,* $p(|u|)$ *RS-steps.*
- *the family* $\mathbf{\Pi}$ *is time-free sound (with respect to* X *); that is, for any time-mapping* e, *the following property holds: if for each instance of the problem* $u \in I_X$ *such that there exists an accepting computation of* $\Pi_u(e)$, *we have* $\Theta_X(u) = 1$.
- *the family* $\mathbf{\Pi}$ *is time-free complete (with respect to* X *); that is, for any time-mapping* e, *the following property holds: if for each instance of the problem* $u \in I_X$ *such that* $\Theta_X(u) = 1$, *every computation of* $\Pi_u(e)$ *is an accepting computation.*

We also say that the family $\mathbf{\Pi}$ provides an efficient *time-free solution* to the decision problem X.

3   Main Results

Theorem 1. SAT *problem can be solved in polynomial RS-steps by a family of polarization P systems with membrane creation with rules of types* (a'), (b'), (c'), (d'), (e') *in a time-free manner, where the correctness of the solution is irrelevant to the times associated with the involved rules.*

Proof. (Sketch) Let us consider a propositional formula $C = C_1 \wedge C_2 \wedge \ldots \wedge C_m$, with $C_i = y_{i,1} \vee \ldots \vee y_{i,p_i}$, for some $m \geq 1, p_i \geq 1$, and $y_{i,j} \in \{x_k, \neg x_k \mid 1 \leq k \leq n\}$, for each $1 \leq i \leq m, 1 \leq j \leq p_i$, where $\neg x_k$ is the negation of a propositional variable x_k, the two connections $\vee, \wedge$ are *or*, *and*, respectively.

For the given propositional formula C, we construct the P system with membrane creation Π solving C according to Definition 5.

Theorem 2. $PsOP^{free}((a),(b),(c),(d),(e)) = PsRE.$

Proof. (Sketch) Consider a matrix grammar $G = (N,T,S,M,F)$ with appearance checking in the binary normal form, with $N = N_1 \cup N_2 \cup \{S, \#\}$. Each matrix of the form $(X \to \lambda, A \to x), X \in N_1, A \in N_2, x \in T^*$, is replaced by $(X \to Z, A \to x)$, where Z is a new symbol. The obtained grammar is denoted by G'. Assume that we have n_1 matrices of the form $(X \to Y, A \to x)$, with $X \in N_1, Y \in N_1 \cup \{Z\}, A \in N_2, x \in (N_2 \cup T)^*$, and n_2 matrices of the form $(X \to Y, A \to \#)$, with $X, Y \in N_1, A \in N_2$.

We construct the time-free P system with membrane creation Π to simulate each matrix. We mention that once the trap object appears in the system, the computation will never stop, the simulation of the matrix $m_i = (X \to Y, A \to \#), n_1 + 1 \le i \le n_1 + n_2$ is successful if and only if the computation will stop. The results of the simulation are the terminal symbols, which are sent out of the system. Thus, system Π exactly simulates the terminal derivations in G', and the object Z cannot evolve. Thus, we have $Ps(L(G)) = Ps(\Pi)$.

4   Conclusions

In this work, the computational efficiency and universality of timed P systems with membrane creation are investigated. The solution to SAT problem in this work is semi-uniform, it remains open how we can construct a uniform time-free solution to SAT problem. The P systems constructed in the proof of Theorem 1 have polarizations on membranes, it remains open how we construct P systems without polarizations on membranes to time-freely solve SAT problem.

In membrane computing, some asynchronous P systems, such as asynchronous P systems with active membrane [5], asynchronous spiking neural P systems [7], asynchronous spiking neural P systems with local synchronization [6] have been proposed. The study on computation efficiency of the asynchronous P systems deserves for further research.

Acknowledgments. The work of L. Pan was supported by National Natural Science Foundation of China (61033003, 91130034, and 61320106005), Ph.D. Programs Foundation of Ministry of Education of China (20100142110072 and 2012014213008), and Natural Science Foundation of Hubei Province (2011CDA027). The work of M.J. Pérez-Jiménez was supported by "Ministerio de Economía y Competitividad" of Spanish government (TIN2012-37434), cofunded by FEDER funds.

References

1. Păun, G.: Computing with Membranes. J. Comput. Syst. Sci. 61(1), 108–143 (2000)
2. Păun, G.: P Systems with Active Membranes: Attacking NP-complete Problems. J. Auto. Langua. Combinat. 6(1), 75–90 (2001)

3. Păun, G., Rozenberg, G., Salomaa, A. (eds.): The Oxford Handbook of Membrane Computing. Oxford University Press (2010)
4. Song, T., Macías-Ramos, L.F., Pan, L., Pérez-Jiménez, M.J.: Time-free Solution to SAT Problem Using P Systems with Active Membranes. Theor. Comput. Sci. 529, 61–68 (2014)
5. Frisco, P., Govan, G., Leporati, A.: Asynchronous P Systems with Active Membranes. Theor. Comput. Sci. 429, 74–86 (2012)
6. Song, T., Pan, L., Păun, G.: Asynchronous Spiking Neural P Systems with Local Synchronization. Information Sciences 219, 197–207 (2013)
7. Cavaliere, M., Ibarra, O.H., Păun, G.: Asynchronous Spiking Neural P Systems. Theor. Comput. Sci. 410(24), 2352–2364 (2009)

A Membrane-Inspired Evolutionary Algorithm Based on Artificial Bee Colony Algorithm

Xiaoxiao Song and Jun Wang

School of Electrical and Information Engineering, Xihua University
Chengdu, Sichuan, P.R. China, 610039
sxx_pippen@163.com, 745257101@qq.com

Abstract. The paper presents a novel membrane-inspired evolutionary algorithm, named artificial bee colony algorithm based on P systems (ABCPS), which combines P systems and artificial bee colony algorithm (ABC). ABCPS uses the evolutionary rules of ABC, the one level membrane structure, and transformation or communication rules in P systems to design its algorithm. Experiments have been conducted on a set of 29 benchmark functions. The results demonstrate good performance of ABCPS in solving complex function optimization problems when compared with ABC.

Keywords: Artificial bee colony algorithm, P system, Function optimization.

1 Introduction

As a young and vigorous branch of natural computing, membrane computing was introduced by Gheorghe Păun [1] in 1998. It is inspired by the structure and the functioning of living cells, which focuses on abstracting computing models and membrane systems. Membrane-inspired evolutionary algorithms (MIEAs) [2, 3] are considered as a class of hybrid optimization algorithms after Nishida [4–6] first proposed this concept by combining P systems and meta-heuristic search methodologies to solve traveling salesman problems. A similar algorithm was also applied to solve the min storage problem [7]. Huang [8, 9] and Cheng [10] combined genetic algorithm and differential evolution with membrane systems to solve some single- and multi-objective optimization problems. Quantum-inspired evolutionary algorithm based on P systems was proposed to solve some classical theory problems [11, 12] and practical problems [13–20]. Also some novel MIEAs based on particle swarm optimization [21] and artificial fish swarm algorithm [22] were proposed. All these investigations support the claim made by Păun and Pérez-Jiménez [23] that the MIEA is a new research direction with a well-defined scope.

In this paper, a novel MIEA, called artificial bee colony algorithm based on P systems (ABCPS), is presented. This is the first attempt to discuss the interaction between artificial bee colony algorithm and P systems. Based on the concepts and principles of artificial bee colony algorithm and P systems, the

L. Pan et al. (Eds.): BIC-TA 2014, CCIS 472, pp. 395–410, 2014.

ABCPS employs the evolutionary rules of artificial bee colony algorithm, the one level membrane structure (OLMS) and transformation or communication rules in P systems. A large number of experiments are carried out on function optimization problems to verify the effectiveness of the ABCPS. Experimental results show that ABCPS performs better than its counterpart artificial bee colony algorithm (ABC).

This paper is organized as follows. In Section 2 first gives a brief introduction of P systems and ABC algorithm, and then discusses ABCPS in detail. Section 3 addresses some discussions with regard to parameter setting and experimental results. Section 4 concludes this paper.

2   ABCPS

This section starts with basic P systems concepts and a presentation of the ABC. The rest of this section is dedicated to a presentation of ABCPS.

2.1   P Systems

P systems could be divided into three groups: cell-like P systems, tissue-like P systems and neural-like P systems [24]. The structure of cell-like P systems is the basic structure of other P systems. The membrane structure of a cell-like P system is shown in Fig. 1. The outermost membrane is the skin membrane. Outside of the skin membrane is the environment. Usually, there are some other membranes inside the skin membrane. We call the spaces between membranes regions. The region just inside the skin membrane is the outermost region, and the region in an elementary membrane is an elementary region. In membrane computing, regions contain multisets of objects and sets of evolution rules.

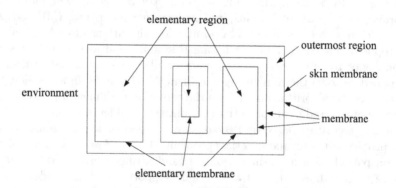

Fig. 1. The membrane structure of a cell-like P system

A cell-like P system is formally defined as follows [1, 25]:

$$\Pi = [V, T, \mu, w_1, \ldots, w_m, R_1, \ldots, R_m, i_0].\tag{1}$$

where:
(i) V is an alphabet; its elements are called objects;
(ii) $T \subseteq V$ is the output alphabet;
(iii) μ is a membrane structure consisting of m membranes; m is called the degree of Π;
(iv) w_i, $1 \leq i \leq m$, are strings representing multisets over V associated with the regions, $1, 2, \ldots, m$ of μ;
(v) R_i, $1 \leq i \leq m$, are finite sets of evolution rules associated with the regions, $1, 2, \ldots, m$ of μ;
(vi) i_0 is a number between 1 and m which specifies the output membrane of Π.

The rules of R_i, $1 \leq i \leq m$, have the form $a \rightarrow v$, where $a \in V$ and $v \in (V \times \{here, out, in\})^*$. The multiset v consists of pairs (b,t), $b \in V$ and $t \in \{here, out, in\}$. *here* means when the rule is used in one region, b will stay in the region; *out* means that b exits the region and *in* means that b will be communicated to one of the membranes contained in the current region.

2.2 ABC

Artificial bee colony algorithm, ABC for short, a successful evolutionary paradigm of swarm intelligence inspired from the behaviors of honey bees, was introduced by Karaboga to optimize multi-variable and multi-modal continuous functions [26]. ABC algorithm was developed based on the model of foraging behavior of honey bee colonies proposed by Tereshko and Loengarov [27]. Numerical comparisons demonstrated that performance of the ABC algorithm is competitive to some other swarm intelligent algorithms [28–30]. For ABC employs fewer control parameters and ease of implementation, it has been applied to solve many practical optimization problems [31–33].

In ABC, the foraging bees are classified into three groups: employed bees, onlookers and scouts. The position of a food source represents a possible solution for the problem and the nectar amount of a food source represents the quality of the associated solution. For every food source, there is only one employed bee. It means that the number of employed bees is equal to the number of food sources. And the number of onlookers is equal to the number of employed bees too.

At the first step, an initial population with SN number of solutions is generated by random approach. Let a D-dimensional vector $x_i = \{x_{i1}, x_{i2}, \ldots, x_{iD}\}$ represents the ith food source in the population. Each food source is generated as follows:

$$x_{ij} = x_{ij,min} + rand(0, 1)(x_{ij,max} - x_{ij,min}) \tag{2}$$

where $i = 1, \ldots, SN$, $j = 1, \ldots, D$, $x_{ij,min}$ and $x_{ij,max}$ are the lower and upper bounds for the dimension j.

An employed bee generates a new neighboring solution around its associated solution as follows:

$$x_{new,j} = x_{ij} + \Phi_{ij}(x_{ij} - x_{kj}) \tag{3}$$

where $i \in \{1, \ldots, SN\}, k \in \{1, \ldots, SN\} \cap k \neq j, j \in \{1, \ldots, D\}$, $x_{new,j}$ is jth dimensional of the new solution and Φ_{ij} is a random number between $[-1, 1]$. Then x_{new} will be evaluated and compared with x_i, and the solution with high quality will be the winner. After that, the employed bee returns to the hive and share information with onlookers.

Onlookers use probability values to select food sources to discover according to the quality of food sources. The probability value for each food source is calculated by the following expression:

$$p_i = \frac{fit_i}{\sum\limits_{n=1}^{SN} fit_n} \tag{4}$$

where fit_i is the fitness value of x_i. The exploit method of onlookers is similar with employed bees.

When a food source is exploited fully, which means the food source cannot be further improved through the predetermined number of trials "$limit$", it is abandoned and the associated employed bee becomes a scout. The food source is replaced with a new food source by the scout.

It is clear from the above explanation that employed bees and onlookers perform exploitation, whereas scouts perform exploration. The main steps of ABC algorithm can be described as follows:

(a): Initialize the population of solutions by using (2);

(b): Produce new solution for each employed bee by using (3) and evaluate it, then apply greedy selection process;

(c): Calculate the probability value p_i by using (4);

(d): After each onlooker selecting their food source, produce a new solution for each onlooker by using (3) and evaluate it, then apply greedy selection process;

(e): Determine whether there are some food sources need to be abandoned, if existed, they are replaced by some new random solutions for scouts;

(f): Memorize the best solution;

(g): Jump to step (b) if the termination condition is not satisfied; otherwise stop the algorithm.

2.3   ABCPS

In this subsection, we use the hierarchical framework of cell-like P systems and ABC algorithm to specify the ABCPS algorithm. And OLMS proposed by Zhang et al. [12] is adopted in ABCPS. The structure of ABCPS is shown in Figure 2.

The P system-like framework will consist of:

(i) a membrane structure $[_0[_1]_1, [_2]_2, \ldots, [_m]_m]_0$ with m elementary membranes and the skin membrane denoted by 0;

(ii) a vocabulary that consists of all the bees;

(iii) a set of terminal symbols, T, consisting of all the bees;

(iv) initial multisets $w_0 = \lambda$,

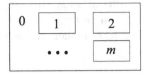

Fig. 2. One level membrane structure

$w_1 = B_1 B_2 \dots B_{n1},$
$w_2 = B_{n1+1} + B_{n1+2} \dots B_{n2},$
$\dots$

$w_m = B_{n(m-1)+1} B_{n(m-1)+2} \dots B_{nm}$
where B_i, $1 \leq i \leq n$, is a employed bee; n_j, $1 \leq j \leq m$, is the number of employed bee in the w_j; $\sum_{j=1}^{m} n_j = SN$,where SN is the total number of employed bees in this computation;
(v) rules which are categorized as

a) each of the compartments 0 to m implements the evolution rules of ABC independently (see the description of ABC);

b) communication rules which send the best food source from each of the m regions into the skin membrane and then the best food source from the skin back to each region to affect the next generation update.

In the ABCPS the initial employed bees are scattered across the membrane structure. The initial population will consist of the multisets $w_1, \dots, w_m$. In each elementary membrane, a employed bee generates a new neighboring solution around its associated solution as follows:

$$x_{new,l} = x_{il} + \Phi_{il}(x_{il} - x_{kl}) \tag{5}$$

where $i \in \{1, \dots, n_j\}, k \in \{1, \dots, n_j\} \cap k \neq i$, $l \in \{1, \dots, D\}$, n_j is the number of employed bee in membrane j, $1 \leq j \leq m$.
The probability value is

$$p_{ij} = \frac{fit_{ij}}{\sum\limits_{n=1}^{n_j} fit_n} \tag{6}$$

where fit_{ij} is the fitness value of x_{ij}, which is the ith employed bee in jth membrane. Detailed description of each step is given below:
(a): Initialization

Initialize the membrane structure and scatter SN employed bees into m elementary membranes in such a random way that guarantees each elementary membrane contains at least two employed bees. Thus, the number of employed bees, n_j, in an elementary membrane varies from 2 to $SN - 2m + 2$. Then assign n_j onlookers to each elementary membrane respectively.

(b): Employed bee phase

Produce new solution for each employed bee in each elementary membrane by using (5) and evaluate it, then apply greedy selection process.

(c): Onlooker phase

Calculate the probability value p_{ij} by using (6), then select food source depending on the probabilities. Produce a new solution for each onlooker in each elementary membrane by using (5) and evaluate it, then apply greedy selection process.

(e): Scout phase

Determine whether there are some food sources need to be abandoned, if existed, they are replaced by some new random solutions for scouts.

(f): First communication rule

The first communication rule is responsible for sending the best food source in each elementary membrane to the skin membrane.

(g): Perform ABC in skin membrane

In this step, employed bee phase and onlooker phase are adopted in skin membrane to update the m food sources. Then erase food sources but the best one in region 0 and memorize it.

(h): Second communication rule

The second communication rule is responsible for sending the best food source in region 0 to all elementary membranes.

(i): Check the termination criteria

Jump to step (b) if the termination condition is not satisfied; otherwise stop the algorithm.

3   Experiments and Results

The performance of the ABCPS is tested on various benchmark functions. First of all, it is discussed how to set the number of elementary membranes and the frequency of communication (FoC) between the skin membrane and the elementary membranes by using 3 benchmark functions. Then 29 benchmarks are applied to compare ABCPS and its counterpart ABC algorithm.

3.1   Parameter Setting

This subsection uses three benchmark functions to discuss how to choose the number m of elementary membranes and FoC. The three benchmarks include one unimodal function *Quartic Function i.e. Noise Function* [34], two multimodal functions *Ackley's Function* [34] and *Shifted Ackley's Function* [35]. The dimensions of three benchmarks are set to be $D = 500$. The population size is 100 and the *limit* is $SN * D$, which are same as those in [29]. The maximum number of generations is set to be 1000. Each of the experiments is repeated 20 times independently. And the performances of ABCPS are evaluated by using the best solutions, the mean of best solutions, standard deviations of the best solutions and mean of elapsed time per run. All the algorithms are coded in C programming language, and tested the algorithms on the platform Microsoft Visual C++ 6.0 by using a PC with 2.4GHz CPU, 2G RAM and Windows 7.

We first investigate the effect of the number of elementary membranes on the ABCPS performance and the parameter m varies from 2 to 20. Experimental results are shown in Fig. 3 - Fig. 8.

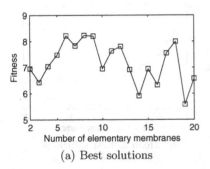
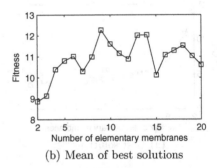

(a) Best solutions   (b) Mean of best solutions

Fig. 3. Experimental results of *Quartic Function i.e. Noise Function* with different membranes

It can be seen from Fig. 3 - Fig. 8, both the best solutions and the mean of best solutions over 20 runs have fluctuant behavior in solving the unimodal function *Quartic Function i.e. Noise Function*, but has a general decrease as m goes up from 2 to 20 in solving the two multimodal functions. The standard deviations of best solutions do not show some clear trend in solving the three benchmarks. At last, the elapsed time per run has a general increase as m goes up from 2 to 20 for all of them. From these experimental results, a trade-of value for solving unimodal and multimodal functions, the parameter m between the quality of solutions and the elapsed time could be about 5.

In what follows we set the number of elementary membranes to 5 to conduct a further investigation on the effects of FoC on the ABCPS performance. FoC means that for every FoC iterations, elementary membranes exchange information with skin membrane. Here we let the FoC vary from 1 to 10. Experimental results are shown in Fig. 9 - Fig. 14.

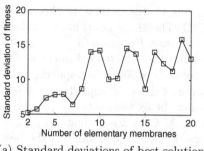
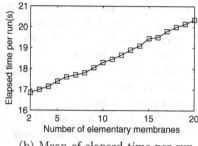

(a) Standard deviations of best solutions

(b) Mean of elapsed time per run

Fig. 4. Experimental results of *Quartic Function i.e. Noise Function* with different membranes

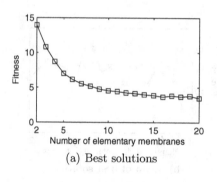
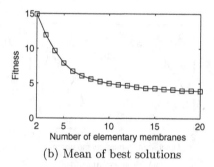

(a) Best solutions

(b) Mean of best solutions

Fig. 5. Experimental results of *Ackley's Function* with different membranes

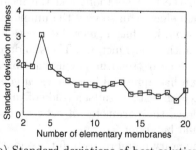
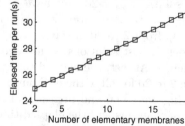

(a) Standard deviations of best solutions

(b) Mean of elapsed time per run

Fig. 6. Experimental results of *Ackley's Function* with different membranes

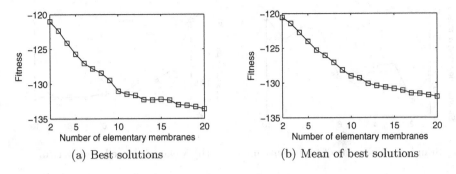

(a) Best solutions

(b) Mean of best solutions

Fig. 7. Experimental results of *Shifted Ackley's Function* with different membranes

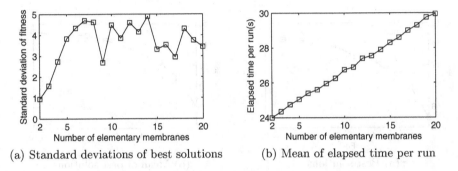

(a) Standard deviations of best solutions

(b) Mean of elapsed time per run

Fig. 8. Experimental results of *Shifted Ackley's Function* with different membranes

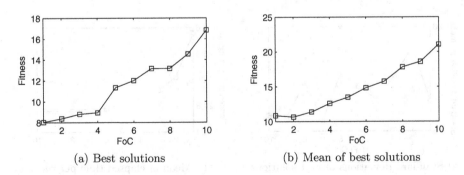

(a) Best solutions

(b) Mean of best solutions

Fig. 9. Experimental results of *Quartic Function i.e. Noise Function* with different FoC

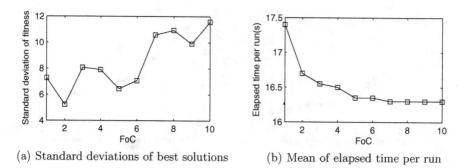

(a) Standard deviations of best solutions   (b) Mean of elapsed time per run

Fig. 10. Experimental results of *Quartic Function i.e. Noise Function* with different FoC

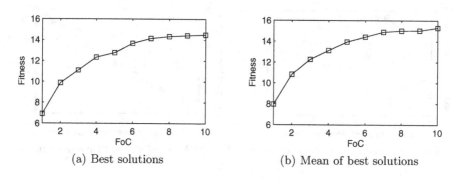

(a) Best solutions   (b) Mean of best solutions

Fig. 11. Experimental results of *Ackley's Function* with different FoC

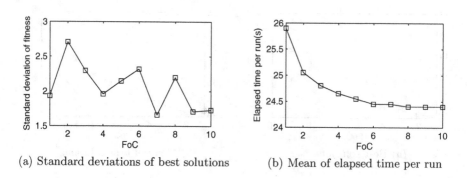

(a) Standard deviations of best solutions   (b) Mean of elapsed time per run

Fig. 12. Experimental results of *Ackley's Function* with different FoC

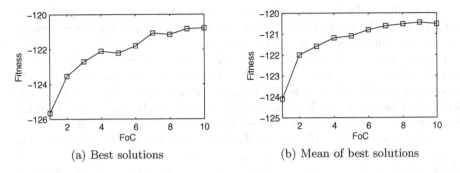

(a) Best solutions   (b) Mean of best solutions

Fig. 13. Experimental results of *Shifted Ackley's Function* with different FoC

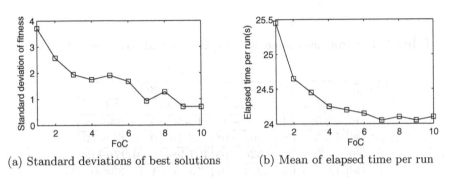

(a) Standard deviations of best solutions   (b) Mean of elapsed time per run

Fig. 14. Experimental results of *Shifted Ackley's Function* with different FoC

Figures 9 to 14 show that the mean of best solutions and the best solutions increase as FoC goes up from 1 to 10 for the three benchmarks. The standard deviations of best solutions also do not show some clear trend in solving all of them. The elapsed time per run has a general decrease as FoC goes up from 1 to 10 for the three benchmarks. The results show that the elapsed time decreases as FoC increases, but these is a rapid fall in the quality of solutions. So Foc is set to 1.

3.2   Experimental Comparisons Between ABCPS and ABC

Twenty-nine benchmark functions are applied to compare ABCPS and its counterpart ABC algorithm. First 23 functions are employed from [34], labeled as $f1$-$f23$. And the last 6 functions are chosen from CEC2008 test suite proposed in [35], denoted as $f24$-$f29$. In the following experiments, the ABCPS and ABC have identical settings for parameters: $SN = 50$, $limit = SN * D$. Each of the experiments is repeated 20 times independently. And the means and standard deviations of the experimental data are given. For clarity, the results of the best algorithm are marked in boldface. The results of first 23 functions are shown in Table 1 in terms of the mean and SD of the solutions.

The results in Table 1 indicate that the number of functions where ABCPS outperforms ABC is much larger than the number of functions where ABC is superior to ABCPS in terms of solution quality.

In order to evaluate the algorithm performance in solving complex benchmark functions, the dimensions of the first 13 functions are set to be 500 (the dimensions of $f14$-$f23$ are fixed). The results of functions $f1$-$f13$ and $f24$-$f29$ with 500 dimensions are shown in Table 2 in terms of the mean and SD of the solutions. The results of the best algorithm are also marked in boldface.

As shown in Table 2, ABCPS significantly outperforms ABC on most of the functions. ABCPS achieves better results on both mean and standard deviations of the errors in 16 functions, while achieves slightly worse result in standard deviations of the errors in only three functions, $f10$, $f28$ and $f29$.

Table 1. Performance comparisons of ABCPS and ABC over $f1$-$f23$

Fun	D	ABC		$ABCPS$	
		$Mean$	SD	$Mean$	SD
$f1$	30	$1.97e-13$	$1.17e-12$	**1.45e-15**	**1.03e-14**
$f2$	30	$1.27e-08$	$1.80e-08$	**4.53e-10**	**6.87e-10**
$f3$	30	$7.47e+03$	$8.32e+03$	**3.73e+03**	**6.97e+03**
$f4$	30	$1.07e+01$	$1.28e+01$	**4.66e-01**	**4.33e-01**
$f5$	30	**7.26e-01**	$4.40e+00$	$1.87e+00$	**1.10e+01**
$f6$	30	0	0	0	0
$f7$	30	$5.35e-02$	$6.78e-02$	**5.32e-02**	**5.18e-02**
$f8$	30	$-9.39e+03$	**5.35e+02**	**-9.45e+02**	$6.63e+02$
$f9$	30	**5.35e-12**	**3.20e-11**	$1.20e-11$	$1.15e-10$
$f10$	30	$5.46e-08$	$8.73e-08$	**6.47e-09**	**2.69e-08**
$f11$	30	$1.08e-08$	$1.67e-07$	**6.31e-11**	**7.56e-10**
$f12$	30	$5.76e-16$	$2.12e-15$	**1.45e-17**	**1.92e-16**
$f13$	30	$1.25e-13$	$5.78e-13$	**1.94e-16**	**1.27e-15**
$f14$	2	$9.98e-01$	$4.97e-16$	$9.98e-01$	$4.97e-16$
$f15$	4	$5.37e-04$	**4.28e-04**	**5.00e-04**	$5.31e-04$
$f16$	2	$-1.03e+00$	$9.93e-16$	$-1.03e+00$	$9.93e-16$
$f17$	2	$3.98e-01$	$0e+00$	$3.98e-01$	$0e+00$
$f18$	2	$3.00e+00$	**3.23e-15**	$3.00e+00$	$4.07e-15$
$f19$	3	$-3.86e+00$	$7.94e-15$	$-3.86e+00$	$7.94e-15$
$f20$	6	$-3.32e+00$	$1.99e-15$	$-3.32e+00$	$1.99e-15$
$f21$	4	$-1.02e+01$	**1.10e-14**	$-1.02e+01$	$1.18e-14$
$f22$	4	$-1.04e+01$	**1.53e-14**	$-1.04e+01$	$1.60e-14$
$f23$	4	$-1.05e+01$	**1.00e-14**	$-1.05e+01$	$1.20e-14$

Table 2. Performance comparisons of ABCPS and ABC over $f1$-$f13$ and $f24$-$f29$

Fun	D	ABC		$ABCPS$	
		$Mean$	SD	$Mean$	SD
$f1$	500	$2.37e+05$	$8.68e+04$	**2.42e+02**	**1.36e+02**
$f2$	500	$1.86e+01$	$3.90e+01$	**1.64e+01**	**4.39e+00**
$f3$	500	$3.48e+06$	$1.29e+06$	**9.70e+01**	**3.40e+00**
$f4$	500	$9.78e+01$	$3.29e+00$	**9.70e+01**	**2.40e+00**
$f5$	500	$5.25e+08$	$6.50e+08$	**1.49e+04**	**9.41e+03**
$f6$	500	$2.34e+05$	$9.97e+04$	**3.14e+02**	**1.42e+02**
$f7$	500	$3.44e+03$	$7.73e+03$	**1.10e+01**	**8.11e+00**
$f8$	500	$-1.15e+05$	$1.34e+04$	**-1.46e+05**	**7.29e+03**
$f9$	500	$3.11e+03$	$3.05e+02$	**4.89e+02**	**1.36e+02**
$f10$	500	$1.80e+01$	**8.01e-01**	**8.01e+00**	$2.04e+00$
$f11$	500	$2.16e+03$	$9.76e+02$	**3.57e+00**	**1.25e+00**
$f12$	500	$5.86e+08$	$1.41e+09$	**9.81e-02**	**1.14e-01**
$f13$	500	$1.65e+09$	$2.86e+09$	**1.41e+01**	**8.25e+00**
$f24$	500	$7.00e+05$	$2.91e+05$	**3.05e+02**	**3.62e+02**
$f25$	500	$-2.83e+02$	$9.39e+00$	**-2.95e+02**	**2.75e+01**
$f26$	500	$2.91e+11$	$3.03e+11$	**8.20e+05**	**1.64e+06**
$f27$	500	$4.14e+03$	$5.92e+02$	**2.20e+02**	**1.98e+02**
$f28$	500	$2.51e+04$	**1.63e+03**	**5.79e+03**	$3.21e+03$
$f29$	500	$-1.20e+02$	**2.92e-01**	**-1.24e+02**	$3.45e+00$

4 Conclusions

This paper first proposes a novel algorithm ABCPS which combines ABC and P systems, and evaluates its performance on a number of benchmark functions. The experimental results show that ABCPS performs better than ABC for both unimodal and multimodal functions, and demonstrates strong competitive capabilities in term of accuracy and robustness.

The possible future work may exploit two aspects. The first is how to select appropriate membrane structures and communication rules for ABCPS to solve different complex problems. The second is adopting some methods, such as improved initial population [36, 37], global best solution [36, 38], improved search equation [37, 39], to improve ABC algorithm within elementary membranes.

Acknowledgments. This work is supported by the National Natural Science Foundation of China (Grant No. 61170030), the Chunhui Plan of Ministry of Education of China (Grant No. Z2012025), the Research Projects of Eduction Department of Sichuan Province (Grant No. 13ZB0017) and the Key Scientific Research Foundation of Xihua University (Grant No. Z1120943). The authors also gratefully acknowledge the helpful comments and suggestions of the reviewers, which have improved the presentation.

References

1. Păun, G.: Computing with Membranes. Journal of Computer and System Sciences 61(1), 108–143 (2000)
2. Zhang, G.X., Cheng, J.X., Gheorghe, M.: Dynamic Behavior Analysis of Membrane-Inspired Evolutionary Algorithms. International Journal of Computers, Communications & Contorl 9(2), 227–242 (2014)
3. Zhang, G.X., Gheorghe, M., Pan, L.Q., Pérez-Jiménez, M.J.: Evolutionary membrane computing: A comprehensive survey and new results. Information Sciences (2014), http://dx.doi.org/10.1016/j.ins.2014.04.007
4. Nishida, T.Y.: An application of P-system: A new algorithm for NP-complete optimization problems. In: 8th World Multi-Conference on Systems, Cybernetics and Informatics, V, Orlando, pp. 109–112 (2004)
5. Nishida, T.Y.: An approximate algorithm for NP-complete optimization problems exploiting P-systems. In: 6th International Workshop on Membrane Computing, Vienna, pp. 26–43 (2005)
6. Nishida, T.Y.: Membrane algorithms: Approximate algorithms for NP-complete optimization problems. Applications of Membrane Computing, pp. 303–314 (2006)
7. Leporati, A., Pagani, D.: A membrane algorithm for the min storage problem. In: Hoogeboom, H.J., Păun, G., Rozenberg, G., Salomaa, A. (eds.) WMC 2006. LNCS, vol. 4361, pp. 443–462. Springer, Heidelberg (2006)
8. Huang, L., He, X.X., Wang, N., Xie, Y.: P systems based multi-objective optimization algorithm. Progress in Natural Science 17(4), 458–465 (2007)
9. Huang, L., Wang, N.: An optimization algorithm inspired by membrane computing. In: Jiao, L., Wang, L., Gao, X.-b., Liu, J., Wu, F. (eds.) ICNC 2006. LNCS, vol. 4222, pp. 49–52. Springer, Heidelberg (2006)
10. Cheng, J.X., Zhang, G.X., Zeng, X.X.: A novel membrane algorithm based on differential evolution for numerical optimization. International Journal of Unconventional Computing 7(3), 159–183 (2011)
11. Zhang, G.X., Liu, C.X., Gheorghe, M., Ipate, F.: Solving satisability problems with membrane algorithm. In: 4th International Conference on Bio-Inspired Computing: Theories and Applications, Beijing, pp. 29–36 (2009)
12. Zhang, G.X., Gheorghe, M., Wu, C.Z.: A quantum-inspired evolutionary algorithm based on P systems for knapsack problem. Fundamenta Informaticae 87(1), 93–116 (2008)
13. Liu, C.X., Zhang, G.X., Zhu, Y.H., Fang, C., Liu, H.W.: A quantum-inspired evolutionary algorithm based on P systems for radar emitter signals. In: 4th International Conference on Bio-Inspired Computing: Theories and Applications, Beijing, pp. 1–5 (2009)
14. Liu, C., Zhang, G., Liu, H., Gheorghe, M., Ipate, F.: An improved membrane algorithm for solving time-frequency atom decomposition. In: Păun, G., Pérez-Jiménez, M.J., Riscos-Núñez, A., Rozenberg, G., Salomaa, A. (eds.) WMC 2009. LNCS, vol. 5957, pp. 371–384. Springer, Heidelberg (2010)
15. Liu, C.X., Zhang, G.X., Liu, H.W.: A memetic algorithm based on P systems for IIR digital filter design. In: 8th IEEE International Conference on Pervasive Intelligence and Computing, Chengdu, pp. 330–334 (2009)
16. Huang, L., Suh, I.H.: Controller design for a marine diesel engine using membrane computing. International Journal of Innovative Computing Information and Control 5(4), 899–912 (2009)

17. Zhang, G.X., Liu, C.X., Rong, H.N.: Analyzing radar emitter signals with membrane algorithms. Mathematical and Computer Modelling 52(11-12), 1997–(2010)
18. Yang, S.P., Wang, N.: A P systems based hybrid optimization algorithm for parameter estimation of FCCU reactor-regenerator model. Chemical Engineering Journal 211-212, 508–518 (2012)
19. Zhang, G.X., Gheorghe, M., Li, Y.Q.: A membrane algorithm with quantuminspired subalgorithms and its application to image processing. Natural Computing 11(4), 701–717 (2012)
20. Zhang, G.X., Cheng, J.X., Gheorghe, M., Meng, Q.: A hybrid approach based on differential evolution and tissue membrane systems for solving constrained manufacturing parameter optimization problems. Applied Soft Computing 13(3), 1528–1542 (2013)
21. Zhang, G.X., Zhou, F., Huang, X.L.: A Novel membrane algorithm based on particle swarm optimization for optimization for solving broadcasting problems. Journal of universal computer science 18(13), 1821–1841 (2012)
22. Tu, M., Wang, J., Song, X.X., Yang, F., Cui, X.R.: An artificial fish swarm algorithm based on P systems. ICIC Express Letters, Part B: Applications 4(3), 747–753 (2013)
23. Păun, G., Pérez-Jiménez, M.J.: Membrane computing: brief introduction, recent results and applications. Biosystems 85(1), 11–22 (2006)
24. Păun, G.: Tracing some open problems in membrane computing. Romanian Journal of Information Science and Technology 10(4), 303–314 (2007)
25. Păun, G., Rozenberg, G.: A guide to membrane computing. Theoretical Computer Science 287(1), 73–100 (2002)
26. Karaboga, D.: An idea based on honey bee swarm for numerical optimization. Technical Report TR06, Erciyes University, Engineering Faculty, Computer Engineering Department (2005)
27. Tereshko, V., Loengarov, A.: Collective decision-making in honeybee foraging dynamics. Computing and Information Systems Journal 9(3), 1–7 (2005)
28. Karaboga, D., Basturk, B.: A powerful and efficient algorithm for numerical function optimization: artificial bee colony (ABC) algorithm. Journal of Global Optimization 39(3), 459–471 (2007)
29. Karaboga, D., Basturk, B.: On The performance of artificial bee colony (ABC) algorithm. Applied Soft Computing 8(1), 687–697 (2008)
30. Karaboga, D., Akay, B.: A comparative study of artificial bee colony algorithm. Applied Mathematics and Computation 214(1), 108–132 (2009)
31. Singh, A.: An artificial bee colony algorithm for the leaf-constrained minimum spanning tree problem. Applied Soft Computing 9(2), 625–631 (2009)
32. Kang, F., Li, J.J., Xu, Q.: Structural inverse analysis by hybrid simplex artificial bee colony algorithms. Computers & Sturctures 87(13-14), 861–870 (2009)
33. Samrat, L., Udgata, S.K., Abraham, A.: Artificial bee colony algorithm for small signal model parameter extraction of MESFET. Engineering Applications of Artificial Intelligence 23(5), 689–694 (2010)
34. Yao, X., Liu, Y., Lin, G.M.: Evolutionary programming made faster. IEEE Transactions on Evolutionary Computation 3(2), 82–102 (1999)
35. Tang, K., Yao, X., Suganthan, P.N., MacNish, C., Chen, Y.P., Chen, C.M., Yang, Z.: Benchmark Functions for the CEC2008 Special Session and Competition on Large Scale Global Optimization, Technical Report, Nature Inspired Computation and Applications Laboratory, USTC, Hefei, China (2007)

36. Gao, W.F., Liu, S.Y., Huang, L.L.: A global best artificial bee colony algorithm for global optimization. Journal of Computational and Applied Mathematics 236(11), 2741–2753 (2012)
37. Gao, W.F., Liu, S.Y.: A modified artificial bee colony algorithm. Computers & Operations Research 39(3), 687–697 (2012)
38. Zhu, G.P., Kwong, S.: Gbest-guided artificial bee colony algorithm for numerical-function optimization. Applied Mathematics and Computation 217(7), 3166–3173 (2010)
39. Gao, W.F., Liu, S.Y.: Improved artificial bee colony algorithm for global optimization. Information Processing Letters 111(17), 871–882 (2011)

The Intelligent Editing Based on Perception for Structuring Digital Ink

Rui Su

Jining Medical University, Jijing 272000, Shandong, China
suruiyaya@aliyun.com

Abstract. With the development of human-computer interface moving in the natural and efficient direction, people pay more and more attentions to the structural analysis and intelligent editing of digital Ink, also known as digital Handwriting. Firstly, we put forward a new method of the multi-level interactional structure analysis and understanding based on context awareness for handwriting, and then we have the intelligent edit operations. The result of experimental evaluation shows that the method has an effective effect for intelligent editing of handwriting.

Keywords: Digital ink, Structure analysis, Intelligent editing.

1 Introduction

With the development of human-computer interface moving in the natural, efficient and integrated direction, digital Ink, also known as digital Handwriting or Online Handwriting, its structural analysis and intelligent editing is paid more and more attentions. Digital handwriting [1,2] is vector data made of strokes left by the pen input device when moving on its writing plane, which has the characteristics of the irregularity. Digital handwriting has its implicit spatial structure relations, but its text implicit structure is difficult to accurately extract. The interaction based on context awareness is core technology. This used to implement implicit interactions. Using the space and time relationship between strokes, especially the constraint relation of the space position, digital handwriting is structurally understood and recognized. After that we can make intelligent editing operations in order to achieve convenient user "non-canonical input, standard output" which is like other electronic document format supporting and convenient editing operation effect.

2 The Structure Understanding and Analysis of Digital Handwriting

It is an important topic in digital handwriting structure understanding for text structure. Free writing has irregular dynamic variable boundary information, which needs to analyze the spatial relationship between strokes and a set of spatial relations between the strokes [3,4]. Generally, text is written line by line,

L. Pan et al. (Eds.): BIC-TA 2014, CCIS 472, pp. 411–415, 2014.

which needs to consider the context information of strokes and distance between strokes. Character segmentation is a key step of handwriting structure understanding when user input strokes [5]. We use the binary classification histogram extract character of strokes. Before and after the interval of the stroke are calculated as histogram data. The optimal threshold of strokes classification is obtained by histogram, and the identifiable character set and the character set to be identified are produced according to the optimal threshold. We can use a recursive algorithm to iterate through all the character space until all the characters are recognized.

The text line correctly extraction is crucial in the structure of handwriting analysis and recognition [6]. Usually when getting the text line that we can extract and identify characters in a line of handwriting; to create such as paragraphs or list of handwriting, also based on the text line structure; text line structure played an essential role in analysis and identification, and also is the basis of handwriting structured editing therefore it is especially important.

The difficulty of handwriting extraction is determined whether the text lines can be written smoothly, specifically whether text lines are parallel each other [7]. For the overall tilting text lines of digital handwriting by using the method of optimal histogram projection, we can extract parallel text lines. Extraction for multiple directions text lines based on the gestalt psychology of the cognitive psychology as the foundation of computing theory, we use the bottom-up strategy to establish a link mesh structure model in order to evaluate all potential text line arrangement, finally we use the global optimization search strategy of branch limit for the link model to obtain the optimal line arrangement.

The understanding of the text lines for digital handwriting lay a solid foundation for paragraph (paragraph is the Ink level is the concept which is made of one or more lines containing handwriting stroke). After understanding of handwriting, paragraph presents three typical organizational structures such as paragraph:

(1) the first line indentation;
(2) the left-aligned cluster structure of the stroke cluster;
(3) a "title-content" outline type.

Paragraph structure extraction is the key to distinguish the line indentation of the first and the last line. Based on line structure, considering each context information, we use decision tree to extract paragraph, the spatial information of stroke, the first blank, the blank at the end of the line, line spacing are main factor.

Through the structure analysis and understanding of handwriting, the seemingly chaotic information form different levels of effective writing organization in order that structured handwriting information can be effectively intelligent editing operation, and also convenient storage and retrieval of handwriting, decrease data compression problem of handwriting. Multi-level structure understanding of handwriting is shown in figure 1.

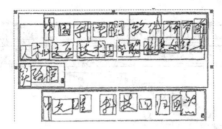

Fig. 1. Multi-level structure understanding of Handwriting

3 The Intelligent Editing of Digital Handwriting

The hierarchical structure of the handwriting maintains the relevance between the handwriting to reduce the burden of the user's cognition, natural and efficient implicit interactions. Three key interaction techniques are used in intelligent editing, such as based on structural understanding, based on the Sketch, based on context awareness. Based on the Sketch of the interactive technology, it reduces people's cognitive load, and usually allows people to operate in the form of freedom. For example; insert function offers users free sketch. Delete operations of Handwriting can also be an example of context-aware interaction. Handwriting can be deleted through the jagged line and the relationship between the deleted handwriting and around it are analyzed, also can cause related handwriting to mobile, as shown in figure 2.

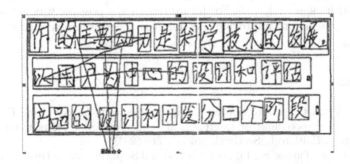

Fig. 2. Using the jagged line to delete characters in different multiple lines

The optimal histogram method with the global feature is used in the extraction of row parallel lines. For the tilted text line extraction, the text lines are rotated the process during the extraction of the lines as shown shown in figure 3.

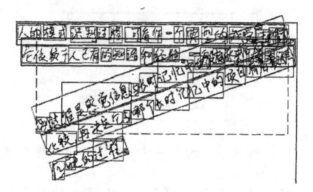

Fig. 3. The rotation process of the parallel lines tilted text line

4   Conclusion

In all kinds of handwriting computing technology, the structural analysis technology is very important, which gives the Pen-based User Interface intelligent, and let the computer can understand the handwriting of the user. The structured expression of handwriting lays the foundation for the structured editing and the specification of the data conversion. In this article, we focus on solving the structural analysis and intelligent editing for the text lines, and good effect is obtained by the experimental evaluation.

In recent works, low-dispersion sequences were used to improve projection based algorithms, see e.g. [10]. For future research, a possible way is using low-dispersion sequences to improve projection based algorithms in handwriting ink recognition.

References

1. Shi, Z., Venu, G.S.: Detection for Complex Document Images Using Fuzzy Run Length. In: Proceedings of International Conference on Document analysis an recognition, Editburgh, Scotland, pp. 715–719 (2003)
2. Feldbach, M., Tnnies, K., Li, D.: Detection and Segmentation in Historical Church Registers. In: Proceedings of International Conference on Document Analysis: An Recognition, Seattle, pp. 743–747 (2001)
3. Christopher, M.B., Markus, S., Geoffrey, E.H.: Distinguishing Text From Graphics in On-Line Handwritten Ink. In: Kimura, F., Fujisawa, H. (eds.) Proceedings of the 9th International Workshop on Frontiers in Handwriting Recognition, F, Tokyo, Japan, pp. 142–147 (2004)
4. Michael, S., Zile, W., Sashi, R., Patrice, S., David, J.: Discerning structure from freeform handwritten notes. In: Proceedings of the 6th International Conference on Document Analyses and Recognition, vol. 1, pp. 60–65 (2003)
5. Su, R., Zhang, X.: Intelligent Handwriting Editing Based on Structure Understanding Of Handwriting. Journal of System Simulation 18, 20–29 (2006)

6. Li, Y., Guan, Z., Wang, H., Dai, G., Ren, X.: Structuralizing Freeform Notes by Implicit Sketch Understanding. In: Proceeding of AAAI Spring Symposium on Sketch Understanding, Palo Alto, California, pp. 113–117 (2002)
7. Lee, S., Ryu, R.: Parameter-Free Geometric Document Layout Analysis. IEEE Transactions on Pattern Analysis and Machine Intelligence 23(11), 1240–1256 (2001)
8. Moran, T., Melle, W., Chiu, W., Kurtenbach, G.: Pen-Based Interaction Techniques for Organizing Material on an Electronic Whiteboard. 45–54 (1997)
9. Xiang, A., Dai, G., Wang, H.: The Extraction for Multi directional Text Lines of the Online Handwriting based on Perception. Journal of Computer Aided Design and Computer Graphics 19 (2007)
10. Wang, X., Miao, Y., Cheng, M.: Finding Motifs in DNA Sequences Using Low-Dispersion Sequences. Journal of Computational Biology 21(4), 320–329 (2014)

Compactly and Weakly Compactly Strongly Exposed Properties in Musielak-Orlicz Sequence Spaces Equipped with the Orlicz Norm

Lihuan Sun

School of Science, AnHui University of Science and Technology,
Huainan 232001, AnHui, China
sunlihuan20040204@126.com

Abstract. In order to improve and generalize the discussion of exposed properties in Musielak-Orlicz function space,in the paper we consider the compactly and weakly compactly strongly exposed properties in Musielak-Orlicz sequence spaces equipped with the Orlicz Norm. First, some criteria for S-property and weakly S-property in Musielak-Orlicz sequence spaces equipped with the Luxemburg norm are given. Second, specific characterizations of compactly strongly exposed property and weakly compactly strongly exposed property in Musielak-Orlicz sequence spaces equipped with the Orlicz norm are given.

Keywords: Compactly strongly exposed property, Weakly compactly strongly exposed property, Musielak-Orlicz sequence space, Orlicz norm.

1   Introduction

X denotes a Banach space, X^*-the dual of X. $S(X), S(X^*)$ are the unit spheres in X and X^*, respectively. For any $x \in S(X)$, we denote by $Grad(x)$ the set of all support functionals at x, that is $Grad(x) = \{f \in S(X^*) : f(x) = ||x||\}$. A Banach space X is said to be compactly strongly exposed (CSE for short)(resp. weakly compactly strongly exposed (resp. WCSE for short)), if for any $x \in S(X)$ and any sequence $\{x_n\}$ in $S(X)$, the condition $f(x_n) \to 1$ for some $f \in Grad(x)$, implies that the sequence $\{x_n : n \in \mathbb{N}\}$ is relatively compact in the norm topology(resp.in the weak topology).

A Banach space X is said to have the S-property (resp.weakly S-property(WS for short)) if for any $x \in S(X)$, $f_n \subset S(X^*)$ and $f_n(x) \to 1$, then the sequence $\{f_n\}$ is relatively compact(resp.$\{f_n\}$ is weakly relatively compact).

Criteria for compactly and weakly compactly strongly exposed properties in Orlicz sequence spaces equipped with the Orlicz norm are given in[9]. More relevant results see[1,2,7,8,4,6].

The sequence $\Phi = (\Phi_i)_{i=1}^{\infty}$ is called a Musielak-Orlicz function provided that for any $i \in \mathcal{N}, \Phi_i : (-\infty, +\infty) \to [0, +\infty]$ is even, convex, left continuous on whole $[0, \infty), \Phi_i(0) = 0$ and there exists $u_i > 0$ such that $\Phi_i(u_i) < \infty$. By $\Psi = (\Psi_i)_{i=1}^{\infty}$, we denote the Musielak-Orlicz function complementary to $\Phi = (\Phi_i)_{i=1}^{\infty}$ in the sense of Young, i.e.

L. Pan et al. (Eds.): BIC-TA 2014, CCIS 472, pp. 416–419, 2014.

$$\Psi_i(v) = \sup\{u|v| - \Phi_i(u) : u \geq 0\}$$

for each $v \in \mathcal{R}$ and $i \in \mathcal{N}$. We say a Musielak-Orlicz function Φ satisfies the δ_2^0-condition($\Phi \in \delta_2^0$ for short), if there exit $a > 0, k > 0, i_0 \in \mathcal{N}$ and a sequence (c_i) of positive numbers, such that $\sum_{i=i_0}^{\infty} c_i < \infty$ and the inequality

$$\Phi_i(2u) \leq k\Phi_i(u) + c_i$$

holds for every $i \geq i_0$ and each $u \in \mathcal{R}$ satisfying $M_i(u) \leq a$.

Let l^0 denote the space of all real sequences $x = (x(i))$. Given any Musielak-Orlicz function $\Phi = (\Phi_i)$, we define on l^0 the convex modular $I_\Phi(x)$ by

$$I_\Phi(x) = \sum_{i=1}^{\infty} \Phi(x(i)), \quad for\ any\ x \in l^0.$$

The liner set $l^\Phi = \{x = (x(i) \in l^0 : I_\Phi(\lambda x) < \infty\ for\ some\ \lambda > 0\}$ endowed with the Luxemburg norm

$$\|x\| = \inf\{\lambda > 0 : I_\Phi(\frac{x}{\lambda}) \leq 1\}$$

or the Orlicz norm

$$\|x\|^0 = \sup\{\sum_{i=1}^{\infty} x(i)y(i) : I_\Psi(y) = \sum_{i=1}^{\infty} \Psi_i(y(i)) \leq 1\} = \inf\{\frac{1}{k}(1+I_\Phi(kx)) : k > 0\}$$

is a Banach space. We call it Musielak-Orlicz space and denote by l_Φ or l_Φ^0, respectively.

The subspace

$$\{x \in l^\Phi : for\ any\ \lambda > 0, there\ exists\ i_0\ such\ that\ \sum_{i>i_0} \Phi_i(\lambda x(i)) < \infty\}$$

endowed with the norm $\|.\|$(or $\|.\|^0$)is also a Banach space, and it is denoted by h_Φ(or h_Φ^0). It is well known that $l_\Phi = h_\Phi$(or $l_\Phi^0 = h_\Phi^0$) if and only if $\Phi \in \delta_2^0$.

For any $x \in l_\Phi^0$(or$x \in l_\Phi$), write

$$dist(x, h_\Phi^0) = \inf\{\|x - y\|^0 : y \in h_\Phi^0\}, dist(x, h_\Phi) = \inf\{\|x - y\| : y \in h_\Phi\},$$

For any $x \in l_\Phi$(or$x \in l_\Phi^0$), we define

$$\theta(x) = inf\{\lambda > 0, there\ exists\ i_0\ such\ that\ \sum_{i>i_0} \Phi_i(\lambda x(i)) < \infty\}.$$

It is clear that $x \in h_\Phi$(or$x \in h_\Phi^0$) if and only if $\theta(x) = 0$ and it has been proved that $\theta(x) = dist(x, h_\Phi) = dist(x, h_\Phi^0)$. $\phi \in (l_\Phi^0)^*$ is a singular functional($\phi \in F$ for short), i.e.$\phi(x) = 0$ for any $x \in h_\Phi^0$. The dual space of l_Φ is represented in the form $(l_\Phi^0)^* = l_\Psi \bigoplus F$, i.e.every $f \in (l_\Phi^0)^*$ has the uniquely represented in the form $f = y + \phi$, where $\phi \in F$ and $y \in L_\Psi$ is the regular functional defined by the formula $y(x) =< x, y >= \sum_{i=1}^{\infty} x(i)y(i)(\forall x = x(i) \in l_\Phi^0)$. For any $x = x(i) \in l_\Phi^0$, we put $suppx = \{i \in \mathcal{N} : x(i) \neq 0\}$.

1.1   Related Lemmas

Lemma 1. *[3] Musielak-Orlicz sequence space l_Φ^0 has H-Property if and only if $\Phi \in \delta_2^0$ or $\sum_{i=1}^\infty \Psi_i(\tilde{B}(i)) \leq 1$.*

Lemma 2. *[9] A Banach space X^* is said to be WCSE, then the dual space X has WS-property.*

Lemma 3. *[9] A Banach space X is said to be CSE if and only if X is said to be WCSE and X has H-property.*

Lemma 4. *[10] If $\Phi \in \delta_2^0, x_n(i) \to 0 (i = 1, 2, ...)$, then $I_\Phi(x_n) \to 0$ implies $||x_n|| \to 0, ||x_n||^0 \to 0$.*

Lemma 5. *[5] If $||x|| = 1, \theta(x) < 1, y_n \in S(l_\Psi^0)$, for any $n \in \mathcal{N}$ and $< x, y_n > \to 1$ as $n \to \infty$, then the condition(1) holds*

$$\lim_{i_0 \to \infty} \sup_n \sum_{i > i_0} \Psi_i(y_n(i)) = 0. \tag{1}$$

2   Main Results

Theorem 1. *For the space h_Φ, the following conditions are equivalent:*
(1)h_Φ has S-property. (2)h_Φ has WS-property. (3) $\Psi \in \delta_2^0$.

Proof. By the definition of S-property and WS-property $(1) \Rightarrow (2)$ is trivial.

Now we need to proof $(2) \Rightarrow (3)$. If $\Psi \notin \delta_2^0$, by Bishop-Phelps theorem, there exist $y \in S(l_\Psi^0 \setminus h_\Psi^0)$ and $x \in S(h_\Phi)$, such that $y(x) = < x, y > = \sum_{i=1}^\infty x(i)y(i) = ||y||^0 = 1$. Put $y_n = (y(1), y(2), ...y(n), 0, ...)(n = 1, 2, ...)$, then $y_n(x) = \sum_{i=1}^n x(i)y(i) \to y(x) = 1$. By Hahn-Banach theorem, there exists a singular function ϕ, such that $\phi(y) \neq 0$. Since $y_n \to y$ coordinate wise, without loss of generality, we assume that $y_n \xrightarrow{w} y$. But

$$\phi(y_n - y) = \phi(y) \neq 0 (n = 1, 2, ...),$$

which contradicts with the assumption, hence the condition (3) is necessary.

$(3) \Rightarrow (1)$. Assume that $x \in S(h_\Phi), \{y_n\} \subset S(l_\Psi^0)$ and $y_n(x) = < x, y_n > \to 1 (n \to \infty)$. By lemma 5 and Young inequality, we get $\lim_{i_0 \to \infty} \sup_n \sum_{i > i_0} x(i)y_n(i) = 0$. By diagonal rule, take a subsequence of $\{y_n\}$(still denoted by $\{y_n\}$)satisfying:

$$\lim_{n \to \infty} y_n(i) = a_i (i = 1, 2, ...). \tag{2}$$

For a sequence $\{a_i\} \in \mathcal{R}$ and for any $\varepsilon > 0$,by the expression (1) and (2), we get $I_\Psi(\frac{y_n - y_m}{2}) \to 0 (n, m \to \infty)$. So by lemma 4, $||\frac{y_n - y_m}{2}||^0 \to 0 (n, m \to \infty)$, which shows that $\{y_n\}$ is relatively compact.

Theorem 2. *For l_Φ^0, the following conditions are equivalent:*
(1)l_Φ^0 is CSE.(2)l_Φ^0 is WCSE. (3)$\Phi \in \delta_2^0$ and $\Psi \in \delta_2^0$.

Proof. By the definition of CSE and WCSE (1) $\Rightarrow$ (2) is trivial.

(2) $\Rightarrow$ (3). We assume that l_Φ^0 is WCSE, then by lemma 2 and theorem 1, we get the condition $\Phi \in \delta_2^0$ holds. Now we need to proof that the condition $\Psi \in \delta_2^0$ also holds. If $\Psi \notin \delta_2^0$, there exists $y \in l_\Psi \setminus h_\Psi$, such that $I_\Psi((1 + \frac{1}{n})y) = \infty, \Psi_i((1 + \frac{1}{n})y(i)) < \infty$ and $I_\Psi(y) \leq 1$. For convenience, we introduce the following notion $[y]_n^m = (0, 0, ...y(n+1), ..., y(m), 0, 0, ...)(n < m)$.

Because $dist(y, h_\Psi) = 1$, hence, $\||[y]_n^\infty\|| \geq 1 (n=1,2,...)$.So we get a sequence $0 < i_1 < i_2 < i_3 < ....$, such that $\||[y]_{i_n}^{i_{n+1}}\|| > 1 - \frac{1}{n}$, for $n = 1, 2, ...$ For each $n \in \mathcal{N}$, there exists $\{x_n\} \subset S(l_\Phi^0)$, such that $< x_n, y > \to 1$, but for any $m, n \in \mathcal{N}, m > n$, we have

$$\|x_m - x_m\|^0 \geq \|x_n\|^0 = 1,$$

which means that the sequence $\{x_n\}$ is not relatively compact. Hence the space l_Φ^0 is not CSE. Therefore by lemma 1 and lemma 3, we know that l_Φ^0 is not WCSE, which is a contradiction.

(3) $\Rightarrow$ (1). Assume that $x \in S(l_\Phi^0), \{x_n\} \subset (l_\Phi^0)$ and $f \in Grad(x), f(x_n) \to 1$. Because $\Phi \in \delta_2^0$ and $\Psi \in \delta_2^0$, so l_Φ^0 is reflexive. Hence, there exists a subsequence $\{x_{n_i}\}$ of $\{x_n\}$ and $x_0 \in l_\Phi^0$, such that $x_{n_i} \overset{w}{\to} x_0$,furthermore, $f(x_0) = 1$. Consequently $\|x_0\|^0 = 1$. By lemma 6, we get $x_{n_i} \to x_0$, which means that the space l_Φ^0 is CSE.

Acknowledgments. I thank the reviewers for their valuable comments and suggestions on this paper.

References

1. Brahmabirth, P., Omparkash, K.: A generalization of local uniform convexity of the norm. J. Math. Anal. App. 52, 300–308 (1975) (in Chinese)
2. Junyi, F., Wenyao, Z.: On weakly compactly locally uniformly rotund spaces. J. Math. 6, 285–290 (1986) (Wuhan, in Chinese)
3. Mingxia, Z., Yunan, C.: H-property in Musielak-Orlicz sequence spaces. J. Nat. Sci. Heilongjiang Univer. 4, 5–10 (2003)
4. Quandi, W., Liang, Z., Tingfu, W.: On CLUR points of Orlicz spaces. Annal. Polon. Math. 2, 147–157 (2000)
5. Shurong, B., Henryk, H., Tingfu, W.: Smooth, very smooth and strongly smooth points in Musielak-Orlicz sequence spaces. Bull. Austral. Math. Soc. 63, 441–457 (2001)
6. Shutao, C.: Geometry of Orlicz spaces.: Dissertationes Mathematicae (1996)
7. Yunan C., Ying L., Chunhui M.: Strong U-points of Orlicz spaces equipped with Orlicz norm. Banyan J. Math. 4, 45–58 (1997)
8. Yunan, C., Henryk, H., Chunhui, M.: On some local gemetry of Orlicz sequence spaces equipped with Luxemburg norm. Acta. Math. 80(1-2), 143–154 (1998) (Hungar)
9. Yunan, C., Henryk, H., Mingxia, Z.: On compactly and weakly compactly strongly exposed properties and criteria for them in Orlicz sequence spaces equipped with Orlicz norm. India J. Pure. Appl. Math. 10, 569–578 (2005)
10. Yunan C., Henryk H., Mingxia Z.: On S-points of Musielak-Orlicz sequence spaces. Acta. Math. Sinica. 5, 1117–1128 (2007)

Extended Extreme Learning Machine for Tensorial Signal Classification

Shuai Sun[1], Bin Zhou[1], and Fan Zhang[2*]

[1] Department of Electric Power Engineering, Zhengzhou Electric Power College,
Zhengzhou, 450000, China
[2] School of Information Engineering,
North China University of Water Resources and Electric Power, Zhengzhou, 450045, China

Abstract. Recently, there are several multilinear methods have been proposed for tensorial data dimensionality reduction (feature extraction). However, there are few new algorithms for tensorial signals classification. To solve this problem, in this paper, a novel classifier as a tensor extension of extreme learning machine for multi-dimensional data recognition is introduced. Due to the proposed solution can classify tensorial data directly without vectorizing them, the intrinsic structure information of the input data can be reserved. It is demonstrated that the new tensor based classifier can get better recognition performance with a faster learning speed.

Keywords: Pattern recognition, Extreme learning machine (ELM), Classification, Tensor object.

1 Introduction

Most of the biometric signals are naturally multi-dimensional objects, such as fingerprint, palmprint, ear, face images and gait silhouettes, which are formally known as tensors. Tensor is a generalization of vectors and matrices but not limit to, vectors are first-order tensors, while matrices are second-order tensors. The elements of a tensor are to be addressed by a number of indices which used to define the order of the tensor object and each index defines one "mode" [1]. There is an increasing interest in the multilinear subspace analysis and many methods have been proposed to operate directly on these tensorial data during the past several years. Such as multilinear principal component analysis (MPCA) [2], a tensor extension of principal component analysis (PCA) [3], applies PCA transformation on each mode of tensors. By the same way, multilinear discriminant analysis (MDA) [4], general tensor discriminant analysis (GTDA) [5], and tensor subspace analysis (TSA) [6], respectively apply linear discriminant analysis (LDA) [7], maximum scatter difference (MSD) [8], and locality preserving projections (LPP) [9] transform each mode of tensors.

For most practical pattern recognition systems, feature extraction and classification methods are equally important. Feature extraction algorithms should retain most if not all of the useful information in the original data while keeping the dimension of the

---

* Corresponding author.

L. Pan et al. (Eds.): BIC-TA 2014, CCIS 472, pp. 420–424, 2014.

features as low as possible. For classification, good generalization is an important character for classifiers. Although there are several tensor based dimensionality reduction (feature extraction) solutions introduced above, there are few tensor based classification algorithms. The classical classifiers include nearest neighbor (NN), feed-forward neural network (FNN) [10], support vector machine (SVM) [11], and so on. Traditional classification methods are usually vector based, such as SVM and FNN. When they are employed to classify an input tensor data, we have to transform tensor data into vector data at first. Moreover, due to the distance between two data with form either tensor or vector is the same, NN classifier can be used to classify the feature tensor objects directly. Therefore, NN classifier is usually applied after many multilinear dimension reduction methods such as in [2]. However, the structure of NN classifier is too simple to achieve satisfying recognition rate. Consequently, it is desirable to propose a novel classifier which can classify tensorial data directly and to preserve the intrinsic structure of input data effectively. Recently, classifiers that representing images as matrices rather than vectors have been introduced. A two-dimensional neural network with random weights (2D-NNRW) algorithm is proposed in [12], which can use matrix data as direct input by employing left and right projecting vectors instead of the usual high dimensional input weight in the single-hidden layer feed forward neural networks (SLFNN). In [13,14], multiple-rank left projecting vectors and right projecting vectors are applied to regress each matix data to its label for efficient image classification. Unfortunately, that classifiers mentioned above focus on dealing with two dimensional data rather than tensor objects with higher order.

As a tensor extension of extreme learning machine (ELM), we introduce a novel tensor based classification method named as tensorial extreme learning machine (TELM) for tensor objects classification. Without converting tensor objects into vectors, TELM can classify them directly. ELM [15] is originally proposed as a new learning algorithm for SLFNN which can be used both in regression and classification with an extremely fast learning speed. ELM randomly assigns the input weights and the bias of neurons in the hidden layer, while the output weights are obtained using the Moore-Penrose (MP) generalized inverse. TELM not only takes the advantage of ELM, but also preserves the natural structure of the input data. Furthermore, with fewer parameters to be calculated, a faster computing speed can be achieved.

The rest of this paper is organized as follows: In section 2, the new classifier TELM is summarized in detail. Finally, the major findings and conclusions are drawn in section 3.

2   The Proposed Method

Following the notation in [16], we denote vectors by lowercase letters, e.g., x; matrices by uppercase boldface, e.g., U; and tensors by calligraphic letters, e.g., $\mathcal{A}$.

It is generally accepted that reshaping tensor data to vector leads to two fundamental limitations: high computational burden and a loss of the potential spatial structure information of the original data. In [12], the traditional projection term $w_i^T x_j$ is replaced by $u_i^T X_j v_i$ to construct a two dimensional classifier. Similarly, one direct way to construct a tensor classifier is to replace $w_i^T x_j$ by its tensor counterpart, such as $\mathcal{X}_j \times_1 u_i^{(1)^T} \times_2 u_i^{(2)^T} \cdots \times_M u_i^{(M)^T}$. Consequently, in order to deal with tensorial data directly, for a set of N tensor data $\{(\mathcal{X}_j, t_j)\}_{j=1}^N$, with $t_j \in \mathbb{R}^C$:

$$
\begin{aligned}
y_j &= \sum_{i=1}^{L} \beta_i g\left(\mathcal{X}_j \times_1 u_i^{(1)^T} \times_2 u_i^{(2)^T} \cdots \times_M u_i^{(M)^T} + b_i\right) \\
&= \sum_{i=1}^{L} \beta_i g\left(\mathcal{X}_j \prod_{m=1}^{M} \times_m u_i^{(m)^T} + b_i\right)
\end{aligned}
\tag{1}
$$

where $\mathcal{X}_j \in \mathbb{R}^{I_1 \times I_2 \times \cdots \times I_M}$ is a Mth-order tensor, $u_i^{(m)} \in \mathbb{R}^{I_m}$ are corresponding transformation vectors for $m = 1, \cdots, M$, $b_i \in \mathbb{R}$, and $\beta_i \in \mathbb{R}^C$, $i = 1, 2, \cdots, L$, and L is the number of hidden nodes.

In order to discuss the relationship, let $\mathcal{X} \in \mathbb{R}^{I_1 \times I_2 \times \cdots \times I_M}$, and $x = Vec(\mathcal{X})$ as the input vector, and the input weight vector w will be a column vector with $I_1 I_2 \cdots I_M$ elements. It is known that the Kronecker product of matrices $A \in \mathbb{R}^{I \times J}$ and $B \in \mathbb{R}^{K \times L}$ is denoted by $A \otimes B$ of size $(IK) \times (JL)$. By the same way, we can define w of size $I_1 I_2 \cdots I_M \times 1$ by

$$
w = u^{(1)} \otimes u^{(2)} \otimes \cdots \otimes u^{(M)}
\tag{2}
$$

where $u^{(m)} \in \mathbb{R}^{I_m}$. Because of the elements in w are randomly determined, the parameters in $u^{(m)}$ can be randomly generated too. Evoked by the above formulation:

$$
\begin{aligned}
y &= Vec(\mathcal{Y}) = Vec(\mathcal{X} \times_1 u^{(1)^T} \times_2 u^{(2)^T} \times \cdots \times_M u^{(M)^T}) \\
&= (u^{(1)} \otimes u^{(2)} \otimes \cdots \otimes u^{(M)})^T Vec(\mathcal{X}) = w^T x
\end{aligned}
\tag{3}
$$

where $u^{(m)}$, $\mathcal{X}$, w, and x are defined as previous. As seen from above derivation, we notice that TELM can be regarded as a special case of ELM, provided that the constraint is $w = u^{(1)} \otimes u^{(2)} \otimes \cdots \otimes u^{(M)}$. More concretely, the corresponding w is determined by only $(I_1 + I_2 + \cdots + I_M)$ variables through TELM while there is $(I_1 I_2 \cdots I_M)$ elements to be calculated for ELM. In a word, the input tensor data sets can be calculated directly without vectoring them. Not only the inner structural information among the elements of the data can be preserved, but also fewer parameters need to be computed.

All the weights and bias will be determined randomly. After confirming the projecting vectors and biases, the output weights β can be determined while the matrix H should be changed as follows

$$
\Phi = \begin{bmatrix}
G\left(\mathcal{X}_1 \prod_{m=1}^{M} \times_m u_1^{(m)^T} + b_1\right) & \cdots & G\left(\mathcal{X}_1 \prod_{m=1}^{M} \times_m u_L^{(m)^T} + b_L\right) \\
\vdots & \ddots & \vdots \\
G\left(\mathcal{X}_N \prod_{m=1}^{M} \times_m u_1^{(m)^T} + b_1\right) & \cdots & G\left(\mathcal{X}_N \prod_{m=1}^{M} \times_m u_L^{(m)^T} + b_L\right)
\end{bmatrix}
\tag{4}
$$

Φ is the hidden output matrix for TELM, then the output weights can be solved by the following optimal

$$
\begin{aligned}
\widehat{\beta} &= \arg\min_{\beta} \sum_{j=1}^{N} \left\| \sum_{i=1}^{L} \beta_i g\left(\mathcal{X}_j \prod_{m=1}^{M} \times_m u_i^{(m)^T} + b_i\right) - t_j \right\| \\
&= \arg\min_{\beta} \|\Phi\beta - T\| = \Phi^\dagger T
\end{aligned}
\tag{5}
$$

where

$$\beta = \begin{pmatrix} \beta_1^T \\ \vdots \\ \beta_L^T \end{pmatrix}, \quad \text{and} \quad T = \begin{pmatrix} t_1^T \\ \vdots \\ t_N^T \end{pmatrix} \tag{6}$$

With the above description, this algorithm is called tensorial extreme learning machine for tensorial data classification.

3 Conclusions

In this paper, a new UMPCA+ELM framework has been proposed for unsupervised dimensionality reduction with tensorial signal. Through a tensor-to-vector projection, the UMPCA algorithm is capable of extracting uncorrelated features directly from tensor based representation. As the features extracted by UMPCA are vectors, then a novel classifier named ELM with fast learning speed is employed for classification. Experiments results on face recognition corroborate our claim that the proposed method achieves improved recognition against existing techniques.

References

1. De Lathauwer, L., De Moor, B., Vandewalle, J.: On the best rank-1 and rank-$(R_1, R_2, \cdots, R_N)$ approximation of higher-order tensors. SIAM J. Matrix Anal. Appl. 4(21), 1324–1342 (2000)
2. Lu, H., Plataniotis, K.N., Venetsanopoulos, A.N.: MPCA: Multilinear principal component analysis of tensor objects. IEEE Trans. on Neural Networks 19(1), 18–39 (2008)
3. Turk, M., Pentland, A.: Eigenfaces for recognition. Journal of Cognitive Neuroscience 3(1), 71–86 (1991)
4. Yan, S., Xu, D., Yang, Q., Zhang, L., Tang, X., Zhang, H.J.: Multilinear discriminant analysis for face recognition. IEEE Trans. on Image Processing 16(1), 212–220 (2007)
5. Tao, D., Li, X., Wu, X., Maybank, S.J.: General tensor discriminant analysis and gabor features for gait recognition. IEEE Trans. on Pattern Analysis and Machine Intelligence 29(10), 1700–1715 (2007)
6. He, X., Cai, D., Niyogi, P.: Tensor subspace analysis. In: Advances in Neural Information Processing Systems, vol. 4(4), pp. 499–506 (2005)
7. Belhumeur, P.N., Hespanha, J.P., Krigman, D.J.: Eigenfaces vs. Fisherfaces: Recognition using class specific linear projection. IEEE Trans. on Pattern Analysis and Machine Intelligence 19(7), 711–720 (1997)
8. Song, F., Zhang, D., Mei, D., Guo, Z.: A multiple maximum scatter difference discriminant criterion for facial feature extraction. IEEE Trans. on Systems, Man, and Cybernetics, Part B: Cybernetics 37(6), 1599–1606 (2007)
9. He, X., Yan, S., Hu, Y., Niyogi, P., Zhang, H.J.: Face recognition using Laplacianfaces. IEEE Trans. on Pattern Analysis and Machine Intelligence 27(3), 328–340 (2005)
10. Er, M.J., Wu, S., Lu, J., Toh, H.L.: Face recognition with radial basis function (RBF) neural networks. IEEE Trans. on Neural Networks 13(3), 697–710 (2002)
11. Qin, J., He, Z.S.: A SVM face recognition method based on Gabor-featured key points. In: Proc. 4th IEEE Conf. on Machine Learning and Cybernetics, pp. 5144–5149 (2005)
12. Lu, J., Zhao, J., Cao, F.: Extended feed forward neural networks with random weights for face recognition. Neurocomputing 136, 96–102 (2014)

13. Hou, C., Nie, F., Yi, D., Wu, Y.: Efficient image classification via multiple rank regres-sion. IEEE Trans. on Image Processing 22(1), 340–352 (2013)
14. Hou, C., Nie, F., Zhang, C., Yi, D., Wu, Y.: Multiple rank multi-linear SVM for matrix data classification. Pattern Recognition 47(1), 454–469 (2014)
15. Huang, G.B., Zhu, Q.Y., Siew, C.K.: Extreme learning machine: theory and applications. Neurocomputing 70, 489–501 (2006)
16. Kolda, T.G., Bader, B.W.: Tensor decompositions and applications. SIAM Review 51(3), 455–500 (2009)

A Report on Uncorrelated Multilinear PCA Plus Extreme Learning Machine to Deal with Tensorial Data

Shuai Sun[1], Bin Zhou[1], and Fan Zhang[2,*]

[1] Department of Electric Power Engineering, Zhengzhou Electric Power College,
Zhengzhou, 450000, China
[2] School of Information Engineering,
North China University of Water Resources and Electric Power, Zhengzhou, 450045, China
zfgh8221@163.com

Abstract. Subspace learning is an important direction in computer vision research. In this paper, a new method of tensor objects recognition based on uncorrelated multilinear principal component analysis (UMPCA) and extreme learning machine (ELM) is proposed. Because of mostly input data sets for pattern recognition are naturally multi-dimensional objects, UMPCA seeks a tensor-to-vector projection that captures most of the variation in the original tensorial input while producing uncorrelated features through successive variance maximization. A subset of features is extracted and the classifier ELM with extremely fast learning speed is then applied to achieve better performance.

Keywords: Pattern recognition, Uncorrelated multilinear principal component analysis (UMPCA), Extreme learning machine (ELM), Classification, Feature extraction.

1 Introduction

In many practical pattern recognition problems, most of the input data sets are intrinsically multi-dimensional and they are formally called tensors. Tensor is a generalization of vectors and matrices but not limit to, such as vectors are first-order tensors and matrices are second-order tensors. Many objects are represented as tensors in the real world. For example, gray-level images are second order tensor, and gray-scale video sequences, color images, 3D objects are third order tensors. If tensor objects are vectorized during calculation projection, their intrinsic structure information will be lost [1]. In order to deal with tensorial data directly without reshaping them, the study on tensor subspace transformation is becoming an important aspect of pattern recognition research field. Multilinear principal component analysis (MPCA) [2], a tensor extension of principal component analysis (PCA) [3], applies PCA transformation on each mode of tensors. Similarly, multilinear discriminant analysis (MDA) [4], general tensor discriminant analysis (GTDA) [5], and tensor subspace analysis (TSA) [6] respectively apply linear discriminant analysis (LDA) [7], maximum scatter difference [8], and locality preserving projections (LPP) [9] to transform each mode of tensors.

---

* Corresponding author.

L. Pan et al. (Eds.): BIC-TA 2014, CCIS 472, pp. 425–429, 2014.

Beyond the multilinear subspace research introduced above, uncorrelated multilinear algorithms have been proposed during the recent years. That uncorrelated multilinear extensions of PCA take an important property of PCA into account that PCA derives uncorrelated features. Since uncorrelated features contain minimum redundancy and ensure linear independence among features, they are highly desirable in many recognition tasks [10]. In [11], a novel uncorrelated multilinear principal component analysis (UMPCA) method is proposed for unsupervised tensor object dimensionality reduction (feature extraction) based on a tensor-to-vector projection (TVP) [1] and it follows the classical PCA derivation of successive variance maximization. During the TVP, a $P \times 1$ vector can be captured that consists of P projections from a tensor to a scalar. In this paper, we use UMPCA algorithm for tensor object feature extraction, and then the $P \times 1$ vector will be the input of classifier to perform better results.

A typical data recognition system must reliably include feature extraction step and recognition step, and both of them are equally important. Feature extraction should retain most if not all of the useful information in the original data while keeping the dimension of the features as low as possible. For classification, good generalization is an important character. Since the features extracted by UMPCA are vectoring sets, one-dimensional classifier can be used for the second step. There are several classical vector-based classifiers such as nearest neighbor (NN), feed-forward neural network (FNN) [12], support vector machine (SVM) [13], and so on. Feed-forward neural networks are ideal classifiers for nonlinear mappings that utilize gradient descent approach for weights and bias optimization [14]. Huang et al. [15] proposed ELM to train a single-hidden layer feed-forward neural network (SLFNN). Unlike those traditional iterative implementations, the values of input weights and hidden biases are randomly computed by ELM while the output weights are analytically determined. As a unified learning method for regression and multiclass classification, ELM tends to have better scalability and achieves similar or much better generalization performance with faster learning speed than traditional classifiers [16]. Extensive experiments have been performed to demonstrate superiority of the proposed method over existing comparative techniques.

2   Uncorrelated Multilinear PCA and Extreme Learning Machine

As a uncorrelated multilinear extension of PCA, UMPCA is used for tensor images feature extraction and then get low dimensionality vectors which are ready for applying classifier. Next, to enhance the discriminability of extracted features and to achieve superior recognition performance, the ELM is implemented to classify the vectorized features.

2.1   Uncorrelated Multilinear Principal Component Analysis

In this section, UMPCA algorithm is introduced in detail based on the analysis introduced in [18]. A set of M tensor object samples $\{\mathcal{X}_1, \mathcal{X}_2, \cdots, \mathcal{X}_M\}$ are available for training and each tensor object $\mathcal{X}_m \in \mathbb{R}^{I_1 \times I_2 \times \cdots \times I_N}$. The objective of the UMPCA is to find a TVP, which consists of P EMPs $\left\{ \mathrm{u}_p^{(n)} \in \mathbb{R}^{I_n \times 1}, n = 1, \cdots, N \right\}_{p=1}^{P}$, mapping from the original space $\mathbb{R}^{I_1} \otimes \mathbb{R}^{I_2} \cdots \otimes \mathbb{R}^{I_N}$ into a vector subspace $\mathbb{R}^P$ (with $P < \prod_{n=1}^{N} I_n$):

$$\mathbf{y}_m = \mathcal{X}_m \times_{n=1}^{N} \left\{ \mathbf{u}_p^{(n)^T}, n = 1, \cdots, N \right\}_{p=1}^{P} \tag{1}$$

The P EMPs $\{\mathbf{u}_p^{(n)^T}, n = 1, \cdots, N\}_{p=1}^{P}$ are determined by maximizing the variance captured while producing features with zero correlation. Thus, the objective function for the Pth EMP is:

$$\left\{ \mathbf{u}_p^{(n)^T}, n = 1, \cdots, N \right\}_{p=1}^{P} = argmax \sum_{m=1}^{M} (\mathbf{y}_m(p) - \bar{\mathbf{y}}_p)^2 = argmax \mathcal{S}_{T_p}^{\mathbf{y}} \tag{2}$$

subject to $\mathbf{u}_p^{(n)^T} \mathbf{u}_p^{(n)} = 1$ and $\frac{g_p^T g_q}{\|g_p g_q\|} = \delta_{pq}, p, q = 1, \cdots, P$, where δ_{pq} is the Kronecker delta defined as:

$$\delta_{pq} = \begin{cases} 1, & \text{if } p = q \\ 0, & \text{otherwise} \end{cases} \tag{3}$$

We follow the successive variance maximization approach. The P EMPs

$$\left\{ \mathbf{u}_p^{(n)^T}, n = 1, \cdots, N \right\}_{p=1}^{P}$$

are sequentially determined in P steps, with the pth step obtaining the pth EMP.

Step 1: Determine the first EMP $\left\{ \mathbf{u}_1^{(n)^T}, n = 1, \cdots, N \right\}_{p=1}^{P}$ by maximizing $\mathcal{S}_{T1}^{\mathbf{y}}$.

Step 2: Determine the second EMP $\left\{ \mathbf{u}_2^{(n)^T}, n = 1, \cdots, N \right\}_{p=1}^{P}$ by maximizing $\mathcal{S}_{T2}^{\mathbf{y}}$ subject to the constraint that $g_2^T g_1 = 0$.

Step 3: Determine the third EMP $\left\{ \mathbf{u}_3^{(n)^T}, n = 1, \cdots, N \right\}_{p=1}^{P}$ by maximizing $\mathcal{S}_{T3}^{\mathbf{y}}$ subject to the constraint that $g_3^T g_1 = 0$ and $g_3^T g_2 = 0$.

Step $p(p = 4, \cdots, P)$: Determine the pth EMP $\left\{ \mathbf{u}_p^{(n)^T}, n = 1, \cdots, N \right\}_{p=1}^{P}$ by maximizing $\mathcal{S}_{Tp}^{\mathbf{y}}$ subject to the constraint that $g_p^T g_q = 0$ for $q = 1, \cdots, p-1$.

In order to solve for the pth EMP $\left\{ \mathbf{u}_p^{(n)^T}, n = 1, \cdots, N \right\}_{p=1}^{P}$, we need to determine N sets of parameters corresponding to N projection vectors, $\mathbf{u}_p^{(1)}, \mathbf{u}_p^{(2)}, \cdots, \mathbf{u}_p^{(N)}$, one in each mode.

2.2 Extreme Learning Machine

For N arbitrary distinct samples $(\mathbf{x}_j, \mathbf{t}_j)$, where $\mathbf{x}_j = [x_{j1}, x_{j2}, \cdots, x_{jn}]^T \in \mathbb{R}^n$ and $\mathbf{t}_j = [t_{j1}, t_{j2}, \cdots, t_{jm}]^T \in \mathbb{R}^m$, standard SLFNN with L neuron nodes and activation function g can be written as follows:

$$\mathbf{y}_j = \sum_{i=1}^{L} \beta_i g_i(\mathbf{x}_j) = \sum_{i=1}^{L} \beta_i g(\mathbf{w}_i^T \cdot \mathbf{x}_j + b_i), j = 1, \cdots, N \tag{4}$$

where $w_i = [w_{i1}, w_{i2}, \cdots, w_{in}]$ is the weight vector connecting the i-th hidden node and the input nodes, $\beta_i = [\beta_{i1}, \beta_{i2}, \cdots, \beta_{im}]^T$ is the weight vector connecting the i-th hidden node and the output nodes, and b_i is the bias of the i-th hidden node.

Considering t_j is the corresponding observation value. The ELM reliably approximates N samples with minimum error

$$\sum_{i=1}^{L} \beta_i g(w_i^T \cdot x_j + b_i) = t_j, j = 1, \cdots, N \tag{5}$$

According to ELM proposed by Huang et al. [15], a random selection of input weights w_i and the hidden layer biases b_i transforms the training of SLFNN into a linear system. Therefore, the output weights β_i can be analytically determined through a simple generalized inverse operation of the hidden layer output matrices are modeled as:

$$\widehat{\beta} = \arg \min_{\beta} \sum_{j=1}^{N} \left\| \sum_{i=1}^{L} \beta_i g(w_i^T \cdot x_j + b_i) - t_j \right\|$$
$$= \arg \min_{\beta} \|H\beta - T\| \tag{6}$$

where

$$H = \begin{bmatrix} G(w_1^T \cdot x_1) + b_1 & \cdots & G(w_L^T \cdot x_1) + b_L \\ \vdots & \ddots & \vdots \\ G(w_1^T \cdot x_N) + b_1 & \cdots & G(w_L^T \cdot x_N) + b_L \end{bmatrix} \tag{7}$$

is called the hidden layer output matrix of the neural network.

3   Conclusions

In this paper, a new UMPCA+ELM framework has been proposed for unsupervised dimensionality reduction with tensorial signal. Through a tensor-to-vector projection, the UMPCA algorithm is capable of extracting uncorrelated features directly from tensor based representation. As the features extracted by UMPCA are vectors, then a novel classifier named ELM with fast learning speed is employed for classification.

Acknowledgments. This work is supported by the Scientific Research Fund of Henan Provincial Education Department No. 14B170012.

References

1. Lu, H., Plataniotis, K.N., Venetsanopoulos, A.N.: A survey of multilinear subspace learning for tensor data. Pattern Recognition 44(7), 1540–1551 (2011)
2. Lu, H., Plataniotis, K.N., Venetsanopoulos, A.N.: MPCA: Multilinear principal component analysis of tensor objects. IEEE Trans. on Neural Networks 19(1), 18–39 (2008)
3. Turk, M., Pentland, A.: Eigenfaces for recognition. Journal of Cognitive Neuroscience 3(1), 71–86 (1991)

4. Yan, S., Xu, D., Yang, Q., Zhang, L., Tang, X., Zhang, H.J.: Multilinear discriminant analysis for face recognition. IEEE Trans. on Image Processing 16(1), 212–220 (2007)
5. Tao, D., Li, X., Wu, X., Maybank, S.J.: General tensor discriminant analysis and gabor features for gait recognition. IEEE Trans. on Pattern Analysis and Machine Intelligence 29(10), 1700–1715 (2007)
6. He, X., Cai, D., Niyogi, P.: Tensor subspace analysis. Advances in Neural Information Processing Systems 4(4), 499–506 (2005)
7. Belhumeur, P.N., Hespanha, J.P., Krigman, D.J.: Eigenfaces vs. Fisherfaces: Recognition using class specific linear projection. IEEE Trans. on Pattern Analysis and Machine Intelligence 19(7), 711–720 (1997)
8. Song, F., Zhang, D., Mei, D., Guo, Z.: A multiple maximum scatter difference discriminant criterion for facial feature extraction. IEEE Trans. on Systems, Man, and Cybernetics, Part B: Cybernetics 37(6), 1599–1606 (2007)
9. He, X., Yan, S., Hu, Y., Niyogi, P., Zhang, H.J.: Face recognition using Laplacianfaces. IEEE Trans. on Pattern Analysis and Machine Intelligence 27(3), 328–340 (2005)
10. Ye, J., Janardan, R., Li, Q., Park, H.: Feature reduction via generalized uncorrelated linear discriminant analysis. IEEE Trans. on Knowledge and Data Engineering 18(10), 1312–1322 (2006)
11. Lu, H., Plataniotis, K.N., Venetsanopoulos, A.N.: Uncorrelated multilinear principal component analysis for unsupervised multilinear subspace learning. IEEE Trans. on Neural Networks 20(11), 1820–1836 (2009)
12. Er, M.J., Wu, S., Lu, J., Toh, H.L.: Face recognition with radial basis function (RBF) neural networks. IEEE Trans. on Neural Networks 13(3), 697–710 (2002)
13. Qin, J., He, Z.S.: A SVM face recognition method based on Gabor-featured key points. In: Proc. 4th IEEE Conf. on Machine Learning and Cybernetics, pp. 5144–5149 (2005)
14. Mohammed, A.A., Minhas, R., Jonathan Wu, Q.M., Sid-Ahmed, M.A.: Human face recognition based on multidimensional PCA and extreme learning machine. Pattern Recognition 44(10), 2588–2597 (2011)
15. Huang, G.B., Zhu, Q.Y., Siew, C.K.: Extreme learning machine: theory and applications. Neurocomputing 70, 489–501 (2006)
16. He, Q., Jin, X., Du, C., Zhuang, F., Shi, Z.: Clustering in extreme learning machine feature space. Neurocomputing 128, 88–95 (2014)
17. Kolda, T.G., Bader, B.W.: Tensor decompositions and applications. SIAM Review 51(3), 455–500 (2009)
18. Lu, H., Plataniotis, K.N., Venetsanopoulos, A.N.: Uncorrelated multilinear principal component analysis through successive variance maximization. In: Proc. 25th IEEE Int. Conf. Machine Learning, pp. 616–623 (2008)

Quantum Statistical Edge Detection Using Path Integral Monte Carlo Simulation

Yangguang Sun[1,2,*]

[1] State Key Laboratory of Software Engineering, Wuhan University,
Wuhan 430072, Hubei, China
[2] School of Computer Science, South-Central University for Nationalities,
Key Laboratory of Education Ministry for Image Processing and Intelligent Control,
Huazhong University of Science and Technology,
Wuhan 430074, Hubei, China
ygsunster@aliyun.com

Abstract. A novel statistical method using path integral Monte Carlo simulation based on quantum mechanics to detect edges of interested objects was proposed in this paper. Our method was inspired by essential characteristics of quantum, and based on the quantum particle movement evolved towards the edge position with high probability density in the gradient-based image potential field. The discussion about computational complexity and parameter settings demonstrated the feasibility and robustness of our method.

Keywords: Statistical method, Edge detection, Path integral Monte Carlo simulation, Quantum mechanics.

1 Introduction

Edge detection is an important task in a variety of applications such as computer vision, image segmentation, and object recognition. Deformable models have been demonstrated to be an efficient edge detection approach widely used in many fields [1,2]; however, there are some shortcomings such as the sensitivity to initialization and difficult to handle topology changes. Although level sets [3] alleviated some of these drawbacks, the initial contour has to be symmetrically initialized with respect to the edge of interested object. Moreover, the inner and outer edge cannot be detected by a single initialization.

To solve these problems, we proposed a novel statistical method using path integral Monte Carlo (PIMC) simulation based on quantum mechanics to detect edge of the interested object of images. Our method was based on quantum mechanics and inspired by the essential characteristics of quantum, namely the quantum discontinuity of nature, and wave function including complete state information about quantum particle. Moreover, as described by Youngs double slit experiment, the probability density of quantum particle appearing at a position is proportional to the square amplitude of its wave function in quantum

---

* Corresponding author.

L. Pan et al. (Eds.): BIC-TA 2014, CCIS 472, pp. 430–434, 2014.
© Springer-Verlag Berlin Heidelberg 2014

mechanics [4,5]. Therefore, the former quantum discontinuity of nature corresponds to the discreteness of image while the later property corresponds to the gray possibility of image. The discussion about computational complexity and parameter settings demonstrated the feasibility and robustness of our method.

2 Proposed Method Using Path Integral Monte Carlo Simulation

2.1 Representation of the Path Integral

In the Schrödinger representation, the probability amplitude of finding the electron at a given position is obtained by solving Schrödinger wave equation, which can be performed by the path integral in Feynman's representation.

In Feynman's theory, the wave function $\Psi(R, t)$ of a quantum particle at position R at time t is equal to the total amplitude contributed from from the previous state at position R' at time t' along all the possible paths. From the normalized wave function, the square amplitude of the wave function is described by the propagator as:

$$|\Psi_0(R)|^2 = \lim_{T \to \infty} K(R, t, R, t')(\int_{-\infty}^{+\infty} K(R, t, R', t')dR)^{-1}. \qquad (1)$$

For a digital image, the gray-level of an image pixel at a point can be considered as the probability that a particle appears at the point. In the proposed method, when a quantum particle moves in an image under the influence of the image gradient field, the probability that the particle appears at a position depends on the gray-level contrast in the image at the position. Thus, the square amplitude of the wave function reflects the objects edge in the image.

2.2 Numerical Discretization of Path Integral

Using time lattice discretization, the path integral is translated from continuum space into discretized space. The sum over all paths connecting the initial and final points in an image is only considered at the nodes on a discretized time axis$[t_a, t_b]$. The interval is divided into M equal segments, called M time slices, $t_n = t_a + n \cdot \varepsilon$, for $n = 0, 1, \ldots, M$, where the time step ε is defined by $(t_b - t_a)/M$.

The state of a quantum particle in an image can be described as the polymer isomorphism introduced by Chandler and Wolynes [6]. Intuitively, each quantum particle is represented by a necklace of beads in Ref.[7]. Time slices corresponds to the number of beads. Now, a path can be interpreted as a polymer represented by a necklace of beads. Using the Trotter formula and the Wick rotation transform $\mu = i\varepsilon$ and letting $\beta = \mu/\hbar$ (i.e. m is the mass of a quantum particle and $\hbar$ is Planck's constant), the propagator in Euclidean space is described as:

$$K(R_0, R_M; \beta) = \left(\frac{m}{2\pi\mu\hbar}\right)^{\frac{M}{2}} \int \prod_{j=1}^{M-1} dR_j \cdot exp[-\frac{\mu}{\hbar}E(R_0, R_1, \ldots, R_M))]. \qquad (2)$$

where the energy function E is defined as $\sum_{j=1}^{M}[\frac{m}{2}(\frac{R_j - R_{j-1}}{\mu})^2 - V(R_{j-1})]$, and a path is described by the location R_j at time t_j.

2.3   Monte Carlo Simulation Based on Metropolis Sampling

Obviously, the integrand is always non-negative and can be interpreted as a probability, an essential property of Monte Carlo simulation. Therefore, an alternative is to construct a Markov chain using Monte Carlo technique by sampling a given probability distribution[8,9]. Now, Eq.(2) can be rewritten as:

$$|\Psi_0(\boldsymbol{R})|^2 = Z^{-1} \int \prod_{j=1}^{M} d\boldsymbol{R}_j exp[-\frac{\mu}{\hbar}E(\boldsymbol{R}, \boldsymbol{R}_1, \boldsymbol{R}_2, \ldots, \boldsymbol{R}_M)]) \tag{3}$$

where Z is defined by $Z = \int \prod_{j=0}^{M} d\boldsymbol{R}_j exp[-\frac{\mu}{\hbar}E(\boldsymbol{R}_0, \boldsymbol{R}_1, \boldsymbol{R}_2, \ldots, \boldsymbol{R}_M)]$.

Therefore, sampling is an essential operation in path integral Monte Carlo method, and will control the beads within the necklaces. Because the sampling distribution is arbitrary, the well-known Monte Carlo technique proposed by Metropolis et al. can be used to sample any known probability distribution and be a powerful tool to handle quantum questions [10,11]. The used Metropolis algorithm is an effective approach sampling a probability distribution.

3   Computational Complexity and Parameter Settings

3.1   Computational Complexity Analysis

The main computational cost of our method occurs at two stages: generating the required samples, and complete the path integration. Sampling a given distribution required using Metropolis algorithm dominates over the overall computational cost. The latter stage, i.e., the average procedure, depends on the length of Markov chains and the number of image pixels. Therefore, the total computational time depends on the chosen parameters, such as time slices, time step, standard deviation, and the length of Markov chains etc.

3.2   Time Slices and Time Step

Two requirements have to be considered in the choice of the time step and time slices. From Trottor formulation, the approximation is exact in the case of infinite time slices. Furthermore, if the time slices, the number of beads in a polymer, is not sufficiently large, the polymer would not spread as much as expected for a given conditions. The detected edges become more intact as the time slices increases.

3.3   Standard Deviation

The random number is generated with the probability Gaussian distribution using the Metropolis-Hasting algorithm based on Metropolis sampling. The efficiency of updating the paths is determined by the standard deviation. When the standard deviation is large, the nodes in the paths will have a large change and most of them will be rejected; if the standard deviation is too small, the changes is too subtitle and most of them are accepted. Both extreme conditions are undesirable because they all produce too small changes on the paths, which lead to a slow convergence.

3.4   Length of Markov Chain

The length of Markov chain is independent. When it increases, the statistical error vanishes, which can ensure that the convergence of the calculation and the detected edges become increasingly more intact as shown in Fig. 1. However, a large computational time is taken. In addition, no matter whatever the variance is chosen, the produced successive paths always have some correlation. Because the paths at the beginning of Markov Chain are usually atypical, therefore, the choice of the length of Markov chain is necessary for the generation of a satisfactory Markov Chain. These optimal values depend upon the application and can be determined by the experiment.

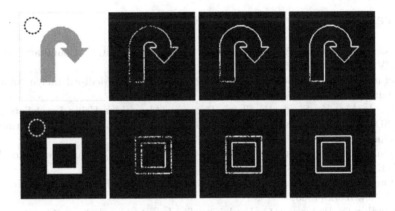

Fig. 1. Effect of parameter settings in our method. First row: original image with initialization (the dotted polymer), the detected edges with the same length of Markov chain as time slices increases respectively; Second row: input image with initialization, the detected edges as the length of Markov chain increases respectively.

4   Conclusions

In conclusion, we described a novel statistical method using path integral Monte Carlo method based on quantum mechanics to detect the edge in this paper. Our method was inspired by essential characteristics of quantum, and based on the quantum particle movement evolved towards the edge position with high probability density in the gradient-based image potential field. The discussion about computational complexity and parameter settings demonstrated the feasibility and robustness of our method.

Acknowledgments. This work is supported by National Natural Science Foundation of China (60672057), Open Foundation of Key Laboratory of Education Ministry of China for Image Processing and Intelligence Control (200906), Natural Science Foundation of South-Central University for Nationalities (YZY10006), Academic Team of South-Central University for Nationalities (XTZ10002), Science and Technique Research Guidance Programs of Hubei Provincial Department of Education of China (B20110802), "the Fundamental Research Funds for the Central Universities", South-Central University for Nationalities (CZY12007, CTZ12023), and Open Foundation of State Key Laboratory of Software Engineering(SKLSE2 0120934), Natural Science Foundation of Hubei Province of China (2012FFB07404).

References

1. Kass, M., Witkin, A., Terzopoulus, D.: Snakes: Active Bound-ary Model. IJCV 1(4), 321–331 (1988)
2. McInerney, T., Terzopoulos, D.: Deformable Models in Medi-cal Image Analysis: A Survey. Medical Image Analysis 1, 91–108 (1996)
3. Suri, J., Liu, K., Singh, S.: Shape Recovery Algorithms Using Level Sets in 2-D/3D Medical Imagery: A State of the Art Review. IEEE Trans. on Information Technology in Biomedicine 6, 8–28 (2002)
4. Feymann, R.P.: Space-time Approach to Non-relativistic Quantum Mechanics. Rev. Mod. Phys. 20, 367–387 (1948)
5. Feynman, R.P., Hibbs, A.R.: Quantum Mechanics and Path Integrals. McGraw-Hill, New York (1965)
6. Chandler, D., Wolynes, P.G.: Exploiting The Isomorphism Between Quantum Theory and Classical Statistical Mechanics of Polyatomic Fluids. J. Chem. Phys. 74(7), 4078–4095 (1981)
7. Brualla Barbera, L.: Path integral Monte Carlo algorithms and applications to quantum fluids. Universitat Politénica de Catalunya, Barcelona (2002)
8. Ceperley, D.M., Manousakis, E.: Path integral Monte Carlo Applications to Quantum Fluids in Confined Geometries. J. Chem. Phys. 115(22), 10111–10118 (2001)
9. Shumway, J., Gilbert, M.J.: Path Integral Monte Carlo Simulations of Nanowires and Quantum Point Contacts. J. Phys. Conf. Ser. 35, 190–196 (2006)
10. Metropolis, N., Rosenbluth, A.W., Rosenbluth, M.N.: Equations of state calculations by fast computing machines. J. Chem. Phys. 21, 1087–1091 (1953)
11. Ceperley, D.M.: Path Integrals in the Theory of Condensed Helium. Rev. Mod. Phys. 67, 279–355 (1995)

Intelligent Model-Based Speed Controller Design for PMSM

Lisi Tian, Yang Liu*, and Jin Zhao

School of Automation, Huazhong University of Science and Technology,
Wuhan 430074, Hubei, China
tianlisi@hust.edu.cn, yangliu30@gmail.com, jinzhao617@163.com

Abstract. An intelligent model-based speed controller of permanent magnet synchronous motors (PMSM) is proposed in this paper, which synthesizes the simplicity of PID controller and the adaptability of artificial neural network based controller. Small signal model of the speed loop as the foundation of the framework of the controller is analyzed. The gradient rule is utilized to update the weights of the neuron inputs, and auxiliary retrain process is used to improve the dynamic performance of the controller. A comprehensive simulation was done to verify the validation of the intelligent speed controller. Comparison with the conventional PID controller demonstrates the outstanding performance and robustness of the proposed controller. The feasibility of implementation of the proposed speed controller on physical platforms is also covered in this paper.

Keywords: Small signal model, Permanent magnet Synchronous motor, Artificial neural network, Speed control.

1 Introduction

Permanent magnet synchronous motor (PMSM) has been in a growing wide use in recent years, especially in application fields where high precision control and fast response are required [1]. PMSM gains reputation for its outstanding characteristics, such as high energy density, low torque ripples, high torque per current rating [2], etc. The most conventional speed control method of PMSM is the PID control, which has been used over decades and in many cases is the first choice of many engineers, benefiting from the distinguished advantages that PID controller is easy to implement and fair satisfied results can be achieved under most circumstances. However, the PID-based speed control is also on the same time criticized for its sensitivity to parameter variations [3,4].

With the rapid development of microprocessors and intelligent control theories, new control approaches emerged, including sliding mode [5], fuzzy logic [6], and artificial neural network (ANN) [4], etc. These mentioned control methods share some common shortcomings, such as the increase of complexity of the whole control system, large amount of computation overhead.

---

* Corresponding author.

L. Pan et al. (Eds.): BIC-TA 2014, CCIS 472, pp. 435–439, 2014.

2 Framework of the Controller

Relationship of the torque and the speed of the PMSM is expressed in equation

$$T_e = T_L + B_m\omega + J_m p\omega \tag{1}$$

The small signal analysis of the dynamic model of the speed loop of PMSM is

$$\Delta T_e = J_m \frac{d(\Delta\omega)}{dt} + B_m\Delta\omega \tag{2}$$

Applying continuous to discrete time domain transform, (2) can be rewritten as

$$\Delta T_e(n) = \frac{J_m}{T_s}\left(\Delta\omega(n+1) - \Delta\omega(n)\right) + B_m\Delta\omega(n+1) \tag{3}$$

Hence, the expected torque is a nonlinear function of the reference speed, the feedback speed and previous feedback speed, as equation (4) suggests.

$$\begin{aligned}
T_e(n) &= \frac{J_m}{T_s}\sum\Delta T_e(n)\\
&= f\left(\Delta\omega(n+1), \Delta\omega(n)\right)\\
&= f\left(\omega^*(n), \omega(n), \omega(n-1)\right)
\end{aligned} \tag{4}$$

On the other hand, the discrete PID controller, as the transfer function (5) indicates, is a nonlinear combination of the speed error and its difference.

$$u(n) = K_P e(n) + K_I\sum e(n) + K_D\Delta e(n) \tag{5}$$

Combining the small signal model of the speed loop and the PID controller, the intelligent model-based speed controller is proposed, as shown in

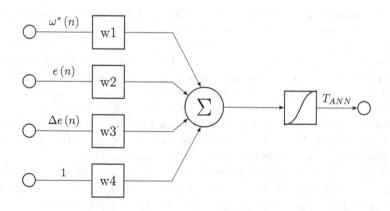

Fig. 1. Framework of the intelligent model-based speed controller

3   Update and Retrain Rule

Back-propagation updating for the four weights, w1, w2, w3 and bias is utilized
to make the controller adaptive. When the speed track error exceeds a preset
threshold (0.1rad/s), the update routine is triggered and executed once in every
sampling time interval. The weights hold themselves when the speed track error
lies in the acceptable limits. Gradient method is used to adjust the weights of
the inputs, and speed track error is the performance index.

To further improve the dynamic performance of the controller, an auxiliary
retrain process is proposed on the basis of an internal generated auxiliary torque
reference. The torque reference is generated based on load estimation and an
arbitrary nonlinear function of the reference speed and speed track error. The
retrain process is only activated when the torque track error exceeds a relative
error as 0.4.

The update and retraining processes, along with a corresponding supervisory
program comprise the whole speed controller. During each sampling period, the
update process is evoked to produce the latest weights and bias, and the permitted range of torque is also generated via the auxiliary torque reference path.
The supervisory routine checks the validity of the present weights and bias by
determining whether the output of the controller lies in the permitted range. If
the output is out of range, the present weights and bias are discarded and the
retraining process is evoked to produce a more rational weights and bias set,
which ensures that the output complies with the its preset path. Otherwise, the
retraining process is bypassed.

4   Simulation Results and Discussion

To verify the validity of the proposed controller, a comprehensive simulation
was carried out on the platform MATLAB/SIMULINK. Fig 2 zooms in the interested details of the simulation result, from which the improvements through
retraining can be viewed clearly. The overshoot deceases from 3.2rad/s (2.1%)
to 1.6rad/s (1.1%), speed dropout deceases from 3.8rad/s (2.5%) to 1.9rad/s
(1.3%), the recovering time decreases from 0.5sec to 0.27sec. Dynamic performance with retrain is much better, while the steady-state performance is the
same because the retraining process is blocked when the motor reaches a steady
state. Throughout the whole simulation, only two retraining events occurred as
expected, one happened at the time when overshoot occurs, the other at the
time when the load changed. The update process and auxiliary reference torque
accommodate each other well.

Additionally, a discrete conventional PID controller is tuned and simulated to
serve as a cross comparison to the proposed speed controller. Forward Euler rule
is used in the discretization process and a low pass filter is put in the differential
path. The clamping anti-windup method is utilized to get a better response. Fig
3 shows the performance of the PID controller, of which the coefficients were
tuned to get a tradeoff between the overshoot and load disturbance transients.

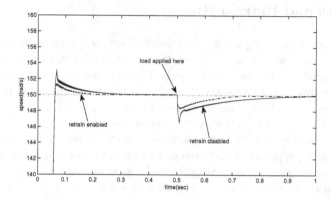

Fig. 2. Performance comparison of the proposed controller with and without retraining

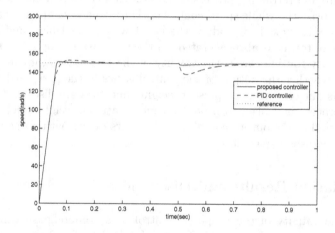

Fig. 3. Performance comparison of the proposed controller with PID controller

The comparison demonstrates that the proposed speed controller offers a better performance. Due to the simplicity of the model-based speed controller, real-time implementation of the controller in physical platforms is feasible. During each control cycle, the update routine executes only once, thus the computation burden is not heavy. In control cycles when retraining is evoked, simulation demonstrates that in most cases, the retraining process can be completed within 4 iterations, and format of the processing data can be fixed-point numbers due to the large error tolerance.

5   Conclusion

In conclusion, the intelligent model-based speed controller is simple and clearly organized, inheriting the neatness of conventional PID controllers and adaptability of artificial neural network based controllers. The dynamic and steady-state performance is satisfactory with the proposed controller, and the computation costs are acceptable. The convergence of the update process is fast and stable, and the auxiliary retrain process functions in the way as expected, improving the dynamic speed response significantly. The simulation results indicate that the controller is adaptive and robust.

Acknowledgments. The Authors gratefully acknowledge the support of National Nature Science Foundation of China (61304034).

References

1. Miller, T.J.E.: Permanent Magnet and Reluctance Motor Drives. Oxford Science Publications, Oxford (1989)
2. Pillay, P., Krishnan, R.: Application characteristics of permanent magnet synchronous and brushless dc motors for servo drives. IEEE Transactions on Industry Applications 27(5), 986–996 (1991)
3. Bose, B.K.: High performance control and estimation in ac drives. In: 23rd International Conference on Industrial Electronics, Control and Instrumentation, IECON 1997, vol. 2, pp. 377–385 (1997)
4. Rahman, M.A., Hoque, M.A.: On-line Adaptive Artificial Neural Network Based Vector Control of Permanent Magnet Synchronous Motors. IEEE Transactions on Energy Conversion 13(4), 311–318 (1998)
5. Zhang, X., Sun, L., Zhao, K., Sun, L.: Nonlinear Speed Control for Pmsm System Using Sliding-Mode Control and Disturbance Compensation Techniques. IEEE Transactions on Power Electronics 28(3), 1358–1365 (2013)
6. Choi, H.H., Jung, J.-W.: Discrete-time fuzzy speed regulator design for pm synchronous motor. IEEE Transactions on Industrial Electronics 60(2), 600–607 (2013)

Phase-Locked Loop (PLL) Type Sensorless Control of PMSM Using Neural Network Filter

Lisi Tian, Jin Zhao*, and Zhenfeng Peng

College of Automation, Huazhong University of Science and Technology,
Wuhan, China
{tianlisi,pengzhenfeng}@hust.edu.cn,
jinzhao617@163.com

Abstract. This paper describes a Phase-Locked Loop (PLL) type sensorless control strategy of permanent-magnet synchronous machines with pulsating high frequency (HF) voltage signal injection. The HF model of the PMSM and the demodulation scheme are analyzed in detail. A neural network (NN) based adaptive filter replaces the common band-pass filter (BPF) to extract the desired frequency signal which includes the rotor position information. The proposed NN filter has an adjustable bandwidth which helps the filter to capture the desired signal even in the presence of high speed estimation errors. The recursive least square (RLS) algorithm is used to update the neuron weights. The simulation results verify the performance of the proposed NN adaptive filter in the sensorless control strategy.

Keywords: Permanent-magnet synchronous motor (PMSM), phase-locked loop (PLL), neural network (NN), sensorless control, recursive least square (RLS) algorithm.

1 Introduction

Permanent-magnet synchronous machines (PMSMs) are widely used especially in many high-performance applications. The control algorithms without speed sensor have been developed in the last two decades. Eliminating the speed sensor on the motor shaft means the absence of relevant mechanical component and sensor cable, bringing benefits of lower cost, reduced hardware complexity and increased reliability[1]. Sensorless control in the low speed range requires signal injection techniques for rotor position estimation. The signal injection methods exploit the anisotropic properties of PMSMs, caused either by the inherent saliency due to machine geometry, or by the saturation of the stator iron[2]. Two different types of carrier signals are usually used for sensorless control: rotating high frequency carrier signal[3] and pulsating high frequency carrier signal[4].

In[5], the speed and position estimation algorithm is interpreted as a PLL whose bandwidth has a clear relationship with the selection of design parameter. In the normal demodulation scheme, the measured current is band-pass filtered (BPF).

---

* Corresponding author.

L. Pan et al. (Eds.): BIC-TA 2014, CCIS 472, pp. 440–446, 2014.

The filtered high frequency current is then demodulated and low-pass filtered to extract the rotor position information. In[6], the classic fixed band BPF is replaced by a neural network (NN) based adaptive variable-band filter. The filter structure is based on a linear neural network (ADALINE)[7]. In[8], the NN filter is used to remove the harmonic estimation error in back-EMF based sensorless control.

This paper presents a PLL-type speed and position estimator based on the work presented in[5]. The structure of NN filter is introduced. The training method using the recursive least square (RLS) algorithm is discussed. The bandwidth of the NN filter is adjusted according to the change of the estimated speed.

2   PLL-type Speed and Position Estimator of PMSM

The PMSM model in the matrix form is expressed as (1) where p represents the differential operator and λ_f represents the permanent-magnet flux linkage.

$$\begin{bmatrix} u_d \\ u_q \end{bmatrix} = \begin{bmatrix} R + pL_d & -\omega L_q \\ \omega L_d & R + pL_q \end{bmatrix} \begin{bmatrix} i_d \\ i_q \end{bmatrix} + \begin{bmatrix} 0 \\ \omega \lambda_f \end{bmatrix} \tag{1}$$

The high frequency model of PMSMs can be simplified as:

$$\begin{bmatrix} u_{cd} \\ u_{cq} \end{bmatrix} \approx \begin{bmatrix} L_d & 0 \\ 0 & L_q \end{bmatrix} \begin{bmatrix} \frac{di_{cd}}{dt} \\ \frac{di_{cq}}{dt} \end{bmatrix} \tag{2}$$

The position error signal used in the sensorless control can be obtained from (3), where θ is the actual rotor position, $\hat{\theta}$ is the estimated rotor position, and K is the application specific gain.

$$\varepsilon = K \sin \left[m \left(\theta - \hat{\theta} \right) \right] \tag{3}$$

The PLL-type speed and position estimation algorithm used in this paper is expressed as (4) and (5), and the error signal is obtained using HF signal injection.

$$\dot{\hat{\omega}} = \gamma_1 \varepsilon \tag{4}$$

$$\dot{\hat{\theta}} = \hat{\omega} + \gamma_2 \varepsilon \tag{5}$$

By properly selecting the gain γ_1 and γ_2 as (6) and (7), a stable speed and position estimator is acquired. The dynamic property is related to the selection of ρ.

$$\gamma_1 = \frac{\rho^2}{mK} \tag{6}$$

$$\gamma_2 = \frac{2\rho}{mK} \tag{7}$$

The block diagram of the proposed speed and position sensorless drive is shown in Fig 1. The essence of the sensorless control algorithm is to extract the saliency position information from the HF current.

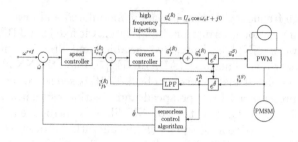

Fig. 1. Block diagram of the proposed sensorless drive

Usually the HF current can be separated from the fundamental current with a band-pass filter (BPF), as in (8).

$$\overrightarrow{i_c}(\hat{R}) = BPF\left(i^{(S)}e^{-j\hat{\theta}}\right) \tag{8}$$

The demodulation process is expressed as (9).

$$i_{\tilde{\theta}} = LPF\left(i_{c\hat{q}}\sin\omega_c t\right) = \frac{U_c}{2\omega_c \Delta L}sin2\tilde{\theta} \tag{9}$$

Comparing formula (9) with (3), $K = \frac{U_c}{2\omega_c \Delta L}$ and $m = 2$ can be applied. Utilizing (4) and (5), the PLL-type speed and position estimator is accomplished.

3   Neural Network Based Filter

The adaptive filter structure is based on a linear neural network (ADALINE). As compared with the fixed band BPF, the NN filter provides an easy way to track the exact frequency by adapting its weights online and the bandwidth of NN filter can be adjusted.

The structure of the NN filter is shown in Fig 2. The inputs of the neuron are two orthogonal signals with amplitude C and frequency ω_0, given by (10) and (11). It is used as a notch adaptive filter in [7] to attenuate 60-Hz noise in electrocardiogram (ECG).

$$x_{1,k} = C\cos\left(k\omega_0 + \phi\right) \tag{10}$$

$$x_{2,k} = C\sin\left(k\omega_0 + \phi\right) \tag{11}$$

In [9], the adaptive filters using LMS algorithm and RLS algorithm are discussed respectively. Compared with the LMS algorithm, the RLS algorithm is more complex and require more computational resources. But the filter order

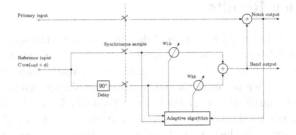

Fig. 2. The structure of NN filter

using the RLS algorithm is much smaller. And the RLS algorithm has a faster convergence velocity and better filtering effect.

The matric operation in the RLS algorithm needs more calculation resources. In order to make the calculation process faster and easier, the update algorithm can be simplified as follows.

$$\begin{cases} w_{1,k} = w_{1,k-1} + g_{1,k}\varepsilon_k \\ w_{2,k} = w_{2,k-1} + g_{2,k}\varepsilon_k \end{cases} \tag{12}$$

The gain vector $G(k)$ is transformed into two gains $g_{1,k}$ and $g_{2,k}$, which can be calculated as (13).

$$\begin{cases} g_{1,k} = \frac{\phi_{1,k}}{\lambda + r_{1,k}\phi_{1,k}} \\ g_{2,k} = \frac{\phi_{2,k}}{\lambda + r_{2,k}\phi_{2,k}} \end{cases} \tag{13}$$

The coefficient λ is the forgetting factor, which is a positive constant close but less than 1. $\phi_{1,k}$ and $\phi_{2,k}$ are the intermediate variables, given as (14), where the diagonal element P_{11} and P_{22} are extracted from the autocorrelation matrix P. The update method of P_{11} and P_{22} can be expressed as (15).

$$\begin{cases} \phi_{1,k} = P_{11,k-1}r_1(k) \\ \phi_{2,k} = P_{22,k-1}r_2(k) \end{cases} \tag{14}$$

$$\begin{cases} P_{11,k} = \frac{P_{11,k-1} - g_{1,k}\phi_{1,k-1}}{\lambda} \\ P_{22,k} = \frac{P_{22,k-1} - g_{2,k}\phi_{2,k-1}}{\lambda} \end{cases} \tag{15}$$

In this paper, the NN adaptive filter using RLS algorithm replaces the fix-band BPF to extract the desired frequency signal. In practical applications, two aspects should be considered.

In order to adjust the bandwidth of NN filter according to the error between the real speed and the estimated speed, the forgetting factor λ can be expressed as (16)

$$\begin{cases} \lambda = \lambda_{\max}, if \; |\omega - \hat{\omega}| \geq \Delta\omega \\ \lambda = \lambda_{\max} - \frac{|\omega - \hat{\omega}|}{\Delta\omega}(\lambda_{\max} - \lambda_{\min}), if \; |\omega - \hat{\omega}| < \Delta\omega \end{cases} \tag{16}$$

4   Simulation Results

The sample is synchronized to the modulation, and both the sample frequency and the switching frequency are 8 kHz. The deadtime is set at $3\mu s$. The Saber Designer environment in used for the simulation. Considering the HF model $u_h = \omega_h L_d I_h$, in order to limit the HF current amplitude within 250mA, the injection voltage amplitude is selected from 20V-60V. It can be observed that the rotor speed tracks the reference speed properly. A relatively large position estimation error exists in the transient region. In steady-state region, the position estimation error is limited within 0.05rad.

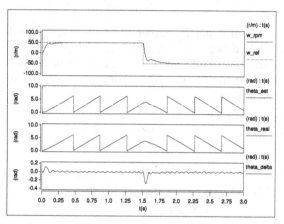

Fig. 3. Simulation results of the rotor speed and the position estimation error with reversal speed reference from 50r/m to −50r/m under 2Nm load

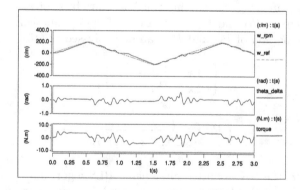

Fig. 4. Simulation results of the rotor speed and the position estimation error using the NN filter with triangular speed reference from 200r/m to −200r/m under 2Nm load

Triangular speed reference test results of control scheme using proposed NN based filter and the common fixed band BPF are shown in Fig 4 and Fig 5 respectively. The triangular speed reference of 200 r/min peak and 0.5Hz frequency, corresponding to an acceleration of 400 r/m/s, has been provided. The rotor speed, the position estimation error and the electromagnetic torque are presented from top to bottom. It is clear that the control strategy using NN based filter has better transient performance. The adaptive bandwidth helps the NN filter to capture the desired signal even in the presence of high speed estimation errors. The position estimation error and the electromagnetic torque waveform is less noisy. So the proposed sensorless control strategy provides better speed tracking performance.

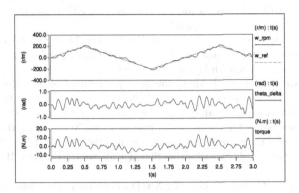

Fig. 5. Simulation results of the rotor speed and the position estimation error using the common fixed band BPF with triangular speed reference from 200r/m to −200r/m under 2Nm load.

5 Conclusion

This paper has presented the PLL-type sensorless control strategy of PMSM. The pulsating HF voltage signal is injected to the d-axis. The NN based adaptive filter replaces the common fixed band BPF to extract the desired frequency current of q-axis. The NN filter provides an easy way to track the exact frequency by adapting its weights online. The bandwidth can be adjusted by changing the forgetting factor of the RLS algorithm. As for the NN filter, the high stop-band attenuation and the wide bandwidth cannot be meet simultaneously. In order to improve the transient performance, the stop band attenuation is sacrificed. The demodulation scheme used in this paper makes up the low frequency attenuation shortage. The simulation investigation has proven that the proposed sensorless control scheme using the adaptive NN filter enables better transient performance than the common fixed band BPF.

Acknowledgments. The Authors gratefully acknowledge the support of National Nature Science Foundation of China (61273174).

References

1. Holtz, J.: Sensorless Control of Induction Motor Drives. In: Proceedings of the IEEE International Conference on Intelligent Computing, pp. 1359–1394 (2002)
2. Jang, J., Sul, S., Ha, J., Ide, K., Sawamura, M.: Sensorless Drive of Surface-mounted Permanent-magnet Motor by High-frequency Signal Injection Based on Magnetic Saliency. IEEE Transactions on Power Electronics 39(4), 1031–1039 (2003)
3. Briz, F., Degner, M.W., Garcia, P., Lorenz, R.D.: Comparison of Saliency-Based Sensorless Control Techniques for Ac machines. IEEE Transactions on Industry Applications 40(4), 1107–1115 (2004)
4. Corley, L.: Rotor Position and Velocity Estimation for a Salient-pole Permanent Magnet Synchronous Machine at Standstill and High Speeds. IEEE Transactions on Industry Applications 34(4), 784–789 (1998)
5. Harnefors, N.H.: A General Algorithm for Speed and Position Estimation of Ac Motors. IEEE Transactions on Industrial Electronics 47(1), 77–83 (2000)
6. Angelo, A., Maurizio, C., Marcello, P., Gianpaolo, V.: Sensorless Control of Pmsm Fractional Horsepower Drives by Signal Injection and Neural Adaptive-Band Filtering. IEEE Transactions on Industrial Electronics 59(3), 1355–1366 (2012)
7. Bernard, W., Samuel, D.S.: Adaptive Signal Processing. Prentice-Hall, Englewood Cliffs (1985)
8. Wang, G., Li, T., Zhang, G., Gui, X., Xu, D.: Position Estimation Error Reduction Using Recursive-Least-Square Adaptive Filter for Model-Based Sensorless Interior Permanent-Magnet Synchronous Motor Drives. IEEE Transactions on Industrial Electronics 61(9), 5115–5125 (2014)
9. Ortolan, R.L., Mori, R.N., Pereira, R.N., Cabral, C.M., Pereira, J.C., Cliquet, A.: Evaluation of Adaptive/Nonadaptive Filtering and Wavelet Transform Techniques for Noise Reduction in Emg Mobile Acquisition Equipment. IEEE Transactions on Neural Systems and Rehabilitation Engineering 11(1), 60–69 (2003)

Facial Expression Recognition Based on Feature Block and Local Binary Pattern

Wencheng Wang[1,2] and Faliang Chang[2]

[1] College of Information and Control Engineering, Weifang University,
Weifang, 261061, China
[2] College of Control Science and Engineering, Shandong University,
Jinan, 250014, China

Abstract. Automatic facial expression recognition (FER) played more and more important role in recent years for its wide range of potential applications. So, as one of the challenging tasks in intelligent system, it still has many questions need to be deeply researched. Taking into account the importance of eyes and mouth for FER and the outstanding performance of local binary pattern (LBP) to extract local textures, a representation model for facial expressions based on feature blocks and LBP descriptor is proposed. The strategies of feature blocks obtaining and LBP feature extracting are analyzed in details and the recognition experiment is conducted. Experimental result shows that this algorithm has good performance.

Keywords: Facial Expression Recognition, Principle Component Analysis, Feature Block, Local Binary Pattern.

1 Introduction

With the development of computer technology, automatic facial expression recognition (FER) has attracted much attentions in recent years for its wide range of potential applications in areas such as image understanding, psychological study, synthetic face animation and intelligent human computer interaction. Several of methods have been proposed to solve this problem, such as the Facial Action Coding System (FACS) [1], Eigenfaces [2], bilinear factorization expression classifier [3], 2D Gabor wavelet representation [4], Artificial Neural Networks (ANN), Support Vector Machines(SVM), Wavelet Analysis, Hidden Markov Model (HMM) and Optical Flow [5–10], etc..

As the appearance feature, local binary pattern is brilliant because of its low computation cost and texture description ability; it have gained increasing attention in facial image analysis due to its robustness to challenges such as pose and illumination changes [11–13]. But during the course of LBP using, it is observed that some local facial regions contain more useful information for expression classification than others in original face images, that is to say, different sub-regions have different contribution to the classification. This motives us to propose a method for facial expression recognition by cropping the feature blocks from original image and extracting LBP features in this paper.

L. Pan et al. (Eds.): BIC-TA 2014, CCIS 472, pp. 447–451, 2014.

2 Local Binary Pattern and Feature Block

2.1 Local Binary Pattern

The original local binary pattern (LBP) operator is a powerful method for texture description; it describes the surroundings of the pixel by generating a bit-code from the binary derivatives of a pixel in an image. At a given pixel position (x_c, y_c), LBP is defined as an ordered set of binary comparisons of pixel intensities between the central pixel and its neighbor pixels. Taking 3×3 pixels for example, the resulting LBP pattern at the pixel can be expressed as follows:

$$LBP(x_c, y_c) = \sum_{n=0}^{7} s(i_n - i_c) \times 2^n \tag{1}$$

2.2 Feature Block

As for the facial expression recognition, the traditional approaches based on whole face are highly sensitive to noise caused by the human face contour, hair, etc.. In order to reduce the influence of such noises, the original image needs pre-processing by cutting off the useless part such as hair, background, contour and reserving the main areas of the pure face only. But the cut face image still has a lot of redundancies.

If we take the human face as an object, then the eyes, nose, mouth, forehead will be the components of the object, and the area which contains different components will be named as a feature block. So the face can be described well by using a few feature blocks and their relations. Suppose a human face could be decomposed to n_b feature blocks and n_r corresponding relations, and then the face can be defined as the model:

$$F = U(B_i, R_j)i = 1, \ldots, n_b \quad j = 1, \ldots, r_j \tag{2}$$

3 Feature Extraction and Dimension Reduction

3.1 Face Image Pre-processing

In order to improve the efficiency of extracting facial features, more facial image pre-processing including feature region localization and face normalization are performed before detecting facial feature points. The ideal output of processing is to obtain pure facial expression images with normalized intensity, uniform size and shape. In this work, all the images have aligned two eyes and mouth with same size, the detailed strategy is as follows. At first, we manually select the two eyes and mouth centers, gain the corresponding coordinates of these 3 points, and keep the left eyes center and right eye center on the same level by rotating.

3.2   Feature Blocks Obtaining

It is observed that some local facial regions contain more useful information for expression classification than others. Considering human eyes and mouth maybe have mainly contribution to the classification based on man-made experience, we mainly crop the eyes region and mouth region as feature blocks. In order to facilitate the operation for calculating LBP features, each face image is divided into possibly several non-overlapping sub-regions firstly. It should be pointed out that there are several of ways for division, the division scheme of LBP operator has some extent influence on the effectiveness of LBP. In this way, we effectively have a description of the facial expression.

3.3   LBP Feature Extraction and Selection

Because a LBP histogram computed over the whole face image encodes only the occurrences of the micro-patterns without any indication about their locations. So in order to consider shape information of faces, face images were divided into small regions equally to extract LBP histograms. The LBP features extracted from each sub-region are concatenated into a single, spatially enhanced feature histogram defined as:

$$H_{ij} = \sum_{x,y} I\{f_l(x,y) = i\}I\{(x,y) \in R_j\} \quad i = 0,\ldots,n-1, j = 0,\ldots,m-1 \quad (3)$$

4   Experimental Results and Analysis

In this section, experiments are performed on international open database to testify the effectiveness of the proposed algorithm for facial expression recognition. The proposed algorithm is implemented in MATLAB2008a with Windows XP platform. Recognition rate is defined as follows:

$$ratio = \frac{Num_{correct}}{Num_{all}} \times 100\% \quad (4)$$

where $ratio$ is the correct recognition rate, $Num_{correct}$ is the number of correct matches, and Num_{all} is the total number of test images.

We test our verification method on the JAFFE database and TFEID database. From what is discussed above, a number of experimental findings can be extracted from the results:

(1) FER performance based on LBP features are much better than those methods based directly on gray level images.

(2) The proposed algorithm works well on JAFFE database, especially on TFEID database with higher recognition rate.

(3) It is clear that the combination of eyes block and mouth block has better performance than each of them woks respectively.

5   Conclusion

Comparing with the nonlinear models algorithm, the proposed algorithm is rather computationally simpler and most likely will not be over-fitting, and it is effective when applied to images with a variety of different illumination conditions. Though the proposed method in this paper can improve the total recognition ratios to some extent, it still needs researching and improving, especially the way how to combine of eyes block with mouth block optimally needs the researchers' efforts. Our next goal is to exploit the method for selecting and cropping the more feature blocks resulting from the feature representation of face images, further search for an optimal joint strategy of feature blocks and applying the method for facial expression classification. Over all, facial expression recognition rates are still relatively low for practical applications, and there is a long way to go for FER.

Acknowledgments. This work is supported by Shandong Provincial Natural Science Foundation, China (No. ZR2013FQ036), Natural Science Foundation of China (No. 61273277), by the Spark Program of China (No. 2013XH06034), by the Spark Program of Shandong Province (No. 2013XH06034) and Technology Development Plan of Weifang City (No. 201301015). We would also like to express our thanks to Brain Mapping Laboratory (National Yang-Ming University), they offer us the TFEID database for testing our method.

References

1. Ekman, P., Friesen, W.V.: Constants Across Cultures in The Face and Emotion. Journal of Personality Social Psychology 17(2), 124–129 (1971)
2. Pantic, M., Rothkrantz, L.: Facial Action Recognition for Facial Expression Analysis From Static Face Images. IEEE Trans. SMC-Part B 34, 1449–1461 (2004)
3. Abboud, B., Davoine, F.: Appearance Factorization for Facial Expression Recognition and Synthesis. In: Proceedings International Conference on Pattern Recognition, pp. 163–166 (2004)
4. Lyons, M., Budynek, J., Akamatsu, S.: Automatic Classification of Single Facial Images. IEEE Trans. PAMI 21(12), 1357–1362 (1999)
5. Domaika, F., Davoine, F.: Simultaneous Facial Action Tracking and Expression Recognition in the Presence of Head Motion. International Jounal of Computer Vision 76(3), 257–281 (2008)
6. Kotsia, I., Pitas, I.: Facial Expression Recognition in Image Sequences Using Geometric Deformation Features And Support Vector Machines. IEEE Transactions on Image Processing 16(1), 172–187 (2007)
7. Valstar, M., Mehu, M.: Meta-Analysis of the First Facial Expression Recognition Challenge. IEEE Transactions on SMC-Part B 42(4), 966–979 (2012)
8. Yu, K., Wang, Z., Hagenbuchner, M.: Spectral Embedding Based Facial Expression Recognition with Multiple Features. Neurocomputing 129, 136–145 (2014)
9. Khan, R.A., Meyera, A., Konika, H., Bouakaza, S.: Framework for Reliable, Real-time Facial Expression Recognition for Low Resolution Images. Pattern Recognition Letters 34(10), 1159–1168 (2013)

10. Wan, S., Aggarwal, J.K.: Spontaneous Facial Expression Recognition: A Robust Metric Learning Approach. Pattern Recognition 47(5), 859–1868 (2014)
11. Zhao, X., Zhang, S.: Facial Expression Recognition Based on Local Binary Patterns and Kernel Discriminant Isomap. Sensors (Basel) 11(10), 9573–9588 (2011)
12. Zhan, Y., Cheng, K.: A New Classifier for Facial Expression Recognition: Fuzzy Buried Markov Model. Journal of Computer Science and Technology 25(3), 641–650 (2010)
13. Wang, W., Chang, F., Zhao, J., Chen, Z.: Automatic Facial Expression Recognition Using Local Binary Pattern. In: WCICA 2010, pp. 6375–6378 (2010)

Multiple Positive Solutions of Nonlinear Fourth-Order Singular P-Laplacian Resonant Problems

Xuchao Wang and Libo Wang*

School of mathematics and statistics, Beihua University,
Jilin 132013, Jilin, China
wlb_math@163.com

Abstract. Nonlinear fourth-order singular P-Laplacian resonant problems is a class of classical problems in mathematics and have lots of applications in engineering practice. In this paper, by using the variational method and Mountain pass lemma, multiple positive solutions of the nonlinear fourth-order singular resonant problems involving the p-Laplace operator were obtained.

Keywords: Mountain pass lemma, Singular, Resonant, Fourth-order, P-Laplace operator.

1 Introduction

The p-Laplace operator appears in many research areas. For instance, in Fluid Mechanics, torsional creep, flow through porous media, nonlinear elasticity and glaciology, see [1] for more details. Recently, fourth-order differential equations involving the p-laplacian attracted increasing attention, see [2,3] and the reference therein. But most of these works studied the nonresonant problems, the resonant problem are seldom considered, see [4,5].

In this paper, we consider the following fourth-order singular p-Laplacian resonant problem

$$
\begin{cases}
(\phi_p(y''))'' = f(t,y), & 0 < t < 1, \\
y(0) = y(1) = 0, & \\
y''(0) = y''(1) = 0,
\end{cases}
\tag{1.1}
$$

where $\phi_p(s) = |s|^{p-2}s, 1 < p < +\infty, \dfrac{1}{p} + \dfrac{1}{q} = 1$, function $f \in C((0,1) \times (0,\infty), [0,\infty))$ may be singular at $y = 0$ and satisfies

$$
2\varepsilon \le f(t,y) \le Cy^{-\gamma}, \quad (t,y) \in (0,1) \times (0, K_\varepsilon),
\tag{1.2}
$$

where $K_\varepsilon := \frac{1}{2}(\frac{1}{4})^q \varepsilon^{q-1}$, $\varepsilon, C > 0$, $\gamma \in (0,1)$ and C depends ε. A typical example is

$$
f(t,y) = y^{-\gamma} + g(t,y),
\tag{1.3}
$$

where $g \in C((0,1) \times [0,\infty), (0,\infty))$.

---

* Corresponding author.

L. Pan et al. (Eds.): BIC-TA 2014, CCIS 472, pp. 452–456, 2014.

Define $f_\varepsilon \in C((0,1) \times R, [0, \infty))$ be

$$f_\varepsilon(t, y) = f(t, (y - \varphi_\varepsilon(t))^+ + \varphi_\varepsilon(t)), \tag{1.4}$$

where $y^\pm = \max\{\pm y, 0\}$, $\varphi_\varepsilon(t) = \int_0^1 G(t,s)\phi_q(\varepsilon s(1-s))ds$ be the solution of the problem

$$\begin{cases} (\phi_p(y''))'' = 2\varepsilon, & 0 < t < 1, \\ y(0) = y(1) = 0, \\ y''(0) = y''(1) = 0, \end{cases} \tag{1.5}$$

and

$$G(t, s) = \begin{cases} t(1-s), 0 \le t \le s \le 1, \\ s(1-t), 0 \le s \le t \le 1. \end{cases}$$

Consider the following problem

$$\begin{cases} (\phi_p(y''))'' = f_\varepsilon(t, y), & 0 < t < 1, \\ y(0) = y(1) = 0, \\ y''(0) = y''(1) = 0. \end{cases} \tag{1.6}$$

From (1.2),

$$2\varepsilon \le f_\varepsilon(t, y) \le C\varphi_\varepsilon(t)^{-\gamma}, \quad (t, y) \in (0, 1) \times (-\infty, K_\varepsilon). \tag{1.7}$$

Lemma 1.1. If y is a solution of (1.6), then $y \ge \varphi_\varepsilon$, $t \in (0, 1)$ and y also be a positive solution of (1.1).

Consider the Banach space $X := W^{2,p}(0, 1) \cap W_0^{1,p}(0, 1)$, the corresponding norm is

$$\|y\| = \left(\int_0^1 |y''(t)|^p dt \right)^{\frac{1}{p}}. \tag{1.8}$$

Define C^1 functional $\Phi : X \to R$ as

$$\Phi(y) = \int_0^1 (\frac{1}{p}|y''(t)|^p - F_\varepsilon(t, y(t))dt, \quad \forall y \in X, \tag{1.9}$$

where $F_\varepsilon(t, y) = \int_{K_\varepsilon}^y f_\varepsilon(t, x)dx$.

From $\varphi_\varepsilon^{-\gamma} \in L^1(0, 1)$ and (1.7), the critical point of Φ is a solution of (1.6), and then a positive solution of (1.1).

Cerami (C) condition: Every sequence $\{y_m\} \subset X$, satisfies

$$\Phi(y_m) \text{ bounded}, \ (1 + \|y_m\|)\|\Phi(y_m)\| \longrightarrow 0, \tag{1.10}$$

$\{y_m\}$ has a convergent subsequence.

2   Existence Results

Assume that
(f) $\exists M > 0$, for all $\lambda \in (0, 1]$, each solution of the problem

$$
\begin{cases}
(\phi_p(y''))'' = \lambda f(t, y), & 0 < t < 1, \\
y(0) = y(1) = 0, \\
y''(0) = y''(1) = 0
\end{cases}
\tag{2.1}
$$

satisfies $\|y\| \neq M$.

Lemma 2.1. If (1.2) and (f) hold, then problem (2.1) has at least one solution.
Assume that

$$
f(t, y) \leq C\phi_p(y), \quad (t, y) \in (0, 1) \times [K_\varepsilon, +\infty),
\tag{2.8}
$$

for some $C > 0$. We say that (1.1) is resonant if

$$
\frac{f(t, y)}{\phi_p(y)} \to \lambda_1, \quad y \to \infty.
\tag{2.9}
$$

where $\lambda_1 = \inf\limits_{y \in X} \dfrac{\int\limits_0^1 |y''|^p dt}{\int\limits_0^1 |y|^p dt}$ be the first eigenvalue of the problem

$$
\begin{cases}
(\phi_p(y''))'' = \lambda \phi_p(y), & 0 < t < 1, \\
y(0) = y(1) = 0, \\
y''(0) = y''(1) = 0.
\end{cases}
\tag{2.10}
$$

Define

$$
H(t, y) = pF_\varepsilon(t, y) - yf_\varepsilon(t, y).
\tag{2.11}
$$

Theorem 2.1. If (1.2) and (2.8) hold, then (1.1) has at least one positive solution
if (2.9) holds,

$$
H(t, y) \leq C, \quad (t, y) \in (0, 1) \times [K_\varepsilon, +\infty),
\tag{2.12}
$$

for some $C > 0$, and

$$
H(t, y) \to -\infty, \quad y \to \infty.
\tag{2.13}
$$

Proof. For $y \geq K_\varepsilon$,

$$
\frac{\partial}{\partial y}\left(\frac{F_\varepsilon(t, y)}{y^p}\right) = -\frac{H(t, y)}{y^{p+1}} \quad \text{and} \quad \frac{F_\varepsilon(t, y)}{|y|^p} \to \frac{\lambda_1}{p}, \quad \text{as } y \to \infty.
\tag{2.14}
$$

From (2.14) and (2.12),

$$
\begin{aligned}
F_\varepsilon(t, y) &= \left(\tfrac{\lambda_1}{p} + \int\limits_y^\infty \tfrac{H(t, x)}{x^{p+1}} dx\right) y^p \\
&\leq \tfrac{\lambda_1}{p} y^p + C,
\end{aligned}
\tag{2.15}
$$

For $y < K_\varepsilon$,

$$\Phi(y) = \frac{1}{p}||y_0||^p - \int\limits_0^1 F_\varepsilon(t, y_0(t))dt \geq 0,$$

by Wirtinger inequality, Φ is bounded below.

In order to verifiy (C), let $\{y_m\}$ satisfy (1.10) and suppose $\rho_m := ||\ y_m\ || \to \infty$. Since $\{y_m^-\}$ is bounded, for a subsequence, $\tilde{y}_m := \frac{y_m}{\rho_m} \rightharpoonup \tilde{y} \geq 0$ in X, $\tilde{y}_m \to \tilde{y}$ in $L^2(0,1)$, and $\tilde{y}_m \longrightarrow \tilde{y}$, a.e. in $(0,1)$. Then

$$\int\limits_0^1 |\tilde{y}_m''(t)|^{p-2}\tilde{y}_m''(t)(\tilde{y}_m''(t) - \tilde{y}''(t))dt = \int\limits_0^1 g_m(t)dt + \frac{< \Phi'(y_m), \tilde{y}_m - \tilde{y} >}{\rho_m^{p-1}}, \quad (2.16)$$

where $g_m(t) = \dfrac{f_\varepsilon(t, y_m(t))}{\rho_m^{p-1}}(\tilde{y}_m(t) - \tilde{y}(t))$. From (1.7) and (2.16),

$$|g_m(t)| \leq C(\varphi_\varepsilon(t)^{-\gamma} + 1)|\tilde{y}_m(t) - \tilde{y}(t)|, \quad (2.17)$$

and $g_m(t) \to 0$, a.e. $t \in (0,1)$, $|g_m| \leq C(\varphi_\varepsilon^{-\gamma} + 1) \in L^1(0,1)$. So passing to the limit in (2.16) gives $||\tilde{y}|| = 1$. In particular, $\tilde{y} \neq 0$.

From (1.7) and (2.12),

$$H(t, y) \leq \begin{cases} C\varphi_\varepsilon(t)^{-\gamma}|y|, & y < 0, \\ 0, & 0 \leq y < K_\varepsilon, \\ C, & y \geq K_\varepsilon, \end{cases} \quad (2.18)$$

Hence by (2.7) and (2.18), $||y_m^-||_0$ is bounded,

$$\int\limits_{\tilde{y}>0} H(t, y_m(t))dt \to -\infty, \quad (2.19)$$

and $\int\limits_{\tilde{y}=0} H(t, y_m(t))dt$ is bounded from above. Hence

$$
\begin{aligned}
< \Phi'(y_m), y_m > -p\Phi(y_m) &= \int\limits_0^1 [|y_m''(t)|^p - f_\varepsilon(t, y_m(t))y_m(t)]dt \\
&\quad -p\int\limits_0^1 [\tfrac{1}{p}|y_m''(t)|^p - F_\varepsilon(t, y_m(t))]dt \\
&= \int\limits_0^1 [pF_\varepsilon(t, y_m) - yf_\varepsilon(t, y_m)]dt \quad (2.20) \\
&= \int\limits_0^1 H(t, y_m(t))dt \\
&= \int\limits_{\tilde{y}>0} H(t, y_m(t))dt + \int\limits_{\tilde{y}=0} H(t, y_m(t))dt \\
&\to -\infty,
\end{aligned}
$$

which contradicts to (1.10).

Theorem 2.2. Assume (1.2), (2.8) and (*f*) hold. Then (1.1) has two positive solutions if (2.9) holds,

$$H(t,y) \geq -C, \ (t,y) \in (0,1) \times [K_\varepsilon, +\infty), \tag{2.21}$$

for some $C > 0$, and

$$H(t,y) \rightarrow +\infty, \ y \rightarrow \infty. \tag{2.22}$$

Proof. The proof is similar to Theorem 2.1, we omitted.

Acknowledgments. The author Libo Wang is supported by the National Natural Science Foundation of China (No. 11201008).

References

1. Ahmad, B., Nieto, J.J.: The Monotone Iterative Technique for Three-Point Second-Order Integro Differential Boundary Value Problems With P- Laplacian, Boundary Value Problems 2007, Article ID 57481 (2007)
2. Jiang, J.Q., Liu, L.S., Wu, Y.H.: Positive Solutions for P-Laplacian Fourth-Order Differential System with Integral Boundary Conditions. Discrete Dynamics in Nature and Society Article ID 293734, 1–19 (2012)
3. Xu, J., Yang, Z.: Positive Solutions for a Fourth Orderp-Laplacian Boundary Value Problem. Nonlinear Analysis 74, 2612–2623 (2011)
4. Lin, X., Du, Z., Ge, W.: Solvability of Multipoint Boundary Value Problems At Resonance for Higher-Order Ordinary Differential Equations. Computers and Mathematics with Applications 49, 1–11 (2005)
5. Liu, S.B., Squassina, M.: On the Existence of Solutions to A Fourth-Order Quasilinear Resonant Problem. Abstract and Applied Analysis 7, 125–133 (2002)

A 3D DNA Self-assembly Model and Algorithm for Minimum Spanning Tree Problem

Zicheng Wang[1,2,*], Lizheng Bian[1,2], Yanfeng Wang[1,2], and Guangzhao Cui[1,2]

[1] School of Electrical and Information Engineering,
Henan Key Lab of Information-based Electrical Appliances,
Zhengzhou University of Light Industry
[2] Department of electric power engineering, Zhengzhou Eelectric Power College,
No.5 Dongfeng Road, Zhengzhou, 450002, China
wzch@zzuli.edu.cn

Abstract. The minimum spanning tree (MST) problem has been widely studied for its wide applicationsin recent years. Because of its outstanding advantages, DNA self-assembly computing has been used to solve MST problem. A new paradigm, called a three dimensional (3D) DNA self-assembly model, is proposed for this type of problem in this paper. The results show that it is efficient in solving MST problem and the algorithm has a high-efficiency.

Keywords: The MST problem, 3D tile, DNA Self-assembly.

1 Introduction

Bio-computing is hot branch in natural computing, mainly include DNA computing [2] and membrane computing [3–5] In 1994, the Hamilton problem with seven vertexes was successfully solved by biology method [2]. Whereafter, based on Wang tiles theory [6], a lot of NP hard problems have been solved with DNA self-assembly tile, see e.g. [7–11]. The 2D DNA computing model was used for Degree Constrained Minimum Spanning Tree Problem [12].

In 2008, a cube structure, which is composed of complementary DNA strands, was used to paired transiently assembly in [13]. It demonstrated in [14] that the symmetric and complementary supra-molecular polyhedra can be fabricated by hierarchical DNA self-assembly. A 3D DNA structure was used in assemble computing in [15]. In 2011, a 3D DNA self-assembly Model was used to solve the Minimum Vertex Cover Problem in [16].

Because of its high automation degree, the 3D DNA self-assembly computing is selected to solve MST problem in this paper. The results shows that the MST problem can be solved successfully with a 3D self-assemble model.

---

[*] Corresponding author.

L. Pan et al. (Eds.): BIC-TA 2014, CCIS 472, pp. 457–462, 2014.

2   The Minimum Spanning Tree Problem

Given a connected, undirected graph $G = (V, E)$, in which V is the set of vertices, and E is the set of edges, a spanning tree of G is a sub-graph, and all the vertices are connected together. The spanning tree whose sum of edge weights is minimized is called the minimum spanning tree.

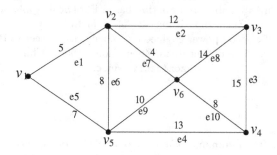

Fig. 1. The simple connected graph

3   The Algorithm for the Minimum Spanning Tree

3.1   Nondeterministic Algorithm

In MST problem solving, two parts are organized as follows: the first one is to make sure whether the sub-graph formation of the randomly input side is a spanning tree, and if it is a spanning tree, then the weights of the spanning tree was calculated, and we can get the spanning tree which has the minimum weights. In the second part, all the weights of the spanning tree were compared, the one of which has the minimum weights is the minimum spanning tree of the graph.

Judgment and Calculation Subsystem
For a given graph $G = (V, E)$, which has n vertexes with a vertex set V and an edge set E, the vertex set and edges set can be respectively expressed as follows: $V = \{v_1, v_2, v_3, \ldots, v_n\}$, $E = \{e_1, e_2 \ldots e_j\}$.

Assuming E_x is the spanning tree of G, the function is defined as follows:

$$e_j = \begin{cases} 1 & e_j \in E_x \\ 0 & e_j \notin E_x \end{cases} \tag{1}$$

Then, the incidence matrix A of the graph G is achieved as follows:

$$A = \begin{vmatrix} 1\ 0\ 0\ 0\ 1\ 0\ 0\ 0\ 0\ 0 \\ 1\ 1\ 0\ 0\ 0\ 1\ 1\ 0\ 0\ 0 \\ 0\ 1\ 1\ 0\ 0\ 0\ 0\ 1\ 0\ 0 \\ 0\ 0\ 1\ 1\ 0\ 0\ 0\ 0\ 0\ 1 \\ 0\ 0\ 0\ 1\ 1\ 1\ 0\ 0\ 1\ 0 \\ 0\ 0\ 0\ 0\ 0\ 0\ 1\ 1\ 1\ 1 \end{vmatrix}$$

Each vertex was randomly compared with and the input edge subset.When the edge in the subset is associated with the vertices, then OK is output; if not, this vertex is still output, and continue.Until the random input subset is the spanning tree.

The Comparison System
All the weights of spanning tree were compared, and we can get the minimum weight spanning tree. The algorithm is described as below:

Step 1. Randomly chose a edge set of G as an input.

Step 2. Check if each vertex of G is associated with the input side, that is, there is at least one edge linked to every vertex in the input set, go to Step 3; otherwise, repeat Step 1.

Step 3. Check if the input set has $(n-1)$ edge (the graph has n vertexes). If so, go to Step 4; otherwise, repeat Step 1.

Step 4. Check if there are loops in input set. If so, go to Step 5; otherwise, repeat Step 1.

Step 5. Calculate the weights of the input edge.

4   DNA Self-assembly Model to Solve the MST Problem

DNA tiles model used in the assembly process is described in this section. The assembly process is composed of two systems, one of which is judgment and calculation systems, and the other is comparison subsystem. A definition for the 3D tiles 6-tuple of form $(\sigma_X, \sigma_{-X}, \sigma_Y, \sigma_{-Y}, \sigma_Z, \sigma_{-Z}) \in \sum$ from [17] is given. The 3D tile model is shown in Figure 2.

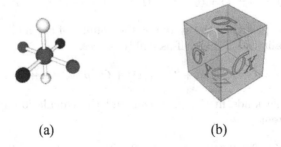

(a)   (b)

Fig. 2. (a) Hexahedron of 3D DNA structure model; (b) Abstraction six sides figure of the map

4.1   The Self-assembly Process

A successful assembly computation is shown in Fig.5. From the Fig.5we know the subset $e1, e2, e5, e7, e10$ is the minimum spanning tree, and the weight is "100100". The 3D tiles was used in the assembly process in Figures 3 and 4.

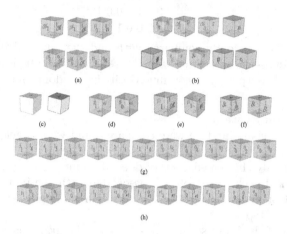

Fig. 3. (a) The transfer tiles;(b) The boundary tiles;(c) The incidence tiles;(d) The input tiles; (e) The judgment tiles;(f) The output tiles;(g) The subtraction tiles;(h) The multiplication and addition tiles

4.2   Analysis and Discussion

The complexity of our 3D DNA self-assembly model is considered in terms of computation time, computation space and the number of distinct tiles. Time complexity: In accordance with the growth trend of self-assembly, the assembly step number from seed configuration to assembly end is $(i + 1) + (n + 1) + (q + 1)) + (p + (q + 1))$, and the time complexity is:

$$T = ((i + 1) + (n + 1) + (q + 1) + (p + (q + 1)) = i + n + p + 2q + 4, \quad (2)$$

The space complexity of the system is the volume of assembly body in space, namely, the totality of tiles in self-assembly process.

$$S = O(2(n + m + 3)(i + 1)) + O((p + 2)(m + 2)). \quad (3)$$

It contains tile kinds in the judgment and the calculation system and the comparison system

$$N = 2 + 2 + 2 + 2 + +6 + 2 + 13 + 5 + 8 + 2 = 43. \quad (4)$$

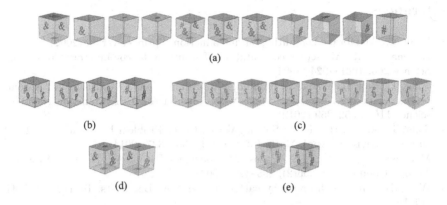

(a)

(b)   (c)

(d)   (e)

Fig. 4. (a)The boundary tiles(b)The comparison tiles (c) The transfer tiles(d) The output tiles (e) The input tiles

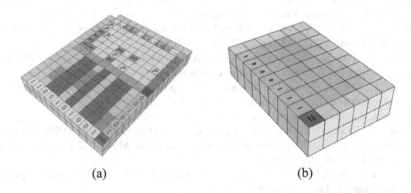

(a)   (b)

Fig. 5. (a) A successful assembly example of judgment and calculation system;(b) A successful assembly example of comparison system with five weights of the spanning tree

5   Conclusions

DNA self-assembly is a new calculation method. It has broad application prospects in the combinatorial optimization problem. In this paper, we construct 3D DNA tiles to solve the MST problem. The 3D DNA structure is the non-solution space index model, thus it can avoid the problems which produce the exponential solution space, and to a certain extent, it also reduces the complexity of the calculation, and the species' number of the tiles in the calculation has nothing to do with the problem scale. Of course, while the DNA self-assembly calculation model improves the calculation ability, it brings huge challenges for biochemical experiment.

References

1. Păun, G.: Membrane computing: an introduction, Springer-verlan (2002)
2. Adleman, L.M.: Molecular computation of solutions to combinatorial problems. Science 266, 1021–1024 (1994)
3. Song, T., Pan, L., Wang, J., Ibrahim, V., Subramanian, K.G., Rosni, A.: Normal Forms of Spiking Neural P Systems with Anti-Spikes. IEEE Trans. on Nanobioscience 11(4), 352–359 (2012)
4. Song, T., Zheng, H., He, J.: Solving Vertex Cover Problem by Tissue P Systems with Cell Division. Appl. Math. Inf. Sci. 8(1), 333–337 (2014)
5. Martın-Vide, C., Păun, G., Pazos, J., Rodrıguez-Patón, A.: Tissue P Systems, Theore. Comput. Sci. 296(2), 295–326 (2003)
6. Wang, H.: Proving theorems by pattern recognition. Bell Systs. Tech. J. 40, 1–41 (1961)
7. Winfree, E.: Algorithmic self-assembly of DNA. California Institute of Technology, California (1998)
8. Zhang, X., Niu, Y., Cui, G., Xu, J.: Application of DNA Self-Assembly on Graph Coloring Problem. J. Comput. Theor. Nanosci. 6, 1–8 (2009)
9. Zhang, X., Niu, Y., Cui, G., Xu, J.: Application of DNA Self-Assembly on 0-1 Integer Programming Problem. J. Comput. Theor. Nanosci. 7, 1–8 (2010)
10. Wang, Y., Hu, P., Cui, G.: DNA Self-Assembly for Graph Vertex 3-Coloring Problem. J. Comput. Theor. Nanosci. 7, 29–38 (2010)
11. Wang, Y., Bai, X., Wei, D., Cui, G.: DNA Self-Assembly for Maximum Weighted Independent Set Problem. Advanced Science Letters 5, 1–6 (2012)
12. Song, T., Pan, L., Păun, G.: Asynchronous Spiking Neural P Systems with Local Synchronization. Information Sciences 219, 197–207 (2013)
13. Crocker, J.: Golden Handshake. Nature 451, 528–529 (2008)
14. Song, T., Wang, X., Zhang, Z., Hong, L.: Detecting Motifs in DNA Sequences by Branching from Neighbors of Qualified Potential Motifs. J. Comput. Theor. Nanosci. 10, 2201–2206 (2013)
15. Jonoska, N., Karl, S., Saito, M.: Three Dimensional DNA Structures in Computing. BioSystems 52, 143–153 (1999)
16. Zhang, X., Song, W., Fan, R., Cui, G.: Three Dimensional DNA Self-Assembly Model for the Minimum Vertex Cover Problem. In: Proceedings of the 4th International Symposium on Computational Intelligence and Design (2011)
17. Lin, M.Q., Xu, J.: 3D DNA Self-Assembly Model for Graph Vertex Coloring. J. Comput. Theor. Nanosci. 7, 1246–1253 (2010)

Multi-digit Logic Operation Using DNA Strand Displacement

Zicheng Wang, Guihua Tian, Yan Wang,
Yanfeng Wang, and Guangzhao Cui*

College of Electrical and Electronic Engineering,
Zhengzhou University of Light Industry,
No. 5, Dongfeng Road, Zhengzhou, 450002, China
wzch@zzuli.edu.cn

Abstract. DNA strand displacement which is an approach of dynamic nanotechnology has been widely used in constructing of molecular logic circuit, molecular automata and nanomedicine and so on. DNA strand displacement is enormous capable of implementation of logical calculation which plays a critical role in the acquirement of bio-computer. In our paper, the multi-digit full adder which is based on the reaction of DNA strand displacement is designed and has been verified by simulation of DSD (DNA strand displacement). The accuracy of simulation result further confirmed DNA strand displacement is a valid method for the research of logical bio-chemical circuit.

Keywords: DNA strand displacement, Logic operation, Visual DSD.

1 Introduction

Bio-computing is hot branch in natural computing, mainly include DNA computing [2] and membrane computing [1, 3–5] The applications of DNA as an excellent nanoscale engineering material have extensively involved in molecular devices [6], logic circuits [7], nano-network [8], autonomous molecular walks [9, 10], nanomedicine [11] and so on. DNA strand displacement emerged as a new method of DNA self-assembly, which has a series of advantages.

In [12], Georg Seelig et al. designed AND, OR, and NOT gates by using single-strand nucleic acids as input and output, and demonstrated signal restoration function. Lederman H et al. developed three-input logic gates based on deoxyribozyme and constructed molecular full adder which consists of a seven logic gate array in [13]. In 2010, some Boolean circuits with series of properties were proposed, in which the simulations of a latch circuit and a D flip-flop are exhibited. Qian and Winfree presented a simple and universal method of building logic gates in [15], made the simulation about a 74–85 standard 4-bit magnitude comparator [12] and tested the logic circuit [16] of the square root of a four-bit binary number. Zhang and Seelig described the performing of logic AND gate

---

* Corresponding author.

L. Pan et al. (Eds.): BIC-TA 2014, CCIS 472, pp. 463–467, 2014.
© Springer-Verlag Berlin Heidelberg 2014

through two grades reaction of strand displacement in [17]. In [18], Zhang et al. suggested the pattern of logic AND gate and OR gate and confirmed by experiment.

2   The Background of DNA Strand Displacement and Logic Calculation

The strand displacement reaction is a process through which one single strand served as input signal replaces another bounding single strand from complex served as output signal. It is initialed in a toehold, then processing branch migration to release output strand. Since input and output strand possess the same structure: toehold domain (short and usually consists of 4~6 base sequences) see, e.g. [19–21], the previous output could serve as input of the next logic operation. It provides advantage to construct cascade between front and back gates.

Boolean logic that used to determine the relationship of two numbers is a computing method, in which two states are defined: digit "0" usually expresses that the event is false, as well as digit "1" often represents that the event is true. There are three kinds of logical operationlogic "AND", logic "OR" and logic "NOT".

The electronically logic circuit can be transformed into an equivalent biochemical circuit through a certain corresponding rules. The description above is concerning Boolean logic in the electronic digital circuit, while Boolean values will be represented through high or low concentration of DNA strands.

3   Binary Multi-digit Adder and the Simulation in DSD

We previously designed one-bit half adder and one-bit full adder, but it is unlikely to meet the demand of implementing complex computing instructions of bio-computer. Therefore, it is necessary strongly to design the complicated logic operation. Here we take two-bit full adder as an example, which takes two numbers as input and produces an output which is in the form of three-bit. According to the calculating principle of multi-digit addition operation, the corresponding logic circuit, which has a certain relationship with bio-chemical circuit and can be transformed equivalently into it, is designed as Figure 3. Working from left to right in Figure 3, so x_1, x_2, y_1, y_2 which are located at the left side all indicate input signal, s_1, s_2 and c_2 which are located at the right side denotes severally the sum of low-level bit, the sum of high-level bit and the highest level carry bit.

The simulation results of multi-digit addition operation which consist of 16 kinds of combination from 00-00 to 11-11 are shown as figure 4. In the plot, there are three kinds of output signal and every one has two kinds of state, which is described using the curve in different colors: the red curve and green curve indicate the logic OFF and logic ON of s_1, respectively; the blue curve and yellow curve denote the logic OFF and logic ON of s_2, respectively; the orange curve and purple curve represent the logic OFF and logic ON of c_2, respectively.

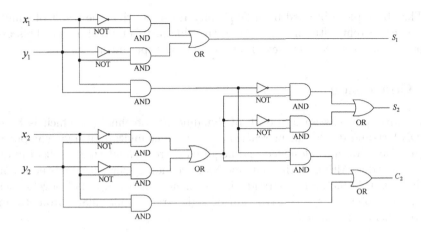

Fig. 1. Logic Circuit of Multi-digit Addition Operation

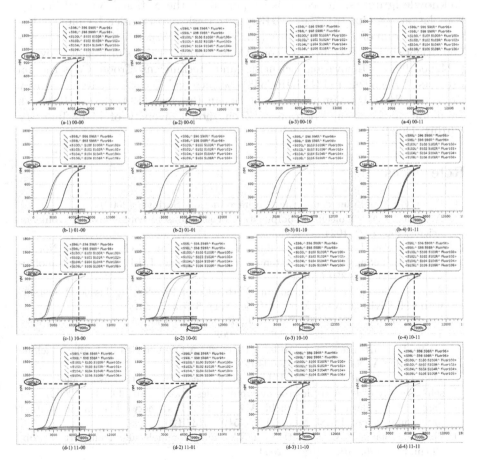

Fig. 2. Simulation Result in DSD

The above plot obtained from DSD software shows that the result of simulation is consistent with the value of truth table of two-bit full adder. This also strongly confirms the accuracy of our simulation experiment.

4 Conclusion

This paper presents an approach of dynamic Nanotechnology which is based on DNA strand displacement reaction to construct multi-digit logic computing circuit. Here, we have designed and acquired correct simulating result of multi-digit full adder. Although the dynamic Nanotechnology currently faces enormous challenges, this method of strand displacement still has a broad development prospect applied in the construction of logic circuit, molecular automata and nanomedicine and so on.

Acknowledgments. Research is supported by the National Natural Science Foundation of China (61272022, U1304620), Basic and Frontier Technology Research Program of Henan Province (122300413211, 132300410183), and Innovation Scientists and Technicians Troop Construction Projects of Henan Province (124200510017). Innovation Scientists and Technicians Troop Construction Projects of Zhengzhou (131PLJRC648). Science and Technology Research Key Project of the Education Department Henan Province (13A413371). Research Fund for the Doctoral Program of Zhengzhou University of Light Industry (2010BSJJ002).

References

1. Păun, G.: Membrane computing: an introduction. Springer (2002)
2. Adleman, L.M.: Molecular computation of solutions to combinatorial problems. Science 266, 1021–1024 (1994)
3. Song, T., Pan, L., Wang, J., Ibrahim, V., Subramanian, K.G., Rosni, A.: Normal Forms of Spiking Neural P Systems with Anti-Spikes. IEEE Trans. on Nanobioscience 11(4), 352–359 (2012)
4. Song, T., Zheng, H., He, J.: Solving Vertex Cover Problem by Tissue P Systems with Cell Division. Appl. Math. Inf. Sci. 8(1), 333–337 (2014)
5. Martın-Vide, C., Păun, G., Pazos, J., Rodrıguez-Patón, A.: Tissue P Systems. Theore. Comput. Sci. 296(2), 295–326 (2003)
6. Yurke, B., Turberfield, A.J., Mills, A.P., et al.: A DNA-fuelled molecular machine made of DNA. Nature 406, 605–608 (2000)
7. Mao, C., LaBean, T.H., Reif, J.H., et al.: Logical computation using algorithmic self-assembly of DNA triple-crossover molecules. Nature 407, 493–496 (2000)
8. Santini, C.C., Bath, J., Turberfield, A.J., et al.: A DNA network as an information processing system. Int. J. Mol. Sci. 13, 5125–5137 (2012)
9. Shin, J., Pierce, N.A.: A synthetic DNA walker for molecular transport. J. Am. Chem. Soc. 126, 10834–10835 (2004)
10. Lund, K., Manzo, A.J., Dabby, N., et al.: Molecular robots guided by prescriptive landscapes. Nature 465, 206–210 (2010)

11. Rahul, C., Jaswinder, S., Yan, L., Sherri, R., Hao, Y.: DNA Self-assembly for Nanomedicine. Adv. Drug. Deliver. Rev. 62, 617–625 (2010)
12. Seelig, G., Soloveichik, D., Zhang, D.Y., Winfree, E.: Enzyme-free nucleic acid logic circuits. Science 314, 1585–1588 (2006)
13. Lederman, H., Macdonald, J., Stephanovic, D., Stojanovic, M.N.: Deoxyribozyme-based three-input logic gates and construction of a molecular full adder. Biochemistry 45, 1194–1199 (2006)
14. Chiniforooshan, E., Doty, D., Kari, L., Seki, S.: Scalable, Time-Responsive, Digital, Energy-Efficient Molecular Circuits using DNA Strand Displacement. DNA Computing and Molecular Programming. Springer (2011)
15. Qian, L., Winfree, E.: A simple DNA gate motif for synthesizing large-scale circuits. J. R. Soc. Interface. 8, 1281–1297 (2011)
16. Qian, L., Winfree, E.: Scaling up digital circuit computation with DNA strand displacement cascades. Science 332, 1196–1201 (2011)
17. Zhang, D.Y., Seelig, G.: Dynamic DNA nanotechnology using strand-displacement reactions. Nat. Chem. 3, 103–113 (2011)
18. Zhang, C., Ma, L.N., Dong, Y.F., et al.: Molecular logic computing model based on DNA self-assembly strand branch migration. Chinese. Sci. Bull. 58, 32–38 (2013)
19. Zhang, D.Y., Winfree, E.: Control of DNA strand displacement kinetics using toehold exchange. J. Am. Chem. Soc. 131, 17303–17314 (2009)
20. Song, T., Pan, L., Wang, J., Ibrahim, V., Subramanian, K.G., Rosni, A.: Normal Forms of Spiking Neural P Systems with Anti-Spikes. IEEE Trans. on Nanobioscience 11(4), 352–359 (2012)
21. Song, T., Zheng, H., He, J.: Solving Vertex Cover Problem by Tissue P Systems with Cell Division. Appl. Math. Inf. Sci. 8(1), 333–337 (2014)

Existence of Multiple Positive Solutions of Nonlinear Singular Fourth-Order Problems Involving the P-Laplacian

Ying Wei[1,*], Min Wang[2], and Libo Wang[2]

[1] College of Computer Science and Technology,
Beihua University, Jilin 132013, Jilin, China
[2] School of Mathematics and Statistics, Beihua University,
Jilin 132013, Jilin, China
wlb_math@163.com

Abstract. Nonlinear fourth-order singular P-Laplacian resonant problems is a class of classical problems in mathematics and have lots of applications in engineering practice. In this paper, by using the variational method, the existence of multiple solutions for some nonlinear singular fourth-order p-Laplacian problems were obtained.

Keywords: Varitional method, Singular, Fourth-order, P-Laplacian.

1 Introduction

Fourth-order differential equations appears in many research areas, such as beam theory[1, 2], ice formation[3, 4], fluids on lungs [5], brain warping [6, 7], designing special curves on surfaces[8]. we refer the reader to the work [9–11] for more background and applications. Recently, fourth-order differential equations involving the p-laplacian attracted increasing attention, see [12, 13] and the refenrence therein.

Motivated by above works, in this paper, we consider the following nonlinear singular fourth-order p-Laplacian problem

$$\begin{cases} (\phi_p(y''))'' = f(t, y), & 0 < t < 1, \\ y(0) = y(1) = 0, \\ y''(0) = y''(1) = 0, \end{cases} \tag{1.1}$$

where $\phi_p(s) = |s|^{p-2}s, 1 < p < +\infty, \dfrac{1}{p} + \dfrac{1}{q} = 1$, function $f \in C((0,1) \times (0,\infty), [0,\infty))$ may be singular at $y = 0$ and satisfies

$$2\varepsilon \le f(t, y) \le Cy^{-\gamma}, \quad (t, y) \in (0,1) \times (0, K_\varepsilon), \tag{1.2}$$

where $K_\varepsilon := \frac{1}{2}(\frac{1}{4})^q \varepsilon^{q-1}$, $\varepsilon, C > 0$, $\gamma \in (0,1)$ and C depends ε.

---

* Corresponding author.

L. Pan et al. (Eds.): BIC-TA 2014, CCIS 472, pp. 468–472, 2014.

Define $f_\varepsilon \in C((0,1) \times R, [0, \infty))$ be

$$f_\varepsilon(t, y) = f(t, (y - \varphi_\varepsilon(t))^+ + \varphi_\varepsilon(t)), \tag{1.3}$$

where $y^\pm = \max\{\pm y, 0\}$, $\varphi_\varepsilon(t) = \int\limits_0^1 G(t, s)\phi_q(\varepsilon s(1 - s))ds$ be the solution of the problem

$$\begin{cases} (\phi_p(y''))'' = 2\varepsilon, & 0 < t < 1, \\ y(0) = y(1) = 0, \\ y''(0) = y''(1) = 0, \end{cases} \tag{1.4}$$

and

$$G(t, s) = \begin{cases} t(1 - s), 0 \le t \le s \le 1, \\ s(1 - t), 0 \le s \le t \le 1. \end{cases}$$

Consider the following problem

$$\begin{cases} (\phi_p(y''))'' = f_\varepsilon(t, y), & 0 < t < 1, \\ y(0) = y(1) = 0, \\ y''(0) = y''(1) = 0. \end{cases} \tag{1.5}$$

From (1.2),

$$2\varepsilon \le f_\varepsilon(t, y) \le C\varphi_\varepsilon(t)^{-\gamma}, \quad (t, y) \in (0, 1) \times (-\infty, K_\varepsilon). \tag{1.6}$$

Lemma 1.1. If y is a solution of (1.6), then $y \ge \varphi_\varepsilon$, $t \in (0, 1)$ and y also be a positive solution of (1.1).

Consider the Banach space $X := W^{2,p}(0, 1) \cap W_0^{1,p}(0, 1)$, the corresponding norm is

$$\|y\| = (\int\limits_0^1 |y''(t)|^p dt)^{\frac{1}{p}}.$$

Lemma 1.2. If $y \in X$, then $\|y\|_0 \le \|y\|$.

Define C^1 functional $\Phi : X \to R$ as

$$\Phi(y) = \int\limits_0^1 (\frac{1}{p}|y''(t)|^p - F_\varepsilon(t, y(t))dt, \ \forall y \in X,$$

where $F_\varepsilon(t, y) = \int\limits_{K_\varepsilon}^y f_\varepsilon(t, x)dx$.

From $\varphi_\varepsilon^{-\gamma} \in L^1(0, 1)$ and (1.7), the critical point of Φ is a solution of (1.6), and then a positive solution of (1.1).

Cerami (C) condition: Every sequence $\{y_m\} \subset X$, satisfies

$$\Phi(y_m) \text{ bounded}, \ (1 + \|y_m\|)\|\Phi(y_m)\| \longrightarrow 0,$$

$\{y_m\}$ has a convergent subsequence.

Remark. To prove (C) condition hold, it is enough to prove $\{y_m\}$ is bounded.

2   Existence Results

Assume that

(f) $\exists M > 0$, for all $\lambda \in (0, 1]$, each solution of the problem

$$\begin{cases} (\phi_p(y''))'' = \lambda f(t, y), & 0 < t < 1, \\ y(0) = y(1) = 0, \\ y''(0) = y''(1) = 0 \end{cases} \tag{2.1}$$

satisfies $\|y\| \neq M$.

Theorem 2.1. If (1.2) and (f) hold, then problem (1.1) has at least one positive solution.

Proof. The proof is similiar to the Theorem 2.1 of [14], we omitted it.

Assume that

$$f(t, y) \leq C\phi_p(y), \quad (t, y) \in (0, 1) \times [K_\varepsilon, +\infty), \tag{2.2}$$

for some $C > 0$. We set $\lambda_1 = \inf\limits_{y \in X} \dfrac{\int\limits_0^1 |y''|^p dt}{\int\limits_0^1 |y|^p dt}$ be the first eigenvalue of the problem

$$\begin{cases} (\phi_p(y''))'' = \lambda \phi_p(y), & 0 < t < 1, \\ y(0) = y(1) = 0, \\ y''(0) = y''(1) = 0. \end{cases} \tag{2.3}$$

Define

$$H(t, y) = pF_\varepsilon(t, y) - yf_\varepsilon(t, y). \tag{2.4}$$

Theorem 2.2. If (1.2) and (2.2) hold, then (1.1) has at least one positive solution if

$$f(t, y) \leq a\phi_p(y) + C, \quad (t, y) \in (0, 1) \times [K_\varepsilon, +\infty), \tag{2.5}$$

for some $a < \lambda_1$ and $C > 0$.

Proof. From (1.7) and (2.5), $\forall y \in R$,

$$F_\varepsilon(t, y) \leq \begin{cases} 0, & y < K_\varepsilon, \\ \frac{a}{p}|y|^p + Cy, & y \geq K_\varepsilon. \end{cases} \tag{2.6}$$

From $a < \lambda_1$ and Wirtinger inequality, Φ is bounded from below and coericive, and hence satisfies (C). Then Φ admits a global minimizer.

Theorem 2.3. Assume (1.2), (2.2) and (f) hold. Then (1.1) has two positive solutions if there exist $b > \lambda_1$ and $d > 0$ such that

$$f(t, y) \geq b\phi_p(y) - d, \quad (t, y) \in (0, 1) \times [K_\varepsilon, +\infty). \tag{2.7}$$

Proof. From the proof of Theorem 2.1, Φ has a local minimizer $y_0 \in int(B)$ and $\inf \Phi(B) = \Phi(y_0)$.

Next we'll show that (C) holds and $\Phi(R\varphi_1) \leq \inf \Phi(B)$ if $R > M$ is sufficiently large, where $\varphi_1 > 0$ is the normalized eigenfunction associated with λ_1. Then from the mountain pass lemma, we can get a second critical point at the level

$$c := \inf_{\gamma \in \Gamma} \max_{y \in \gamma([0,1])} \Phi(y), \tag{2.8}$$

where

$$\Gamma = \{\gamma \in C([0,1], E) : \gamma(0) = y_0, \gamma(1) = R\varphi_1\} \tag{2.9}$$

is the class of paths joining y_0 and $R\varphi_1$.

Let $\{y_m\} \subset X$ be such that (1.12) holds. Since $\{y_m^-\}$ is bounded, we assume $y_m \geq 0$. For some $0 < \theta < \frac{b-\lambda_1}{C-\lambda_1}$ and $M > 0$,

$$M \leq\ < \Phi'(y_m), y_m > -\theta p \Phi(y_m)$$
$$= (\int_0^1 |y_m''(t)|^p - f_\varepsilon(t, y_m(t))y_m(t))dt) - \theta(\int_0^1 |y_m''(t)|^p - \theta p F_\varepsilon(t, y_m(t))dt)$$
$$= (1-\theta)\int_0^1 |y_m''(t)|^p dt + \int_0^1 \theta p F_\varepsilon(t, y_m(t)) - f_\varepsilon(t, y_m(t))y_m(t)dt$$
$$= (1-\theta)\int_0^1 |y_m''(t)|^p dt + \int_{0 \leq y_m < K_\varepsilon} \theta p F_\varepsilon(t, y_m(t))dt$$
$$\quad + \int_{y_m \geq K_\varepsilon} \theta p F_\varepsilon(t, y_m(t))dt - \int_{0 \leq y_m < K_\varepsilon} f_\varepsilon(t, y_m(t))y_m(t)dt$$
$$\quad - \int_{y_m \geq K_\varepsilon} f_\varepsilon(t, y_m(t))y_m(t)dt$$
$$\leq (1-\theta)\int_0^1 |y_m''(t)|^p dt + \int_{y_m \geq K_\varepsilon} \theta p \frac{C}{p} |y_m(t)|^p dt$$
$$\quad -2\varepsilon \int_{0 \leq y_m < K_\varepsilon} y_m(t)dt - \int_{y_m \geq K_\varepsilon} (b\phi_p(y_m(t)) - d)y_m(t)dt$$
$$\leq (1-\theta)\int_0^1 |y_m''(t)|^p dt + \theta C \int_{y_m \geq K_\varepsilon} |y_m(t)|^p dt$$
$$\quad -b \int_{y_m \geq K_\varepsilon} |y_m(t)|^p dt + d \int_{y_m \geq K_\varepsilon} |y_m(t)| dt$$
$$= (1-\theta)\int_0^1 |y_m''(t)|^p dt + (\theta C - b) \int_{y_m \geq K_\varepsilon} |y_m(t)|^p dt + d \int_{y_m \geq K_\varepsilon} |y_m(t)| dt$$
$$\leq (1-\theta)\int_0^1 |y_m''(t)|^p dt + (\theta C - b) \int_0^1 |y_m(t)|^p dt + d \int_0^1 |y_m(t)| dt$$
$$\leq (1-\theta)\int_0^1 |y_m''(t)|^p dt + \frac{\theta C - b}{\lambda_1} \int_0^1 |y_m''(t)|^p dt + d \int_0^1 |y_m(t)| dt$$
$$= \frac{\lambda_1 - C}{\lambda_1}(\frac{b-\lambda_1}{C-\lambda_1} - \theta) \int_0^1 |y_m''(t)|^p dt + d \int_0^1 |y_m(t)| dt$$
$$\leq \frac{\lambda_1 - C}{\lambda_1}(\frac{b-\lambda_1}{C-\lambda_1} - \theta)||y_m||^p + dC_1||y_m||$$
$$\to -\infty, \tag{2.10}$$

then $\{y_m\}$ is bounded.

From (1.7),(2.7), $b > \lambda_1$ and (2.11), it is easy to see that $\Phi(R\varphi_1) \to -\infty$, $R \to \infty$.

Assume
$$0 < \theta F_\varepsilon(t,y) \leq yf(t,y), \quad (t,y) \in (0,1) \times [y_0, \infty), \tag{2.12}$$
for some $\theta > p$ and $y_0 > K_\varepsilon$.

Theorem 2.4. If (1.2), (2.12) and (f) hold, then (1.1) has two positive solutions.

Proof. The proof is similiar to the Theorem 2.3, we omitted it.

References

1. Bernis, F.: Compactness of The Support in Convex and Nonconvex Fourth Order Elasticity Problems. Nonlinear Analysis 6(11), 1221–1243 (1982)
2. Zill, D.G., Cullen, M.R.: Differential Equations and Boundary Value Problems, 5th edn. Computing and Modeling. Brooks Cole (2001)
3. Myers, T.G., Charpin, J.P.F.: A Mathematical Model for Atmospheric Ice Accretion and Water Flow on a Cold Surface. International Journal of Heat and Mass Transfer 47(25), 5483–5500 (2004)
4. Myers, T.G., Charpin, J.P.F., Chapman, S.J.: The Flow and Solidification of a Thin Fluid Film on An Arbitrary Three-dimensional Surface. Physics of Fluids 14(8), 2788–2803 (2002)
5. Halpern, D., Jensen, O.E., Grotberg, J.B.: A Theoretical Study of Surfactant and Liquid Delivery Into the Lung. Journal of Applied Physiology 85, 333–352 (1998)
6. Mémoli, F., Sapiro, G., Thompson, P.: Implicit Brain Imaging. NeuroImage 23(supple. 1), S179–S188 (2004)
7. Toga, A.: Brain Warping, Academic Press, New York (1998)
8. Hofer, M., Pottmann, H.: Energy-minimizing Splines in Manifolds. In: Proceedings of the ACM Transactions on Graphics, pp. 284–293 (2004)
9. Timoshenko, S.P.: Theory of Elastic Stability. McGraw-Hill, New York (1961)
10. Soede W.: Vibrations of Shells and Plates. Marcel Dekker, New York (1993)
11. Dulcska, E.: Soil Settlement Effects on Buildings of Developments in Geotechnical Engineering, Amsterdam, The Netherlands (1992)
12. Jiang, J.Q., Liu, L.S., Wu, Y.H.: Positive Solutions for p-Laplacian Fourth-Order Differential System with Integral Boundary Conditions.Discrete Dynamics in Nature and Society, Article ID 293734, 1–19 (2012)
13. Xu, J., Yang, Z.: Positive Solutions for a Fourth Order p-Laplacian Boundary Value Problem. Nonlinear Analysis 74, 2612–2623 (2011)
14. Agarwal, R.P., Kanishka, P., O'Regan, D.: Multiple Positive Solutions of Singular Problems by Variational Methods. Proc. Amer. Math. Soc. 134, 817–824 (2005)

Real-Time Surgery Simulation Systems Based on Collision Detection

Chang Wen[1,*] and Kai Xie[2]

[1] School of Computer Science, Yangtze University,
Jingzhou 434102, China
[2] School of Electronic Information, Yangtze University,
Jingzhou 434102, China
pami2010@163.com

Abstract. In this paper, we present a novel collision detection approach for surgery simulation. Each model is represented as a clustered hierarchy of sphere tree (CHST). GPU-based occlusion queries were used for fast collision culling between massive models. Furthermore, we are able to generate these hierarchies and perform collision queries using out-of-core techniques on all triangulated models. Experimental results show that our algorithm performs real-time collision detection between massive bones and implant models, consisting of millions of triangles at interactive rates on a commodity PC.

Keywords: Collision detection, GPU, Triangles, Implant models.

1 Introduction

Fast and reliable collision detection is of great importance in areas like real-time graphics, virtual reality, games, computer animation, CAD, robotics and manufacturing. With the rapid development of computer and network technology, there is an urgent necessity to realistically simulate the physical world and interact with computers in real time. Real-time collision detection is one of the key issues simulating real objects and their motions. Meanwhile, with three-dimensional objects growing more and more complicated; it becomes increasingly time-critical for the computational overhead of collision detection tasks. Collision detection is the key technologies in surgery simulation system [1,2], which can avoid incorrect intersection.

2 Theory Foundation

The problem of collision detection has been well studied in the literature. Most of the commonly used techniques to accelerate collision detection between two objects utilize spatial data structures, including bounding volume and spatial

---

* Corresponding author.

L. Pan et al. (Eds.): BIC-TA 2014, CCIS 472, pp. 473–477, 2014.

partitioning hierarchies. Some of the commonly used bounding volume hierarchies (BVHs) include sphere-trees [3], AABB-trees [4], OBB-trees [5,6], etc. These representations are used to cull away portions of each object that are not in close proximity. Recently, GPU-based accelerated techniques have also been proposed for fast collision detection. Their accuracy is governed by the frame-buffer or image-space resolution. Recently, Govindaraju et al. [7] have presented a reliable GPU-based collision culling algorithm that overcomes these precision problems due to limited frame-buffer resolution.

3   Our Method

We present a hierarchical collision detection algorithm based on the sphere-tree, several culling techniques are used to improve its performance. The overall algorithm for collision detection between two colliding objects is shown in Figure 1(a). We compute the colliding front of the bounding volume test tree (BVTT) using the culling operations. The colliding front contains pairs of clusters from the two objects that are in collision. For each of these cluster pairs, we perform an exact collision test. The cluster collision test uses a further culling algorithm that relies on GPU occlusion queries. Exact collision tests are performed after this additional culling step.

1.Construction of the binary tree of spheres: Our approach uses the sphere-tree structure. Figure 1(b) shows the sphere-tree construction algorithm. The idea is to find an almost balanced binary tree, where the leaf spheres completely contain the surface of the object and node-spheres completely contain the spheres of its descendant nodes.

2.Bounding Volume Test Tree (BVTT): We use the concept of the bounding volume test tree (BVTT)[8] to accelerate the computation of collision. In the CHST representation, the cluster hierarchy is also a BVH. We traverse the bounding volume hierarchies (BVHs) of both the objects and compute the BVTT. A node (a,b) in the BVTT represents a test between clusters a and b from objects A and B, respectively. If the test determines that the objects are non-colliding then the node is a leaf of the BVTT and no further tests are needed between the subtrees of A and B rooted at a and b. Otherwise, there is a potential collision between a and b.

3.GPU-based Culling: Performing all pairwise tests between triangles of two clusters can be an expensive operation as the clusters may contain around 1K triangles. To further reduce the potentially colliding set of triangles, we employ GPU based culling similar to [7]. Triangles in the mesh selected from each cluster are randomly partitioned into "sub-objects" of size k triangles. For each triangle of a sub-object we construct a bounding volume (BV) dilated by. Since these BVs must be constructed quickly at runtime, we use axis aligned bounding boxes. We use GPU-based occlusion queries to cull the subobjects between the two clusters. After rendering some geometric primitives, an occlusion query returns the number of pixels that pass the depth buffer test. We use these queries to perform a 2.5D overlap test between bounding volumes along the three orthogonal axes.

4. Triangle Collision Test: We perform exact collision detection for triangles pairs that pass sub-object culling. Each triangle of an object represents a set of triangles of the original model. In order to conservatively meet the error bound, an oriented bounding box (OBB) is constructed for each triangle that contains the triangle plus the original mesh triangles that were simplified into it. Triangles whose enclosing OBBs are overlapping are reported as colliding.

5. Out-of-Core Computation: Our goal is to perform collision detection between models that cannot be stored in main memory. The CHST representation also serves as a mechanism for out-of-core management. At runtime we keep the CHST hierarchy for each object in the main memory, while the progressive meshes (PMs) for each cluster reside on the disk. A working set of PMs is kept in memory for collision detection. For each pair of colliding objects, we keep PMs for nodes on the BVTT front in main memory as well as their parents and children.

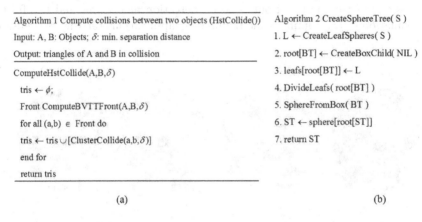

Algorithm 1 Compute collisions between two objects (HstCollide())

Input: A, B: Objects; δ: min. separation distance

Output: triangles of A and B in collision

ComputeHstCollide(A,B,δ)

tris $\leftarrow \phi$;

Front ComputeBVTTFront(A,B,δ)

for all (a,b) $\in$ Front do

tris $\leftarrow$ tris $\cup$ [ClusterCollide(a,b,δ)]

end for

return tris

Algorithm 2 CreateSphereTree(S)

1. L $\leftarrow$ CreateLeafSpheres(S)

2. root[BT] $\leftarrow$ CreateBoxChild(NIL)

3. leafs[root[BT]] $\leftarrow$ L

4. DivideLeafs(root[BT])

5. SphereFromBox(BT)

6. ST $\leftarrow$ sphere[root[ST]]

7. return ST

(a)   (b)

Fig. 1. (a) global collision query. Triangles separated by less than this distance are in collision. (b) Algorithm for building the hierarchical representation of objects with bounding spheres.

4 Results and Analysis

In this section, we explain the implementation issues of our collision detection algorithm and analyze its performance. A useful system is presented to simulate nose augmentation surgical operation. The three-dimensional reconstruction results of skull and implant models are shown in Figure 2(a). According to middle axis plane of skull model, implant model is moved until two middle axis planes are in a same plane, the result is shown in Figure 2(b). During the moving of implant model, there are collisions between two models, we adjust the position of implant model until two models completely joint, the results of joint are shown in Figure 2(c) and Figure 2(d). Our algorithm has been implemented on a 2.4GHz Pentium-IV PC, with 512MB of RAM and a GeForce FX 6600 Ultra GPU.

Testing scenarios have been created to test our algorithm in comparison with other related algorithms like RECODE [9] and RAPID [7]. The time cost(t_i) for collision detection at each iteration and the average time cost(t_n) for collision detections among 1000 iterations are recorded. Figures 3(a) demonstrate the variation of with increment of the complexity of the testing scene. From these, it is obvious that our algorithm is superior to RECODE and RAPID for the testing cases. Figures 3(b) show the variety of the time cost for the testing case. The x-axis represents the frame number in the collision detection process, while the y-axis is the variety:

$$\eta = (t_i - t_n)/t_n. \tag{1}$$

From the experimental data shown in Figure 4, we can find that our algorithm has demonstrated the stability with the time cost, i.e. at each iteration of the run-time collision detection phase, the time cost remains almost constant, which is one of the merits of our collision detection algorithms and helpful to the estimation of the running time required by applications relating to collision detection.

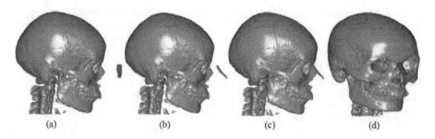

Fig. 2. Experiment of skull and implant models quick joint. (a) 3D reconstruction of skull and implant model. (b) Middle axis of implant model. (c) Reset of implant model, lateral result of joint. (d) Result of joint in other angle.

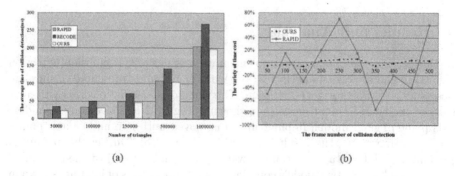

Fig. 3. (a)The comparison of the test results of the scene in PC.(b)The comparison chart of the collision detection time change rate in the scene.

5   Conclusions

A collision detection algorithm for surgery simulation has been presented. The algorithm uses a hierarchical sphere-tree representation of objects. The results show that our algorithm is suitable for real-time surgery simulation systems.

Acknowledgments. This work has been partially supported by National Natural Science Foundation of China (10JJ2045).

References

1. Larsen, E., Gottschalk, S., Lin, M., Manocha, D.: Fast distance queries with rectangular swept sphere volumes. In: IEEE Conf. on Rob. and Auto., pp. 121–128. IEEE Press, New York (2000)
2. Baciu, G., Wong, S., Sun, H.: RECODE: An image-based collision detection algorithm. Journal of Visualization and Computer Animation 10(4), 181–191 (1999)
3. Chang, J.-W., Kim, M.-S.: Efficient triangle – triangle intersection test for OBB based collision detection. Computers Graphics 33(3), 235–240 (2009)
4. Beckmann, N., Kriegel, H., Schneider, R., Seeger, B.: An efficient and robust access method for points and rectangles. ACM SIGMOD Record 19(2), 322–331 (1990)
5. Govindaraju, N., Lin, M., Manocha, D.: OBB-Tree: Fast and Reliable Collision Detection Using Graphics Hardware. In: Proc. ACM VRST, pp. 161–168. IEEE Press, New York (2004)
6. Hubbard, P.: Interactive collision detection. In: Proceedings of the IEEE Symposium on Research Frontiers in Virtual Reality, pp. 24–31. IEEE Press (1993)
7. Robison, R.A., Liu, C.Y., Apuzzo, M.L.J.: Man, Mind, and Machine: The Past and Future of Virtual Reality Simulation in Neurologic Surgery. World Neurosurgery 76(5), 419–430 (2011)
8. Gottschalk, S., Lin, M., Manocha, D.: OBB-Tree: A Hierarchical Structure for Rapid Interference Detection. In: the Proceedings of ACM SIGGRAPH 1996, pp. 171–180. IEEE Press, New York (1996)
9. Lin, Y., Wang, X., Wu, F., Chen, X., Wang, C., Shen, G.: TDevelopment and validation of a surgical training simulator with haptic feedback for learning bone-sawing skill. Journal of Biomedical Informatics. Journal of Biomedical Informatics (in Press, 2013)

Fuzzy RBF Neural PID Control to Simulation Turntable Servo System

Yanmin Wu, Guangzhao Cui, and Xuncai Zhang

School of Electrical and Information Engineering,
Zhengzhou University of Light Industry,
450002, Zhengzhou, China
yanmin1020@126.com

Abstract. Simulation turntable servo system is highly nonlinear and uncertainty plants. Up to now, various kinds of nonlinear PID controllers have been designed in order to satisfactorily control this system and some of them applied in actual systems with different degrees. Given this background, the simulation experiments are carried out based on MATLAB/SIMULINK tools to evaluate the performances of four different turntable servo controllers, including the conventional PID, the fuzzy self-tuning PID, the neural network PID and the fuzzy RBF neural network PID controller. The simulation results show that the simulation turntable servo system with fuzzy RBF neural PID controller exhibits robustness and good adaptation capability.

Keywords: Turntable, Servo System, Fuzzy Neural Control, RBF Network.

1 Introduction

Simulation turntable is an important part of the seeker pre-install test system [1]. The precision and control performance of simulation turntable servo system have a significant impact for successfully completing seeker performance testing and inspection.

Traditionally, conventional PID controller is extensively used in the simulation turntable servo system, because of its simplicity of operation, ease of design, inexpensive maintenance, low cost, and so on [2,3]. However, its control performance is difficult to guarantee when the parameters change or the disturbance exists. In order that the servo system can have good accuracy and control performance in more running mode, more recently, intelligent control and conventional PID control methods are combined to design the position controller of turntable servo system.

Although, various methods have been proposed to design the position controller of the turntable servo system, there are not comparative analysis on performance and accuracy of these position controllers. This paper fully considers the characteristics of fuzzy control and neural network control, combines the fuzzy RBF neural network control with conventional PID control and designs

L. Pan et al. (Eds.): BIC-TA 2014, CCIS 472, pp. 478–482, 2014.

fuzzy RBF neural network PID controller of the servo system. The simulation models are built based on the Matlab/Simulink RTW tools, and the step input, sinusoidal input simulation tests are carried out. The simulation results are analyzed comparing with the conventional PID controller, fuzzy self-tuning PID and the neural network PID controller. The comparison results show that the fuzzy RBF neural network PID controller has better performances in the stability and robust of the simulation turntable servo system.

2   Model of Simulation Turntable Servo System

Each axis of the simulation turntable is individually controlled by double-loop control structure. The single-axis position control block diagram is shown as Fig. 1. For this control system, the inner velocity loop is controlled by conventional PID controller and the outer position loop is controlled by the fuzzy RBF neural network PID method.

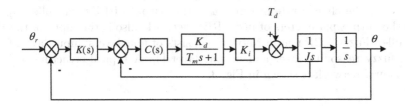

Fig. 1. Position control block diagram of simulation turntable

In Fig. 1, $K(s)$ is the main controller of the outer position loop; $C(s)$ is the secondary controller of the inner velocity loop. $\frac{K_d}{T_m s+1}$ is the transfer function of AC servo motor and its driver, where, K_d is the transfer coefficient of driver-motor device, measuring out through experiment; T_m is the electromechanical time constant of driver-motor device. K_i is the transfer function of the reducer, $\frac{1}{Js^2}$ is the transfer function of turntable platform. T_d is the total load torque viz. disturbance torque. θ_r is the set input value of turntable corner; θ is the actual value measured by the optical encoder.

According to the element parameters of servo system, the open-loop transfer function can be calculated as equation (1):

$$G(s) = \frac{0.29s + 13.2}{0.0000682s^3 + 0.022s^2 + 2.77s + 126.1} \tag{1}$$

3   Configuration of Fuzzy RBF Neural PID Controller

The configuration of fuzzy RBF neural network PID controller is shown in Fig. 2.

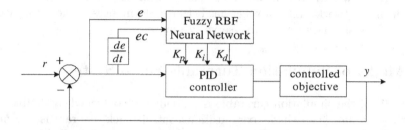

Fig. 2. Configuration of Fuzzy RBF Neural Network PID Controller

In Fig. 2, r is the set input value; y is the output value of system. e is the error, ec is the change rate of error, u is the output of PID controller. k_p, k_i, k_d is the output parameters of fuzzy RBF network, also is the input of the PID controller. Fuzzy RBF neural Network consists of four layers: input layer, fuzzy layer, fuzzy reasoning layer and output layer [4]. A typical structure of fuzzy RBF neural network is shown in Fig. 3.

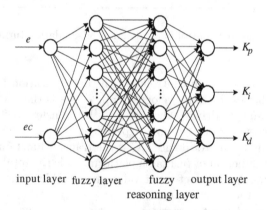

Fig. 3. Structure of fuzzy RBF neural network

Layer 1 is input layer. Each neuron in this layer represents an input variable, and passes the input value to the next level [5]. Here use error e and error change rate ec as the input variables. The output of layer 1 is $f_1(x_i) = x_i$, viz.$x_1 = e(t)$, $x_2 = ec(t)$.

Layer 2 is fuzzy layer. Each neuron in this layer is used to analog a membership function of input variables. The role of fuzzy layer is to calculate fuzzy set membership function for each input language variable [6].

According to the characteristics of simulation turntable servo system, here use Gaussian function as the membership function. Its expression is:

$$f_2(i,j) = \exp[-\frac{(x_i - m_{ij})^2}{\sigma_{ij}^2}] \tag{2}$$

Layer 3 is fuzzy reasoning layer. Each node represents a fuzzy rule, and its action is completing the fuzzy matching of fuzzy rules by connecting the fuzzy layer, or obtaining the corresponding activation strength by combining every fuzzy node. The output of node j can be expressed as equation (3).

$$f_3(j) = \prod_{j=1}^{N} f_2(i,j) \tag{3}$$

Layer 4 is output layer. The layer output f_4 is the tuning results of k_p, k_i, k_d, can be induced as equation (4).

$$f_4(i) = w \cdot f_3 = \sum_{j=1}^{N} w(i,j) \cdot f_3(j) \tag{4}$$

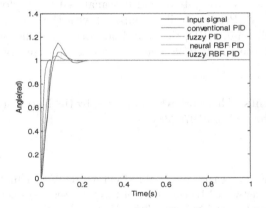

Fig. 4. Comparison of step response curves

4   Simulations and Research

In order to compare the performance of the four controllers: conventional PID controller, Fuzzy Self-tuning PID Controller, RBF neural network PID controller and fuzzy RBF neural network PID controller, the simulation experiment based on MATLAB/SIMULINK kit has been carried out. The output responses curls of step signal are indicated as Fig. 4, the tracking curves of 2Hz sinusoidal signal are shown in Fig. 5.The comparison results show that the fuzzy RBF neural network PID controller has better performances and good robust.

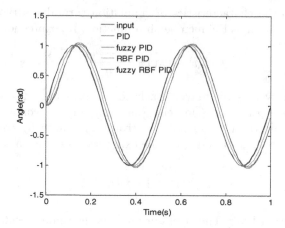

Fig. 5. Comparison of 2Hz sinusoidal signal tracking curves

5   Conclusions

This paper has proposed a fuzzy RBF neural network PID controller of simulation turntable servo system, and has analyzed the performance of fuzzy RBF neural network PID controller compared with the conventional PID control, the fuzzy self-tuning PID, the neural network PID. The simulation results have shown that the fuzzy RBF neural network PID controller has stronger robustness.

Acknowledgments. This work was supported by the National Natural Science Foundation of China (No: 61070238).

References

1. Wu, Y.M., Huang, C., Deng, W., et al.: MATLAB RTW tool application to configure RBF neural network PID controller of turntable servo system. J. International Review on Computers and Software. 7(5), 2750–2755 (2012)
2. Tang, K.S., Man, K.F., Chen, G.R., et al.: An optimal fuzzy PID controller. IEEE Transactions on Industrial Electronics, 757–765 (2001)
3. Piao, H.G., Wang, Z.X.: Simulation research of fuzzy-PID synthesis yaw vector control system of wind turbine. WSEAS Transactions on Systems and Control, 469–476 (2007)
4. Mao, B.Q., Wang, F., Xu, L., et al.: PID controller of robot weapon station servo system based on fuzzy-neural network. J. Ordnance Industry Automation. 29(9), 75–78 (2010)
5. Huang, W., Wu, Q.: Fuzzy-PID controller of parameter based auto-tuning and its application. J. Hydromechatronics Engineering. 41(6), 81–86 (2013)
6. Leng, G., Ginnity, T.M., Prasad, G.: An approach for on-line extraction of fuzzy rules using a self-organising fuzzy neural network. J. Fuzzy Sets and Systems. 150(2), 211–243 (2005)

Three-Input Molecular Logic
Based on Light-Control System

Yuhui Xia[1], Shanshan Liu[1], Xiangxiang Chen[2], Ming Song[1],
and Yafei Dong[1,2,*]

[1] College of Life Science, Shaanxi Normal University, Xi'an 710119, China
[2] Department of Computer Science, Shaanxi Normal University, Xi'an 710119, China
dongyf@snnu.edu.cn

Abstract. In biomolecular programming, the control of interaction among biomolecules is harnessed for computational purposessuch as proteins and nucleic acids. Recently, a new kind of biocompution system has drew considerable attention. Rational designing and engineering of biological computing systems can promote our ability to control biological processes. In this paper we construct a multi-input logic circuit based on photoreceptor protein, which aims to achieve spatial regulation of gene expression in the tissue level. It is a certain inspiration for applying to tissue engineering.

Keywords: Multi-input, Logic gate, Light, Protein.

1 Introduction

Operation of the computer consist of three stereotypical parts: sensors, processors and actuators. Sensors can sense signals both from internal and external environment and deliver information to the processor, processor translate information and determine how to respond. Then, the actuators carry such a response out[1]. Computation is manifest even in single-input-single output systems, such as a conditional transgene in a mouse [2]or an inducible expression vector [3]. Because the relationship between the inducer and the gene expression is integrated, which implies a certain mapping relationship between them. However, more intricate multiple-input and multiple-output computations that are able to trigger multiple processes are needed [4–6]. Thus the application of biomolecular engineering is expanded [7–9].

Using biomolecular methods to compute dates decade back [10]researchers try to use DNA and RNA to solve certain problems that are difficult for mathematical methods, such as the satisfactory ability problem, the graph coloring problem, the maximal clique problem, and the maximum independent set problem [11–13]. DNA was implemented to operate parallel computing by the principle of complementary base pairing [14–16]. Stojanovic and Stefanovic constructed a DNA computer capable of encoding a tic-tac-toe game[17]. DNA molecule has

---

* Corresponding author.

L. Pan et al. (Eds.): BIC-TA 2014, CCIS 472, pp. 483–488, 2014.

a powerful parallel computing capacity. For a long time, DNA computing and self-assembly model have drew much attention and got great progress. Most of computation based on the principle of DNA strand displacement. Recently, gene circuit and signal transduction pathway could be implemented even in a single cell [18]. Potential applications including tissue engineering, disease diagnosis, drug screening, environmental monitoring [19].

Chemical molecules as an input signal in logic pathway has been widely studied [20–22]. Whereas most of the chemical molecules are easy to diffuse and hard to eliminate from organisms, sometimes they are even toxic. On the contrary ,light could be an ideal inducer with many advantages,such as non-toxic, highly tunable, easy to manipulate and allowing spatial and temporal control of gene expression. Therefore, optical signal as an input is a promising tool to control physiological processes. We developed an AND logic circuit based on light-switchable gene expression system which aims to control spatiotemporal gene expression in multicellular organisms precisely.

2   Logic Gate and Materials

In boolean logic gates, the input information is mathematically conversed into digital signal. This signal is codes representing a sequence of discrete values. In the case of a binary code, the basic unit of information is denoted as a series of 0 and 1 digits to represent the two states of the logic circuit. Usually, a threshold is adopted to define the input and output range. Then , the value of either 0 or 1 depends on the threshold set in place.

Photoreceptor proteins or Light-sensitive proteins, are a kind of proteins that can perceive light signal and control physiological processes, which are of great physiological significance in circadian regulation, cell signal transduction etc.The adoption of light-sensitive proteins to control gene expression is a combinational method of optical technology and genetic technology. This field is called optogenetics[23].In recent years, analytic and functional studies on the light-sensitive proteins structures as well as in its application have experienced a big booming [24–26].

3   The Logic Gate Based on Light-Control System

The light oxygen or voltage (LOV) family of PAS proteins can bind flavin adenine dinucleotide (FAD) or flavin mononucleotide (FMN) [27]. The Neurospora crassa LOV protein VIVID (VVD) allows adaptations to constant or increasing light levels and circadian rhythms. TetR is a dipolymer with each monomer composed of an N-terminal DNA-binding domain and a C-terminal tetracycline binding domain (TBD). In order to create a DNA-binding domain that could be activated by light, we remove C-terminal TBD of TetR and keep the part that can bind to tetO sequence. To avoid conformational antagonism, we add linker between TetR and VVD. Then we fused a transactivation domains VP16 to the C terminus of TetR -VVD. Herein, we can test theirlight-dependent impacts on transcriptional activity of a GFP reporter driven by tetO binding sites after transient transfection in HEK293 cells. We reasoned that the DNA-binding property of a TetR-VVD chimeric protein would be light-switchable, as light could induce dimerization of the fusion protein, enhance TetR bind to the tetO sequence and activate transcription. Removing the light result in gradual dissociation of the dimers, downstream DNA transcription will be stoped(Fig. 1).

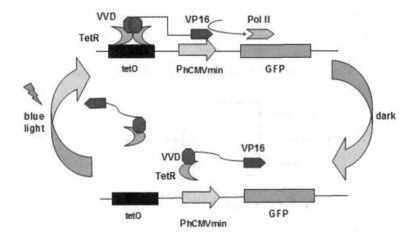

Fig. 1. mechanism of light-control system

We construct two plasmids to accomplish the design of logic gate. In this logic gate, we assume that providing light (L) as input "1", whereas the dark is defined as " 0 ". The transfected of plasmid 1 or plasmid 2 (P1, P2) is defined as " 1 " , otherwise "0". When providing illumination and transfecting the plasmid1 and plasmid2 into the cells ,the input is (1,1,1). If the GFP gene express and the detection of fluorescence intensities overpass the threshold , then the output is defined as 1. When there are only two inputs, the input is (1,1,0) , (1,0,1) or (0,1,1). Because the lack of necessary conditions of gene expression, the output is 0 . When there is only one input , the input is (1,0,0), (0,1,0) or (0,0,1) , due to the insufficient conditions, the expression of the gene can not be detected ,so the output is 0 too. Finally, if all three inputs are absent, the input is (0, 0, 0), neither the templates of gene expression nor the activated conditions are provided, so the output is still 0. In conclusion, only when all three inputs are 1, can the output be 1.

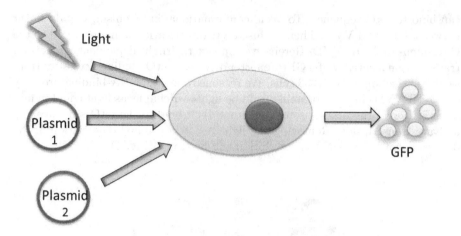

Fig. 2. Schematic diagram of Light-switchable system

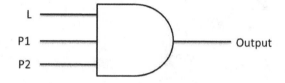

Fig. 3. Three-input logic electrical symbol

4   Conclusion

Light control system appears advantages. However, there are also some limitations, for example, its computing speed is not fast enough. whats more, it takes
some time for proteins to decompose and aggregate. Besides, there is still some
background transcription. Now,it is believed that the most promising application of bio-computer may be medical treatment. Computational Biology now
targets the recognition of cancer cells and can discriminate tumor cells from
normal cells. If we replace the GFP gene with apoptosis activating factor gene
in light-control system, it can promote programmed cell death of cancer cells.
Another application is to regulate the tissue differentiation. Computational Biology is in its infancy, but research in this field will promote the development
of its applications. So there will be a good prospect in the future, especailly in
pathology, biomedicine, environmental science and computer science.

References

1. Biomolecular Computing Systems: Principles, Progress and Potential. Nat. Rev. Genet. 13(7), 455–468 (2012)
2. Bockamp, E., et al.: Conditional Transgenic Mouse Models: from the Basics to Genome-Wide Sets of Knockouts and Current Studies of Tissue Regeneration. Regen. Med. 3, 217–235 (2008)
3. Kartsson, M., Weber, W., Fussenegger, M.: Methods in Enzymology: Synthetic Biology, Part A. In: Voigt, C. (ed.) Methods for Part/Device Characterization and Chassis Engineering, vol. 497, pp. 239–253 (2011)
4. Kramer, B.P., Fischer, C., Fussenegger, M.: BioLogic gates enable logical transcription control in mammalian cells. Biotechnol. Bioeng. 87, 478–484 (2004)
5. Leisner, M., Bleris, L., Lohmueller, J., Xie, Z., Benenson, Y.: Rationally Designed Logic Integration of Regulatory Signal Sin Mammalian Cells. Nat. Nanotechnol. 5, 666–670 (2010)
6. Rinaudo, K., Bleris, L., Maddamsetti, R., Subramanian, S., Weiss, R., Benenson, Y.: A Universal RNAi-based Logic Evaluator that Operates in Mammalian Cells. Nat. Biotechnol. 25, 795–801 (2007)
7. Win, M.N., Smolke, C.D.: Higher-Order Cellular Information Processing with Synthetic Rna Devices. Science 322, 456–460 (2008)
8. Xie, Z., Wroblewska, L., Prochazka, L., Weiss, R., Benenson, Y.: Multi-input RNAi-Based Logic Circuit For Identification of Specific Cancer Cells. Science 333, 1307–1311 (2011)
9. Nissim, L., Bar-Ziv, R.H.: A Tunable Dual-Promoter Integrator for Targeting of Cancer Cells. Mol. Syst. Biol. 6, 444 (2010)
10. Sugita, M.: Functional Analysis of Chemical Systems in Vivo Using A Logical Circuit Equivalent. J. Theor. Biol. 1, 415–430 (1961)
11. Adleman, L.M.: Molecular Computation of Solutions to Combinatorial Problems. Science 266, 1021–1024 (1994)
12. Lipton, R.J.: DNA Solution of Hard Computational Problems. Science 268, 542–545 (1995)
13. Faulhammer, D., Cukras, A.R., Lipton, R.J., Landweber, L.F.: Molecular computation: RNA solutions to chess problems. Proc. Natl Acad. Sci. USA 97, 1385–1389 (2000)
14. Benner, S.A., Sismour, A.M.: Synthetic biology. Nature Rev. Genet. 6, 533–543 (2005)
15. Baker, D., et al.: Engineering life: building a fab for biology. Sci. Am. 294, 44–51 (2006)
16. Tan, C.M., Song, H., Niemi, J., You, L.C.: A synthetic biology challenge: making cells compute. Mol. Biosyst. 3, 343–353 (2007)
17. Stojanovic, M.N., Stefanovic, D.: A deoxyribozyme-based molecular automaton. Nat. Biotechnol. 21, 1069–1074 (2003)
18. Auslander, S., Auslander, D., Muller, M., Wieland, M., Fussenegger, M.: Programmable single-cell mammalian biocomputers. Nature 487(7405), 123–127 (2012)
19. Sinha, J., Reyes, S.J., Gallivan, J.P.: Reprogramming bacteria to seek and destroy an herbicide. Nat. Chem. Biol. 6, 464–470 (2010)
20. Iyer, S., Karig, D.K., Norred, S.E., et al.: Multi-input regulation and logic with t7 promoters in cells and cell-free systems. PloS One 8(10), e78442 (2013)

21. Yokobayashi, Y., Weiss, R., Arnold, F.H.: Directed evolution of a genetic circuit. Proceedings of the National Academy of Sciences 99(26), 16587–16591 (2002)
22. Bronson, J.E., Mazur, W.W., Cornish, V.W.: Transcription factor logic using chemical comple-mentation. Mol. BioSyst. 4(1), 56–58 (2007)
23. Deisseroth, K., Feng, G., Majewska, A.K., Miesenboek, G., Ting, A., Sehnitzer, M.J.: Next Generation Optical Technologies for Illuminating Genetieally Targeted Brain Circuits. J. Neuro. Sci. (26), 10380–1038 (2006)
24. Heintzen, C., Loros, J.J., Dunlap, J.C.: The PAS Protein VIVID Defines a Clock-Associated Feedback Loop that Represses Light Input, Modulates Gating, and Regulates Clock Resetting. Cell 104, 453–464 (2001)
25. Cheng, P., He, Q., Yang, Y., Wang, L., Liu, Y.: Functional Conservation of Light, Oxygen, or Voltage Domains in Light Sensing. Proc. Natl. Acad. Sci. USA 100, 5938–5943 (2003)
26. Lee, C.-T., Malzahn, E., Brunner, M., Mayer, M.P.: Light-induced Differences in Conformational Dynamics of The Circadian Clock Regulator Vivid. Journal of Molecular Biology (2013) ISSN: 0022-2836
27. Crosson, S., Moffat, K.: Photoexcited Structure of a Plant Photoreceptor Domain Reveals a Light-Driven Molecular Switch. The Plant Cell Online 14, 1067 (2002)

The Reconstruction of 3D Human Face Based on the Post-Plastic Surgery

Kai Xie[1,*], Bo Liu[1], Ningjun Ruan[1], and Jun Chen[2]

[1] School of Computer Science, Yangtze University, 434023 Jingzhou, China
[2] School of Electronic Information and Electrical Engineering,
Shanghai Jiaotong Univ., 200030 Shanghai, China
pami2009@163.com

Abstract. In medical area, the technology of 3D visualization has been widely used and the method of high-quality synthesizing of human face is of great importance. In this paper, we present a method to synthesize a high-quality human face. We employ three 2D digital color photos to obtain high-resolution textures and take advantages of 3D face model reconstructed from CT data for flexible deformation of finite elements. We get the accurately projective parameters from 3D face model to 2D photos via the iterative algorithm of DSM. We use multi-texture mapping of OpenGL to avoid splicing crack and accelerate the whole fusing process due to GPU-based parallel processing. Experimental results show that our method can synthesize a high-definition and realistic human face on standard PC hardware.

Keywords: Realistic rendering, Multi-texture mapping, 3D human face model, Plastic surgery, OpenGL.

1 Introduction

In the past decade, the technology of 3D visualization has been widely used in the field of medicine. Among that, realistic human face rendering plays an important role in predicting the effects of post-plastic-surgical patients. Although the information of geometry and texture can be accurately acquired utilizing 3D laser scanner, it is not suitable for predicting the post-surgical effect. Because the prediction of the post-surgical effect involves the deformation of soft tissue, which requires the internal structure information of the object, but laser scanner simply provides the information of the surface. Due to the limitation of the sampling rate, the texture obtained is relatively rough and it is far from the high resolution digital photos. Therefore, its an ideal way to predict post-surgical effect using the patients CT data and high-resolution digital photos. That is to say, the deformation of finite element can be easily realized by utilizing the CT data and more precise texture information can be obtained by digital photos. The principle of two-step mapping is usually used for mapping between the texture

---

* Corresponding author.

L. Pan et al. (Eds.): BIC-TA 2014, CCIS 472, pp. 489–493, 2014.

of digital photo and 3D human face. Firstly, digital photos is synthesized by seamless montagethen it is mapped to 3D human face by cylinder. However, this method will produce lots of deformation. We briefly survey earlier work on Medical image processing. Zha H B [4] utilizes an adaptive method to make registration from 3D to 2D with numerous pictures. However, only the color of the vertices of triangular facets on 3D model is taken into account in the latter two methods, thus getting rougher texture. Recently, significant work is being conducted in the field of 3D face fusing. Wang [3] use the algorithm based on Sub-regional difference to obtain face model. Li [1] generates realistic wrinkle for 3D face model by extracted curves and shape control function. Liao [2] reconstructs the 3D face by fusing of SFS and LMM.

2 Method

The feature points are selected in this paper as follows: four positive eye corner points, two lip corner points and a top tip point, by the side, a eye corner point, a lip corner point and the intersecting point of two auricle lines (Fig. 1). The coordinate value should be reserved after the feature points are selected. First of all, it must be made sure that the triangle strip of 3D human face is mapped by which one or two photo correspondingly. The rules selected in this paper is as follows : the front right part (A) choosing the right and the positive photos to map , the former left side (B) choosing the left and the positive photos , the back left side (C) and the back right(D) respectively choosing the mapping of left photos and the mapping of right (Fig. 2). Each texture image created by three photos corresponds to one texture unit. After confirming the mapping photos of each triangle strips, the coordinates of each vertex of triangle strips mapping to the corresponding picture are calculated according to the projective parameters obtained by the mapping of 3D human face to each picture in the previous, then the texture coordinates of corresponding texture unit will be obtained after normalizing it. If a triangle strips have two mapping photos, you need to fuse the corresponding texture, and the function of fusion can be set by

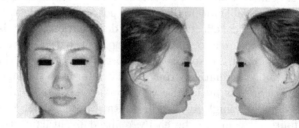

Fig. 1. Selection of landmark points

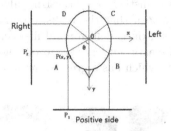

Fig. 2. Projection directions of vertices on 3D face model

using the texture combined function. The method of fusion used by this article can be expressed as follows:

$$C(p) = C(p1)\cos^2\theta + C(p2)\sin^2\theta, \tag{1}$$

among them, C (p) expresses the color of p. p, p1, p2 and are shown in Fig. 4. Because the coordinates of the original 3D human face model are normalized to the interval [-1,1] and the original point is located in the center of model. , can be approximately respectively expressed by the coordinates of x, y of point p. Thus it simplifies the calculation of trigonometric function and the simplified formula (2) can be expressed as follows:

$$\eta = C(p2)x^2 + C(p1)y^2. \tag{2}$$

3   Experiment Analysis and Result

We have implemented our realistic face synthesizing algorithm using Visual C++, OpenGL 4.0 and measure its performance on a dual-core 2.3 GHz Conroe PC equipped with NVIDIA GeForce GT 610M (48 cores). The Fig.3 shows the 3D face model synthesized by the method of Marching Cubes.

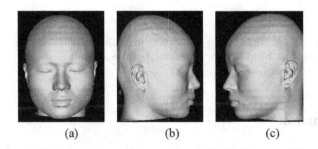

(a)   (b)   (c)

Fig. 3. 3D face model reconstructed by CT data

The performance of our realistic face synthesizing algorithm is shown in Fig.4. From the figure, it can be seen that the realistic human face of multi-texture mapping is great; the facial skin is delicate and lifelike. It can be used to accurately predict the effect of plastic surgery and accordingly the patient can decide whether do surgery or not, which has a great value in clinical application.

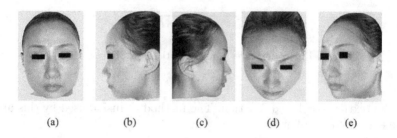

    (a)   (b)   (c)   (d)   (e)

Fig. 4. Results of photorealistic rendering based on multi-texture mapping. (a), (b), (c) are the results of observation from the positive, the left and the right side respectively. (d) and (e) are the result of observation from other arbitrary angle respectively.

Fig.5 shows the results of comparison when using the method of standard texture mapping in OpenGL and the method of multiple texture mapping in OpenGL .The left is the result for the standard texture mapping and the right is for the multiple texture mapping. From the figure, it is clear that it produces significant splicing crack in the transition zone with the method of OpenGL standard texture mapping, which has serious influence on the effect of drawing. But it can be avoided by using the OpenGL multiple texture mapping.

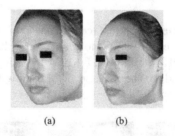

    (a)   (b)

Fig. 5. Comparison of results from simple texture mapping and multi-texture mapping of OpenGL. (a) The result of the standard texture mapping. (b) The result of the method of multi-texture mapping.

4   Conclusions

In this paper, we have presented a face synthesizing algorithm which obtains photorealistic 3D human face. And it proves that our synthesizing algorithm is superior to others by comparing the synthesizing method. These datasets are often used in clinical medicine to predict the effect of plastic surgery. By taking advantage of Multi-texture of OpenGL and visibility testing, we can synthesize high-definition realistic 3D human face at real-time performance on standard PC hardware.

Acknowledgments. This work has been partially supported by National Natural Science Foundation of China (10JJ2045) and University Students' innovative undertaking training projects (104892013013).

References

1. Li, L., Liu, F., Li, C.: Realistic Wrinkle Generation for 3D Face Modeling Based on Automatically Extracted Curves and Improved Shape Control Functions. Computers Graphics 35(1), 175–184 (2011)
2. Liao, H., Chen, Q., Zhou, Q.: Rapid 3D Face Reconstruction by Fusion of Sfs and Local Morphable Model. Journal of Visual Communication and Image Representation 23(6), 924–931 (2012)
3. Wang, H., Wang, W., Chang, Y.: 3D Face Modeling Research Based on Deformation Model. In: International Conference on Opto-Electronics Enginering and Information Science, Houston, pp. 254–265 (2011)
4. Zha, H.B., Wang, P.: Realistic Face Modeling by Registration of A 3-D Mesh Model and Multi-View Color Images. In: Proceedings of the 8th International Conference on CAD/Graphics, New York, pp. 171–180 (2003)

PSO Application in Power System: Low-Frequency Oscillation Fault Analysis

Wei Xiong[1,*], Xiaoya Hu[1], Zhuguo Li[1], and Lejiang Guo[2]

[1] School of Automation, Huazhong University of Science & Technology,
1037 Luoyu Road, Wuhan 430074, Hubei, China
icyrainxw@gmail.com
[2] Department of Early Warning Surveillance Intelligence,
Air Force Radar Academy, Wuhan 430074, Hubei, China
radar_boss@163.com

Abstract. Low-frequency oscillation is an important problem in modern power systems, the system monitoring and realtime analysis operation are the most basic and important part of the system stability. This paper introduces the main issues of the detection of power system low-frequency oscillation and the fundamental principles of particle swarm optimization (PSO) technique. Point out the lack of the ordinary signal analysis methods in low-frequency oscillations detection, and discuss the feasibility of using the PSO algorithm to detect low-frequency oscillation in power system.

Keywords: Low-frequency oscillation, PSO, Power system stability.

1 Introduction

In modern power systems, low-frequency oscillation problem is one of the major issues currently threaten the safety and stability of the interconnected power grid and capacity of power grid transmission [1]. In the early 1960s, when the Northwest and Southwest system of the North American MAPP were testing interconnection, the low-frequency oscillations of power lines have been reported in [2]. In 1996 a major failure occurred in the Western Systems Coordinating Council (WSCC), system resulting in break-up into four islands, with loss of 30,390 MW of load, affecting 7.49 million customers in western of North America in [3]. Especially in 2003 and 2006, large power failures which causing huge economic losses occurred in the North American power grid and western European power grid, are caused by a single fault of power oscillation, which cause a ripple effect at last and the system finally splitting instability [4]. Thus, low-frequency oscillation has great harm to the stability of the grid in large interconnected power system.

2 Particle Swarm Optimization Technique

Particle swarm optimization (PSO) algorithm has roots in two main component methodologies: artificial life and evolutionary computation. Long time ago

---

* Corresponding author.

L. Pan et al. (Eds.): BIC-TA 2014, CCIS 472, pp. 494–498, 2014.

many scientists simulate the biological behavior of birds and fish on the computer, which is more famous are Reynolds, Hepper and Grenander's simulations of the birds. With CG Reynolds simulate the complex group behavior of birds [5], he builds this behavior with three simple rules: away from the nearest neighbor, close to the target and close to the center of group. The five fundamental principles of swarm intelligence are:

- Adaptability: can change their behaviors at the appropriate time in the amount of attainable calculation;
- Diverse response: should not be activity in too narrow scope;
- Proximity: must be able to perform a simple calculation of space and time;
- Quality: must be able to react to the quality factor of the surrounding environment;
- Stability: should not change their behaviors every time when the environment change.

In the PSO algorithm, each individual is called a particle represents a potential solution. In a D-dimensional search space, each particle is a point of the space. The group is formed by M particles. M also known as population size, which too large M will affect the algorithm computing speed and convergence. $X_i = (X_1, X_2, X_3, \ldots, X_D)$ is the D-dimensional vector position of the particle $i(i = 1, 2, 3, \ldots, M)$. According to pre-set fitness function calculate the current value of X_i, which can measure the position quality of the particle. $V_i = (V_{i1}, V_{i2}, V_{i3}, \ldots, V_{iD})$ is the flight speed of the particle i, which is the distance that the particle moves, $P_i = (P_{i1}, P_{i2}, P_{i3}, \ldots, P_{iD})$ is the optimal position of the particle so far searched, $P_g = (P_{g1}, P_{g2}, P_{g3}, \ldots, P_{gD})$ is the optimal position for the entire particle swarm so far searched. During each iteration, each particle update velocity and position according to $Eq.1$ and $Eq.2$.

$$V_{id}^{k+1} = V_{id}^k + c_1 r_1 (P_{id} - X_{id}^k) + c_2 r_2 (P_{gd} - X_{id}^k) \tag{1}$$

$$X_{id}^{k+1} = X_{id}^k + V_{id}^{k+1} \tag{2}$$

where $i = 1, 2, 3, \ldots, M$, $d = 1, 2, 3, \ldots, D$, k is the number of iterations, r_1 and r_2 are random numbers between $[0, 1]$ which can remain population diversity. c_1 and c_2 are learning factors which also called accelerated factor. So the particle has the learning ability from self-summary and the other outstanding particles, thus to get close to the optimal point of itself and the group. The two parameters can be adjusted to reduce the local minima problems, and to accelerate the convergence rate. Because there is no actual algorithm mechanism in PSO to control the particle velocity, it is necessary to restrict the maximum speed as V_{max}. This parameter is very important, the optimal solution is skipped, when it is too large, the search is not sufficient in space when it is too small. The minimum speed limit of V_i is V_{min}, X_i position values are between X_{min} and X_{max}.

The second part of $Eq.1$ is the cognition part, behalf of learning on the particle itself. The third part is the social part, behalf of the cooperation between particles. So based on the last speed, current location, best experience of itself and best experience of the group, the particle update its speed, and fly to the new position.

3   Oscillation Signal Simulation

After removing DC signal the main ingredient of low-frequency oscillation is attenuated sine function. The PSO algorithm can search the optimum value of each parameter in the given range, and find the variable combinations which best fit to the raw data. There is an example to illustrate the implementation process. Given signal as Eq.3:

$$y = 10\sin(x + \frac{\pi}{3})e^{-0.08x} \tag{3}$$

Assume that the signal amplitude, frequency, attenuation coefficient, and phase is unknown, the following steps show how to solve parameters by using PSO algorithm.

First is initialization of the parameters. Set the signal frequency, amplitude, attenuation and phase as unknown parameters. Each particle is a group of solutions. c_1 and c_2 all set 1, r_1 and r_2 are random numbers between $(0, 1)$. The signal amplitude, frequency, phase and attenuation are the component 1 to component 4 of the particle, and the value ranges are $(0, 20)$, $(0, 2)$, $(0, 2\pi)$ and $(-1, 0)$.

And then, the number of particles set 300; iterations is 800. Calculate the fitness value of each particle. Sampling interval dt takes 0.5s, the number of total sampling points n takes 40, the original values of the sampling points are $(z_1, z_2, z_3, \ldots, z_n)$, the sinusoidal signal values consists of the four components of each particle are $(y_1, y_2, y_3, \ldots, y_n)$. The four components of particle i are $X_{i1}, X_{i2}, X_{i3}, X_{i4}$, the y_k is shown in Eq.4.

$$y_k = X_{i1}\sin(X_{i2} \times 2\pi kdt + X_{i3})e^{X_{i4}kdt} \tag{4}$$

Fitness values formula is Eq.5.

$$F(X_i) = \sum_{k=1}^{n}(y_k - z_k)^2 \tag{5}$$

This fitness value describes the difference between the original signal and signal of each component of current particles. If the $F(X_i)$ is small, the difference is small. At last, according to calculation procedure of PSO algorithm described in the previous section, we can find the optimal solution.

The PSO analysis result is shown in Fig.1 and Table 1. In the oscillogram, the blue wave is the theoretical value, the red one is the analysis result. According to the results of the analysis, frequency, amplitude, attenuation and phase analysis results are very close to the theoretical value, fitted curve are almost coincident with the original curve, the analytical results is accurate and reliable.

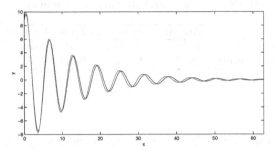

Fig. 1. PSO analysis result and comparison with theoretical value

Table 1. PSO analysis result

	Amplitude	Frequency	Phase	Attenuation
Theoretical value	10	0.159	1.047	-0.080
Analysis result	10.327	0.156	1.051	-0.081

After adding Gaussian white noise to the signal, use the same method to analyze the signal described in Eq.6. The part of $rand()$ generate a random number between (0,1).

$$y = 10\sin(x + \frac{\pi}{3})e^{-0.08x} + rand() \tag{6}$$

The result of PSO analysis with Gaussian white noise is shown in Fig.2 and Table 2. In the oscillogram, the blue wave is the theoretical value, the red one is the analysis result. The fitted curve is also coincident with the original curve.

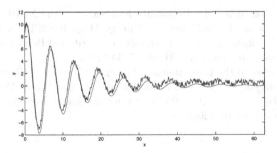

Fig. 2. PSO analysis with Gaussian white noise

Table 2. PSO analysis with Gaussian white noise

	Amplitude	Frequency	Phase	Attenuation
Theoretical value	10	0.159	1.047	-0.080
Analysis result	10.518	0.161	0.911	-0.081

4   Conclusions

In this work, we using PSO algorithm to extract the principal character of low-frequency oscillation. Based on the mode of oscillation signal we determine the amplitude, frequency, phase and attenuation coefficient of the oscillation. Simulation and analysis of the measured data illustrate that the PSO algorithm can be applied in low-frequency oscillation detection. It can provide accurate and effective information which is use for analysis and control of low-frequency oscillations.

Acknowledgments. This work was supported by National Natural Science Foundation of China (60802002, 60773190) and the Fundamental Research Funds for the Central Universities (2013TS127).

References

1. Zhu, F., Zhao, H.G., Liu, Z.H., Kou, H.Z.: The Influence of Large Power Grid Interconnected on Power System Dynamic Stability. Proceedings of the CSEE 1, 1–7 (2007)
2. Schleif, F.R., White, J.H.: Damping for the Northwest-Southwest Tieline Oscillations-An Analog Study. IEEE Transactions on Power Apparatus and Systems (12), 1239–1247 (1966)
3. Kosterev, D.N., Taylor, C.W., Mittelstadt, W.A.: Model Validation for the August 10, 1996 WSCC System Outage. IEEE Transactions on Power Systems 14(3), 967–979 (1999)
4. Sulzberger, V., Gallagher, T.: Reliability and Security: the NERC New Standards Development Process. IEEE Power and Energy Magazine 2(2), 56–61 (2004)
5. Reynolds, C.W.: Flocks, Herds and Schools: A Distributed Behavioral Model. ACM SIGGRAPH Computer Graphics 21(4), 25–34 (1987)
6. Boyd, R.: Culture and the Evolutionary Process. University of Chicago Press (1988)
7. Mingqi, D., Dongjun, Y., Yong, H.: Simulation of Regional Low Frequency Oscillation Based on Data Measured by Wams of Central China Power Grid. Power System Technology 33(13), 64–69 (2009)

Interference Avoidance Scheme for Relay-Based Device-to-Device Communication System in LTE Network

Jianbin Xue* and Supan Wei

School of Computer and Communication, LanZhou University of Technology,
Langongping, 287, Qilihe district, LanZhou 730050, Gansu, China
nothing137club@gmail.com

Abstract. In this paper, we propose an interference avoidance scheme for relay-based D2D communication system. First reach a relay trigger condition of D2D communication through the analyze of outage probability, and then a relay selection algorithm that based on optimal capacity is proposed. Simulations demonstrate that, compared with traditional cellular communication, D2D communication with relay can make full use of the idle resource of the cell so as to increase the users' capacity effectively and improve system performance as well.

Keywords: D2D communication, Relay technology, Interference avoidance, Optimal capacity.

1 Introduction

D2D (device - to - device) communication is a new type of mobile cellular network which based on end-to-end communication directly. It is a short distance communication service, which can achieve data transmission directly under the control of cellular network [1]. In the D2D communication, in order to guarantee the reliability and effectiveness of communication, interference problem becoming one of the hottest issues in recent research. There are many articles discuss the interference avoidance and coordination from the aspects of resource management and allocation. But most interference suppression scheme above are reserched under the environment that have no relay. In fact, if before the D2D has been completed communication on the connection which has been established, channel fading can't meet the requirements of system communication's speed. We need for a certain processing.

In order to solve the problems above. We propose a D2D interference suppression scheme based on relay technology, research how to choose the appropriate user in free cellular users as a relay to limit the interference caused by D2D communication. Through the performance analysis of cellular communication model, D2D communication model and D2D communication with relay model, obtain

---

* Corresponding author.

L. Pan et al. (Eds.): BIC-TA 2014, CCIS 472, pp. 499–504, 2014.

this three models' interrupt probability. Finally the simulation results not only show the occurrence probability of three models, but also show the average total capacity of D2D communication with relay model is greater than the cellular communication model.

2   Model of the System and Outage Probabilities Analysis

In Figure 1(a), we assume all channel gain obey the Independent Gaussian Distribution. $D2D_T$ transmit signal x_t to $D2D_R$. CUE_k transmit signal x_c to BS. Then, the signal-to-interference-and-noise-ratio(SINR) transmitting to BS and the SINR of D2D communication can be formulated by Equations (1) and (2), respectively.

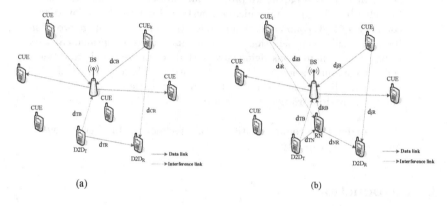

(a)   (b)

Fig. 1. (a):The model without relay, reuse a cellular user's uplink resources; (b):The model with relay, reuse two different users' uplink resources respectively

$$SINR_{BS} = \frac{|h_{CB}|^2 P_C d_{CB}^{-\alpha}}{|h_{TB}|^2 P_D d_{TB}^{-\alpha} + N_0} \qquad (1)$$

$$SINR_{D2D_R} = \frac{|h_{TR}|^2 P_D d_{TR}^{-\alpha}}{|h_{CR}|^2 P_C d_{CR}^{-\alpha} + N_0} \qquad (2)$$

The outage probability of CUE_k transmitting to BS which equals the Cumulative Distribution Function (CDF) can be formulated as Equation (3),

$$P_{out}^C = 1 - \frac{P_C d_{CB}^{-\alpha}}{P_C d_{CB}^{-\alpha} + \xi P_D d_{TB}^{-\alpha}} exp(-\frac{\xi N_0}{P_C d_{CB}^{-\alpha}}) \qquad (3)$$

The outage probabilities of D2D communication is given by Equation (4),

$$P_{out}^D = 1 - \frac{P_D d_{TR}^{-\alpha}}{P_D d_{TR}^{-\alpha} + \tau P_C d_{CR}^{-\alpha}} exp(-\frac{\tau N_0}{P_D d_{TR}^{-\alpha}}) \qquad (4)$$

In Figure 1(b), compared with D2D communication mode, D2D communication with relay mode is an extension of D2D communication, i.e. two hops with D2D communication.

3   Interference Avoidance Scheme for Relay-Based in D2D Communication

The relay triggers condition is Equation (5):

$$SINR_{D2D_R} = \frac{|h_{TR}|^2 P_{D\_max} d_{TR}^{-\alpha}}{|h_{CR}|^2 P_C d_{CR}^{-\alpha} + N_0} \leq SINR_{D\_Th} \tag{5}$$

For D2D equipment which satisfy the D2D relay trigger condition, select the optimal relay in the K candidate relay users. Selection criteria as Equation (6):

$$P_{out}^{RN} = \min_i \{max\{min\{P_{out}^{D_1}\}, min\{P_{out}^{D_2}\}\}\} \tag{6}$$

If the optimal relay exist, Equation (7) gives the total system throughput,

$$C_{sum\_RN}^{D2D,C_i,C_j} = \frac{1}{2}(1 - P_{out}^{RN})log_2(1 + \sigma) \tag{7}$$

In a similar way, Equation (8) show system total throughput of D2D communication which reuse uplink frequency spectrum resources of cellular user.

$$C_{sum\_cell}^{D2D,C_i,C_j} = \frac{5}{2}log_2(1 + \varepsilon) \tag{8}$$

If $C_{sum\_RN}^{D2D,C_i,C_j} \geq C_{sum\_cell}^{D2D,C_i,C_j}$, D2D use relay to communicate, on the contrary, D2D communicate with each other directly by reuse cellular users' uplink resources.

4   Results of Simulation and Performance Analysis

In Figure 2(a), with the increasing of the number of cellular users, the occurrence probability of D2D communication model is grown. In addition ,it also leads to the probability of candidate relay increasing. Therefore, the occurrence probability of D2D communication model with relay is increased, and the occurrence probability of cellular communication between two D2D UEs is descendant. In Figure 2(b), as the cell radius increases, the probability that D2D UEs located in the cell edge also increases. So the disturbance that caused by D2D users to base station decreases and the probability that users choose D2D communication increases. Thus, the D2D UEs may cause less interference to the BS than them located near by the BS, and the probabilities that the D2D UEs select D2D communication is increased. Besides that, the distances among UEs and the distances between UEs and BS become large, and they affect the outage probability of D2D communication with relay mode. According to Equation (11), the probability of D2D communication with relay goes down.

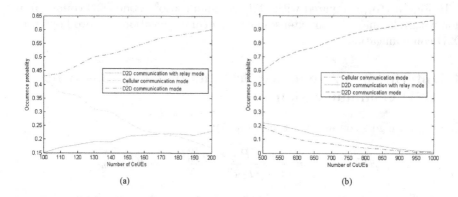

(a)   (b)

Fig. 2. (a):Occurrence probabilities with the number of CeUEs increasing; (b): Occurrence probabilities with the radius of cell increasing

In Figure 3(a), the exceeding average sum-capacity raises in general. It is because the candidate relays is incremental as the number of CeUEs increases, and the outage probability of D2D communication with relay mode is reduced. In Figure 3(b), the increasing cell radius enables the distances from paired CeUEs to BS and to D2D UEs become large, so the link gains of paired CeUE decrease accordingly. Hence, on the basis of (6), the outage probability of D2D communication with relay mode is raised. Therefore, the exceeding average sum-capacity is diminished with the cell size increasing.

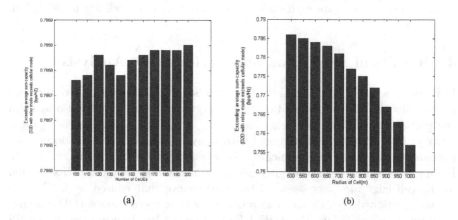

(a)   (b)

Fig. 3. (a):Average sum-capacity that D2D with relay exceeds cellular mode with the number of CeUEs increasing; (b):Average sum-capacity that D2D with relay exceeds cellular mode with the radius of cell increasing

5   Conclusion

This paper proposes a D2D interference suppression scheme based on relay technology. First introduce the D2D communication consist with cellular model, consider the path loss, calculates the interrupt probability when using relay. In order to further improve the system performance, this paper puts forward the relay selection algorithm based on the optimal capacity. The simulation results show that the proposed algorithm can effectively improve the system capacity and improve the system performance. But this paper only consider the one-way transmission. In real system, no matter terminal direct communication or small cellular collaborative access, communication is a two-way channel. Therefore, designing perfect interference suppression scheme based on relay technology for two-way communication will be the further research.

Acknowledgments. This work was supported by the National Science Foundation of China (61062002).

References

1. 3GPP, 3rd Generation Partnership Project, Technical Specification Group SA; Feasibility Study for Proximity Services (ProSe) (release 12), 3GPP TR 22.803 V1.0.0 (2012)
2. Fodor, G., Dahlman, E., Mildh, G., Parkvall, S., Reider, N., Mikl, G., Turanyi, Z.: Design Aspects of Network Assisted Device-To-Device Communications. IEEE Communications Magazine 50(3), 170–177 (2012)
3. Corson, M., Laroia, R., Li, J., Park, V., Richardson, J., Tsirtsis, G.: Toward Proximity-aware Internetworking. IEEE Wireless Communications 17(6), 26–33 (2010)
4. Yu, C.H., Tirkkonen, O., Doppler, K., Ribeiro, C.: On the Performance of Device-to-device Underlay Communication with Simple Power Control. In: Proceedings of the IEEE Vehicular Technology Conference, pp. 1–5 (2009)
5. Yu, C.H., Doppler, K., Ribeiro, C., Tirkkonen, O.: Resource Sharing Optimization for Device-to-device Communication Underlaying Cellular Networks. IEEE Transactions on Wireless Communications 10(8), 2752–2763 (2011)
6. Gu, J., Bae, S.J., Choi, B.G., Chung, M.Y.: Dynamic Power Control Mechanism for Interference Coordination Of Device-To-Device Communication In Cellular Networks. In: Proceedings of the 3rd International Conference on Ubiquitous and Future Networks, pp. 71–75 (2011)
7. Xiao, X., Tao, X., Lu, J.: A Qos-Aware Power Optimization Scheme in Ofdma Systems With Integrated Device-To-Device (D2D) Communications. In: Proceedings of IEEE Vehicular Technology Conference, pp. 1–5 (2011)
8. Lei, L., Zhong, Z., Lin, C., Shen, X.: Operator Controlled Deviceto-Device Communications In Lte-Advanced Networks. IEEE Wireless Communications 19(3), 96–104 (2012)
9. Lee, J., Andrews, J.G., Hong, D.: Spectrum-Sharing Transmission Capacity. IEEE Transactions on Wireless Communications 10(9), 3053–3063 (2011)
10. Lin, X., Andrews, J.G.: Optimal Spectrum Partition and Mode Selection in Device-To-Device Overlaid Cellular Networks. Submitted to IEEE Globecom (2013)

11. Foschini, G., Miljanic, Z.: A Simple Distributed Autonomous Power Control Algorithm and Its Convergence. IEEE Transactions on Vehicular Technology 42(4), 641–646 (1993)
12. Moltchanov, D.: Distance Distributions in Random Networks. Ad Hoc Networks 10(6), 1146–1166 (2012)
13. Heath, R.W., Kountouris, M.: Modeling Heterogeneous Network Interference Using Poisson Point Processes. Submitted to IEEE Transactions on Signal Processing (July 2012), http://arxiv.org/abs/1207.2041

Power Control Research Based on Interference Coordination for D2D Underlaying Cellular Networks

Jianbin Xue*, Bing Wen, and Supan Wei

School of Computer and Communication,
Lanzhou University of Technology, Lanzhou 730050, Gansu, China
nothing137club@gmail.com

Abstract. This paper considers a device-to-device (D2D) underlaying cellular network where an uplink cellular user communicates with the base station while multiple direct D2D links share the uplink spectrum. This paper proposes a random network model based on stochastic geometry and develops centralized power control algorithm. The goal of the proposed power control algorithm is two-fold: ensure the cellular users have sufficient coverage probability by limiting the interference created by underlaid D2D users, while also attempting to support as many D2D links as possible. This paper adopts the two level control strategy: Cellular link SINR(signal-to-interference-plus noise ratio) and sum rate maximization, to ensure the cellular communication and improve the coverage probability of D2D and cellular links. Numerical results show the gains of the proposed power control algorithm and accuracy of the analysis.

Keywords: Power control, Stochastic geometry, Poisson point process, Coverage probability.

1 Introduction

Underlaying cellular networks, D2D communication allow direct communication between mobile users [1]. D2D is an attractive approach for dealing with local traffic in cellular networks. The initial motivation for incorporating D2D communication in cellular networks is to support proximity-based services [2]. Assuming that there are proximate communication opportunities, introducing D2D communication can increase area spectral efficiency, improve cellular coverage, reduce end-to-end latency, or reduce handset power consumption [3]. Due to the difficulty of interference management, the coexistence problem between D2D and cellular communication in the same spectrum is challenging. Specifically, the underlaid D2D signal becomes a new source of interference. As a result, cellular links experience cross-tier interference from the D2D transmissions whereas the D2D links need to combat the inter-D2D interference and the cross-tier interference. Therefore, effective interference management is essential

---

* Corresponding author.

L. Pan et al. (Eds.): BIC-TA 2014, CCIS 472, pp. 505–519, 2014.
© Springer-Verlag Berlin Heidelberg 2014

to ensure successful coexistence of cellular and D2D links. Power control is an effective approach to mitigate interference in cellular networks and currently it is broadly used.

In this paper, we propose power control methods for interference coordination and analyze their performance in D2D underlaying cellular networks. In particular, we consider stochastic geometry as a hybrid random network model and develop a power control algorithm for the proposed network model. With a carefully designed power control technique, we show that multiple D2D links may communicate successfully while guaranteeing reliable communication for the existing cellular link. This indicates that applying the power control technique contributes to increase the network sum-throughput without causing unacceptable performance degradation to existing cellular links.

1.1 Related Work

Now there has been a lot of power control methods for D2D in cellular networks. In [4], a simple power control scheme was proposed for a single-cell scenario and deterministic network model, which regulates D2D transmit power to protect the existing cellular links. And in [5], a D2D transmit power allocation method was proposed to maximize the sum rate of the network for the deterministic network model. A dynamic power control mechanism for a single D2D link communication was proposed in [6], which adjusts the D2D transmit power via base station (BS) to protect cellular users targets and improve the cellular system performance by mitigating the interference generated by D2D communication. A power minimization solution with joint subcarrier allocation, adaptive modulation, and mode selection was proposed to guarantee the quality-of service demand of D2D and cellular users in [7]. In [8], D2D power control strategies are developed and evaluated in a deterministic D2D link deployment scenario. In [9,10], for a random network model, spectrum sharing between ad-hoc and cellular networks was studied but power control has not been addressed. Most studiers are based on the determined distribution model without fully considering the randomness of users in the network. In our paper, based on Stochastic geometry distribution model, we propose a power control algorithm and analyze their performance in the D2D communication underlaying cellular network.

1.2 Contributions

In this paper, we consider N D2Ds underlaying cellular network in which M uplink cellular users want to communicate with the BS while multiple D2D links coexist in the common spectrum. In such a network, we model the D2D users locations using a spatial Poisson point process (PPP). This model is motivated by the fact that D2D users are distributed randomly over the network like ad hoc nodes. In the D2D underlaying cellular network, we propose a two stage filtration power control algorithm. The main idea of the algorithm is to design the transmit power of mobile users so as to maximize the SINR of the cellular link while satisfying the individual target SINR constraints for D2D links. Using the fact that the power allocation problem is convex, we solve it with a feasibility set increment technique. One main observation is that the power control approach can significantly improve the overall cellular network throughput due to the newly underlaid D2D links while guaranteeing the coverage probability of pre-existing cellular links. For this power control method, we derive expressions including the coverage probabilities of both cellular and D2D links using stochastic geometry.

The remainder of this paper is organized as follows. In Section II, the proposed model for D2D underlaid cellular networks is described. The proposed power control algorithms are presented in Section III. In Section IV, the analytical expressions for the cellular user coverage probability and the typical D2D link coverage probability are derived when the centralized power control method is applied. Simulation results are provided in Section V to demonstrate the effectiveness of the proposed algorithms and in Section VI we validate the analytical results, which are followed by our conclusions.

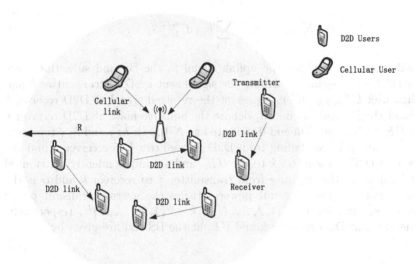

Fig. 1. A single-cell cellular system: M Cellular users and N D2D pairs in a circular disk centered at the BS and with radius R

2   Problem Formulation

2.1   System Model

In this section, we present the system model and describe network metrics that will be used in this paper. We consider a D2D underlaying cellular network, as shown in Figure 1. In this model, let the circular disk C with radius R denotes the coverage region of BS centered at the origin. We assume that on M cellular uplink users are uniformly located in this region. Further, we assume that the locations of the D2D transmitters are distributed in the whole R^2 plane according to a homogeneous PPP Φ with density λ.

For a given D2D transmitter, its associated receiver is located at a fixed distance away with isotropic direction. Under the given assumptions, the N D2D transmitters in C is a Poisson random variable with mean $E[N] = \lambda \pi R^2$. Given one realization of the PPP Φ, the received signals at D2D receiver k and the Cellular UE_i at base station end are given by

$$y_k = h_{k,k} d_{k,k}^{-\alpha/2} S_k + \sum_{i=1}^{M} h_{k,i} d_{k,i}^{-\alpha/2} S_i + \sum_{l=1, l \neq k}^{N} h_{k,l} d_{k,l}^{-\alpha/2} S_l + n_k. \tag{1}$$

$$y_i = h_{i,i} d_{i,i}^{-\alpha/2} S_i + \sum_{k=1}^{N} h_{i,k} d_{i,k}^{-\alpha/2} S_k + n_i, \tag{2}$$

where subscript i is used for the uplink signal to the BS and subscript k are used for D2D links; s_k and s_i denote the signal sent by D2D transmitter k and the uplink user UE_i; y_k and y_i represent the received signal at D2D receiver k and UE_i at the BS end; n_k and n_i denote the additive noise at D2D receiver k and the UE_i at base station end distributed as $N(0, \sigma^2)$; $h_{k,l}$ and $h_{i,k}$ represent the distance-independent fading from D2D transmitter l to receiver k and the channel from D2D transmitter k to the UE_i, and are independently distributed as $N(0, 1)$. denotes the distance from transmitter j to receiver k and α is the path-loss exponent. The transmit power satisfies the average transmit power constraint, i.e., and for $i \in \{1, 2, \ldots, N\}^C, k \in \{1, 2, \ldots, M\}^D$, respectively. Then the SINR at D2D receiver k and UE_i at the BS end are given by

$$SINR_k(N, \boldsymbol{P}) = \frac{|h_{k,k}|^2 d_{k,k}^{-\alpha} p_k^D}{\sum_{i=1}^{M} |h_{k,i}|^2 d_{k,i}^{-\alpha} p_i^C + \sum_{l \neq k}^{N} |h_{k,l}|^2 d_{k,l}^{-\alpha} p_l^D + \sigma^2} \geq \beta_k. \tag{3}$$

$$SINR_i(M, \boldsymbol{P}) = \frac{|h_{i,i}|^2 d_{i,i}^{-\alpha} p_i^C}{\sum_{k=1}^{N} |h_{i,k}|^2 d_{i,k}^{-\alpha} p_k^D + \sigma^2} \geq \beta_i. \tag{4}$$

where $\boldsymbol{P} = [p_i^C, p_1^D, p_2^D, \ldots, p_N^D]$ denotes transmit power profile vector with p_i^C and p_k^D respectively being the transmission power of UE_i and $D2D_k$.

2.2 Evaluation Parameters

According to the above formula, the transmit power of the D2Dk transmitter S_k is derived as

$$P_k^D \geq \frac{\beta_k(\sum_{i=1}^{M}|h_{k,i}|^2 d_{k,i}^{-\alpha}p_i^C + \sum_{l \neq k}^{N}|h_{k,i}|^2 d_{k,l}^{-\alpha}p_l^D + \sigma^2)}{|h_{k,k}|^2 d_{k,k}^{-\alpha}} \quad (5)$$

$$p_k^D \leq \frac{|h_{i,i}|^2 d_{i,i}^{-\alpha}p_i^C - \sigma^2 \beta_i}{\beta_i \sum_{k=1}^{N}|h_{i,k}|^2 d_{i,k}^{-\alpha}} \quad (6)$$

From the above formulas, the transmission power of $D2D_k$ is influenced by its own link attenuation and interference from other users, and it is also related to cellular link, because the power control algorithm is to achieve the maximum SINR of cellular user, which limits the D2D transmission power, protecting the cellular communication equality. The interference caused by $D2D_k$ transmitter S_k at base station end is expressed as

$$I_{i,k} = \sum_{k=1}^{N}|h_{i,k}|^2 d_{i,k}^{-\alpha}p_k^D + \sigma^2 \quad (7)$$

In addition to the above parameters, we are interested in the coverage probability of Cellular links and D2D links, the cellular link coverage probability can be defined as

$$\bar{P}_{cov}^C = E[P_cov^C] = P(E[SINR_i \geq \beta_i]) \quad (8)$$

And the coverage probability of D2D link can be expressed as

$$\bar{P}_{cov}^D = E[P_cov^D] = P(E[SINR \geq \beta_k]) \quad (9)$$

Further, the sum rate of D2D links and Cellular links are formulated as

$$R^C = E[\sum_{i=1}^{M} log_2(1 + SINR_i(M, \boldsymbol{P}))] \quad (10)$$

$$R^D = E[\sum_{i=1}^{N} log_2(1 + SINR_k(M, \boldsymbol{P}))] \quad (11)$$

3 Power Control Algorithm

A main difference between ad hoc networks and underlaid D2D cellular networks is that centralized power control is possible when the D2D links are managed by the BS. For other management strategies, centralized power control can provide an upper bound on what can be achieved with more decentralized algorithms.

Suppose that the BS has global channel state information (CSI). Under this assumption, the centralized power control problem is formulated as

$$To \quad determine \qquad \boldsymbol{p} = [p_i^C, p_1^D, p_2^D, P_3^D, ..., p_N^D] \tag{12}$$

$$To \quad maxmize \qquad SINR_i^C = \frac{G_{i,i}^C p_i^C}{\sum_{k=1}^N G_{i,k} p_k^D \sigma^2} \tag{13}$$

$$To \quad minimize \qquad I_{i,k} = \sum_{k=1}^N G_{i,k} p_k^D + \sigma^2 \tag{14}$$

$$Subject \quad to \qquad \frac{G_{k,k}^D p_k^D}{\sum_{l \neq k}^N G_{k,l} p_l^D + \sigma^2} \geq \beta_k \tag{15}$$

$$0 \leq p_i^C \leq p_{avg}^C \tag{16}$$

$$0 \leq p_k^D \leq p_{avg}^D \tag{17}$$

Where $k, l \in \{0, 1, 2, 3, ..., N\}$ (0 denotes the UE_i) and $|h_{i,i}|^2 d_{i,i}^{-\alpha}$. This optimization problem can be compactly written in a vector form as

$$To \quad maximize \qquad \frac{g_i^T \boldsymbol{P}}{g_i^{CT} \boldsymbol{P} + \sigma^2} \tag{18}$$

$$To \quad minimize \qquad g_i^{CT} \boldsymbol{P} \tag{19}$$

$$Subject \quad to \qquad (1 - \boldsymbol{F})\boldsymbol{P} \geq \boldsymbol{b} \tag{20}$$

$$0 \leq \boldsymbol{P} \leq \boldsymbol{P}_{avg} \tag{21}$$

Where i denotes the i-th cellular user. $g_i^T = [G_{i,i}^T, 0, 0, ..., 0]$, $g_i^{CT} = [G_{i,1}^C, G_{i,2}^D, ..., G_{i,N}^D]$, $P_{avg} = [p_{avg}^C, p_{avg}^D, p_{avg}^D, ..., p_{avg}^D]^T$ and the normalized channel gain matrix $\boldsymbol{F}$ and target SINR vector b are defined as

$$\boldsymbol{F} = \begin{pmatrix} 0 & \frac{\beta_0 G_{0,1}}{G_{0,0}} & \frac{\beta_0 G_{0,2}}{G_{0,0}} & \cdots & \frac{\beta_0 G_{0,N}}{G_{0,0}} \\ \frac{\beta_1 G_{1,0}}{G_{1,1}} & 0 & \cdots & \cdots & \frac{\beta_1 G_{1,N}}{G_{1,1}} \\ \frac{\beta_2 G_{2,0}}{G_{0,0}} & \cdots & 0 & \cdots & 0 \\ \cdots & \cdots & \cdots & 0 & \frac{\beta_{N-1} G_{N-1,N}}{G_{N-1,N-1}} \\ \frac{\beta_N G_{N,0}}{G_{N,N}} & \frac{\beta_N G_{N,1}}{G_{N,N}} & \cdots & \frac{\beta_N G_{N,N-1}}{G_{N,N}} & 0 \end{pmatrix}_{N+1N+1} \tag{22}$$

$$\boldsymbol{b} = [\frac{\beta_i^C \sigma^2}{G_{0,0}^C}, \frac{\beta_1^D \sigma^2}{G_{1,1}^D}, \frac{\beta_2^D \sigma^2}{G_{2,2}^D}, ..., \frac{\beta_N^D \sigma^2}{G_{N,N}^C}] \tag{23}$$

The above matrix can be described as: when $k \neq l, F_{k,l} = \frac{\beta_k G_{k,l}}{G_{k,k}}$, and when $k = l, F_{k,l} = 0$. Since the objective function(13) is quasi-convex and the constraint set is convex with respect to power profile vector p, the optimal solution can be obtained by using standard convex programming tools, provided that the feasible set is nonempty. Note that the matrix $F = [f_0, f_1, ..., f_N]$ is comprised of nonnegative elements and is irreducible because all the active D2D links interfere each other. By the Perron-Frobenious theorem, the following well-known lemma proved in [11] gives a necessary and sufficient condition on the feasibility of the optimization problem.

Solution: in [11] the constraint set in the optimization problem (13) is nonempty if and only if the maximum modulus eigenvalue of F is less than one, i.e., $(F) < 1$, where $\rho()$ denotes the spectral radius of a matrix. We next describe our proposed centralized algorithm to solve the optimization problem (13). First we assume that D2D receivers can feedback all the perfect normalized channel gains $G_{i,k}$ and target SINR information $_i$ to the BS. Using this assumption, the BS then computes the transmit power used for both D2D transmitters and the uplink user. Note that the feasible set should be nonempty to obtain the optimal solution, i.e., $\rho(F) < 1$. Since the normalized channel gains $G_{i,k}$, however, are random variables, there exists a nonzero probability that the power control solution is infeasible, i.e., $P(\rho(F) \geq 1) \neq 0$, especially when the number of D2D links N is large. When the solution is infeasible, an admission control method is needed in conjunction with the power control algorithm to provide a feasible solution to the power control problem by selecting a subset of D2D links. And the solving process is as follows:

Step1: Set initial F^l for $l = 0$, assuming K D2D links are all active.
Step2: Test feasibility condition $(F^l) \leq 1$. If this condition is satisfied, go to Step 5. Otherwise, go to Step2.
Step3: Pick the column of F^l such that $k = argmax_{k \in K/\{0\}} ||f_k^l||_2$.
Step4: Generate a reduced matrix F^l by removing the $k - th$ column and row vectors in F^l.
Step5: Update $F^l = F^{l-1}$. Go to Step1.

Through the above optimization process , we can get a first-order power matrix, which denotes all active D2Ds have a optimal power selection. And for M Cellular users, we can get a $M * N$ matrix, indicating that there existing M optimal power selections for each D2D pair. For each D2D pair, it is the focus of our research to find the best value. We hope to ensure cellular performance at the same time, to obtain the maximum throughput.

$$max \sum_{i}^{M} log_2(1 + SINR_i) + \sum_{i=1}^{N} log_2(1 + SINR_k) \qquad (24)$$

$$I_{i,k} \leq I_{max} \qquad (25)$$

In order to guarantee the fairness of users, and make the performance of the system, we use the greedy search algorithm, traverse the transmission power of each pair of D2D used in UE_i, and calculate the interference caused by the D2D, while meets the interference threshold preset value, ultimately determine which one to use for the D2D, so every scheduling needs to calculate $(M * NlogN)$ times.

4   Coverage Probability Analysis for Proposed Power Control

In this section, we derive the cellular link coverage probability, propose an optimal power control strategy for the cellular link under the average transmit power constraint, and derive the D2D link coverage probability. The coverage probability is computed using stochastic geometry. To enable the stochastic geometric analysis, we assume that the distribution $d_{i,i}$ of $h_{i,i}$ and are independent.

4.1   Cellular Link Coverage Probability

Assume that the BS is located at the origin. The SINR of the typical uplink is given by

$$SINR_i = \frac{p_i^C |h_{i,i}|^2 d_{i,i}^{-\alpha}}{\sum_{k \in \Phi} p_k^D |h_{i,k}|^2 d_{i,k}^{-\alpha} + \sigma^2} \tag{26}$$

Further, since the cellular users location is distributed uniformly in the circle with radius R, the distribution function of the distance $d_{0,0}$ of the cellular link is given by

$$F_{d_{i,i}}(r) = \begin{cases} 0, & \text{if } r < 0; \\ \frac{r^2}{R^2}, & \text{if } 0 \le r \le R; \\ 1, & \text{if } r \ge R. \end{cases} \tag{27}$$

The following theorem provides an analytical formula for the uplink coverage probability.

We are interested in the coverage probability of the cellular link and D2D links. The cellular coverage probability is defined as

$$P_{cov}^C = E[P_{cov}^C(\boldsymbol{P})] = E[P(SINR_i(N, \boldsymbol{P}) \ge \beta_i)] \tag{28}$$

where β_i represents the minimum SINR value for reliable uplink connection.

$$
\begin{aligned}
P_{cov}^C &= P(SINR_i \ge \beta_i) \\
&= P(\frac{p_i^C |h_{i,i}|^2 d_{i,i}^{-\alpha}}{\sum_{k \in \Phi} p_k^D |h_{i,k}|^2 ||x_k||^{-\alpha} + \sigma^2} \ge \beta_i) \\
&= P(|h_{i,i}|^2 \ge (p_i^C)^{-1} d_{i,i}^{\alpha} \beta_i (\sum_{k \in \Phi} p_k^D |h_{i,k}|^2 ||x_k||^{-\alpha} + \sigma^2)) \\
&= E[e^{-(p_i^C)^{-1} d_{i,i}^{-\alpha} \beta_i \sigma^2}] E[e^{-(p_i^C)^{-1} d_{i,i}^{\alpha} \beta_i \sum_{k \in \Phi} p_k^D |h_{i,k}|^2 ||x_k||^{\alpha}}]
\end{aligned}
\tag{29}
$$

Where in the second last equality we use the fact that $|h_{i,i}|^2 \sim Exp(1)$ and thus $P(|h_{i,i}|^2 \geq x) = e^{-x}$. Conditioned on the Transmit power of the typical uplink transmitter the distance $d_{i,i} = d$ from the cellular transmitter to BS. To this end, we need the Laplace transform $Ł_{\phi(S)} = E[e^{-s(\sum_{k \in \phi} p_k^D |h_{i,i}|^2 ||x_k||^{-\alpha})}]$ given as

$$Ł_{\phi(s)} = e^{-\frac{(2/\alpha)\pi^2}{sin(2\pi/\alpha)}(p_k^D)^{2/\alpha} \lambda s^{2/\alpha}} \tag{30}$$

Using the above transform, we can get

$$P_{cov/d_{i,i}=d}^C = e^{-\sigma^2 \beta_i (p_i^C)^{-1} d^\alpha} e^{-\frac{(2/\alpha)\pi^2}{sin(2\pi/\alpha)} \lambda \beta_i^{1/\alpha} (p_k^D)^{2/\alpha} d^2 (p_i^C)^{-2/\alpha}} \tag{31}$$

De-conditioning with respect to $d_{i,i}$ yields the uplink coverage probability P_{cov}^C. Let $\Phi(x) = e^{-a_1 x - a_2 x^{\frac{2}{\alpha}}}$. We compute the first and second derivation of $\Phi(x) = e^{-a_1 x - a_2 x^{\frac{2}{\alpha}}}$ as follows:

$$\phi'(x) = e^{-a_1 x - a_2 x^{\frac{2}{\alpha}}} (a_1 + a_2 \frac{2}{\alpha} x^{\frac{2}{\alpha}-1}) \tag{32}$$

$$\phi''(x) = e^{-a_1 + a_2 \frac{2}{\alpha} x^{\frac{2}{\alpha}}} (a_1 + a_2 \frac{2}{\alpha} x^{\frac{2}{\alpha}-1})^2 + e^{-a_1 x - a_2 x^{\frac{2}{\alpha}}} a_2 \frac{2}{\alpha} (1 - \frac{2}{\alpha}) x^{\frac{2}{\alpha}-2} \tag{33}$$

When $\alpha \geq 2$, $\phi''(x) \geq 0$, for $x \geq 0$ and thus $\phi(x)$ is convex for $x \geq 0$. Applying Jensens inequality, we obtain

$$P_{cov}^C = E_X[e^{-a_1 X - a_2 X^{frac2\alpha}}] \geq e^{a_1 E[X] - a_2 E[X]^{\frac{2}{\alpha}}} \tag{34}$$

Where $E[X] = E[d_{i,i}^\alpha]$, and $E[d_{i,i}^\alpha]$ can be computed explicitly.

$$E[d_{i,i}^\alpha] = \int r^\alpha dF_{d_{i,i}}(r) = \int_0^R r^\alpha \frac{2r}{R^2} dr = \frac{2}{2+\alpha} R^\alpha \tag{35}$$

$$P_{cov}^C \geq e^{-\frac{2}{2+\alpha} R^\alpha (p_i^C)^{-1} \beta_i \sigma^2} e^{-(\frac{2}{2+\alpha})^{\frac{2}{\alpha}} R^2 - \frac{(2/\alpha\pi^2)}{sin(2\pi/\alpha)} \lambda \beta_i^{\frac{2}{\alpha}} p_k^{2/\alpha} (p_i^C)^{-2/\alpha}} \tag{36}$$

4.2   D2D Link Coverage Probability

The D2D coverage probability is defined as

$$P_{cov}^D = E[P_{cov}^D(\mathbf{P})] = E[P(SINR_k(N, \mathbf{P}) \geq \beta_k)] \tag{37}$$

where β_k represents the minimum SINR value for reliable D2D link connections. We derive an expression for the coverage probability for the typical D2D link. Consider an arbitrary communication D2D pair k and assume that the D2D receiver is located at the origin. Then,

$$SINR_k = \frac{p_k^D |h_{k,k}|^2 d_{k,k}^{-\alpha}}{\sum_{x \in \Phi/k} p_i^C |h_{k,i}|^2 ||x_i||^{-\alpha} + p_i^C |h_{k,i}|^2 d_{k,i}^{-\alpha} + \sigma^2}, \tag{38}$$

where $\|x_i\| = d_{k,i}$. Using the same approach, we need to compute two Laplace transforms $E[e^{-s|h_{k,i}|^2 d_{k,i}^{-\alpha}}]$ and $E[e^{-\sum_{x \in \phi/k} |h_{k,i}|^2 d_{k,i}^{-\alpha}}]$ to derive the distribution of $SINR_k$. First let us focus on $E[e^{-s|h_{k,i}|^2 d_{k,i}^{-\alpha}}]$. As we assume the uplink user and the D2D receiver are randomly positioned in the disk with radius R, the pdf $f_{d,i}(r)$ is given by [12].

$$f_{d_{k,i}}(r) = \frac{2r}{R^2}(\frac{2}{\pi}\cos^{-1}(\frac{r}{2R}) - \frac{r}{\pi R}\sqrt{1 - \frac{r^2}{4R^2}}, \tag{39}$$

where $0 \leq r \leq 2R$ Besides, $|h_{k,i}|^2$ Exp(1). Noting further that $|h_{k,i}|^2$, and $d_{k,i}$ are independent, we have

$$E[e^{-s|d_{k,i}|^2 d_{k,i}^{-\alpha}}] = \int_0^\infty \int_0^{2R} e^{-shr^{-\alpha}-h} f_{dk,i}(r) dr dh \tag{40}$$

Since (32) is complicated and gives little insight, we use the Gamma approximation for the distribution of $|h_{k,i}|^2 d_{k,i}^{-\alpha}$ is inspired by[13]. Using the Gamma approximation, the Laplace transform of $Y = |h_{k,i}|^2 d_{k,i}^{-\alpha}$ is approximated as

$$Ł_{Y(S)} = (1 + \theta S)^{-k}, \tag{41}$$

where $k = \frac{E^2[d_{k,i}^{-\alpha}]}{2E[d_{k,i}^{-\alpha}] - E^2[d_{k,i}^{-\alpha}]}, \theta = \frac{2E[d_{k,i}^{-\alpha}]}{E[d_{k,i}^{-\alpha}]} - E[d_{k,i}^{-\alpha}]$. Note that the D2D coverage probability has a penalty term compared with that of the cellular user due to the $\hat{L}_Y(S)$ interference coming from the cellular users. Intuitively, the coverage performance of the D2D links decreases as increasing the average transmit power used by the cellular user.

5   Simulation and Analyze

In this section, we provide numerical results of the proposed power control algorithm. From our simulation results, we first show the performance gain of the proposed methods compared to the no power control case in terms of the cellular user and the D2D user coverage probability. Further, to show the sum rate gain. Simulation scenario is as follows: the BS is located at the center position $(0,0)$ in R^2 plane and the cellular user is uniformly dropped within the range of $R = 500m$. The D2D transmitters are dropped according to PPP with the density parameter $\lambda \in 0.00002, 0.00006$ so that the average number of D2D links are $E[N] = \pi R^2 \lambda \in 15, 47$. Further, for a given D2D transmitters location, the corresponding D2D receiver is isotropically dropped at a fixed distance $d_{k,k} = 50m$ away from the D2D transmitter. Since the D2D communication are supposed to be of short range compared to the cellular link, we assume that the average transmit power of the cellular user and D2D links are equal to $P_{avg,c} = 100mW$ and $P_{avg,d} = 0.1mW$. Since the number of D2D links N is a random variable and we evaluate the coverage probability and sum rate performance of the proposed algorithms by averaging 103 independent realizations. Simulation parameters are showed in Table.

Table 1. Simulation parameters

Parameters	value
Cell radius(R)	500m
The D2D link range($d_{k,k}$)	50(m)
The D2D link density(λ)	0.00002 and 0.00006
Average number Cellular links(M)	20-40
Average number D2D links(N)	15-47
Target SINR threshold(β)	-3,3,9,12,15(dB)
The average transmit power of the cellular user	p^C_{avg}=100mW
The average transmit power of the D2D transmitters	p^C_{avg}=0.1mW
Noise variance()for 1MHZbandwidth	-143.97(dbm)
Path-loss exponent(α)	4
The number of realizations	10^3 times

Table 2. The performance summary of proposed power control algorithm

Target SINR	-3dB	6dB	9dB	12dB	15dB
Cellular link coverage numbers	40	40	40	39	38
$|S|_{\lambda=0.00006} = E[NP^D_{cov}(\boldsymbol{P})]$	32	24	21	18	14
$|S|_{\lambda=0.00002} = E[NP^D_{cov}(\boldsymbol{P})]$	14	12	11	10	9

As shown in Figure 2. that when $\lambda = 0.00002$, the sparse D2D link deployment scenario where the average number of D2D links in the cell equals $E[N] = \pi R^2 \lambda = 15.7$. In this scenario, we compare the coverage probability of the cellular link and the D2D links under different power control algorithms. We observe that the proposed power control methods improve the cellular user coverage probability. The proposed power control methods also provide increased D2D link coverage probability compared to the no power control case, especially in the low target SINR regime. This implies that the power control methods are efficient to mitigate both intra-D2D and cross-tier interference. In particular, one remarkable observation is that the centralized power control achieves nearly perfect cellular user coverage probability performance, while successfully supporting a large number of active D2D links when target SNIR $\beta = 3dB$. Meanwhile, the proposed power control method yields performance gains for both cellular and D2D links compared to that of no power control case when the target SINR is larger than 9 dB.

Suppose a dense D2D link deployment scenario where the average number of D2D links in the cell equals $E[N] = \pi R^2 \lambda = 47.1$. For the dense D2D link deployment, as shown in Figure 3, we observe similar trends as in the sparse D2D link deployment case. One interesting point is that the cellular users coverage probability is not degraded as the number of D2D links increases when the centralized power allocation method is applied because the proposed admission control ensures that the uplink user is protected. This implies that the centralized power control method is able to support reliable uplink performance

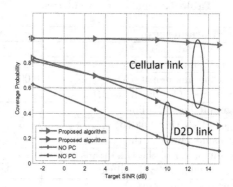

Fig. 2. Coverage probability performance of both the cellular and D2D links according to different power control methods when the D2D links are sparse,i.e., $\lambda = 0.00002$

regardless of the density of D2D links. Meanwhile, the D2D user coverage probability performance becomes deteriorated because of the increased intra-D2D link interference. It is notable that the proposed power control method improves the D2D link coverage probability performance compared to that of no power control case in a more broad range of the target SINR. Although the D2D user coverage probability performance decreases in the dense scenario, the total number of successful D2D transmissions is large than that of the sparse D2D link deployment scenario as shown Table 2.

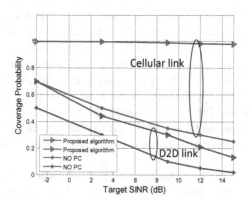

Fig. 3. Coverage probability performance of both the cellular and D2D links according to different power control methods when the D2D links are sparse,($\lambda = 0.00006$)

As shown in Figure 4, the D2D link sum rate performance behaves differently than the D2D link coverage performance. In the case of no power control, the sum rate of D2D does not change in the target SINR as the D2D transmission power is independent of the target SINR. The interesting point is that the centralized power control method provides the poor D2D sum rate. This is because it was designed to maximize the coverage probability, implying that many D2D links are inactive to guarantee the uplink user coverage. In spit of the poor sum rate, the coverage probability of D2D and cellular links is improved while satisfying with the communication of D2D pairs and cellular users in the network.

As shown in Figure 5, the cellular link sum rate performance differently than that of the D2D link. From the figure, we can find that the cellular link sum rate with the proposed algorithm is obviously larger than no power control.

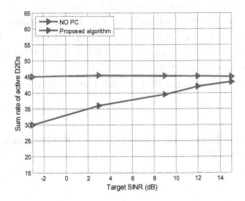

Fig. 4. Sum rate performance of D2D links when the D2D links are dense,($\lambda = 0.00005$)

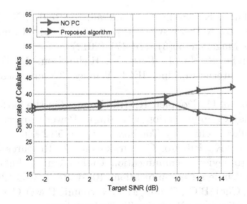

Fig. 5. Sum rate performance of cellular links when the D2D links are dense,($\lambda = 0.00005$)

And when target SINR is smaller than 9dB, the growth is slow, but more than 9dB, compared with no power control algorithm, the proposed algorithm keeps the sum rate of the cellular links high growth. Because when target SINR is larger than 9dB, the coverage probability decreases, however, the total number of D2D increases,to bring more interference to the cellular users, and resulting in decreased sum rate. The proposed algorithm uses the power control with coordination of interference caused by D2D, to ensure the interference limited in a reasonable range.

6   Conclusions

In this paper, we proposed a new network model for a D2D underlaid cellular system based on stochastic geometry. In this system, we proposed a centralized power control algorithm. The results we observed is that the proposed centralized power control approach leads to improve the cellular network throughput performance due to the additional underlaid D2D links while supporting reliable communication for the uplink cellular user. And to ensure the coverage probability of two different links of D2D underlaied cellular network. In addition, this control method is relatively simple, which can save more control command consumption. Future work could investigate the effect of other adjacent cell interference.

Acknowledgments. This work was supported by the National Science Foundation of China (61062002).

References

1. 3GPP, 3rd generation partnership project; technical specification group SA; feasibility study for proximity services (ProSe) (release 12), 3GPP TR 22.803 V1.0.0 (2012)
2. Fodor, G., Dahlman, E., Mildh, G., Parkvall, S., Reider, N., Mikl, G., Turanyi, Z.: Design Aspects of Network Assisted Device-To-Device Communications. IEEE Communications Magazine 50(3), 170–177 (2012)
3. Corson, M., Laroia, R., Li, J., Park, V., Richardson, J., Tsirtsis, G.: Toward Proximity-aware Internetworking. IEEE Wireless Communications 17(6), 26–33 (2010)
4. Yu, C.H., Tirkkonen, O., Doppler, K., Ribeiro, C.: On the Performance of Device-to-device Underlay Communication with Simple Power Control. In: Proceedings of the IEEE Vehicular Technology Conference, pp. 1–5 (2009)
5. Yu, C.H., Doppler, K., Ribeiro, C., Tirkkonen, O.: Resource Sharing Optimization for Device-to-device Communication Underlaying Cellular Networks. IEEE Transactions on Wireless Communications 10(8), 2752–2763 (2011)
6. Gu, J., Bae, S.J., Choi, B.G., Chung, M.Y.: Dynamic Power Control Mechanism for Interference Coordination Of Device-To-Device Communication In Cellular Networks. In: Proceedings of the 3rd International Conference on Ubiquitous and Future Networks, pp. 71–75 (2011)

7. Xiao, X., Tao, X., Lu, J.: A Qos-Aware Power Optimization Scheme in Ofdma Systems With Integrated Device-To-Device (D2D) Communications. In: Proceedings of IEEE Vehicular Technology Conference, pp. 1–5 (2011)

8. Lei, L., Zhong, Z., Lin, C., Shen, X.: Operator Controlled Device to-Device Communications in Lte-Advanced Networks. IEEE Wireless Communications 19(3), 96–104 (2012)

9. Lee, J., Andrews, J.G., Hong, D.: Spectrum-Sharing Transmission Capacity. IEEE Transactions on Wireless Communications 10(9), 3053–3063 (2011)

10. Lin, X., Andrews, J.G.: Optimal Spectrum Partition and Mode Selection in Device-To-Device Overlaid Cellular Networks. Submitted to IEEE Globecom (2013)

11. Foschini, G., Miljanic, Z.: A Simple Distributed Autonomous Power Control Algorithm and Its Convergence. IEEE Transactions on Vehicular Technology 42(4), 641–646 (1993)

12. Moltchanov, D.: Distance Distributions In Random Networks. Ad Hoc Networks 10(6), 1146–1166 (2012)

13. Heath, R.W., Kountouris, M.: Modeling Heterogeneous Network Interference Using Poisson Point Processes. Submitted to IEEE Transactions on Signal Processing (July 2012), http://arxiv.org/abs/1207.2041

The Molecular Beacons Self-assembly Model of the Dislocation Permutation Problem

Jing Yang[1], Zhixiang Yin[1], Mingqiang Chen[2], and Jianzhong Cui[3]

[1] School Science, Anhui University of Science and Technology,
Huainan, Anhui Province, China
[2] School of Chemical Engineering, Anhui University of Science and Technology,
Huainan, Anhui Province, China
[3] Huainan Union University Huainan
Anhui Province, China
{jyangh82,zxyin66}@163.com, mqchen@aust.edu.cn

Abstract. Special "hairpin" structure of molecular beacon makes it with strong specificity, high sensitivity, fast reaction and fluorescence labeling and so on. In this paper, we choose to use a special structure design of self-assembled tile.Compared with DX tiles, TX tile, its special "hairpin" structure makes the ring and stem cadres can express different information, in order to design the assembly module can reduce the complexity, reduce the use of the module, lower assembled depth.The paper uses molecular beacons in self-assembled tile to try and resolve a derangement-wide issues to verify the feasibility of its design.

Keywords: Molecular beacons, The dislocation permutation problem, Self-assembly models.

1 Introduction

Molecular self-assembly is a new kind of calculation model. It is based on DNA molecule with biological enzyme,and so on, as the basic material, using self-assembly technology, through controlled biochemical reaction for information processing. Self-assembled calculation process is essentially a process of constant choice and eliminate, and biological molecules synthesis process from simple to complex, combination of DNA computing, Tiling theory in the thoughts [1] and DNA nanotechnology [2]. In 1994, Adleman solved 7 vertex directed Hamilton path problem with DNA computing methods which abstracts computing models [3]. Adleman encoded in the experiment well all vertices and edges in the test tube to a massive self-assembled, then get all possible paths. Since then research on self-assembly model begins,calculation model of molecular self-assembly is using a cluster of branch structure of DNA crossover molecules as DNA tile [4]. Molecular structure of the tiles are mainly DX cross [5] ,TX cross [6], cross structure[7] and so on [8–11]. DX cross has 4 binding domains. TX cross molecule structure has 6 binding domains.

L. Pan et al. (Eds.): BIC-TA 2014, CCIS 472, pp. 520–524, 2014.

2   Molecular Beacon Tile

Molecular beacon [12] generally includes three parts: (1) ring district, can combine with specific target molecules; (2) beacon stem area, the thermodynamic equilibrium relationship of stem area and hybrid ring area target molecules between the double chain structure, make the hybridization specificity of molecular beacon was obviously higher than that of conventional linear probe; (3) the fluorescent groups and quenching groups, fluorescent groups usually connected in the 5' end of the molecular beacon,quenching groups connected to the 3' end.

Here we still use similar DX tiles representation method, molecular beacon tile is abstracted into a square. S, E side represents the input; W, S represents output.

3   The Dislocation Permutation Problem

The dislocation permutation is also "the wrong envelope problem". It is by the mathematician John Bernoulli's son, Daniel Bernoulli mentioned: "one person wrote n different letter and corresponding n different envelope, he put it n letters are wrong envelope, asking all the wrong envelope method with how many?". Famous mathematician Euler called it a good topic for combinatorial number theory, and it is an important NP-complete problem in combinatorial mathematics, also known as the matching problem or fixed point permutation. It is described as:the set 1, 2, 3, 4of the dislocation permutation $i_1, i_2, \cdots, i_n$ is the permutation that it meets the conditions of $i_j \neq j (1 \leq j \leq n)$. Namely any element of the set 1, 2, 3, 4 are not on position in their natural order. The algorithm of dislocation permutation, and they are generally classified according to the restrictive conditions, or using the recursive relations to solve, or using chessman polynomial to solve, or using the true and false value determinant calculation. There are also using surface of DNA computing model and DNA chip calculation model to solve. Here we try to take advantage of molecular beacon self-assembled model to solve the dislocation permutation problem.

4   Simulation Experiment

We use the set 1, 2, 3, 4 as an example of the dislocation permutation problem that the set 1, 2, 3, 4 of dislocation permutation must satisfy the following four conditions: (1) the number 1 is not the first position; (2) the number 2 is not in the second position; (3) the number 3 is not in the third position; (4) the number 4 is not in the fourth position.Let i_j be show on the jth position is i. And the set1, 2, 3, 4 of the dislocation permutation is to satisfy the permutation of $i \neq j$. ALL permutation of1, 2, 3, 4 have , as 1234, 1243, 1432, 1423, 1342, 1324, 2134, 2143, 2314, 2341, 2413, 2431, 3214, 3241, 3142, 3124, 1421, 3412, 4123, 4132, 4213, 4231, 4312, 4321. The algorithm is to list all permutation, and gradually remove the solution of $i = j$, to get its solution. Next, we introduce the self-assembly of dislocation permutation system.

Let $S_S = \langle T_S, g_S, \tau_S \rangle$ be a tile system of the dislocation permutation. For self-assembly system of the dislocation permutation problem. The tile with $\sigma_E, \sigma_W, \sigma_S,$ σ_N indicate its on the east, west, south, north of binding domains information. Usually, binding strength function takes constant value 1, as $g_S = (\sigma, \sigma')$, and τ_S also take a constant value, just $\tau_S = 2$, in $\sigma \in t$, $\sigma' \in t'$. The "T" realize information exchange, through the growth to a certain pattern of tile self-assembly to form a new pattern that a process, so as to complete the calculation of solving the problem. Here we specified σ_E and σ_S as input of information, σ_W and σ_N as the output of the information. Before computing, we introduce the seed tile. Here we are still using the L-configuration of border tile form as a framework of seed. For basic operators, there are subsystems of comparison, transmission, input and output.

4.1   The Subsystem of Comparison

To determine whether A combination of the dislocation permutation and combination, the first is to compare the relationship between i_j and j. There will be an integer into a binary number. Compare subsystem can detect input two binary number are equal or whether. If the same output " = ", or output " ≠ ".

4.2   The Subsystem of Transmission

The 4 tiles are input transmission tile, and the 4 tiles are in-output transmission tile. The 'N' direction of in-output transmission tile is passing up the input data, and the 'E' direction is passing up the output result. After the two binary number is complete, the in-output transmission tile will pass it to the left.

4.3   The Subsystem of Output

If $i = j$, 'times' will be output, or "$\sqrt{}$" will be output. We link fluorescence groups and quenching groups in the four sticky end of output tile. When the comparison of the array was finished, if the transitive result is " ≠ ", we mark with red fluorescencehe . When the comparison of the array was finished, if the transitive result is " = ", we mark with blue fluorescencehe. We can be read using fluorescence spectrometer to solution of the problem.

Here we give the example to test 2134, 2341 whether for dislocation permutation.

The complexity of this model is generally consider from two aspects :the time complexity of the algorithm, and the size of the algorithm. Firstly, we analyze the number of tile types of the self-assembly system as Num (.).

For the dislocation permutation problem system $S_S = \langle T_S, g_S, \tau_S \rangle$, it needs of tile according to the executive function different, mainly divided into six types: the set of comparison tile T_1, the set of transmission tile T_2, the set of output tile T_3, the set of border tile T_4. For tile T_1, $Num(T_1) = 4 = \Theta(1)$. For tile T_2, $Num(T_2) = 8 = \Theta(1)$. For tile T_3, $Num(T_3) = 4 = \Theta(1)$, and $Num(T_4) = \Theta(1)$.

Thus the number of tiles types for the system is $Num(T) = \sum Num(T_i) = \Theta(1)$, has nothing to do with the problem size, for constant.

Next, we discuss the issue the required by the self-assembly of time. Yuriy Brun provided the lemma in his paper [13]. The assembly time of the dislocation permutation problem is $Tim(S_1) = (m + 1) \times (n \times m + 1) = \Theta(n)$, n is the size of the problem and m is a binary number every integer, and $Tim(S_1)$ is the time needed for the self-assembly to determine each permutation. All the permutation for determining is parallel, so the time needed for model is still linear function.

5   Conclusion

In this paper, we presented the model of the dislocation permutation problem based on molecular beacon tile to solve. Each permutation of the problem was mapped for DNA tile in the model. Through proper encoding the sticky end on the tile, molecules will be carried out in accordance with the principle of complementary hybridization, thus parallelism and determine whether each group permutation for dislocation permutation. Compared with the previous calculation model, the model may solve all dislocation permutation problems of the set1, 2,..., n in polynomial time, by using molecular beacon tile self-assembly technology. For each group of judgement by self-assembly, so it can realize the automation of model. Molecular beacon self-assembled model can decrease the rate of DNA computing produce the wrong solution for this kind of problem.This paper also tries to embody the potential value of the molecular beacon self-assembly technique in the study of computation by solving the simple questions.

Acknowledgment. This work was supported by National Natural Science Foundation of China (61170172).

References

1. Grunbaum, B., Shephard, G.C.: Tilings and Patterns. Freeman, New York (1986)
2. Seeman, N.C.: Biochemistry and Structural DNA Nanotechnology: An Evolving Symbiotic Relationship. Biochemistry 42(24), 7259–7269 (2003)
3. Adlenlan, L.: Molecular Computation of Solutions to Combinatorial Problems. Science 266(11), 1021–1024 (1994)
4. Winfree, E., Liu, F., Wenzler, L.A.: Design and Self-Assembly of Two-Dimensional DNA Crystals. Nature 394, 539–544 (1998)
5. Seeman, N.C.: DNA Nicks and Nodes and Nanotechnology. Nano Lett. 1, 22–26 (2001)
6. LaBean, T., Yan, H., Kopatsch, J.: The Construction, Analysis, Ligation and Self-Assembly of DNA Triple Crossover Complexes. Journal of the American Chemical Society 122(9), 1848–1860
7. Yan, H., Park, S.H., Finkelstein, G.: DNA-Templated Self-Assembly of Protein Arrays and Highly Conductive Nanowires. Science 301, 1882–1884 (2003)
8. Rothemund, P.W.K.: Folding DNA to Create Nanoscale Shapes and Patterns. Nature 440, 297–302 (2006)

9. Du, S.M., Stollar, B.D., Seeman, N.C.: A Synthetic DNA Molecule in Three Knotted Topologies. Journal of the American Chemical Society 117, 1194–1200 (1995)
10. Mao, C., Sun, W., Seeman, N.C.: Construction of Borromean Rings from DNA. Nature 386, 137–138 (1997)
11. Chen, J., Seeman, N.C.: The Synthesis from DNA of a Molecule with the Connectivity of a Cube. Nature 350, 631–633 (1991)
12. Tyagi, S., Kramer, F.R.: Molecular Beacon: Probes that Fluoresce Upon Hybridization. Nat. Biotechnol. 14, 303–308 (1996)
13. Brun, Y.: Arithmetic Computation in the Tile Assembly Model: Addition and Multiplication. Theoretical Computer Science 378, 17–31 (2007)

Detecting Bots in Follower Markets

Wu Yang*, Guozhong Dong, Wei Wang, Guowei Shen,
Liangyi Gong, Miao Yu, Jiguang Lv, and Yaxue Hu

Information Security Research Center, Harbin Engineering University,
Harbin, China 150001
{yangwu,dongguozhong,w_wei,shenguowei,gongliangyi,
yumiao,lvjiguang,huyaxue}@hrbeu.edu.cn

Abstract. Along with the widely using of microblog, third party services such as follower markets sell bots to customers to build fake influence and reputation. However, the bots and the customers that have large numbers of followers usually post spam messages such as promoted messages, messages containing malicious links. In this paper, we propose an effective approach for bots detection based on interaction graph model and BP neural network. We build an interaction graph model based on user interaction and design robust interaction-based features. We conduct a comprehensive set of experiments to evaluate the proposed features using different machine learning classifiers. The results of our evaluation experiments show that BP neural network classifier using our proposed features can be effectively used to detect bots compared to other existing state-of-the-art approaches.

Keywords: Follower market, Bots detection, Interaction-based feature, Neural network.

1 Introduction

Microblog services, such as Twitter and Sina Microblog are more and more popular over the last few years. As microblog users grow, the influence and reputation of accounts play an important role in information propagation and are associated with the number of a user's followers [1]. As a result, some follower markets sell followers to the "customers" who want to quickly increase the number of followers, such as celebrities and organizations. There are two ways to produce followers in follower markets. One way is to create fake accounts that imitate real users. On the other hand, follower markets promise some legitimate accounts free followers and compromise their accounts to add them as new followers each other [2]. The compromised and fake accounts that are manipulated by follower markets are named as bots in this paper. There are several studies that have addressed the detection of spammers and spam messages in social media, rather than focusing on the detection of bots in follower markets. Two main approaches have been studied in spam detection: classification and

---

* Corresponding author.

L. Pan et al. (Eds.): BIC-TA 2014, CCIS 472, pp. 525–530, 2014.
© Springer-Verlag Berlin Heidelberg 2014

anomaly detection approaches. In the classification approaches, one of the most important problems is the identification of spammers' features. In the first work focusing on spam detection, Wang et al.[3,4] studied the spam behaviours in Twitter and proposed novel content-based and graph-based features to facilitate spam detection. Based on an in-depth analysis of the evasion tactics utilized by Twitter spammers, Yang et al.[5] proposed more robust features to detect Twitter spammers whose work is the first work to study and evaluate the effect of evasion tactics utilized by Twitter spammers. Han et al.[6] proposed an efficient detection method for detecting content polluters operating on Twitter. Miller et al.[7] viewed spammer detection as an anomaly detection problem and proposed two stream-based clustering algorithm to facilitate spam identification. Chu et al.[8] measured and characterized the behaviours of humans, bots, and cyborgs on Twitter and designed an automated classification system. Stringhini et al.[2,9] presented a detailed study of Twitter follower markets and analyzed the characteristics of followers and customers. Based on the analysis of collected dataset, a detection system that uses follower dynamics was developed to detect the customers of follower markets. However, the problem of detecting bots in follower markets is not presented in previous work. In this paper, we focus on detecting bots including fake accounts and compromised accounts that aim at following and participating in marketing campaigns in follow markets. To detect bots in follower markets, we collected and analyzed bots as well as their followers. Then we described and analyzed the features that used to detect spammers in existing state-of-the-art approaches on our collected dataset. Based on the in-depth analysis of collected dataset, we designed robust interaction-based features that have lower computational complexity than existing graph-based features. An interaction graph model based on the interaction between users is proposed and some novel interaction-based features extracted from interaction graph are designed. Finally, we conducted our evaluation by using different machine learning classifiers. The results of our evaluation experiments show that BP neural network classifier with our proposed features can be effectively used to detect bots compared to other machine learning classifiers.

The remainder of the paper is organized as follows. In section 2 we presents our novel interaction-based features and describes the bots detection approach. Section 3 shows the experimental results on classification of normal accounts and bots. Finally, Section 4 concludes this paper.

2   Detecting Bots with Interaction-Based Features

For ease of the following presentation, we propose the concept of interaction graph and define the basic notations used in the interaction graph. The basic notations used in the interaction-based features are defined as follows.

Definition 1 (Interaction action) Given two users i and j, if i takes initiative in communicating with j (such as comment, repost). This kind of one-way user interaction is defined as active interaction, where i as an active user and j as a passive user. If user j responds to i (such as reply), the user interaction is called passive interaction and the one-way user interaction changes to two-way interaction.

Definition 2 (Interaction graph) The interaction graph is an undirected weighted graph, denoted as $G = (U, E, W)$, where U is the set of users and E is the set of undirected edges. The weight of each edge $w_{ij} \in W$ is defined as the interaction frequency of two users i and j.

Definition 3 (Interaction quality) A user i has interaction index r if r of his/her N neighbor nodes in graph G has at least r two-way interactions each, and the other $(N - r)$ neighbor nodes have no more than r two-way interactions each.

Based on these definitions, we next introduce the interaction graph model. We focus on the two types of interaction-based features: the feature of one-way interaction and the feature of two-way interaction.

2.1 The Features of One-Way Interaction

We designed two one-way interaction-based features: the average of one-way interaction in original messages and the average of one-way interaction in non-original messages.

The average of one-way interaction in original messages, denoted as $A_o(i)$, can be computed as:

$$A_o(i) = \frac{1}{|M_o(i)|} \sum_{m \in M_o(i)} rc(m) \tag{1}$$

where $M_o(i)$ denotes the original message set of user i and $rc(m)$ denotes the sum of comments and reposts of m.

The average of one-way interaction in non-original messages, denoted as $A_{no}(i)$, can be computed as:

$$A_{no}(i) = \frac{1}{|M_{no}(i)|} \sum_{m \in M_{no}(i)} rc(m) \tag{2}$$

where $M_{no}(i)$ denotes the non-original message set of user i and $rc(m)$ denotes the sum of comments and reposts of m.

2.2 The Features of Two-Way Interaction

Given the interaction graph of user i denoted as G_i, the interaction degree of user i is computed as:

$$N(i) = \sum_{j \in U_i} w_{ij} \tag{3}$$

where U_i is the set of neighbor nodes that have two-way interaction with user i in the interaction graph.

The interaction quality of user i is computed as:

$$Q(i) = r_i \tag{4}$$

where r_i is the interaction index of user i.

2.3   The Features of Two-Way Interaction

Our approach for bots detection based on interaction graph model is presented in this section. The main innovation is the combination of proposed features and machine learning methods for accurate and reliable bots detection. It contains three functional modules, each of which has a specific task: crawling and storing data, feature extraction and classifier. First, we crawled the necessary information used in our approach and stored the dataset. Second, Parsing program is utilized to extract interaction-based features. Finally, the classier analyzes the extracted features and makes a decision: bots or normal accounts. As for the classifier, we compared the performance of several automatic classification methods, including decision trees, random forest, Bayesian network and BP neural network. Through the comparative analysis, BP neural network was selected for its better performance.

3   Experiments

We conduct extensive experiments to evaluate the performance of our approach for bots detection and perform a validation by comparing it with state-of-the-art method.

3.1   Performance Experiment with Different Classifiers

In this experiment, we compare the performance of our features with different classifiers: BP neural network, random forest, Bayesian network and decision trees. The neural network has 1 hidden layer with 3 neurons and 2 output neurons corresponding to bots and normal accounts.

Table 1. Comparision with different classifiers

Classifier	Accuracy	F-1 Measure
BP neural network	0.986	0.933
Random forest	0.931	0.904
Bayesian network	0.912	0.889
Decision trees	0.906	0.875

The result of performance experiment with different classifiers is shown in table 1. As is shown in table 1, our bots detection approach using our proposed feature has higher accuracy and F-1 value and BP neural network outperforms than other classifiers. The result validates that our proposed features is more effective to detect bots and BP neural network is more accurate to solve the problem of bots detection.

3.2   Comparison with Other Approaches

As there is no works that focus on studying the problem of bots detection, in this experiment, we compare the performance of our work with two existing works[5,8] that study the problem of spammer detection which are very similar to our work. To better describe the results, we label the work[5] as DS(detect spammers), the work[8] as DA(detect automation) and our work as DB(detect bots).

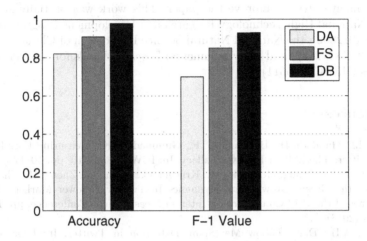

Fig. 1. The comparison of accuracy

In order to achieve effective comparison results, we extracted the necessary features and used the best classification in their papers. In order to reduce time and space costs, we randomly select 200 followers when the number of account's followers larger than 200 during the process of extracting interaction-based features in our work. The experimental result is shown in Fig. 1. As seen in Fig. 1, our work has higher accuracy and F-1 value than DS and DA. According to the analysis based on the categorized result, we found that some high level bots were classified as normal accounts in DS and DA. Besides, since interaction-based features can be extracted through local network structure, our work has lower computational complexity than existing work based on network structure graph.

4   Conclusion

In this paper, we have addressed the problem of bots detection in microblog. We present an effective approach for bots detection based on interaction graph model and BP neural network. Based on empirical analysis of collected dataset, we build a interaction graph model based on user interaction and propose robust interaction-based features. Our proposed features can distinguish more intelligent bots from normal accounts. We conduct a comprehensive set of experiments to evaluate the proposed features using different machine learning classifiers. The results of our evaluation experiments show that BP neural network classifier using our proposed features can be effectively used to detect bots compared with other existing state-of-the-art approaches.

Acknowledgement. The authors would like to thank the reviewers for suggesting many ways to improve the paper. This work was partially supported by the National High Technology Research and Development Program of China (2012AA012802), the National Natural Science Foundation of China (61170242, 61101140, 61272537) and the Fundamental Research Funds for the Central Universities (HEUCF100611).

References

1. Cha, M., Haddadi, H., Benevenuto, F., Gummadi, P.K.: Measuring User Influence in Twitter: The Million Follower Fallacy. In: ICWSM, vol. 10, pp. 10–17 (2010)
2. Stringhini, G., Wang, G., Egele, M., Kruegel, C., Vigna, G., Zheng, H., Zhao, B.Y.: Follow the Green: Growth and Dynamics In Twitter Follower Markets. In: Proceedings of the 2013 Conference on Internet Measurement Conference, pp. 163–176. ACM (2013)
3. Wang, A.H.: Don't Follow Me: Spam Detection in Twitter. In: Proceedings of the 2010 International Conference on Security and Cryptography (SECRYPT), pp. 1–10. IEEE (2010)
4. Lea, D.: Detecting Spam Bots in Online Social Networking Sites: A Machine Learning Approach. In: Foresti, S., Jajodia, S. (eds.) Data and Applications Security and Privacy XXIV. LNCS, vol. 6166, pp. 335–342. Springer, Heidelberg (2010)
5. Yang, C., Harkreader, R., Gu, G.: Empirical Evaluation and New Design for Fighting Evolving Twitter Spammers. IEEE Transactions on Information Forensics and Security 8(8), 1280–1293 (2013)
6. Han, J.S., Park, B.J.: Efficient Detection of Content Polluters in Social Networks. In: IT Convergence and Security 2012, pp. 991–996 (2013)
7. Miller, Z., Dickinson, B., Deitrick, W., Hu, W., Wang, A.H.: Twitter Spammer Detection Using Data Stream Clustering. Inform. Sciences (2013)
8. Chu, Z., Gianvecchio, S., Wang, H., Jajodia, S.: Detecting Automation of Twitter Accounts: Are You a Human, Bot, or Cyborg? IEEE Transactions on Dependable and Secure Computing 9(6), 811–824 (2012)
9. Stringhini, G., Egele, M., Kruegel, C., Vigna, G.: Poultry Markets: on the Underground Economy of Twitter Followers. In: Proceedings of the 2012 ACM Workshop on Online Social Networks, pp. 1–6. ACM (2012)

Digital TV Program Recommendation System Based on Collaboration Filtering

Fulian Yin[1,2], Jianping Chai[1], Hanlei Wang[1], and Ya Gao[1]

[1] Information Engineering School, Communication University of China,
Beijing, China
[2] Collaborative Innovation Center of Communication Ability Construction,
Communication University of China, Beijing, China
{yinfulian,jp_chai,gaoya}@cuc.edu.cn, wanghanlei0703@sina.com

Abstract. In order to solve the problem of information overload brought by over abundant digital television (TV) program resources, this paper proposed a digital TV program recommendation system based on collaborative filtering (CF) which contains information inputting unit, system analysis unit and recommendation sending unit. The audience behavior analysis proposed in this paper was based on two forms: personalized audience behaviour analysis and group audience behaviour analysis, which can recommend interesting TV programs suited for the particular individual or group. The result of simulation proves the feasibility of algorithms.

Keywords: Digital television, Audience behaviour analysis, Personalized behaviour analysis, Group behaviour analysis.

1 Introduction

With the wide spread of digital TV, the audience are facing the similar severe problem of information overload as internet users. The Electronic Program Guide (EPG) cannot automatically recommend TV program to audience by their own interests and regularities now, nor can it automatically track the changes in digital TV audience's interests. What it can do is no more than searching the required digital TV program. Under this circumstance, this paper proposed a new digital TV program recommendation system to provide a personalized service designed for particular individual or group audience helping to find the interesting programs swiftly and accurately.

The core of the recommended algorithm lies in combining the information of both users and items. Application of neighbourhood is one of the basic algorithms in recommendation system [6] [4]. Containing User Collaborative Filtering (UserCF) [1] and Item Collaborative Filtering (ItemCF) [5], CF has already been widely applied to business field like the Internet. While UserCF is used firstly in spam filtering system, Amazon, Hulu and Youtube are good examples of using ItemCF as core of their own recommendation systems. Similar algorithms are tentatively applied to digital TV program recommendation system [2] [3], but

L. Pan et al. (Eds.): BIC-TA 2014, CCIS 472, pp. 531–538, 2014.
© Springer-Verlag Berlin Heidelberg 2014

all of them are based on the program contents only. In order to better reflect the features of user' interests, this paper proposed a integrated structure of digital TV program recommendation system and new analysis methods based on CF of both personalized behaviour and group behaviour.

2   Model of Recommendation System

2.1   The Structure of Recommendation Systemfigures

As shown in Figure 1, the structure of digital TV program recommendation system contains three parts: information inputting unit, system analysis unit and recommendation sending unit. Both man-machine interface component and database are included in the information inputting unit. Needed parameters and commands for digital TV program recommendation system can be input through man-machine interface component while database contains all kinds of information and data relating to digital TV, which include user base preserving the background of user, program base recording both digital TV programs and their attributes, and audience behaviour base containing the audience behaviour record of users. System analysis unit is the most important part of this digital TV program recommendation system. Using the parameters and commands input through information inputting unit as well as the information from database, it generates the personalized program list to recommend to the particular audience. Recommendation sending unit puts personalized program list through Short Message Service (SMS) platform recommendation and mail platform recommendation which analysis unit has identified.

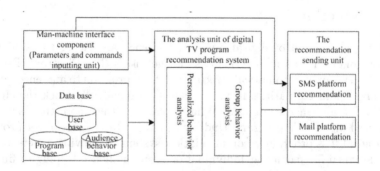

Fig. 1. The structure of digital TV program recommendation system

2.2   Data Preparation

The digital TV program recommendation system proposed in this paper requires preserving the background of digital TV audience, the audience behaviour record of user and the broadcasting information of programs.

At the same time, jurisdiction user should be allowed to inquire and use all these data. Figure 2 shows the E-R diagram of data management in digital TV program recommendation system. In the diagram, according to the sampling theory, this paper collects 628 samples from Chengde (Hebei Province, China) as background data of digital TV audience and an entire month of sample users' digital TV viewing data, about 210 thousand channel changing records as audience behaviour record. An entire month of broadcasting data of all kinds of programs relating to users' viewing records also be collected as broadcasting information, including data about channel and program. This paper classifies the total population of viewing group into 17 parts according to different professions: real estate/construction, service industry, manufacture/mining industry, broadcast TV/culture and arts, computer-related (IT/Internet), communication/transportation, education/training, finance (banking/securities/insurance), hotel/tourism/catering, trade/import and export, media/advertisement/consulting, agriculture/aquaculture, healthcare/pharmacy/health industry, government agency, student, retired people and other professions.

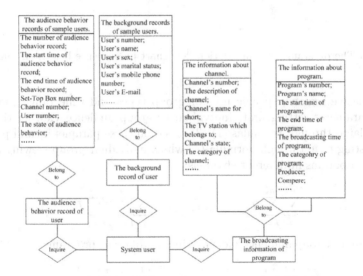

Fig. 2. The E-R diagram of data management in digital TV program recommendation system

3   Audience Behaviour Analysis Based on CF

Application of neighbourhood is the basic algorithm in recommendation system which has already been widely applied in both academics and industry. In this paper, two methods of audience behaviour analysis in digital TV program recommendation system are proposed: personalized behaviour analysis which based on

ItemCF and group behaviour analysis which based on UserCF. For personalized behaviour analysis, when an audience needs the personalized digital TV program recommendation, the system will find the audience group having similar interests with him/her at first, then recommend the program that favoured by this group yet has not been chosen by this particular audience. For group behaviour analysis, it analyses the audience groups with similar attributes, then recommends the digital TV program which favoured by this group before or other similar programs. This method doesn't utilize the similarity between different digital TV programs but analyses the audience viewing behaviour records of audience through the calculated similarity between different digital TV programs. Figure 3 shows the program recommendation flow chart by audience behaviour analysis.

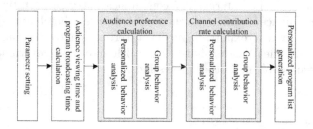

Fig. 3. The program recommendation flow chart by audience behaviour analysis

Alternative regions, specific user or group types and time range should be set in parameter setting unit. Individual or group audience viewing time can be calculated through Formulas (1) (3) based on these parameters and program broadcasting time through Formula (4) which individual/group viewing time of different programs in different channels:

$$T_{i,n,N} = \sum_{j=1}^{n1}\sum_{k=1}^{n3} T_{i,j,k,n,N}; T_{i,M,N} = \sum_{j=1}^{n1}\sum_{n=1}^{n2}\sum_{k=1}^{n3} T_{i,j,k,n,M,N} \qquad (1)$$

Individual/Group audience viewing time in different programs:

$$T_{n,N} = \sum_{j=1}^{n1}\sum_{k=1}^{n3}\sum_{i=1}^{n4} T_{i,j,k,n,N}; T_{M,N} = \sum_{j=1}^{n1}\sum_{n=1}^{n2}\sum_{k=1}^{n3}\sum_{i=1}^{n4} T_{i,j,k,n,M,N} \qquad (2)$$

Individual/Group total audience viewing time in all kinds of programs:

$$T_{n} = \sum_{j=1}^{n1}\sum_{k=1}^{n3}\sum_{i=1}^{n4}\sum_{N=1}^{n5} T_{i,j,k,n,N}; T_{M} = \sum_{j=1}^{n1}\sum_{n=1}^{n2}\sum_{k=1}^{n3}\sum_{i=1}^{n4}\sum_{N=1}^{n5} T_{i,j,k,n,M,N} \qquad (3)$$

Different broadcasting time of program in different channels and total broadcasting time of all the programs:

$$T'_{i,N} = \sum_{j=1}^{m1}\sum_{k=1}^{m3} T_{i,j,k,N}; T'_N = \sum_{j=1}^{m1}\sum_{k=1}^{m3}\sum_{i=1}^{m4} T'_{i,j,k,N} \tag{4}$$

Where i is the serial number of channel; j is the nth user in the Mth group view the N'^{th} program in the Nth type that day; k is the day collected the samples of digital TV viewing preference; $n1$ is the total number of programs which the th user viewed in the nth type that day; $n2$ is the total number of users viewed the Nth type program of the ith channel; $n3$ is the total number of days collected the samples of digital TV viewing preference; $n4$ is the total number of channels the nth user viewed in that day; $n5$ is the total number of program types user n viewed in that day; $m1$ is the total number of programs type N contained that day; $m3$ is the total number of days collected the program broadcasting; $m4$ is the total number of channels.

In the calculation unit of viewing preference and contribution rate of certain channel, this paper proposed a basic algorithm based on normalized audience viewing time and loyalty to a certain program as the measurement. Normalized audience viewing time measures the user viewing time in a kind of programs with the total time of viewing all the programs. The more a program occupies, this particular audience would pay more attention to it. Loyalty measures the user viewing time of a kind of program with the total program broadcasting time of the same kind of program. It would be a normal condition which cannot reflect the preference of audience for daily shows or programs which have longer program broadcasting time to get a longer audience viewing time while weak shows or programs having rather shorter program broadcasting time to get a limited audience viewing time. But it can never deny that even for a shorter audience viewing time, if the audience watched the entire program from the beginning to the very end, obviously, it can reflect the audience's preference to this program. It is an efficient way to reduce the effect caused by different program broadcasting time in users' loyalty. Finally, recommendation system generates the personalized program list sending to selected individual or group.

3.1   Personalized Behaviour Analysis Based on ItemCF

Individual normalized audience viewing time:

$$\psi_s = \frac{T_{n,N}}{T_n} \tag{5}$$

Contribution rate of a certain channel to individual normalized audience viewing time:

$$\xi_s = \frac{T_{i,n,N}}{T_{n,N}} \times 100\% \tag{6}$$

Individual loyalty:

$$\psi_s = \frac{T_{n,N}}{T'_N} \tag{7}$$

Contribution rate of a certain channel to individual loyalty:

$$\xi_s = \frac{T_{i,n,N}}{T'_{i,N}} \tag{8}$$

3.2   Group Behaviour Analysis Based on UserCF

Group normalized audience viewing time:

$$\psi_g = \frac{T_{M,N}}{T_M} \tag{9}$$

Contribution rate of a certain channel to group normalized audience viewing time:

$$\xi_g = \frac{T_{i,M,N}}{T'_{M,N}} \tag{10}$$

Group loyalty:

$$\psi_g = \frac{T_{M,N}}{T'_N \times N_{>1min}} \tag{11}$$

Contribution rate of a certain channel to group loyalty:

$$\xi_g = \frac{T_{i,M,N}}{T'_{i,N} \times N_{>1min}} \tag{12}$$

Where $N_{>1min}$ represents the number of users whose audience viewing time is longer than 1 minute.

4   Simulation and Performance Analysis

Audience behaviour analysis requires data that include sample background of user, record of watching program as well as information about channel and program. Figure 4 shows the histogram of normalized audience viewing time and Figure 5 shows channel contribution rate to normalized audience viewing time, which both through personalized behaviour analysis. Individual loyalty and contribution rate to individual loyalty are showed respectively in Figure 6 and Figure 7, which both through personalized behaviour analysis as well. According to the results, the digital TV program recommendation system can choose the program with highest contribution rate to generate the final personalized program list, and then send to the selected individual audience. Similarly, Figure 8 and Figure 9 show the histogram of normalized audience viewing time and contribution rate to group normalized audience viewing time, which both through group behaviour analysis. According to the results, digital TV program recommendation system could choose the program with highest contribution rate to generate the final personalized program list, and then send to the selected group audience. The analysis methods proposed in this paper have the general applicability, but figures are highly connected with the selected database, cannot represent all the circumstances.

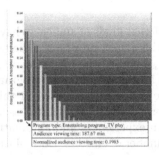

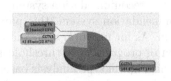

Fig. 4. The histogram of normalized audience viewing time through personalized behaviour analysis

Fig. 5. Channel contribution rate to normalized audience viewing time through personalized behaviour analysis

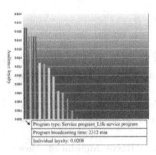

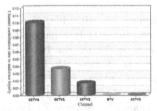

Fig. 6. The histogram of audience loyalty through personalized behaviour analysis

Fig. 7. Contribution rate to audience loyalty through personalized behaviour analysis

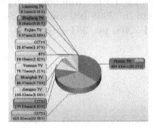

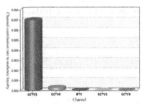

Fig. 8. Channel contribution rate to normalized audience viewing time through group audience behaviour analysis

Fig. 9. Contribution rate to audience loyalty through group behaviour analysis

5   Conclusion

Digital TV media are flourishing these days, but different kinds of audiences have their own particular interests. In this condition, this paper proposed a digital TV program recommendation system based on CF, analysed the requirement of program recommendation system and constructed a basic structure of program recommendation system, this paper explained the collected data used in this system. As for program type analysis, this paper proposed the artificial classification of program type threshold analysis based on experiences and automatic cluster program type analysis based on arbitrary number of clusters. Both of the methods can effectively be proved by simulations.

Acknowledgement. Sponsored by State Administration of Radio, Film and Television. Sponsored by Communication University of China.

References

1. Chunshan, M., Huaying, S.: User activity-based CF Algorithm in Value-Added Services. In: 2011 International Conference on Management Science and Industrial Engineering, MSIE, pp. 793–798 (2011)
2. Eunhui, K., Shinjee, P., Park, E.: An automatic Recommendation Scheme of TV program Contents for (IP)TV Personalization. IEEE Transaction on Broadcasting 57(3), 674–684 (2011)
3. Hongguang, Z., Shibao, Z.: Personalized TV Program Recommendation Based on TV-Anytime Metadata. In: Proceedings of the Ninth International Symposium on Consumer Electronics, ISCE 2005, pp. 242–246 (2005)
4. Linting, G., Hailing, L.: Recommend Items for User in Social Networking Services with CF. In: 2012 International Conference on Computer Science & Service System, CSSS 2012, pp. 1347–1350 (2012)
5. Tiraweerakhajohn, C., Pinngern, O.: Finding Item Neighbours in Item-Based Collaborative Filtering by Adding Item Content. In: 8th International Conference on Control, Automation, Robotics and Vision, ICARCV, vol. 3, pp. 1674–1678 (2004)
6. XiaoYan, S., HongWu, Y., SongJie, G.: A Personalized Recommender Integrating Item-Based and User-Based Collaborative Filtering. In: 2008 International Seminar on Business and Information Management, ISBIM 2008, pp. 264–267 (2008)

A Variable Multidimensional Fuzzy Model and Its Application to Online Tidal Level Prediction

Jianchuan Yin[1] and Nini Wang[2]

[1] Navigation College, Dalian Maritime University, Dalian 116026, China
[2] Institute of Geographic Science and Natural Resources Research,
Chinese Academy of Sciences, 100101 Beijing, China
yinjianchuan@dlmu.edu.cn, wangnini2008@gmail.com

Abstract. To represent the time-varying dynamics of nonlinear systems, a variable multidimensional fuzzy model is online constructed by the Delaunay triangulation method. Construction and adjustment of model is based on the learning of samples in a real-time updated sliding data window (SDW). The proposed fuzzy model is combined with harmonic method and the resulted modular model is implemented for real-time tidal level prediction where the harmonic method is used to represent the periodic changes of tidal level caused by celestial movement and the variable fuzzy model is used to give predictions caused by water temperature and air pressure. The measured tidal data at the port of Honolulu is implemented for the online tidal level prediction and the results demonstrate the feasibility and effectiveness of the proposed variable multidimensional fuzzy model and the modular prediction method.

Keywords: Fuzzy prediction, Variable structure, Tidal prediction, Modular model, Multidimensional fuzzy model.

1 Introduction

Precise tidal prediction is vital for navigational safety, such as stipulating ship voyage plan of navigating through shallow waters or under bridge. The conventional harmonic prediction method represents the relative location of celestial bodies as well as coastal topography like coastline shape and sea floor profile. However, it cannot represent influences caused by time-varying meteorological factors such as atmospheric pressure, wind, rainfall and ice.

Fuzzy modeling has been approved to be an efficient approach for identifying nonlinear systems. semantic-driven modeling approaches represent knowledge semantically and is convenient to set up rules manually [1]. However, under some circumstances, expert knowledge is not sufficient or even not available thus may result in the phenomenon of "curse of dimensionality". In contrast, data-driven modeling attracts much attention because it has been proved to be able to approximate system input-output mapping at arbitrary approximation

L. Pan et al. (Eds.): BIC-TA 2014, CCIS 472, pp. 539–543, 2014.

accuracy and avoid the phenomenon of "curse of dimensionality" [2]. In this study, those membership functions are obtained by Delaunay triangulation [3].

To represent system's time-varying dynamics, in this study, a SDW is introduced to represent the time-varying dynamics. Based on the studying of samples in SDW, fuzzy rules and connecting parameters of resulted fuzzy model are both determined online. To achieve better prediction accuracy as well as stable prediction result, a modular tidal level prediction system is constructed by combining mechanism model and an online identification model. The mechanism module is performed by conventional harmonic tidal prediction, and the identification module is performed by variable fuzzy identification model based on SDW.

2   Variable Fuzzy Model with Sliding Data Window

2.1   Fuzzy Model with Multi-dimensional Membership Functions

Different from conventional zero-order Takagi-Sugeno fuzzy model, in the multi-dimensional fuzzy sets, the input space is partitioned by piece-wise linear multivariable fuzzy sets $\mathbf{p}_j = [p_{j,1}, p_{j,2}, \ldots, p_{j,n}]\mathrm{T}$ with $j = 1, \ldots, n_p$. n_p is the number of fuzzy node. The fuzzy sets are defined with membership degrees at these nodes: $A_i = \{u_{i,j}/\mathbf{P}_j\}$. This enables that the sum of membership functions to be 1 for entire antecedent domain: $\sum_{i=1}^{n_r} A_i(z) = 1$. Hence the fuzzy model can be written as:

$$y = \sum_{i=1}^{n_r} A_i(z)d_i = \mathbf{A}(z)^{\mathrm{T}}d, \qquad (1)$$

with $A(z)$ and d being vectors of antecedent membership degrees and the consequent parameters, respectively. $A(z)$ is defined by linear interpolation of the membership degrees of selected nodes. The partition of input space is performed by Delaunay triangulation and the interpolation is performed by barycentric coordinates of the obtained polytope which is also referred to as simplices. It has been proven that the piecewise approximation based on the Delaunay triangulation has the smallest error of all triangulations and has been widely used [4,5]. The simplices are represented by $\mathbf{P}$ whose s-th row contains the indices of the nodes that form simplex T_s: $T_s = \mathrm{conv}(\mathbf{p}_{v_{s,1}}, \cdots, \mathbf{p}_{v_{s,n+1}})$.

For $z \in T_s$, the membership function $A_i(\mathbf{z})$ is defined through barycentric coordinates $\mathbf{b}_s = [b_{s,1}, , b_{s,n+1}]$ of $\mathbf{z}$: $\mathbf{bs} = Z_s^{-1} z'$, where $z' = [z_1, \ldots, z_n, 1]^{\mathrm{T}}$ is the extended regression vector, and $\mathbf{Z}_s = \begin{pmatrix} \mathbf{P}_{v_{s,1}} & \cdots & \mathbf{P}_{v_{s,n+1}} \\ 1 & \cdots & 1 \end{pmatrix}$.

The vector of membership degrees of fuzzy set A_i at the nodes forming simplex T_s is denoted as $\mu_{s,i} = [\mu_{i,v_{s,1}}, \ldots, \mu_{i,v_{s,n+1}}]^{\mathrm{T}}$. By arranging $\mu_{s,i}$ into the matrix $\mathbf{U}_s = [\mu_{s,1}, \ldots, \mu_{s,nr}]$, the vector of membership degree of z for all the membership functions can be determined: $\mathbf{A}(\mathbf{z}) = \mathbf{U}_s^{\mathrm{T}} \mathbf{b}_s = \mathbf{U}_s^{\mathrm{T}} \mathbf{Z}_s^{-1} z'$.

The mapping of the fuzzy model can be achieved [5]:

$$y = \mathbf{A}(\mathbf{z})^{\mathrm{T}} \mathbf{d} = (\mathbf{U}_s^{\mathrm{T}} \mathbf{Z}_s^{-1} z')^{\mathrm{T}} \mathbf{d} = \mathbf{d}^{\mathrm{T}} \mathbf{U}_s^{\mathrm{T}} \mathbf{Z}_s^{-1} z'. \qquad (2)$$

In the stepwise rule construction algorithm, first insert the samples in the n-dimensional domain of z as initial nodes, and compute the model response to each training data. The modeling error of each simplex is computed and more nodes would be inserted for the complex with the largest modeling error.

2.2 Variable Fuzzy Model Based on Sliding Data Window (SDW)

The method constructs the variable-structure fuzzy model by learning information underlying samples in the first-in-first-out sliding data window (SDW):

$$W_{\mathrm{SD}} = [(x_{t-N+1}, y_{t-N+1}), \ldots, (x_t, y_t)], \tag{3}$$

where N denotes the window width. The current dynamic of system is represented by the input matrix $\mathbf{X} = [x_{t-N+1}, x_t]$ and the output matrix $\mathbf{Y} = [y_{t-N+1}, y_t]$, with n and m are the dimensions of input and output, respectively.

At each step, when the data in the sliding window is updated, the fuzzy model is constructed by the Delaunay triangulation method based on the current data in SDW. The simplexes are formed by Delaunay triangulation and the interpolation is performed by barycentric coordinates method. At the time of t, a discrete-time nonlinear system with two input variables can be described as $y(t) = f(u_1(t-1), \ldots, u(t-n_{u_1}), u_2(t-1), \ldots, u(t-n_{u_2})) + e(t)$, where $u(t)$, $y(t)$ and $e(t)$ are the system input, output and noise; n_{u_1} and n_{u_2} are the maximum time lags in the two inputs, respectively; and f is the unknown nonlinear mapping to be identified, which can be realized by various method.

In prediction process, for instance, in one-step-ahead prediction, the model output of the next step is acquired by substituting the t with $t+1$, thus the prediction model is realized by variable multi-dimensional fuzzy sets in the following form: R_i : If $\mathbf{z}$ is $A_i(\mathbf{z})$ then $y(t+1)$ is d_i ,with $\mathbf{z} = [u_1(t), \ldots, y(t-n_{u_1}+1), u_2(t), \ldots, y(t-n_{u_2}+1)]$.

3 Modular Prediction Based on Variable Fuzzy Model

Two steps are conducted during identification process. Firstly, the harmonic method is implemented and the prediction of y is denoted as y_M. y_R denotes the residual between $y(t)$ and y_M. In this study, u is composed of the water temperature T and air pressure P, with n_T and n_P are the orders of the T and P, respectively. Residual information is considered as determined by environmental changes. To construct variable fuzzy model, we set $y_R(t)$ as output, $T(t-1), \ldots, T(t-n_T)$ and $P(t-1), \ldots, P(t-n_P)$ as inputs, respectively:

$$y_R(t) = f(T(t-1), \ldots, T(t-n_T), P(t-1), \ldots, P(t-n_P)) + e(t). \tag{4}$$

The modular prediction model is achieved by combing the SDW-based fuzzy model with the harmonic method. Once the identification is completed, $T(t)$, $T(t-n_T+1)$ and $P(t), \ldots, P(t-n_P+1)$ are then set as input and the $y_R(t+1)$ would be the prediction of the influence of environment to the tidal levels:

$$y_R(t+1) = f(T(t), \ldots, T(t-n_T+1), P(t), \ldots, P(t-n_P+1)). \tag{5}$$

Predictions generated by the two modules are combined together to form the final prediction result.

4   Simulation of Online Tidal Level Prediction

Tidal level data of port of Honolulu, measured from GMT0000 April 1 to GMT2300 April 30, 2014, is implemented to evaluate the feasibility and effectiveness of the proposed model. All the measurement data are achieved from web site of American National Oceanic and Atmospheric Administration: http://co-ops.nos.noaa.gov. Using harmonic method, the largest prediction error of is larger than 0.6m and the prediction RMSE is 0.1816801m .

The modular prediction method is implemented and the parameters are set as follows: width of sliding data window N is 15, the number limit of nodes for the fuzzy model is 10, and the running step is 700. The achieved fuzzy model is variable and the fuzzy input-output map in the final step is depicted in Fig. 1.

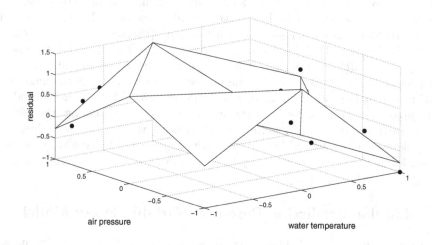

Fig. 1. Input-output map of the fuzzy model

The dots in Fig. 1 denote samples in the SDW, and the curved surface constructed by various planes representing the input-output mapping. Identification RMSE is 0.0022372m and prediction RMSE is 0.0343591m, which is less than 20% of the 0.1816801m using harmonic method alone. The results prediction of modular prediction system is illustrated in Fig. 2, together with measured ones.

It can be seen in Fig. 2 that the predicted tidal level coincide with the actually measured ones well. This shows that the proposed modular tidal level prediction models as well as variable fuzzy model can online generate accurate predictions. Furthermore, the total running time for 700 steps is 14.928776s, and it spends only about 0.02s for each step. The fast processing speed facilitates the practical applications of proposed prediction method.

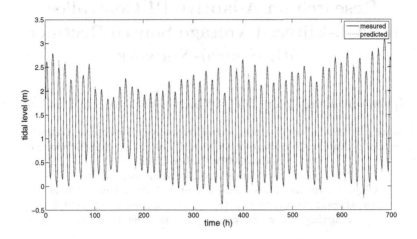

Fig. 2. Prediction result of tidal level by using modular prediction

5 Conclusion

A variable multidimensional fuzzy model is proposed which is online constructed based on the learning of the samples in a sliding data window. The real-time adjustment of the fuzzy model enables its representing ability for time-varying dynamics. The combination of parametric harmonic method and nonparametric variable fuzzy model takes both advantages of mechanism model and identification model, and the simulation result of tidal level prediction demonstrates the feasibility, effectiveness and fastness of the proposed tidal prediction method.

Acknowledgement. This work is supported by the Applied Basic Research Fund of the Chinese Ministry of Transport (2014329225010), and Fundamental Research Funds for the Central Universities (3132014028).

References

1. Agard, B., Barajas, M.: The Use of Fuzzy Logic in Product Family Development: Literature Review and Opportunities. J. Intel. Manuf. 23, 1445–1462 (2012)
2. Ma, Z.M., Li, Y.: A Literature Overview of Fuzzy Conceptual Data Modeling. J. Inform. Sci. Eng. 26, 427–441 (2010)
3. Devillers, O.: Delaunay Triangulation of Imprecise Points: Preprocess and Actually Get a Fast Query Time. J. Comput. Geom. 2(1), 30–45 (2011)
4. Benderskaya, E.N., Zhukova, S.V.: Clustering by Chaotic Neural Networks with Mean Field Calculated via Delaunay Triangulation. In: Corchado, E., Abraham, A., Pedrycz, W. (eds.) HAIS 2008. LNCS (LNAI), vol. 5271, pp. 408–416. Springer, Heidelberg (2008)
5. Abonyi, J.: Fuzzy Model Identification for Control. Birkhäuser, Boston (2002)

Research on Adaptive PI Controller
of LCL-Filtered Voltage Source Rectifier
with Neural-Network

Quan Yin[1], Ronghui Lu[1], Qingyi Wang[2,*], Hui Luo[1], and Hu Guo[1]

[1] State Key Laboratory of Multispectral Information Processing Technology,
School of Automation, Huazhong University of Science and Technology,
Wuhan 430074, Hubei, China
[2] Faculty of Mechanical and Electronic Information,
China University of Geosciences, Wuhan 430074, Hubei, China
yinquan@email.hust.edu.cn, {rh_lu_1016,guohu_email}@163.com,
wangqingyi@cug.edu.cn, keyluo@mail.hust.edu.cn

Abstract. In this paper, a neural-network-based adaptive PI current controller of voltage source rectifier (VSR) is proposed. Complex vector PI decoupling scheme can eliminate the voltage coupling completely, and the neural network algorithm can tune the parameters of current regulator online. The novel controller has a fast dynamic response, strong adaptability to those occasions such as the nonlinear model and variable load. A double loop control strategy with an outer dc link voltage control based on traditional PI controller and inner current control based on the novel controller is discussed in this paper. Simulation results verify the correctness and feasibility of the neural-network-based PI controller.

Keywords: Complex Vector Model, LCL Filter, PI Control, Neural Network.

1 Introduction

Three-phase grid-connected pulse width modulation (PWM) rectifiers provide constant controllable dc bus voltage, nearly sinusoidal input current, controllable power factor and regenerating capability. Because of these features, they are widely used in regenerative energy systems and adjustable-speed drives. To damp the switching harmonics, LCL-filters are increasing being used to connect the rectifier with the grid, because they are more cost-effective compared to simple L-filters as smaller inductors can be used to achieve the same damping effect [1].

The difficulty in controlling the LCL-filtered converter is mainly due to the nonlinearity of the system. In the conventional control system design, a classical PI control structure is adopted and designed [2] according to the linearized mathematical model. The parameters of PI controller can be tuned in accordance with the engineering optimum design method [3]. Nevertheless, the calculation

---

* Corresponding author.

L. Pan et al. (Eds.): BIC-TA 2014, CCIS 472, pp. 544–548, 2014.

of the parameters should be based on the precise system parameters and the robustness of the system is poor.

Neural networks (NN) have been introduced into power electronics circuits successfully in recent years, because they have the ability to approach an arbitrary non-linear function with a high degree of fault tolerance [4]. In [5], an artificial intelligent neural network algorithm is used to compute the switching patterns and duty cycles with space vector pulse-width modulation (SVPWM) algorithm. An off-line neural network algorithm is used in uninterruptible power supply (UPS) to reduce the total harmonic distortion (THD) of the current in [6]. In [7], conventional PI control, neural network PI control and direct power control of current are compared under different load conditions. All of these approaches show that the neural network algorithm exhibits an excellent performance to the nonlinear system.

In this paper, a neural-network-based complex vector PI controller is designed in the three-phase ac/dc PWM converter, and the parameters of controller are tuned through self-learning and self-adjusting weights of the neural network online. To validate the performance of the proposed controller, simulation studies have been performed. The results show that the current tracks rapidly to the reference value without overshoot and steady errors. Furthermore, load variations are rapidly tracked and the changes of the converter parameters are fairly well dealt with.

2 Traditional Complex Vector Control System of Three-Phase VSR

The analyzed system topology is shown in Fig. 1, $T_1 - T_6$ are the three-leg power switches. The three-phase VSR is connected to the grid through a LCL filter, including the grid-side inductor L_g, the bridge-side inductor L, the filter capacitor C_f, the grid-side inductance parasitic equivalent resistance R_g, and the bridge-side inductance parasitic equivalent resistance R, the PWM converter is loaded by a resistor.

To simplify the analysis and computation, this paper only considers the fundamental component of the grid voltage and current. In the two-phase stationary $\alpha\beta$ coordinate, $M_{\alpha\beta}$ represents electromagnetic complex vector of the system.

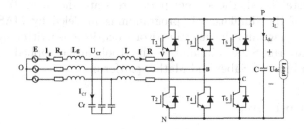

Fig. 1. Topology of the LCL-filtered VSR system

Applying Kirchhoff's laws and the coordinate transformation theory, the complex vector mathematical model of the three-phase LCL filter in two-phase stationary $\alpha\beta$ coordinate can be derived.

$$\begin{cases} p\boldsymbol{I}_{g,\alpha\beta}L_g = (-R_g - j\omega_0 L_g)\boldsymbol{I}_{g,\alpha\beta} + \boldsymbol{E}_{\alpha\beta} - \boldsymbol{U}_{cf,\alpha\beta} \\ p\boldsymbol{U}_{cf,\alpha\beta}C_f = -j\omega_0 C_f \boldsymbol{U}_{cf,\alpha\beta} + \boldsymbol{I}_{g,\alpha\beta} - \boldsymbol{I}_{\alpha\beta} \\ p\boldsymbol{I}_{\alpha\beta}L = (-R - j\omega_0 L)\boldsymbol{I}_{\alpha\beta} + \boldsymbol{U}_{cf,\alpha\beta} - \boldsymbol{V}_{\alpha\beta} \end{cases} \quad (1)$$

where, p is the differential operator, ω_0 is the fundamental angular frequency of the grid voltage.

3   BP Neural-Network-Based Adaptive PI Controller System

A three-layer neural network control system can be constructed. The input-layer has 3 neurons, the hidden-layer has 5 neurons, and the output-layer has 2 neurons. The inputs of input-layer are the given current amount $i_{ref}(k)$, the feedback current $i(k)$, and the error between them $e(k)$. The outputs of output-layer are the PI controller parameters. The control block diagram of current loop control in $\alpha\beta$ coordinate is shown in Fig. 2.

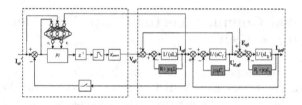

Fig. 2. Neural-network-based PI closed-loop current control block diagram in $\alpha\beta$ coordinate

4   Simulation Analysis

While a four-quadrant PWM 22kW rectifier model based on Saber Designer platform is established, the system parameters are shown in Table ?? . The control part of the simulation is programming modeled by MAST hardware description language and the neural network algorithm is written by M function in Matlab platform. Saber Simulink Cosim Tool can be applied to achieve the co-simulation between Saber and Matlab platform.

4.1   Start-Up Process

Fig. 3 shows the K_p, K_i curves during the start-up process when a neural-network-based adaptive complex vector PI controller is applied in the closed-loop current control. During t=0-20ms, PI controller is not involved in the closed-loop control, and the three-phase VSR works in un-controlled rectifier state. At t=20ms, the closed-loop regulation of the three-phase VSR is applied. The algorithm can automatically adjust its weights according to the current error, and the parameters of controller can reach stable within 10ms. It is clear that the neural network algorithm has a fast learning process.

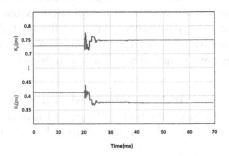

Fig. 3. Parameters curves of neural-network-based complex vector PI during start-up process

4.2 Load Variation

Fig. 4 shows the electrical parameters curves when a neural-network-based PI controller is applied during load variation. At t = 20ms, the load changes from 50% to rated load. (a) shows the parameters curves of neural network adaptive PI controller, (b) indicates the dc bus voltage waveform, (c) and (d), respectively, represent the grid-side and bridge-side current waveform. Due to the neural network algorithm can adjust the parameters of controller during the load variation, the three-phase current maintain stability within 10ms. A fast dynamic response process and small steady state error can be obtained during the load variation.

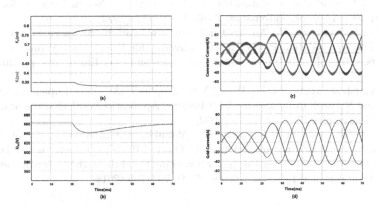

Fig. 4. Electrical parameters curves of neural-network-based PI control during the load variation

5   Conclusion

Due to the poor adaptability of the parameters of traditional PI current controller in the three-phase voltage source rectifier, a neural-network-based adaptive complex vector PI controller is proposed and analyzed in this paper. The parameters of the controller are tuned online through the neural network algorithm according to the variation of system parameters. Simulation results show that the adjustment of the parameters of neural-network-based controller is extremely fast. Moreover, the parameters can be self-adjusted according to the variation of load. Simulation results demonstrate the desired performances of the novel controller in both dynamic and static conditions.

Acknowledgement. This work was supported in part by the National Natural Science Foundation of China under Project 61374049 and supported by the Fundamental Research Funds for the Central Universities CUGL120242, HUST:2014QN169.

References

1. Dannehl, J., Wessels, C., Fuchs, F.W.: Limitations of Voltage Oriented PI Current Control of Grid-connected PWM Rectifiers With LCL Filters. IEEE Transcations on Industrial Electronics 56(2), 380–388 (2009)
2. Dannehl, J., Fuchs, F.W., Hansen, S., Thogersen, P.B.: Investigation of Active Damping Approaches for PI-Based Current Control of Grid-Connected Pulse Width Modulation Converters With LCL Filters. IEEE Transcations and Industrical Applications 46(4), 1509–1517 (2010)
3. Wessels, C., Dannehl, J., Fuchs, F.W.: Active Damping of LCL Filter Resonance Based on Virtual Resistor For PWM Rectifiers Stability Analysis With Different Filter Parameters. In: Proceeding of Power Electronics Specialists Conference, pp. 3532–3538 (2008)
4. Hunt, K.J., Sbarbaro, D., Zbikowski, R., Gawthrop, P.J.: Neural Networks for Control System-A survey. Automatica 29(6), 1083–1112 (1992)
5. Bhat, A.H., Agarwal, P.: An Artificial Neural-network-based Space Vector PWM of A Three-phase High Power Factor Converter for Power Quality Improvement. In: Proceeding of India International Conference on Power Electronics, pp. 309–314 (2006)
6. Sun, X., Chow, M.H., Xu, D., Wang, Y.S., Lee, Y.-S.: Analogue Implementation of A Neural Network Controller for UPS Inverter Applications. IEEE Transcations on Power Electronics 17(3), 305–313 (2002)
7. Li, S., Fairbank, M., Johnson, C., Wunsch, D.C., Alonso, E.: Artificial Neural Network for Control of A Grid-Connected Rectifier/Inverter under Disturbance, Dynamic And Power Converter Switching Conditions. IEEE Transcations on Neural Network and Learning System 25(4), 738–750 (2014)

A DNA Computing Model on Triple-Stranded for Minimum Spanning Tree Problem

Zhixiang Yin[1], Xia Sun[1], Feng Xu[1], Xianwen Fang[1,*], and Hui Xu[2]

[1] School of Science, Anhui University of Science and Technology,
Huainan, China
[2] School of Computer Science and Engineering,
Anhui University of Science and Technology, Huainan, China
zxyin66@163.com, mqchen@aust.edu.cn

Abstract. Single-strand DNA can match with homologous double-stranded into a triple-stranded structure mediated by RecA protein. The paper provides a triple-stranded DNA computing model for minimum spanning tree problem. DNA fragments corresponding to edges are coded by double-stranded DNA, wrong hybridization does not take place and hairpin structure does not form. The single-strand DNA probe is bond with RecA protein, so the rate of wrong solution will reduce. And in this way, encoding complexity and the errors in computation will be decreased.

Keywords: Triple-stranded DNA, Antigen intermediary, Minimum spanning tree problem.

1 Introduction

In recent years with the improvement of the experiment technology, many researchers have confirmed in experiments that the molecule can exist with other structures, such as triple-stranded DNA. Three-stranded structure that has been found includes triple helix structure and three strand braid structure. In three-stranded DNA molecules, base sequence is the same type of purine or pyrimidine, that the whole base are purine or pyrimidine. In the three chains, one is the purine strand, and the others are the pyrimidine strands. The third interacts to the chain in double helix structure through hoogsteen and trans-hoogsteen hydrogen bond, and their directions are consistent [1]. It is proved that three-stranded molecules mediated by RecA protein is fairly stable, it can be used to extract the target DNA sequence, and the method is feasible.

Some researchers tried to use three-stranded DNA solve some NP problems, such as Gang Fang [2] presented the DNA model to solve 3-SAT problem and that of three vertex coloring problem, Jing Yang [3] gave the DNA model to solve 0-1 integer programming problem, Xia Sun [4] established DNA computing model of whole error permutation problems etc. Minimum spanning tree problem is one of

---

* Corresponding author.

L. Pan et al. (Eds.): BIC-TA 2014, CCIS 472, pp. 549–551, 2014.

the important contents of operational research, the common method is Krustal. Zhixiang Yin [5] gave the model for this problem, but the vertices and edges are coded with single-stranded that are easy to form the secondary structure and the hairpin structure.

2 Preliminary Knowledge

Graph G is a two-dimensional array $G = \langle V, E \rangle$, the set of vertices is recorded as $V = \{v_1, v_2, \cdots, v_n\}$, the set of edges is labeled as $E = \{e_1, e_2, \cdots, e_n\}$. G is known as a weighted graph in which each edge is assigned a non-negative real number known as the edge weight. The sequence $\Gamma = v_1 - e_1 - v_2 - e_2 - \cdots - e_1 - v_1$ of alternating vertices and edges, if v_i, v_{i+1} are the endpoints of e_1, is known as a pathway from v_1 to v_1. If $v_1 = v_1$, vertices and edges both are different, the pathway is a cycle. If any two different vertices in G have a pathway, it is called a connected graph. If there is not more than one link with any two different vertices and different two points have connection, G is called a simple graph. A spanning tree of G is the tree which is contained in G and contains all the vertices. Obviously there must be a spanning tree in connected graph. For the connected weighted simple graph, the addition of all edges weight is called the right of the spanning tree. A spanning tree with minimum weight is named the minimum spanning tree.

2.1 A DNA Computing Model On Triple-Stranded for Minimum Spanning Tree Problem

The basic idea of the algorithm [6,7] is as follows: first, pick the edge of the minimum weight out, and get a tree; second, extend the tree with the minimal weight, that is to say, add an edge and a vertex to a new tree (always maintaining the edge number = the number of vertices -1), causing the increased weight is minimum; until it can no longer extend (the number of vertices is limited).

2.2 Algorithm

(1) Basic Algorithm Step1:select the edge with the minimum weight from E, which is credited as $e_1 = v_1 v_2$ $E_2 = \{e_1\} V_2 = \{v_1, v_2\}$ $n = 2$ Step2: if $n = |V|, T = (V_n, E_n)$ is the minimum spanning tree, or turn to step3; Step3: select the edge with the minimum weight from $E \setminus E_n$, that must associate two vertices from V_n and V/V_n, which is labeled as $e_n = v_n v_{n+1}$, $V_{n+1} = V_n \cup \{v_{n+1}\}$, $E_{n+1} = E_n \cup \{e_{n+1}\}$; put $n + 1$ into n, then turn to step2.

(2) Biological Algorithm Step1: vertices, edges and edge weight of G are encoded into single strand. For single-stranded is easy to form the secondary structure, the single chains corresponding to the coded edges are amplified to double chains, and RecA protein is added to the 5' end of the single strand corresponding to the vertex, then which is denoted with biotin. These single chains are mixed with antigen proteins in the solution containing ATP_γ, and RecA protein

-DNA complex is generated under the proper conditions, at last the strands are used to make DNA probes as template;

Step2: by electrophoresis, seek out the DNA fragment corresponding to the minimum weight edge;

Step3: sequencing and record the fragment, find the vertices and edges of the segment which is credited as $e_1 = v_1v_2$ $E_2 = \{e_1\}V_2 = \{v_1, v_2\}n = 2$.If $n = |V|, T = (V_n, E_n)$, is the minimum spanning tree, or turn to step4;

Step4: capture all edges by using the probe, and then using electrophoresis identify the edge of the minimum weight. Turn to step1.

3   Conclusion

On the basis of the nature that single-strand DNA can match with homologous double-stranded into a stable three-stranded structure mediated by RecA protein, the paper proposes a new DNA computing model to solve the minimum spanning tree problem. Because DNA fragments corresponding to edges are coded by double-stranded, wrong hybridization does not take place and hairpin structure does not form. The single-strand DNA probe is bond with RecA protein, so these errors do not occur. Encoding complexity and the errors in computation will be decreased.

Acknowledgment. This work was supported by National Natural Science Foundation of China Acknowledgment (61170172).

References

1. Zang, H., Jue, J., Mukherjee, B.: A Review of Routing and Wavelength Assignment Approaches for Wavelength-routed Optical WDM Networks. Opt. Netw. Mag 1, 47–60 (2000)
2. Fang, G., Zhang, S., Zhu, Y., Xu, J.: The DNA Computing Based on Triple Helix Nucleic Acid. China Journal of Bioinformatics 7(3), 181–185 (2009)
3. Yang, J., Yin, Z.: 0-1 Integer Programming Problem Based on Reca-Mediated Triple-Stranded DNA Structure. Computer Engineering and Applications 44(2), 76–79 (2008)
4. Sun, X., Yin, Z., Zhao, Q., Xu, F.: DNA Computing Model on Triple-stranded of the Whole Error Permutation Problems. Journal of Chuzhou University 14(2), 18–20 (2012)
5. Yin, Z., Zhang, F., Xu, J.: DNA Computing in Graph Theory and Combinatorial Optimization. Science Press (2004)
6. Ye, L.: A DNA Computing Algorithm for Solving the Knapsack Problem. In: Qu, X., Yang, Y. (eds.) IBI 2011, Part II. CCIS, vol. 268, pp. 84–90. Springer, Heidelberg (2012)
7. Zhou, X., Li, K., Yue, G., Yang, Z.: A Volume Molecular Solution for The Maximum Matching Problem on DNA-Based Computing. Computer Research and Development 48(11), 2147–2154 (2011)
8. Xu, J., Qiang, X., Yang, Y., Wang, B., Yang, D., Luo, L., Pan, L., Wang, S.: An unenumerative DNA computing model for vertex coloring problem. IEEE Transactions on Nanobioscience 10(2), 94–98 (2011)

An Adaptive Unimodal and Hysteresis Thresholding Method

Yin Yu[1,2], Zhen Li[1,2], Bing Liu[1,2], and Xiangdong Liu[1,2]

[1] School of Automation, Beijing Institute of Technology, Beijing, China
[2] Key Laboratory for Intelligent Control & Decision on Complex Systems,
Beijing Institute of Technology, Beijing, China

Abstract. This paper addresses the unimodal and hysteresis thresholding, where a pair of low and high thresholds is under investigation targeted with the unimodal image histogram. The novel *bowstring* is introduced to make an accurate *priori*-measurement of the overall tendency of the histogram. The dual-threshold is further computed by adaptively searching two tangent points corresponding to the properly defined transitional characteristics over the whole histogram. The effectiveness of this proposed algorithm is evaluated using the Baddeley's discrepancy.

Keywords: Unimodal thresholding, hysteresis thresholding, Adaptive thresholding, Image histogram, Canny edge detector.

1 Introduction

Thresholding is one of the most fundamental techniques in image processing since its simplicity and effectiveness. Over the years, many thresholding methods have been established in the image segmentation. Ref. [1] gave a historical overview of these thresholding methods.

The image thresholding problem is traditionally treated as an optimal problem. Over the decades, the bio-inspired optimal theory has been significantly developed, such as fuzzy methods, artificial neural networks, evolutionary, particle swarming optimization (PSO), differential evolution (DE), and artificial bee colony (ABC) algorithms, and so on. These bio-inspired optimal methods were extended to image thresholding spontaneously [2,3,4,5]. In Ref. [6], comparison of PSO, DE and ABC algorithms for image thresholding have been explored.

This paper focuses on the unimodal and hysteresis thresholding, where the low and high thresholds are searched under the condition that the image histogram is unimodal. The unimodal thresholding study was reviewed in [7,8,9,10]. Moreover, the hysteresis thresholding is of necessity and has the significant boost of performance in many applications. Compared with the unimodal thresholding, the hysteresis thresholding is more complicated, which needs to acquire dual thresholds simultaneously. Recent works had progresses targeting with this difficulty [11,12,13,14,15,16] .

In this paper, an adaptive hysteresis thresholds computation method is proposed in an unimodal image histogram context. Firstly, the shape feature of

L. Pan et al. (Eds.): BIC-TA 2014, CCIS 472, pp. 552–556, 2014.

 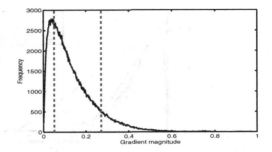

Fig. 1. Typical image and its gradient magnitude histogram. The maximum of gradient magnitude is normalized to 1 and the number of categories is set to 500.

unimodal image histogram is analyzed in different applications. And then two lines, called long and short *bowstring*, are introduced to provide a description of the global tendency characteristics of the image histogram. The hysteresis thresholds are determined by translating the bowstrings when minimizing the intercepts in the histogram coordinate plane.

2 Hysteresis Thresholds Adaptive Computation: Derivation and Algorithm

The gradient magnitude histogram (GMH) is of typical unimodality. A typical GMH is shown in Fig. 1. The unimodal histogram is made up of three parts, which are sketched by two vertical red dash line and called IRP, RFP and STP respectively from left to right. As a matter of fact that the edge points (or signal area) always have the greater magnitude than the high threshold, the criteria to determine the high threshold must be a tendency transition point separating RFP and STP of histogram. Therefore, the selection criteria of the high threshold point should be guaranteed as the closest to the origin.

Let the set of $\{(M(i), F(i)) | i=1, 2, \ldots, N\}$ represents the discrete points of histogram. Its peak point is denoted by $(M(i_{\max}), F(i_{\max}))$, where $F(i_{\max})$ is the maximum frequency of histogram. The *almost zero point* (AZP) is thus introduced with the denotation of $(M(i_0), F(i_0))$, where $F(i_0)$ is a minute fraction of $F(i_{\max})$ and non-negative, e.g. $F(i_0) = 0.01F(i_{\max})$, and the index of i_0 is the first point in RFP and STP area with the frequency equal to $F(i_0)$. The *bowstring* is thus defined as the line passing through both the peak point and the AZP, i.e. *long bowstring*. The high threshold transition point is the resultant tangent point of the parallel to the *long bowstring* as shown in Fig.2.

The low threshold is the counterpart of high threshold and can be derived in a similar way. The low threshold *bowstring* is selected as the line passing through the peak point and the high threshold transition point, which is further referred as *short bowstring*, as depicted in Fig.2. Finally, the high and low thresholds are adaptively determined step by step.

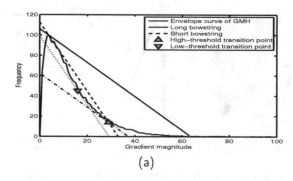

(a)

Fig. 2. Derivation of hysteresis thresholds. The maximum of gradient magnitude and frequency are all normalized to 100.

3   Simulation Results and Discussion

The 200 training image in BSD500 of the Berkeley Segmentation Dataset, found in Ref. [17], is used in this testing. Firstly, the low and high thresholds are applied to image thresholding to verify their performance in unimodal thresholding application. Secondly, the dual thresholds are applied to Canny edge detector simultaneously to verify the performance in the hysteresis application. In the first set of verification, the method proposed in the experiment of Ref. [9] is used to evaluate the performance. The Baddeley's discrepancy are calculated for four kinds of binary edge images from low threshold of the proposed method, high threshold of the proposed method, MSA [8], Medina-Carnicer's [9] methods. The result is shown in Fig. 3. According to the summary of Ref. [9], the high threshold of the proposed method performs best for case 2, while the low threshold of the proposed method has the optimal performance for case 3. It is reasonable to apply the twin thresholds to the hysteresis thresholding and achieve the performance in the complementary way.

In the second set of verification, the proposed hysteresis thresholding method is under investigation in the case of the application for the Canny edge detector. The Otsu's method is also included for the evaluation as comparison. The results of the second set of experiment are divide into 4 categories: (1) $T_h^{adp} >= T_h^{ots}$, $T_l^{adp} >= T_l^{ots}$; (2) $T_h^{adp} >= T_h^{ots}$, $T_l^{adp} < T_l^{ots}$; (3) $T_h^{adp} < T_h^{ots}$, $T_l^{adp} >= T_l^{ots}$; (4) $T_h^{adp} < T_h^{ots}$, $T_l^{adp} < T_l^{ots}$, where T_h^{adp}, T_l^{adp}, T_h^{ots}, T_h^{ots} are the high and low threshold of the proposed adaptive and Otsu's method, respectively. The simulation results indicate the statistics of the four category is 42, 8, 22, 128. The detailed threshold statistics are listed in Tab. 1. As shown in the table, each row corresponds to the mean values of category 1, 2, 3, 4 and all images. The proposed method prefers to selecting relatively lower thresholds, while the Otsu's method has the inclination to high thresholds. The other significant advantage of the proposed method is that the high-/low-threshold ratio is evidently adjustable for various images.

Table 1. Hysteresis thrshold statistics

	Proposed Method			Otsu's Method		
	T_H^{adp}	T_L^{adp}	T_L^{adp}/T_H^{adp}	T_H^{ost}	T_L^{ost}	T_L^{ost}/T_H^{ost}
C1	0.2571	0.1349	0.5277	0.2018	0.0807	0.4000
C2	0.2128	0.0608	0.2961	0.1877	0.0751	0.4000
C3	0.1733	0.0970	0.5605	0.2055	0.0822	0.4000
C4	0.1158	0.0458	0.4022	0.2050	0.0820	0.4000
Total	0.1897	0.0846	0.4466	0.2000	0.0800	0.4000

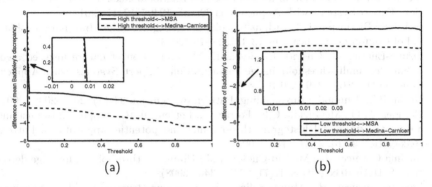

(a)   (b)

Fig. 3. Results of unimodal thresholding experiment. (a) the mean discrepancy difference of high threshold; (b) the mean discrepancy difference of low threshold.

4   Conclusion

In this paper, a novel thresholding method is raised, targeting with determining a couple of thresholds for hysteresis thresholding in the case of unimodal histogram. The *bowstring* is introduced to explore two tangent points on the envelope curve of unimodal histogram. Two testing experiments are performed to verify the unimodal and hysteresis thresholding performance, respectively. The comparisons of the proposed method with MSA and Medina-Carnicer's method indicate that the high threshold and low threshold have complementary functions to each other. The comparison of the proposed method with Otsu's method shows that the proposed method prefers to selecting the lower thresholds and offering the adjustment of the ratio between low and high threshold, by which a proper trade-off can be made between true and fake detected edge points. Therefore, it can be concluded that the proposed unimodal and hysteresis thresholding method has a relative good performance.

References

1. Sezgin, M., Sankur, B.C.: Survey over image thresholding techniques and quantitative performance evaluation. Journal of Electronic Imaging 13(1), 146–168 (2004)
2. Tobias, O.J., Seara, R.: Image segmentation by histogram thresholding using fuzzy sets. IEEE Transactions on Image Processing 11(12), 1457–1465 (2002)
3. Tao, W.B., Tian, J.W., Liu, J.: Image segmentation by three-level thresholding based on maximum fuzzy entropy and genetic algorithm. Pattern Recognition Letters 24(16), 3069–3078 (2003)
4. Ghamisi, P., Couceiro, M.S., Benediktsson, J.A., Ferreira, N.M.F.: An efficient method for segmentation of images based on fractional calculus and natural selection. Expert Systems with Applications 39(16), 12407–12417 (2012)
5. Nebti, S.: Bio-inspired algorithms for color image segmentation. International Journal of Computer Applications 73(18), 11–16 (2013)
6. Osuna-Enciso, V., Cuevas, E., Sossa, H.: A comparison of nature inspired algorithms for multi-threshold image segmentation. Expert Systems with Applications 40(4), 1213–1219 (2013)
7. Rosin, P.L.: Unimodal thresholding. Pattern Recognition 34(11), 2083–2096 (2001)
8. Baradez, M.O., McGuckin, C.P., Forraz, N., Pettengell, R., Hoppe, A.: Robust and automated unimodal histogram thresholding and potential applications. Pattern Recognition 37(6), 1131–1148 (2004)
9. Medina-Carnicer, R., Madrid-Cuevas, F.J.: Unimodal thresholding for edge detection. Pattern Recognition 41(7), 2337–2346 (2008)
10. Medina-Carnicer, R., Munoz-Salinas, R., Carmona-Poyato, A., Madrid-Cuevas, F.J.: A novel histogram transformation to improve the performance of thresholding methods in edge detection. Pattern Recognition Letters 32(5), 676–693 (2011)
11. Hancock, E.R., Kittler, J.: Adaptive estimation of hysteresis thresholds. In: Proc. IEEE Computer Society Conference on Computer Vision and Pattern Recognition, pp. 196–201. IEEE (1991)
12. Medina-Carnicer, R., Madrid-Cuevas, F.J., Munoz-Salinas, R., Carmona-Poyato, A.: Solving the process of hysteresis without determining the optimal thresholds. Pattern Recognition 43(4), 1224–1232 (2010)
13. Medina-Carnicer, R., Munoz-Salinas, R., Yeguas-Bolivar, E., Diaz-Mas, L.: A novel method to look for the hysteresis thresholds for the canny edge detector. Pattern Recognition 44(6), 1201–1211 (2011)
14. Medina-Carnicer, R., Carmona-Poyato, A., Munoz-Salinas, R., Madrid-Cuevas, F.J.: Determining hysteresis thresholds for edge detection by combining the advantages and disadvantages of thresholding methods 19(1), 165–173 (2010)
15. Yitzhaky, Y., Peli, E.: A method for objective edge detection evaluation and detector parameter selection 25(8), 1027–1033 (2003)
16. Medina-Carnicer, R., Madrid-Cuevas, F.J., Carmona-Poyato, A., Munoz-Salinas, R.: On candidates selection for hysteresis thresholds in edge detection. Pattern Recognition 42(7), 1284–1296 (2009)
17. Arbelaez, P., Maire, M., Fowlkes, C., Malik, J.: Contour detection and hierarchical image segmentation. IEEE Trans. Pattern Anal. Mach. Intell. 33(5), 898–916 (2011)

An Artificial Immune System Approach for Malware Detection

Jinquan Zeng[1] and Weiwen Tang[2]

[1] School of Computer Science & Engineering,
University of Electronic Science and Technology of China 610054 Chengdu, China
[2] Sichuan Communication Research Planning & Designing Co., Ltd.,
610041 Chengdu, China
zengjq@uestc.edu.cn, tangww@sctele.com

Abstract. Artificial immune system(AIS) is an efficient solution for network security. In this paper, an artificial immune system approach for malware detection is proposed, which is referred to AISMD. In AISMD, the method to build the profile of benign executables in computer systems is given. Based on the built model of benign executable, the detectors are generated to detect malware. Experimental results show that AISMD is an efficient method to build the profile of benign executable and extract the characteristics of the executable, and has better detecting ability than that of the previous techniques.

Keywords: Artificial immune system, Negative selection algorithm, Malware.

1 Introduction

With the development of Internet, more and more computers and mobile smart devices connect to the Internet. The growing connectivity of computers and mobile smart devices through the Internet makes an hacker launch attacks easily. McAfee threats report [1] said that they gathered only 792 mobile threat samples in 2011, but at the first quarter 2013, the number of mobile malware reached 50926 and the number of general malwares was more than 128 million. In order to defense malwares, many researchers begin to study malwares detection [2].

In order to detect unknown malwares, some detection techniques were proposed, including behavior-based method [3], Data mining method [4], based on Artificial immune system (AIS) method [5], et al. AIS generally includes clonal selection based algorithms, negative selection based algorithms and artificial immune network models. One of the major algorithms developed within AIS is the Negative Selection Algorithm (NSA). The initial NSA was proposed by Forrest et al. and early works in NSAs used the problem in binary representation [5]. Recently, more research focuses on real-valued negative selection algorithm (RNS) [6]. Another important variation among RNSs, is V-detector [7]. Zhang et al. [8] proposed a malware detection model, named NSAPF. The researchers of this paper has done some related works in the anti-virus field and achieved

L. Pan et al. (Eds.): BIC-TA 2014, CCIS 472, pp. 557–561, 2014.

some [8]. The main related work is that benign and malicious program are both used to construction instruction library. But zhang et al. only uses two-bytes instruction, we adopt real-valued negative selection algorithm and many bytes instruction.

2   Proposed Approach

2.1   Antibody Gene

Define the binary strings extracted from benign executables as antibody gene, and let Agd_l devote the antibody gene set given by:

$$Agd_l = \{ad \,|ad \in D_l, |ad| = l, l \in N \,\} \tag{1}$$

where l is the length of antibody gene (the number of bytes), N is the natural number and D_l is the binary strings extracted from the benign executables. D_l is described by the equation (2), where the function $f_e(b, i, l)$ extracts the binary string from the benign executable $b(b \in B)$, B is the benign executable set, i is the extracted position and l is the number of extracted bytes, respectively.

$$D_l = \bigcup_{b \in B} \bigcup_{l \in N, i=0}^{|b|} \{f_e(b, i, l)\} \tag{2}$$

$$ad_g = \frac{ad_g^b / B_g}{ad_g^b / B_g + ad_g^m / M_g} \tag{3}$$

$$ad_f = \frac{ad_f^b / B_f}{ad_f^b / B_f + ad_f^m / M_f} \tag{4}$$

$$\sqrt{ad_g^2 + ad_f^2} \geq \delta \tag{5}$$

In order to select the fit antibody gene, the antibody gene ad satisfies the equation (5),where ad_g describes its occurrence frequency on gene sequence(described by the equation (3),where ad_g^b is the number of ad occurrence count in the benign executable, B_g is the total gene number in the benign executables, ad_g^m is the number of ad occurrence count in the malwares, and M_g is the total gene number in the benign executable.),ad_f describes its occurrence frequency on files (described by the equation (4),where ad_f^b is the file number of ad occurrence count in the benign executable, B_f is the total file number in the benign executable,ad_f^m is the file number of ad occurrence count in the malwares, and M_f is the total file number in the benign executable.), and δ is the threshold value.

Let Agd denote the antibody gene library given by:

$$Agd = Agd_{l_1} \cup Agd_{l_2} \cup, \cdots, \cup Agd_{l_n} \tag{6}$$

where $l_i \in N, i = 1 \cdots n$ is the length of antibody gene, and N is the natural number.

2.2 Antigen Presenting

Antigens are defined as the executables and the characteristics of the executables are extracted by the antibody gene library Agd. Let C devote the set of executable characteristics given by:

$$C = \{\langle x_{l_1}, x_{l_2}, \cdots, x_{l_n} \rangle \,|\, 0 \le x_{l_i} \le 1,\ x_{l_i} = f_c(e, Agd_{l_i}), i = 1, \cdots, n\} \qquad (7)$$

where $x_{l_i}, i = 1, \cdots, n$ is the characteristic of the executable e extracted by the antibody gene set Agd_{l_i} , and n is the dimension; the function $f_c(e, Agd_{l_i})$ counts the characteristic of the executable e in the antibody gene set Agd_{l_i} , described by the equation (8) . The equation (8) shows that the state vector of the executable is made up of the characteristics extracted from the whole antibody gene set Agd_{l_i}, $i = 1, \cdots, n$.

$$f_c(e, Agd_{l_i}) = \frac{\left| Agd_{l_i} \cap \left\{ \bigcup_{l_i \in N, j=0}^{|e|} \{f_e(e, j, l_i)\} \right\} \right|}{\left| \bigcup_{l_i \in N, j=0}^{|e|} \{f_e(e, j, l_i)\} \right|} \qquad (8)$$

2.3 Self Elements

Let S denote the benign executables set given by:

$$S = \{\langle ch, rd \rangle \,|\, ch \in C_b, rd \in R\} \qquad (9)$$

where ch is the characteristics of the benign executables, C_b is the set of the characteristics of the benign executables, rd is the self radius of benign executables, and R is the real number, respectively.

2.4 Detectors

Let D denote the detector set given by:

$$D = \{\langle ch, rd \rangle \,|\, ch \in U, rd \in R\} \qquad (10)$$

where ch is the characteristics of the detectors, $U = [0, 1]^n$, rd is the detection radius of the detectors, and R is the real number, respectively. D is subdivided into immature and mature detectors. Immature detectors are newly generated ones given by:

$$I = \{\langle x_{l_1}, x_{l_2}, \cdots, x_{l_n} \rangle \,|\, 0 \le x_{l_i} \le 1, i = 1, \cdots, n\} \qquad (11)$$

Mature detectors are the ones that are tolerant to S given by:

$$\begin{aligned} M = \{x \,|\, &\forall s \in S,\ f_d(s, x) > s.rd, \exists s' \in S, \forall s'' \in S, \\ &f_d(s', x) < f_d(s'', x),\ x.rd = f_d(s', x) - s'.rd\} \end{aligned} \qquad (12)$$

The equation (12) shows that a detector is tolerant to S if the detector does not lie within S. Furthermore, the detection radius of the detectors is decided by the nearest benign executable in S and $f_d(x, y)$ is the Euclidean distance between x and y.

2.5 Immune Surveillance

After the characteristics c of an executable e is extracted, its characteristics are presented to the detectors for detecting and the detecting process is given by:

$$f_{detect}(c) = \begin{cases} 0, & \text{iff } \forall m \in M \wedge f_d(c,m) > m.ra \\ 1, & \text{iff } \exists m \in M \wedge f_d(c,m) \leq m.ra \end{cases} \qquad (13)$$

if the executable lies within the detection radius of a detector, the function $f_{detect}(c)$ returns 1 and then the executable is malicious. Otherwise, the function $f_{detect}(c)$ returns 0 and then the executable is benign.

3   Simulations and Experimental Results

To study the property and possible advantages of AISMD, we compared AISMD with the methods used by Schultz [4] and Peng [9]. we performed the experiments with our dataset, which was gathered from a freshly installed Windows XP running MSOffice 2000 and Visual C++. The number of the benign executables was 480. The number of the malicious executables was 812. There were no duplicate programs in the data set and every example in the set was labeled either malicious or benign by the commercial virus scanner. All labels were assumed to be correct. The 234 benign executables and 243 malicious executables were used to construct gene library and other benign executables and malicious executables are used to test. Table 1 shows the comparison for detection performance, where self radius is 0.009, the selecting threshold is 0.6 and the number of detectors is 3800 in AISMD. Table 1 shows the signature-based method has the worst true-positive rate, the learning-based methods have better detection performance than that of signature-based methods, and Naive Bayes, Multi-Naive Bayes and SVM have almost same overall accuracy; our proposed approach, AISMD, has higher detection performance than that of Naive Bayes, Multi-Naive Bayes and SVM.

Table 1. The comparison for detection performance of Schultz[4],Peng[9] and AISMD

	TP	TN	FP	FN	Detection Rate	False Positive Rate
Signature Method [4] -Bytes	1102	1000	0	2163	33.75%	0%
RIPPER [4] -DLLs used	22	187	19	16	57.89%	9.22%
-DLL function calls	27	190	16	11	71.05%	7.77%
-DLLs with counted function calls	20	195	11	18	52.63%	5.34%
Naive Bayes [4] -Strings	3176	960	41	89	97.43%	3.80%
Multi-Naive Bayes [4] -Bytes	3191	940	61	74	97.76%	6.01%
SVM [9]	3188	938	63	77	97.64%	6.29%
AISMD	563	44	2	6	98.95%	4.35%

4   Conclusion

Traditional signature-based method cannot detect unknown malicious executables or its variants. In order to detect unknown malware, an artificial immune system approach for malware detection is proposed in this paper, which is referred to AISMD. In AISMD, the method to build the model of benign executable is given. In order to avoid covering the malware space, malwares are used to build the model of benign executable. Based on the built model of benign executable, the detectors are generated to detect malware. Experimental results show that AISMD is an efficient method to build the profile of benign executable and extract the characteristics of the executable, and has better detecting ability than that of the previous techniques.

Acknowledgments. This work is supported by 863 High Tech Project of China under Grant No. 2013AA01A213, special technology development fund for research institutes of the Ministry of Science and Technology of China (2011EG126038 and 2013EG126063) and Applied Basic Research Program of Sichuan Provincial Science and Technology Department (2014JY0140).

References

1. McAfee Threats Report: First Quarter (2013), http://www.mcafee.com/au/resources/reports/rp-quarterly-threat-q1-2013.pdf
2. Fan, W.Q., Lei, X., An, J.: Obfuscated Malicious Code Detection with Path Condition Analysis. Journal of Networks 9(5), 1208–1214 (2014)
3. Iker, B., Urko, Z., Simin, N.T.: Crowdroid: Behavior-Based Malware Detection System for Android. In: Proceedings of the 1st ACM Workshop on Security and Privacy in Smartphones and Mobile Devices, pp. 15–26 (2011)
4. Schultz, M., Eskin, E., Zadok, E., Stolf, S.: Data Mining Methods for Detection of New Malicious Executables. In: Proceedings of IEEE Symposium on Security and Privacy, pp. 38–49. IEEE Computer Society (2001)
5. Forrest, S., Perelson, A.S., Allen, L., Cherukuri, R.: Self-nonself Discrimination in a Computer. In: Proceedings of the 1994 IEEE Symposium on Research in Security and Privacy (1994)
6. Gonzalez, F.A., Dasgupta, D.: Anomaly Detection Using Real-Valued Negative Selection. Genetic Programming and Evolvable Machines 4, 383–403 (2003)
7. Ji, Z., Dasgupta, D.: Real-valued Negative Selection Algorithm with Variable-Sized Detectors. In: Deb, K., Tari, Z. (eds.) GECCO 2004. LNCS, vol. 3102, pp. 287–298. Springer, Heidelberg (2004)
8. Zhang, P.T., Wang, W., Tan, Y.: A malware Detection Model Based on A Negative Selection Algorithm with Penalty Factor. Science China Information Sciences 53(12), 2461–2471 (2010)
9. Peng, H., Wang, J.: Research of Malicious Executables Detection Method Based on Support Vector Machine. Acta Electronica Sinica 33(2), 276–278 (2005)

Time-Free Tissue P Systems for Solving the Hamilton Path Problem

Xiangxiang Zeng[1], Ningxiang Ding[1], Fei Xing[2], and Xiangrong Liu[1,3,*]

[1] Department of Computer Science,
Xiamen University, Xiamen 361005, China
{xzeng,xrliu}@xmu.edu.cn, sunnydnx@gmail.com
[2] Department of Aeronautics, Xiamen University, Xiamen, China
f.xing@xmu.edu.cn
[3] Shenzhen Research Institute of Xiamen University, Shenzhen, China

Abstract. Tissue P systems are distributed and parallel computing models inspired by the communication behavior of living cells in tissues. Theoretically, tissue P systems can generate exponential working space in linear time, which makes it feasible to solve computational hard problems in polynomial time. In traditional tissue P systems, the execution of each rule takes exactly one time unit, thus making the system work synchronously. However, the restriction does not correspond with the biological fact, since biochemical reactions may vary in unpredicted conditions. In this work, we define the timed tissue P systems by adding a time mapping to each rules to specify the execution time for them. Furthermore, a uniform and time-free solution to Hamilton Path Problems is obtained by a family of such systems, where the execution time of rules can change and the output produced is always correct. *abstract environment.*

Keywords: Membrane computing, Tissue P systems, Time-free solution, Hamilton Path Problem.

1 Introduction

Membrane computing, an innovative branch of natural computing, was initially introduced by G. Păun in the late 20th century [12]. Inspired by the division behavior of living cells, as well as the structure of cells in tissues, or even other higher organs, P systems provide distributed and parallel computing models. Most of the variants of P systems are described during the past years, and people defined them as four classes – cell-like P systems, tissue-like P systems, neural-like P systems, and population P systems. Many variants have also been investigated during the past years, and most of them are proved to be computationally universal (equal in power to Turing machines). A series of applications of P systems, in biology, economics, graphics, optimization, fault diagnosis, image processing etc., were reported. An overview of the field can be found in [2],

---

* Corresponding author.

L. Pan et al. (Eds.): BIC-TA 2014, CCIS 472, pp. 562–565, 2014.
© Springer-Verlag Berlin Heidelberg 2014

[11] and [13], with up-to-date information available at the membrane computing website (http://ppage.psystems.eu).

In tissue P systems, the membrane structure is a directed graph and cells are placed in the nodes of it. Each cell contains several objects and some rules. Cells can communicate with others through the edges. It has been proved that the tissue P systems can solve some computational hard problems in polynomial or even linear time [3–5, 7–10].

In traditional tissue P systems, rules are used in a non-deterministic parallel way. In this paper, timed tissue P systems, the tissue P systems without a constraint on time, are proposed. And time-free tissue P systems, which can produce correct output with a changeable execution time of rules, are a special type of timed P systems. In [1], time-free tissue P system was first proposed. Soon afterwards, some other time-free tissue P systems were investigated in [6, 14]. In this paper, we consider a time-free solution for the Hamilton Path Problems by constructing a family of recognizer tissue P systems.

2   Solving the Hamilton Path Problem with Time-Free Tissue P System

Hamiltonian path is a path of length n that visits all nodes in α once, and only once. In a Hamilton Path Problem, we find out if there is a Hamiltonian path in graph α. We consider an directed graph $\alpha = (N, E)$, in which $N = \{n_1, n_2, \ldots, n_n\}$ is the set of vertices, and E is the set of edges. And we construct a family of time-free tissue P systems:

$$\Pi(n, f) = (\Gamma, \Omega, \omega_1, \omega_2, R, i_{in}, i_{out}, f),$$

where

- $\Gamma = \sum \bigcup \{a_{i,j}, b_i, N_i \mid 1 \leq i, j \leq n\} \bigcup \{t, yes, no\}$.
- $\Omega = \Gamma - \{yes, no\}$.
- $\omega_1 = \{b_1, \ldots, b_n, f\}, \omega_2 = \{yes, no\}$.
- $i_{in} = 1$ is the input cell.
- $i_{out} = 0$ is the environment.
- $f \colon R \to \mathbb{N}$ is the time mapping from R to natural numbers.
- R is the set of rules.
- $\Sigma = \{e_{i,j} \mid$ for all $1 \leq i, j \leq n\}$, there is not an edge between n_i and n_j.

Three stages are followed to explain how the system $\Pi(n, f)$ works to compute the Hamilton Path Problem.

Generating stage:

$g_1 : (2, no/\lambda, 0)$

$g_{2,i} : [B]_i \to [a_{i,1}]_1[N_{i,1}]_1$, for $1 \leq i \leq n$

$g_{3,ij} : [N_{i,j}]_1 \to [a_{i,j+1}]_1[N_{i,j+1}]_1$, for $1 \leq i \leq n, 1 \leq j \leq n - 3$

$g_{4,ij} : [N_{i,j}]_1 \to [a_{i,j+1}]_1[a_{i,j+2}]_1$, for $1 \leq i \leq n, j = n - 2$

$g_{5,ivh} : (1, a_{i,v}a_{i+1,h}e_{v,h}/\lambda, 0)$, for $0 \leq i \leq n - 1, 1 \leq v \leq n, 1 \leq h \leq n$

Checking stage:

$\mathfrak{c}_1 : [a_{x,i}]_i \to [a]_{1+i}[a]_{1+i}$, for $1 \leq i \leq n - 1$, $1 \leq x \leq n$ is arbitrary

$\mathfrak{c}_2 : [a_{x,n}]_n \to [t]_n[t]_n$ $1 \leq x \leq n$ is an arbitrary number

Outputting stage:

$\mathfrak{o}_1 : (n, t/yes, 2))$

$\mathfrak{o}_2 : (n, yes/no, 0)$

With the maximally parallel way, at the beginning of the first stage, object no is sent to the environment by rule $\mathfrak{g}_1$. After that, with rule $\mathfrak{g}_2$, $\mathfrak{g}_3$ and $\mathfrak{g}_4$, we can create n^n new cells and each cell describes one n-length path with n objects $a_{i,j}$. This process will be completed in $f(\mathfrak{g}_2) + f(\mathfrak{g}_3) + f(\mathfrak{g}_4)$ time units, and it takes n valid steps to complete it. Then, $\mathfrak{g}_5$ starts to work. And, $e_{v,h}$ over Σ Thus, the edges which are not in directed graph α will be removed. This process will cost $n - 1$ valid steps at most. Checking stage begins afterwards to find out if there is a hamiltonian path. It will take at most n valid steps in this stage.

If at least one Hamilton path exists to visit all nodes exactly once, we get object yes from the environment and the result of the computation is positive.

We can easily prove that the system above $\Pi(n, f)$ can be built in polynomial time with respect to n, which means the number of nodes in the graph α.

Theorem 1. *A family of timed tissue P system $\Pi = \{\Pi(n, f)|u \in I_x\}$ can be constructed as a uniform time-free solution to the Hamilton Path Problem. For any time mapping f, the execution time of the rules does not influence the results of the system.*

Proof. It is easy to prove that the systems constructed above is time-free sound, time-free complete, and time-free polynomially bounded. Therefore, it is a time-free solution to the Hamilton Path Problem.

References

1. Cavaliere, M., Sburlan, D.: Time and Synchronization in Membrane Systems. Fundamenta Informaticae 64(1), 65–77 (2005)
2. Ciobanu, G., Păun, G., Pérez-Jiménez, M.J.: Applications of Membrane Computing. Springer (2006)
3. Díaz-Pernil, D., Gutiérrez-Naranjo, M.A., Pérez-Jiménez, M.J., Riscos-Núñez, A.: A Linear-Time Tissue P System Based Solution for the 3-Coloring Problem. Theoretical Computer Science 171(2), 81–93 (2007)
4. Díaz-Pernil, D., Gutiérrez-Naranjo, M.A., Jesús Pérez-Jímenez, M., Riscos-Núñez, A.: Solving Subset Sum in Linear Time by Using Tissue P Systems with Cell Division. In: Mira, J., Álvarez, J.R. (eds.) IWINAC 2007. LNCS, vol. 4527, pp. 170–179. Springer, Heidelberg (2007)
5. Díaz-Pernil, D., Gutiérrez-Naranjo, M.A., Pérez-Jimenez, M.J., Riscos-Nunez, A.: Solving the Partition Problem by Using Tissue-Like P Systems with Cell Division. In: Proceedings of the Third International Conference on Bio-Inspired Computing: Theories and Applications, pp. 43–47 (2008)
6. Pan, L., Zeng, X., Zhang, X.: Time-free Spiking Neural P Systems. Neural Computation 23(5), 1320–1342 (2011)

7. Song, T., Macías-Ramosb, L.F., Pan, L., Pérez-Jiménez, M.J.: Time-free solution to SAT Problem Using P Systems with Active Membranes. Theoretical Computer Science 529, 61–68 (2014)
8. Pan, L., Alhazov, A., Ishdorj, T.O.: Further Remarks on P Systems with Active Membranes, Separation, Merging, and Release Rules. Journal of Parallel and Distributed Computing 66(6), 867–872 (2006)
9. Wang, J., Hoogeboom, H.J., Pan, L., Păun, G., Pérez-Jiménez, M.J.: Spiking Neural Systems with Weights. Neural Computation 22(10), 2615–2646 (2010)
10. Zhang, X., Wang, S., Niu, Y., Pan, L.: Tissue P Systems with Cell Separation: Attacking the Partition Problem. Science China 54(2), 293–304 (2011)
11. Păun, G., Rozenberg, G., Salomaa, A.: The Oxford handbook of Membrane Computing. Oxford University Press (2010)
12. Păun, G.: Computing with Membranes. Journal of Computer and System Sciences 61(1), 108–143 (2000)
13. Păun, G.: Membrane Computing. An Introduction. Springer, Berlin (2002)
14. Song, T., Wang, X., Zheng, H.: Time-free Solution to Hamilton Path Problems Using P Systems with D-Division. Journal of Applied Mathematics (2013)

Face Classification via a Novel Two-Dimensional Extreme Learning Machine

Fan Zhang[1,2,*], Lin Qi[1], and Enqing Chen[1]

[1] School of Information Engineering, Zhengzhou University, Zhengzhou, 450052, China
[2] School of Information Engineering,
North China University of Water Resources and Electric Power, Zhengzhou, 450045, China
zfgh8221@163.com

Abstract. Because of face images are naturally two-dimensional data, there have been several 2D feature extraction methods to deal with facial images while there are few 2D effective classifiers. In this work, by using a linear tensor projection, a new two-dimensional classifier based on extreme learning machine is introduced. Due to the proposed algorithm can classify matrix data directly without vectorizing them, the intrinsic structure information of the input data can be reserved. It is demonstrated that the proposed 2D-ELM achieves better recognition performance.

Keywords: Face recognition, Feature extraction, Extreme learning machine, Classification.

1 Introduction

On account of face image is the most common visual pattern in our surrounding life, face recognition has attracted much attention from researchers over the past several years. It seems that facial image recognition being regarded as a fundamental field of biometrics which has been applied to various areas. Generally, there are two main steps in a typical face recognition system [1]. In the first step, methods of feature extraction are usually used to derive an effective representation of the facial images. These features include abundant information of the image for future classification, and a high-dimensional data can be set into a low-dimensional equivalent representation. The second step is to classify a new face image with the chosen representation. Principal component analysis (PCA) [2] and liner discriminative analysis (LDA) [3] are two of the most popular classical subspace learning methods in many existing dimensionality reduction algorithms. The PCA is a unsupervised algorithm supports to find the most useful image representation while LDA takes the label information into account. Both of them operate on vector rather than higher order tensor. Due to the fact that grey-scale images of face are naturally two-dimensional tensor, these tensor objects have to be reshaped into vectors first for PCA and LDA. It is generally accepted that this reshaping breaks the potential spatial structure of the original data and leads high computational burden. To address these issues, many algorithms which treat the input image

---

* Corresponding author.

L. Pan et al. (Eds.): BIC-TA 2014, CCIS 472, pp. 566–570, 2014.

as a 2D matrix without vectorizing them are proposed, such as 2DPCA [4], 2DLDA [5], $(2D)^2$PCA [6], and $(2D)^2$LDA [7]. Furthermore, in order to solve the higher order tensor data, several multilinear methods which can deal with the input data based on tensor representation are designed too. For example, Multilinear principal component analysis (MPCA) [8], a tensor version of PCA, applies PCA transformation on each mode of tensors while multilinear discriminant analysis (MDA)[9] applies LDA to transform each dimensionality of tensors. Hence, the natural structure of the objects will be reserved and a better performance will be achieved.

On the other hand, for the classification step, the classical image classifiers with good generalization include nearest neighbor (NN), artificial neural network (ANN), support vector machine (SVM) [10], and so on. With the same limitation, traditional classification methods are usually vector-based, such as SVM and ANN. When they are employed to classify an input image, we have to transform matrix data into vector data at first. Besides, due to the distance between two data with form either tensor or vector is the same, NN classifier can be used to classify the feature matrices directly. Therefore, NN classifier is usually applied after many multilinear dimension reduction methods just as in [8]. However, the structure of NN classifier is too simple to obtain satisfying recognition rate. Consequently, it is desirable to propose a novel classifier which can classify matrix data directly and to preserve the intrinsic structure effectively.

Extreme learning machine (ELM) [11,12] is originally proposed as a new learning algorithm for single-hidden layer feed forward neural networks (SLFNs) which can be used both in regression and classification with an extremely fast learning speed. This method randomly assigns the input weights and the bias of neurons in the hidden layer, while the output weights are obtained using the Moore-Penrose (MP) generalized inverse. In [13,14], a new classifier which employs left projecting vectors and right projecting vectors to regress each matrix data set to its label for each category has been introduced for matrix data classification. Evoked by the above model, in this paper, an extend ELM method is designed for image classification by using left and right projection vectors instead of the input weights matrix, which named two-dimensional extreme learning machine (2D-ELM). Compared with traditional vector based classification approaches, the new classifier keeps the natural structure of input data and has a faster learning speed.

As mentioned above, feature extraction should retain most of the useful information in input data while keeping the dimension of the features as low as possible. In this paper, MPCA is used for feature extraction from facial images with two (left and right) projection matrices to maximize the captured variation. Then the extracted feature matrixes are put into the proposed 2D-ELM for classify. Several experiments on different face databases are presented for illustration.

2   Two-Dimensional Extreme Learning Machine

Following the notation in [15], we denote vectors by lowercase letters, e.g., x; matrices by uppercase boldface, e.g., U; and tensors by calligraphic letters, e.g., $\mathcal{A}$. Tensor is a generalization of vector and matrix. Vectors are first-order tensors, and matrices are second-order tensors. An Nth-order tensor is denoted as $\mathcal{A} \in \mathbb{R}^{I_1 \times I_2 \times \cdots \times I_N}$. It is addressed by N indices i_n, and each i_n addresses the n-mode of $\mathcal{A}$.

2.1   Theoretical Foundation of the Proposed 2D-ELM

As the definition of ELM in [12], the data through input layer to hidden layer is a linear transformation of the input data x with model of $w_i x$ where x should be reformulated to a vector by connecting each row (or column) of a tensor firstly. There have been several precedents of putting a vector-based approach to a tensor-based method for matrix data analysis, such as $(2D)^2$PCA and 2DLDA are the 2D extension of PCA and LDA. As the description in [5], a set of N labeled matrix samples $\{X_1, X_1, \cdots, X_N\}$ are available for training, and each matrix sample $X_i \in \mathbb{R}^{I_1 \times I_2}$, the 2DLDA objective is to find two linear transformations $U^{(1)} \in \mathbb{R}^{I_1 \times P_1}(P_1 \leqslant I_1)$ and $U^{(2)} \in \mathbb{R}^{I_2 \times P_2}(P_2 \leqslant I_2)$ that project a sample X_i to

$$Y_i = U^{(1)^T} X_i U^{(2)} = X_i \times_1 U^{(1)^T} \times_2 U^{(2)^T} \in \mathbb{R}^{P_1 \times P_2} \tag{1}$$

where $U^{(1)}$, $U^{(2)}$ can be calculated according to the corresponding objective functions.

Motivated by the above linear conversion, one direct way to construct a two-dimensional ELM based classifier is to replace the traditional projection term $w_i x_j$ by its tensor counterpart, such as $u_i^T X_j v_i$, where u_i and v_j are the left and right projection vectors. Consequently, for a set of N matrix features $\{(X_j, t_j)\}_{j=1}^N$, with $X_j \in \mathbb{R}^{m \times n}$, $t_j \in \mathbb{R}^C$, we can have

$$y_j = \sum_{i=1}^L \beta_i g(u_i^T X_j v_i + b_i) \tag{2}$$

where $u_i \in \mathbb{R}^m$, $v_i \in \mathbb{R}^n$, $b_i \in \mathbb{R}$, and $\beta_i \in \mathbb{R}^C$, $i = 1, 2, \cdots, L$, and L is the number of hidden nodes. With the formula (2), the vector w_i contains mn elements is replaced by $v_i \otimes u_i$ that consists of $m + n$ parameters, the input data X can be treated with the form of matrix without vectoring them. As the random selection of input weights w_i, the value of u_i and v_i can be randomly determined too. Moreover, it is demonstrated that ELM is insensitive to the values of input layer weights and the hidden layer biases [12].

According to the derivation in [13,14], there is $\|w_i\| = w_i^T w_i = Tr(w_i w_i^T)$, and then we can have

$$\begin{aligned} u_i^T X v_i &= Tr(u_i^T X v_i) = Tr(X v_i u_i^T) = Tr((u_i v_i^T)^T X) \\ &= (Vec(u_i v_i^T))^T Vec(X) = w_i x \end{aligned} \tag{3}$$

Here $Vec(u_i v_i^T)$ and $Vec(X)$ is the vectorization of matrix $u_i v_i^T$ and X. In Equation (3), it is demonstrated that $u_i^T X v_i$ equals to $w_i x$ and Equation (2) can get the same result.

Utilizing the tensor based conversion in Equation (2), the input matrix image data can be calculated directly without vectoring them. Not only the inner structural information among the elements of the image can be preserved, but also fewer parameters need to be computed. For the same image $X \in \mathbb{R}^{m \times n}$, there are only $(m + n + 1 + c)L$ parameters need to be calculated for 2D-ELM, while $(mn + 1 + c)L$ for ELM.

All the weights and bias will be determined randomly. After confirming the projecting vectors and biases, the output weights β_i can be determined while the matrix H should be changed as follows

$$H = \begin{bmatrix} G(u_1^T X_1 v_1 + b_1) & \cdots & G(u_L^T X_1 v_L + b_L) \\ \vdots & \ddots & \vdots \\ G(u_1^T X_N v_1 + b_1) & \cdots & G(u_L^T X_N v_L + b_L) \end{bmatrix} \tag{4}$$

H is the hidden output matrix for 2D-ELM, then the output weights can be solved by the following optimal

$$\widehat{\beta} = \arg\min_{\beta} \sum_{j=1}^{N} \| \sum_{i=1}^{L} \beta_i g(u_i^T X_j v_i + b_i) - t_j \|$$

$$= \arg\min_{\beta} \|H\beta - T\| \tag{5}$$

where

$$\beta = \begin{pmatrix} \beta_1^T \\ \vdots \\ \beta_L^T \end{pmatrix}, \quad \text{and} \quad T = \begin{pmatrix} t_1^T \\ \vdots \\ t_N^T \end{pmatrix} \tag{6}$$

With the above description, this algorithm is called two-dimensional extern learning machine, where two-dimensional represents that it is designed for the matrix input data.

Applying the proposed 2D-ELM method for face recognition, for a new tensor input $\mathcal{X} \in \mathbb{R}^{m \times n \times Q}$, where $m \times n$ is the dimension of each face image, and Q is the amount of the input images. The output of the proposed 2D-ELM can be computed in Equation (2), and the obtained y_j should be compared with the real corresponding class label value t_j to check the effectiveness of the learning algorithm.

3 Conclusions

In this paper, a new 2D-ELM classification is designed to classify matrix data directly for face recognition. For the proposed algorithm, instead of using the high dimensional input weight vector in hidden layer, a left and right projecting vector with random values are applied to preserve the natural structure information of the input two-dimensional data. There are two advantages of using 2D-ELM for face image classification, one is higher recognition rate can be obtained by classifying matrix data directly, the other is faster computing speed can be achieved benefits by much less parameters to be calculated with 2D-ELM than the traditional ELM. In the future research, we can extend ELM to higher order for more widely application.

Acknowledgments. This work is supported by the National Natural Science Foundation of China under grant No. 61331021.

References

1. Zong, W., Huang, G.B.: Face Recognition Based on Extreme Learning Machine. Neurocomputing 74(16), 2541–2551 (2011)
2. Turk, M., Pentland, A.: Eigenfaces for Recognition. Journal of Cognitive Neuroscience 3(1), 71–86 (1991)
3. Belhumeur, P.N., Hespanha, J.P., Krigman, D.J.: Eigenfaces vs. Fisherfaces: Recognition Using Class Specific Linear Projection. IEEE Trans. on Pattern Analysis and Machine Intelligence 19(7), 711–720 (1997)
4. Yang, J., Zhang, D., Frangi, A.F., Yang, J.Y.: Two-dimensional PCA: A New Approach to Appearance-Based Face Representation and Recognition. IEEE Trans. on Pattern Analysis and Machine Intelligence 26(1), 131–137 (2004)
5. Li, M., Yuan, B.Z.: 2D-LDA: A Statistical Linear Discriminant Analysis for Image Matrix. Pattern Recognition Letters 26(5), 527–532 (2005)
6. Zhang, D., Zhou, Z.H.: (2d)2pca: 2-directional 2-dimensional pca for Efficient Face Representation and Recognition. Neurocomputing 29, 224–231 (2005)
7. Noushath, S., Hemantha Kumar, G., Shivakumara, P.: (2d)2lda: An Efficient Approach for Face Recognition. Pattern Recognition 39, 1396–1400 (2006)
8. Lu, H., Plataniotis, K.N., Venetsanopoulos, A.N.: MPCA: Multilinear Principal Component Analysis of Tensor Objects. IEEE Trans. on Neural Networks 19(1), 18–39 (2008)
9. Yan, S., Xu, D., Yang, Q., Zhang, L., Tang, X., Zhang, H.J.: Multilinear Discriminant Analysis for Face Recognition. IEEE Trans. on Image Processing 16(1), 212–220 (2007)
10. Qin, J., He, Z.S.: A SVM Face Recognition Method Based on Gabor-Featured Key Points. In: Proc. 4th IEEE Conf. on Machine Learning and Cybernetics, pp. 5144–5149 (2005)
11. Huang, G.B., Zhou, H., Ding, X., Zhang, R.: Extreme Learning Machine for Regression and Multiclass Classification. IEEE Trans. on Systems, Man, and Cybernetics, Part B: Cybernetics 42(2), 513–529 (2012)
12. Huang, G.B., Zhu, Q.Y., Siew, C.K.: Extreme Learning Machine: A New Learning Scheme of Feedforward Neural Networks. In: Proc. Int. Joint Conf. Neural Networks (IJCNN 2004), Budapest, Hungary, vol. 2, pp. 25–29 (2004)
13. Huang, G.B., Zhu, Q.Y., Siew, C.K.: Extreme Learning Machine: Theory and Applications. Neurocomputing 70, 489–501 (2006)
14. Hou, C., Nie, F., Yi, D., Wu, Y.: Efficient Image classification via multiple rank regression. IEEE Trans. on Image Processing 22(1), 340–352 (2013)
15. Lu, J., Zhao, J., Cao, F.: Extended Feed Forward Neural Networks with Random Weights for Face Recognition. Neurocomputing 136, 96–102 (2014)

Prediction Nucleic Acid Secondary Structure with Planar Pseudoknots and Genetic Algorithm

Kai Zhang[1,2,*], Xinquan Huang[1,2], Wei Hu[1,2], and Jun Liu[1,2]

[1] School of Computer Science, Wuhan University of Science and Technology,
Wuhan 430081 P.R. China
[2] Hubei Province Key Laboratory of Intelligent Information Processing
and Real-time Industrial System
zhangkai@wust.edu.cn

Abstract. In recent years, DNA and RNA molecules have shown great potential as a design medium for the construction of nanostructures and the programmed assembly of molecular computing. In this paper, we propose a novel genetic algorithm to predict nucleic acid secondary structure with planar pseudoknots. In our algorithm, the free energy and the number of continues base pairs stacking are used as fitness function to evaluate the individuals. We have compared the results obtained by our algorithm with RNAStructure. As will be discussed, our algorithm can efficiently predict the planar pseudoknots with lower free energy and more continues base pairs stacking.

Keywords: Secondary structure prediction, Genetic algorithm, Minimum free energy, Dynamic programming, Pseudoknots.

1 Introduction

In the past few decades, bio-computing has become a hot branch in natural computing [19, 2, 3]. DNA and RNA molecules have also shown great potential as a design medium for the construction of nanostructures and the pro-grammed assembly, such as 3D nanostructure design [4, 5], molecular computing and membrane computing [2, 6–9], DNA chips [10]. In these fields, it is very important to select nucleic acid sequences with required secondary structure.

In recent years, several dynamic programming algorithms have been proposed to predict secondary structures of DNA or RNA sequences. Zuker proposed an algorithm for prediction of RNA secondary structure [11]. The time complexities of the algorithms is $O(n^4)$. Andronescu et al. developed the PairFold algorithm for secondary structure prediction of minimum free energy [12]. Different dynamic programming algorithms with different scoring functions for predicting secondary structures [13–15]. Some improved algorithms based dynamic programming were proposed by Rivas in [16], Dirks in [17], and Reeder in [18]. But in practice, these algorithms cannot be applied to large sequences due to high computational complexity.

---

* Corresponding author.

L. Pan et al. (Eds.): BIC-TA 2014, CCIS 472, pp. 571–577, 2014.
© Springer-Verlag Berlin Heidelberg 2014

In this article, we propose a novel genetic algorithm to predict nucleic acid secondary structure with planar pseudoknots. The minimum free energy and the number of continues base pairs stacking are used as fitness function. Moreover, in order to validate our proposal, we have compared the results obtained by our algorithm with the results obtained by RNAStructure. Our algorithm can generate more stable nucleic acid secondary structure with lower free energy and more continues base pairs stacking.

2   Definition of the Problem

Single-stranded nucleic acid molecules can fold back onto itself to reduce their energy and form a stable structure like double helix, hairpin loops, internal loops, bulge loops, pseudpoknots etc. The stability of the duplex structure is based on the perfect fit of G $\equiv$ C and A=T (in DNA) or A=U (in RNA) base pairs into the Watson-Crick double helix structure.

In this paper, we use planar graph to represent the nucleic acid secondary structures, where the nodes are the individual nucleotides and the edges are the connections between neighbors from the backbone and the base pairs. The planar graph representation is shown in figure 1.

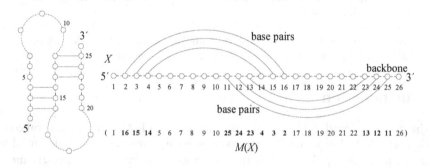

Fig. 1. The planar graph representation of nucleic acid secondary structures

Given a DNA string X=5'-$x_1x_2...x_n$-3' of length n, $M(X)$ is the one to one mapping of base-pairs of X, $M(X) = (m_1, m_2, ...m_i, ...m_n)$. If x_i bonds with x_j, the value of m_i are assigned to j and the value of m_j is assigned to i. If x_i do not bonds with any other bases, the value of m_i is assigned to i. An example of the $M(X)$ is shown in figure 1.

It is assumed that a structure with more number of base-pairs is more stable than that with fewer base-pairs. So if $M(X)$ contains more number of bonded base pairs, the corresponding secondary structure should be an candidate optimal solution. In order to predicted planar pseudoknots, we give three definitions of base pairs bonds.

Definition 1. Positive Bond: A base pairs (x_i, x_j) is Positive Bond if and only if they are bonded above the nucleic acid backbone, and the bond could not intersect any other existing above positive bonds, as shown in Figure 2, part A.

Definition 2. Negative Bond: A base pairs (x_i, x_j) is Negative Bond if and only if they are bonded below the nucleic acid backbone, and the bond could not intersect any other existing below negative bonds, as shown in Figure 2, part B.

Definition 3. Invalid Bond: If a base pairs (x_i, x_j) intersect with another existing positive bond, it could not to be assigned a positive bond. Then the algorithm should checks whether the base pairs can be assigned negative bond. If a base pairs (x_i, x_j) is neither Positive Bond nor Negative Bond; instead, it is an Invalid Bond, as shown in Figure 2.

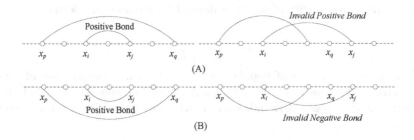

Fig. 2. Example of Positive Bond and Negative Bond

3   Genetic Algorithm for Nucleic Acid Secondary Structure Prediction

3.1   Evaluate Strategy and Fitness Function

Let $M(X) = (m_1, m_2, ...m_i, ...m_n)$ be a candidate individual. Firstly, our algorithm statistics continuous base-pair stacking, then the results are sorted in descending order. Secondly, every mi should be assigned positive bond or negative bond from the largest continuous base-pair stacking to the smallest, as shown in figure 3.

After all positive bonds and negative bonds are clearly assigned, the invalid bonds would be neglected. The fitness function is the accumulation of free energy, which contribute by continuous base-pair stacking. The fitness function be calculated as following:

$$f(M_k) = \sum \Delta G_{Stack(m_i, m_j)} \tag{1}$$

where M_k is the k-th individual in population, $\Delta G_{Stack(mi,mj)}$ is the free energy change of continuous base-pair stacking from position i to position j in M_k.

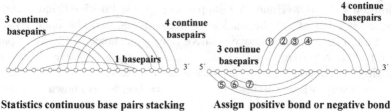

Statistics continuous base pairs stacking   Assign positive bond or negative bond

Fig. 3. Assign positive bonds or negative bonds in descending order

3.2   Roulette Wheel Selection

Roulette wheel method is adopted as the selection operation in this work. M_i is selected with a probability of p_i which defined by the following formula.

$$p_i = \frac{f_i}{\sum_{i=1}^{n} f_i} \tag{2}$$

where n is the number of population size. Selection is the method of tends to be chosen high fitness M_i. Low fitness M_i would be chosen a few. Selection works that high fitness individuals survive, while low fitness individuals become extinct.

3.3   Crossover Operator

The crossover operator exchanges parts of the genes from two parent individuals to generate two new individuals. In this paper, we have improved PMX as a secondary structure crossover operator. First, two crossover points i and j are chosen randomly, as shown in figure 4.

Subsequently, the offspring directly inherits the crossover sections from parents between i and j section. The section of the first parent which is copied directly to the offspring preserves position and adjacency bonds. Swap its genes section with those of another individual and produce two individual of descendants where position less than i or position greater than j.

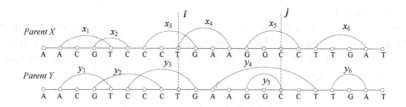

Fig. 4. Example of Crossover operator

Exchange the redundant genes according to the selected section, then find that exclusive base pair $y3$, $x2$, and $x3$ in the left chromosome and base pair $y5$, $x5$, and $x6$ in the right one are assigned to bond the wrong base pairs. Then, the exclusive base pairs are removed, as shown in figure 5.

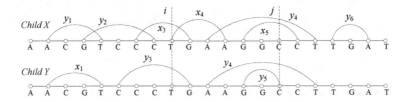

Fig. 5. Remove the wrong base pairs bond

3.4 Mutation Operator

The algorithm choose two points p and q randomly. There are two possibilities for crossing points p, in the first case base p paired with s and in the second case base p is alone. Another base q should be considered in similar situations.

3.5 Algorithm Flow

Step 1: Initializing the population, according to the input nucleic acid sequence X, generate *popsize* sequences M_1 to $M_{popsize}$ as chromosomes randomly;

Step 2: Calculate the fitness of each chromosome based on the current fitness of each one in the population, according to the formula (1);

Step 3: Execute the roulette wheel selection operator, and carry out crossover operation with probability $P_{crossover}$;

Step 4: Carry out mutation operator with probability $P_{mutation}$;

Step 5: Put the children chromosome that have generated through above operations into chromosome pool, and calculate their fitness values again. If the number of the chromosomes exceeds the pools capacity, delete the chromosomes of smaller fitness values.

Step 6: Determine whether the evolution of the entire population of complete maximum genetic operations. If the condition are satisfied, the algorithm continue down to step 7, otherwise, jump back to step 3;

Step 7: According to the results of fitness values output the optimal solution.

4   Results and Discussion

To verify the superiority of this algorithm, we compare the prediction results obtained by our algorithm against RNAStructure. The nucleic acid sequence is 5'-TTTTTGGGGGGGGGGGGAAAAAAAAAACCCCC-3', the comparison result is shown in Figure 6.

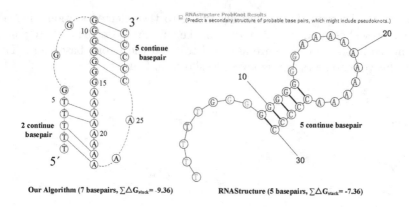

Fig. 6. Comparison with pseudoknots

Our sequences show more continues stacking value 7 base pairs better than RNA Structure value 5 base pairs. In addition, our algorithm show lower stacks free energy -9.36 better than RNAStructure value -7.36. Obviously, our algorithm predict the pseudoknots successful, however, the RNAStructure has no correct result.

5 Conclusions

In this paper, we propose a novel genetic algorithm to predict nucleic acid secondary structure with planar pseudoknots. In our algorithm, the thermodynamic free energy and the number of continues base pairs stacking are used as fitness function. A novel crossover and mutation operators are also designed to generate new children individuals efficiently. Finally, the performance of our algorithm is compared with RNAStructure. The comparison result shows that our algorithm can efficiently predict secondary structure with planar pseudoknots, which is more stable due to the lower free energy and more continues base pairs stacking.

In recent works, low-dispersion sequences were used to improve projection based algorithms, see e.g. [19]. For future research, a possible way is using low-dispersion sequences to improve the algorithms in predictions of secondary structure of DNA sequences.

Acknowledgments. This work was supported by the National Natural Science Foundation of China (Grant Nos. 61100055, 61033003, 60974112 and 31201121).

References

1. Păun, G.: Membrane Computing: An Introduction. Springer (2002)
2. Adleman, L.M.: Molecular Computation of Solutions to Combinatorial Problems. Science 266, 1021–1024 (1994)

3. Song, T., Pan, L., Păun, G.: Asynchronous Spiking Neural P Systems with Local Synchronization. Information Sciences 219, 197–207 (2013)
4. Ke, Y., Ong, L., Shih, W., Yin, P.: Three-dimensional Structures Self-Assembled from DNA Bricks. Science 338, 1177–1183 (2012)
5. Han, D., Pal, S., Yang, Y.: DNA Ridiron Nanostructures Based on Four-Arm Junctions. Science 339, 1412–1415 (2013)
6. Faulhammer, D., Cukras, A.R., Lipton, R.J.: Molecular Computation: RNA Solutions to Chess Problems. Proceedings of the National Academy of Sciences 97(4), 1385–1389 (2000)
7. Song, T., Pan, L., Wang, J., Ibrahim, V., Subramanian, K.G., Rosni, A.: Normal Forms of Spiking Neural P Systems with Anti-Spikes. IEEE Trans. on Nanobioscience 11(4), 352–359 (2012)
8. Song, T., Zheng, H., He, J.: Solving Vertex Cover Problem by Tissue P Systems with Cell Division. Appl. Math. Inf. Sci. 8(1), 333–337 (2014)
9. Martın-Vide, C., Păun, G., Pazos, J., Rodrıguez-Patón, A.: Tissue P Systems. Theore. Comput. Sci. 296(2), 295–326 (2003)
10. Shoemaker, D.D., Lashkari, D.A., Morris, D., Mittman, M., Davis, R.W.: Quantitative Phenotypic Analysis of Yeast Deletion Mutants using a Highly Parallel Molecular Barcoding Strategy. Nature. Genet. 16, 450–456 (1996)
11. Zuker, M., Stiegler, P.: Optimal Computer Folding Of Large RNA Sequences Using Thermodynamics and Auxiliary Information. Nucl. Acids Res. 9, 133–148 (1981)
12. Andronescu, M., Zhang, Z.C., Condon, A.: Secondary Structure Prediction of Interacting RNA Molecules. J. Mol. Biol. 4, 987–1001 (2005)
13. Pervouchine, D.D.: IRIS, Intermolecular RNA Interaction Search. Genome Inform. 15, 92–101 (2004)
14. Alkan, C., Karakoç, E., Nadeau, J.H., Sahinalp, S.C., Zhang, K.: RNA-RNA Interaction Prediction and Antisense RNA Target Search. J. Comput. Biol. 13, 267–282 (2006)
15. Kato, Y., Akutsu, T., Seki, H.: A Grammatical Approach to RNA-RNA Interaction Prediction. Pattern Recognition 42, 531–538 (2009)
16. Rivas, E., Eddy, S.R.: A Dynamic Programming Algorithm For RNA Structure Prediction Including Pseudoknots. J. Mol. Biol. 285(5), 2053–2068 (1999)
17. Dirks, R.M., Lin, M., Winfree, E., Pierce, N.A.: Paradigms for Computational Nucleic Acid Design. Nucleic Acids Res. 32(4), 1392–1403 (2004)
18. Reeder, J., Giegerich, R.: Design Implementation And Evaluation of A Practical Pseudoknot Folding Algorithm Based On Thermodynamics. BMC Bioinformatics 5(104), 2053–2068 (2004)
19. Wang, X., Miao, Y., Cheng, M.: Finding Motifs in DNA Sequences Using Low-Dispersion Sequences. Journal of Computational Biology 21(4), 320–329 (2014)

Accelerating Genetic Algorithm for Solving Graph Coloring Problem Based on CUDA Architecture

Kai Zhang*, Ming Qiu, Lin Li, and Xiaoming Liu

[1] School of Computer Science, Wuhan University of Science and Technology,
Wuhan 430081, Hubei, China
[2] Hubei Province Key Laboratory of Intelligent Information Processing
and Real-time Industrial System
zhangkai@wust.edu.cn

Abstract. Graph coloring problem (GCP) is a well-known NP-hard combinatorial optimization problem in graph theory. Solution for GCP often finds its applications to various engineering fields. So it is very important to find a feasible solution quickly. Recent years, Compute Unified Device Architecture (CUDA) show tremendous computational power by allowing parallel high performance computing. In this paper, we present a novel parallel genetic algorithm to solve the GCP based on CUDA. The initialization, crossover, mutation and selection operators are designed parallel in threads. Moreover, the performance of our algorithm is compared with the other graph coloring methods using standard DIMACS benchmarking graphs, and the comparison result shows that our algorithm is more competitive with computation time and graph instances size.

Keywords: Graph coloring problem, Genetic algorithm, CUDA.

1 Introduction

The graph coloring problem (GCP) is a well-known NP-hard combinatorial optimization problem in graph theory. The GCP is interesting not only because it is computationally intractable, but also because it has numerous practical applications, such as register assignment in timetabling [1], scheduling [2], register allocation [3], frequency assignment [4], and noise reduction in VLSI circuits [5].

In recent years, a wide variety of algorithms has been proposed. There are a limited number of exact algorithms for GCP [6, 7] presented in literature. Experimental results show that most of exact coloring algorithms are able to solve in-stances limited of 100 nodes sizes for random graphs [8, 9] which are small when compared to those generated by many real world applications. Another kind of algorithms for GCP is heuristic algorithms including constructive

---

* Corresponding author.

L. Pan et al. (Eds.): BIC-TA 2014, CCIS 472, pp. 578–584, 2014.

methods [10], iterative methods [11], genetic algorithms [12], local search methods [13], taboo techniques [14], ant system algorithms [15], etc. These heuristic techniques have been designed to solve large instances at the cost of regularly suboptimal solutions. This is clearly unsatisfactory for many applications, where a solution is required in a limited amount of time.

Currently, GPU architectures have hundreds of cores with the ability to run thousands of threads in parallel [16]. The NVidias CUDA is a new hardware and software architecture for issuing and managing computations on GPUs. Providing orders of magnitude more performance and simplifying software development by using the standard C language, CUDA enables developers to create innovative solutions for data-intensive problems.

In this paper, a novel parallel genetic algorithm for GCP is proposed. The algorithm is based on CUDA. The algorithm provides parallel initialization population, selection, crossover and mutation operators, which are the most important processes for genetic algorithm. Moreover, our algorithm has been implemented on Visual Studio 2013 and tested using benchmark graphs provided by the COLOR04 web site http://mat.gsia.cmu.edu/COLOR/instances.html. These are the graphs of the DIMACS Second Challenge. The performance of our algorithm is very encouraging.

2   Parallel Genetic Algorithm for GCP

2.1   Graph Color Problem

Given a graph $G=(V, E)$ with n vertices and m edges, a coloring of G is an assignment of colors to each vertex such that the endpoints of any edge have different colors. A k-coloring of G is a coloring that uses k colors. The chromatic number of G is the smallest number of colors needed to color G and is denoted by $\chi(G)$. The coloring problem is to determine $\chi(G)$ and to find a coloring of G that uses $\chi(G)$ colors.

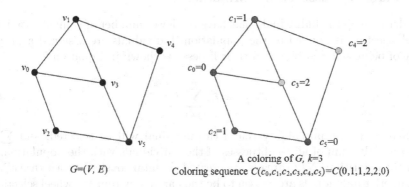

$G=(V, E)$ A coloring of G, $k=3$

Coloring sequence $C(c_0,c_1,c_2,c_3,c_4,c_5)=C(0,1,1,2,2,0)$

Fig. 1. The Graph G has 6 vertices and can be colored with 3 colors

The algorithm starts with an undirected graph G with n vertices and m edges. Vertex numbers range from 1 through n. The algorithm try to color n vertices with given k colors, numbered $\{0, 1, ..., k-1\}$. These k numbers are encoded for each graph vertex. If v_i is a vertex, c_i is a variable that means vertex v_i has color c_i, $c_i \in \{0, 1, ..., k-1\}$. A proper coloring formula as sequence $C(c_1, c_2, ..., c_n)$, a simple example is shown in Figure 1.

The coloring sequence $C(c_1, c_2, ..., c_n)$ should guarantee that each vertex v_i must receive exactly one color c_i. And each sequence must be checked with all edges constraints conditions $c_i \neq c_j$, if $e(i, j) \in E$.

2.2 Fitness Function

The fitness function $f(C_p)$ is the number of conflicting edges present in that individual C_p. The mathematical description is as shown in Equation 1.

$$f(C_p) = \sum_{e(i,j) \in E} equal(c_i, c_j)$$
$$equal(c_i, c_j) = \begin{cases} 1, \text{if } c_i = c_j \\ 0, \text{else } c_i \neq c_j \end{cases} \tag{1}$$

where C_p is the p-th individual in population. The aim of the optimizing process is to minimize $f(C_p)$ until reaching $f(C_p) = 0$ for a fixed k colors, which corresponds to a valid k-coloring.

2.3 Parallel Population Initialization

Given population size N, each individual in the population is generated by a CUDA thread. In each thread, the coloring sequence $C_p(c_1, c_2, ..., c_n)$ is generated for Population P_0, and the value of each color c_i drawn from $[1, \chi(G)]$ randomly. After each individual is generated, our algorithm calculate the fitness value within the same thread.

2.4 Parallel Crossover and Mutation

In order to keep the individuals that have the lower number of conflicts, roulette wheel selection is applied to the population. Individuals are assigned a probability of being selected based on their fitness, as shown in Equation 2.

$$p_i = f_i / \sum_{j=1}^{N} f_j \tag{2}$$

where p_i is the probability that i-th individual will be selected, and $\sum f_j$ represents the sum of all the fitnesses of the individuals with the population.

In the algorithm, $N/2$ threads are created simultaneously. In each threading, two superior individuals are chosen to be the parents by roulette wheel selection.

Secondly, a crossover probability P_{random} is generated randomly, if the probability is smaller than given $P_{crossover}$, the two-point crossover operator is adapted to generate two child individuals. Furthermore, a mutation probability P_{random} is generated randomly, if the probability is smaller than given $P_{mutation}$, the child individual would then be carried out mutation operator.

The mutation operator is to do some change to disturb the individual, which aimed at enrich the diversity of whole population, and at the same time to help the algorithm get out of local optimal solution. After choosing a child coloring sequence $C_p(c_1, c_2, ..., c_n)$, the algorithm search for the most conflicts color c_i from c_1 to c_n. Then the color ci should be replaced by another different color from $[1, \chi(G)]$ randomly. The crossover and mutation process in CUDA architecture is shown in Figure 2.

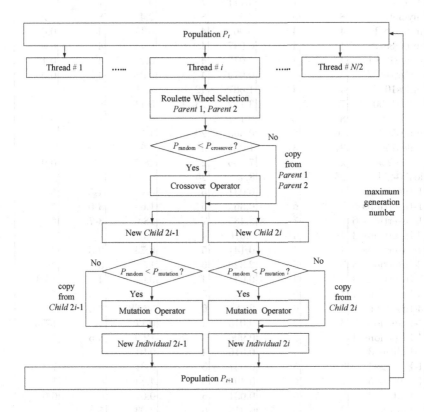

Fig. 2. Crossover and mutation on CUDA Architecture

3   Results and Discussion

The algorithm has been implemented on C++ language of Visual Studio 2013. In this section, the compute results of our algorithm are presented on 36 benchmark graphs given by DIMACS. Information about these graphs is summarized in Table 1. The 'Best Known' columns indicate the best known upper bound on the chromatic number. A '?' indicates an unknown value. The parameters of genetic algorithm, the probability $P_{crossover}$ and $P_{mutation}$, are set to be 0.8 and 0.05, respectively. In addition, the size of population is set to be 300, and the number of maximum iterations is set to be 2000.

Table 1. Comparision results on DIMACS graph coloring challenge instances

Graph Instances	Best Known	Our Colors	Our Time	ABAC Colors	ABAC Time	LDC Colors	LDC Time
myciel6	7	7	0.171	7	0.56	7	3
myciel7	8	8	0.5	8	2.49	8	53
mugg88-1	4	4	0.062	4	0.17	4	0.0
mugg88-25	4	4	0.047	4	0.16	4	0.0
mugg100-1	4	4	0.078	4	0.25	4	0.1
mugg100-25	4	4	0.079	4	0.35	4	0.0
miles1000	42	43	1.687	42	2.55		
miles1500	73	73	3.172	73	5.11		
miles250	8	8	0.187	8	0.57	8	0.0
miles500	20	20	0.563	20	1.53		
miles750	31	31	1.031	31	1.95		
le450-25a	25	26	7.765	25	28.71	25	0.0
le450-25b	25	25	8.438	25	27.14		
1-Insertions-4	4	5	0.031	5	0.1	4-5	*
1-Insertions-5	?	6	0.36	6	1.64	3-6	*
1-Insertions-6	?	7	3.485	7	18.6	3-7	*
2-Insertions-3	4	4	0.016	4	0.02		
2-Insertions-4	4	5	0.141	5	0.74	3-5	*
2-Insertions-5	?	6	2.328	6	17.82	3-6	*
3-Insertions-3	4	4	0.031	4	0.07	4	23.3
3-Insertions-4	?	5	0.343	5	4.69	3-5	*
3-Insertions-5	?	6	20.813	6	36.68	3-6	*
4-Insertions-3	3	4	0.015	4	0.17	4	1774
4-Insertions-4	?	5	0.906	5	12.9	3-5	*
1-FullIns-3	?	4	0.016	4	0.01	4	0
1-FullIns-4	?	5	0.047	5	0.31	5	7.3
1-FullIns-5	?	6	0.496	6	4.54	4-6	*
2-FullIns-3	?	5	0.031	5	0.07	5	0.0
2-FullIns-4	?	6	0.313	6	2.03	5-6	*
2-FullIns-5	?	7	7.922	7	29	5-7	*
3-FullIns-3	?	6	0.031	6	0.22	6	0.0
3-FullIns-4	?	7	0.954	7	11.22	3-7	*
4-FullIns-3	?	7	0.109	7	0.73	7	0.0
4-FullIns-4	?	8	4.281	8	22.53	4-8	*
5-FullIns-3	?	8	0.141	8	1.38	8	0.0
5-FullIns-4	?	9	15.046	9	33.5	3-9	*

In this paper, NVidia GeForce GTX 480 and CUDA SDK 5.0 are used. The GPU has 480 cores each having 700 MHz of frequency and access to total 1536MB of global memory. The algorithm is implemented and runs on Microsoft 64-bit Windows 8.1 operating system.

The algorithm is compared with the recent results of the exact LDC algorithm of Lucet et al. [6], and ant-based algorithm of Thang et al. [15]. The results of experiments are reported in Table 1. Results of the ant-based algorithm are listed in ABAC columns. Another exact algorithm results are reported in LDC columns. Comparing their time results for the same 36 benchmark graphs, our algorithm seems to run faster than their algorithms. In addition, the algorithm can solve graph instances with larger sizes than previews exact graph coloring methods.

4   Conclusions

In this paper, we present a novel parallel genetic algorithm to solve the GCP on CUDA. The GA initialization, crossover, mutation and selection operators are designed parallel in CUDA architecture. The algorithm provides parallel initialization population, selection, crossover and mutation operators, which are the most important processes for genetic algorithm. Moreover, the performance of our algorithm is compared with the other graph coloring methods using 36 DIMACS benchmarking graphs, and the comparison result shows that our algorithm is more competitive with computation time and graph instances size.

Acknowledgments. This work was supported by the National Natural Science Foundation of China (Grant Nos. 61100055, 31201121 and 61273225).

References

1. Hertz, A., Werra, D.: Using Tabu Search Techniques for Graph Coloring. Computing 39, 345–351 (1987)
2. Lucet, C., Mendes, F., Moukrim, A.: An Exact Method for Graph Coloring. Computers and Operations Research 33(8), 2189–2207 (2006)
3. Morgenstern, C.: Distributed Coloration Neighborhood Search. In: Cliques, Coloring and Satis-fiability – Second DIMACS Implementation Challenge 1993, vol. 26, pp. 335–358. American Mathematical Society (1996)
4. Brelaz, D.: New Methods to Color the Vertices of a Graph. Communications of the ACM 22(4), 251–256 (1979)
5. De, W.D.: An Introduction to Timetabling. European Journal of Operational Research 19, 151–162 (1985)
6. Luebke, D., Santa, C.: CUDA Scalable Parallel Programming for High-Performance Scientific Computing. In: Proceedings of the 5th IEEE International Symposium on Biomedical Imaging: From Nano to Macro, pp. 836–838 (2008)
7. Hermann, F., Hertz, A.: Finding the Chromatic Number by Means of Critical Graphs. ACM Journal of Experimental Algorithms 7(10), 1–9 (2002)

8. Shi, X., Lu, W., Wang, Z.: Programmable DNA Tile Self-assembly Using a Hierarchical Sub-tile Strategy. Nanotechnology 25(7), 075602 (2014)
9. Culberson, J., Luo, J.: Exploring the k-colorable Landscape with Iterated Greedy. Cliques. In: Coloring and Satisfiability - Second DIMACS Implementation Challenge, American Mathematical Society, vol. 26, pp. 245–284 (1996)
10. Smith, K., Palaniswami, M.: Static and Dynamic Channel Assignment Using Neural Networks. IEEE J. Select. Areas Commun. 15, C238–C249 (1997)
11. Bianco, L., Caramia, M., Dell'Olmo, M.: Solving a Preemptive Scheduling Problem Using Coloring Technique. In: Project Scheduling Recent Models, Algorithms and Applications. Kluwer Academic Publishers (1998)
12. Caramia, M., DellOlmo, M.: Iterative Coloring Extension of a Maximum Clique. Naval Research Logistics 48, 518–550 (2001)
13. Noise Reduction in VLSI Circuits using Modified GA Based Graph Coloring. International Journal of Control and Automation 3(2) (2010)
14. Kannan, S., Proebsting, T.: Register allocation in structured programs. Journal of Algorithms 29, 223–237 (1998)
15. Thang, N., Bui, T.H., Nguyen, C.M.P., Kim-Anh, T.P.: An Ant-based Algorithm for Coloring Graphs. Discrete Applied Mathematics 156, 190–200 (2008)
16. White, T., Pagurek, B., Oppacher, F.: Improving the Ant System by Integration with Genetic Algorithms. In: Proceedings of the 3rd Conference on Genetic Programming, vol. 7, pp. 610–617 (1998)

Parallel Genetic Algorithm with OpenCL for Traveling Salesman Problem

Kai Zhang*, Siman Yang, Li li, and Ming Qiu

[1] School of Computer Science, Wuhan University of Science and Technology,
Wuhan 430081, Hubei, China
[2] Hubei Province Key Laboratory of Intelligent Information Processing
and Real-time Industrial System
zhangkai@wust.edu.cn

Abstract. In the past few years, CUDA and OpenCL are developed in full use of the GPU, which is a significant topic in high performance computing. In this paper, we have proposed an implementation of the genetic algorithm for the traveling salesman problem on the parallel OpenCL architecture. Population initialization, fitness evaluation, selection, crossover and mutation operators are implemented on the GPU by using individual to thread mapping. Moreover we have evaluated our algorithm using a set of benchmark instances from the TSPLIB library. The comparison results shows that GPU computations provide better performance than traditional CPU implementation.

Keywords: Traveling salesman problem, Genetic algorithm, OpenCL.

1 Introduction

The Traveling Salesman Problem (TSP) is a well-known NP-complete combinatorial optimization problem. The objective of TSP is to find the shortest Hamilton cycle in a weighted complete graph. Although it is very easily described, there is no known deterministic optimal search algorithm that runs in polynomial time [1].

In recent years, a wide variety of algorithms has been proposed. There are a limited number of exact algorithms like Branch & Cut are also able to solve larger instances of some of these problems in a reasonable time [2,3]. Most algorithms for TSP are heuristic algorithms including ant colony optimization [4], simulated annealing [5], genetic algorithms [6], taboo techniques [7], etc. However, enormous amount of computation time still unsatisfactory for many applications, where a solution is required in a limited amount of time.

In the past few years, Compute Unified Device Architecture (CUDA) [8] a nd Open Computing Language (OpenCL) [9,10] are developed in full use of the Graphics Processing Unit (GPU), which is a significant topic in high performance computing. However, CUDA currently works only on NVidia GPUs. OpenCL

---

* Corresponding author.

L. Pan et al. (Eds.): BIC-TA 2014, CCIS 472, pp. 585–590, 2014.

is a more open standard maintained by the non-profit technology consortium Khronos Group. OpenCL deliver higher peak computational throughput than latency-oriented CPUs, thus offering tremendous potential performance uplift on massively parallel problems.

In this paper, an efficient parallel genetic algorithm for TSP is proposed. The algorithm is based on OpenCL. By using individual to thread mapping, the algorithm provides massively parallel population initialization, selection, crossover and mutation operators on GPU threads, which reduce time cost significantly. Moreover we have evaluated our implementation using a set of benchmark instances from the TSPLIB library. The GPU performance is compared with the corresponding CPU implementation, and the results shows that the performance of our GPU algorithm is very encouraging.

2   Parallel Genetic Algorithm for TSP on OpenCL

A salesman visits n cities, and makes a tour visiting each city exactly once to try to find the shortest possible tour. The instance of TSP can be conveniently represented by means of a complete graph of n nodes, where the nodes represents the cities and the weights of each pair of nodes represents the distances between cities, respectively. Let v_0, $v_1, \ldots, v_{n-1}$ be vertices that represent n cities, and (x_i, y_i) be the location coordinates of v_i, as shown in Figure 1, part A.

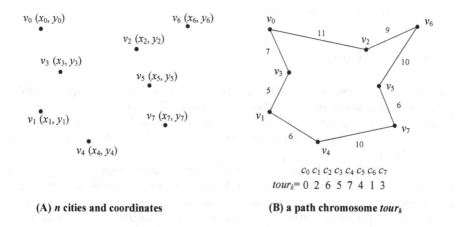

$$c_0\ c_1\ c_2\ c_3\ c_4\ c_5\ c_6\ c_7$$
$$tour_k = 0\ 2\ 6\ 5\ 7\ 4\ 1\ 3$$

(A) *n* cities and coordinates   (B) a path chromosome *tour_k*

Fig. 1. Example of 8 cities TSP and a tour

A tour is represented as the sequence of cities. The i-th city must be visited on the i-th position in the order. For example, the tour in Figure 1, part B is represented as follows.

In our genetic algorithm, the tour is a candidate chromosome, which can be represented as Equation 1.

$$tour_k = (c_1 c_2 c_3 \ldots c_i \ldots c_n) \tag{1}$$

where c_i is the city which must be visited on the i-th position in the order.

2.1 Evaluation Function

The fitness gives main pressure for convergence of evolution process. It is calculated by the evaluation function. Let d (c_i, c_j) be the distance between v_i and v_j. In this paper, we assume that the distance between two cities is their Euclidean distance. Given a tour $tour_k$, the evaluation function $f(tour_k)(k = 1, 2, \ldots, popsize)$ is defined as:

$$f(tour_k) = \sum_{i=1}^{n} d(c_i, c_{i+1}) + d(c_n, c_1)$$
$$d(c_i, c_j) = \sqrt{x_i - x_j}^2 + y_i - y_j^2 \tag{2}$$

Each distance $d(c_i, c_j)$ between cities i and j, and the fitness of each tour chromosome k in Equation 2 is computed. The sum distance is used to be the fitness, the smaller the fitness is, and the better the individual is.

2.2 Population Initialization

In this paper, we implement genetic algorithm on GPU to accelerate the performance by using OpenCL. The population and finesses are placed in global device memory. The population initialization, fitness evaluation, selection, crossover and mutation operators are executed by a large amount of parallel workitems.

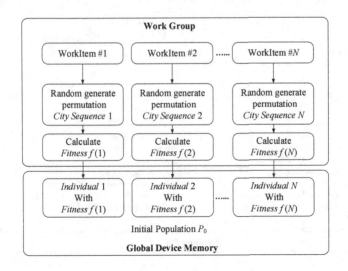

Fig. 2. Initial population P_0 on OpenCL architecture

Given population size N, the initial individuals in population P_0 are generated by N OpenCL workitems simultaneously. In each workitem, the tour sequence $(c_1 c_2 c_3 \ldots c_i \ldots c_n)$ is generated randomly. Then our algorithm calculates the fitness value within the same thread. The process is shown in Figure 2.

2.3   Crossover and Mutation

In the i-th work item, two individuals are chose by roulette wheel selection as parent1 and parent2. Then a crossover probability P_{ran} is generated randomly, if the probability is smaller than given threshold P_{cross}, the PMX crossover operator is adapted to generate two child individuals. Otherwise, the child individuals are copied from the parents directly without crossover. Each individual would be mutated with a probability. There is variable Pmutation which is the threshold

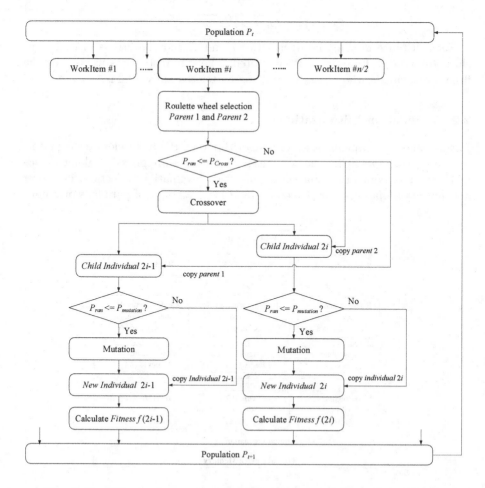

Fig. 3. Parallel selection, crossover and mutation operators in GPU threads

to judge whether the individual to mutate or not, when random probability P_{ran} is less than $P_{mutation}$, it will mutate. The process of parallel workitems is shown in Figure 3.

3   Results and Discussion

In order to verify the performance of our algorithm, we have implemented GA for the TSP on OpenCL, which use AMD Radeon HD 5970 with 1600 processing cores running in 725MHz and 2GB memory. We have evaluated our implementation using a set of benchmark instances from the TSPLIB library [11]. Each TSPLIB name consists of the name of the instance and the number of cities. The parameters of genetic algorithm, the probability P_{cross} and $P_{mutation}$, are set to be 0.9 and 0.1, respectively. In addition, the size of population is set to be 200, and the number of maximum iterations is set to be 1500. Table 1 shows the comparison results of GPU and CPU implements for various TSPLIB instances.

The results in Table 1 indicate that the GPU version of the GA implementation is accelerated apparently. As the number of cities grows, GPU shows more and more apparent advantages of time saving and efficiency. In addition, because

Table 1. Comparison results on TSPLIB challenge instances

Instance	CPU(s)	GPU(s)	Speed-up	Distance(CPU)	Distance(GPU)
a280	18	10	1.8	3021	2997
berlin52	1	1	0	7737	7542
bier127	3.09	1.9	1.63	143798.23	123710
ch130	3.1	1	3.1	7069.37	6345.03
ch150	4	2	2	8565.08	6869.6
d198	15	8	1.875	16187	16052
eil51	5	3	1.67	428	463.4
eil76	2.18	2	0	585	570.6
eil101	2	1	2	721.38	684
gil262	16	3	5.3	4797	2687
kroA100	3	2	1.5	24247.6	23551.73
kroE100	2.4	1.3	1.85	23924.09	23341
kroA200	8.58	2.3	3.73	43258.05	33769
kroB100	2.9	1	2.9	24166.81	22779
kroC100	2.9	1	2.9	27744.06	22592
kroD100	3.5	1	3.5	27803.78	23555
lin318	28	10	2.8	48668.3	47573
nrw1379	434	59	7.36	67822.5	67253
pcb442	51	11	4.64	58199.1	57901
pr2392	1238	91	13.6	378062.83	378062
pr107	4.26	1	4.26	50656.42	46295
pr299	72	2.5	28.8	58475.7	56804
pr1002	154	14	11	309830.8	309413
rat783	121	11	11	10651	10239
tsp225	15	8	1.875	4550.7	4476

of the massively OpenCL parallel threads, the GPU model reduce the population scales influence on convergence speed of genetic algorithm.

4   Conclusions

Genetic algorithm belongs to the family of population-based metaheuristics that has been successfully applied to many NP-complete problems. In this paper, we have proposed an implementation of the genetic algorithm for the traveling salesman problem on the parallel OpenCL architecture. This approach enhances the performance by increasing parallelism on GPU. Population initialization, fitness evaluation, selection, crossover and mutation operators are implemented on GPU by using individual to thread mapping. Moreover, GPU performance is compared with the corresponding CPU implementation with TSPLIB instances, and the results shows that GPU computations provide better performance than traditional CPU implementation.

Acknowledgments. This work was supported by the National Natural Science Foundation of China (Grant Nos. 61100055, 61033003, 60974112 and 31201121).

References

1. Papadimitriou, C.H.: The Euclidean Traveling Salesman Problem is NP-complete. Theoretical Computer Science 4(3), 237–244 (1977)
2. Grotschel, M., Holland, O.: Solution of Large-Scale Travelling Salesman Problems. Mathematical Programming 51(2), 141–202 (1991)
3. Hernández-Pérez, H., Salazar-González, J.: A Branch-and-Cut Algorithm for a Traveling Salesman Problem with Pickup and Delivery. Discrete Applied Mathematics 145(1), 126–139 (2004)
4. Anuraj, M., Remya, G.: A Parallel Implementation of Ant Colony Optimization for TSP based on MapReduce Framework. International Journal of Computer Applications 88(8), 9–12 (2014)
5. Klaus, M.: Simulated Annealing versus Metropolis for a TSP instance. Information Processing Letters 104(6), 216–219 (2007)
6. Wang, X., Song, T., Wang, Z.: MRPGA: Motif Detecting by Modified Random Projection Strategy and Genetic Algorithm. J. Comput. Theor. Nanosci. 10, 1209–1214 (2013)
7. He, Y., Qiu, Y., Liu, G., Lei, K.: A Parallel Adaptive Tabu Search Approach for Traveling Salesman Problems. In: Proceedings of IEEE International Conference on Natural Language Processing and Knowledge Engineering, pp. 796–801 (2005)
8. Hofmann, J., Limmer, S., Fey, D.: Performance Investigations of Genetic Algorithms on Graphics Cards. Swarm and Evolutionary Computation 12, 33–47 (2013)
9. Lan, Q., Xun, C., Wen, M.: Improving Performance of GPU Specif-ic OpenCLProgram on CPUs. In: Proceedings of 13th International Conference on Parallel and Distributed Computing, Applications and Technologies, pp. 356–360 (2012)
10. Shen, J., Fang, J., Sips, H., Varbanescu, A.L.: An Application-centric Evaluation of OpenCL on Multi-core CPUs. Parallel Computing 39(12), 834–850 (2013)
11. Shi, X., Lu, W., Wang, Z.: Programmable DNA Tile Self-assembly Using a Hierarchical Subtile Strategy. Nanotechnology 25(7), 075602 (2014)

Multiobjective Genetic Algorithm for Optimized DNA Sequences for DNA Self-assembly

Kai Zhang*, Jiaren Yi, Jun Liu, and Wei Hu

[1] School of Computer Science, Wuhan University of Science and Technology,
Wuhan 430081, Hubei, China
[2] Hubei Province Key Laboratory of Intelligent Information Processing
and Real-time Industrial System
zhangkai@wust.edu.cn

Abstract. DNA sequence design is a very important task for DNA self-assembly technologies, including DNA computing, complex 3D nanostructures and nano-devices design. These experimental DNA molecules must satisfy several combinatorial, thermodynamic and secondary structure criteria, which aim to avoid undesired hybridizations and make the molecular experiment more re-liable and stable. In this paper, the DNA sequence design problem is formulated as a multi-objective optimization problem and solving it using multi-objective genetic algorithm. Moreover, the performance of our algorithm is compared with the other sequence design methods, and the comparison result shows that our algorithm is able to generate higher quality DNA sequences than previously published studies which consider same criteria.

Keywords: DNA self-assembly, Multi-objective optimization, DNA sequence design, Genetic algorithm.

1 Introduction

DNA self-assembly has advanced extensively in recent years, from Adelman DNA computing experiment to the current designs and experimental implementations of complex nanostructures and nanodevices. Recent developments in the field include complex 3D nanostructure design [1,2], robotic motors designs [3], DNA strand displacement cascades [4], nucleic acid sensors [5] and potential drug delivery [6]. DNA sequences design algorithms are likely to play an increasing role in exploring these DNA self-assembly fields.

There has been a great deal of previous work in designing DNA sequences [7-9]. Existing techniques for DNA sequence design include genetic algorithms, dynamic programming, and heuristic methods. In particular, Frutos et al. [10] proposed the template-map method for DNA word design. Arita et al. [11] developed a DNA sequence design system using genetic algorithm. Deaton et al. [12] presented a dynamic programming algorithm for generating DNA strands.

---

* Corresponding author.

L. Pan et al. (Eds.): BIC-TA 2014, CCIS 472, pp. 591–597, 2014.

Tanaka et al. [13] designed DNA sequences by a simulated annealing. Shin et al. [14] proposed several sequence fitness criteria, and generated the sequence using multi-objective evolutionary algorithm.

In this paper, multi-objective genetic algorithm is adopt to solve DNA sequence design problem, which takes thermodynamic, combinatorial, and secondary structure design criteria into account, such as similarity, h-measure, hairpin secondary structure, melting temperature. Moreover, the results are compared that obtained by our algorithm with other algorithms. As will be discussed, the algorithm can generate more reliable DNA sequences than other approaches previously published in the literature.

2   DNA Sequence Design Problem

2.1   Multi-objective DNA Sequence Design Criteria

The design of reliable DNA sequences involves several conflicting design constraints which have to be considered simultaneously. In mathematical terms, DNA sequence design problem can be formulated as a multi-objective optimization problem as follows.

$$Minimize\, F(x) = (f_1(x), f_2(x), ..., f_n(x)) \qquad (1)$$

where $f_i(x)$ is the evaluate criterion fitness function. Several typical biochemical design criteria is chosen that other relevant authors use to evaluate and generate reliable DNA libraries. The formal definition for each design criteria is provided in the following subsections.

2.2   Melting Temperature Criterion

In order to improve the efficiency of DNA self-assembly, the melting temperature for each DNA molecular and its complement must be in a uniform range. The mathematical description for this measure, calculated by using the Nearest-Neighbor method, is provided in Equation (2).

$$f_{Tm}(L) = \sum_{i=1}^{N} |TM(X_i) - TM_{Target}|$$
$$TM(X_i) = \frac{\Delta H^\circ}{\Delta S^\circ + R\ln(|C_T|/4)} \qquad (2)$$

where R is a gas constant and $|CT|$ is the total DNA sequence concentration. ΔH and ΔS refer to predicted enthalpies and entropies. Those values are constant values and they were taken from the work by Santa Lucia [15].

2.3   GC Content Criterion

The GC content is the percentages of bases which are either G or C. If all these words will assure similar GC content, all DNA sequences must have similar thermodynamic characteristics which can reduce the probability of occurring non-specific hybridization effectively. These evaluation functions are described in Equation (3).

$$f_{GC}(L) = \sum_{i=1}^{N} |GC(X_i) - GC_{Target}|$$
$$GC(X_i) = \frac{\sum G + \sum C}{\sum A + \sum T + \sum G + \sum C} \tag{3}$$

2.4 Continuity Criterion

The continuity criterion tests the repeated run of identical bases. If the same base appears continuously, an unstable secondary structure can be formed and the reaction is not easy to control. The mathematical definition for this criterion is provided in Equation (4).

$$f_{Continuity}(L) = \sum_{i=1}^{N} Continuity(X_i)$$
$$Continuity(X_i) = \sum Con(x_i)^2 \; if x_i \neq x_{i+1} \; and \; Con(x_i) \geq 3$$
$$Con(x_i) = eq(x_i) \times [eq(x_i) + Con(x_{i-1})]$$
$$eq(x_i) = \begin{cases} 1, x_i = x_{i-1} \\ 0, x_i \neq x_{i-1} \end{cases} \tag{4}$$

2.5 Hairpin Secondary Structure Criterion

Hairpin is an undesirable DNA secondary structure in some DNA self-assembly models, because it can hybridize itself. Given the hairpin settings are Watson-Crick stem length p and loop length r. Equation (5) provide a formal description of minimum hairpins with Rmin loop and Pmin base pairs stem at position i in the sequence x, in case that more than half bases in the subsequence $x_{i-p}...x_i$ hybridize with the subsequence $x_{i+r}...x_{i+r+p}$.

$$f_{Hairpin}(L) = \sum_{i=1}^{N} Hairpin(X_i)$$
$$Hairpin(X_i) = \sum_{p=P_{min}}^{l-R_{min}/2} \sum_{r=R_{min}}^{l-2p} \sum_{i=1}^{l-2p-r} HP$$
$$HP = \begin{cases} \sum_{j=1}^{pinlen(p,r,i)} bp(x_{p+i+j}, x_{p+i+r+j}), \; if \; greater than \; \frac{pinlen(p,r,i)}{2} \\ 0, \; else \end{cases} \tag{5}$$

where $pinlen(p, r, i) = min(p + i, l - r - i - p)$ and represents the maximum number of basepairs when a hairpin with centre in $p + i + r/2$ is formed.

2.6 Similarity Criterion

The similarity criterion is used to describe the similar degree between two DNA sequences. The constraint computes the same nucleic acid bases to keep each sequence as unique as possible including position shift. Equation (6) defines mathematically this design criterion:

$$f_{similarity}(L) = \sum_{i=1}^{N} \sum_{j=1}^{N} Similarity(X_i, X_j) \tag{6}$$

The function is divided into two terms, expanded as indicated in Equation (7). One term represents the overall discrete discontinuous similarity, and the other calculates the penalty for the identical continuous subsequence.

$$Similarity(X,Y) = Max_{g,i}(s_{dis}(x,\ shift[y(-)^g y, i]\ ) + s_{con}(x,\ shift[y(-)^g y, i]))$$

$$s_{dis}(x,\ y) = \begin{cases} \sum_{i=1}^{l} eq(x_i, y_i),\ if\ greater than\ S_{dis} \times length_{nb}(y) \\ 0,\ \ else \end{cases}$$

$$s_{con}(x,\ y) = \begin{cases} \sum_{j=1}^{l} ceq(x_i, y_i, i),\ if\ greater than\ S_{con} \\ 0,\ \ else \end{cases}$$

$$\tag{7}$$

where S_{dis} and S_{con} are given by user. S_{dis} is a floating point number between 0 and 1, and S_{con} is an integer number between 1 and l. $ceq(x, y, i)$ indicates the length of continuous same subsequence starting in the ith base of sequence x.

2.7   H-measure Criterion

The h-measure criterion which considers two sequences as complementary ones. H-measure computes how many nucleotides are complementary between the given sequences to prevent cross-hybridization. Equation (8) shows the mathematical definition for this criterion.

$$f_{H\ measure}(L) = \sum_{i=1}^{N} \sum_{j=1}^{N} H{-}measure(X_i, X_j) \tag{8}$$

H-measure is also divided into two terms. One term provides the penalty for the continuous complementary region and the other term indicates the overall complementarily. Formally, this objective is expressed in Equation (9).

$$H{-}measure(X,Y) = Max_{g,i}(\ h_{dis}(x,\ shift[y(-)^g y, i]\ )$$
$$+ h_{con}(x,\ shift[y(-)^g y, i]\ )\ )$$

$$= h_{dis}(x,\ y) = \begin{cases} \sum_{i=1}^{l} bp(x_i, y_i),\ if\ greater than\ H_{dis} \times length_{nb}(y) \\ 0,\ \ else \end{cases}$$

$$h_{con}(x,\ y) = \begin{cases} \sum_{j=1}^{l} cbp(x_i, y_i, i),\ if\ greater than\ H_{con} \\ 0,\ \ else \end{cases}$$

$$\tag{9}$$

where H_{dis} and H_{con} are given by user. H_{dis} is a floating point number between 0 and 1, and H_{con} is an integer number between 1 and l. $cbp(x, y, i)$ indicates the length of continuous base pair from the ith base of sequence x.

3   Multi-objective Genetic Algorithm for DNA Sequence Design

The goal of our algorithm is to design a set of DNA words with equal-length l, satisfying certain combinatorial criteria and thermodynamic criteria. Let N be the DNA sequences population size, and *maxstep* is the specified in number of generations.

The algorithm starts with the random generation of the initial population P_0 of N size. Each of the N sequences of each individual is randomly generated with l bases (A, C, G or T). Then, the original population P_t is sorted according to non-domination criterion for ranking these individuals. Furthermore, the crowding distance sorting were adopt to keep diversity. The algorithm flow graph is depicted in Fig. 1.

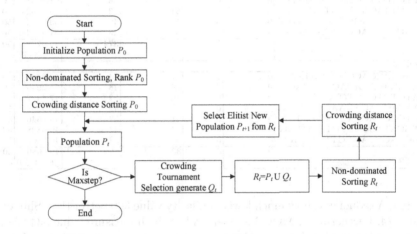

Fig. 1. Algorithm flow graph of multi-objective genetic algorithm

In each generation for P_t, the crowding tournament selection, crossover, and mutation operators are used to create an offspring population Q_t of size N. Then, the combined population $R_t = P_t \cup Q_t$ is sorted according to non-domination criterion by creating different Pareto fronts of non-dominated solutions.

At the end of each iteration, if termination criteria *maxstep* are reached, the evolution stops. Otherwise the new created population P_{t+1} is used to restart the evolutionary cycle. In order to choose exactly the N ranked population R_t members, the solutions are ordered using the crowded-comparison operator in descending order. Pareto fronts that exceed the size of the new population will be removed, and in case that there are solutions of the last front that cannot be accommodated in the new population.

4   Results and Discussion

We compare the quality of the sequences obtained by our proposal (MOGA) against the quality of the sequences obtained in other relevant studies in terms of each design criterion separately, such as similarity, h-measure, continuity, hairpin secondary structure, melting temperature and GC content. Sequences are taken from the results of Shin et al. [14] shown in Table 1.

Table 1. Comparison of the sequences provided by Shin et al.[14] and MOGA

Sequence(5'-3')	Continuity	Hairpin	H-measure	Similarity	Tm	GC
Shin et al.[18]						
CTCTTCATCCACCTCTTCTC	0	0	43	58	46.6803	50
CTCTCATCTCTCCGTTCTTC	0	0	37	58	46.9393	50
TATCCTGTGGTGTCCTTCCT	0	0	45	57	49.1066	50
ATTCTGTTCCGTTGCGTGTC	0	0	52	56	51.3381	50
TCTCTTACGTTGGTTGGCTG	0	0	51	53	49.9252	50
GTATTCCAAGCGTCCGTGTT	0	0	55	49	50.7224	50
AAACCTCCACCAACACACCA	9	0	55	43	51.4734	50
Sum	9	0	338	374	49.0768 (±2.3965)	50 (±0)
MOGA						
CCACCACCACCACCAATAAT	0	0	41	54	49.6425	50
CACACACACACACACACACA	0	0	34	48	51.2945	50
AATCTCTCTCTCTCTCTGCC	0	0	46	52	47.4427	50
TAACAGAACAGAACAGGCCG	0	0	53	49	49.9252	50
CCTCCGCACTACAAGTCTTA	0	0	51	57	48.7546	50
TTGCATTCCTTCCTTCCTGG	0	0	54	47	49.6828	50
CGCCAGCCAGCCTATATTAA	0	0	55	53	49.5507	50
Sum	0	0	334	360	49.3686 (±1.9259)	50 (±0)

MOGA sequences show much lower similarity value 360 better than Shin et al. value 374. Furthermore, MOGA sequences has the h-measure value 334 slightly less than Shin et al. value 338. This implies the sequences generated by MOGA are more reliable, and have much higher probability to hybridization with its correct complementary sequences. The secondary structure is more prohibited due to the lower continuity and hairpin values, so any pair of DNA molecules cannot form a stable double stranded structure to prevent the occurrence of non-specific hybridization. In addition, MOGA show more uniform melting temperature around 49.3686(±1.9259), which are more uniform in TM than Shin et al. value 49.0768(±2.3965).

5   Conclusions

In this paper a multi-objective genetic algorithm is proposed to generate highly reliable DNA sequences for reliable DNA self-assembly. The algorithm fulfills several conflicting bio-chemical requirements which have to be considered simultaneously. The algorithm can obtain sets of sequences which simultaneously minimize multiobjects similarity, h-measure, continuity, hairpin, melting temperature and GC content. Finally, the sequences generated by MOGA are compared with the result obtained from other relevant studies. The comparison result shows that MOGA is able to generate higher quality DNA sequences than previously published studies which consider same design criteria.

Acknowledgments. This work was supported by the National Natural Science Foundation of China (Grant Nos. 61100055, 61033003, 60974112 and 31201121).

References

1. Shi, X., Lu, W., Wang, Z.: Programmable DNA Tile Self-assembly Using a Hierarchical Sub-tile Strategy. Nanotechnology 25(7), 075602 (2014)
2. Han, D., Pal, S., Yang, Y.: DNA Gridiron Nanostructures Based on Four-Arm Junctions. Science 339, 1412–1415 (2013)
3. Zhang, Olsen, E.M., Kryger, M.: A DNA Tile Actuator with Eleven Discrete States. Angew. Chem. 50, 3983–3987 (2011)
4. Qian, L., Winfree, E.: Scaling up Digital Circuit Computation with DNA Strand Displacement Cascades. Science 332, 1196–1201 (2011)
5. Liu, J., Cao, Z., Lu, Y.: Functional Nucleic Acid Sensors. Chem. Rev. 109, 1948–1998 (2009)
6. Li, J., Pei, H., Zhu, B., Liang, L.: Self-assembled Multivalent DNA Nanostructures for Non-invasive Intracellular Delivery of Immune Stimulatory CpG Oligonucleotides. ACS Nano 5, 8783–878 (2011)
7. Hartemink, A.J., Gifford, D.K.: Automated Constraintbased Nucleotide Sequence Selection for DNA Computation. In: Proceedings of the 4th DIMACS Workshop DNA Based Compution, pp. 227–235 (1998)
8. Penchovsky, R., Ackermann, J.: DNA Library Design for Molecular Computation. Journal of Computational Biology 10(2), 215–229 (2003)
9. Marathe, A., Condon, A.E., Corn, R.M.: On Combinatorial DNA Word Design. In: Proceedings of the 5th DIMACS Workshop DNA Based Computation, pp. 75–89 (1999)
10. Frutos, A.G., Liu, Q.H., Thiel, A.T.: Demonstration of a Word Design Strategy for DNA Computing on Surface. Nucleic Acids Research 25, 4748–4757 (1997)
11. Arita, M., Nishikawa, A., Hagiya, M.: Improving Sequence Design for DNA Computing. In: Proceedings of the Genetic and Evolutionary Computation Conference, pp. 875–882 (2000)
12. Deaton, R., Chen, J., Bi, H.: A Software Tool for Generating Noncrosshybridization Libraries of DNA Oligonucleotides. In: The Proceedings of the 8th International Workshop DNA Based Computing, pp. 252–261 (2003)
13. Tanaka, F., Kameda, A., Yamamoto, M.: Design of Nucleic Acid Sequences for DNA Computing Based on a Thermodynamic Approach. Nucleic Acids Research 33(3), 903–911 (2005)
14. Shin, S.-Y., Lee, I.-H., Dongmin, K.: Multiobjective Evolutionary Optimization of DNA sequences for Reliable DNA Computing. IEEE Transactions on Evolutionary Computation 9(2), 143–158 (2005)
15. Santa, L.: A Unified View of Polymer, Dumbbell, and Oligonucleotide DNA Nearest Neighbor Thermodymamics. Proc. Natl. Acad. Sci. 95, 1460–1465 (1998)

Sufficient Conditions for Nonsingular $H-$matrices

Lijun Zhang and Min Li*

School of Mathematics and Statistics, Beihua University,
JiLin 132013, Jinlin, P.R. China
bhulimin@163.com

Abstract. For many applications of numerical analysis, control theory, economic mathematics and so on, it is very useful to know whether a matrix is a nonsingular matrix or not. In this paper, by using the theory of diagonally dominant matrices, we discuss some criteria for nonsingular matrices according to partition for the index set of diagonal dominance. A set of sufficient conditions for nonsingular matrices are given. These results are illustrated by using a numerical example.

Keywords: Diagonally dominant matrices, $\alpha-$diagonally dominant matrices, Sufficient condition, $H-$matrices.

1   Introduction

$H-$matrices play an important role in matrix theory, numerical analysis, control theory, economic mathematics, see [1, 2]. Some criteria of determining $H-$matrices is necessary and have been investigated in some papers in [3–6]. In this work, we introduce a set of sufficient conditions for $H-$matrices. In practice, advantages are illustrated by one numerical example.

Let $C^{n \times n}$ be the set of all n by n complex matrices. Let $A = (a_{ij}) \in C^{n \times n}$ and $R_i(A) = \sum_{j \neq i} |a_{ij}|$, $C_i(A) = \sum_{j \neq i} |a_{ji}|$, $\forall i \in N = \{1, 2, \cdots, n\}$. If $|a_{ii}| > R_i(A), \forall i \in N$, then A is said to be a strictly diagonally dominant matrix and is denoted by $A \in D$. If there exists a positive diagonally matrix $X = diag(d_1, d_2, \cdots, d_n)$, where $d_i > 0, i \in N$, such that $AX \in D$ (i.e., $d_i|a_{ii}| > \sum_{j \neq i} d_j|a_{ij}|, i \in N$), then A is said to be a generalized strictly diagonally dominant matrix and is denoted by $A \in D^*$.

It is well known that A is a nonsingular $H-$matrix if and only if A is a generalized strictly diagonally dominant matrix (i.e., $A \in D^*$). So we always assume that all diagonal entries of A, $R_i(A)$, and $C_i(A)$ are nonzero throughout the paper.

---

* Corresponding author.

L. Pan et al. (Eds.): BIC-TA 2014, CCIS 472, pp. 598–605, 2014.
© Springer-Verlag Berlin Heidelberg 2014

2   Main Results

Definition 1. *Let* $A = (a_{ij}) \in C^{n \times n}$, *if there exists* $\alpha \in (0,1)$ *such that*

$$|a_{ii}| > [R_i(A)]^\alpha [C_i(A)]^{1-\alpha}, \ i \in N,$$

then A is said to be a strictly α−diagonally dominant matrix and is denoted by $A \in D(\alpha)$.

Definition 2. *Let* $A = (a_{ij}) \in C^{n \times n}$, *if there exists a positive diagonally matrix X such that $AX \in D(\alpha)$, then A is said to be a generalized strictly α−diagonally dominant matrix and is denoted by* $A \in D^*(\alpha)$.

Lemma 1. *Let* $A = (a_{ij}) \in C^{n \times n}$. *$A$ is a generalized strictly diagonally dominant matrix if and only if it is a generalized strictly α−diagonally dominant matrix.*

Remark 1. $A \in D^*(\alpha) \Leftrightarrow A \in D^* \Leftrightarrow A$ *is a nonsingular H−matrix.*

Theorem 1. *Let* $A = (a_{ij}) \in C^{n \times n}$, *if*

$$\sum_{i \in N} \frac{\varepsilon_i}{1 + \varepsilon_i} < 1. \tag{1}$$

Then A is a nonsingular H−matrix. Where there exists $\alpha \in (0,1)$ such that ε_i satisfies either

$$\varepsilon_i = \frac{(\max_{j \neq i} |a_{ij}|)(C_i(A))^{\frac{1-\alpha}{\alpha}}}{|a_{ii}|^{\frac{1}{\alpha}}}, \tag{2}$$

or

$$\varepsilon_i = \frac{[R_i(A)(C_i(A))^{\frac{1-\alpha}{\alpha}}]^q}{(|a_{ii}|^{\frac{1}{\alpha}})^q}, \tag{3}$$

in the equality (3), q satisfies that $q \geq 1$.

Proof. For $\forall i \in N$, take

$$\sigma = \sum_{i \in N} \frac{\varepsilon_i}{1 + \varepsilon_i},$$

then $\sigma < 1$.

Case 1. If ε_i satisfies (2),we take

$$d_i = \frac{\varepsilon_i}{1 + \varepsilon_i} + \frac{1 - \sigma}{n}, \ i \in N. \tag{4}$$

Obviously, $d_i > 0$, $\forall i \in N$ and $\sum_{i \in N} d_i = 1$. From (2) and (4),

$$d_i > \frac{\varepsilon_i}{1 + \varepsilon_i} = \frac{(\max_{j \neq i} |a_{ij}|)(C_i(A))^{\frac{1-\alpha}{\alpha}}}{|a_{ii}|^{\frac{1}{\alpha}} + (\max_{j \neq i} |a_{ij}|)(C_i(A))^{\frac{1-\alpha}{\alpha}}}, \quad \forall i \in N.$$

This implies

$$d_i > \frac{(\max_{j \neq i} |a_{ij}|)(C_i(A))^{\frac{1-\alpha}{\alpha}}}{|a_{ii}|^{\frac{1}{\alpha}}}(1 - d_i), \ i \in N.$$

For $\forall i \in N$,

$$\begin{aligned}
\frac{(C_i(A))^{\frac{1-\alpha}{\alpha}}}{|a_{ii}|^{\frac{1}{\alpha}}}(\sum_{j \neq i} |a_{ij}|d_j) &\leq \frac{(C_i(A))^{\frac{1-\alpha}{\alpha}}}{|a_{ii}|^{\frac{1}{\alpha}}}(\sum_{j \neq i} (\max_{j \neq i} |a_{ij}|)d_j) \\
&= \frac{(\max_{j \neq i} |a_{ij}|)(C_i(A))^{\frac{1-\alpha}{\alpha}}}{|a_{ii}|^{\frac{1}{\alpha}}}(\sum_{j \neq i} d_j) \\
&= \frac{(\max_{j \neq i} |a_{ij}|)(C_i(A))^{\frac{1-\alpha}{\alpha}}}{|a_{ii}|^{\frac{1}{\alpha}}}(1 - d_i) \\
&< d_i.
\end{aligned}$$

$$|a_{ii}|^{\frac{1}{\alpha}} d_i > (C_i(A))^{\frac{1-\alpha}{\alpha}}(\sum_{j \neq i} |a_{ij}|d_j), \quad \forall i \in N.$$

This implies

$$|a_{ii}|d_i > (\sum_{j \neq i} |a_{ij}|d_j)^{\alpha}(\sum_{j \neq i} |a_{ji}|d_i)^{1-\alpha}, \ i \in N. \tag{5}$$

Case 2. If ε_i satisfies (3), we take

$$d_i = \{\frac{\varepsilon_i}{1 + \varepsilon_i} + \frac{1 - \sigma}{n}\}^{\frac{1}{q}}, \ i \in N. \tag{6}$$

$$d_i^q = \frac{\varepsilon_i}{1 + \varepsilon_i} + \frac{1 - \sigma}{n}, \ i \in N. \tag{7}$$

Obviously, $d_i > 0$, $\forall i \in N$ and $\sum_{i \in N} d_i^q = 1$.

Case 2.1. When $q > 1$, it is similar to the proof of case 1. From (3) and (7),

$$d_i^q > \frac{[R_i(A)(C_i(A))^{\frac{1-\alpha}{\alpha}}]^q}{(|a_{ii}|^{\frac{1}{\alpha}})^q}(1 - d_i^q), \ i \in N.$$

i.e.,

$$d_i > \frac{R_i(A)(C_i(A))^{\frac{1-\alpha}{\alpha}}}{(|a_{ii}|^{\frac{1}{\alpha}})}(1 - d_i^q)^{\frac{1}{q}}, \ i \in N.$$

By $q > 1$, let $p = \dfrac{q}{q-1}$, we can obtain $p > 1$, too. Futhermore, p and q satisfy

$$\frac{1}{p} + \frac{1}{q} = 1.$$

Based on the *Hölder* inequality, for $\forall i \in N$,

$$\frac{(C_i(A))^{\frac{1-\alpha}{\alpha}}}{|a_{ii}|^{\frac{1}{\alpha}}}(\sum_{j\neq i}|a_{ij}|d_j) \leq \frac{(C_i(A))^{\frac{1-\alpha}{\alpha}}}{|a_{ii}|^{\frac{1}{\alpha}}}(\sum_{j\neq i}|a_{ij}|^p)^{\frac{1}{p}}(\sum_{j\neq i}d_j^q)^{\frac{1}{q}}$$

$$\leq \frac{(C_i(A))^{\frac{1-\alpha}{\alpha}}}{|a_{ii}|^{\frac{1}{\alpha}}}[(\sum_{j\neq i}|a_{ij}|)^p]^{\frac{1}{p}}(\sum_{j\neq i}d_j^q)^{\frac{1}{q}}$$

$$= \frac{R_i(A)(C_i(A))^{\frac{1-\alpha}{\alpha}}}{|a_{ii}|^{\frac{1}{\alpha}}}(1-d_i^q)^{\frac{1}{q}}$$

$$< d_i.$$

i.e.,

$$|a_{ii}|^{\frac{1}{\alpha}}d_i > (C_i(A))^{\frac{1-\alpha}{\alpha}}(\sum_{j\neq i}|a_{ij}|d_j), \ i \in N.$$

This implies

$$|a_{ii}|d_i > (\sum_{j\neq i}|a_{ij}|d_j)^{\alpha}(\sum_{j\neq i}|a_{ji}|d_i)^{1-\alpha}, \ i \in N. \tag{8}$$

Case 2.2. When $q = 1$, we notice the inequality

$$\sum_{i\in N}\frac{(\max_{j\neq i}|a_{ij}|)(C_i(A))^{\frac{1-\alpha}{\alpha}}}{|a_{ii}|^{\frac{1}{\alpha}} + (\max_{j\neq i}|a_{ij}|)(C_i(A))^{\frac{1-\alpha}{\alpha}}} \leq \sum_{i\in N}\frac{R_i(A)(C_i(A))^{\frac{1-\alpha}{\alpha}}}{|a_{ii}|^{\frac{1}{\alpha}} + R_i(A)(C_i(A))^{\frac{1-\alpha}{\alpha}}}. \tag{9}$$

From the proof of case 1, we have

$$|a_{ii}|d_i > (\sum_{j\neq i}|a_{ij}|d_j)^{\alpha}(\sum_{j\neq i}|a_{ji}|d_i)^{1-\alpha}, \ i \in N. \tag{10}$$

Now, we construct a positive diagonally matrix $X = diag(d_1, d_2, \cdots, d_n)$ (where d_i see (4) or (6)). From (5),(8) and (10), it is easy to see that $AX \in D(\alpha)$, i.e., $A \in D^*(\alpha)$. By the Lemma 1, then A is a nonsingular H−matrix.

We introduce some notations: $N_1 = \{i \in N : |a_{ii}| > R_i(A)\}$, $N_2 = \{i \in N : 0 < |a_{ii}| \leq R_i(A)\}$, $N_{11} = \{i \in N : R_i(A) < |a_{ii}| < C_i(A)\}$, $N_{12} = \{i \in N : |a_{ii}| > R_i(A), |a_{ii}| \geq C_i(A)\}$.

Obviously, if $N_2 = \emptyset$, then $A \in D$. If $N_1 = \emptyset$, then A is not a nonsingular H−matrix. So we always assume that $N_1 \neq \emptyset$, $N_2 \neq \emptyset$.

Theorem 2. *Let $A = (a_{ij}) \in C^{n\times n}$, if $N_{11} = \emptyset$ and there exists $\alpha \in (0, 1)$ such that*

$$\sum_{i\in N_2}\frac{[R_i(A)(C_i(A))^{\frac{1-\alpha}{\alpha}}]^q[1 + \sum_{j\in N_1}(\frac{R_j(A)}{|a_{jj}|})^q]}{(|a_{ii}|^{\frac{1}{\alpha}})^q + [R_i(A)(C_i(A))^{\frac{1-\alpha}{\alpha}}]^q} < 1. \tag{11}$$

Hence, A is a nonsingular H−matrix.

Proof. Case 1. For $q = 1$, we notice the inequality

$$\sum_{i \in N_2} \frac{(\max_{j \neq i} |a_{ij}|)(C_i(A))^{\frac{1-\alpha}{\alpha}}(1 + \sum_{j \in N_1} \frac{R_j(A)}{|a_{jj}|})}{|a_{ii}|^{\frac{1}{\alpha}} + (\max_{j \in N_2, j \neq i} |a_{ij}|)(C_i(A))^{\frac{1-\alpha}{\alpha}}}$$

$$< \sum_{i \in N_2} \frac{R_i(A)(C_i(A))^{\frac{1-\alpha}{\alpha}}(1 + \sum_{j \in N_1} \frac{R_j(A)}{|a_{jj}|})}{|a_{ii}|^{\frac{1}{\alpha}} + R_i(A)(C_i(A))^{\frac{1-\alpha}{\alpha}}},$$

the condition of the Theorem 2 in [4] is satisfied, from (11). By the Theorem 2 in [4], the conclusion holds.

Case 2. When $q > 1$, we take $\tau = \sum_{i \in N_2} \dfrac{[R_i(A)(C_i(A))^{\frac{1-\alpha}{\alpha}}]^q[1 + \sum_{j \in N_1} (\frac{R_j(A)}{|a_{jj}|})^q]}{(|a_{ii}|^{\frac{1}{\alpha}})^q + [R_i(A)(C_i(A))^{\frac{1-\alpha}{\alpha}}]^q}$,

then $\tau < 1$. Let

$$d_i = \{\frac{[R_i(A)(C_i(A))^{\frac{1-\alpha}{\alpha}}]^q[1 + \sum_{j \in N_1} (\frac{R_j(A)}{|a_{jj}|})^q]}{(|a_{ii}|^{\frac{1}{\alpha}})^q + [R_i(A)(C_i(A))^{\frac{1-\alpha}{\alpha}}]^q} + \frac{1 - \zeta}{n_2}\}^{\frac{1}{q}}, \ i \in N_2. \qquad (12)$$

i.e.,

$$d_i^q = \frac{[R_i(A)(C_i(A))^{\frac{1-\alpha}{\alpha}}]^q[1 + \sum_{j \in N_1} (\frac{R_j(A)}{|a_{jj}|})^q]}{(|a_{ii}|^{\frac{1}{\alpha}})^q + [R_i(A)(C_i(A))^{\frac{1-\alpha}{\alpha}}]^q} + \frac{1 - \zeta}{n_2}, \ i \in N_2.$$

(where n_2 is the number of entries in the set N_2). Obviously $\sum_{i \in N_2} d_i^q = 1$ and

$$d_i^q > \frac{[R_i(A)(C_i(A))^{\frac{1-\alpha}{\alpha}}]^q[1 + \sum_{j \in N_1} (\frac{R_j(A)}{|a_{jj}|})^q]}{(|a_{ii}|^{\frac{1}{\alpha}})^q + [R_i(A)(C_i(A))^{\frac{1-\alpha}{\alpha}}]^q}, \quad \forall i \in N_2.$$

From this inequality, for $\forall i \in N_2$

$$|a_{ii}|^{\frac{1}{\alpha}} d_i > \{[R_i(A)(C_i(A))^{\frac{1-\alpha}{\alpha}}]^q[1 + \sum_{j \in N_1} (\frac{R_j(A)}{|a_{jj}|})^q - d_i^q]\}^{\frac{1}{q}}$$

$$= R_i(A)(C_i(A))^{\frac{1-\alpha}{\alpha}}[\sum_{j \in N_1} (\frac{R_j(A)}{|a_{jj}|})^q + 1 - d_i^q]^{\frac{1}{q}}.$$

i.e.,

$$|a_{ii}|^{\frac{1}{\alpha}} d_i > R_i(A)(C_i(A))^{\frac{1-\alpha}{\alpha}}[\sum_{j \in N_1} (\frac{R_j(A)}{|a_{jj}|})^q + \sum_{j \in N_2, j \neq i} d_j^q]^{\frac{1}{q}}, i \in N_2. \qquad (13)$$

Let

$$x_i = \begin{cases} \dfrac{R_i(A)}{|a_{ii}|}, & \text{if } i \in N_1, \\ d_i, & (\text{where } d_i \text{ see } (12)) \text{ if } i \in N_2. \end{cases}$$

Construct a positive diagonally matrix $X = diag(x_1, x_2, \cdots, x_n)$. Next, we will prove $AX \in D(\alpha)$.

Let $B = AX = (b_{ij}) \in C^{n \times n}$, notice $N_{11} = \emptyset$, then $N_1 = N_{12}$. for $i \in N_1 = N_{12}$,

$$|b_{ii}| = |a_{ii}|x_i = |a_{ii}|\frac{R_i(A)}{|a_{ii}|} = R_i(A)$$

$$R_i(B) = \sum_{j \in N_1} |a_{ij}|x_j + \sum_{j \in N_2} |a_{ij}|x_j < \sum_{j \in N_1} |a_{ij}| + \sum_{j \in N_2} |a_{ij}| = R_i(A).$$

$$C_i(B) = \sum_{j \neq i} |a_{ji}|x_i = \sum_{j \neq i} |a_{ji}|\frac{R_i(A)}{|a_{ii}|} = \frac{R_i(A)}{|a_{ii}|}C_i(R) \leq R_i(A).$$

$$(R_i(B))^\alpha (C_i(B))^{1-\alpha} < (R_i(A))^\alpha (C_i(A))^{1-\alpha} = R_i(A) = |b_{ii}|, \quad i \in N_1 = N_{12}.$$

By $q > 1$, it is similar to the proof of the case of the Theorem 1. We can obtain $p = \dfrac{q}{q-1} > 1$. i.e.,

$$\frac{1}{p} + \frac{1}{q} = 1.$$

For $\forall i \in N_2$, from (13) and $H\ddot{o}lder$ inequality, we obtain

$$|a_{ii}|^{\frac{1}{\alpha}}x_i = |a_{ii}|^{\frac{1}{\alpha}}d_i$$
$$> R_i(A)(C_i(A))^{\frac{1-\alpha}{\alpha}}[\sum_{j \in N_1}(\frac{R_j(A)}{|a_{jj}|})^q + \sum_{j \in N_2, j \neq i} d_j^q]^{\frac{1}{q}}$$
$$= (C_i(A))^{\frac{1-\alpha}{\alpha}}R_i(A)[\sum_{j \in N_1}(\frac{R_j(A)}{|a_{jj}|})^q + \sum_{j \in N_2, j \neq i} d_j^q]^{\frac{1}{q}}$$
$$= (C_i(A))^{\frac{1-\alpha}{\alpha}}[(\sum_{j \neq i} |a_{ij}|)^p]^{\frac{1}{p}}[\sum_{j \neq i} x_j^q]^{\frac{1}{q}}$$
$$\geq (C_i(A))^{\frac{1-\alpha}{\alpha}}[\sum_{j \neq i} |a_{ij}|^p]^{\frac{1}{p}}[\sum_{j \neq i} x_j^q]^{\frac{1}{q}}$$
$$\geq (C_i(A))^{\frac{1-\alpha}{\alpha}}(\sum_{j \neq i} |a_{ij}|x_j)$$
$$= (C_i(A))^{\frac{1-\alpha}{\alpha}}R_i(B).$$

The above inequality implies

$$|b_{ii}| = |a_{ii}|x_i > [R_i(B)]^\alpha [C_i(B)]^{1-\alpha}, \quad i \in N_2.$$

We know

$$|b_{ii}| = |a_{ii}|x_i > [R_i(B)]^\alpha [C_i(B)]^{1-\alpha}, \quad i \in N. \tag{14}$$

According to the Definition 1 and (14), we know $B = AX \in D(\alpha)$. Thus $A \in D^*(\alpha)$. By the Lemma 1, then A is a nonsingular H-matrix.

3 Numerical Examples

Example 1. Let

$$A = \begin{pmatrix} 7 & 4 & 4 & 1 \\ 1 & 8 & 3 & 0 \\ 2 & 3 & 7 & 1 \\ 2 & 1 & 0 & 3 \end{pmatrix}$$

So

$$R_1(A) = 9, R_2(A) = 4, R_3(A) = 6, R_4(A) = 3;$$
$$C_1(A) = 5, C_2(A) = 8, C_3(A) = 7, C_4(A) = 2.$$
$$N_{11} = \emptyset, \ N_{12} = N_1 = \{2,3\}, \ N_2 = \{1,4\}.$$

If we take $\alpha = \dfrac{1}{4}$, then from (1) and (2), we know

$$\sigma = \sum_{i \in N} \frac{(\max_{j \neq i} |a_{ij}|)(C_i(A))^{\frac{1-\alpha}{\alpha}}}{|a_{ii}|^{\frac{1}{\alpha}} + (\max_{j \neq i} |a_{ij}|)(C_i(A))^{\frac{1-\alpha}{\alpha}}}$$
$$= \frac{4 \times 5^3}{7^4 + 4 \times 5^3} + \frac{3 \times 8^3}{8^4 + 3 \times 8^3} + \frac{3 \times 7^3}{7^4 + 3 \times 7^3} + \frac{2 \times 2^3}{3^4 + 2 \times 2^3}$$
$$\approx 0.9100 < 1.$$

Taking $q = 2$, then from (1) and (3), we know

$$\sigma = \sum_{i \in N} \frac{[(R_i(A))(C_i(A))^{\frac{1-\alpha}{\alpha}}]^q}{(|a_{ii}|^{\frac{1}{\alpha}})^q + [(R_i(A))(C_i(A))^{\frac{1-\alpha}{\alpha}}]^q}$$
$$= \frac{9^2 \times 5^6}{7^8 + 9^2 \times 5^6} + \frac{4^2 \times 8^6}{8^8 + 4^2 \times 8^6} + \frac{6^2 \times 7^6}{7^8 + 6^2 \times 7^6} + \frac{3^2 \times 2^6}{3^8 + 3^2 \times 2^6}$$
$$\approx 0.8843 < 1.$$

Taking $q = 2$, then from (11), we know

$$\tau = \sum_{i \in N_2} \frac{[R_i(A)(C_i(A))^{\frac{1-\alpha}{\alpha}}]^q[1 + \sum_{j \in N_1} (\frac{R_j(A)}{|a_{jj}|})^q]}{(|a_{ii}|^{\frac{1}{\alpha}})^q + [R_i(A)(C_i(A))^{\frac{1-\alpha}{\alpha}}]^q}$$
$$= \frac{9^2 \times 5^6 \times [1 + (\frac{4}{8})^2 + (\frac{6}{7})^2]}{7^8 + 9^2 \times 5^6} + \frac{2 \times 2^3 \times [1 + (\frac{4}{8})^2 + (\frac{6}{7})^2]}{3^8 + 4^2 \times 2^6}$$
$$\approx 0.6252 < 1.$$

If we take $\alpha = \dfrac{1}{10}$, $q = 1$, then from (1) and (3), we know

$$\sigma = \sum_{i \in N} \frac{R_i(A)(C_i(A))^{\frac{1-\alpha}{\alpha}}}{|a_{ii}|^{\frac{1}{\alpha}} + R_i(A)(C_i(A))^{\frac{1-\alpha}{\alpha}}}$$
$$= \frac{9 \times 5^9}{7^{10} + 9 \times 5^9} + \frac{4 \times 8^9}{8^{10} + 4 \times 8^9} + \frac{6 \times 7^9}{7^{10} + 6 \times 7^9} + \frac{3 \times 2^9}{3^{10} + 3 \times 2^9}$$
$$\approx 0.8788 < 1.$$

Therefore, A is a nonsingular $H-$matrix.

Acknowledgement. The author thanks an anonymous referee for his helpful comments which improved the paper. In this paper, the research was supported by the National Science Foundation of China (Project No. 11171103) and the Scientific Research Fund of Jilin Provincial Education Department of China (Project No. 2012-152).

References

1. Varga, R.S.: On Recurring Theorems on Diagonal Dominance. Linear Algebra Appl. 13, 1–9 (1976)
2. Plemmons, R.J., Berman, A.: Nonnegative Matrices in the Mathmatical Sciences. SIAM Press, Philadelphia (1994)
3. Sun, Y.: An Improvement on a Theorem by Ostrowski and Its Applications. Northeastern Math. J. 7(4), 497–502 (1991)
4. Li, M., Li, Q.: New Criteria Nonsingular H-matrices. Chinese Journal of Engineering Mathematics 29, 715–719 (2012)
5. Gan, T.B., Huang, T.Z.: Simple Criteria for Nonsingular H-matrices. Linear Algebra Appl. 374, 317–326 (2003)
6. Huang, T.Z., Xu, C.X.: Generalized α-diagonal Dominance. Computers and Mathematics With Applications 45, 1721–1727 (2003)
7. Gao, Y.M., Wang, X.H.: Criteria for Generalized Diagonally Dominant Matrices and M-matrices. Linear Algebra Appl. 248(2), 339–353 (1996)
8. Li, M., Sun, Y.: Practical Criteria for H-matrices. Applied Mathematics and Computation 211, 427–433 (2009)
9. Bru, R., Corral, C., Gimenez, I., Mas, J.: Classes of General H-matrices. Linear Algebra and Its Applications 429, 2358–2366 (2008)

PBIL Algorithm for Signal Timing Optimization of Isolated Intersection

Qingbin Zhang, Wenlei Dong, and Xianfang Xing

Shijiazhuang Institute of Railway Technology, Shijiazhuang 050041, China
zqbin2002@sina.com

Abstract. In the research of Webster delay model, Genetic Algorithm (GA), Ant colony algorithm (ACO) and Particle Swarm Optimization algorithm (PSO) have been used to solve the signal timing problem. However, the performances of these algorithms depend heavily on determination of the operators and the choice of related parameters. In this paper, an improved PBIL algorithm is proposed to solve the signal timing problem of an isolated intersection. The experimental results show that the algorithm can get rational signal timing effectively with more insensitive to the parameters setting.

Keywords: Signal timing, Intersection, PBIL, Total delay.

1 Introduction

Optimizing signal timing of intersections is to seek signal timing scheme which can decrease the delay time or (and) stop frequency of the vehicles passing through the intersections and then increase the traffic capacity of the intersections [1]. Based on the Webster delay model [2], GA, ACO and PSO have been used to solve the signal control of urban intersections [3–7]. However, the past researches have also shown that the performances of the algorithms depend heavily on the operators and the related parameters [8–10]. In this paper, we adopted an integer code PBIL to solve the signal timing problem.

2 Traffic Signal Control of Isolated Intersection

In Webster delay model, the average delay per vehicle on particular arm of the intersection is

$$d = \frac{C(1-\lambda)^2}{2(1-\lambda x)} + \frac{x^2}{2q(1-x)}, \tag{1}$$

where C stands for signal cycle, λ stands for green split, which is the ratio of effective green time g_e to the signal cycle time, q stands for traffic flow, and x stands for the degree of saturation, which is the ratio of the actual flow to the maximum flow which can be passed through the intersection and is given by $x = \frac{q}{\lambda s} = \frac{Cq}{sg_e}$, in which s means the saturation flow.

L. Pan et al. (Eds.): BIC-TA 2014, CCIS 472, pp. 606–610, 2014.

Then, for the typical four-phase intersection, we use the minimum total delay as the objective function which can be defined as the following[3]

$$\min D = \min \sum_{i=1}^{4} \sum_{j=1}^{2} \{[\frac{C(1-\lambda_i)^2}{2(1-\lambda_i x_{ij})} + \frac{x_{ij}^2}{2q_{ij}(1-x_{ij})}]q_{ij}\}. \tag{2}$$

The three constraints must be satisfied are

$$\begin{cases} t_1 + t_2 + t_3 + t_4 = C - L, \\[2mm] t_{min} \leq t_i \leq C - L - t_{\min} \times 3 \quad (i = 1, \cdots, 4), \\[2mm] t_i = g_{ei} \geq \frac{Cy_{i\,\max}}{x_{\max}} \quad (i = 1, \cdots, 4), \end{cases} \tag{3}$$

where q_{ij} denotes traffic volume at phase i and entrance lane j; likewise, x_{ij} denotes saturation at phase i and entrance lane j; λ_i denotes green split at phase i; C denotes the signal cycle; L denotes the total lost time in a signal cycle; y is the ratio of traffic flow q to the saturation flow s, $y_{i\,\max}$ is the higher value of y at phase i; t_1, t_2, t_3 and t_4 mean the green time of each phase.

3 The PBIL Algorithm

The initial PBIL uses a binary code in which the population is represented by a probability vector $p_l(x) = (p_l(x_1), p_l(x_2), \cdots, p_l(x_n))$ and $p_l(x_i)$ refers to the probability of obtain a value 1 in the ith gene position in the lth generation [11, 12].

At each generation during the evolution process, M solutions are generated based upon the probabilities specified in the current probability vector $p_l(x)$. The solutions are then evaluated and N best solutions ($N \leq M$) are selected as the best solutions set. We denote them by $x_{1m}^l, \cdots, x_{im}^l, \cdots, x_{NM}^l, (i = 1, \cdots, N)$.

These selected best solutions are used to update the probability vector by using a Hebbian inspired rule:

$$p_{l+1}(x) = (1-a)p_l(x) + a\frac{1}{N}\sum_{k=1}^{N} x_{kM}^l, \tag{4}$$

where a is the learning rate.

After the probability vector is updated, a new set of solutions are generated by sampling from the new probability vector $p_{l+1}(x)$, and the cycle is repeated until some termination condition is satisfied.

In the permutation or integer code PBIL, the probability vector represented the direction of the evolution in binary PBIL is expanded to be a probability matrix P.

Suppose the solution of a permutation optimization problem is represented by an integer string, the length of the integer string is n and the value range is from 1 to m, then an element p_{ij} in P represents the probability which the value is j in the ith gene $(1 \le i \le n; l \le j \le m)$ [13].

The initial value of the probability matrix is a uniform distribution. During the evolution, the values of the p_{ij} is updated by the formula (4) and roulette method is used to sample the probability matrix in order to get the solutions of the problem.

4   Experiments and Results

Suppose the traffic flow and the saturation flow of the intersection with four phases are shown in table 1, and suppose the signal cycle is 130s, the total lost time is 10s and the minimum green time is 10s at each phase, the x_{max} is set to be 0.9. Furthermore, we suppose that the lost time equals to the time of yellow light, and then the effective green time is the real green time [3].

Table 1. The traffic flow of the experimental intersection

phase		q	s	y	$y_{i\,max}$
Phase1	E	270	1500	0.18	0.18
	W	240	1500	0.16	
Phase2	E	60	500	0.12	0.12
	W	60	500	0.12	
Phase3	S	400	2000	0.20	0.20
	N	240	2000	0.12	
Phase4	S	80	800	0.10	0.15
	N	120	800	0.15	

There are only three basic parameters in the PBIL, where a is the learning rate. M is the parameter just like the population size as in the GA or the number of the ants in ACO. The N is the number of selected best solutions used to guide the evolution directions. In the experiments, M is set to be 200, the learning rate a is set to be 0.02, and the selected best solutions N is set as $0.10 * M$. The total delay D can be gotten easily which is 59236s, and the green time of four phases is $(30, 17, 51, 22)$s.

In order to compare the influence of different parameters setting on the total delay of the experimental problem, 20 independent runnings of different N with the learning rate a is 0.02 and 20 independent runnings of different a with N is $0.10 * M$ are executed. The average generations needed to be executed before convergence are showed in Table 2 and Table 3.

From Table 2 we can see that although more better solutions are used to update the probability matrix, the more generations need to evolution, all running can get the optimization solution 59236 s. In the Table 3, it can be concluded that with the increase of the learning rate a , the convergence speed is also improved and all the experiments can get the optimization total delay.

Table 2. The average solution of different N with the learning rate a is 0.02

N	average generations	total delay
$0.02 * M$	6.9	59236
$0.05 * M$	11.2	59236
$0.10 * M$	17.2	59236

Table 3. The average solution of different a with N is $0.10 * M$

a	average generations	total delay
0.02	17.2	59236
0.05	8.0	59236
0.10	7.7	59236

5   Conclusion

In this paper, an integer code PBIL is proposed to solve the signal timing problem of an isolated intersection. Experimental results show that the proposed algorithm can get rational signal timing effectively with more insensitive to the parameters setting.

Acknowledgments. This work was supported by Talents Cultivation Engineering Research Project of Hebei Province (No. 2013-12) and Science and Technology Research Project of Hebei Education Department (No. Q2012138).

References

1. Hua, H., Gao, Y., Yang, X.: Multi–objective Optimization Method of Fixed–Time Signal Control of Isolated Intersections. In: Proceedings of IEEE International Conference on Computational and Information Sciences, pp. 1281–1284 (2010)
2. Webster, F.V.: Traffic Signal Settings. Road Research Technical Paper No. 39. London: HMSO (1958)
3. Chen, Q.: Research on Signal Control of Urban Intersection Based on Genetic Algorithms. In: Second International Conference on Intelligent Computation Technology and Automation, pp. 193–196 (2009)
4. Leena, S.: Time Optimization for Traffic Signal Control Using Genetic Algorithm. International Journal of Recent Trends in Engineering 2(2), 4–6 (2009)
5. Dong, C., Huang, S., Xue, X.: Comparative Study of Several Intelligent Optimization algorithms for Traffic Control applications. In: International Conference on Electronics, Communications and Control, pp. 4219–4223 (2011)
6. Jiajia, H., Zaien, H.: Ant Colony Algorithm for Traffic Signal Timing Optimization. Advances in Engineering Software 43, 14–18 (2012)
7. Wang, X., Song, T.: MRPGA: Motif Detecting by Modified Random Projection Strategy and Genetic Algorithm. J. Comput. Theor. Nanosci. 10, 1209–1214 (2013)
8. Goldberg, D.E.: The design of innovation–lessons from and for competent genetic algorithms. Kluwer Academic Publishers, Norwell (2002)

9. M. Samrout, R. Kouta, F. Yalaoui, E. Châtelet, N. Chebbo.: Parameter's setting of the ant colony algorithm applied in preventive maintenance optimization. Journal of Intelligent Manufacturing 18(6), 663–677 (2007)

10. Erik, M., Pedersen, H.: Good Parameters for Particle Swarm Optimization. Hvass Laboratories,Technical Report no. HL1001 (2010)

11. Baluja, S.: Population–Based Incremental Learning: A Method for Integrating Genetic Search Based Function Optimization and Competitive Learning, Carnegie Mellon University (1994)

12. Larrañaga, P., Lozano, J. A.: Estimation of Distribution Algorithms: A New Tool for Evolutionary Computation. Kluwer Academic Publishers (2002)

13. Zhang, Q., Cai, M., Zhou, F., Nie, H.: An Improved PBIL Algorithm for Path Planning Problem of Mobile Robots. In: Yin, H., Tang, K., Gao, Y., Klawonn, F., Lee, M., Weise, T., Li, B., Yao, X. (eds.) IDEAL 2013. LNCS, vol. 8206, pp. 85–92. Springer, Heidelberg (2013)

Application to Logic Circuits Using Combinatorial Displacement of DNA Strands

Xuncai Zhang, Weiwei Zhang, Yanfeng Wang, and Guangzhao Cui

School of Electrical and Information Engineering,
Henan Key Lab of Information-based Electrical Appliances,
Zhengzhou University of Light Industry,
No.5 Dongfeng Road, Zhengzhou, 450002, China
zhangxuncai@163.com

Abstract. The toehold and branch migration domain of traditional DNA strand displacement are covalently connected, such a structure cannot be changed during the execution of the circuit, so to some extent it limits the construction of DNA circuits. To solve this problem, we use combinatorial displacement of DNA strands technology where toehold and branch migration domains are located in different strand, these two domains must be firstly linked by hybridization of linking domains that can occur strand displacement reaction, this paper is to design an Inhibit and a XOR based on this principle which is theoretically possible.

Keywords: DNA strand displacement, DNA logic gate, Inhibit, XOR.

1 Introduction

Since 2000, Yurke et al. [1] first used strand displacement technology to control nano-mechanical switches open and close, people started using it to build dynamic nature of engineering systems, such as: circuits [2, 3], catalytic amplifiers [4], molecular motors [5–7], reconfigurable and autonomous nanostructures [8, 9].

DNA strand displacement technology is very suitable for the logic circuits. In 2007, Ghadiri et al. [2] used this scheme to design a set of logic gates AND, OR, and AND-NOT, and then integrated into a multi-stage circuit for performing XOR function. In 2011, Winfree et al. [10] published a paper based on the DNA strand displacement cascade reaction, which can calculate the square root of an integer less than 15. In 2013, Yan et al. [3] proposed a strand displacement-based 3 input -1 output logic circuit, the circuit can be switched between "AND" gate and "OR" gate. On the basis of majority gate described here author designed a complex five-input logic gate. In the same year, Wang et al. [11] also designed a 3-input model based on the combination strand displacement and used this model to select the composite number represented by excess-three code from 0 to 9.

This paper design an "Inhibit" gate and a "XOR" gate based on the "Inhibit" gate using combinatorial displacement of DNA strands.

L. Pan et al. (Eds.): BIC-TA 2014, CCIS 472, pp. 611–615, 2014.

2 Combinatorial Displacement of DNA Strands

2.1 The Mechanism of Combinatorial Strand Displacement

The toehold and branch migration domain of combinatorial strand displacement are located in different strands. A "⊥" type DNA complex [12] firstly formed by a linking domain hybridized, which we call displacing complex, can react with other strands (reporter strand) in strand displacement fashion. The below illustration (Fig. 1) explains the process of combinatorial strand displacement [13]. The toehold domain (TH) is shown as red lines, and branch migration domain (BM) is shown as black lines, gray lines show bulgy domains, green lines indicate the linking domains, the direction of arrow indicate the 5' to 3' direction, the displacing complex can reaction with the reporter strand in strand displacement fashion, and an output strand is be displaced. In this paper, a single-stranded DNA contained BM is defined BM strand, a single-stranded DNA contained TH is defined TH strand. The displacing complex cannot effectively trigger the strand displacement reaction, but adding two bulged thymidines (bulgy domain) can accelerate obviously the strand displacement reaction [14].

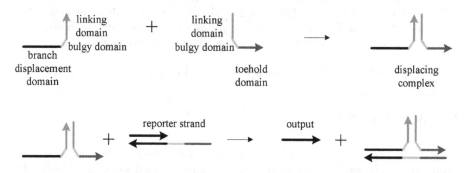

Fig. 1. The process of combinatorial strand displacement

3 Application to Logic Circuits Using Combinatorial Displacement of DNA Strands

3.1 An "Inhibit" Logic Gate Design

Here we design an "Inhibit" $(A\overline{B})$ gate, and the corresponding logical relationship is: if and only if A is present, there will be output, otherwise no output exists.

An "Inhibit" logic gate based on combinatorial strand displacement is shown below, in the logic gate, each input which has a same linking domain contains only a single strand, input A is a BM strand, input B is perfectly complementary with a TH strand, the TH strand and reporter strand compose the "Inhibit"

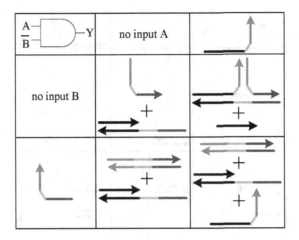

Fig. 2. A design of "Inhibit" logic gate using combinatorial displacement

logic gate. Similarly, the presence of specific DNA strand indicate logical "1", the inexistent DNA strand represent logical "0". The first row and column of Fig. 2 show the inputs states.

The displacing complex is formed only when input A exist and then react strand displacement with reporter strand, input B and the TH strand from the logic gate are perfectly complementary, the binding strength between input B and the TH strand is stronger than input A and TH strand's, in ideal circumstances, as long as input B is present, unformed displacing complex lead to nothing happened, there is not a single-strand DNA being displaced.

3.2   A "XOR" Logic Gate Design

A "XOR" logic gate has two inputs and one output, if only one of the inputs is "true", the output is "true". The output is "false" if both inputs are "false" or if both inputs are "true". Here we design a "XOR" gate based on the integration of "Inhibit" gate.

Each input contains a BM strand and a strand which is perfectly complementary with a TH strand from the logic gate that the linking domain are different, the two inputs have the same toehold and branch migration domain, the "XOR" logic gate is comprise of reporter strand and two TH strands with the same toehold domain and different linking domain, as shown in Fig. 3.

When either, but not both, of the inputs are exist, the displacing complexes is formed because of the BM strand in input A or B presence and the react with reporter strand, while the other strand from the input is paired with TH strand perfectly. When both of inputs exist, no displacing complexes formed lead to the output absence.

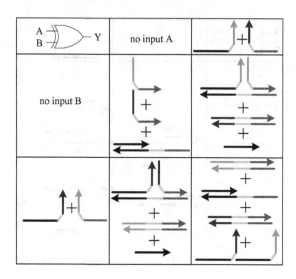

Fig. 3. A design of "XOR" logic gate using combinatorial strand displacement

4   Conclusion

In this paper, we designed an "Inhibit" logic gate and a "XOR" logic gate using combinatorial displacement. That's all right in theory, but in practice it may exists some error, for example different kinds of single-strand DNA can show the same logic but various binding strength with other strands have an effect on the kinetics of displacement reaction, in addition, the yield of displacing complexes would have a influence on the subsequent displacement reaction happened. To reduce these errors, it is necessary to design DNA sequence and to set reaction condition reasonably. A flexible between BM strand and TH strand can achieve the function of certain strands reprogrammable compared with the traditional DNA strand displacement. In addition to this paper suggested the logic gate, the combinatorial displacement also can be used in other building block of digital circuits, such as AND, OR, multi-channel input gate and so on.

Acknowledgment. This work is supported by the Natural Science Foundation of China (61076103, 61070238), the Basic and Frontier Technology Research Program of Henan Province (142300413214) and the Young Backbone Teachers Project of Henan province (2013GGJS-106).

References

1. Yurke, B., Turberfield, A.J., Mills, A.P., et al.: A DNA-fuelled Molecular Machine Made of DNA. J. Nature 406(6796), 605–608 (2000)
2. Frezza, B.M., Cockroft, S.L., Ghadiri, M.R.: Modular Multi-level Circuits from Immobilized DNA-based Logic Gates. J. Journal of the American Chemical Society 129(48), 14875–14879 (2007)
3. Li, W., Yan, H., Liu, Y., et al.: Three-Input Majority Logic Gate and Multiple Input Logic Circuit Based on DNA Strand Displacement. J. Nano Letters 13(6), 2980–2988 (2013)
4. Zhang, D., Turberfield, A.J., Yurke, B., et al.: Engineering Entropy-driven Reactions and Networks Catalyzed by DNA. J. Science 318(5853), 1121–1125 (2007)
5. Sherman, W.B., Seeman, N.C.: A Precisely Controlled DNA Biped Walking Device. J. Nano Letters 4(7), 1203–1207 (2004)
6. Shin, J.S., Pierce, N.A.: A Synthetic DNA Walker for Molecular Transport. J. Journal of the American Chemical Society 126(35), 10834–10835 (2004)
7. Gu, H., Chao, J., Xiao, S.J., et al.: A Proximity-Based Programmable DNA Nanoscale Assembly Line. J. Nature 465(7295), 202–205 (2010)
8. Yan, H., Zhang, X.P., Shen, Z.Y., et al.: A Robust DNA Mechanical Device Controlled by Hybridization Topology. J. Nature 415(6867), 62–65 (2002)
9. Ding, B.Q., Seeman, N.C.: Operation of a DNA Robot Arm Inserted Into A 2D DNA Crystalline Substrate. J. Science 314(5805), 1583–1585 (2006)
10. Qian, L.L., Winfree, E.: Scaling Up Digital Circuit Computation with DNA Strand Displacement Cascades. J. Science 332(6034), 1196–1201 (2011)
11. Zhu, J.B., Zhang, L.B., Wang, E.K., et al.: Four-way junction-driven DNA strand displacement and its application in building majority logic circuit. J. Journal of the American Chemical Society Nano 7(11), 10211–10217 (2013)
12. Duckett, D.R., Lilley, D.M.: The Three-Way DNA Junction is A Y-Shaped Molecule in which There is No Helix-Helix Stacking. J. The EMBO Journal 9(5), 1659 (1990)
13. Genot, A.J., Bath, J., Turberfield, A.J.: Combinatorial Displacement of DNA Strands: application to matrix multiplication and weighted sums. J. Angewandte Chemie International Edition 52(4), 1189–1192 (2013)
14. Chen, X.: Expanding the Rule Set of DNA Circuitry with Associative Toehold Activation. J. Journal of the American Chemical Society. 134(1), 263–271 (2011)

Microscan Imager Logging Data Compression Using improved Huffman Algorithm

Yanhui Zhang[1,2], He Zhang[1], Jun Shi[3], and Xiaozheng Yin[3]

[1] School of Mechanical Engineering,
Nanjing University of Science and Technology, Nanjing, 210094, China
[2] School of Mechanical Engineering, Henan Institue of Engineering,
No.1 Xianghe Road, Longhu Town, Zhengzhou, 451191, China
[3] School of Electrical Engineering, Zhengzhou University of Light Industry,
No.5 Dongfeng Road, Zhengzhou, 450002, China
306584016@qq.com

Abstract. The conflict between ever-increasing volumes of microscan imager logging data and limited cable transmission bandwidth intensifying day by day. In this paper, an improved lossless data compression algorithm is proposed. Specifically, according to the characteristics of the micro resistivity imaging logging data, it is proved that Hex character encoding has better compressibility than decimal character encoding. Then, it analyzed that traditional quaternary Huffman algorithm does not be fully applicable to microscan imager logging data. Lastly, it employed improved quaternary Huffman algorithm for logging data compression so as to enhance the data compression ratio. The experiment comparsions show that ,compared to the convention quaternary algorithm and the improved compressed Huffman encoding, Both elapsed time and compression ratio are a great improvement.

Keywords: Microscan imager logging, Logging data, Lossless data compression, Huffman algorithm.

1 Introduction

The signal needs to be measured in microscan imager logging system is the 10kHz sine wave signal with current of 0-3A, which is extracted from intensely noisy background [1–3]. The current intensity emitted by each electrode varies with different rocks and conditions of the borehole wall it leans against. The microscan imager logging system has more than one hundred signal sources and high-density acquisition, to make the data volume enormous. However, the unceasingly growing logging data is limited by real-time transmission bandwidth, which hinders the improvement of transmissibility and promotes researchers to constantly seek various approaches to improve the transmission efficiency. Then the Huffman coding will be used for lossless data compression [4–7]. Huffman algorithm is the foundation of the most common compression programs and often as a step in the process of compression. At present the algorithm has been constituted the core of today's compression softwares. How to make the improvement of Huffman algorithm is still a key direction of the study.

L. Pan et al. (Eds.): BIC-TA 2014, CCIS 472, pp. 616–620, 2014.

2   Huffman Coding with Different Systems

The principle of the Huffman[8, 9] coding can be described as follows: supposing the characters are expressed by set $J = \{j_1, j_2, \cdots, j_n\}$, in which j_i represents different characters, if the frequency of character j_i is F and the coding length is L, its required to determine the coding scheme to make the ΣFL value minimum to achieve the shortest total coding length of source file. According to data compression theory and the definition of information entropy, in the worst circumstance (occurrence probabilities of each character are equal), the information entropy presented with decimal character is $F = -10 \times (1/10) \times \log_2(1/10) \approx 3.3219$. With the same conditions, the information entropy presented with hexadecimal character is $F = -16 \times (1/16) \times \log_2(1/16) = 4$. Since the logging data is stored by double byte, each double-byte data will need five decimal digit characters and one sign symbol for presentation, thereby the shortest data length that the corresponding Huffman coding needed is $M = 3.3219 \times 6 \times 2 \times L/8 \approx 4.9829L$ (bytes). If four hexadecimal digit characters are used for presentation, the shortest data length that the corresponding Huffman coding needed is $M = 4 \times 5 \times 2 \times L/8 = 4.1524L$ (bytes). With sampling frequency of 320KHz and fundamental frequency of 10KHz, the original circumferential borehole microscan imager logging signal is able to collect 64,000 samples in 0.2 seconds. Usually, the original logging signal is coded based on decimal character, each sample has five digitals and one sign bit 64,000 samples are totally expressed as 384,000 characters. If hexadecimal character is adopted for coding, each sample will be expressed as four digits and one sign bit and 64,000 samples will be totally expressed as 320,000 characters. From the comparison of sampling probabilities, we know that the logging data is characterized by large amount of information, high repetition rate of characters and small difference in occurrence probabilities of various characters. Under the circumstance of the same (or slightly different) probability of occurrence of various characters [10], compared with decimal character coding, the application of hexadecimal character coding has more advantages in enhanceing compression ratio.

3   Improved Quaternary Huffman Algorithm

3.1   Traditional Huffman Algorithm

Huffman algorithm in lossless data compression is the foundation of numerous data compression algorithms. Normally, the compression ratio of text data by Huffman coding is typically around 2-3. The rate of executable file and waveform data is about 1-2 [11].Traditional quaternary Huffman algorithm is unable to guarantee that all nodes with greater weight are included in the higher level of nodes. If there are not four uncoded nodes remaining in the end, the number of child nodes in the root will be deficiency, which means no use of the nodes with minimum weight but the application of the nodes with maximum weight. Then the average code length will be increased and coding efficiency decreased, resulting in waste. For example, there are 12 characters (A, B, C, D, E, F, G, H,

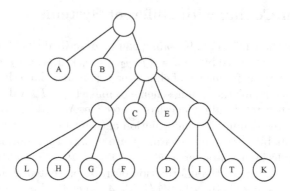

Fig. 1. Quaternary Traditional Huffman tree

I, J, K, L) with respective probabilities of (0.25, 0.23, 0.105, 0.02, 0.12, 0.07, 0.08, 0.04, 0.025, 0.015, 0.015, 0.03). The result of traditional quaternary algorithm is shown in Fig.1. The average code length is 3.70 and coding efficiency is 83.08%.

3.2   The Proposed Quaternary Huffman Algorithm

Different with traditional quaternary Huffman algorithm, the improved quaternary Huffman algorithm gives priority to the nodes with greater weight. These nodes will be shifted up, closest to the root, so as to make sure both the tree root and high-level node possess of 4 child nodes, with vacancy only in the lowest level. The algorithm process is as follows:

(1) Compute the total number of nodes based on J characters.

(2) Compute the number of child nodes which cannot form a collection of four by set as k.

(3) If $k = 0$, execute Step(5), otherwise execute Step(4).

(4) First, k child nodes with the minimum weight are used to generate their father node by set as K. Then k nodes are deleted from the node collection and the father node K is added to constitute node collection by set as J^*.

(5) Construct the rest of Huffman tree based on the traditional quaternary algorithm with J^*.

As shown in Fig.2, there has been an increase in layers of new Huffman tree after improvement. The average code length is reduced to 3.28 and coding efficiency is raised to 97.3%. Since the compression ratio has been improved, the elapsed time for compression and decoding is correspondingly decreased.

3.3   Algorithm Comparison and Analysis

Five sets of measured raw logging data have been randomly intercepted and respectively coded with hexadecimal and decimal characters by using of matlab language. Both the traditional quaternary Huffman compression algorithms and

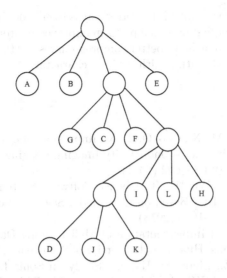

Fig. 2. Improved Quaternary Huffman tree

Table 1. Traditional Huffman algorithm and new Huffman algorithm

Source	Traditional Huffman			Improved Huffman			Improved percentage	
file/b	C/b	R	ET/s	C/b	R	ET/s	Com	ER
4431873	5074429	1.144985	0.7129	4123634	1.074749	0.6446	18.73698	9.580586
16103967	17665428	1.096961	2.666	13606291	1.183568	2.368	22.97786	11.17779
34320370	38457272	1.120538	5.816	30011078	1.14359	4.999	21.96254	14.04746
330895360	380603556	1.150223	74.9692	309902603	1.06774	62.8822	18.57601	16.12262
2817888	1965029	0.697341	0.4046	1617725	1.741883	0.3072	17.67424	24.07316

improvement are used to compress these data. The comparison between their compression ratio and time have been conducted with the results and shown in Table1.

It can be seen from Table1 that no matter which coding method is chose, decimal or hexadecimal method, there will be always a situation that the number of four child nodes is zero in quaternary Huffman compression in accordance with the logging datas features. Compared with traditional one, the improved quaternary Huffman algorithm shows a significant improvement in compression ratio and time. In addition, through the comparison with binary coding, hexadecimal coding has higher efficiency.

4   Conclusion

By the analysis on features of raw microscan imager logging data, this paper proposes an application of hexadecimal coding for logging data and verifies the superiority of hexadecimal coding over binary coding in data file processing. Moreover, it has discussed the deficiencies of traditional quaternary Huffman coding in data compression. And the better way is to encode the logging data with hexadecimal character first and then perform improved quaternary Huffman data compression, whith will achieve better compression results than using traditional quaternary Huffman algorithm with decimal character.

References

1. Xu, F., Xiao, H., Ma X., Cao, Q., Li X.: Improvement of Digital Phase Sensitivity Detection in Micro-conductivity Imaging Logging Tool. Well Logging Technology 35(S0), 688–692 (2011)
2. Yang, X., Ju, X., Wu W.: Test-bench Software System Development for Imaging Logging Tool Based on C/S Mode. Science Technology and Engineering 13(7), 1936–1940 (2013)
3. Liu, J.: Design and Implementation of MCI Logging Data Acquisition and Processing Systems, Huazhong University of Science and Technology, (2010)
4. Zou, X., Feng, Z., Zhang S., Han F.: Study on Sonic Logging Data Compression Based on LZW Algorithm. Well Logging Technology 37(3), 294–296 (2013)
5. Sharma, M.: Compression Using Huffman Coding. International Journal of Computer Science and Network Security 10(5), 133–141 (2010)
6. Yan, C., Liu, J., Yang, Q.: A Real-Time Data Compression & Reconstruction Method Based on Lifting Scheme. In: 2005/2006 IEEE PES proceeding of Transmission and Distribution Conference and Exhibition, pp.863–867. IEEE Press, New York (2005)
7. Hsieh, C. T., Huang, S. -J.: Disturbance Data Compression of A Power System Using the Huffman Coding Approach with Wavelet Transform Enhancement. IEE Proceedings-Generation, Transmission and Distribution 150(1), 7–14 (2003)
8. Huffman, D. A.: A Method for the Construction of Minimum-Redundancy Codes. Proceedings of the IRE 40(9), 1098–1101 (1952)
9. Shi, P., Li, M., Yu, T., Zhao, L., Wang, J.: Design and Application of an XML Data Compression Algorithm Based on Huffman Coding. Journal of Beijing University of Chemical Technology (Natural Science) 40(4), 120–124 (2013)
10. Bi, Y.: Study on Electric System Data Compression Algorithms and Communication Network Simulation, Shandong University, (2007)
11. Hu, Z., Yin, X., Lu, L.: An Improved Quaternary Huffman Algorithm, Microcomputer and its Applications 31(10), 65–66, (2012)

Decision-Making Strategies for Multi-Objective Community Detection in Complex Networks

Yu Zhang, Xingyi Zhang*, Jin Tang and Bin Luo

Key Lab of Intelligent Computing and Signal Processing of Ministry of Education,
School of Computer Science and Technology, Anhui University, Hefei 230039, China
ahuzhangyu@126.com, {xyzhanghust,ahhftang}@gmail.com, luobin@ahu.edu.cn

Abstract. Multi-objective optimization algorithms have demonstrated their effectiveness and efficiency in detecting community structure in complex networks, by which a set of trade-off partitions of networks are obtained instead of a single partition. The large number of partitions lead to a challenging problem for decision makers: how to obtain an ideal partition from the set of trade-off partitions of networks. In this paper, we present two decision-making strategies for obtaining the ideal partition, one is based on the knee points and the other is based on the majority voting. Experimental results on random networks and real-world networks illustrate that the presented two strategies are very competitive for obtaining an ideal partition of networks.

Keywords: complex network, community detection, multi-objective optimization, decision-making strategy.

1 Introduction

There exist a large number of complex networks in real-world, such as social networks, biological networks and the Internet. One of the hot topics in complex networks is to detect community structure, which aims to divide a network into several sets of closely connected nodes. Briefly, a community of a network refers to a set of nodes in the network such that nodes in the set are closely connected, while nodes in the set and nodes outside the set are loosely connected. In order to efficiently detect community structure in networks, different strategies and approaches have been proposed. Among these methods, optimization based approaches were proved to be very effective for detecting community structure. In the past years, a large number of single objective optimization algorithms have been developed for detecting communities, in which the modularity was usually adopted as the criterion function, such as GN [4], GAS [8] and JSACO [7]. Experimental results illustrated that the single objective optimization algorithms based on modularity can well detect communities with a large size, while may fail to identify communities smaller than a scale even in cases where communities are unambiguously defined. Actually, similar problems also exist in the single objective optimization algorithms based on other criterion functions.

---

* Corresponding author.

L. Pan et al. (Eds.): BIC-TA 2014, CCIS 472, pp. 621–628, 2014.

To address the problems in single objective optimization algorithms, researchers from different areas start to consider multi-objective optimization algorithms for detecting communities, such as MOGA-Net [10], MOCD [11] and MOEA/D-Net [6]. Different from the case in single objective optimization algorithms, multi-objective optimization algorithms simultaneously optimize multiple criterion functions which conflict with each other. Due to the conflicting nature of objectives, multi-objective optimization algorithms usually do not find a single optimal partition, but rather a set of trade-off partitions of networks. This means that decision makers should obtain an ideal partition from the large number of partitions, which is a very challenging problem for decision makers. Up to now, much work has been done to design multi-objective optimization algorithms for finding a good set of partitions, while little work focuses on the problem of how to provide decision makers with a strategy for obtaining their ideal partition from the set of partitions. In complex networks, the widely adopted strategy is to identify the partition with the largest modularity as the ideal partition. Lots of studies illustrated that, the partition with the largest modularity is usually not the ideal partition of complex networks, despite that it is better than the partitions with a quite small modularity.

In this paper, we present two decision-making strategies for obtaining an ideal partition from the large number of partitions: (1) a strategy based on knee points, (2) a strategy based on majority voting. The first strategy is to select the knee point from the set of partitions. A knee point in a set refers to the partition in which a small deterioration in one objective will cause a large improvement in the other one [1]. Compared with other partitions in the set, the knee point is of course very interesting for decision makers. So, the first strategy will select the knee point from the large number of partitions and provide it to decision makers. The second strategy is to use the majority voting. This means that two nodes are considered in the same community if most partitions in the set indicate that the two nodes are in the same community. So, the second strategy will generate a new partition of networks based on all partitions found by multi-objective optimization algorithms. Experimental results on random networks and real-world networks confirm that the proposed two strategies are effective to obtain an ideal partition of complex networks.

The rest of this paper is organized as follows. In Section 2, we briefly review the notion of community and the multi-objective optimization algorithm used in the experiments. Section 3 presents the two proposed strategies for decision-making, with the experimental results given in Section 4. Finally, conclusions and remarks are given in Section 5.

2   Prerequisites

It is assumed that readers have some familiarity with complex networks, as well as multi-objective optimization. We here directly introduce the notions used in the following sections.

Let $G = (V, E)$ be an undirected network with $|V| = n$ nodes and $|E| = m$ edges. A partition of network G with k communities is defined as $S = \{V_1, \ldots, V_k\}$, such that $V_i \subseteq V$, $V_i \cap V_j = \emptyset$, $1 \leq i, j \leq k$ and $\cup_{i=1}^{k} V_i = V$.

In complex networks, two criterion functions are usually used as optimization objectives of multi-objective optimization algorithms for community detection, which can be defined as follows:

$$\begin{cases} \min f_1 = -\sum_{i=1}^{k} \frac{L(V_i,V_i)}{|V_i|} \\ \\ \min f_2 = \sum_{i=1}^{k} \frac{L(V_i,\overline{V_i})}{|V_i|} \end{cases} \tag{1}$$

where $S = \{V_1,\ldots,V_k\}$ is a partition of network $G = (V,E)$, $|V_i|$ denotes the number of nodes in V_i, $\overline{V_i} = V - V_i$, $L(V_i,V_j) = \sum_{p\in V_i,q\in V_j} a_{pq}$, and $A = (a_{pq})_{n\times n}$ is the adjacency matrix of G. Objective f_1 characterizes the strength of connections between nodes in each community of the partition, while f_2 indicates the strength of connections between nodes in a community and nodes outside the community. Therefore, the larger the strength of connections between nodes in each community, the better the partition will be, but the smaller the strength of connections between nodes in a community and nodes outside it is, the better the partition will be.

In the following experiments, we will use the above two criterion functions as optimization objectives, and adopt the non-dominated sorting genetic algorithm (NSGA-II) [3] as the multi-objective optimization algorithm. We should stress that, the proposed two decision-making strategies are also effective for other objective functions and multi-objective optimization algorithms.

3   The Proposed Decision-Making Strategies

In this section, we present two strategies for decision makers to obtain an ideal partition from the large number of partitions found by multi-objective optimization algorithms.

3.1   A Knee Point Based Strategy

A knee point in a set of trade-off solutions refers to the solution with the maximum marginal rate of return, which means that a small improvement on one objective of the solution is accompanied by a severe degradation in another. It is obvious that knee points are quite different from the other solutions in the set. For that reason, we argue that a partition of a network which corresponds to the knee point is more likely to be the ideal one in the large number of partitions found by multi-objective optimization algorithms. So, we here suggest the decision-making strategy based on knee points to obtain the ideal partition of networks.

Specifically, a knee point in the large number of partitions can be obtained by the following four steps (we assume that $p_1,\ldots,p_n$ are the n trade-off solutions found by a multi-objective optimization algorithm and that each solution corresponds to a partition of a network):

(1) find the two solutions which have the minimal value on the first objective and the second objective, respectively;

(2) construct an extreme line based on the two solutions;
(3) calculate the distance between each solution and the extreme line;
(4) find the solution with the maximal distance to the extreme line, and identify
    it as the knee point of the n solutions (if there are more than one solution
    with the maximal distance, then the solution with the maximal distance and
    the maximal modularity is identified as the knee point).

Fig. 1 illustrates an example of finding the knee point in a large number of solutions, where s_1 denotes the solution with the minimal value on the first objective f_1, s_2 denotes the solution with the minimal value on the second objective f_2, and L denotes the extreme line between the two solutions s_1 and s_2. From this figure, it is not difficult to find that the solution marked by star is the knee point of the 10 solutions. Note that if we assume that the extreme line L is defined as $ax + by + c = 0$, then the distance from a solution $A(x_A, y_A)$ to the extreme line L can be simply calculated by the following formula:

$$d(A, L) = \frac{|ax_A + by_A + c|}{\sqrt{a^2 + b^2}} \qquad (2)$$

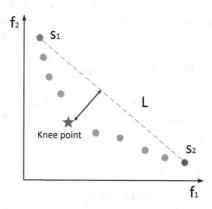

Fig. 1. An illustration of finding the knee point in a set

3.2   A Majority Voting Based Strategy

The main idea of majority voting based strategy is to obtain a new partition of networks by using the information of all partitions found by multi-objective optimization algorithms. If two nodes belong to the same community in most of the partitions, then these two nodes are considered in the same community. In this way, any pair of nodes in a network can be checked whether they are in the same community and thus a new partition of the network is obtained.

Specifically, the majority voting based strategy is performed as follows (we assume that $p_1, \ldots, p_n$ are the n trade-off solutions found by a multi-objective optimization algorithm and that each solution corresponds to a partition of a network):

(1) for each solution p_i ($1 \leq i \leq n$), construct a matrix $A_i = (a_{kl}^{(i)})_{m \times m}$, where m is the number of nodes in the network and $a_{kl}^{(i)}$ indicates whether node k and node l belong to the same community in p_i; if they belong to the same community in p_i, then $a_{kl}^{(i)} = 1$, otherwise $a_{kl}^{(i)} = 0$;

(2) construct a matrix $B = (b_{kl})_{m \times m}$ by using the n matrices $A_1, \ldots, A_n$, where b_{kl} is calculated by the formula

$$b_{kl} = \frac{\sum_{i=1}^{n} a_{kl}^{(i)}}{n} \tag{3}$$

(3) compare each element b_{kl} of matrix B with a given threshold T, and replace it with 1 if $b_{kl} >= T$, otherwise replace it with 0;

(4) obtain a partition based on matrix B: if $b_{kl} = 1$, then two nodes k and l belong to the same community.

4 Experimental Results and Analysis

In this section, we validate the performance of the proposed two decision-making strategies by empirically comparing them with the strategy based on maximal modularity (termed as $Max - Q$) and three single objective optimization algorithms for community detection, i.e., GN, GAS and JSACO. The multi-objective optimization algorithm NSGA-II for finding a set of partitions is set as follows: the population size $size_P = 100$, the crossover probability $p_c = 0.9$ and the mutation probability $p_m = 0.05$. The experiments are conducted on random networks and real-world networks. All simulation results reported in this paper are obtained by averaging over 10 independent runs. Two widely used metrics, modularity Q [4] and normalized mutual information NMI [2], are used to evaluate the quality of the obtained partition. In what follows, we consider the experiments on random networks and real-world networks, respectively.

4.1 Experiments on Random Networks

The random networks used in the experiments are generated by Newman model $RN(C, s, d, P_{in})$ [9], where C is the number of communities, s is the number of nodes in each community, d is the degree of nodes and P_{in} is the density of communities. The larger the value of P_{in} is, the more clear the community structure becomes.

Fig. 2 shows the average modularity and NMI obtained by the proposed two strategies and the four compared methods on the random networks $RN(4, 32, 16, P_{in})$ in which P_{in} varies from 0.4 to 0.9 with an increment of 0.05, resulting in

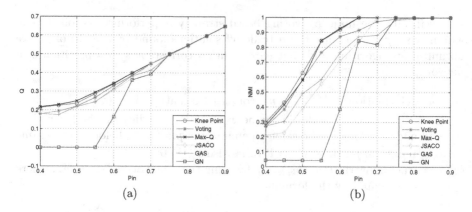

Fig. 2. Modularity and NMI obtained by different approaches on random networks

11 random networks. From this figure, we can find the following results: (1) the performance of all the six methods increases with an increment of P_{in} in terms of both modularity and NMI, and all the considered methods can find the correct partition when $P_{in} > 0.8$; (2) the strategy based on maximal modularity obtains higher modularity value than the knee point based strategy and the majority voting based strategy when $P_{in} < 0.7$ and $P_{in} < 0.8$, respectively, due to the fact that the strategy based on maximal modularity is to select a partition with the maximal modularity; (3) the proposed strategy based on knee point obtains higher NMI value than the other two decision-making strategies when $P_{in} < 0.55$, this means that the knee point based strategy outperforms the other two strategies, since NMI which reflects the similarity between the true partition and the detected one can correctly characterize the quality of a partition (when calculating NMI, the true partition should be known); (4) the partitions obtained by the three decision-making strategies are better than those obtained by the three single objective optimization algorithms (JSACO, GAS and GN), which illustrates that multi-objective optimization algorithm is a very promising approach for detecting communities of complex networks.

Overall, the proposed two strategies are effective for decision makers to obtain an ideal partition from the large number of partitions found by multi-objective optimization algorithms.

4.2   Experiments on Real-World Networks

Three popular real-world networks are used in the experiments, i.e., Zackary Karate Club (34 nodes, 78 edges and 2 communities), Dolphins social network (62 nodes, 159 edges and 2 communities) and American college football network (115 nodes, 613 edges and 12 communities) [5].

Fig. 3 illustrates the average modularity and NMI obtained by the proposed two strategies and the four compared methods on the three real-world networks. From this figure, we can find the following results: (1) the knee point based

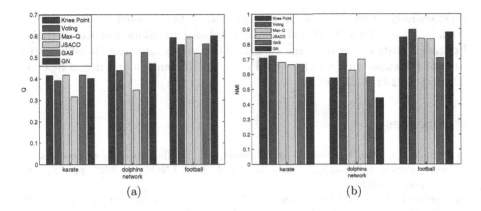

Fig. 3. Modularity and NMI obtained by different approaches on real-world networks

strategy and the maximal modularity based strategy obtain higher modularity value than the other compared methods on the three real-world networks; (2) the modularity obtained by the majority voting based strategy is not very good among those obtained by the six considered methods on the three real-world networks (it only has a better modularity value than JASCO), but the majority voting based strategy can obtain the best partition from the perspective of NMI; this result confirms that the solution with the largest modularity does not always correspond to the best partition of networks; (3) this fact also occurs in the three compared single objective optimization algorithms for community detection; although the modularity obtained by JSACO is quite bad, it can find a better partition than the other two single objective optimization algorithms.

Overall, the proposed two decision-making strategies are competitive on the three real-world networks. Moreover, it seems that the majority voting based strategy is well suitable for detecting community structure of real-world networks.

5   Conclusions and Remarks

In this paper, we present two strategies for decision-makers to obtain an ideal partition from the large number of partitions found by multi-objective optimization algorithms. Experimental results on both random networks and real-world networks confirm that these two strategies are promising for decision makers to obtain an ideal partition. There still remain many problems which need to be further investigated. One of the most interesting problems is to consider the multi-objective optimization algorithms which only focus on finding the potentially ideal partitions of networks instead of all possible partitions. In this way, no strategy will be needed for decision-makers to obtain the ideal partition.

Acknowledgment. This work was supported by National Natural Science Foundation of China (61272152), Natural Science Foundation of Anhui Higher Education Institutions of China (KJ2012A010 and KJ2013A007), MOE (Ministry of Education in China) Youth Project of Humanities and Social Sciences (Project No.14YJCZH169).

References

1. Branke, J., Deb, K., Dierolf, H., Osswald, M.: Finding knees in multi-objective optimization. In: Yao, X., et al. (eds.) PPSN 2004. LNCS, vol. 3242, pp. 722–731. Springer, Heidelberg (2004)
2. Danon, L., Diaz-Guilera, A., Duch, J., Arenas, A.: Comparing community structure identification. Journal of Statistical Mechanics: Theory and Experiment 2005(09), P09008 (2005)
3. Deb, K., Pratap, A., Agarwal, S., Meyarivan, T.: A fast and elitist multiobjective genetic algorithm: NSGA-II. IEEE Transaction on Evolutionary Computation 6(2), 182–197 (2002)
4. Girvan, M., Newman, M.E.: Community structure in social and biological networks. Proceedings of the National Academy of Sciences 99(12), 7821–7826 (2002)
5. Gong, M.G., Cai, Q., Chen, X.W., Ma, L.J.: Complex network clustering by multiobjective discrete particle swarm optimization based on decomposition. IEEE Transaction on Evolutionary Computation 18(1), 82–97 (2014)
6. Gong, M.G., Ma, L.J., Zhang, Q.F., Jiao, L.C.: Community detection in networks by using multiobjective evolutionary algorithm with decomposition. Physica A: Statistical Mechanics and its Applications 391(15), 4050–4060 (2012)
7. Lei, X.-J., Huang, X., Wu, S., Guo, L.: Joint strength based ant colony optimization clustering algorithm for PPI networks. Acta Electronica Sinica 40(4), 695–702 (2012)
8. Li, S.Z., Chen, Y.H., Du, H.F., Feldman, M.W.: A genetic algorithm with local search strategy for improved detection of community structure. Complexity 15(4), 53–60 (2010)
9. Newman, M.E., Girvan, M.: Finding and evaluating community structure in networks. Physical Review E 69(2), 026113 (2004)
10. Pizzuti, C.: A multi-objective genetic algorithm for community detection in networks. In: 21st International Conference on Tools with Artificial Intelligence, ICTAI 2009, pp. 379–386 (2009)
11. Shi, C., Yan, Z.Y., Cai, Y.N., Wu, B.: Multi-objective community detection in complex networks. Applied Soft Computing 12(2), 850–859 (2012)

A New Graphical Representation of Protein Sequences Based on Dual-Vector Model

Zhujin Zhang[1,4,*], Xiangxiang Zeng[2], Zhihua Chen[3], and Eric Ke Wang[4,5]

[1] School of electrical engineering and information,
Sichuan University, Chengdu 610065, China
[2] Department of Computer Science, Xiamen University, Xiamen 361005, China
[3] School of Automation, Huazhong University of Science & Technology,
Wuhan 430074, Hubei, China
[4] Shenzhen Graduate School, Harbin Institute of Technology, Shenzhen 518055, China
[5] Shenzhen Key Laboratory of Internet Information Collaboration, Shenzhen 518055, China

Abstract. Graphical representation of protein sequences is an important method of sequences analysis. We propose a new graphical representation of protein sequences with Virtual DNA Codon and DV-Curve. With virtual DNA codon, we successfully retranslate a protein sequence to a virtual DNA sequence. And then we use DV-Curve to visualize the virtual DNA sequence. The new graphical representation avoids degeneracy and loss of information. It also has good visualization even sequences are long, and avoids the difficulty of observing in multi-dimensional graph.

Keywords: Graphical representation, Protein sequence, Degeneracy, Loss of information.

1 Introduction

About 30 years ago Hamori and Ruskin [1, 2] first proposed a 3D graphical representation for DNA sequences, as an efficient ways to intuitively inspect and analyze DNA sequences. Since then, graphic tools of DNA sequences are improved by a large number of scholars in various aspects, such as degeneracy problem [3–7], loss of information problem, compact[8–11], and good visualization [12].

It was only recent years that the first graphical representations of proteins were proposed by Randić [13, 14]. After the first graphical representation of proteins, several approaches followed, such as [15]. Randić [15, 16] introduced graphical representations, which are compact but having degeneracy.

By virtual DNA codon, we successfully use DV-Curve[12] to visualize and analyze protein sequences. The new protein tool, DV-Protein, avoids degeneracy and loss of information, and has good visualization even sequences are long, and avoids the difficulty of observing in multi-dimensional graph.

---

* Corresponding author.

L. Pan et al. (Eds.): BIC-TA 2014, CCIS 472, pp. 629–632, 2014.

2 DV-Protein

2.1 DV-Curve of DNA Sequences

DV-Curve [12] is an outstanding two-dimensional graphical representation for DNA sequences.

Several advanced properties of DV-Curve have been proved: (i) There is no circuit and degeneracy in DV-Curve. (ii) The correspondence between DNA sequences and DV-Curves is one to one, and no loss of information results from such graphical constructions. (iii) The X-coordinate value of the end point of DV-Curve indicates the length of DNA sequence. (iv) DV-Curve can represent long DNA sequences with good visualization.

Table 1. The codon of 20 basic amino acids

Amino Acid	Virtual RNA codon [13]	Virtual DNA codon
Alanine	GCG	GCG
Arginine	CGG	CGG
Aspargine	AAC	AAC
Aspartic acid	GAU	GAT
Cysteine	UGC	TGC
Glutamine	CAG	CAG
Glutamic acid	GAA	GAA
Glycine	GGC	GGC
Histidine	CAU	CAT
Isoleucine	AUC	ATC
Leucine L	CUC	CTC
Lysine	AAG	AAG
Methionine	AUG	ATG
Phenylalanine	UUC	TTC
Proline	CCA	CCA
Serine	UCU	TCT
Threonine	ACA	ACA
Tryptophan	UGG	TGG
Tyrosine	UAU	TAT
Valine	GUU	GTT

2.2 Virtual DNA Codon

From the knowledge of biology, we know that in gene expression, a DNA is transcribed to an RNA (message RNA), and then this RNA is translated to a protein. So it is reasonable to find the original DNA sequence to represent a protein. The virtual DNA codon is used to retranslate a protein sequence to a virtual DNA sequence.

In translation, the mechanism is much more complicated, and the relationship between RNA and protein is multiple to one. The assigned triplet is one of several triplets that may appear in RNA sequence for the particular amino acid. Amino acid Aspargine is synthesized by AAU, AAC and we selected AAC. The results are shown in Table 1 column 2.

In transcription the relationship between DNA and RNA is one to one. Every 'T' in DNA sequence is transcribed as 'U'. For example, A coding DNA strand reading ATG is transcribed as AUG in RNA. In this work, we retranscribed 'U' as 'T'. For example, Aspartic acid's virtual RNA codon is GAU, we retranscribe it as GAT. 20 virtual RNA codons are retranscribed, shown in Table 1 column 3.

2.3 Visualization of Protein Sequence

By virtual DNA codon, we can retranslate a protein sequence to a virtual DNA sequence. In this subsection, we illustrate visualization of protein sequence on two shorter segments of protein of yeast *Saccharomyces cerevisiae*, already used in the literature [15]:

Protein I WTFESRNDPAKDPVILWLNGGPGCSSLTGL
Protein II WFFESRNDPANDPIILWLNGGPGCSSFTGL

These two protein sequences are retranslated to two corresponding virtual DNA sequences. Take Protein I as an example. The first amino acid is 'W', the virtual DNA codon is TGG. The second amino acid is 'T', so the corresponding the virtual DNA codon is ACA. After retranslating all the amino acids, we connect them as a virtual DNA sequence. The corresponding virtual DNA sequence is 3 times longer than a protein.

After getting virtual DNA sequences, we can use DV-Curve to visualize them. Take a close look at these two figures, we can find that DV-Curve for protein sequence has the same property for DNA sequence. The correspondence between DNA sequences and DV-Curves is one to one, and no loss of information. The X-coordinate value of the end point of DV-Curve indicates the length of protein sequence. That is $n = X_{end}/6$. DV-Curve can represent long protein sequences with good visualization.

3 Conclusion

With virtual DNA codon, we successfully retranslate a protein sequence to a virtual DNA sequence. In this contribution, DV-Curve can be used to visualize proteins. So we build a new graphical representation of protein sequences — DV-Protein. DV-Protein avoids degeneracy, and avoids loss of information. It also has good visualization even sequences are long, and avoids the difficulty of observing in multi-dimensional graph.

Acknowledgment. The work was supported by National Natural Science Foundation of China (61272385), China Postdoctoral Science Foundation (2012M511485, 2013T60374), and Shenzhen Strategic Emerging Industries Program (ZDSY20120613125016389).

References

1. Hamori, E., Ruskin, J.: H Curves, A Novel Method of Representation of Nucleotide Series Especially Suited for Long DNA Sequences. Journal of Biological Chemistry 258(2), 1318–1327 (1983)
2. Hamori, E.: Novel DNA Sequence Representations. Nature 314(6012), 585–586 (1985)
3. Gates, M.A.: Simpler DNA Sequence Representations. Nature 316(6025), 219 (1985)
4. Nandy, A.: A New Graphical Representation and Analysis of DNA Sequence Structure: I. Methodology and Application to Globin Genes. Current Science 66, 309–314 (1994)
5. Guo, X., Randić, M., Basak, S.: A Novel 2-D Graphical Representation of DNA Sequences of Low Degeneracy. Chemical Physics Letters 350(1-2), 106–112 (2001)
6. Wu, Y., Liew, A., Yan, H., Yang, M.: DB-Curve: a Novel 2D Method of DNA Sequence Visualization and Representation. Chemical Physics Letters 367(1-2), 170–176 (2003)
7. Zhang, Y., Liao, B., Ding, K.: On 2D Graphical Representation of DNA Sequence of Non-degeneracy. Chemical Physics Letters 411(1-3), 28–32 (2005)
8. Jeffrey, H.: Chaos Game Representation of Gene Structure. Nucleic Acids Research 18(8), 2163–2170 (1990)
9. Randić, M., Vračko, M., Zupan, J., Novič, M.: Compact 2-D Graphical Representation of DNA. Chemical Physics Letters 373(5-6), 558–562 (2003)
10. Randic, M.: Graphical Representations of DNA as 2-D Map. Chemical Physics Letters 386(4-6), 468–471 (2004)
11. Randic, M., Lers, N., Plavsic, D., Basak, S., Balaban, A.: Four-color Map Representation of DNA or RNA Sequences and Their Numerical Characterization. Chemical Physics Letters 407(1-3), 205–208 (2005)
12. Zhang, Z.: DV-Curve: a Novel Intuitive Tool for Visualizing and Analyzing DNA sequences. Bioinformatics 25(9), 1112–1117 (2009)
13. Randić, M.: 2-D Graphical Representation of Proteins Based on Virtual Genetic Code. SAR and QSAR in Environmental Research 15(3), 147–157 (2004)
14. Randić, M., Zupan, J., Balaban, A.: Unique Graphical Representation of Protein Sequences Based on Nucleotide Triplet Codons. Chemical Physics Letters 397(1-3), 247–252 (2004)
15. Randić, M., Butina, D., Zupan, J.: Novel 2-D Graphical Representation of Proteins. Chemical Physics Letters 419(4-6), 528–532 (2006)
16. Randić, M., Novič, M., Vikić-Topić, D., Plavšić, D.: Novel Numerical and Graphical Representation of DNA sequences and Proteins. SAR and QSAR in Environmental Research 17(6), 583–595 (2006)

New Fuzzy Probability Spaces and Fuzzy Random Variables Based on Gradual Numbers

Caili Zhou[1,*] and Peng Wang[2]

[1] College of Mathematics and Computer Science,
Hebei University, Baoding 071002, China
[2] College of Physics Science and Technology,
Hebei University, Baoding 071002, Hebei, China
pumpkinlili@163.com

Abstract. In this paper, we deal with special generalization of probability measures and random variables by considering their values in the set of gradual numbers. Firstly, the concept of gradual probability measures is introduced and some of its properties are discussed. And then, the concept of gradual random variables is introduced and weak law of large numbers for gradual random variables on a gradual probability space is obtained.

Keywords: Gradual number, Gradual probability space, Gradual random variable, Law of large numbers.

1 Introduction

Motivated by the applications in several areas of applied science, such as mathematical economics, fuzzy optimal, process control and decision theory, much effort has been devoted to the generalization of different probabilistic concepts and classical results to the case when outcomes of a random experiment are represented by fuzzy sets, such as the concept of fuzzy (probability) measures [2, 17, 20–22, 26], the concept of fuzzy random variables [9, 14], expected values and variances of fuzzy random variables and limit theorems for fuzzy random variables [4,25]. In above literatures, the most often proposed fuzzy sets are fuzzy numbers or fuzzy real numbers. But it is well known that fuzzy numbers generalize intervals, not numbers and model incomplete knowledge, not the fuzziness per se. Also fuzzy arithmetics inherit algebraic properties of interval arithmetics, not of numbers. In particular, addition does not define a group on such fuzzy numbers. There are some authors who tried to equip fuzzy numbers with a group structure. This kind of attempt suggests a confusion between uncertainty and gradualness. Hence the name fuzzy number used by many authors is debatable. On the other hand, a different view of a fuzzy real number, starting with Hutton [10], which is usual defined as a non-increasing upper-semicontinuous function $\tilde{z} : \mathbb{R} \to [0, 1]$ such that $\sup \tilde{z}(x) = 1$ and $\inf \tilde{z}(x) = 0$, the arithmetic

---

* Corresponding author.

L. Pan et al. (Eds.): BIC-TA 2014, CCIS 472, pp. 633–643, 2014.

operations are also defined by the extension principle, it is much more complicated than ordinary arithmetics, in particular what concerns inverse operations like subtraction and division.

In order to model the essence of fuzziness without uncertainty, the concept of gradual numbers has been proposed by Fortin *et al.* [7]. Gradual numbers are unique generalization of the real numbers, which are equipped with the same algebraic structures as real numbers (addition is a group, etc.). The authors claimed that the concept of gradual numbers is a missing primitive concept in fuzzy set theory. In the brief time since their introduction, gradual numbers have been employed as tools for computations on fuzzy intervals, with applications to combinatorial fuzzy optimization [8, 11] and monotonic (or non-monotonic) function evaluation [7, 23] and others [1, 3, 15, 16, 18, 27]. Hence, it is an interesting question whether a probability measure or a random variable can be introduced with value in the set of gradual numbers. This is the motivation of current work.

In the present paper, the concept of gradual probability measures is introduced, which is a generalization of classical probability measures. And then the concept of gradual random variables and its expected value on gradual probability spaces are presented and their properties are discussed. Finally, weak law of large numbers for gradual random variables on a gradual probability space is obtained. The organization of the paper is as follows. In section 2, we state some basic concepts about gradual numbers. In section 3, gradual probability measures and gradual random variables are introduced. Weak law of large numbers for gradual random variables on a gradual probability space is obtained.

2 Preliminaries

We state some basic concepts about gradual numbers. All concepts and signs not defined in this paper may be found in [7, 19, 27].

Definition 2.1. [7] A gradual real number (or gradual number for short) $\tilde{r}$ is defined by an assignment function

$$A_{\tilde{r}} : (0, 1] \to \mathbb{R}.$$

Naturally a nonnegative gradual number is defined by its assignment function from $(0, 1]$ to $[0, +\infty)$.

In the following, $\tilde{r}(\alpha)$ may be substituted for $A_{\tilde{r}}(\alpha)$. The set of all gradual numbers (resp. nonnegative gradual numbers) is denoted by $\mathbb{R}(I)$ (resp. $\mathbb{R}^*(I)$).

A crisp element $b \in \mathbb{R}$ has its own assignment function $\tilde{b}$ defined by $\tilde{b}(\alpha) = b$, $\forall \alpha \in (0, 1]$. We call such elements in $\mathbb{R}(I)$ constant gradual numbers. Obviously, there is a bijection between the set of all constant gradual numbers and $\mathbb{R}$, hence $\mathbb{R}$ can be regarded as a subset of $\mathbb{R}(I)$ if we do not distinguish $\tilde{b}$ and b. In particular, $\tilde{0}$ (resp. $\tilde{1}$) denotes constant gradual number defined by $\tilde{0}(\alpha) = 0$ (resp. $\tilde{1}(\alpha) = 1$), $\forall \alpha \in (0, 1]$.

Definition 2.2. [7] Let $\tilde{r}, \tilde{s} \in \mathbb{R}(I)$ and $\gamma \in \mathbb{R}$. The arithmetics of $\tilde{r}$ and $\tilde{s}$ are defined as follows:

(1) $(\tilde{r} + \tilde{s})(\alpha) = \tilde{r}(\alpha) + \tilde{s}(\alpha), \forall \alpha \in (0, 1]$;

(2) $(\tilde{r} - \tilde{s})(\alpha) = \tilde{r}(\alpha) - \tilde{s}(\alpha), \forall \alpha \in (0, 1]$;

(3) $(\tilde{r} \cdot \tilde{s})(\alpha) = \tilde{r}(\alpha) \cdot \tilde{s}(\alpha), \forall \alpha \in (0, 1]$;

(4) $\left(\dfrac{\tilde{r}}{\tilde{s}}\right)(\alpha) = \dfrac{\tilde{r}(\alpha)}{\tilde{s}(\alpha)}$, if $\tilde{s}(\alpha) \neq 0, \forall \alpha \in (0, 1]$;

(5) $(\gamma \tilde{r})(\alpha) = \gamma \tilde{r}(\alpha), \forall \alpha \in (0, 1]$.

Definition 2.3. [19] Let $\tilde{r}, \tilde{s} \in \mathbb{R}(I)$. The relations between $\tilde{r}$ and $\tilde{s}$ are defined as follows:

(1) $\tilde{r} = \tilde{s}$ if and only if $\tilde{r}(\alpha) = \tilde{s}(\alpha), \forall \alpha \in (0, 1]$;

(2) $\tilde{r} \succeq \tilde{s}$ if and only if $\tilde{r}(\alpha) \geq \tilde{s}(\alpha), \forall \alpha \in (0, 1]$;

(3) $\tilde{r} \preceq \tilde{s}$ if and only if $\tilde{r}(\alpha) \leq \tilde{s}(\alpha), \forall \alpha \in (0, 1]$;

(4) $\tilde{r} \succ \tilde{s}$ if and only if $\tilde{r}(\alpha) > \tilde{s}(\alpha), \forall \alpha \in (0, 1]$;

(5) $\tilde{r} \prec \tilde{s}$ if and only if $\tilde{r}(\alpha) < \tilde{s}(\alpha), \forall \alpha \in (0, 1]$.

Definition 2.4. [27] Let $\tilde{r}, \tilde{s} \in \mathbb{R}(I)$. The mapping $|\tilde{r}| : (0, 1] \to \mathbb{R}^*(I)$ defined by

$$|\tilde{r}|(\alpha) = |\tilde{r}(\alpha)|, \forall \alpha \in (0, 1]$$

is called the absolute value of $\tilde{r}$. $|\tilde{r} - \tilde{s}|$ is called the distance between $\tilde{r}$ and $\tilde{s}$.

Definition 2.5. [27] Let $\{\tilde{r}_n\} \subseteq \mathbb{R}(I)$ and $\tilde{r} \in \mathbb{R}(I)$.

(1) $\{\tilde{r}_n\}$ is said to converge to $\tilde{r}$ if for each $\alpha \in (0, 1]$,

$$\lim_{n \to \infty} \tilde{r}_n(\alpha) = \tilde{r}(\alpha),$$

and it is denoted as $\lim_{n \to \infty} \tilde{r}_n = \tilde{r}$ or $\tilde{r}_n \to \tilde{r}$, if there is no such an $\tilde{r}$, the sequence $\{\tilde{r}_n\}$ is said to be divergent;

(2) if $\lim_{n \to \infty} \sum_{i=1}^{n} \tilde{r}_i$ exists, then the infinite sum of sequence $\{\tilde{r}_n\}$ is defined by

$$\sum_{i=1}^{\infty} \tilde{r}_i = \lim_{n \to \infty} \sum_{i=1}^{n} \tilde{r}_i,$$

if $\lim_{n \to \infty} \sum_{i=1}^{n} \tilde{r}_i$ does not exist, then the infinite sum of sequence $\{\tilde{r}_n\}$ is said to be divergent.

3 Gradual Probability Measures and Gradual Random Variables

In this section, the concept of gradual probability measures is introduced and some of its properties are discussed. And then the concept of gradual random variables is introduced, familiar concepts such as independence and expected value of a gradual random variable are available and their properties are discussed. Finally, weak law of large numbers for gradual random variables on the gradual probability space is obtained.

Definition 3.1. Let $(\Omega, \mathscr{A})$ be a measurable space. A mapping $\tilde{\pi} : \mathscr{A} \to \mathbb{R}^*(I)$ is called a gradual probability measure if it satisfies the following conditions:

(1) $\tilde{\pi}(\Omega) = \tilde{1}$;

(2) if $A_1, A_2, \ldots$ are in $\mathscr{A}$, with $A_i \cap A_j = \emptyset$ for $i \neq j$, then

$$\tilde{\pi}\left(\bigcup_{i=1}^{\infty} A_i\right) = \sum_{i=1}^{\infty} \tilde{\pi}(A_i).$$

The second condition is called countable additivity of the gradual probability measure $\tilde{\pi}$ and we say that $(\Omega, \mathscr{A}, \tilde{\pi})$ is a gradual probability space.

Theorem 3.2. *Let $(\Omega, \mathscr{A}, \tilde{\pi})$ be a gradual probability space.*

(1) $\tilde{\pi}(\emptyset) = \tilde{0}$;

(2) *if $A_1, A_2, \ldots, A_n$ are in $\mathscr{A}$, with $A_i \cap A_j = \emptyset$ for $i \neq j$, then $\tilde{\pi}\left(\bigcup_{i=1}^{n} A_i\right) = \sum_{i=1}^{n} \tilde{\pi}(A_i)$;*

(3) *if A, B are in $\mathscr{A}$ and $A \subseteq B$, then $\tilde{\pi}(B \setminus A) = \tilde{\pi}(B) - \tilde{\pi}(A)$ and $\tilde{\pi}(B) \succeq \tilde{\pi}(A)$;*

(4) *if A, B are in $\mathscr{A}$, then $\tilde{\pi}(A \cup B) + \tilde{\pi}(A \cap B) = \tilde{\pi}(A) + \tilde{\pi}(B)$;*

(5) *if $A_1, A_2, \ldots$ are in $\mathscr{A}$, then $\tilde{\pi}\left(\bigcup_{i=1}^{\infty} A_i\right) \preceq \sum_{i=1}^{\infty} \tilde{\pi}(A_i)$.*

Proof. (1) Combining

$$\Omega = \Omega \cup \emptyset \cup \emptyset \cup \cdots \text{ and } \Omega \cap \emptyset = \emptyset,$$

we obtain that

$$\tilde{\pi}(\Omega) = \tilde{\pi}(\Omega \cup \emptyset \cup \emptyset \cup \cdots) = \tilde{\pi}(\Omega) + \tilde{\pi}(\emptyset) + \tilde{\pi}(\emptyset) + \cdots = \tilde{1} + \tilde{\pi}(\emptyset) + \tilde{\pi}(\emptyset) + \cdots = \tilde{1}.$$

It follows that $\tilde{\pi}(\emptyset) = \tilde{0}$.

(2) Since $\bigcup_{i=1}^{n} A_i = \bigcup_{i=1}^{n} A_i \cup \emptyset \cup \emptyset \cdots$, by conclusion (1), we can conclude that

$$\tilde{\pi}\left(\bigcup_{i=1}^{n} A_i\right) = \sum_{i=1}^{n} \tilde{\pi}(A_i).$$

(3) If $A \subseteq B$, then $B = A \cup (B \setminus A)$ and $A \cap (B \setminus A) = \emptyset$. By conclusion (2), we obtain that $\tilde{\pi}(B) = \tilde{\pi}(A) + \tilde{\pi}(B \setminus A)$. This implies that $\tilde{\pi}(B \setminus A) = \tilde{\pi}(B) - \tilde{\pi}(A)$. Aslo, since $\tilde{\pi}(B \setminus A) = \tilde{\pi}(B) - \tilde{\pi}(A) \succeq \tilde{0}$, it follows that $\tilde{\pi}(B) \succeq \tilde{\pi}(A)$.

(4) Since $A \cup B = A \cup (B \setminus A)$ and $A \cap (B \setminus A) = \emptyset$, we obtain that

$$\tilde{\pi}(A \cup B) = \tilde{\pi}(A) + \tilde{\pi}(B \setminus A).$$

Also, since $A \cap B = A \setminus (A \setminus B)$ and $(A \setminus B) \subseteq A$, by conclusion (3), we have

$$\tilde{\pi}(A \cap B) = \tilde{\pi}(A) - \tilde{\pi}(A \setminus B).$$

Combining the above two inequalities, we get

$$\tilde{\pi}(A \cup B) + \tilde{\pi}(A \cap B) = \tilde{\pi}(A) + \tilde{\pi}(B).$$

(5) Note that the family of sets

$$B_1 = A_1, \ B_2 = A_2 \setminus A_1, \ B_3 = A_3 \setminus (A_1 \cup A_2), \ldots, B_n = A_n \setminus \left(\bigcup_{i=1}^{n-1} A_i \right)$$

is disjoint and $\bigcup_{i=1}^n B_i = \bigcup_{i=1}^n A_i$. Also, since $B_i \subseteq A_i$, by conclusion (3) we have that

$$\tilde{\pi}(B_i) \preceq \tilde{\pi}(A_i).$$

Thus

$$\tilde{\pi}\left(\bigcup_{i=1}^n A_i \right) = \tilde{\pi}\left(\bigcup_{i=1}^n B_i \right) = \sum_{i=1}^n \tilde{\pi}(B_i) \preceq \sum_{i=1}^n \tilde{\pi}(A_i).$$

Now we can repeat the argument for the infinite family using countable additivity of gradual probability. This completes the proof. $\qquad\square$

Theorem 3.3. *Let $(\Omega, \mathscr{A})$ be a measurable space and $\tilde{\pi} : \mathscr{A} \to \mathbb{R}^*(I)$ a mapping. For each $\alpha \in (0,1]$, we define $\tilde{\pi}_\alpha : \mathscr{A} \to [0, +\infty)$ by*

$$\tilde{\pi}_\alpha(A) = \tilde{\pi}(A)(\alpha), \ \forall A \in \mathscr{A},$$

then $\tilde{\pi}$ is a gradual probability if and only if $\{\tilde{\pi}_\alpha : \alpha \in (0,1]\}$ is a family of classical probabilities on $(\Omega, \mathscr{A})$.

Proof. Necessity. Suppose that $\tilde{\pi}$ is a gradual probability. According to Definition 3.1, for each $\alpha \in (0,1]$, the following two conclusions hold:

(1) $\tilde{\pi}_\alpha(\Omega) = \tilde{\pi}(\Omega)(\alpha) = 1$.

(2) If $A_1, A_2, \ldots$ be in $\mathscr{A}$ with $A_i \cap A_j = \emptyset$ for $i \neq j$, then

$$\tilde{\pi}_\alpha\left(\bigcup_{i=1}^\infty A_i \right) = \tilde{\pi}\left(\bigcup_{i=1}^\infty A_i \right)(\alpha) = \left(\sum_{i=1}^\infty \tilde{\pi}(A_i) \right)(\alpha) = \sum_{i=1}^\infty \tilde{\pi}(A_i)(\alpha) = \sum_{i=1}^\infty \tilde{\pi}_\alpha(A_i).$$

Therefore, for each $\alpha \in (0,1]$, $\tilde{\pi}_\alpha$ is a gradual probability.

Sufficiency. If $\{\tilde{\pi}_\alpha : \alpha \in (0,1]\}$ is a family of classical probabilities on $(\Omega, \mathscr{A})$, then

(1) for each $\alpha \in (0,1]$, we have

$$\tilde{\pi}(\Omega)(\alpha) = \tilde{\pi}_\alpha(\Omega) = 1.$$

This implies that $\tilde{\pi}(\Omega) = \tilde{1}$.

(2) For each $\alpha \in (0,1]$, we have

$$\tilde{\pi}\left(\bigcup_{i=1}^\infty A_i \right)(\alpha) = \tilde{\pi}_\alpha\left(\bigcup_{i=1}^\infty A_i \right) = \sum_{i=1}^\infty \tilde{\pi}_\alpha(A_i) = \left(\sum_{i=1}^\infty \tilde{\pi}(A_i) \right)(\alpha).$$

It follows that $\tilde{\pi}(\bigcup_{i=1}^\infty A_i) = \sum_{i=1}^\infty \tilde{\pi}(A_i)$. Thus $\tilde{\pi}$ is a gradual probability. This completes the proof. $\qquad\square$

In the following, we introduce the concept of gradual random variables.

Definition 3.4. A mapping $\tilde{\xi} : \Omega \to \mathbb{R}(I)$ is said to be gradual random variable associated with a measurable space $(\Omega, \mathscr{A})$ if and only if for each $\alpha \in (0, 1]$, the real-valued mapping $\tilde{\xi}_\alpha : \Omega \to \mathbb{R}$, defined by

$$\tilde{\xi}_\alpha(\omega) = \tilde{\xi}(\omega)(\alpha), \ \forall \omega \in \Omega,$$

is a classical random variable associated with $(\Omega, \mathscr{A})$.

Remark 3.5. Evidently, a classical random variable must be a particular case of gradual random variables if $\mathbb{R}$ is regarded as a subset of $\mathbb{R}(I)$.

Definition 3.6. Let $\tilde{\xi}, \tilde{\eta} : \Omega \to \mathbb{R}(I)$ be two gradual number-valued functions. Define
  (1) $(\gamma + \tilde{\xi})(\omega) = \gamma + \tilde{\xi}(\omega), (\gamma\tilde{\xi})(\omega) = \gamma\tilde{\xi}(\omega), \forall \gamma \in \mathbb{R}, \forall \omega \in \Omega$;
  (2) $(\tilde{\xi} * \tilde{\eta})(\omega) = \tilde{\xi}(\omega) * \tilde{\eta}(\omega), \forall \omega \in \Omega$, where $* \in \{+, -, \times, \div\}$;
  (3) $\max\{\tilde{\xi}, \tilde{\eta}\}(\omega) = \max\{\tilde{\xi}(\omega), \tilde{\eta}(\omega)\}, \min\{\tilde{\xi}, \tilde{\eta}\}(\omega) = \min\{\tilde{\xi}(\omega), \tilde{\eta}(\omega)\}, \forall \omega \in \Omega$;
  (4) $|\tilde{\xi}|(\omega) = |\tilde{\xi}(\omega)|, \forall \omega \in \Omega$.

Theorem 3.7. *If $\tilde{\xi}$ and $\tilde{\eta}$ are gradual random variables associated with a measurable space $(\Omega, \mathscr{A})$, then*
  (1) *for each $\gamma \in \mathbb{R}$, $\gamma + \tilde{\xi}$ and $\gamma\tilde{\xi}$ are gradual random variables;*
  (2) *$\tilde{\xi} \pm \tilde{\eta}$, $\tilde{\xi}\tilde{\eta}$ and $\frac{\tilde{\xi}}{\tilde{\eta}}$ are gradual random variables;*
  (3) *$\max\{\tilde{\xi}, \tilde{\eta}\}$, $\min\{\tilde{\xi}, \tilde{\eta}\}$ and $\left|\tilde{\xi}\right|$ are gradual random variables.*

Proof. Suppose $\tilde{z} = \gamma + \tilde{\xi}$. We need to prove that for each $\alpha \in (0, 1]$, $\tilde{z}_\alpha$ is a classical random variable. For all $\omega \in \Omega$, we have

$$\tilde{z}_\alpha(\omega) = \tilde{z}(\omega)(\alpha) = (\gamma + \tilde{\xi})(\omega)(\alpha) = \gamma + \tilde{\xi}_\alpha(\omega).$$

We know that for each $\alpha \in (0, 1]$, $\tilde{\xi}_\alpha$ is a classical random variable, so is $\tilde{z}_\alpha$. Using the same method, we can show that $\gamma\tilde{\xi}$ is also a gradual random variable.
  By Definition 3.4 and 3.6, it is easy to see that

$$(\tilde{\xi} + \tilde{\eta})_\alpha = \tilde{\xi}_\alpha + \tilde{\eta}_\alpha, \ (\tilde{\xi}\tilde{\eta})_\alpha = \tilde{\xi}_\alpha\tilde{\eta}_\alpha, \ \left(\frac{\tilde{\xi}}{\tilde{\eta}}\right)_\alpha = \frac{\tilde{\xi}_\alpha}{\tilde{\eta}_\alpha},$$

$$(\max\{\tilde{\xi}, \tilde{\eta}\})_\alpha = \max\{\tilde{\xi}_\alpha, \tilde{\eta}_\alpha\}, \ (\min\{\tilde{\xi}, \tilde{\eta}\})_\alpha = \min\{\tilde{\xi}_\alpha, \tilde{\eta}_\alpha\}, \ |\tilde{\xi}|_\alpha = |\tilde{\xi}_\alpha|.$$

By properties of classical random variables, we obtain conclusions (2) and (3). This completes the proof.   □

Definition 3.8. Let $\{\tilde{\xi}_n\}$ be a sequence of gradual random variables on the gradual probability space $(\Omega, \mathscr{A}, \tilde{\pi})$. $\{\tilde{\xi}_n\}$ is called independent and identically distributed if for each $\alpha \in (0, 1]$, $\{\tilde{\xi}_{n\alpha}\}$ is an independent and identically distributed classical random variables sequence on the probability space $(\Omega, \mathscr{A}, \tilde{\pi}_\alpha)$.

Definition 3.9. Let $\tilde{\xi}$ be a gradual random variable defined on a gradual probability space $(\Omega, \mathscr{A}, \tilde{\pi})$. If for each $\alpha \in (0, 1]$, the expected value $E_{\tilde{\pi}_\alpha}(\tilde{\xi}_\alpha)$ of $\tilde{\xi}_\alpha$

on the probability space $(\Omega, \mathscr{A}, \tilde{\pi}_\alpha)$ exists, then we call that the expected value of $\tilde{\xi}$ on the gradual probability space $(\Omega, \mathscr{A}, \tilde{\pi})$ exists and is a gradual number $E_{\tilde{\pi}}(\tilde{\xi})$ defined by

$$E_{\tilde{\pi}}(\tilde{\xi})(\alpha) = E_{\tilde{\pi}_\alpha}(\tilde{\xi}_\alpha), \forall \alpha \in (0,1].$$

Theorem 3.10. Let $\tilde{\xi}, \tilde{\eta}$ be gradual random variables defined on a gradual probability space $(\Omega, \mathscr{A}, \tilde{\pi})$. Then

(1) $E_{\tilde{\pi}}(\tilde{r}) = \tilde{r}$, where $\tilde{r}$ denote the gradual random variable which have the same outcome $\tilde{r}$ for all $\omega \in \Omega$, i.e., $\tilde{r}(\omega) = \tilde{r}, \forall \omega \in \Omega$;

(2) $E_{\tilde{\pi}}(\gamma\tilde{\xi} + \lambda\tilde{\eta}) = \gamma E_{\tilde{\pi}}(\tilde{\xi}) + \lambda E_{\tilde{\pi}}(\tilde{\eta}), \forall \gamma, \lambda \in \mathbb{R}$.

Proof. (1) Since for all $\omega \in \Omega$, we have $\tilde{r}(\omega) = \tilde{r}$. Thus for each $\alpha \in (0,1]$ and $\omega \in \Omega$, we have $\tilde{r}_\alpha(\omega) = \tilde{r}(\alpha)$, i.e., $\tilde{r}_\alpha$ is constant-valued random variable. It follows that $E_{\tilde{\pi}_\alpha}(\tilde{r}_\alpha) = \tilde{r}(\alpha)$, i.e., for each $\alpha \in (0,1]$,

$$E_{\tilde{\pi}}(\tilde{r})(\alpha) = E_{\tilde{\pi}_\alpha}(\tilde{r}_\alpha) = \tilde{r}(\alpha).$$

Therefore, we have $E_{\tilde{\pi}}(\tilde{r}) = \tilde{r}$.

(2) For each $\alpha \in (0,1]$, we have

$$\begin{aligned}
E_{\tilde{\pi}}(\gamma\tilde{\xi} + \lambda\tilde{\eta})(\alpha) &= E_{\tilde{\pi}_\alpha}[\gamma\tilde{\xi}_\alpha + \lambda\tilde{\eta}_\alpha] \\
&= \gamma E_{\tilde{\pi}_\alpha}(\tilde{\xi}_\alpha) + \lambda E_{\tilde{\pi}_\alpha}(\tilde{\eta}_\alpha) \\
&= \gamma E_{\tilde{\pi}}(\tilde{\xi})(\alpha) + \lambda E_{\tilde{\pi}}(\tilde{\eta})(\alpha) \\
&= [\gamma E_{\tilde{\pi}}(\tilde{\xi}) + \lambda E_{\tilde{\pi}}(\tilde{\eta})](\alpha).
\end{aligned}$$

It follows that $E_{\tilde{\pi}}(\gamma\tilde{\xi} + \lambda\tilde{\eta}) = \gamma E_{\tilde{\pi}}(\tilde{\xi}) + \lambda E_{\tilde{\pi}}(\tilde{\eta})$. This completes the proof. $\square$

In the rest of this section, we come up with weak law of large numbers for gradual random variables on a gradual probability space. Firstly, we present the concept of convergence in gradual probability.

Definition 3.11. Let $\{\tilde{\xi}_n\}$ and $\tilde{\xi}$ be gradual random variables defined on the same gradual probability space $(\Omega, \mathscr{A}, \tilde{\pi})$ and $\tilde{r} \in \mathbb{R}(I)$.

(1) We say that $\{\tilde{\xi}_n\}$ converges in gradual probability $\tilde{\pi}$ to $\tilde{\xi}$ (write $\tilde{\xi}_n \xrightarrow[n\to\infty]{\tilde{\pi}} \tilde{\xi}$) if for any $\tilde{\varepsilon} \succ \tilde{0}$, we have

$$\lim_{n\to\infty} \tilde{\pi}\left\{\omega : \left|\tilde{\xi}_n(\omega) - \tilde{\xi}(\omega)\right| \succeq \tilde{\varepsilon}\right\} = \tilde{0}.$$

(2) We say that $\{\tilde{\xi}_n\}$ converges in gradual probability $\tilde{\pi}$ to $\tilde{r}$ (write $\tilde{\xi}_n \xrightarrow[n\to\infty]{\tilde{\pi}} \tilde{r}$) if for any $\tilde{\varepsilon} \succ \tilde{0}$, we have

$$\lim_{n\to\infty} \tilde{\pi}\left\{\omega : \left|\tilde{\xi}_n(\omega) - \tilde{r}\right| \succeq \tilde{\varepsilon}\right\} = \tilde{0}.$$

Theorem 3.12. Let $\{\tilde{\xi}_n\}$ and $\tilde{\xi}$ be gradual random variables defined on the same gradual probability space $(\Omega, \mathscr{A}, \tilde{\pi})$ and $\tilde{r} \in \mathbb{R}(I)$. If for each $\alpha \in (0, 1]$, $\{\tilde{\xi}_{n\alpha}\}$ converges in probability $\tilde{\pi}_\alpha$ to $\tilde{\xi}_\alpha$ (resp. $\tilde{r}(\alpha)$), then $\{\tilde{\xi}_n\}$ converges in gradual probability $\tilde{\pi}$ to $\tilde{\xi}$ (resp. $\tilde{r}$).

Proof. We only prove that $\{\tilde{\xi}_n\}$ converges in gradual probability $\tilde{\pi}$ to $\tilde{\xi}$. $\{\tilde{\xi}_n\}$ converges in gradual probability $\tilde{\pi}$ to $\tilde{r}$ have the similar proof. For any $\tilde{\varepsilon} \succ \tilde{0}$ and $\alpha \in (0, 1]$, we have

$$\left\{\omega : \left|\tilde{\xi}_n(\omega) - \tilde{\xi}(\omega)\right| \succeq \tilde{\varepsilon}\right\} = \bigcap_{\alpha \in (0,1]} \left\{\omega : \left|\tilde{\xi}_{n\alpha}(\omega) - \tilde{\xi}_\alpha(\omega)\right| \geq \tilde{\varepsilon}(\alpha)\right\}$$

$$\subseteq \left\{\omega : \left|\tilde{\xi}_{n\alpha}(\omega) - \tilde{\xi}_\alpha(\omega)\right| \geq \tilde{\varepsilon}(\alpha)\right\}.$$

It follows that

$$\tilde{\pi}_\alpha \left\{\omega : \left|\tilde{\xi}_n(\omega) - \tilde{\xi}(\omega)\right| \succeq \tilde{\varepsilon}\right\} \leq \tilde{\pi}_\alpha \left\{\omega : \left|\tilde{\xi}_{n\alpha}(\omega) - \tilde{\xi}_\alpha(\omega)\right| \geq \tilde{\varepsilon}(\alpha)\right\}.$$

Since $\{\tilde{\xi}_{n\alpha}\}$ converges in probability $\tilde{\pi}_\alpha$ to $\tilde{\xi}_\alpha$, we have

$$\lim_{n \to \infty} \tilde{\pi}_\alpha \left\{\omega : \left|\tilde{\xi}_{n\alpha}(\omega) - \tilde{\xi}_\alpha(\omega)\right| \geq \tilde{\varepsilon}(\alpha)\right\} = 0.$$

It follows that

$$\lim_{n \to \infty} \tilde{\pi}_\alpha \{\omega : \left|\tilde{\xi}_n(\omega) - \tilde{\xi}(\omega)\right| \succeq \tilde{\varepsilon}\} = 0,$$

i.e., for each $\alpha \in (0, 1]$, we have

$$\lim_{n \to \infty} \tilde{\pi}_\alpha \left\{\omega : \left|\tilde{\xi}_{n\alpha}(\omega) - \tilde{\xi}_\alpha(\omega)\right| \geq \tilde{\varepsilon}(\alpha)\right\} = \lim_{n \to \infty} \tilde{\pi} \left\{\omega : \left|\tilde{\xi}_n(\omega) - \tilde{\xi}(\omega)\right| \succeq \tilde{\varepsilon}\right\}(\alpha)$$

$$= \tilde{0}(\alpha).$$

This implies that $\lim_{n \to \infty} \tilde{\pi}\{\omega : \left|\tilde{\xi}_n(\omega) - \tilde{\xi}(\omega)\right| \succeq \tilde{\varepsilon}\} = \tilde{0}$. Thus $\{\tilde{\xi}_n\}$ converges in gradual probability $\tilde{\pi}$ to $\tilde{\xi}$. This completes the proof. □

Theorem 3.13. *Let $\{\tilde{\xi}_n\}$ be a sequence of independent and identically distributed gradual random variables on a gradual probability space $(\Omega, \mathscr{A}, \tilde{\pi})$ and $\tilde{\xi}_n, n = 1, 2, \ldots$ have the same expected value. Then $\{\tilde{\xi}_n\}$ converges in gradual probability $\tilde{\pi}$ to $E_{\tilde{\pi}}(\tilde{\xi}_1)$, i.e., for any $\tilde{\varepsilon} \succ \tilde{0}$, we have*

$$\lim_{n \to \infty} \tilde{\pi} \left\{\omega : \left|\frac{1}{n}\sum_{i=1}^{n} \tilde{\xi}_i(\omega) - E_{\tilde{\pi}}(\tilde{\xi}_1)\right| \succeq \tilde{\varepsilon}\right\} = \tilde{0}.$$

Proof. Note that for any $\tilde{\varepsilon} \succ \tilde{0}$ and $\alpha \in (0, 1]$, we have

$$\left\{\omega : \left|\frac{1}{n}\sum_{i=1}^{n} \tilde{\xi}_i(\omega) - E_{\tilde{\pi}}(\tilde{\xi}_1)\right| \succeq \tilde{\varepsilon}\right\} = \bigcap_{\alpha \in (0,1]} \left\{\omega : \left|\frac{1}{n}\sum_{i=1}^{n} \tilde{\xi}_{i\alpha}(\omega) - E_{\tilde{\pi}_\alpha}(\tilde{\xi}_{1\alpha})\right| \geq \tilde{\varepsilon}(\alpha)\right\}$$

$$\subseteq \left\{\omega : \left|\frac{1}{n}\sum_{i=1}^{n} \tilde{\xi}_{i\alpha}(\omega) - E_{\tilde{\pi}_\alpha}(\tilde{\xi}_{1\alpha})\right| \geq \tilde{\varepsilon}(\alpha)\right\}.$$

It follows that

$$\tilde{\pi}_\alpha \left\{ \omega : \left| \frac{1}{n} \sum_{i=1}^{n} \tilde{\xi}_i(\omega) - E_{\tilde{\pi}}(\tilde{\xi}_1) \right| \succeq \tilde{\varepsilon} \right\} \leq \tilde{\pi}_\alpha \left\{ \omega : \left| \frac{1}{n} \sum_{i=1}^{n} \tilde{\xi}_{i\alpha} - E_{\tilde{\pi}_\alpha}(\tilde{\xi}_{1\alpha}) \right| \geq \tilde{\varepsilon}(\alpha) \right\}.$$

Since $\{\tilde{\xi}_n\}$ is a sequence of independent and identically distributed gradual random variables, according to Definition 3.8, for each $\alpha \in (0, 1]$, $\{\tilde{\xi}_{n\alpha}\}$ is a sequence of independent and identically distributed classical random variables on the probability space $(\Omega, \mathscr{A}, \tilde{\pi}_\alpha)$ and $E_{\tilde{\pi}_\alpha}(\tilde{\xi}_{n\alpha}) = E_{\tilde{\pi}_\alpha}(\tilde{\xi}_{1\alpha})$. Therefore, by classical Khintchine law of large numbers, we have

$$\lim_{n \to \infty} \tilde{\pi}_\alpha \left\{ \omega : \left| \frac{1}{n} \sum_{i=1}^{n} \tilde{\xi}_{i\alpha} - E_{\tilde{\pi}_\alpha}(\tilde{\xi}_{1\alpha}) \right| \geq \tilde{\varepsilon}(\alpha) \right\} = 0.$$

It follows that

$$\lim_{n \to \infty} \tilde{\pi}_\alpha \left\{ \omega : \left| \frac{1}{n} \sum_{i=1}^{n} \tilde{\xi}_i(\omega) - E_{\tilde{\pi}}(\tilde{\xi}_1) \right| \succeq \tilde{\varepsilon} \right\} = 0.$$

This implies that

$$\lim_{n \to \infty} \tilde{\pi} \left\{ \omega : \left| \frac{1}{n} \sum_{i=1}^{n} \tilde{\xi}_i(\omega) - E_{\tilde{\pi}}(\tilde{\xi}_1) \right| \succeq \tilde{\varepsilon} \right\} = \tilde{0}.$$

This completes the proof.   □

4   Conclusions

This paper first introduces a new concept of fuzzy probability measures which we call gradual probability measure. It is a generalization of classical probability measures. Secondly, we introduce the concept of gradual random variables and obtain weak law of large numbers of gradual random variables on a gradual probability space. Future research will focus on the special properties of gradual probability measures and gradual random variables.

Acknowledgments. This research is supported by the National Natural Science Foundation of China (41201327), Natural Science Foundation of Hebei Province (A2013201119), Education Department of Hebei Province (QN20131055) and Science and Technology Bureau of Baoding (14ZF058). Their financial support is gratefully acknowledged.

References

1. Aiche, F., Dubois, D.: Possibility and Gradual Number Approaches To Ranking Methods For Random Fuzzy Intervals. Communications in Computer and Information Science 299, 9–18 (2012)

2. Ban, J.: Radon Nikodym Theorem and Conditional Expectation for Fuzzy Valued measures and variables. Fuzzy Sets and Systems 34, 383–392 (1990)
3. Boukezzoula, R., Galichet, S.: Optimistic Arithmetic Operators for Fuzzy and Gradual Intervals - Part II: Fuzzy and Gradual Interval Approach. Communications in Computer and Information Science 81, 451–460 (2010)
4. Deiri, E., Sadeghpour, B.G., Yari, G.H.: Dominated Convergence for Fuzzy Random Variables. Int. J. Industrial Mathematics 2, 89–96 (2010)
5. Dubois, D., Kerre, E., Mesiar, R., Prade, H.: Fuzzy Interval Analysis. Fundamentals of Fuzzy Sets, pp. 483–581. Kluwer (2000)
6. Dubois, D., Fortin, J., Zieliński, P.: Interval PERT and its Fuzzy Extension. Studies in Fuzziness and Soft Computing 252, 171–199 (2010)
7. Fortin, J., Dubois, D., Fargier, H.: Gradual Numbers and Their Application to Fuzzy Interval Analysis. IEEE Transactions on Fuzzy Systems 16, 388–402 (2008)
8. Fortin, J., Kasperski, A., Zielinski, P.: Some Methods for Evaluating the Optimality of Elements in Matroids. Fuzzy Sets and Systems 160, 1341–1354 (2009)
9. Gil, M.Á., LÓpez-Díaz, M.: Overview on the Development of Fuzzy Random Variables. Fuzzy Sets and Systems 157, 2546–2557 (2006)
10. Hutton, B.: Normality in Fuzzy Topological Spaces. J. Math. Anal. Appl. 50, 74–79 (1975)
11. Kasperski, A., Zieliński, P.: Using gradual numbers for solving fuzzy-valued combinatorial optimization problems. In: Melin, P., Castillo, O., Aguilar, L.T., Kacprzyk, J., Pedrycz, W. (eds.) IFSA 2007. LNCS (LNAI), vol. 4529, pp. 656–665. Springer, Heidelberg (2007)
12. Kruse, R., Meyer, K.D.: Statistics with Vague Data. Reidel Publ. Co., Dordrecht (1987)
13. Kwakernaak, H.: Fuzzy Random Variables. Part I: Definitions and Theorems. Inform. Sci. 15, 1–29 (1978)
14. Kwakernaak, H.: Fuzzy Random Variables. Part II: Algorithms and Examples for the Discrete Case. Inform. Sci. 17, 253–278 (1979)
15. Lietard, L., Rocacher, D.: Conditions with Aggregates Evaluated Using Gradual Numbers. Control and Cybernetics 38, 395–417 (2009)
16. Lodwick, W.A., Untiedt, E.: A Comparison of Interval Analysis Using Constraint Interval Arithmetic and Fuzzy Interval Analysis Using Gradual Numbers. In: Annual Meeting of the North American Fuzzy Information Processing Society, NAFIPS 2008, pp. 1–6 (2008)
17. Puri, M.L., Ralescu, D.A.: Convergence Theorem for Fuzzy Martingale. J. Math. Anal. Appl. 160, 107–122 (1991)
18. Sadeqi, I., Azart, F.Y.: Gradual Normed Linear Space. Iranian Journal of Fuzzy Systems 8, 131–139 (2011)
19. Stock, E.A.: Gradual Numbers and Fuzzy Optimization. Ph.D. Thesis, University of Colorado Denver, Denver. America (2010)
20. Stojaković, M.: Fuzzy Valued Measure. Fuzzy Sets and Systems 65, 95–104 (1994)
21. Stojaković, M.: Decomposition and Representation of Fuzzy Valued Measure. Fuzzy Sets and Systems 112, 251–256 (2000)
22. Stojaković, M.: Imprecise Set and Fuzzy Valued Probability. Journal of Computational and Applied Mathematics 235, 4524–4531 (2011)
23. Untiedt, E., Lodwick, W.: Using Gradual Numbers to Analyze Non-Monotonic Functions of Fuzzy Intervals. In: Annual Meeting of the North American Fuzzy Information Processing Society, NAFIPS 2008, pp. 1–6 (2008)
24. Shi, X., Lu, W., Wang, Z.: Programmable DNA Tile Self-assembly Using a Hierarchical Sub-tile Strategy. Nanotechnology 25(7), 075602 (2014)

25. Wu, H.C.: The Laws of Large Numbers for Fuzzy Random Variables. Fuzzy Sets and Systems 116, 245–262 (2000)
26. Xue, X., Ha, M.: On the Extension of the Fuzzy Number Measures in Banach Spaces: Part I. Representation of the Fuzzy Number Measures. Fuzzy Sets and Systems. 78, 347–354 (1996)
27. Zhou, C., Zhou, Y., Bao, J.: New Fuzzy Metric Spaces Based on Gradual Numbers. In: 2013 10th International Conference on Fuzzy Systems and Knowledge Discovery (FSKD), pp. 1–5. IEEE Press, New York (2013)

Protein Structure Prediction Based on Improved Multiple Populations and GA-PSO

Changjun Zhou*, Tianyun Hu, and Shihua Zhou

Key Laboratory of Advanced Design and Intelligent Computing,
Dalian University, Ministry of Education, Dalian, China
zhouchangjun@dlu.edu.cn

Abstract. Predicted amino acid sequence of the protein through its spatial structure can be attributed to a multivariable multi extreme global optimization problem. Based on AB off lattice model, a novel hybrid algorithm-MPGPSO which brings together the idea of multiple populations with the improved genetic algorithm and particle swarm optimization algorithm is presented in this paper for searching for the ground state structure of protein. The new algorithm taking advantages of the idea of best of best to enhance the algorithm's search capability. Experimental results are effective when it is applied to predict the best 3D structure of real protein sequences.

Keywords: Off-lattice AB model, Multiple populations, Random disturbance factor.

1 Introduction

Protein structure prediction (PSP) [1] problem is also known as protein folding problem. The shape of the protein folding structure in largely determines its biological function [2]. Controlling the structural information of the protein for studying its function and effect is of great importance. Protein structure prediction, therefore, has become an important research question to bioinformatics.

The protein molecule is a very complex system, and understanding the folding of natural protein remains one of the most challenging objectives in bioinformatics research. Based on the minimum free-energy theory [3], In recent years many researchers have developed various theoretical computing methods to search for the structures of proteins, such as conformational space annealing (CSA) [4], energy landscape paving minimizer (ELP)[5], pruned-enriched-Rosenbluth method (PERM) [6].

This paper presents a hybrid algorithm of the multi-population based on improved GA-PSO [7] to search for the natural structure of the protein. The algorithm uses the concept of multiple species to increase the population diversity, at the same time, the use of improved genetic particle swarm optimization in various populations can speed up the search efficiency of the algorithm which guarantees the search of the algorithm is global.

---

* Corresponding author.

L. Pan et al. (Eds.): BIC-TA 2014, CCIS 472, pp. 644–647, 2014.
© Springer-Verlag Berlin Heidelberg 2014

2   Materials and Methods

Based on the algorithmic thought of multiple populations [8],[9], we propose a new algorithm MPGPSO. The algorithm structure is shown in Fig.1.

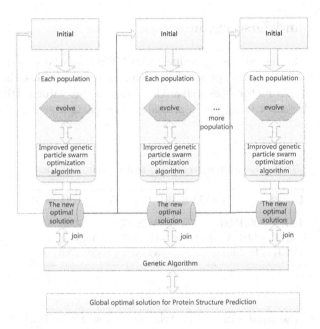

Fig. 1. The algorithm structure of multiple populations

In this algorithm, we use the improved GA-PSO to evolve the various populations independently. In the process of search, we do not allowed communication among populations , until the algorithm gets the local optimal solution from each population. Then all the local optimal solutions are regarded as an individual of the new population. At last, the GA is applied to the new population, and then we pick out the global optimal solution compared with the local optimum solution. The algorithm process is as follows:

Step1: Initialize the parameters, and Randomly generate the initial population.

Step2: Initialize the velocities and positions of particles.

Step3: Compute energy of particles and sort it from lowest to highest.

Step4: Use the improved GA using stochastic liner crossover and PSO which using a stochastic disturbance to obtain the local optimal solution.

Step5: Repetitive operation from Step1 to Step4, and obtain the minimum energy value.

Step6: Utilize the obtained results to generate a new population.

Step7: Perform the standard crossover and mutation operations for the new population.

Step8: Compute energy values of particles in the population and save the minimum energy value.

Step9: Compare the values obtained by Step8 and Step5, get the minimum energy and the global optimal solution.

3   Results and Discussion

Table 1 shows the lowest energy value E(MPGPSO) of the protein based on AB non-lattice model in this paper. For comparison, we also list the minimum energy value of other methods as well as the lowest energy value getting from the algorithm which simply using the improved genetic particle swarm optimization (GA-PSO)[7].

Table 1. Running results of real protein sequence

Length	E(PSO)	E(LPSO)	E(GAPSO)	E(MPGPSO)
1CRN	-20.1826	-28.7591	-35.9267	-43.9339
2KAP	-8.0448	-15.9988	-17.3197	-18.9513
1PCH	-18.4408	-	-34.9700	-38.2766

Table 1 gives the results of real protein sequences. From Table 1 we can see our results are much lower than the previous results. So our algorithm is more effective and much better than other algorithms.

4   Conclusion

According to the characteristics of 3D protein structure prediction of multiple variables and multiple extremism, this paper proposes a GA-PSO algorithm based on the idea of multiple group. At the beginning of the algorithm, we initializes multiple populations and search each population independently with GA-PSO to obtain the local optimal solution from each population , then all local optimal solutions can regroup to a new population. At last, the GA operation is used on this population to obtain the global optimal solution.

Based on the improved genetic particle swarm optimization the algorithm fuses the idea of multiple populations to achieve the best optimization among the different populations, which strengthens the exchanges among different populations. The global search and local search could ensure the diversity and convergence of search, making the result to be certain of optimality. In AB off lattice model, experiments on Fibonacci sequence, the results show that the algorithm is superior to other methods, meanwhile reflects the real protein characteristics in a certain extent.

In recent works, low-dispersion sequences were used to improve projection based algorithms, see e.g. [11]. For future research, a possible way is using low-dispersion sequences to improve the algorithms in predictions of secondary structure of RNA.

Acknowledgments. This work is supported by the National Natural Science Foundation of China (No.31170797, 61103057, 31370778 and 61370005), the Program for Changjiang Scholars and Innovative Research Team in University (No.IRT1109), the Key Project of Chinese Ministry of Education (No.211036),the Project Supported by Scientific Research Fund of Liaoning Provincial Education Department (No. L2011218), the Project is sponsored by "Liaoning BaiQianWan Talents Program" (No.2013921007), the Project is supported by the Natural Science Foundation of Liaoning Province(No. 2014020132).

References

1. Lee, J.Y., Wu, S., Zhang, Y.: AB Initio Protein Structure Prediction, From Protein Structure to Function with Bioinformatics, pp. 3–25. Springer, Heidelberg (2009)
2. Zhou, H.B., Lv, Q., We, W.: Stochastic Perturbation PSO Algorithm for Toy Model-based Folding Problem. Computer Engineering and Application 47(18), 234–236 (2011)
3. Anfinsen, C.B.: Principles That Govern The Folding Of Protein Chains. Science 181, 223 (1973)
4. Kim, S.Y., Lee, S.B., Lee, J.: Structure Optimization By Conformational Space Annealing In An Off-Lattice Protein Model. Phys. Rev. E 72, 011916 (2005)
5. Bachmann, M., Arkin, H., Janke, W.: Multicanonical Study Of Coarse-Grained Off-Lattice Models For Folding Heteropolymers. Phys. Rev. E 71, 031906 (2005)
6. Hsu, H.P., Mehra, V., Grassberger, P.: Structure Optimization in an Off-lattice Protein Model. Phys. Rev. E. 68, 037703 (2003)
7. Zhou, C.J., Hou, C.X., Zhang, Q., Wei, X.P.: Enhanced Hybrid Search Algorithm for Protein Structure Prediction Using the 3D-HP Lattice Model. Journal of Molecular Modeling 19(9), 3883–3891 (2003)
8. Sereni, B., Krahenbuhl, L.: Fitness Sharing and Niching Methods Revisited. IEEE Trans. on Evolutionary Computation 2(3), 972–1106 (1998)
9. Cohoon, J.P., Martin, W.N., Richards, D.S.: A Multi-Population Genetic Algorithm for Solving the K-Partition Problem on Hyper-Cubes. ICGA 91, 244–248 (1991)
10. Zhou, H.B., Lv, Q.: A Study on Applying Particle Swarm Optimization Algorithm, Soochow University (2009)
11. Wang, X., Miao, Y., Cheng, M.: Finding Motifs in DNA Sequences Using Low-Dispersion Sequences. Journal of Computational Biology 21(4), 320–329 (2014)

A Multi-population Discrete Firefly Algorithm to Solve TSP

Lingyun Zhou[1,2], Lixin Ding[1,*], and Xiaoli Qiang[2]

[1] State Key Laboratory of Software Engineering, Computer School,
Wuhan University, Wuhan 430072, Hubei, China
[2] College of Computer Science, South-Central University for Nationalities,
Wuhan 430074, Hubei, China
{zhouly,qiangxl}@mail.scuec.edu.cn, lxding@whu.edu.cn

Abstract. In this paper, the Firefly algorithm (FA) is improved and a multi-population discrete firefly algorithm is presented combined with k-opt algorithm to solve the traveling salesman problem (TSP). The proposed algorithm is tested on some instances and the performance of the proposed algorithm is compared with the other discrete firefly algorithm for TSP. The results of the tests show that the proposed algorithm performs better in terms of convergence rate and solution quality.

Keywords: Metaheuristics, Discrete firefly algorithm, Traveling salesman problem, Multi-population.

1 Introduction

The traveling salesman problem (TSP) is an well-known combinatorial optimization problem which can be described that the salesman visits a number of cities exactly once and returns to the starting city as trying to obtain a closed tour in finding a shortest route within minimum span of time. [2]. During the past years, artificial intelligence based metaheuristic algorithms are becoming powerful in solving optimization problems. Many of them have been applied to solve TSP and have been effective methods [2-9]. Recently, a metaheuristic algorithm which named firefly algorithm (FA) has been brought up by Xin-She Yang [15]. FA provided effective results for multimodal functions in comparison with both genetic algorithms (GA) and particle swarm optimization (PSO) [16]. The FA literature has expanded significantly with several hundred papers published. Most of them are for continuous optimization problems [12-14]. However, it can also solve discrete optimization problems. A discrete firefly algorithm was proposed by Gilang Kusuma Jati to solve TSP named EDFA, which incorporates evolutionary operations of mutations and selections [5], however, it can also easily be trapped into local optimum solutions for some instances.

A number of research works have demonstrated that using multi-swarm would have more exploration and exploitation abilities than one swarm [16-17]. This

---

* Corresponding author.

L. Pan et al. (Eds.): BIC-TA 2014, CCIS 472, pp. 648–653, 2014.
© Springer-Verlag Berlin Heidelberg 2014

idea can be applied to FA. In this paper, a multi-population discrete firefly algorithm combined with k-opt algorithm is proposed, in which premature convergence is more likely to be avoided.

2 Firefly Algorithm

FA is one of the recent nature inspired metaheuristic algorithm. The basic steps of the FA can be found in the reference [16].From a mathematical perspective, the FA optimization mechanism can be described as follows.

The attractiveness β_{ij} between firefly i and firefly j is calculated by the equation

$$\beta_{ij} = \beta_0 e^{-\gamma r_{ij}^2} \tag{1}$$

where β_0 is a constant and presents the attractiveness at the source. γ is the light absorption coefficient which can be taken as a constant.

The distance r_{ij} between any two fireflies i and j , is the Cartesian distance, can be defined as

$$r_{ij} = \|x_i - x_j\|_2 = \sqrt{\sum_{k=1}^{d}(x_{ik} - x_{jk})^2} \tag{2}$$

where d denotes the dimensionality of the problem.

The movement of a firefly i that is attracted to another more attractive firefly j at the tth iteration is determined by

$$x_i(t) = x_i(t-1) + \beta_{ij}(x_j(t-1) - x_i(t-1)) + \alpha(rand - 0.5) \tag{3}$$

where α is a randomness scaling factor and $rand$ is a random number.

3 Multi-population Discrete Firefly Algorithm (MDFA)

3.1 Representation and Initialization

In the MDFA, a TSP solution is represented by a firefly in the population. The initial population is generated at random included with a greedy solution. By putting one relatively good solution among the random solutions would probably contribute to better exploitation of the search space.

3.2 Discrete Distance and the Moving in the Search Space

In the MDFA, the distance between any two fireflies i and j at x_i and x_j , respectively, is the Hamming's distance.

$$r_{ij} = hamming(x_i, x_j) \tag{4}$$

In the MDFA, the k-opt move method [3] is used to change the order of visited cities, which represent the movements of fireflies. Each firefly i will move to a new position towards another firefly j having higher fitness value based on:

$$k = random(2, r_{ij}) \tag{5}$$

$$x_i(t) = kOpt(x_i(t-1), k) \tag{6}$$

Where $kOpt$ represents a function that uses a k-opt trial move. The k-opt algorithm is a local search algorithm and k is the neighboring components of the solution that will be reversed. The value of k will be randomly selected from 2 to r_{ij}. The $kOpt$ function is defined to detect k neighboring nodes in a tour, exchanging them of the current solution and then evaluating the generated new solutions to find the optimum one.

3.3   Elitist Strategy: Movement of the Lightest Firefly

The brightest firefly is a firefly at current global best position. If this brightest firefly moves randomly as in the standard firefly algorithm, its fitness may decrease depending on the direction. This leads to the decrement of the performance of the algorithm in that particular iteration. However, if this highest fitness firefly is allowed to move only if in a direction in which its fitness improves, it will not decrease the performance of the algorithm in terms of global best solution for the solutions in that particular iteration [13]. To determine the movement direction of the brightest firefly, the proposed improvement considers the following method:

$$x_b(t) = bestkOpt(x_b(t-1), k) \tag{7}$$

Where $x_b(t)$ is the brightest firefly at generation t. $bestkOpt$ is the function which calls the $kOpt$ function, in which the value of k is from 2 to 3. When a new tour is achieved, its expected length is calculated. If it is less than the expected length of the current tour, then the new tour is considered as the current tour and the procedure continues from this one. The method may be more likely to improve the fitness of the brightest firefly.

General scheme of MDFA

The general scheme of MDFA is demonstrated by the following pseudo code.

Algorithm 1. Multi-population Discrete Firefly Algorithm (MDFA)

```
t = 0;
Initialize population of fireflies x(t);
Evaluate the population;
while(not termination condition)
   t= t+1;
   Divide population, select fireflies for each swarm at random;
   for each subpopulation
     Rank subpopulation by their lightness;
```

```
    for i = 1:the number of fireflies in subpopulation
      for j = 1:i
        if(Ij>Ii)
          Compute distance based on (4);
          Move firefly i towards j based on (5,6);
        end
      end
    end
    Update the brightness firefly of each subpopulation
    based on (7)
  end
  Merge sub-population;
  Evaluate the new population;
  Rank the fireflies and find the current best;
End
```

4 Computational Experiments and Results

To test the performance of the MDFA, computational experiments are carried out. The computational procedures described above have been implemented in a MATLAB computer program on an Intel Core 3.20 GHz CPU, 4GB RAM computer. The performance of MDFA is tested on some TSP instances including some randomly generated instances and the known TSP instances downloaded from TSPLIB. The MDFA will be compared with the EDFA [5].

The parameter settings used in the experiments are shown in Table 1. In each case study, 30 independent runs of the algorithms are carried out and each simulation is with maximum number of iterations (MaxGeneration) as a termination criterion.

Table 1. Parameter settings for the algorithms in the comparisons

Parameters	EDFA	MDFA
Number of population	1	3
Population size	15	15
m	8	-
MaxGeneration	200	200

Tables 2 summarizes the results, where the column 'Ave' shows the mean solution length of the 30 independent runs of each algorithm. The column 'PDb(%)' gives the percentage deviation of the best solution length over the optimal solution length of 30 runs, the column 'PDav(%)' denotes the percentage deviation of the average solution length over the optimal solution length of 30 runs. The

Table 2. Comparison of EDFA and MDFA

Instance	Opt	EDFA				MDFA			
		Best	Ave	PDb(%)	PDav(%)	Best	Ave	PDb(%)	PDav(%)
city10	-	262	262	-	-	262	262	-	-
city20	-	360	363	-	-	360	361	-	-
city30	-	464	483	-	-	454	460	-	-
bays29	2020	2020	2066	0	2.28	2020	2036	0	0.79
eil51	426	497	540	16.67	26.76	432	443	1.41	3.99
berlin52	7542	8752	9135	16.04	21.12	7681	7933	1.84	5.81
st70	675	985	1039	45.93	53.93	682	706	1.04	4.59

percentage deviation of a solution to the best known solution is defined by the formula[10]:

$$PDsolution(\%) = \frac{solutionlength - bestknownsolutionleggth}{bestknowsolutionlength} \times 100 \qquad (8)$$

5 Discussion and Conclusion

In this paper, the original firefly algorithm is modified and a multi-population discrete firefly algorithm (MDFA) for solving TSP has been implemented. There are three main modifications in the proposed algorithm. One of the main modifications is combined with k-opt local search. The second is identifying the best direction in which the brightness of the brightest firefly increases. The third characteristic is using multiple population technique. Some small not extremely difficult TSP instances are chosen to conduct a series of experiments in order to see the benefits of the MDFA. According to the results, it outperforms the EDFA for solving TSP.

Acknowledgments. The authors thank the financial support for the work from Chinese National Natural Science Foundation (61379059, 61370105), the Fundamental Research Funds for the Central Universities (CZY14011, CZZ13003).

References

1. Aarts, E.H.L., Korst, J.H.M., van Laarhoven, P.J.M.: A Quantitative Analysis of The Simulated Annealing Algorithm: A Case Study For The Traveling Salesman Problem. Journal of Statistical Physics 50(1-2), 187–206 (1988)
2. Applegate, D.L.: The Traveling Salesman Problem: A Computational Study. Princeton University Press, Princeton (2006)

3. Chandra, B., Karloff, H., Tovey, C.: New Results on the Old K-Opt Algorithm for the Traveling Salesman Problem. SIAM Journal on Computing 28(6), 1998–2029 (1999)
4. Dorigo, M., Gambardella, L.M.: Ant Colonies for the Travelling Salesman Problem. Bio Systems 43(2), 73–81 (1997)
5. Jati, G.K.: Evolutionary Discrete Firefly Algorithm for Travelling Salesman Problem. Adaptive and Intelligent Systems, pp. 393–403. Springer, Heidelberg (2011)
6. Krasnogor, N., Smith, J.: A Memetic Algorithm With Self-Adaptive Local Search: TSP as A Case Study. In: GECCO 2000, pp. 987–994 (2000)
7. Łukasik, S., Żak, S.: Firefly algorithm for continuous constrained optimization tasks. In: Nguyen, N.T., Kowalczyk, R., Chen, S.-M. (eds.) ICCCI 2009. LNCS, vol. 5796, pp. 97–106. Springer, Heidelberg (2009)
8. Marinakis, Y., Marinaki, M.: A hybrid multi-swarm particle swarm optimization algorithm for the probabilistic traveling salesman problem. Computers and Operations Research 37(3), 432–442 (2010)
9. Niasar, N.S., Shanbezade, J., Perdam, M.M., et al.: Discrete Fuzzy Particle Swarm Optimization for Solving Traveling Salesman Problem. In: Information and Financial Engineering 2009, pp. 162–165. IEEE Press, New York (2009)
10. Ouaarab, A., Ahiod, B., Yang, X.S.: Discrete Cuckoo Search Algorithm for the Travelling Salesman Problem. In: Neural Computing and Applications, pp. 1–11 (2013)
11. Potvin, J.Y.: Genetic Algorithms for the Traveling Salesman Problem. Annals of Operations Research 63(3), 337–370 (1996)
12. Shi, X.H., Liang, Y.C., Lee, H.P., et al.: Particle Swarm Optimization-Based Algorithms for Tsp and Generalized Tsp. Information Processing Letters 103(5), 169–176 (2007)
13. Tilahun, S.L., Ong, H.C.: Modified Firefly Algorithm. Journal of Applied Mathematics (2012)
14. Xue-Hui, L., Ye, Y., Xia, L., Solving, T.S.P.: with Shuffled Frog-Leaping Algorithm. In: Eighth IEEE Intelligent Systems Design and Applications, pp. 228–232. IEEE Press, New York (2008)
15. Yang, X.S.: Nature-inspired Metaheuristic Algorithms. Luniver Press (2008)
16. Yang, X.-S.: Firefly algorithms for multimodal optimization. In: Watanabe, O., Zeugmann, T. (eds.) SAGA 2009. LNCS, vol. 5792, pp. 169–178. Springer, Heidelberg (2009)
17. Yang, X.S.: Firefly Algorithm, Stochastic Test Functions and Design Optimisation. International Journal of Bio-Inspired Computation 2(2), 78–84 (2010)
18. Yang, X.S.: Multiobjective Firefly Algorithm for Continuous Optimization. Engineering with Computers 29(2), 175–184 (2013)
19. Yao, J., Kharma, N., Grogono, P.: A Multi-Population Genetic Algorithm for Robust and Fast Ellipse Detection. Pattern Analysis and Applications 8(1-2), 149–162 (2005)

Study and Application of DNA Cellular Automata Self-assembly

Shihua Zhou*, Bin Wang, Xuedong Zheng, and Changjun Zhou

Key Laboratory of Advanced Design and Intelligent Computing
of Ministry of Education, Dalian University, Dalian 116622, Liaoning, China
shihuajo@gmail.com

Abstract. Because DNA self-assembly technique has its unique molecular function and control of nanomaterials synthesis, DNA computing model based on the self-assembly owns great prospects for development. At present, humans have been widely used image to record and express the objective world, and image also becomes a kind of extremely important multimedia information storage and transmission format. In order to enhance the security of image, people have started to use DNA self-assembly to study DNA cryptography-based image encryption. In this paper, design of image encryption-oriented DNA self-assembly is introduced. The paper gives the self-assembly definition of elementary XOR-DNA cellular automata and elementary T-shaped XOR-DNA cellular automata. Combined with the characteristics of image encryption, the design of image encryption self-assembly is given by the definition of elementary T-shaped DNA cellular automata.

Keywords: DNA cellular automata, Self-assembly, Image encryption.

1 Introduction

In 1994, Adleman presented his paper "Molecular Computation of Solutions to Combinatorial Problems" in Science [1], in which he solved successfully Hamiltonian Path Problem by DNA sequences. Since then, DNA computing [2] that is a new discipline has come into being. Because DNA self-assembly technique has its unique molecular function and control of nanomaterials synthesis, DNA computing model based on the self-assembly owns great prospects for development. Winfree et al. [3] first came up with the idea of computing by self-assembly tiles. From the mid-1990s, many researchers [4] have done large theoretical and experimental work. Image encryption [5] is usually used to protect the important image information from usurping. The traditional image encryption algorithms except for the one-time pad own only computational security. Therefore, people try to search the safer and more effective encryption method. With the fast development of the genetic engineering techniques and DNA computing, people have started to use them to study DNA cryptography-based image encryption

---

* Corresponding author.

L. Pan et al. (Eds.): BIC-TA 2014, CCIS 472, pp. 654–658, 2014.

[6]. In the paper, we give the self-assembly design of DNA cellular automata. Combined with the characteristics of image encryption, the design of image encryption self-assembly is given.

2   DNA Cellular Automata

A DNA sequence contains four nucleic acid bases, namely A (adenine), C (cytosine), G (guanine) and T (thymine), where A and T is complement, C and G is complement. We define the one-dimensional DNA cellular automata, and it is consisted of a line of cells. A given node s can be the one of four state values, $s \in S = \{A, C, G, T\}$, and the neighborhood radius is r. The closet nodes to node s are those to its left and right. In that case, one node s can have a local neighborhood of $2r$ cells, $f : s^{2r+1} \to s$ is the transfer function at discrete time. The state of s at time $t + 1$ will be determined by the states of the cells within its neighborhood at time t.

$$s_i^{t+1} = f(s_{i-r}^t, ..., s_{i-1}^t, s_i^t, s_{i+1}^t, ..., , s_{i+r}^t). \tag{1}$$

s_i^{t+1} represents the state of the ith cell, at discrete time $t + 1$. In general, a rule is needed, that will be used to synchronously calculate the state s_i^{t+1} from the states of the cells in the neighborhood at the ith time level.

In particular, elementary XOR-DNA cellular automata is a type of one-dimensional DNA cellular automata that the number of state values is $k = 4$ and the neighborhood radius is $r = 1$. At discrete time t, the state of the ith cell is s_i^t, and the states of its neighborhood are s_{i-1}^t and s_{i+1}^t. Here, the transfer function $f : s^3 \to s$ is as follow:

$$s_i^{t+1} = f(s_{i-1}^t, s_i^t, s_{i+1}^t). \tag{2}$$

We define a T-shaped DNA cellular automata that is consisted of one cell and the neighborhood cells in three directions (namely left, right and bottom). At discrete time $t + 1$, a given node s can be determined by the states of itself and neighborhood cells in three directions. For T-shaped XOR-DNA cellular automata, every node s can be the one of four state values, $s \in S = \{A, C, G, T\}$, and the neighborhood radius is r. In that case, one node s can have $3r$ neighborhood cells, $f : s^{3r+1} \to s$ is the transfer function at discrete time. In particular, elementary T-shaped XOR-DNA cellular automata is a T-shaped DNA cellular automata that the number of state values is $k = 4$, the neighborhood radius is $r = 1$ and the new state is gained by XOR operation among the states of cells. At discrete time t, the state of the cell in the location (i, j) is $s_{i,j}^t$. The states of its three neighborhood are $s_{i,j-1}^t$, $s_{i,j+1}^t$ and $s_{i+1,j}^t$ respectively. Here, the transfer function $f : s^4 \to s$ is as follow:

$$s_{i,j}^{t+1} = f(s_{i,j-1}^t, s_{i,j}^t, s_{i,j+1}^t, s_{i+1,j}^t). \tag{3}$$

3   Design of Image Encryption-Based Cellular Automata Self-assembly

In this section, image encryption is implemented by the above definition of elementary T-shaped XOR-DNA cellular automata. Through one example, the process of this self-assembly is introduced in detail.

3.1   Design of Key Self-assembly

One natural DNA sequence is selected as secret keys for image encryption, and secret keys are implemented by synthetic random tiles. Fig.1 is an example of secret keys self-assembly. In this example, the selected DNA sequence is $\{C, T, A, T, G, T, C, T\}$, and two boundaries are $\{G\}$ and $\{G\}$. From left to right,the information of upper right sticker ends are $\{G\}$, $\{C\}$, $\{T\}$,$\{A\}$,$\{T\}$,$\{G\}$, $\{T\}$,$\{C\}$, $\{T\}$ and $\{G\}$. From left to right, the information of upper left sticker ends are $\{C\}$, $\{T\}$,$\{A\}$,$\{T\}$,$\{G\}$,$\{T\}$,$\{C\}$,$\{T\}$ and $\{G\}$.

Fig. 1. The example of secret keys self-assembly

3.2   Design of Plaintext Tiles and Self-assembly

The original image is expressed by initial tiles self-assembly. First of all, every pixel of the original image is converted into four bases, and each a bases is expressed by an initial tile. Assuming that the image is composed of two pixels, gray values are 132 and 76 respectively. They are converted to a DNA sequence that is $\{G, A, C, A, C, A, T, A\}$. Boundary conditions are gained by the underlying transmission, and the upper layer is gained in Fig.2. From left to right,the information of upper right sticker ends are $\{C\}$, $\{C\}$, $\{C\}$,$\{G\}$,$\{T\}$,$\{T\}$,$\{G\}$,$\{G\}$,$\{A\}$ and $\{T\}$. From left to right, the information of upper left sticker ends are $\{G\}$, $\{A\}$,$\{C\}$,$\{A\}$,$\{C\}$,$\{A\}$,$\{T\}$,$\{A\}$ and $\{G\}$.

Fig. 2. The example of plaintext self-assembly

3.3   Design of Encryption Self-assembly

The encryption self-assembly is implemented by process tiles, and Fig.3 shows the structure of the encryption self-assembly. The figure shows two rounds of self-assembly process, which is the result that the original image is encrypted twice. This process is done by process tiles self-assembly , and doesn't need any manual intervention. After two rounds of self-assembly, the states of the cells are $\{C, A, T, C, A, A, G, G\}$.

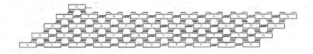

Fig. 3. The example of encryption self-assembly

3.4   Design of Ciphertext Self-assembly

Final tiles are used to extract the encrypted information, and Fig.4 shows the overall process of image encryption by elementary T-shaped XOR-DNA cellular automata. The example is that two pixels are encrypted via four rounds of self-assembly. From the top layer, the encrypted information are $\{T, T, T, C, A, T, T, G\}$, and the new pixel values are 253 and 62. Pixel values of the original image pixel that is 132 and 76 are different from the new pixel values, and the purpose of encryption is achieved. Here is just an examples, and the number of tiles and encryption is not limited in practice.

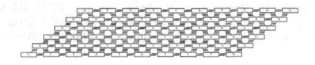

Fig. 4. The example of cipertext self-assembly

The processes of decryption and encryption are reverse, but the basic principle is the same. In the process of decryption, the states of the cells at the time t_n are regarded as the connection of random tiles, and the ones at the time t_{n-1} are regarded as the connection of initial tiles. Process tiles are self-assembled via the same number of rounds, and the original image information are gained.

4   Conclusions

In this paper, the self-assembly of DNA cellular automata is designed. The paper gives the self-assembly definition of elementary XOR-DNA cellular automata and elementary T-shaped XOR-DNA cellular automata. Combined with the characteristics of image encryption, the design of image encryption self-assembly is given by the definition of elementary T-shaped DNA cellular automata. The self-assembled model includes four parts, namely design of key self-assembly, design of plaintext tiles and self-assembly, design of encryption self-assembly and design of ciphertext self-assembly. Through the designed model, image encryption can been implemented accurately.

Acknowledgments. This work is supported by the National Natural Science Foundation of China (No.31170797, 61103057, 31370778, 61370005), the Program for Changjiang Scholars and Innovative Research Team in University (No.IRT1109), the Key Project of Chinese Ministry of Education (No.211036), the Project Supported by Scientific Research Fund of Liaoning Provincial Education Department (No. L2011218), the Project is sponsored by "Liaoning BaiQianWan Talents Program" (No.2013921007), the Project is supported by the Natural Science Foundation of Liaoning Province (No. 2014020132).

References

1. Adleman, L.M.: Molecular Computation of Solutions to Combinatorial Problems. Science 266(5187), 1021–1024 (1994)
2. Hossein, E., Majid, D.: Application of DNA Computing in Graph theory. Artificial Intelligence Review 38(3), 223–235 (2012)
3. Winfree, E., Liu, F., Wenzler, L., Seeman, N.: Design and Self-assembly of Two-dimensional DNA Crystals. Nature 394(6693), 539–544 (1998)
4. Lin, C., Liu, Y., Rinker, S., Yan, H.: DNA Tile Based Self-assembly: Building Complex Nanoarchitectures. Chemphyschem. 7(8), 1641–1647 (2006)
5. Mirzaei, O., Yaghoobi, M., Irani, H.: A New Image Encryption Method: Parallel Sub-image Encryption with Hyper Chaos. Nonlinear Dynamics 67(1), 557–566 (2012)
6. Zhang, Q., Guo, L., Wei, X.: Image Encryption Using DNA Addition Combining with Chaotic Map. Mathematical and Computer Modelling 52, 2028–2035 (2011)

Fixed Point in Fuzzy Metric Spaces

Yinying Zhou*

Department of Mathematics and Information Sciences
Langfang Teacher's College, Langfang, Hebei 065000, China
zhouyinying_hbu@163.com

Abstract. In this paper, we propose a new definition of generalized fuzzy contractive mapping,which is a generalization of the fuzzy contractive mapping in the sense of Yonghong Shen. and prove some convergence theorems by different contractive conditions in fuzzy metric space. Our results improve and extend the corresponding results in [5,6,8].

Keywords: Fuzzy metric space, Fuzzy contractive mapping, Fixed point.

1 Introduction

Fuzzy metric space was initiated by Kramosil and Michalek [1] ,which can be regarded as a generalization of the statistical metric space. Many authors introduce and investigate the different types of fuzzy contractive mappings. They extended the Banach contraction theorem to G-complete fuzzy metric spaces and obtained some fixed point theorems for contractive mappings in G-complete fuzzy metric spaces.

2 Preliminaries

Throught the paper N denotes the set of all positive integers. We start with the definition of continuous t-norm. It is an important role in fuzzy metric spaces. Now,we recall some basic definations and the properties.

Definition 2.1. [1] A binary operation $* : [0,1] \times [0,1] \to [0,1]$ is called a continuous t-norm if it satisfies the following conditions:
$(T1)*$ is commuative and associative;
$(T2)*$ is continuous;
$(T3)a * 1 = a$ for every $a \in [0,1]$;
$(T4)a * b \leq c * d$ whenever $a \leq c, b \leq d$ for all $a, b, c, d \in [0,1]$.

Definition 2.2. [1] A triple $(X, M, *)$ is called a fuzzy metric space if X is a nonempty set,* is a continuous t-norm and $M : X \times X \times (0, +\infty) \to [0,1]$ is a fuzzy set satisfying the following conditions:

---

* Corresponding author.

L. Pan et al. (Eds.): BIC-TA 2014, CCIS 472, pp. 659–663, 2014.

$(GV1)M(x, y, 0) = 0;$
$(GV2)M(x, y, t) = 1 \Leftrightarrow x = y;$
$(GV3)M(x, y, t) = M(y, x, t);$
$(GV4)M(x, z, t + s) \geq M(x, y, t) * M(y, z, s);$
$(GV5)M(x, y, \cdot) : (0, \infty) \to [0, 1]$ is left continuous, for all $x, y, z \in X, s, t > 0.$

Definition 2.3. [5] Let $(X, M, *)$ is a fuzzy metric space,then:
(i) A sequence $\{x_n\}$ is said to converge to x in X,denoted by $x_n \to x$ if and only if $\lim_{n \to \infty} M(x_n, x, t) = 1$ for any $t > 0$.that is for each $r \in (0, 1), t > 0$,there exists a positive integers N_0 such that $M(x_n, x, t) > 1 - r(\forall n \geq N_0)$;
(ii) A sequence $\{x_n\}$ is an $M-$Cauchy sequence if and only if for each $\epsilon > 0, t > 0$,there exists a positive integers N_0 such that $M(x_n, x_m, t) > 1 - \epsilon \ (\forall m, n \geq N_0)$;
(iii) Fuzzy metric space $(X, M, *)$ is called M-complete if every M-Cauchy sequence is convergent.

3   The Main Results

In this section,we will introduce a new concept of generalized fuzzy contractive mapping and prove some fixed point theorems by different contractive conditions in fuzzy metric space.

Denote by $\mathcal{H}$ a family of mappings $\varphi : (0, 1] \to [0, +\infty)$ satisfying the following two conditions:
$(P1)$ φ is strictly decreasing and left continuous;
$(P2)$ $\varphi(\lambda) = 0$ if and only if $\lambda = 1$.

Definition 3.1. Let $(X, M, *)$ is a fuzzy metric space,A mapping $T : X \to X$ is said to be a generalized fuzzy contractive mapping with respect to $\varphi \in \mathcal{H}$,if there exists a decreasing function $a_i(t) : [0, +\infty) \to [0, 1)(i = 1, 2, 3, 4, 5), \sum_{i=1}^{3} a_i(t) + 2a_4(t) < 1, \sum_{i=1}^{5} a_i(t) < 1, (\forall t > 0)$ satisfies the following condition:

$$\varphi(M(Tx, Ty, t)) \leq a_1(t)\varphi(M(x, y, t)) + a_2(t)\varphi(M(x, Tx, t)) +$$
$$a_3(t)\varphi(M(y, Ty, t))a_4(t)\varphi(M(x, Ty, t)) + a_5(t)\varphi(M(y, Tx, t)) \tag{1}$$

Proposition 3.2. Let $(X, M, *)$ is a fuzzy metric space,$\varphi \in \mathcal{H}$,a sequence $\{x_n\}$ is said M-Cauchy if and only if for $\forall \epsilon > 0, \forall t > 0$,there exists a positive integers N_0,such that $\varphi(M(x_m, x_n, t)) < \epsilon(\forall m, n \geq N_0)$.

Proposition 3.3. Let $(X, M, *)$ is a fuzzy metric space,$\varphi \in \mathcal{H}$,a sequence $\{x_n\}$ is convergent to x if and only if $\lim_{n \to \infty} \varphi(M(x_n, x, t)) = 0$ for any $t > 0$.
Now we can state the main result of the paper.

Theorem 3.4. Let $(X, M, *)$ is a M-Complete fuzzy metric space,$T : X \to X$ is a generalized fuzzy contractive mapping with respect to $\varphi \in \mathcal{H}$ such that

$r * s > 0 \Rightarrow \varphi(r * s) \leq \varphi(r) + \varphi(s)$ for all $r, s \in \{M(x, Tx, t) : x \in X, t > 0\}$, then T has unique fixed point x^* and $\{x_n\}$ converges to x^* .

Proof. Let $x_0 \in X$, define $x_{n+1} = Tx_n$ and $\tau_n(t) = M(x_n, x_{n+1}, t), (n \in N \bigcup\{0\}, t > 0)$. Now we first prove that T has a fixed point.

Case 1. If there exists $n^* \in N \bigcup\{0\}$ such that $x_{n^*+1} = x_{n^*}$, then it follows that x_{n^*} is a fixed point of T.

Case 2. We assume that $0 < \tau_n(t) < 1$,by (1) and $(GV4)$,for any $t > 0, n \in N \bigcup\{0\}$, we obtain

$$
\begin{aligned}
\varphi(\tau_n(t)) = \varphi(M(x_n, x_{n+1}, t)) \leq\ & a_1(t)\varphi(M(x_{n-1}, x_n, t)) + \\
& + a_2(t)\varphi(M(x_{n-1}, Tx_{n-1}, t)) \\
& + a_3(t)\varphi(M(x_n, Tx_n, t)) + \\
& + a_4(t)\varphi(M(x_{n-1}, Tx_n, t)) \\
& + a_5(t)\varphi(M(x_n, Tx_{n-1}, t)) \\
= [a_1(t) + a_2(t)]\varphi(\tau_{n-1}&(t)) + a_3(t)\varphi(\tau_n(t)) + a_4(t)\varphi(M(x_{n-1}, Tx_n, t)) \\
\leq [a_1(t) + a_2(t)]\varphi(\tau_{n-1}&(t)) + a_3(t)\varphi(\tau_n(t)) + a_4(t)\varphi(M(x_{n-1}, x_n, \frac{t}{2})) \\
& + a_4(t)\varphi(M(x_n, x_{n+1}, \frac{t}{2}))
\end{aligned}
$$

so

$$\varphi(\tau_n(t)) \leq \frac{a_1(t) + a_2(t) + a_4(t)}{1 - a_3(t) - a_4(t)} \varphi(\tau_{n-1}(t)) \qquad (2)$$

Since φ and $\frac{a_1(t)+a_2(t)+a_4(t)}{1-a_3(t)-a_4(t)}$ is strictly decreasing ,it is easy to show that $\{\tau_n(t)\}$ is an increasing sequence for $t > 0$ with respect to n.we put $\lim\limits_{n \to \infty} \tau_n(t) = \tau(t)$ and suppose that $0 < \tau(t) < 1$.As $n \to \infty$,by (2) and the left continuous of φ ,we have

$$\varphi(\tau(t)) \leq \frac{a_1(t) + a_2(t) + a_4(t)}{1 - a_3(t) - a_4(t)} \varphi(\tau(t)) < \varphi(\tau(t)),$$

which is a contradiction,hence $\tau(t) = 1$,that is $\lim\limits_{n \to \infty} \tau_n(t) = 1$.

Next,we claim that $\{x_n\}$ ia a M-Cauchy sequence.Suppose that it is not,then there exists a $\epsilon > 0$ and two sequences $\{p(n)\}, \{q(n)\}$,such that for every $n \in N \bigcup\{0\}, t > 0, p(n) > q(n) \geq n$,

$M(x_{p(n)}, x_{q(n)}, t) \leq 1 - \epsilon; \qquad M(x_{p(n)-1}, x_{q(n)-1}, t) > 1 - \epsilon;$

$M(x_{p(n)-1}, x_{q(n)}, t) > 1 - \epsilon. \qquad (3)$

Let $s_n(t) = M(x_{p(n)}, x_{q(n)}, t)$,then

$$
\begin{aligned}
1 - \epsilon \geq s_n(t) = M(x_{p(n)}, x_{q(n)}, t) &\geq M(x_{p(n)-1}, x_{p(n)}, \frac{t}{2}) * M(x_{p(n)-1}, x_{q(n)}, \frac{t}{2}) \\
&> \tau_{p_n}(\frac{t}{2}) \cdot (1 - \epsilon)
\end{aligned}
$$

since $\lim_{n \to \infty} \tau_n(\frac{t}{2}) = 1$, so $\lim_{n \to \infty} s_n(t) = 1 - \epsilon$. moreover, we know

$$\varphi(M(x_{p(n)}, x_{q(n)}, t)) \leq \frac{a_1(t) + a_2(t) + a_4(t)}{1 - a_3(t) - a_4(t)} \varphi(M(x_{p(n)-1}, x_{q(n)-1}, t))$$
$$< \varphi(M(x_{p(n)-1}, x_{q(n)-1}, t))$$

According to the strictly monotonicity of φ and (3), we have

$$1 - \epsilon \geq M(x_{p(n)}, x_{q(n)}, t) > M(x_{p(n)-1}, x_{q(n)-1}, t) > 1 - \epsilon$$

Clearly, this leads to a contradiction.

We consider another case, that is, there exists a positive integers N_0, such that

$$M(x_m, x_n, t) \leq 1 - \epsilon (\forall m, n \geq N_0)$$

so $M(x_{N_0+p+2}, x_{N_0+p+1}, t) \leq 1 - \epsilon$, by the strictly monotonicity of φ, we see that $\{M(x_{N_0+p+2}, x_{N_0+p+1}, t)\}_{p \geq 1}$ is monotone, so there exists a constant $b \in (0, 1-\epsilon]$ such that $\lim_{p \to \infty} M(x_{N_0+p+2}, x_{N_0+p+1}, t) = b$, by(1), we know

$$\varphi(M(x_{N_0+p+2}, x_{N_0+p+1}, t)) \leq \frac{a_1(t) + a_2(t) + a_4(t)}{1 - a_3(t) - a_4(t)} \varphi(M(x_{N_0+p+1}, x_{N_0+p}, t))$$

as $p \to \infty$,

$\varphi(b) \leq \frac{a_1(t)+a_2(t)+a_4(t)}{1-a_3(t)-a_4(t)} \varphi(b)$, so $\varphi(b) \leq 0$, this leads to a contradiction. By Proposition 3.1, $\{x_n\}$ is a M-Cauchy sequence. By the M-comppleteness of X, there exists $x^* \in X$, such that $\lim_{n \to \infty} x_n = x^*$.

Due to Proposition 3.2, $\lim_{n \to \infty} \varphi(M(x_n, x^*, t)) = 0, (\forall t > 0)$

$$\varphi(M(Tx^*, x_{n+1}, t)) = \varphi(M(Tx^*, Tx_n, t)) \leq a_1(t)\varphi(M(x^*, x_n, t))$$
$$+ a_2(t)\varphi(M(x^*, Tx^*, t)) + a_3(t)\varphi(M(x_n, Tx_n, t))$$
$$+ a_4(t)\varphi(M(x^*, Tx_n, t)) + a_5(t)\varphi(M(x_n, Tx^*, t))$$

as $n \to \infty$, we have

$$\varphi(M(Tx^*, x^*, t)) \leq a_1(t)\varphi(M(x^*, x^*, t)) + a_2(t)\varphi(M(x^*, Tx^*, t))$$
$$+ a_3(t)\varphi(M(x^*, Tx^*, t)) + a_4(t)\varphi(M(x^*, Tx^*, t))$$
$$+ a_5(t)\varphi(M(x^*, Tx^*, t))$$

so $\varphi(M(x^*, Tx^*, t)) = 0$, that is $x^* = Tx^*$.

Furthermore, we claim that x^* is the unique fixed point of T. Suppose that there exists a $y^* \in X, y^* \neq x^*$ such that $Ty^* = y^*$.

$$\varphi(M(x^*, y^*, t)) \leq a_1(t)\varphi(M(x^*, y^*, t)) + a_2(t)\varphi(M(x^*, Tx^*, t))$$
$$+ a_3(t)\varphi(M(y^*, Ty^*, t)) + a_4(t)\varphi(M(x^*, Ty^*, t))$$
$$+ a_5(t)\varphi(M(y^*, Tx^*, t))$$

$[1 - a_1(t) - a_4(t) - a_5(t)]\varphi(M(x^*, y^*, t)) \leq 0$, so $y^* = x^*$.

Corollary 3.5. Let $(X, M, *)$ is a M-Complete fuzzy metric space,let $a(t)$: $(0 + \infty) \to (0, 1)$,$T : X \to X$ is a fuzzy contractive mapping with respect to $\varphi \in \mathcal{H}$ such that $\varphi(M(Tx, Ty, t)) \le a(t)\varphi(M(x, y, t))$,then T has unique fixed point x^* and $\{x_n\}$ converges to x^*.

Acknowledgements. We would like to thank the referee for comments which lead to the improvement of this paper. This research is supported by the Foundation of Langfang Teachers College (LSZY201307).

References

1. Kramosil, I., Michalek, J.: Fuzzy Metric and Statistical Metric Spaces. Kybernetika 11, 336–344 (1975)
2. Fanf, J.X.: On Fixed Point Theorems in Fuzzy Metric Spaces. Fuzzy Sets and Systems 46, 107–113 (1992)
3. George, A., Veeramani, P.: On Some Results in Fuzzy Metric Spaces. Fuzzy Sets and Systems 64, 395–399 (1994)
4. Vasuki, R., Veeramani, P.: Fixed Point Theorems and Cauchy Sequences in Fuzzy Metric Spaces. Fuzzy Sets and Systems 135, 415–417 (2003)
5. Shen, Y., Qiu, D., Chen, W.: Fixed Point Theorems in Fuzzy Metric Spaces. Appl. Math. Lett. 25, 138–141 (2012)
6. Wardowski, D.: Fuzzy Contractive Mappings and Fixed Points in Fuzzy Metric Spaces. Fuzzy Sets and Systems 222, 108–114 (2013)
7. Gregori, V., Morilas, S., Sapena, A.: Examples of Fuzzy Metric and Applications. Fuzzy Sets and Systems 170, 95–111 (2011)
8. Sharma, S.: Common Fixed Point Theorems in Fuzzy Metric Spaces. Fuzzy Sets and Systems 127, 345–352 (2002)
9. Mihet, D.: On Fuzzy Contractive Mappings in Fuzzy Metric Spaces. Fuzzy Sets and Systems 158, 915–921 (2007)
10. Schweizer, B., Sklar, A.: Statistical Metric Spaces. Pacific J. Math. 10, 314–334 (1960)

Shortest Path Problem with k-Intermediate Vertex Constraints

Chun Liu and Kang Zhou*

School of Math and Computer,
Wuhan Polytechnic University, Wuhan, China
zhoukang_wh@163.com

1 Introduction

In urban transit network inquiry system, the optimal scheme of bus line having excessive transfers requires us to consider limiting the number of transfers when to compute the optimal scheme of bus line [1], which can come down to shortest path problem limiting the number of intermediate vertex. And support system of QoS (Quality-of-Service) is playing a more and more important role in communication network. QoS routing problem [2] is to choose transmission path meeting the requirements of QoS service to hop counts, bandwidth, latency, packet loss rate etc. and ensuring effective use of global network resources, which can come down to multi-constrained shortest path problem limiting the number of intermediate vertex. Shortest path problem limiting the number of intermediate vertex is shortest path problem with k-intermediate vertex constraints.

In theoretical research on network analysis [3], to vary and expand shortest path problem and to study the corresponding algorithms are important research directions of shortest path problem [4]. The main research direction of variation of shortest path problem focuses on adding several constraints of vertex weight or constraints of edge weight, such as, shortest path problem with constraints of vertex cost [5] and shortest path problem with constraints [6]. Shortest path is divided into six types [7], however, we haven't found shortest path problem limiting the number of intermediate vertex and its exact algorithms, which is also the theme of our research in this paper. Our research about shortest path problem limiting the number of intermediate vertex and its exact algorithms can have a positive impact on development of the research in the field of network analysis. The complexity and real-time responsiveness of the distributed network system, such as urban public transport network system and communication network system, require to improve computational efficiency of shortest path problem as possible, therefore, it is one of the research contents of this paper.

Shortest path problem with k-intermediate vertex constraints, put forward in this paper, is a variation of shortest path problem limiting the number of intermediate vertex. And based on Dijkstra algorithm, an exact algorithm of shortest path problem with k-intermediate vertex constraints is given, which

---

* Corresponding author.

L. Pan et al. (Eds.): BIC-TA 2014, CCIS 472, pp. 664–668, 2014.
© Springer-Verlag Berlin Heidelberg 2014

has the same complexity with Dijkstra algorithm for given k value. This exact algorithm is the single source and single sink, so search of each iteration of this algorithm is in the neighboring area so as to compress the size of computing.

2   Shortest Path Problem with k-Intermediate Vertex Constraints and Background

Consider a positive weight directed network $D = (V, A, W)$, where $V(D) = \{v_i | i = 1, 2, \cdots, n\}$ is vertex set of network D, $A(D) = \{a_{ij} | v_i \in V(D) \wedge v_j \in V(D)\}$ is arc set of network D, $W(D) = \{w_{ij} | a_{ij} \in A(D) \wedge w_{ij} \in R^+\}$ is weight set of network D.

In a positive weight directed network $D = (V, A, W)$, a sequence of vertex and arc aternating is called a chain, a chain whose vertex does not repeat and whose arc is end to end is called a path. Let L be a path from vertex v_1 to vertex v_n, $W(L) = \sum_{a_{ij} \in L} w_{ij}$ is called weight [2,3] of path L. A path with minimum weight is shortest path. Shortest path problem with k-intermediate vertex constraints is to choose a shortest path from vertex v_1 to vertex v_n which has no more than k intermediate vertexes.

For a positive weight directed network $D = (V, A, W)$, an algorithm for shortest path problem with single source vertex v_1 and single sink vertex v_n (**algorithm 1**) is as follows:

Step 1. Let $P = \{v_1\}$, $T = \emptyset$, $S = V - \{v_1\}$, $l_1 = 0$, $p = \lambda_1 = 1$.

Step 2. Compute $(P, S) = \{a_{ij} | v_i \in P \wedge v_j \in S\}$, if $(P, S) = \emptyset$, then there is no shortest path from vertex v_1 to vertex v_n, end.

Step 3. Compute $R = \{v_i | a_{pi} \in (P, S)\}$, if $R = \emptyset$, then return to step 5.

Step 4. For $\forall v_i \in R$, compute l_i and λ_i.
If $v_i \bar{\in} T$, then $l_i = l_p + w_{pi}$, $\lambda_i = p$, $T = T \cup \{v_i\}$;
otherwise, if $l_i > l_p + w_{pi}$, then $l_i = l_p + w_{pi}$, $\lambda_i = p$.

Step 5. Compute $l_q = \min\{l_i | v_i \in T\}$, let $P = P \cup \{v_q\}$, $T = T - \{v_q\}$, $S = S - \{v_q\}$.

Step 6. If $v_n \in P$, then obtain a shortest path from vertex v_1 to vertex v_n by means of tracing back, end; otherwise, let $p = q$, return to step 2.

For Dijkstra algorithm, search and compute in set S; and for algorithm 1, search and compute in set T; and $T \subseteq S$, so algorithm 1 is more practical for complex and large network, even though complexity of the algorithm is the same between Dijkstra algorithm and algorithm 1.

It is design idea of algorithm 1 to determine shortest path from the near to the distant. However, the shortest path getting by algorithm 1 can not control the number of intermediate vertices. In order to solve this problem, it is necessary to record the number of intermediate vertices of distance l_i. So new ideas of algorithm design is put forward, which is the concept of virtual vertex and the generalized triangle inequality of shortest distance. According to the characteristics of shortest path problem with k-intermediate vertex constraints, the concept of virtual vertex is introduced.

Definition 1. In a positive weight directed network $D = (V, A, W)$, for $\forall r \forall i (r \in \{0, 1, 2, \cdots, k\} \land i \in \{2, 3, \cdots, n\})$, let $l_i^{(r+1)}$ be shortest distance from vertex v_1 to vertex v_i containing r intermediate vertices at most, the vertex corresponding to shortest distance $l_i^{(r+1)}$ of vertex v_i is called virtual vertex of vertex v_i, and denoted by $v_i^{(r+1)}$. Set $V' = \{v_i^{(r+1)} | i = 2, 3, \cdots, n - 1 \land r = 0, 1, 2, \cdots, k - 1\} \cup \{v_n^{(r+1)} | r = 0, 1, 2, \cdots, k\} \cup \{v_1\}$ is called virtual vertex set of set V.

The generalized triangle inequality of shortest distance is as follows.

Theorem 1 (Fundamental Theorem of Algorithm). In a positive weight directed network $D = (V, A, W)$, let $l_i^{(r+1)}$ be shortest distance from vertex v_1 to vertex v_i containing r intermediate vertices at most,

(1) For $i(i \in \{2, 3, \cdots, n\})$, $\forall r \forall s (0 \leq r \leq s \leq k) \Rightarrow l_i^{(s+1)} \leq l_i^{(r+1)}$;

(2) For $r(r \in \{1, 2, \cdots, k\})$, $\forall i \forall j (1 \leq i \leq j \leq n \rightarrow l_i^{(r)} \leq l_j^{(r)}) \Rightarrow l_i^{(r+1)} = \min\{l_s^{(r)} + w_{si} | s < i\}$.

Conclusion (2) of Theorem 1 is generalized triangle inequality of shortest distance.

Proof. (1) For $i(i \in \{2, 3, \cdots, n\})$, the path from vertex v_1 to vertex v_i containing s intermediate vertices at most contains the path from vertex v_1 to vertex v_i containing r intermediate vertices at most, so if $r < s$, then according to the implications of $l_i^{(r+1)}$, $l_i^{(s+1)} \leq l_i^{(r+1)}$, conclusion (1) is established.

(2) $l_s^{(r)} + w_{si}$ is shortest distance from vertex v_1 to vertex v_i containing r intermediate vertices at most and through vertex v_s, so $\min\{l_s^{(r)} + w_{si} | s \neq i\}$ is shortest distance from vertex v_1 to vertex v_i containing r intermediate vertices at most, namely, $l_i^{(r+1)} = \min\{l_s^{(r)} + w_{si} | s \neq i\}$. And $l_s^{(r)} \geq l_i^{(r)} (s > i)$, namely, $l_s^{(r)} + w_{si} > l_i^{(r)} \geq l_i^{(r+1)}$, so $l_i^{(r+1)} = \min\{l_s^{(r)} + w_{si} | s \neq i\} = \min\{l_s^{(r)} + w_{si} | s < i\}$. Conclusion (1) is established.

According to Theorem 1, key points of design of shortest path problem with k-intermediate vertex constraints are as follows:

(1) In virtual vertex set V', the general idea to compute shortest path from vertex v_1 to virtual vertex is to determine in turn shortest path from the near to the distant according to distance from vertex v_1 to virtual vertex.

(2) For $s > r$, if shortest path of virtual vertex $v_i^{(r+1)}$ is determined, then vertex virtual $v_i^{(s+1)}$ can be deleted from set T and set S. (This key point can reduce the computing scale.)

(3) For $i \neq n$, shortest path of virtual vertex $v_i^{(k+1)}$ is irrelevant to shortest path of virtual vertex $v_n^{(k+1)}$. So vertex virtual $v_i^{(k+1)}$ can be deleted from virtual vertex set V'. (This key point can reduce the computing scale.)

(4) Shortest path problem with k-intermediate vertex constraints can be converted into the problem to compute shortest path from vertex v_1 to virtual vertex of set $\{v_n^{(r+1)} | r = 0, 1, 2, \cdots, k\}$, and shortest path of this virtual vertex is the first computed by the algorithm. (This key point is termination condition of the algorithm.)

According to the above key points of design and algorithm 1, exact algorithm for shortest path problem with k-intermediate vertex constraints is designed.

3   Exact Algorithm for Shortest Path Problem with k-Intermediate Vertex Constraints

In a positive weight directed network $D = (V, A, W)$, $V(D) = \{v_i | i = 1, 2, \cdots, n\}$ is vertex set of network D, $A(D) = \{a_{ij} | v_i \in V(D) \wedge v_j \in V(D)\}$ is arc set of network D, $W(D) = \{w_{ij} | a_{ij} \in A(D) \wedge w_{ij} \in R^+\}$ is weight set of network D. Exact algorithm for shortest path problem with k-intermediate vertex constraints (**algorithm 2**), where the shortest path is from vertex v_1 to vertex v_n, is as follows:

Step 1. Let $P = \{v_1\}$, $T = \emptyset$, $S = V' - \{v_1\}$, $l_1^{(0)} = 0$, $p = \lambda_1 = 1$, $r = 0$.

Step 2. Compute $(P, S) = \{a_{ij} | v_i \in P \wedge v_j \in S\}$, if $(P, S) = \emptyset$, then there is no shortest path from vertex v_1 to vertex v_n, end.

Step 3. Compute $R = \{v_i^{(r+1)} | a_{pi} \in (P, S)\}$.

If $r = k - 1$, then compute $R = \{v_n^{(r+1)} | a_{pn} \in A \wedge v_n^{(r+1)} \in S\}$;

otherwise, compute $R = \{v_i^{(r+1)} | a_{pi} \in A \wedge v_i^{(r+1)} \in S\}$.

If $R = \emptyset$, then return to step 5.

Step 4. For $\forall v_i^{(r+1)} \in R$, compute $l_i^{(r+1)}$ and $\lambda_i^{(r+1)}$.

If $(v_i^{(r+1)} \bar{\in} T) \vee (l_i^{(r+1)} > l_p^{(r)} + w_{pi})$, then $l_i^{(r+1)} = l_p^{(r)} + w_{pi}$, $\lambda_i^{(r+1)} = p$;

if $v_i^{(r+1)} \bar{\in} T$, then $T = T \cup \{v_i^{(r+1)}\}$.

Step 5. Compute $l_q^{(u+1)} = \min\{l_i^{(j+1)} | v_i^{(j+1)} \in T\}$, let $P = P \cup \{v_q^{(u+1)}\}$, $T = T - \{v_q^{(r+1)} | r \geq u\}$, $S = S - \{v_q^{(r+1)} | r \geq u\}$.

Step 6. If $q = n$, namely, $v_n^{(u+1)} \in P$, then return to step 7; otherwise, let $p = q$, $r = u + 1$, return to step 2.

Step 7. (Means of tracing back) For $t = u, \cdots, 1, 0$, compute $\lambda_{p(t+1)}^{(t+1)} = p(t)$, and obtain a sequence: $1 = p(0), p(1), \cdots, p(u), p(u + 1) = n$, then obtain a shortest path from vertex v_1 to virtual vertex $v_n^{(u+1)} : 1 \mapsto p(1) \mapsto \cdots \mapsto p(u) \mapsto n$ and the shortest distance $l_n^{(u+1)}$ from vertex v_1 to virtual vertex $v_n^{(u+1)}$.

Theorem 2. The complexity of algorithm 2 is $O((k \times n)^2)$.

Proof. It is well known that the complexity of algorithm 1 is $O(n^2)$.

The main calculation of algorithm 2 is in Step 4 and Step 5, where the calculated amount of comparison operation of set T is the maximum calculated amount of algorithm 2, so the calculation scale n of algorithm 1 can replace the scale of the maximum set T in the iteration. Therefore, the complexity of algorithm 2 is $O((\max |T|)^2)$. Determine $(\max |T|)$ as follows:

The first iteration, $|T| \leq n - 1$; the second iteration, $|T| \leq 2(n - 2)$; the third iteration, $|T| \leq (n - 2) + 2(n - 3)$; $\cdots$; the kth iteration, $|T| \leq (n - 2) + (n - 3) + \cdots + 2(n - k) = k \times n + C_0$, where C_0 is constant, and $|T|$ is maximum. So, $|T| \leq O(k \times n)$. Therefore, the complexity of algorithm 2 is $O((k \times n)^2)$.   □

Acknowledgments. Kang Zhou is corresponding author. The work is supported by the National Natural Science Foundation of China (61179032, 11301405).

References

1. Zhang, X.F., Li, R.M., Li, H.F., Shi, Q.X.: A Traffic Assignment Problem and Model for Partially-Controlled Road Network. Highway Engineering 36, 11–14, 54 (2011)
2. Wang, X.W., Qin, P.Y., Huang, M.: ABC Supporting Qos Unicast Routing Scheme Based on The Artificial Fish Swarm. Chinese Journal of Computers 33, 718–725 (2010)
3. Zhou, K., Chen, J.: Simulation Dna Algorithm of Set Covering Problem. Applied Mathematics and Information Sciences 8, 139–144 (2014)
4. Hu, Y.M., Liu, W.M.: Multi-constrained Shortest Path Model and Solving. Journal of Hunan University of Science and Technology (Natural Science Edition) 25, 87–90 (2010)
5. Li, B.Y., He, Y., Yao, E.Y.: Shortest Path Problem with Constraints of Node'S Cost. Appl. Math. J. Chinese Univ. Ser. A. 15, 93–96 (2000)
6. He, F.G., Qi, H., Fan, Q.: Model and Algorithm of Random Shortest Path Problem with Constraints. Journal of Wuhan University of Technology (Transportation Science and Engineering) 32, 1125–1128 (2008)
7. She, X.Y.: The Shortest Path Algorithm With Constraints. Computer Applications and Software 26, 236–238, 265 (2009)

Author Index